DISCARDED

BEST PRACTICES FOR SOCIAL WORK
WITH REFUGEES AND IMMIGRANTS

BEST PRACTICES FOR SOCIAL WORK WITH REFUGEES AND IMMIGRANTS

MIRIAM POTOCKY-TRIPODI

COLUMBIA UNIVERSITY PRESS NEW YORK

COLUMBIA UNIVERSITY PRESS
Publishers Since 1893
New York   Chichester, West Sussex
Copyright © 2002 Columbia University Press
All rights reserved

Library of Congress Cataloging-in-Publication Data

Potocky-Tripodi, Miriam.
Best practices for social work with refugees and immigrants / Miriam Potocky-Tripodi.
p.   cm.
Includes bibliographical references and index.
ISBN 0-231-11582-2 (cl.)—ISBN 0-231-11583-0 (pa.)
1. Social work with immigrants—United States.   2. Refugees—Services for—United States.
3. Immigrants—Services for—United States.   I. Title.

HV4010 .P67 2002
362.87'0973—dc21
2001058111

∞

Casebound editions of Columbia University Press books are printed
on permanent and durable acid-free paper.
Printed in the United States of America
c 10 9 8 7 6 5 4 3 2 1
p 10 9 8 7 6 5 4 3 2 1

To my parents

CONTENTS

List of Tables xi
Preface xv
Acknowledgments xix

PART I
CONTEXT FOR SOCIAL WORK WITH REFUGEES AND IMMIGRANTS 1

CHAPTER 1 Introduction 3

1.1 Definitions of Immigrants and Refugees 4
1.2 Causes of International Migration 13
1.3 Stages of Migration 17
1.4 Scope of Immigrant and Refugee Populations 20
1.5 Demographic and Socioeconomic Characteristics of Immigrants and Refugees 30
1.6 Program and Service Utilization Patterns of Immigrants and Refugees 36
1.7 History and Characteristics of Major Immigrant and Refugee Groups 38
1.8 Summary 52

CHAPTER 2 Immigration and Refugee Policies 53

2.1 International Law 53
2.2 United States Immigration and Refugee Policies 57

CHAPTER 3 Service Delivery Systems 96

3.1 Service Delivery Organizations 96
3.2 Service Delivery Personnel 113
3.3 Service Delivery Strategies and Techniques 117

PART II
BEST PRACTICES 121

CHAPTER 4 Culturally Competent Social Work Practice 123

4.1 Terminology for Culturally Competent Practice 124
4.2 Attitudes and Beliefs for Culturally Competent Practice 131
4.3 Knowledge for Culturally Competent Practice 137
4.4 Skills for Culturally Competent Practice 152
4.5 Conclusion 181

CHAPTER 5 Health 183

5.1 Health and Health Care Problems 183
5.2 Best Practices 209
5.3 Case Study Exercises 253

CHAPTER 6 Mental Health 256

6.1 Mental Health and Mental Health Care Problems 257
6.2 Best Practices 272
6.3 Case Study Exercises 307

CHAPTER 7 Family Dynamics 310

7.1 Family Dynamics Issues 311
7.2 Best Practices 329
7.3 Case Study Exercises 353

CHAPTER 8 Language, Education, and Economic Well-Being 356

8.1 Research Findings on Language, Education, and Economic Well-Being 356
8.2 Best Practices 384
8.3 Case Study Exercises 414

CHAPTER 9 Interethnic Relations 416

9.1 Key Issues in Interethnic Relations 417
9.2 Best Practices 428
9.3 Case Study Exercises 477

CHAPTER 10 Summary and Conclusions 479

10.1 The Context of Social Work Practice with Refugees and Immigrants 479
10.2 Problem Areas and Best Practices 482
10.3 Synthesis of Best Practice Approaches 488
10.4 Recommendations for Future Practice and Research 489

References 493
Index 525

LIST OF TABLES

TABLE 1.1 Classification of Individuals as Citizens and as Documented or Undocumented Noncitizens of the United States 6
TABLE 1.2 Definitions of Major Legal Categories and Terms 9
TABLE 1.3 Contrasts Between Refugees and Immigrants 12
TABLE 1.4 Stage-of-Migration Framework 18
TABLE 1.5 World Region of Birth and Year of Entry Into the U.S. of the Foreign Born, by Citizenship Status 2000 21
TABLE 1.6 Immigration, 1981–1996: Top Ten Countries of Birth 22
TABLE 1.7 Refugees, 1981–1996: Top Ten Countries of Applicants Approved 22
TABLE 1.8 Illegal Alien Population, 1996: Top Ten Countries of Birth (Estimates) 23
TABLE 1.9 Temporary Workers, 1996: Top Ten Countries of Citizenship 24
TABLE 1.10 Students, 1996: Top Ten Countries of Citizenship 24
TABLE 1.11 Immigrants Admitted, 1998: Top Ten Countries of Birth 25
TABLE 1.12 Refugees Admitted, 2000: Top Ten Countries of Nationality 26
TABLE 1.13 Foreign-Born, 1990 Census: Top Ten States of Residence 27
TABLE 1.14 Legal Permanent Residents, 1996: Top Ten States (Estimates) 28
TABLE 1.15 Refugees and Asylees Granted Permanent Residence, 1996: Top Ten States 28
TABLE 1.16 Illegal Alien Population, 1996: Top Ten States (Estimates) 29
TABLE 1.17 Immigrants Admitted, 1998: Top Ten Metropolitan Areas of Intended Residence 29
TABLE 1.18 Age and Gender of Native-Born and Foreign-Born Population, 2000 (in percent) 30
TABLE 1.19 Demographic Characteristics of the Native Population and Foreign-Born Population by World Region of Birth, 2000 31

TABLE 1.20 Socioeconomic Characteristics of Native-Born and Foreign-Born Population, 2000 (In Percent) 32
TABLE 1.21 Socioeconomic Characteristics of the Native Population and Foreign-Born Population by World Region of Birth, 2000 34
TABLE 1.22 Highest and Lowest Percent Naturalized: 1977 Immigrant Cohort, Through 1995 35
TABLE 1.23 Percent of Households Receiving Public Benefits, by Citizenship and Immigration Status of Household Head, 1997 37
TABLE 2.1 Major United Nations Human Rights, Humanitarian, and Refugee Instruments Pertinent to Immigrants and Refugees 55
TABLE 2.2 Articles of the Universal Declaration of Human Rights 56
TABLE 2.3 Major Historical United States Immigration and Refugee Policies 62
TABLE 2.4 Major Contemporary United States Immigration and Refugee Policies 64
TABLE 2.5 Legal Immigration Admission Preference System 73
TABLE 2.6 General Naturalization Requirements 75
TABLE 2.7 Key Terms in Immigrant Welfare Reform 83
TABLE 2.8 Alien Eligibility for Public Benefits 87
TABLE 3.1 Major Private International Relief Organizations Involved with Immigrants and Refugees 100
TABLE 3.2 Major Advocacy Organizations Involved with Immigrants and Refugees in International Arena 104
TABLE 3.3 Major United States National Refugee Resettlement Agencies 109
TABLE 3.4 Major National Immigrant and Refugee Advocacy Organizations 110
TABLE 3.5 Strategies and Techniques of Service Delivery to Refugees and Immigrants in the Resettlement Phase 118
TABLE 4.1 Two-Dimensional Model of Acculturation 127
TABLE 4.2 Attitudes and Beliefs for Culturally Competent Practice 132
TABLE 4.3 Knowledge for Culturally Competent Practice 138
TABLE 4.4 Common Contrasts Between Helping Professionals and Refugee or Immigrant Clients 149
TABLE 4.5 Skills for Culturally Competent Practice 153
TABLE 5.1 Personal and Cultural Factors Influencing Health Care Access and Treatment Adherence 194
TABLE 5.2 Examples of Folk Illnesses 199
TABLE 5.3 Social Work Services in Health Care 210
TABLE 5.4 Best Practices for Effective Health Care Policy Advocacy 214
TABLE 5.5 Best Practices for Effective Community Health Policy and Program Planning 218

TABLE 5.6 Standards for Effective Public Health Information Programs 223
TABLE 5.7 Best Practices for Effective Public Health Information Programs 224
TABLE 5.8 Formats for Community Health Educational Materials 226
TABLE 5.9 Best Practices for Effective Health Education Materials 227
TABLE 5.10 Best Practices for Effective Health Promotion through Special Events 228
TABLE 5.11 Best Practices for Culturally and Linguistically Appropriate Health Care Services 229
TABLE 5.12 Best Practices for Culturally Competent Health Care with Immigrants and Refugees 232
TABLE 5.13 Principles of Continuous Quality Improvement for Health Care Organizations 237
TABLE 5.14 Best Practice Principles for Improving the Health Care Provider/Client Relationship Across Cultures 238
TABLE 5.15 Best Practices for Ensuring Quality Service Coordination 241
TABLE 5.16 Best Practices for Effective Case Advocacy 242
TABLE 5.17 Best Practices for Culturally Competent Case Management 243
TABLE 5.18 Best Practices for Providing Case Management Services with an Interpreter 244
TABLE 5.19 Best Practices for Effective Health Education and Counseling 248
TABLE 6.1 Resettlement Stages, Refugee Tasks, and Treatment Issues 259
TABLE 6.2 Best Practice Principles of Mental Health Care for Immigrants and Refugees 273
TABLE 6.3 Overall System Best Practice Standards for Mental Health Care for Immigrants and Refugees 278
TABLE 6.4 Clinical Best Practice Standards for Mental Health Care for Immigrants and Refugees 281
TABLE 7.1 Conflicts Across Three Generations of Immigrant and Refugee Families 316
TABLE 8.1 Best Practice Macro Interventions to Enhance Academic Achievement of Immigrant and Refugee Students 389
TABLE 8.2 Components of Effective School Programs for Immigrant and Refugee Students 391
TABLE 8.3 Core Features of Programs for Limited English Proficiency Students 393
TABLE 8.4 Program Alternatives for Limited English Proficiency Students 394
TABLE 8.5 Best Practice Principles for Instructional Practice with Refugee and Immigrant Students 396
TABLE 8.6 Best Practices for Identifying and Serving Gifted Immigrant and Refugee Students 399

TABLE 8.7 Best Practices for Assessment of Immigrant and Refugee Students 401
TABLE 9.1 Key Findings of National Survey on Interethnic Relations 423
TABLE 9.2 General Principles for Policy Development Related to Immigrants and Refugees 432
TABLE 9.3 Legislation Regarding Employment Discrimination Based on National Origin 433
TABLE 9.4 Local Ordinances and Policies to Prevent Ethnic Conflict 434
TABLE 9.5 Best Practices for Fostering Positive Interactions Among Immigrant and Refugee Newcomers and Established Residents 439
TABLE 9.6 Best Practices for Community Initiatives to Improve Relations among Immigrant and Refugee Newcomers and Established Residents 440
TABLE 9.7 Best Practices to Prevent Hate Crimes from Escalating Ethnic Tensions 442
TABLE 9.8 Best Practices for Creating Positive Community Responses to Hate 444
TABLE 9.9 Characteristics of Effective Interethnic Dialogue 451
TABLE 9.10 Steps in Organizing an Interethnic Dialogue 451
TABLE 9.11 Best Practices for Conducting an Effective Interethnic Dialogue 454
TABLE 9.12 Best Practices for the Interethnic Dialogue Leader 458
TABLE 9.13 Principles of Conflict Resolution 460
TABLE 9.14 Fundamental Negotiation Abilities 461
TABLE 9.15 Interest-Based Negotiation Process 463
TABLE 9.16 Best Practices for Mediation 467
TABLE 10.1 Future Agenda for Research on the Psychosocial Wellness of Refugees and Immigrants 490

PREFACE

THIS BOOK had its genesis in the late 1970s when I was in high school, although I didn't know that at the time. My younger brother and his friends had gotten into some trouble with the law, and as part of his juvenile diversion program, the entire family, consisting of us two siblings and our parents, was court-ordered into family therapy. As it turned out, this became one of the worst experiences of my young life.

Every week we piled into the family car and dragged ourselves to these sessions. We would shuffle into the office and seat ourselves in a row, with my brother and me on the inside and our parents on the outside, my mother on my side and my father on my brother's. The sessions were conducted by two co-therapists, a man and a woman. When I was asked to speak I invariably began by complaining that I didn't understand why I had to be there, since it was obviously my brother who had the problem.

If the reader has a knowledge of family systems theory, he or she has certainly identified some "red flags" at this point: the physical distancing of the parents at opposite ends, with the children creating a literal buffer between them; the alignment of parents with children along gender lines; and the presence of the family member who serves as the "scapegoat." But, how did this family get to this point, and what did these therapists do about it?

Some ten years earlier, my family had come to America as refugees from what was then Czechoslovakia. Could there possibly be any connection between this experience and what was happening now? Apparently, the therapists didn't think so, if they thought at all. Basically, they seemed pretty bewildered by what confronted them: a mother who didn't speak English after ten years of living in the U.S.; a son who refused to speak Czech and therefore did not speak with his mother at all; a daughter who continually translated both language and American norms; a family that didn't talk about feelings.

I don't remember much of what these therapists did during these sessions, but I certainly remember what they did not do: they didn't say anything about stresses of adjusting to life in a new country; they didn't ask anything about Czech norms or Czech culture; they didn't ask about who or what was left behind; they didn't ask my brother or me about what it was like to live in one world at home and another one outside. Today I know that it was these very factors that were the major elements of my family life at that point; but it sure would have helped if those therapists had known that, and had helped me know it then.

Instead of helping, these family sessions only added more trauma on top of what we had already experienced. We were told to talk about feelings; today I know that that is not a Czech cultural norm. I was used as a translator between the therapists and my mother; today I know that that gave the child inappropriate power over the parent. We were told to connect with the local Czech American club; but they didn't consider that those club members, the descendants of Czech immigrants who came to America in the 1860s, had little in common with the political refugees who came in the late 1960s. We were made to feel even worse about ourselves than when we came in—I knew those therapists didn't have a clue what to do with us, because we were so "weird"—and their bewilderment only reinforced that feeling of alienation.

So, every week when we left those sessions, we really breathed a sigh of relief, knowing that it was over till next week. And we engaged in a little ritual that, I know now, was an attempt to recover from those "helping" sessions, to restore ourselves as a family. We went home every week and watched "Mork and Mindy" on TV.

That show brought us together and made us laugh. Here was Mork from the planet Ork, and he lived in Colorado. We lived in Colorado too, and to me it seemed like we were from a different planet too. But Mork gave me hope—if he could somehow fit in, maybe someday my family and I could too.

Although this experience occurred more than twenty years ago, I suspect similar events still happen today within the helping professions. While it is certainly true that there has been progress in educating practitioners for cultural competence, it is also true that refugee and immigrant families still encounter problems within the systems that are supposed to help them. To many helping professionals, "aliens" are still very much that—alien. It is for this reason that I wrote this book—to help social workers and other helping professionals be more effective in working with and for refugees, immigrants, and their families. It is my hope that in the future, refugees and immigrants who need help will find their best hopes among helping professionals—rather than among fictional aliens from another planet.

P.S. Thank you, Robin Williams.

ACKNOWLEDGMENTS

I THANK MY HUSBAND, Tony Tripodi, for his patience, support, and nurturing of me as a "writer in residence." I thank my father, Pavel Potocky, and my friend Gail Ukockis for assistance with literature retrieval. Finally, I thank Florida International University for granting a sabbatical leave in Fall 1999 to allow me to work full time on this book.

BEST PRACTICES FOR SOCIAL WORK
WITH REFUGEES AND IMMIGRANTS

PART I
CONTEXT FOR SOCIAL WORK WITH REFUGEES AND IMMIGRANTS

CHAPTER 1

INTRODUCTION

MANY SOCIAL WORKERS practice in settings that serve immigrant and refugee clients as part of their caseloads. Most social workers can expect to encounter such clients at some time in their careers. The population of immigrants and refugees in the United States is growing rapidly. It is estimated that by 2040, immigrants and refugees and their offspring will account for over one-quarter of the U.S. population (Fix & Passel 1994). And immigrants and refugees will account for 65 percent of the country's population growth by 2050 (Doyle 1999). Thus it is essential that social workers be prepared to work effectively with this population.

Social work practice with refugees and immigrants requires specialized knowledge of the unique issues of these populations. It also requires specialized adaptations and applications of mainstream services and interventions. This book provides a comprehensive perspective of social work practice with refugees and immigrants—a perspective that entails examination of the multiple factors that affect immigrants and refugees at the micro, meso, and macro levels, and relevant practice approaches at each of those levels.

Additionally, rather than focusing on specific immigrant or refugee groups, this book adopts a "pancultural" perspective that focuses on the common experiences of and practice approaches for working with all immigrants and refugees. It has been argued that "multicultural social work must offer a pancultural perspective, which encompasses the various ethnic groups and also the dominant . . . culture in which they must coexist . . . . Fundamental to the pancultural perspective is the conviction that the culture and ethnicity of *all* people are important factors in the helping process" (Lum 2000, p. 97).

The book focuses primarily on practice in the United States, although it draws upon literature from around the world. Because of the great diversity of populations, policies, and practices in different countries, the issues addressed in this book may or may not be applicable outside of the United States. Thus, readers in other countries should use their own knowledge and judgment to adapt this information to their own local contexts.

This book is divided into two parts. Part I sets forth the context for social work practice with immigrants and refugees. This includes descriptions of the populations, relevant policies, and service delivery systems. Part II addresses specific problem areas within a biopsychosocial perspective. For each problem area, assessment and intervention techniques are discussed. The book focuses on empirically based practice approaches. This refers to assessment and intervention techniques that have been scientifically validated at least to some degree. It also refers to the social worker evaluating his or her own practice. Based on this, each chapter in part II delineates the "best practices" for the given problem area. It is recommended that the chapters be read in sequential order, since each one builds upon material presented in preceding chapters.

This first chapter discusses who immigrants and refugees are and why they migrate. The process of migration is described. The chapter provides statistics on these populations, their demographic characteristics, and service utilization patterns. Finally, each major group of immigrants and refugees is briefly described.

1.1 DEFINITIONS OF IMMIGRANTS AND REFUGEES

DEFINITIONS OF IMMIGRANTS and refugees differ depending on whether one is using social science definitions, legal definitions, or self-definitions (i.e., how immigrants and refugees identify themselves). At the most fundamental level, immigrants and refugees are people who were born in one country and have relocated to another. In the social science literature, these people are collectively referred to as the *foreign-born population*. People leaving a country to live elsewhere are called *emigrants* and people entering a country to settle there are called *immigrants*.

The fundamental distinction between immigrants and refugees is that *immigrants* leave their countries voluntarily (usually in search of better economic opportunities) whereas *refugees* are forced out of their countries because of human rights violations against them. Therefore, immigrants are also sometimes referred to as *voluntary migrants* or *economic migrants*, and refugees may be referred to as *involuntary migrants* or *forced migrants*. Refugees are also sometimes referred to, or refer to themselves, as *exiles* or *émigrés*.

The social science literature contains further distinctions within these broad categories of immigrants and refugees. These distinctions are based on the purpose and methodology of each particular study. Therefore, there tends to be inconsistency and lack of clarity in social science definitions (Loue 1998). Thus, it is more fruitful to turn to legal definitions.

Legally, anyone who is not a citizen of the United States is termed an *alien*. Aliens are further classified as immigrants and nonimmigrants, and as documented or undocumented (Loue 1998). In this classification, an *immigrant* is a person who has been legally admitted into the United States and granted the privilege to be a permanent resident (a "green card" holder). A *nonimmigrant* is a foreign-born person who is in the United States temporarily, such as a tourist, a student, or a journalist. Nonimmigrants also include temporary, or seasonal, workers, who come to the United States to work during certain periods of the year and return to their countries during the rest of the year. This typically refers to agricultural laborers.

A *documented alien* is one who has been granted a legal right to be in the United States. This legal right is determined by admissions policy. The admissions policy details many categories of people who are eligible to be legally admitted. It also specifies how many people from each country may be legally admitted into the U.S. each year. This policy is described further in the next chapter.

An *undocumented alien* is one who does not have a legal right to be in the United States. These people are also sometimes referred to as *illegal immigrants*. They are also referred to as *deportable aliens*, because if discovered by immigration authorities, they are subject to deportation, or forcible return to their countries of origin. There are two ways in which people become undocumented aliens. One is by entering the U.S. illegally. This means that the person has not received authorization to enter the United States. For example, people who cross the border from Mexico without going through immigration authorities are undocumented aliens. The second way that people become undocumented aliens is by entering the U.S. legally, but then violating the terms of their visa (the authorization to stay in the U.S.). For example, a tourist may be granted a visa to stay in the United States for a limited period of time. If the person stays after that time period has expired, then that person becomes an undocumented alien. Or, a student may be granted a visa to attend school in the U.S. If that student stops attending school and begins working, that person becomes an undocumented alien. The various categories of citizens and documented and undocumented aliens are summarized in table 1.1.

TABLE 1.1 CLASSIFICATION OF INDIVIDUALS AS CITIZENS AND AS DOCUMENTED OR UNDOCUMENTED NONCITIZENS OF THE UNITED STATES

UNITED STATES CITIZENS

- Persons born in the United States.
- Persons born outside of the United States after 12/12/52 and before 11/14/86 to one U.S. citizen parent; second parent may be citizen or noncitizen; U.S. citizen parent resided in the U.S. for at least 10 years prior to birth of respondent, at least 5 of which were after parent was 14 years old.
- Persons born outside of the United States after 11/14/86 to one U.S. citizen parent; second parent may be citizen or noncitizen of U.S.; U.S. citizen parent resided in U.S. for at least 5 years before birth of respondent, at least 2 of which were after parent was 14 years old.
- Persons born outside of U.S. and its territories to parents both of whom are U.S. citizens; one parent resided in U.S. prior to respondent's birth.
- Individuals who obtained U.S. citizenship through the process of naturalization.
- Individuals who obtained citizenship through the naturalization of their parent(s).

NONCITIZENS OF THE UNITED STATES

Documented
- Lawfully admitted permanent resident ("green card" holder).
- Individuals admitted as refugees.
- Nonimmigrants who have not done anything to violate that status and who entered legally (e.g., tourists, students, journalists).
- Individuals granted an extraordinary administrative immigration remedy (parole, deferred action, extended voluntary departure).
- Individuals who have applied for legal status under amnesty or special agricultural worker programs, whose applications are pending.

Undocumented
- Individuals who have entered the United States illegally.
- Individuals who entered the United States legally, but violated the terms of their visa. This can include employment without authorization, failing to attend school if admitted as a student, or overstaying the length of time granted to stay in the U.S.

Source: Loue, 1998.

It is also important to distinguish legally between an immigrant and a refugee. As stated above, immigrants leave their countries voluntarily, whereas refugees leave because of human rights violations against them. Refugees are very specifically defined by international law. That law is the United Nations Convention Relating to the Status of Refugees, which was established in 1951. This law is also sometimes referred to as the Geneva Convention, because it was adopted by the United Nations at Geneva, Switzerland. This law states that a *refugee* is "a person who is outside his / her country and is unable or unwilling to return to that country because of a well-founded fear that she / he will be persecuted because of race, religion, nationality, political opinion, or membership in a particular social group" (U.S. Department of State, 1996).

It is important to note that some people are in circumstances that appear similar to refugees, but they are not refugees as defined above. These are referred to as *refugee-like situations*. For example, a person may have moved from one part of his or her own country into another part of that same country because of the same fear of persecution as described above. This frequently happens in civil wars. Although such people may have suffered from the same human rights violations as refugees, and have been forced to move out of their homes like refugees, they have not actually left their countries. Therefore, they are not refugees, since the refugee definition refers to people who are outside their countries. Instead, such people are referred to as *internally displaced persons*.

Another refugee-like situation occurs when people are forced to leave their countries because of natural disasters such as widespread droughts that have led to starvation. Like refugees, these people are referred to as *forced migrants*. However, they are not refugees because they were forced to leave by acts of nature and not acts of persecution by humans.

It is also important to remember that the refugee definition is an international one. Although the United States uses the same definition in its national refugee policy, this does not mean that everyone who qualifies as a refugee under the international law can be admitted into the United States as a refugee. The United States policy sets limits on how many refugees can be admitted each year. Additionally, the United States has had a historical tendency to be more favorable in granting admission to refugees from certain countries and less favorable to refugees from other countries. In particular, the U.S. has been much more favorable toward admitting refugees from Communist and formerly Communist countries; it has been much less favorable toward admitting refugees from non-Communist countries (Loescher 1993; Portes and Rumbaut 1990).

The process of determining whether someone is eligible to be legally admitted to the United States as a refugee is frequently lengthy. Therefore, several categories exist that describe people who are in different stages of this process. People who are outside of their country and who are applying to be recognized and admitted as refugees by another country are called *asylees*. They are seeking political asylum, or protection from their persecutors. (People who seek asylum after arriving in the U.S. are termed asylees; people who arrive in the U.S. after first being granted asylum in another country are termed refugees). People who have been allowed to enter the United States under emergency humanitarian conditions pending a final decision are termed *parolees*. Another term that sometimes arises in relation to refugees is *entrants*. This refers specifically to people from Cuba and Haiti who entered the United States illegally during certain time periods but have resided continuously in the U.S. since 1982. These people are eligible to adjust to permanent residence status under a law passed in 1986.

In addition to all of the various primary legal statuses described above, many aliens derive their legal status through their relationship to another alien. For example, one member of a family may be recognized and admitted as a refugee under the refugee definition. Typically, that person's spouse and children would also be admitted as refugees even though they themselves may not meet the definition per se. A similar situation applies to the various categories of immigrant admissions.

One final type of foreign-born person is worth noting, even though this person does not have a distinct legal status. This is a person who essentially has permanent residence in two or more countries. Typically, such people spend substantial amounts of time in each country. They generally commute back and forth. They may have dual citizenship. These people are referred to in the social science literature as *transnationals* (Basch, Schiller, and Blanc 1994). They differ from other foreign-born persons in that both countries are "home" to them. In contrast, most foreign-born people consider either their native country or their new country to be "home." Transnationalism is a fairly recent phenomenon and the number of transnationals is growing due to the increasing accessibility of air travel and the technological advances in worldwide communications.

A foreign-born person's legal status can, and usually does, change over time. This is referred to as *adjustment of status*. After one year of residence, a refugee is eligible to become a permanent resident. Permanent residents (including those who were formerly refugees and immigrants) may be eligible to become U.S. citizens after five years of residence. Once they obtain U.S. citizenship, they are referred to as *naturalized citizens*. Undocumented aliens may sometimes become eligible to become legal permanent residents. For example, a law passed in 1986 allowed a large number of undocumented aliens to change to legal status.

Certain undocumented aliens and documented aliens who have a temporary visa are at times allowed to remain in the U.S. under special circumstances. Such circumstances include Temporary Protected Status and Deferred Enforced Departure. *Temporary Protected Status* may be granted to persons from a particular country if the United States has determined that conditions in that country pose a danger to personal safety due to ongoing armed conflict or an environmental disaster. *Deferred Enforced Departure* status may be granted to persons from a particular country if the United States has judged conditions in that country to be unstable or uncertain, or to have shown a pattern of denial of rights. In these circumstances, such persons are granted protection from deportation during the time that the status is in effect. The major legal definitions are summarized in table 1.2.

TABLE 1.2 DEFINITIONS OF MAJOR LEGAL CATEGORIES AND TERMS

ALIEN Any person not a citizen or national of the United States.

ASYLEE An alien in the United States or at a port of entry unable or unwilling to return to his or her country of nationality, or to seek the protection of that country because of persecution or a well-founded fear of persecution. Persecution or the fear thereof may be based on the alien's race, religion, nationality, membership in a particular social group, or political opinion. . . . Asylees are eligible to adjust to lawful permanent residence after one year of continuous presence in the United States.

BENEFICIARIES Those aliens who receive immigration benefits from petitions filed with the U.S. Immigration and Naturalization Service. Beneficiaries generally derive privilege or status as a result of their relationship . . . to a U.S. citizen or lawful permanent resident.

CUBAN / HAITIAN ENTRANT Status accorded (1) Cubans who entered the United States illegally between April 15 and October 10, 1980 and (2) Haitians who entered the country illegally before January 1, 1981. Cubans and Haitians meeting these criteria

TABLE 1.2 *(continued)*

who have continuously resided in the United States since before January 1, 1982, and who were known to the INS before that date, may adjust to permanent residence.

DEFERRED ENFORCED DEPARTURE (DED) A special temporary provision granted administratively to designated national groups physically present in the United States because the U.S. State Department judged conditions in the countries of origin to be "unstable" or "uncertain" or to have shown a pattern of "denial of rights." Aliens in DED status are temporarily allowed to remain in the United States until conditions in their home country change.

DEPORTABLE ALIEN Any alien illegally in the United States, regardless of whether the alien entered the country illegally or entered legally but subsequently violated the terms of his or her visa.

DERIVATIVE CITIZENSHIP Citizenship conveyed to children through the naturalization of parents or, under certain circumstances, to spouses of citizens at or during marriage or to foreign-born children adopted by U.S. citizen parents, provided certain conditions are met.

IMMIGRANT An alien admitted to the United States as a lawful permanent resident. Immigrants are those persons lawfully accorded the privilege of residing permanently in the United States.

LEGALIZED ALIENS Certain illegal aliens who were eligible to apply for temporary resident status under the legalization provision of the Immigration Reform and Control Act of 1986. To be eligible, aliens must have continuously resided in the United States in an unlawful status since January 1, 1982, not be excludable, and have entered the United States either (1) illegally before January 1, 1982 or (2) as temporary visitors before January 1, 1982, with their authorized stay expiring before that date or with the Government's knowledge of their unlawful status before that date. Legalization consists of two stages—temporary and then permanent residency. In order to adjust to permanent status aliens must have had continuous residence in the United States, be admissible as an immigrant, and demonstrate at least a minimal understanding and knowledge of the English language and U.S. history and government.

NATIONAL A person owing permanent allegiance to a state.

NONIMMIGRANT An alien who seeks temporary entry to the United States for a specific purpose. The alien must have a permanent residence abroad . . . and qualify for the nonimmigrant classification sought. The nonimmigrant classifications are foreign government officials, visitors for business and for pleasure, aliens in transit through the United States, treaty traders and investors, students, international representatives, temporary workers and trainees, representatives of foreign information media, exchange visitors, fiancé(e)s of U.S. citizens, intracompany transferees, and NATO offi-

TABLE 1.2 *(continued)*

cials. Most nonimmigrants can be accompanied or joined by spouses and unmarried minor (or dependent) children.

PAROLEE An alien, appearing to be inadmissible to the inspecting officer, allowed to enter the United States under emergency (humanitarian) conditions or when that alien's entry is determined to be in the public interest. Parole does not constitute a formal admission to the United States and confers temporary admission status only, requiring parolees to leave when the conditions supporting their parole cease to exist.

PRINCIPAL ALIEN The alien from whom another alien derives a privilege or status under immigration law or regulations (usually spouses or minor children).

REFUGEE Any person who is outside his or her country of nationality who is unable or unwilling to return to that country because of persecution or a well-founded fear of persecution. Persecution or the fear thereof may be based on the alien's race, religion, nationality, membership in a particular social group, or political opinion. Refugees are eligible to adjust to lawful permanent residence after one year of continuous presence in the United States.

TEMPORARY PROTECTED STATUS (TPS) Establishes a legislative base to the administrative practice of allowing a group of persons temporary refuge in the United States. Under a provision of the Immigration Act of 1990, the Attorney General may designate nationals of a foreign state to be eligible for TPS with a finding that conditions in that country pose a danger to personal safety due to ongoing armed conflict or an environmental disaster.

Source: United States Immigration and Naturalization Service, 1997.

As the preceding discussion suggests, definitions and categorizations of foreign-born persons are quite complex and can be confusing. As noted above, in addition to legal definitions, there are also social science definitions and self-definitions. These are often inconsistent with each other. For example, "transnational" is a social science term that does not have a legal counterpart; and persons in this circumstance may not use the term to refer to themselves. Another example, which is very common, is when a person defines him- or herself as a refugee, and may even be defined as a refugee under the international law, but is not recognized as a refugee by the United States. Depending on the circumstances, such a person may be admitted as a legal immigrant in some other category, or may be an undocumented alien subject to deportation. Another common occurrence is that naturalized citizens are often considered immigrants in the social science literature and also may think of themselves as immigrants, even though legally they are no longer immigrants but citizens. To further complicate matters, lay people and the popular media, such as newspapers, frequently refer to all foreign-born persons as immigrants without making distinctions among the various categories.

For the purposes of social work practice with foreign-born persons, it is important for the social worker to be familiar with social science, legal, and self-definitions. The social science definitions are important because they are often linked with psychological and social phenomena. For example, immigrants and refugees tend to have quite different outlooks, feelings, and experiences from each other, as shown in table 1.3, and as will be further discussed throughout the book. Thus, a person who is legally defined as an immigrant may in fact have the perspective of a refugee and would be defined as such from a social science standpoint. Therefore, knowledge of these social science definitions would be helpful to the social worker in understanding the client.

TABLE 1.3 CONTRASTS BETWEEN REFUGEES AND IMMIGRANTS

CHARACTERISTIC	REFUGEES	IMMIGRANTS
Motivation	Pushed out	Pulled out
Source	Political pressure	Own aspirations
Homeland	Rejected by it	Rejects it
Decision	Involuntary	Voluntary
Departure	Sudden	Planned
Context	Tumult, loss	Planful, hopeful
Visit home	Cannot	Can
Control	Loses it	Gains it
Time orientation	Past	Future
Social network	Other expatriates	Local natives
Expectations	Liberation of homeland	Work, graduation
Control of destiny	Others control	Self controls

Source: Westermeyer, 1990. Copyright © 1990, Hogg Foundation for Mental Health. Reprinted with Permission.

Legal definitions are important because a client's legal status determines eligibility for publicly funded social service assistance, and also influences help-seeking behavior. For example, refugees are eligible for far more publicly funded assistance than are immigrants. And undocumented aliens are very unlikely to seek help for fear of being reported and deported. Finally, it is important for the social worker to find out how a client defines him- or herself. For example, someone may be considered a refugee both legally and by social science definitions. However, one such person may think of the United States as "home" and consider him- or herself an American now, while another may think of the old country as "home" and base his or her identity on being from that country. The client's viewpoint in this regard has important implications for many aspects of his or her life, and such information can be gained only from the client. Thus, when beginning work with a foreign-born client, the social worker should determine the client's legal status as well as the social science definitions and the client's self-definition. A good starting point is to find out why the client came to the United States. There are several common causes of migration, as discussed below.

1.2 CAUSES OF INTERNATIONAL MIGRATION

MANY THEORIES HAVE BEEN DEVELOPED to explain why people migrate from one country to another. The classical theory of international migration is referred to as the *push-pull theory* (Lee 1966). It posits that people migrate in response to "push" factors in the country of origin and / or "pull" factors in the country of destination. "Push" factors are generally negative, such as poor economic conditions, lack of opportunity, discrimination, political oppression, and war. "Pull" factors are generally positive, such as better economic opportunity, political freedom, and favorable reception toward immigrants. Often, refugees are viewed as being "pushed" out of their countries by oppression and war, whereas immigrants are viewed as being "pulled" into the destination country by the prospect of economic improvement (Loescher 1993). However, migration can be a result of both "push" and "pull" factors.

Another element of the classical theory of international migration is *neoclassical economic theory* (Malmberg 1997). Neoclassical economic theory assumes that people's behavior is always based on rational and utilitarian decisions. This means that people contemplating international migration will weigh the relative economic advantages and disadvantages of staying versus moving, decide which option yields the most economic benefit, and act accordingly. This aspect of the classical theory of international migration has been widely criticized as being an inadequate explanation of migration (Malmberg 1997). One of its most obvious shortcomings is that it fails to explain why most people do not migrate (Faist 1997; Fischer, Martin, and Straubhaar 1997). The world consists of relatively few wealthy nations and far more relatively poorer nations. The rational model of behavior implies that most people in the poor nations will move to the wealthy nations. However, this does not occur. Only about 2 percent of the world's population are international migrants (Faist 1997; Fischer, Martin, and Straubhaar 1997). Therefore, there must be other explanations for why people stay in or leave their countries.

Consequently, more complex theories have recently been developed. The more comprehensive theories recognize that international migration is a result of factors operating at three levels: the *macro or structural level*, which entails political, economic, cultural, and geographic forces in the international arena, the country of origin, and the country of destination; the *meso or relational level*, which entails the relationships between potential movers and stayers in both the country of origin and the country of destination; and the *micro or individual level*, which entails personal characteristics and the individual's freedom to make autonomous decisions about moving or staying (Faist 1997; Malmberg 1997).

The macro level forces are those which are addressed by the push-pull theory. Political forces include elements such as political stability, war, persecution, human rights, emigration policies of the country of origin, immigration policies of the country of destination, and the availability of organized assistance for the move and settlement in the new country. Economic forces include elements such as living standards, jobs, working conditions, unemployment rates, and wages in the countries of origin and destination. Geographic forces include elements such as the distance between the two countries, environmental disasters, and climate. Cultural forces include elements such as the ethnic compositions, languages, and predominant religions of the two countries.

People who are considering moving to another country use a complex decisionmaking process to consider the advantages and disadvantages of these political, economic, and cultural factors. This decisionmaking process is influenced by the availability of information about the country of destination. People are more likely to migrate to countries that they already have a lot of accurate information about, or can easily obtain such information (Fischer, Martin, and Straubhaar 1997). Generally, people are more likely to migrate to a country that has more political freedom and stability, favorable immigration policies, better economic conditions, relative geographic proximity, and similar cultural elements to the country of origin. However, decisions about these macro factors are mediated by the meso and micro factors.

The meso level concerns an individual's family and social network, including ties to kinship groups, friends, neighbors, coworkers, acquaintances, and ethnic, religious, and political associations in both the sending and receiving countries (Faist 1997). Generally, the stronger these ties are in the country of origin, both in terms of actual social contact and emotional attachment, the less likely the person is to move. Thus, for example, single people generally are more likely to migrate than married people with children. On the other hand, sometimes family ties are a stimulus for moving, such as when refugee families leave in order to provide a better life for their children in another country.

People who already have family, friends, or acquaintances in the country of destination are more likely to go there than people who do not know anyone in the new country. This often results in what is called "chain migration," where more and more members of a family or social group migrate to a country, following those who came earlier (Faist 1997). Again, decisions about the relative importance of maintaining or disrupting family and social ties are mediated by the macro and micro forces.

The micro forces include personal characteristics such as age, ethnicity, religion, education, and financial assets. For example, older people are less likely to migrate than younger people because they have more and stronger ties in the country of origin, and because it would be more difficult for them to adapt to a new life. Ethnic and religious minorities within a country are more likely to migrate because they are more likely to have been persecuted. In terms of education, potential migrants must consider the economic opportunities available to them in the new country in relation to their educational level. In some cases, particularly refugees, highly educated people often are not able to transfer their education and skills into the job market in the new country, and must take lower-level jobs. The prospect of this might serve as a deterrent to migration. Financial assets are critical because money is required for the move. Thus, extremely poor people are less likely to migrate, unless they receive assistance from family members in the receiving country, or from humanitarian organizations. On the other hand, refugees usually must abandon most of their assets when leaving their country. This can serve as a deterrent to leaving.

Personality characteristics are also very influential in decisions to migrate. Among these characteristics are risk-taking level, time orientation, and emotional ties to geographic places. Moving to another country entails a major risk, since it means embarking on a largely unknown new life. Thus, people who do not like to take risks are less likely to migrate. An international move also means making an investment in the future. Thus, people who are more present-oriented are less likely to migrate (Fischer, Martin, and Straubhaar 1997). Some people have strong emotional ties to physical places such as their homes or neighborhoods, or may have a strong sense of identity with their country of origin. Such people are less likely to leave (Malmberg 1997).

Finally, whether people move or not also depends on whether they have the ability to make autonomous decisions about the move. For example, some countries do not allow most people to emigrate. This was particularly the case in Communist countries during the Cold War. Leaving in this case may entail a life-threatening border crossing. As another example, children do not have autonomous decisionmaking ability. The decision to migrate is made by their parents or other adults.

People who are contemplating moving to another country take into consideration all of these macro, meso, and micro factors in making their decisions. Within each level there are advantages and disadvantages. The individual must weigh these out both within and across the levels. Often, the factors within one level predominate over another level. In the case of refugees, the macro factors usually predominate. In this case, the necessity of escaping war or political oppression outweighs such considerations as disrupting family ties and losing all assets. This is why refugees are forced migrants, because in the absence of these negative macro-level factors, they probably would not have chosen to leave their countries. For economic migrants, the macro and micro levels may outweigh the meso level. That is, the prospect of improvement in living conditions combined with personal risk-taking initiative may outweigh the force of family ties. On the other hand, for the vast majority of people who choose not to leave their countries despite poor economic conditions, family and individual factors are probably the overriding consideration.

The decision to leave one's country of birth is a monumental, life-altering step. As can be seen, people's reasons for choosing to leave are not simple. Also as can be seen, leaving means making some sacrifices, such as leaving behind family, possessions, or a place in society. These losses continue to affect immigrants' and refugees' lives in the new country.

1.3 STAGES OF MIGRATION

THE PROCESS OF MOVING out of one country and settling in another consists of three major stages (Drachman 1992). These are *premigration and departure, transit,* and *resettlement.* Table 1.4 shows the critical variables, or issues, that characterize each stage.

The premigration and departure stage entails the decisionmaking process described above. It also entails losses, including loss of family and friends, and loss of a familiar environment. Generally, the losses are greater and the premigration and departure experience is more traumatic for refugees than for immigrants. Because refugees live in politically oppressive conditions or in the midst of war, they may have been subject to discrimination, ostracization, imprisonment, violence, rape, torture, and death of family members.

Refugees often leave under hurried, chaotic, and dangerous conditions. In many cases refugees flee in the midst of armed conflict. They may be victims of violence during this time or they may witness violence, rape, torture, or killing. In some cases refugees leave in mass movements, with hundreds or thousands of people. In some cases, as mentioned above, countries do not allow their citizens to leave. In these cases refugees have had to sneak across borders or onto boats to go out to sea. These borders are guarded by armed guards and therefore the refugees risk being shot, or captured and imprisoned. Because refugees flee under these chaotic or unauthorized conditions, they usually must leave almost all their possessions behind. Thus, they lose their homes and other assets. Further, refugees do not know when, if ever, they will be able to return to their countries. Thus, leaving behind family and friends is particularly painful since they know they may never see them again.

In contrast, immigrants typically are able to plan their departure well in advance and they leave under relatively calm conditions. The departure is not life-threatening. They do not have to abandon their possessions; they can take some assets, especially money, with them, and they retain owner-

TABLE 1.4 STAGE-OF-MIGRATION FRAMEWORK

STAGE OF MIGRATION	CRITICAL VARIABLES
Premigration and departure	Social, political, and economic factors
	Separation from family and friends
	Decisions regarding who leaves and who is left behind
	Act of leaving a familiar environment
	Life-threatening circumstances
	Experiences of violence
	Loss of significant others
Transit	Perilous or safe journey of short or long duration
	Refugee camp or detention center stay of short or long duration
	Act of awaiting a foreign country's decision regarding final relocation
	Immediate and final relocation or long wait before final relocation
	Loss of significant others
Resettlement	Cultural issues
	Reception from host country
	Opportunity structure of host country
	Discrepancy between expectations and reality
	Degree of cumulative stress throughout migration process

Source: Drachman, 1992. Copyright © 1992, National Assocation of Social Workers, Inc. Reprinted with permission.

ship of their property. Typically, there are no political barriers to prevent them from returning to their country, so they know they can return, even though it may not be for a long time. Nonetheless, the separation from home and family is painful.

Not all refugees and immigrants experience all of the losses and traumas that can occur during this stage. The experience differs for all individuals. However, some degree of loss occurs in all cases. The experiences during this stage influence the later stages of the migration process. In particular, these experiences affect people's health and mental health later. Thus, it is often important for the social worker to learn about a client's experiences in the country of origin and during the departure.

The transit stage involves the actual physical move from one country to another. Again, this experience is usually more traumatic for refugees than immigrants. The experience also differs between legal and illegal immigrants. For legal immigrants to the United States, the transit usually entails arrival by plane or by car at the border. It is typically not traumatic. However, for refugees, the transit may be dangerous or life-threatening. Refugees may be passing through areas of armed conflict and may be subject to or witness the same atrocities as in the premigration and departure stage. They may undertake a lengthy journey on foot during which they may face starvation, dehydration, hypothermia, or other physical ailments. Many refugees leave by boat. Often these boats are in poor condition and are overloaded. Sinking, drowning, and illness or death due to sun exposure are not uncommon. In many cases refugees are placed in refugee camps in neighboring countries before they are sent to a permanent home in a third country such as the United States. These camps usually consist of tent cities. They are often overcrowded and have poor sanitary conditions. Diseases and violence in the camps are not uncommon. Refugees may remain in such camps for years before obtaining permission to enter the United States, or being returned to their country of origin. Refugees who arrive directly in the United States requesting asylum may be placed in a detention center while their case is decided. In some cases, these individuals have remained in the detention center for months or years.

Immigrants who enter the United States illegally often experience a dangerous transit. The most common illegal point of entry is at the Mexican border. Frequently, illegal immigrants hire a smuggler, or "coyote" to get them across the border. These smugglers charge very large amounts of money. Sometimes they assault the immigrants and steal their money without leading them across the border. Other times they take the immigrants only to the border and not across. At other times, the immigrants are crowded and hidden in trucks, where they sometimes die of heat and suffocation. Some immigrants try to cross over the Rio Grande River and may drown. Smuggling also occurs by boat from Cuba and Haiti into Florida. These illegal immigrants are subject to the same dangerous conditions such as assault, theft, and drowning.

Again, not all legal immigrants, refugees, and illegal immigrants have the same transit experiences. And again, trauma experienced during the transit can affect the person's adaptation in the later stage, resettlement.

Resettlement is the last stage of the migration process. This stage can be seen as lasting throughout the people's stay in the new country, which may be the rest of their lives. This is the stage during which social workers in the United States will encounter and work with immigrants and refugees. Therefore, part II of this book is devoted to the issues and problems that immigrants and refugees encounter during this stage. Such issues include adaptation to the cultural norms of the new country; health and mental health problems; language, education, and employment issues; changing family dynamics; and relations between the newcomers and established residents.

1.4 SCOPE OF IMMIGRANT AND REFUGEE POPULATIONS

WORLDWIDE, approximately 2 percent of the population are immigrants and refugees (Faist 1997; Fischer, Martin, and Straubhaar 1997). This is approximately 120 million people. Of these, the number of refugees worldwide has been about 13 million to 18 million each year during the past ten years (U.S. Committee for Refugees 1998). In 1997, the figure was 13.6 million. This figure does not include those refugees who have been permanently resettled in another country.

Some countries are traditionally thought of as immigrant countries because they have accepted relatively large numbers of immigrants throughout their history, and continue to do so. These countries include the United States, Canada, Australia, and Israel. However, all nations have some proportion of immigrants and refugees among their populations. In many countries, this proportion is increasing, and consequently, so is the need to address the multitude of issues that arise for both the immigrants and the native populations.

In the United States, there were more than 28 million foreign-born persons in 2000 (U.S. Bureau of the Census 2001). This represents approximately 10 percent of the U.S. population. The number of foreign-born people in the U.S. as a percentage of the total population has varied during the past century, ranging from a high of 14.8 in 1910 to a low of 4.7 in 1970 (U.S. Immigration and Naturalization Service 1998). Thus, the current 10 percent figure is around the middle of this historical range.

Table 1.5 shows the world regions of birth of the current population of foreign-born people, as well as the distributions of naturalized citizens, noncitizens, and years of entry into the U.S. As seen in the table, the largest population of foreign-born people in the United States is from Latin America. The majority of people from Latin America are from Mexico (U.S. Bureau of the Census 2001). About two-thirds of all foreign-born people are not U.S. citizens. Further, more than 80 percent of foreign-born people entered the U.S. since 1970, and nearly 40 percent entered since 1990. As seen in the table, the longer that people have been in the United States, the greater the proportion of naturalized citizens.

The foreign-born population includes legal immigrants, refugees, undocumented aliens, and nonimmigrants such as students and temporary workers. Tables 1.6 to 1.10 show the major countries of origin of people in each of these categories. As can be seen in table 1.6, the countries of origin of immigrants admitted between 1981 and 1996 closely reflect the world regions of birth of the foreign-born population as a whole (table 1.5). How-

TABLE 1.5 WORLD REGION OF BIRTH AND YEAR OF ENTRY INTO THE U.S. OF THE FOREIGN BORN, BY CITIZENSHIP STATUS, 2000

	TOTAL FOREIGN-BORN		NATURALIZED CITIZEN		NOT U.S. CITIZEN	
	NUMBER	PERCENT	NUMBER	PERCENT	NUMBER	PERCENT
REGION OF ORIGIN						
All regions	28,379,000	100.0	10,622,000	100.0	17,758,000	100.0
Europe	4,355,000	15.3	2,264,000	21.3	2,090,000	11.8
Asia	7,246,000	25.5	3,415,000	32.2	3,831,000	21.6
Latin America	14,477,000	51.0	4,098,000	38.6	10,379,000	58.4
Other Areas	2,301,000	8.1	844,000	7.9	1,457,000	8.2
CAME TO THE UNITED STATES						
All years of entry	28,379,000	100.0	10,622,000	100.0	17,758,000	100.0
Before 1970	4,547,000	16.0	3,655,000	34.4	892,000	5.0
1970–1979	4,605,000	16.2	2,851,000	26.8	1,754,000	9.9
1980–1989	8,022,000	28.3	3,118,000	29.4	4,904,000	27.6
Since 1990	11,206,000	39.5	997,000	9.4	10,209,000	57.5

Source: U.S. Bureau of the Census, 2001.

ever, as seen in table 1.7, refugees come from very different countries than do immigrants. Of the top ten countries of refugee applicants approved between 1981 and 1996, four are countries of the former Communist Soviet Union and Soviet Bloc (Romania, Poland, Bosnia-Herzegovina); three are countries in Communist Southeast Asia (Vietnam, Cambodia, Laos); two are former Communist countries in Africa (Ethiopia) and Asia (Afghanistan); and one is a totalitarian country in Asia (Iran). This is consistent with the definition of refugees as people who flee politically oppressive countries.

TABLE 1.6 IMMIGRATION, 1981–1996: TOP TEN COUNTRIES OF BIRTH

COUNTRY	NUMBER
All countries	13,484,275
Mexico	3,304,682
Philippines	843,741
Vietnam	719,239
China	539,267
Dominican Republic	509,902
India	498,309
Korea	453,018
El Salvador	362,225
Jamaica	323,625
Cuba	254,193

Source: U.S. Immigration and Naturalization Service, 1998.

TABLE 1.7 REFUGEES, 1981–1996: TOP TEN COUNTRIES OF APPLICANTS APPROVED

COUNTRY	NUMBER
All countries	1,412,573
Vietnam	420,178
Soviet Union	413,862
Laos	147,530
Cambodia	109,914

COUNTRY	NUMBER
Iran	41,276
Romania	38,567
Poland	37,996
Bosnia-Herzegovina	35,172
Ethiopia	34,138
Afghanistan	30,952

Source: U.S. Immigration and Naturalization Service, 1998.

Since illegal immigrants are undocumented, then by definition there are no accurate statistics on them. Therefore, the size of this population can only be estimated. Table 1.8 indicates that there are estimated to be a total of 5 million illegal aliens in the United States. Thus, the illegal alien population comprises about one-fifth of the total foreign-born population. More than half of the illegal aliens are from Mexico. Of the remaining top nine countries, six are in Central America or the Caribbean.

TABLE 1.8 ILLEGAL ALIEN POPULATION, 1996: TOP TEN COUNTRIES OF BIRTH (ESTIMATES)

COUNTRY	NUMBER
All countries	5,000,000
Mexico	2,700,000
El Salvador	335,000
Guatemala	165,000
Canada	120,000
Haiti	105,000
Philippines	95,000
Honduras	90,000
Bahamas	70,000
Nicaragua	70,000
Poland	70,000

Source: U.S. Immigration and Naturalization Service, 1998.

Tables 1.9 and 1.10 show the numbers of two classes of nonimmigrants—temporary workers and students. Together, these two groups amount to more than 1 million people. It can be seen that the top ten countries for both of these groups are quite similar. Additionally, these countries are quite different from the legal immigrant, refugee, and illegal immigrant countries.

TABLE 1.9 TEMPORARY WORKERS, 1996: TOP TEN COUNTRIES OF CITIZENSHIP

COUNTRY	NUMBER
All countries	610,359
United Kingdom	74,645
Canada	47,915
Japan	45,904
Germany	43,149
India	36,999
Mexico	35,949
France	29,599
China	20,581
Russia	16,860
Brazil	14,847

Source: U.S. Immigration and Naturalization Service, 1998.

TABLE 1.10 STUDENTS, 1996: TOP TEN COUNTRIES OF CITIZENSHIP

COUNTRY	NUMBER
All Countries	426,903
Japan	66,699
Korea	45,413
China	39,225
India	17,354
Germany	13,191
Thailand	12,259

COUNTRY	NUMBER
Brazil	11,286
Mexico	10,887
Indonesia	10,579
United Kingdom	10,224

Source: U.S. Immigration and Naturalization Service, 1998.

The number of legal immigrants and refugees admitted into the United States varies from year to year, based on admissions limits set by Congress and the President. Between 1995 and 1998, the average number of legal immigrants admitted annually was approximately 774,000. In 1998, 660,477 immigrants were admitted as legal permanent residents. Of these, 357,037 became legal permanent residents immediately upon entry into the United States during the year. The remaining 303,440 had already been living in the U.S. for an average of three years as nonpermanent residents, and they adjusted their status to permanent residents. These included former undocumented aliens, refugees, and asylees (INS 1999). Table 1.11 shows the major countries of the immigrants admitted in 1998. It can be seen that these are generally the same as the top countries for the 1981–1996 period shown in table 1.6.

TABLE 1.11 IMMIGRANTS ADMITTED, 1998: TOP TEN COUNTRIES OF BIRTH

COUNTRY	NUMBER
All countries	660,477
Mexico	131,575
China	36,884
India	36,482
Philippines	34,466
Dominican Republic	20,387
Vietnam	17,649
Cuba	17,375
Jamaica	15,146

COUNTRY	NUMBER
El Salvador	14,590
Korea	14,268

Source: U.S. Immigration and Naturalization Service, 1999.

The average number of refugees admitted annually between 1995 and 2000 was 80,000. The total admitted in 2000 was 72,515. The major countries of origin of refugees admitted in 2000 are shown in table 1.12. As seen, these countries differ quite a bit from the top countries of admitted refugees for the period 1981–1996 (table 1.7). Of the top ten countries in 2000, three are African countries that did not appear on the list for 1981–1996. Additionally, Bosnia is the top country for 2000, overtaking Vietnam and the former Soviet Union. These figures reflect changing political conditions around the world. As political situations in various countries lead to refugee outflows, the population of refugees admitted into the U.S. changes.

TABLE 1.12 REFUGEES ADMITTED, 2000: TOP TEN COUNTRIES OF NATIONALITY

COUNTRY	NUMBER
All countries	72,515
Bosnia	19,027
Former Soviet Union	14,542
Somalia	6,026
Iran	5,100
Vietnam	3,845
Sudan	3,833
Cuba	3,184
Iraq	3,152
Croatia	2,995
Liberia	2,613

Source: U.S. Committee for Refugees, 2000.

Immigrants and refugees tend to be concentrated in certain states. Tables 1.13 to 1.16 show the top ten states of residence of the foreign-born as a whole, legal permanent residents, refugees, and illegal aliens. As can be seen, the top states are generally the same for all categories of immigrants and refugees, with California, New York, Texas, and Florida being the top four states in all cases. Immigrants and refugees also tend to live in urban areas rather than rural areas. Table 1.17 shows the top ten metropolitan areas of intended residence of immigrants admitted in 1998. These ten metropolitan areas account for almost half of all immigrant residents.

In summary, there are currently more than 28 million foreign-born people in the U.S. They come from a wide variety of countries. The major countries vary markedly depending on the category of foreign-born person. Over the past several years, immigrants have been admitted as legal permanent residents at the rate of approximately 774,000 annually, and refugees have been admitted at the rate of approximately 80,000 annually. Immigrants and refugee populations are concentrated in major metropolitan areas in several states.

TABLE 1.13 FOREIGN-BORN, 1990 CENSUS: TOP TEN STATES OF RESIDENCE

STATE	NUMBER
All states	19,767,316
California	6,458,825
New York	2,851,861
Florida	1,662,601
Texas	1,524,436
New Jersey	966,610
Illinois	952,272
Massachusetts	573,733
Pennsylvania	369,316
Michigan	355,393
Washington	322,144

Source: U.S. Immigration and Naturalization Service, 1998.

TABLE 1.14 LEGAL PERMANENT RESIDENTS, 1996: TOP TEN STATES (ESTIMATES)

STATE	NUMBER
All states	10,525,000
California	3,717,000
New York	1,498,000
Texas	825,000
Florida	790,000
New Jersey	462,000
Illinois	457,000
Massachusetts	310,000
Virginia	183,000
Maryland	178,000
Washington	174,000

Source: U.S. Immigration and Naturalization Service, 1996.

TABLE 1.15 REFUGEES AND ASYLEES GRANTED PERMANENT RESIDENCE, 1996: TOP TEN STATES

STATE	NUMBER
All states	128,565
New York	24,625
Florida	23,535
California	20,233
Texas	6,415
Washington	5,271
Illinois	5,040
Minnesota	3,787
New Jersey	3,665
Massachusetts	3,445
Michigan	3,001

Source: U.S. Immigration and Naturalization Service, 1998.

TABLE 1.16 ILLEGAL ALIEN POPULATION, 1996: TOP TEN STATES (ESTIMATES)

STATE	NUMBER
All states	5,000,000
California	2,000,000
Texas	700,000
New York	540,000
Florida	350,000
Illinois	290,000
New Jersey	135,000
Arizona	115,000
Massachusetts	85,000
Virginia	55,000
Washington	52,000

Source: U.S. Immigration and Naturalization Service, 1998.

TABLE 1.17 IMMIGRANTS ADMITTED, 1998: TOP TEN METROPOLITAN AREAS OF INTENDED RESIDENCE

METROPOLITAN AREA	NUMBER
All metropolitan areas	660,477
New York, NY	82,175
Los Angeles, CA	59,598
Chicago, IL	30,355
Miami, FL	28,853
Washington, DC	24,032
San Francisco, CA	14,540
Oakland, CA	13,437
Houston, TX	13,183
Boston, MA	12,725
San Jose, CA	12,656

Source: U.S. Immigration and Naturalization Service, 1999.

1.5 DEMOGRAPHIC AND SOCIOECONOMIC CHARACTERISTICS OF IMMIGRANTS AND REFUGEES

TABLE 1.18 SHOWS some basic demographic characteristics of foreign-born persons compared to the native-born U.S. population. It also breaks down the foreign-born by naturalized citizens and noncitizens. As can be seen, the foreign-born population has a smaller proportion of children and a larger proportion of working-age adults (age 18–64) compared to the native-born population. Among the foreign-born, naturalized citizens have a larger proportion of older adults (age 45 and over), whereas noncitizens have a larger proportion of younger adults (ages 20–34). This is consistent with the fact that naturalization rates increase with length of time in the U.S. and consequently, with age. Table 1.18 also shows that the proportions of men and women are approximately equal across all the groups.

TABLE 1.18 AGE AND GENDER OF NATIVE-BORN AND FOREIGN-BORN POPULATION, 2000 (IN PERCENT)

	NATIVE-BORN CITIZEN	ALL FOREIGN-BORN	NATURALIZED CITIZEN	NONCITIZEN
Age (years)				
Under 5	7.9	1.0	0.5	1.3
5-14	15.8	6.0	1.9	8.6
15-19	7.5	5.7	2.0	7.9
20-24	6.5	8.3	3.4	11.3
25-29	6.3	10.2	5.7	12.9
30-34	6.6	11.4	8.3	13.3
35-44	15.7	22.0	22.9	21.4
45-64	21.7	24.3	34.7	18.1
65 and over	11.9	11.0	20.6	5.2
Percent male	48.7	50.0	47.8	51.4

Source: U.S. Bureau of the Census, 2001.

Table 1.19 shows some demographic characteristics broken down by world region of birth. As can be seen, there is considerable variation across regions in regard to median age and household size. Overall, the foreign-born are slightly older on average than the native-born. The median age is lowest for people from Latin American countries, and highest for people from European countries. This is related to the length of time these groups have been in the U.S. (Heer 1996). Most Latin Americans arrived in the U.S. more recently than most Europeans, so they are younger on average. In regard to household size, in general the foreign-born have a higher proportion of large households (five or more persons) than the native-born. People from Latin American and Asian countries have high proportions of large households, whereas people from Europe have a small proportion.

TABLE 1.19 DEMOGRAPHIC CHARACTERISTICS OF THE NATIVE POPULATION AND FOREIGN-BORN POPULATION BY WORLD REGION OF BIRTH, 2000

NATIVITY AND REGION OF BIRTH	MEDIAN AGE	PERCENT MALE	PERCENT OF HOUSEHOLDS WITH FIVE OR MORE PERSONS
Native-born	34.5	48.7	9.1
Foreign-born	38.1	50.0	20.9
Europe	50.0	48.6	6.6
Asia	39.2	47.8	17.4
Latin America	35.3	50.9	29.8
Other Areas	38.5	54.1	13.7

Source: U.S. Bureau of the Census, 2001.

Table 1.20 shows some socioeconomic characteristics of the native-born and foreign-born. Again, the foreign-born are further broken down into naturalized citizens and noncitizens. It can be seen that overall, the foreign-born population has a greater proportion of people with less than a high school education, and a smaller proportion of high school graduates, compared to the native-born population. The proportions of college graduates

TABLE 1.20 SOCIOECONOMIC CHARACTERISTICS OF NATIVE-BORN AND FOREIGN-BORN POPULATION, 2000 (IN PERCENT)

	NATIVE-BORN CITIZEN	ALL FOREIGN-BORN	NATURALIZED CITIZEN	NONCITIZEN
EDUCATIONAL ATTAINMENT (PERSONS 25 AND OVER)				
Not a high school graduate	13.4	33.0	23.8	40.2
HS graduate or some college	61.0	41.2	45.5	37.8
Bachelor's degree	17.2	16.1	18.8	14.1
Graduate/professional degree	8.4	9.7	11.9	7.9
EMPLOYMENT				
Percent of labor force unemployed	4.3	4.9	3.3	5.9
EARNINGS OF YEAR-ROUND FULL-TIME WORKERS				
$1-$9,999 or loss	4.2	5.7	3.5	7.3
$10,000-$19,999	17.1	30.6	19.7	38.5
$20,000-$34,999	32.8	30.0	31.1	29.2
$35,000-$49,999	21.2	14.6	19.5	11.0
$50,000 or more	24.6	19.1	26.2	14.0
POVERTY STATUS				
Below poverty	11.2	16.8	9.1	21.3
HOME OWNERSHIP				
Own home	69.5	48.8	66.5	33.5

Source: U.S. Bureau of the Census, 2001.

and people with postgraduate degrees are approximately the same between the native-born and foreign-born. However, among the foreign-born, naturalized citizens have a much higher educational level on average than noncitizens. Nearly half of noncitizens are not high school graduates, whereas almost one-third of naturalized citizens have a bachelor's or graduate degree. In fact, among naturalized citizens, the proportion of people with a bachelor's or graduate degree is higher than among the native-born population.

Overall, the foreign-born have a higher unemployment rate, lower earnings, a higher poverty rate, and a lower rate of home ownership, compared to the native-born. Again, substantial differences arise between naturalized citizens and noncitizens. The unemployment rate of noncitizens is almost twice as high as that of naturalized citizens, whose rate is actually lower than that of the native-born. Nearly one-half of noncitizens have earnings below $20,000 compared to about one-fourth of naturalized citizens. At the highest income level, over $50,000, the proportion of naturalized citizens exceeds that of the native-born. Conversely, the poverty level among naturalized citizens is lower than among the native-born, but the poverty level of noncitizens is much higher; nearly one-fourth of noncitizens live below the poverty level. The rate of home ownership among naturalized citizens is similar to that of the native born, but the rate among noncitizens is only about half that of the other groups.

Table 1.21 shows the socioeconomic data broken down by world region of birth. As can be seen, educational attainment, unemployment rates, family income, and poverty rates vary substantially across the different regions. In general, socioeconomic status is lower for people from Latin America and higher for people from Europe and Asia.

Thus, the socioeconomic data show that overall the foreign-born are less educated and have lower economic status than the native born. However, this generalization can be misleading since there are substantial differences between the people from different countries, and between naturalized citizens and noncitizens. Naturalized citizens have a much higher educational level and much better economic status than noncitizens, in some cases exceeding the native-born. Much of these differences are likely due to the fact

TABLE 1.21 SOCIOECONOMIC CHARACTERISTICS OF THE NATIVE POPULATION AND FOREIGN-BORN POPULATION BY WORLD REGION OF BIRTH, 2000

NATIVITY AND REGION OF BIRTH	H.S. GRAD OR HIGHER*	BACHELOR'S DEGREE OR HIGHER*	PERCENT OF LABOR FORCE UNEMPLOYED	MEDIAN FAMILY INCOME	PERCENT OF PERSONS IN POVERTY
Native-born	86.6	25.6	4.3	$51,179	11.2
Foreign-born	67.0	25.8	4.9	$39,897	16.8
Europe	81.3	32.9	2.3	$50,948	9.3
Asia	83.8	44.9	3.5	$59,479	12.8
Latin America	49.6	11.2	6.6	$31,274	21.9
Other Areas	86.6	36.8	2.9	$48,440	11.0

*Persons age 25 and over.

Source: U.S. Bureau of the Census 2001.

that on average, naturalized citizens have been in the U.S. longer than noncitizens. It is also possible that people who are more highly educated and better off economically are more likely to become citizens.

However, the majority of foreign-born people in the U.S. have not become naturalized citizens. Naturalization entails several requirements, including a minimum of five years of residence in the U.S. (three years in some cases). However, many immigrants and refugees who are eligible for naturalization choose not to do so. It is estimated that of the 10.5 million legal permanent residents residing in the U.S. in 1996, 5.8 million were eligible for naturalization, but had not done so. Additionally, approximately 687,000 children were estimated to be eligible to derive their citizenship through their parents' naturalization (U.S. Immigration and Naturalization Service 1996). The rates of naturalization differ for immigrants from different countries. The highest and lowest rates of naturalization for the cohort of immigrants admitted in 1977 and tracked through 1995 are shown in table 1.22. These figures show that generally, immigrants from Asia (with the exception of Japan) are most likely to naturalize, whereas immigrants from Western Europe, Australia, Japan, and Canada are least likely to do so.

TABLE 1.22 HIGHEST AND LOWEST PERCENT NATURALIZED: 1977 IMMIGRANT COHORT, THROUGH 1995

COUNTRY	PERCENT
Highest	
Taiwan	78.1
Hong Kong	76.4
Macau	73.4
Vietnam	70.2
Bangladesh	68.9
Tanzania	68.4
Burma	68.0
Romania	67.7
Egypt	67.2
China	65.5
Average (all countries)	45.9
Lowest	
Australia	8.9
Norway	11.3
Sweden	13.6
Denmark	15.2
Japan	16.7
Germany	16.8
Finland	17.3
Austria	17.8
Canada	18.1
Netherlands	18.4

Source: U.S. Immigration and Naturalization Service, 1998.

It is important to remember that there are substantial differences in demographic and socioeconomic characteristics among individual immigrants and refugees. Thus, although the data presented here can be helpful for an overall perspective, it is important for social work practitioners to obtain information about the demographic, educational, and economic status of each individual client.

1.6 PROGRAM AND SERVICE UTILIZATION PATTERNS OF IMMIGRANTS AND REFUGEES

IN GENERAL, foreign-born people tend to have a higher utilization rate of public welfare benefits compared to native-born people. Again, however, these rates vary substantially based on the category of immigrant or refugee. Table 1.23 shows the national utilization rates of welfare (including Temporary Assistance to Needy Families, Supplemental Security Income [SSI], and General Assistance [GA]), food stamps, and Medicaid. It can be seen that for all these public benefits, the utilization rates of naturalized citizens are not substantially different from those of native-born citizens. The rates are substantially higher for noncitizens, and a great deal higher for refugees. This is due in large part to the fact that refugees have far more eligibility for these and other benefits than do other immigrant groups, due to the humanitarian concerns pertaining to refugees. (Specific eligibility criteria for all groups are discussed in the next chapter.) Overall, the rates of public benefit utilization by noncitizens are higher because noncitizen households are more likely to be below the poverty level and to contain children, which are two major eligibility criteria for receiving these benefits (Fix and Passel 1999).

In regard to utilization of health and mental health services, research has consistently shown that in general, foreign-born people underutilize these services compared to the native-born population (Chung and Lin 1994; Ell and Castañeda 1998; Tran, Dhooper, and McInnis-Dittrich 1997; Yamashiro and Matsuoka 1997). Again, however, utilization rates vary depending on people's characteristics, such as health and mental health status, age, gender, education, English speaking ability, length of time in the U.S., financial status, household composition, and legal status (Chung and Lin 1994; Drachman 1995; Ell and Castañeda 1998; Jang, Lee, and Woo 1998; LeClere, Jensen, and Biddlecom 1994; Portes, Kyle, and Eaton 1992; Riedel 1998; Tran, Dhooper, and McInnis-Dittrich 1997). Foreign-born people who have poorer health and mental health, are elderly, female, or live alone, are more likely to utilize services. On the other hand, people who have lower education, lower

English ability, have been in the U.S. a shorter period of time, are poor, or are undocumented aliens, are less likely to utilize services.

TABLE 1.23 PERCENT OF HOUSEHOLDS RECEIVING PUBLIC BENEFITS, BY CITIZENSHIP AND IMMIGRATION STATUS OF HOUSEHOLD HEAD, 1997

	NATIVE-BORN CITIZEN	ALL FOREIGN-BORN	NATURALIZED CITIZEN	REFUGEE	NONCITIZEN*
Benefit			*Percent*		
Welfare	6.6	9.2	6.9	24.5	9.0
Food Stamps	6.8	9.3	5.4	22.1	10.8
Medicaid	12.5	18.7	13.6	35.8	20.8

*Excludes refugees and nonimmigrants

Source: Fix and Passel, 1999.

In addition to these personal characteristics, structural characteristics are also important in determining utilization of health and mental health services. (Chung and Lin 1994; Ell and Castañeda 1998; Portes, Kyle, and Eaton 1992; LeClere, Jensen, and Biddlecom 1994; Riedel 1998; Tran, Dhooper, and McInnis-Dittrich 1997; Yamashiro and Matsuoka 1998). These include factors such as health beliefs and practices in the country of origin, the availability of informal health and mental health services, the accessibility and cost of formal services, and the cultural appropriateness of service delivery.

Thus, in general, foreign-born people utilize more public welfare benefits but less health and mental health services than the native-born population. Again, however, such a general statement can be misleading since utilization rates vary greatly depending on numerous factors. Much of social work practice with immigrants and refugees is aimed at decreasing their welfare usage, or increasing their access to health and mental health services. Strategies pertaining to these goals are addressed in part II of this book.

1.7 HISTORY AND CHARACTERISTICS OF MAJOR IMMIGRANT AND REFUGEE GROUPS IN THE UNITED STATES

THE FOLLOWING DISCUSSION presents some very brief descriptions of the major refugee and immigrant groups in the United States. These descriptions are introductory only. The various nationalities will be referred to again throughout the remainder of the book. Further, not all of the many nationalities can be addressed here. There are extensive bodies of literature pertaining to each of these groups. Social workers should consult these sources to learn more about their clients from specific countries.

When considering a group of people from a particular country, it is important to beware of stereotyping, or not viewing people as individuals. It is important to remember that some experiences are common to all immigrants and refugees, some are unique to people from particular countries, and some are unique to individuals. Thus, the following background information can be helpful as a general guideline, but the best sources of information are usually clients themselves.

1.7.1 LATIN AMERICAN COUNTRIES

IMMIGRANTS AND REFUGEES from Latin America share some ethnic, cultural, and demographic commonalities. Most Latin American immigrants and refugees are descended from Spanish colonizers and the native Indians of the Americas. Culturally, Latin Americans place a high value on family and child rearing. Family obligations are a strong force (Harper and Lantz 1996). There is high respect for the elderly, and youth are placed in a lower position of authority than older family members. Families tend to be male-dominated, and women generally assume the caregiving responsibilities. Extended families serve as a major social support and informal helping system. Interpersonal exchanges are often characterized by free emotional expression of warmth, and by physical affection. Expressions of anger, particularly toward family members in authority, are discouraged (Harper and Lantz 1996). The predominant religion is Roman Catholicism.

The demographic data presented earlier indicate that on average, Latin American immigrants and refugees have a low educational level, low income, large households, and a high poverty rate. All of these risk factors highlight a need for social work intervention with this population.

MEXICANS As noted earlier, people from Mexico constitute the largest proportion of foreign-born people in the U.S., both legal and illegal. Mexicans have a long history in the United States. Much of the southwestern United States was previously Mexican territory before being conquered by the United States. Thus, the people who lived in that territory became "foreigners in their own land" (Portes and Rumbaut 1990, p. 225). Later, rapid economic growth in the U.S. led to active recruitment of Mexicans to come north to work in agriculture and the railroads. "Mexican immigration thus originated in deliberate recruitment by [United States] interests and was not a spontaneous movement" (Portes and Rumbaut 1990, p. 225). Immigration from Mexico continues due both to economic motivations and extended family networks.

Because of the long history of Mexicans in the U.S., there is a substantial population of U.S.-born Mexican-Americans, in addition to the foreign-born population. Consequently, many Mexican immigrants have family ties that extend across both Mexico and the U.S. Mexican migration to the U.S. is strongly influenced by the presence of family members who migrated previously (Portes and Rumbaut 1990). A substantial proportion of Mexican migrants are seasonal workers, who travel back and forth between Mexico and the U.S. The vast majority of Mexican immigrants reside in five southwestern states: Arizona, California, Colorado, New Mexico, and Texas.

CENTRAL AMERICANS El Salvador, Guatemala, Nicaragua, and Honduras are among the top sources of undocumented aliens in the U.S. In general, these people were forced to leave their countries due to civil wars. From a social science definition and an international legal perspective, most of these people would be recognized as refugees; however, they have not been granted refugee status by the U.S. (Portes and Rumbaut 1990). El Salvador endured a civil war from 1980 to 1992 (Bowen, et al. 1992; U.S. Committee for Refugees 1998). During this time there were attacks against civilians, the use of psychological and physical repression, "disappearances," killings, rapes, tortures, and other human rights abuses (Bowen, et al. 1992).

Even though the war officially ended in 1992, political repression and terrorism have continued. In Guatemala, a 36-year civil war ended in 1997. The war resulted in hundreds of thousands of people dead, "disappeared," widowed, and orphaned (U.S. Committee for Refugees 1998). Atrocities similar to those in El Salvador were widespread (Light 1992). Many Guatemalan refugees are Mayan Indians, and thus they differ in culture, language, and background from other Latin Americans. Nicaragua was engaged in a civil war between the Sandinistas and the Contras from the late 1970s until the early 1990s. And Honduras was often embroiled in the conflicts in neighboring El Salvador and Nicaragua.

These political upheavals caused many people to flee these countries. Because these refugees were not recognized by the U.S., they entered the country illegally. In 1997, the Nicaraguan and Central American Relief Act was passed, allowing some of these illegal aliens to adjust to lawful status (U.S. Committee for Refugees 1998). In working with people from Central America, social workers should keep in mind the traumas they may have experienced in their countries of origin and as illegal aliens, and how these might continue to affect them.

1.7.2 CARIBBEAN COUNTRIES

FOUR CARIBBEAN COUNTRIES are major sources of immigrants and refugees in the U.S.: Cuba, the Dominican Republic, Jamaica, and Haiti. These countries vary substantially in population, language, and culture, due to their varied colonial histories: Cuba and the Dominican Republic were Spanish colonies, Jamaica was a British colony, and Haiti was a French colony. All of them are now independent nations. The reasons for emigration from these countries also vary substantially.

CUBANS Although there were Cuban communities in the United States in the nineteenth century, massive migration of Cubans into the U.S began in 1959, following the revolutionary overthrow of the government by Communist Fidel Castro. Castro instituted a repressive political regime that still persists. As in other Communist countries, human rights such as freedom of speech, freedom of the press, free elections, and freedom to leave the country are severely violated in Cuba. Perceived anti-government activities are punished by imprisonment.

Thus, people from Cuba are generally considered to be refugees. Because of the United States' historical preference to grant refugee status to people fleeing Communist regimes, Cubans were generally granted blanket asylum during the Cold War era. However, that changed in the mid-1990s when new procedures were implemented that required Cuban asylum-seekers to establish on a case-by-case basis that they had a well-founded fear of persecution. Consequently, many Cubans who are intercepted at sea on their way to the U.S. are now returned to Cuba (U.S. Committee for Refugees 1998). Currently, the U.S. and Cuba have a migration agreement according to which Cuba is to prevent its citizens from attempting to leave by boat or raft, and in return, the U.S. is to admit at least 20,000 Cubans yearly directly from Cuba (U.S. Committee for Refugees 1998).

Many Cubans continue to attempt to leave by sea. In the mid-1990s, makeshift rafts were common, and today the most common method of escape is by paying smugglers who transport people in high-powered boats. These people endure dangerous conditions at sea, and risk death by sun exposure or drowning. If they reach the U.S., they are placed in detention pending a decision to admit them into the U.S. or to return them to Cuba (U.S. Committee for Refugees 1998). Although in general, Cubans are refugees by international and social science definitions, their legal status upon admission to the U.S. varies—they may be admitted as refugees, immigrants, or parolees (U.S. Committee for Refugees 1998; U.S. Department of State 1998a).

Cubans have left their country in distinct historical waves. The earliest arrivals in the early 1960s were the country's elite. Generally, they were well-educated professionals from the upper class. Subsequent waves generally consisted of less-educated, lower-class members of the society (Queralt 1984). In 1980, an extremely large wave of Cubans left the port of Mariel by boat. They became known as "boat people" or "Marielitos." This wave consisted of a disproportionately large number of people who were mentally ill, felons, disabled, or uneducated (Harper and Lantz 1996; Queralt 1984).

Ethnically, most Cubans are of Spanish descent, with a minority of African descent. Unlike most Latin Americans, Cubans do not have an Indian heritage. Cuban cultural values and traits are similar to those of Latin Americans, as described above. The dominant religion is Catholicism, but religious beliefs are also influenced by African-based beliefs, resulting in a combined religion called "santeria," which is used by some Cubans to deal with emotional, spiritual, and personal problems (Queralt 1984). Cuban refugees have a strong anti-Communist political activist orientation and have a significant influence on U.S. foreign policy toward Cuba (Portes and Rumbaut 1990). Many profess an intention to return to Cuba after the fall of Castro.

Demographically, Cuban-born people in the U.S. are diverse in terms of education, occupation, and income. On average, their socioeconomic status is higher than that of Latin American immigrants (U.S. Bureau of the Census 1993). The vast majority of Cuban-born people have settled in Miami, making Cubans one of the most densely concentrated populations of foreign-born people in the U.S. (Portes 1990). Cuban communities also exist in New York, New Jersey, and California.

DOMINICANS People from the Dominican Republic began arriving in the U.S. in large numbers following U.S. intervention to suppress a popular leftist revolt in 1965, and subsequent U.S. military occupation (Castex 1994; Portes 1990). Many Dominicans entered the U.S. as illegal immigrants and were able to legalize their status later (Portes and Rumbaut 1990). Demographically, Dominicans have a quite low socioeconomic status on average (U.S. Bureau of the Census 1993). Most Dominicans have settled in the New York City area. In terms of language and culture, they are similar to Cubans and Latin Americans.

JAMAICANS Jamaicans are English-speaking people, mostly of African descent. The current population of Jamaican-born people in the U.S. began arriving after changes in U.S. immigration law in 1965 opened up admissions to large numbers of people based on labor skills or family reunification. In general, Jamaicans come to the U.S. for educational and economic opportunities (Baptiste, Hardy, and Lewis 1997). Most are legal immigrants. Some are seasonal laborers. A common migration pattern is for one member of a family to immigrate to the U.S., followed later by a spouse, children, and extended family members (Baptiste, Hardy, and Lewis 1997). Thus, nuclear families are often separated for lengthy periods.

Jamaican immigrants usually have extended families that serve as sources of social support. Jamaican women tend to be strong and independent. Jamaicans place a high value on education, viewing it as the means for upward mobility (Gopaul-McNicol 1993). Jamaicans also value property, particularly home ownership. Consequently, they often work multiple jobs in the U.S. in order to acquire property (Gopaul-McNicol 1993; Sewell-Coker, Hamilton-Collins, and Fein 1985). Some Jamaican immigrants subscribe to the Rastafari movement, which is a religious movement that affirms

African identity and actively opposes the oppression of black people (Gopaul-McNicol 1993). Jamaican immigrants' socioeconomic status is relatively high (U.S. Bureau of the Census 1993). This is often a result of their multiple-job strategy. Most Jamaican immigrants have settled in the New York City and Miami areas.

HAITIANS Haitian immigration to the United States is a consequence of persistent political instability in Haiti. Haitians began arriving in the U.S. in the 1960s during the oppressive Duvalier regime, which continued through the 1970s and 1980s. The Duvaliers ruled by corruption and intimidation, and tortured and killed political opponents (Chamberlain 1997; Paquin 1983). The Duvalier regime was overthrown in 1986 and a democratically elected president was installed in 1990. However, he was overthrown the following year and the country was under martial rule until the U.S. invaded in 1994. In the late 1990s Haiti was occupied by United Nations peacekeeping forces. These events caused continued emigration throughout the 1990s.

Because of these political factors, Haitian emigrants would be considered refugees by social science definitions and international law definitions. However, in most cases Haitians have not been recognized as refugees by the United States, since the U.S. has been biased against granting refugee status to people from non-Communist countries. In general, the U.S. has argued that Haitian emigrants are economic migrants, because Haiti is the poorest country in the Western Hemisphere. In 1994, 85 percent of the Haitian population was unemployed or underemployed, and the gross national product per capita $220 (Chamberlain 1997). Haiti has one of the highest population densities in the world, and infectious diseases and malnourishment are widespread. Therefore, Haitian emigrants may be viewed as economic migrants, but it is necessary to realize that much of Haiti's economic situation is due to political corruption (Loescher 1993).

Because the U.S. does not recognize most Haitians as refugees, many have illegal immigrant status in the U.S. However, many that arrived in the 1960s entered legally, and many others have been able to adjust to legal status under a law passed in 1986. The earliest arriving Haitians were the educated elite, followed by the lower socioeconomic class. Currently, Haitian emigrants attempt to leave by sea. This leads to many deaths from exposure and drowning. If they are intercepted at sea by the U.S. Coast Guard, they are returned to Haiti.

Haitians are primarily people of African descent. Although their official language is French, most speak Creole, a unique language that does not have a written history. Consequently, many Haitians are not literate. In terms of cultural values, Haitian families are predominantly matriarchal and authoritarian (Holcomb, et al. 1996). Corporal punishment of children is considered normal, and sometimes leads to allegations of child abuse. The elderly are highly respected, and serve as advisors to the family. Decisions tend to be made by the family as a whole. Most Haitians are Catholic, but many also practice voodoo, which is founded in African beliefs and practices.

Most Haitian immigrants and refugees have settled in the New York City and Miami areas. The major issues facing Haitians in the U.S. are poverty, lack of education, and their associated problems. This, combined with the illegal status of many, is a major area for social work intervention.

1.7.3 ASIAN COUNTRIES

SOME COMMON CULTURAL VALUES of people from Asia include "dignity, meditation, family honor, hierarchy of levels in families and businesses, good of family and not self, and experience and wisdom" (Harper and Lantz 1996, p. 62). Others are "filial piety, parent-child interaction in which communication flows essentially from parent to child, self-control and restraint in emotional expression, respect for authority, well-defined social roles and expectations, shame as a behavioral influence, middle position virtue, awareness of social milieu, fatalism, communal responsibility, inconspicuousness, high regard for the elderly, and the centrality of family relationships and responsibilities" (Chung 1992, p. 28). However, beyond these general commonalities, Asian immigrants and refugees are extremely diverse in regard to their backgrounds, religions, and demographic and socioeconomic characteristics.

FILIPINOS Immigrants from the Philippines have been in the U.S. since the early 1900s. However, they began arriving in large numbers after changes in U.S. immigration law in 1965 opened up admissions. These immigrants come for economic advancement, and to join relatives already in the U.S. (Okamura and Agbayani 1991). The Philippines were a Spanish colony for three centuries. This heritage influenced their culture, so that Filipinos share some cultural affinities with Hispanics (Root 1997). Most Filipinos are Catholic. The Philippines were later a possession of the U.S. before becoming independent in 1946. Thus, Filipinos also have familiarity with traditional American culture (Root 1997). Traditional Filipino families are egalitarian or matriarchal (Okamura and Agbayani 1991; Root 1997). Socioeconomically, Filipino immigrants have relatively high status. Almost half are college graduates, a large proportion are employed in professional, managerial, or government positions, and their average family income is high (U.S. Bureau of the Census 1993). Most Filipino immigrants live in California.

CHINESE Chinese immigrants have a relatively long history in the United States, dating to the mid-nineteenth century. Thus, there were already well-established Chinese communities when the current large wave of immigrants began arriving after the immigration law change of 1965. A peculiarity of U.S. immigrant and refugee admission practice is that even though China is a Communist state, the Chinese are not considered refugees, but immigrants. Nonetheless, some Chinese immigrants are likely to have experienced the same political persecution as refugees from other Communist countries.

Culturally, Chinese immigrants have many of the traditional Asian values described above. Their beliefs are based in Confucian philosophy. Buddhism and Taoism are dominant religions. In terms of socioeconomics, Chinese immigrants on average are in the middle of the spectrum. While almost one-third are college graduates, 40 percent do not have a high school diploma. Average family income is moderate, but almost three-fourths do not speak English well (U.S. Bureau of the Census 1993). Most Chinese immigrants live in California and New York, many of them in "Chinatown" ethnic enclaves.

KOREANS Like many other immigrants, large-scale migration of Koreans into the U.S. began after 1965. Koreans' primary reasons for immigration are economic advancement for themselves and better educational opportunities for their children (Rhee 1996). "Although the Korean culture and traditions are built on the teachings of Confucianism and Buddhism, more than 80% of Koreans claim to be Christians. They maintain a Judeo-Christian lifestyle in the United States" (Kim and Kim 1992, p. 228). In general, Korean immigrants have a high level of education. Their median family income is moderate. One noteworthy occupational feature of Koreans is their high rate of self-employment. Almost 20 percent are self-employed, the highest of any immigrant group, and much higher than the rate for the native-born population (U.S. Bureau of the Census 1993). Many of these self-employed people own small family businesses such as liquor stores or grocery stores, often located in impoverished, inner-city neighborhoods (Rhee 1996). Often, family members work in more than one full-time job (Kim and Kim 1992). Most Korean immigrants live in West Coast states and New York City.

INDIANS Most immigrants from India (sometimes referred to as South Asians or Asian Indians) have entered the U.S. since 1965. These immigrants are diverse in ethnicity, culture, language, and religion. Major religions of India include Hinduism, Islam, Christianity, Sikhism, and Buddhism (Das and Kemp 1997). Most Indian immigrants come from the Westernized, educated elite, and speak English fluently. Many received their higher education in American universities, and hold professional positions (Das and Kemp 1997). However, more lower-class Indian immigrants are now entering the U.S to be reunited with family members (Pettys and Balgopal 1998). Many Indian cultural beliefs and behaviors are similar to those described above for Asians as a whole (Das and Kemp 1997). Families are characterized by hierarchical authority structure, and are often male-dominated. Marriages are often arranged. Overall, Indian immigrants are very highly educated and have high incomes, although a substantial proportion live in poverty (U.S. Bureau of the Census 1993).

SOUTHEAST ASIANS People from Vietnam, Cambodia, and Laos are often referred to collectively as Southeast Asians or Indochinese. These people are refugees who began arriving in the U.S. after the end of the Vietnam War in 1975. In the late 1970s, an extensive, comprehensive program was established to permit hundreds of thousands of these refugees into the U.S. and to assist them with resettlement. A modified version of that program continues today, as some refugees still remain in refugee camps, awaiting a permanent solution.

Like most war refugees, many Southeast Asians endured traumatic experiences in their countries of origin, such as torture, imprisonment, rape, loss of family members, and witnessing atrocities or being forced to commit atrocities. For many, the transit experience was also traumatic, involving hasty departures in overcrowded boats and long stays in refugee camps.

As is characteristic of refugee movements, the earliest arriving refugees were the educated elite, followed successively by the lower socioeconomic classes. While Southeast Asians in general have many of the traditional Asian values described above, people from the different Southeast Asian countries differ from each other in some ways. In general, the Vietnamese in their country of origin were more Westernized and educated, whereas many Cambodians and Laotians lived in isolated villages, had little education, and some were illiterate. These differences are reflected in the socioeconomic status of these different groups in the U.S. Overall, the economic status of Southeast Asians is poor, with many living in poverty; the situation is even worse for Cambodians and Laotians than for Vietnamese (U.S. Bureau of the Census 1993). Most Southeast Asians have resettled in California, but there are also substantial numbers in other parts of the U.S. In working with this population, important issues for social workers are dealing with past traumas and enhancing socioeconomic status.

1.7.4 MIDDLE EAST COUNTRIES

IN THE MIDDLE EAST, Afghanistan, Iran, and Iraq are major sources of refugees coming to the U.S. Massive refugee movements out of Afghanistan began following a Soviet invasion in 1979. Internal warfare has continued since then. The Soviets withdrew in 1990, but fighting has continued between internal groups (Krumm 1998). The country is currently under the rule of the Taliban, a Muslim fundamentalist group. The Taliban are extremely oppressive to women and ethnic minorities. They have revoked women's rights to employment, education, and health care (Krumm 1998). These factors are the cause of continuing admission of Afghan refugees.

Iranians started entering the U.S. after the overthrow of the Shah by the Ayatollah Khomeini in 1978. Khomeini instituted a repressive Islamic regime. The earliest Iranian refugees were those who had been allied with the Shah and were thus in danger under the new regime. "The Islamic government restricts religious freedom and subjects certain religious minorities to widespread discrimination and harassment. Members of these groups . . . often face legal penalties and persecution" (U.S. Department of State 1998b, p. 1). For these reasons, refugees continue to flee Iran.

Refugees from Iraq fled during the Persian Gulf War in 1990–1991. After the end of the war, many remained in refugee camps, fearing persecution if they returned. These included ethnic and religious minorities and people who participated in the uprising against the Iraqi regime (U.S. Department of State 1998b). The U.S. continues to resettle these refugees.

Culturally, people from these countries are diverse. In general, they have been influenced by Islamic traditions. Families tend to be authoritarian and male-dominated. In regard to socioeconomic status, Afghan refugees are generally at the lower end of the income spectrum, although many are highly educated former professionals (Portes and Rumbaut 1990). Iranian refugees in general are highly educated, have a high proportion of people employed in professional and managerial positions, and have relatively high family incomes (U.S. Bureau of the Census 1993). Because Iraqis are very recent arrivals, little information is available yet about their socioeconomic status.

1.7.5 EUROPEAN COUNTRIES

THE MAJOR EUROPEAN COUNTRIES that are sources of immigrants and refugees in the U.S. are Great Britain, the former Soviet Union, and countries of Eastern Europe. People from these countries vary widely in culture, language, background, and socioeconomic status.

BRITISH People from Great Britain are immigrants who have come to the U.S. for employment purposes or to reunite with family members. Due to the long shared history of the U.S. and Britain, British people are quite similar to the majority U.S.-born population in regard to language, culture, and beliefs. Socioeconomically, British immigrants on average are highly educated, have a high proportion employed in professional and managerial positions, have a high family income, and low poverty and unemployment rates (U.S. Bureau of the Census 1993).

SOVIETS AND FORMER SOVIETS The Soviet Union was under Communist rule from 1917 to 1989. In 1991, the Soviet Union broke up into a dozen independent democratic republics, the largest of which is Russia. During the Cold War, which lasted from the late 1940s to the late 1980s, hundreds of thousands of Soviet refugees were admitted into the United States, with particularly large numbers entering after 1975. These were people fleeing political repression. Under Communism, human rights such as freedom of speech, freedom of press, and free elections were not permitted. People who opposed the government were punished by execution or imprisonment, and were denied access to educational and employment opportunities. Most Soviet refugees were Jews who had been subjected to anti-Semitism. Since the fall of Communism, hundreds of thousands of people from the former Soviet Union have continued to be admitted. Primarily, these are members of religious minorities, such as Jews and Christian Evangelicals, who continue to have a well-founded fear of persecution in their home country (U.S. Department of State 1998c).

In understanding cultural characteristics of Soviets, the influence of the authoritarian state is paramount. Soviets tend to be wary of authority figures. They tend not to express personal thoughts and feelings, other than to family or close friends. Although most Soviet refugees are Jewish, most are not religious or observant. Like other immigrants and refugees, Soviets rely on extended networks of family and friends for support and assistance. Friendship is highly valued and is characterized by warmth and giving (Ivry 1992).

In terms of socioeconomic characteristics, Soviets are in the mid-range among foreign-born people in general. Almost two-thirds are high school graduates and more than one-fourth are college graduates. However, their median family income is fairly low, and one-fourth live below the poverty level (U.S. Bureau of the Census 1993). Most Soviets have settled in New York City, Chicago, and Los Angeles.

EAST EUROPEANS Major East European sources of refugees in the U.S. are Poland, Romania, and Bosnia-Herzegovina. Others include Hungary, the former Czechoslovakia, Bulgaria, and recently, Kosovo. All of these regions were part of the Soviet bloc from shortly after World War II until 1989. Thus, they were Communist countries under Soviet control. People in these countries were subject to the same political repression as

Soviets. Consequently, these people were similarly admitted to the U.S. as refugees.

The number of refugees from Poland, Romania, Hungary, Czechoslovakia, and Bulgaria dropped substantially after 1992, following the establishment of democracy in those countries (U.S. Committee for Refugees 2000). At the same time, however, there was a new influx of refugees from Bosnia-Herzegovina. These people fled an ethnic civil war during which mass executions, tortures, rapes, and other atrocities were committed. Many of these refugees were Muslims who had been subjected to religious persecution. Currently, tens of thousands of Bosnian refugees continue to be admitted to the U.S. annually (U.S. Committee for Refugees 2000). The most recent refugees from East Europe are Kosovars. Several thousand Kosovar refugees arrived in the U.S. in 1999 following NATO attacks on Kosovo (U.S. Department of State 1998d). Like Bosnians, these refugees had been victims of ethnic and religious persecution, including the same atrocities that had been committed in Bosnia.

Like Soviets, refugees from East Europe have settled primarily in New York City and Chicago, although they are also dispersed throughout the U.S. The cultural, demographic, and socioeconomic characteristics of people from East European countries vary considerably. Some are highly educated whereas others are not, and some are highly religious whereas others are not. Some came from modern, urban areas, whereas others came from less developed, rural areas. Additionally, they have all been influenced by the authoritarian state in the same manner as Soviets. Another issue to bear in mind when working with these refugees is that some older refugees may have been victims of the Nazi Holocaust, and younger refugees may have had parents or grandparents who were such victims. These experiences may continue to influence these refugees' lives.

1.7.6 AFRICAN COUNTRIES

AFRICAN IMMIGRANTS ACCOUNTED for only about 2 or 3 percent of all immigrants in the early 1990s (Kamya 1997). However, in 1998, African countries constituted four of the top ten countries of refugees admitted. Thus, there has been a significant shift in the African-born population in the U.S. Although people from different African countries are diverse in terms of background, culture, and language, there are some cultural commonalities. In general, African beliefs are strongly spiritual and communal (Kamya 1997). These beliefs influence how African refugees cope with their experience in the U.S.

The four major countries of origin of African refugees in the U.S. are Ethiopia, Somalia, Liberia, and Sudan. Ethiopia was under Communist rule from 1974 to 1991, and during the 1980s and early 1990s was engaged in civil war between the Communists and rebel forces. During this time, tens of thousands of refugees fleeing Communism and the war were admitted into the U.S. Since that time, additional Ethiopians have been admitted into the U.S. as relatives of those admitted earlier (U.S. Committee for Refugees 1998; U.S. Department of State 1998e).

"Civil war and factional fighting have embroiled Somalia since 1988, causing up to a half-million deaths. Conditions were particularly severe during 1991–1992, when violence and widespread population displacement produced famine" (U.S. Committee for Refugees 1998, p. 92). Consequently, thousands of Somalian refugees began arriving in the U.S. in 1991 (U.S. Committee for Refugees 2000).

"Liberia's armed conflict began in late 1989 when [rebel forces] attacked government forces. Fighting quickly degenerated into largely inter-ethnic massacres. Most factions . . . pursued sustained warfare, exploitation of natural resources, and looting" (U.S. Committee for Refugees 1998, p. 75). This civil war is ongoing and has been the source of several thousand Liberian refugees in the U.S. since 1990 (U.S. Committee for Refugees 2000).

"Sudan has long experienced conflict . . . because of racial, cultural, religious, and political differences. The current phase of Sudan's civil war has persisted for 14 years . . . Civilian populations have been targeted and exploited by all sides in the war" (U.S. Committee for Refugees 1998). These events have been the source of several thousand Sudanese refugees in the U.S. since 1990 (U.S. Committee for Refugees 2000).

In regard to socioeconomic characteristics, Ethiopian refugees have a high proportion of highly educated professionals; however, their average income is low, since many have been unable to acquire professional positions in the U.S. (Portes and Rumbaut 1990). Little is known about the socioeconomic characteristics of the other African refugee groups because they have been in the U.S. a relatively short time.

1.8 SUMMARY

THE UNITED STATES has a large and growing population of immigrants and refugees from an extremely diverse variety of countries. Understanding an immigrant or refugee client's background, cultural beliefs, reasons for migration, socioeconomic status, and legal status are all important starting points for effectively helping members of these populations.

CHAPTER 2

IMMIGRATION AND REFUGEE POLICIES

IMMIGRATION AND REFUGEE POLICIES provide the legal context for social work practice with these populations. These policies include international law and national laws. International law provides guidelines about how countries should treat their citizens and aliens. National laws determine which aliens are eligible for admission, and which aliens are eligible to receive public services and benefits after arrival. These laws have changed over time, and will continue to do so. The following discussion presents the major historical and contemporary immigration and refugee policies, and examines their causes and consequences. An understanding of these policies and the social, political, and economic forces that have shaped them is a necessary prerequisite to effectively serving these populations.

2.1 INTERNATIONAL LAW

INTERNATIONAL LAW "consists of rules and principles which govern the relations and dealings of nations with each other. . . . [It] concerns itself with questions of rights between several nations or nations and the citizens or subjects of other nations" (Legal Information Institute 1999, p. 1). International law is a part of United States law pertaining to international rights and duties, unless there is some statute or treaty to the contrary. "International law imposes upon the nations certain duties with respect to individuals. It is a violation of international law to treat an alien in a manner which does not satisfy the international standard of justice" (Legal Information Institute 1999, p. 2). A major source of international law is *conventional law*, which consists of conventions and treaties agreed to by nations.

The branches of international law that are most pertinent to immigrants and refugees are international human rights law, international humanitarian law, international refugee law, and international migrant worker law, all of which are codified in a number of conventions (Barutciski 1998; Good, et al. 1995). *International human rights law* concerns the protection of basic rights of people within nations. *International humanitarian law* concerns the protection and treatment of victims of war. *International refugee law* concerns the protection of people who have fled their countries because human rights law or humanitarian law have already been violated. *International migrant worker law* concerns the rights and treatment of migrant workers.

International human rights law is pertinent to immigrants because it concerns the fundamental rights of all people, including aliens, within nations. Both international human rights law and international humanitarian law are pertinent to refugees because it is violations of these laws within their own countries that cause people to become refugees. And these laws, as well as international refugee law, also guide how refugees should be treated by other nations once they have fled their own nations. Finally, international migrant worker law is pertinent to immigrants who migrate for employment purposes.

The conventions which codify international human rights law, international humanitarian law, international refugee law, and international migrant worker law have been developed and adopted by the United Nations. Many of these laws were developed in the aftermath of World War II, in an effort to prevent future atrocities such as those that were widespread in that war. Numerous other such laws have been developed more recently. These conventions have been adopted as resolutions by the UN General Assembly, of which most nations are members. After adoption, member states ratify the conventions and treaties, signifying that they willingly bind themselves to the legal obligations contained in the document. Not all member states have ratified all of the conventions, and nonratifying states are not legally bound by the conventions. However, if the UN acts consistently on a resolution, eventually even the nonratifying member states are deemed to have acquiesced to the resolution. Nonetheless, the fact remains that there is really no completely effective mechanism for enforcing international human rights, humanitarian, and refugee laws.

The major UN human rights, humanitarian, and refugee instruments that are pertinent to immigrants and refugees are listed in table 2.1. The fundamental human rights document is the *Universal Declaration of Human*

TABLE 2.1 MAJOR UNITED NATIONS HUMAN RIGHTS, HUMANITARIAN, AND REFUGEE INSTRUMENTS PERTINENT TO IMMIGRANTS AND REFUGEES

INTERNATIONAL HUMAN RIGHTS LAW

- Universal Declaration of Human Rights (1948)
- Convention on the Prevention and Punishment of the Crime of Genocide (1948)
- Convention Relating to the Status of Stateless Persons (1954)
- Convention on the Elimination of All Forms of Racial Discrimination (1965)
- Covenant on Civil and Political Rights (1966)
- Covenant on Economic, Social, and Cultural Rights (1966)
- Convention on Elimination of all Forms of Discrimination Against Women (1979)
- Convention Against Torture and Other Cruel, Inhuman, or Degrading Treatment or Punishment (1984)
- Convention on the Rights of the Child (1989)

INTERNATIONAL HUMANITARIAN LAW

- Geneva Convention (I) for the Amelioration of the Condition of the Wounded and Sick in Armed Forces in the Field (1949)
- Geneva Convention (II) for the Amelioration of the Condition of Wounded, Sick, and Shipwrecked Members of the Armed Forces at Sea (1949)
- Geneva Convention (III) Relative to the Treatment of Prisoners of War
- Geneva Convention (IV) Relative to the Protection of Civilian Persons in Time of War (1949)

INTERNATIONAL REFUGEE LAW

- Convention Relating to the Status of Refugees (1951)
- Protocol Relating to the Status of Refugees (1967)

INTERNATIONAL MIGRANT WORKER LAW

- Migration for Employment Convention (1949)
- Migrant Workers Convention (1975)
- Convention on the Protection of the Rights of All Migrant Workers and Members of Their Families (1990)

Sources: Good, Jensen, Thompson, and Webster 1995; Legal Information Institute, 1999; Rogers and Copeland, 1993; United Nations, 1996; United Nations High Commissioner for Refugees, 1999a.

Rights. It specifies 30 basic rights to which all people are entitled (table 2.2). This declaration is not legally binding, but many of its provisions are incorporated in the *Covenant on Economic, Social, and Cultural Rights* and the

TABLE 2.2 ARTICLES OF THE UNIVERSAL DECLARATION OF HUMAN RIGHTS

Article 1. Right to Equality
Article 2. Freedom from Discrimination
Article 3. Right to Life, Liberty and Personal Security
Article 4. Freedom from Slavery
Article 5. Freedom from Torture and Degrading Treatment
Article 6. Right to Recognition as a Person before the Law
Article 7. Right to Equality before the Law
Article 8. Right to Remedy by Competent Tribunal
Article 9. Freedom from Arbitrary Arrest and Exile
Article 10. Right to a Fair Public Hearing
Article 11. Right to be Considered Innocent Until Proven Guilty
Article 12. Freedom from Interference with Privacy, Family, Home, and Correspondence
Article 13. Right to Free Movement in and out of the Country
Article 14. Right to Asylum in other Countries from Persecution
Article 15. Right to a Nationality and Freedom to Change It
Article 16. Right to Marriage and Family
Article 17. Right to Own Property
Article 18. Freedom of Belief and Religion
Article 19. Freedom of Opinion and Information
Article 20. Right of Peaceful Assembly and Association
Article 21. Right to Participate in Government and in Free Elections
Article 22. Right to Social Security
Article 23. Right to Desirable Work and to join Trade Unions
Article 24. Right to Rest and Leisure
Article 25. Right to Adequate Living Standard
Article 26. Right to Education
Article 27. Right to Participate in the Cultural Life of Community
Article 28. Right to Social Order assuring Human Rights
Article 29. Community Duties Essential to Free and Full Development
Article 30. Freedom from State or Personal Interference in the above Rights

Source: United Nations High Commissioner for Refugees, 1999b.

Covenant on Civil and Political Rights, both of which are legally binding (United Nations 1996). The Universal Declaration also laid the foundation for all of the other human rights conventions listed in table 2.1, all of which are legally binding.

Humanitarian law addresses the treatment and protection of victims of war, in particular the wounded, sick and shipwrecked, prisoners of war, and civilians. Humanitarian law is codified in four *Geneva Conventions*. These conventions are particularly pertinent to refugees, since refugees are often victims of war.

Refugees have certain specific rights under refugee law, which is codified in the *Convention and Protocol Relating to the Status of Refugees*. These documents provide the international definition of a refugee, as presented in the previous chapter. They also specify who is not a refugee. For example, people who have participated in massive violations of international humanitarian or human rights law cannot be considered refugees. Nor can people who have fled their countries to escape prosecution for nonpolitical crimes, but who have not been persecuted for other reasons. For people who do meet the refugee definition, a fundamental right that is specified in refugee law is the right to *non-refoulement*. This is a French term meaning "no forcible return." The principle of *non-refoulement* means that refugees have the right not to be forcibly returned back to a place where they could be persecuted (U.S. Committee for Refugees 1998a).

Finally, migrant worker law stipulates that immigrants should receive the same treatment as citizens in regard to wages, trade union memberships, collective bargaining, accommodations, basic necessities of living, schooling, and public benefits related to poverty and unemployment. Migrant worker law is codified in several conventions, the first of which is the *Migration for Employment Convention*.

2.2 UNITED STATES IMMIGRATION AND REFUGEE POLICIES

WHILE INTERNATIONAL LAW addresses the fundamental rights of all immigrants and refugees, national laws address admissions and assistance to immigrants and refugees within a particular country. United States immigration and refugee policies have changed drastically over time. These changes in immigration and refugee policies have resulted from a combination of *domestic, foreign policy,* and *humanitarian* considerations (McBride 1999). Domestic considerations include economic concerns and the general public's attitudes toward foreigners. Often, immigration policies are influenced by the interests of domestic employers, such as the manufacturing and agriculture sectors, which benefit from immigrant labor (DeSipio and de la Garza 1998). Foreign policy considerations are involved when refugees from specific countries are admitted in order to embarrass or weaken the governments of those countries. And humanitarian considerations guide the admission of refugees on the basis of commitment to promoting human rights.

U.S. immigration and refugee policies can be divided into two major time periods: historical and contemporary. A major shift in U.S. immigration policy occurred in 1965. Contemporary policy dates from the 1965 legislation. All prior legislation is no longer in effect, but is important from a historical perspective because it laid the foundations for contemporary policies.

2.2.1 HISTORICAL POLICIES

IT IS WELL KNOWN that the United States is a country founded upon immigration. For the first hundred years of the country's existence, immigration was generally unrestricted and unregulated. Two factors influenced this: America's need for new citizens to promote the country's geographic, economic and political growth; and an ideological perception of the U.S. (by both citizens and foreigners) as a place of refuge for the oppressed of other nations (Congressional Research Service 1991). During this period, massive numbers of immigrants from Northern and Western Europe entered the U.S. They came for economic, political, and religious reasons. There was no distinction between immigrants and refugees at that time. Additionally, involuntary migrants were brought from Africa as slaves.

In general, immigrants during this period were viewed positively because they served the nation's needs. However, strong anti-immigrant sentiments also arose periodically. These were rooted in various feelings such as anti-Catholicism, a perceived link between immigration and crime and poverty, and concerns about the economic and political impact of immigrants (Congressional Research Service 1991). These sentiments led to the enactment of the first general immigration statute, the *Immigration Act of 1882*. This law excluded the admission of convicts, paupers, and people deemed mentally defective. They were excluded because they were thought likely to become "public charges"—that is, dependent upon public funds for their financial support.

In the same year, the first law excluding people based on national origin was enacted, the *Chinese Exclusion Act of 1882*. Although people from China had been actively recruited to come to the U.S. during the 1840s to make up for labor shortages, by the 1870s the country was in an economic recession and Chinese immigrants were vilified (Fix and Passel 1994). The Chinese Exclusion Act stopped Chinese immigration for ten years, denied Chinese immigrants the right to become U.S. citizens, and provided for deportation of Chinese illegal immigrants. In 1943, the act was repealed in order to improve relations with China, which was then an ally in World War II (McBride 1999), providing one illustration of how foreign policy interests have influenced immigration policies.

As a result of an economic depression during the 1880s, laws were passed prohibiting the immigration of contract laborers. Thus, the early immigration policies of the 1880s contained three elements—individual qualifications of immigrants, national origin, and protection of U.S. labor—that formed the basis of most later policies (Congressional Research Service 1991). These policies were fundamentally restrictive and supplanted the traditional U.S. stance that had granted asylum, or open immigration, to all.

During the late nineteenth and early twentieth centuries, immigration from Northern and Western Europe decreased, but immigration from Southern and Eastern Europe increased dramatically. These new immigrants were viewed with ambivalence. On the one hand, they supplied needed labor for the industrial revolution. On the other hand, many citizens believed that these immigrants adversely affected the wages and working conditions of U.S.-born workers. Additionally, they came to be associated with urban problems such as crime and poverty. Many were illiterate, and this was also viewed as undesirable. Consequently, the *Immigration Act of 1917* barred immigrants who were illiterate in any language, which was specifically intended to bar these Southern and Eastern European immigrants. The same act also extended the bar on Chinese to other Asians. These developments grew not only out of economic concerns, but also from wartime nationalism and isolationism during World War I (Congressional Research Service 1991).

In addition to these concerns, eugenics theories, which held that some races were biologically superior to others, became popular during the 1920s. All of these factors led to the first legislation that placed quantitative, or numerical, restrictions on immigration, rather than the qualitative restrictions based on individual characteristics. The *Immigration Act of 1924* limited European immigration to 150,000 per year and continued the immigration ban against Asian countries (Congressional Research Service 1991; Fix and Passel 1994). It also established a national origins quota system whereby admissions were "based on the proportion of national origin groups that were present in the United States according to the census of 1890. Because this Census preceded the large-scale immigrations from Southern and Eastern Europe, this provision represented an explicit effort to ensure that future immigration flows would be largely composed of immigrants from Northern and Western Europe" (Fix and Passel 1994, p. 10). After 1927, the 1920 Census was used as the basis for setting quotas. Additionally, this legislation established for the first time a preference system that gave admissions preference within each quota to relatives of U.S. citizens and to immigrants who were skilled in agriculture.

Immigrants from the Western Hemisphere were exempt from the quota. This was due to a desire to attract cheap labor from those countries, and to promote good relations with countries in close proximity to the U.S. (McBride 1999). The national origins quota system remained in force until 1965.

As a result of the 1924 act, immigration admissions dropped drastically in the 1930s and 1940s. The rise of Nazism in Europe in the 1930s again brought humanitarian concerns forward. Between 1933 and 1941, the U.S. admitted a quarter-million refugees from Nazi persecution. However, efforts to liberalize the immigration law in order to admit more of these refugees were defeated, because the country was in the greatest economic depression of its history (Congressional Research Service 1991). Consequently, many more refugees from Nazism were turned away. After World War II, there were huge numbers of refugees in displaced persons camps in Europe. Based on humanitarian concerns, the U.S. enacted the *Displaced Persons Act of 1948*, which was the first refugee legislation in the nation's history. This act allowed for the admission of hundreds of thousands of refugees by borrowing from future immigration quotas (Congressional Research Service 1991).

While restricting permanent immigration, the U.S. encouraged the admission of temporary foreign laborers. In 1942, the Mexican "bracero" program was established, which authorized the entry of almost five million temporary agricultural workers. Additional temporary workers were admitted from several Caribbean countries (Congressional Research Service 1991).

The next major legislation was the *Immigration and Nationality Act of 1952 (INA)*. This was a comprehensive statute that brought together the multiple immigration laws that had been enacted previously. It barred discrimination in admissions on the basis of race and gender. However, it continued the national origins quota system, with a modification of the quota formula. Thus, it still placed substantial limitations on immigration from Southern and Eastern Europe. This legislation was influenced by then-popular sociological theories about cultural assimilation (Congressional Research Service 1991). Essentially, the continuation of the national origins quota system was defended by the view that Western and Northern Europeans would assimilate more easily into American society. However, restrictions on Asian immigration were slightly relaxed. Immigration from Western Hemisphere countries remained unrestricted.

In addition to maintaining the quota system, the 1952 act established a preference system based on employment skills and family relationships. This was the antecedent to the current immigrant admissions system, which is based on employment and family member preference categories. The 1952 system consisted of four categories. Within each national quota, first preference was given to people with high education or urgently needed skills, and three other preference categories were established for relatives of U.S. citizens and permanent residents.

Many people were opposed to the 1952 legislation because its national origin quotas precluded the admission of refugees from Eastern Europe, which by that time was under Communist rule. Thus, the legislation was viewed as incompatible with traditional U.S. humanitarian concerns, as well as with foreign policy, which was strongly anti-Communist. Consequently, several pieces of legislation were soon enacted to permit the admission of these refugees outside of the quota system. The *Refugee Relief Act of 1953* specifically authorized the admission of escapees from Communist countries of Eastern Europe. The *Refugee-Escapee Act of 1957* extended the definition of refugees and escapees to include people fleeing persecution in Middle East countries. It also repealed the quota deductions that had been required by the Displaced Persons Act of 1948. These anti-Communist refugee laws also laid the foundation for the subsequent admission of refugees from Communist Cuba through various legal means (Congressional Research Service 1991).

In summary, historical U.S. immigration and refugee policies evolved from open admissions to gradually more restricted admissions. At different points in time, different groups of immigrants were effectively denied admission. At first this was accomplished by excluding people based on characteristics such as national origin and educational and skill levels, and later by imposing numerical quotas based on national origin. Illegal immigrants and deportation were addressed beginning with the very first immigration legislation. The distinction between immigrants and refugees was not made in policy until after World War II. These shifts in immigration and refugee policy were influenced by a combination of factors including the state of the domestic economy, humanitarian concerns, foreign policy, and popular beliefs about racial superiority and assimilation. The major historical policies are summarized in table 2.3.

TABLE 2.3 MAJOR HISTORICAL UNITED STATES IMMIGRATION AND REFUGEE POLICIES

CHINESE EXCLUSION ACT OF 1882

- Restricted Chinese immigration
- Barred Chinese immigrants from naturalization
- Provided for deportation of Chinese illegal immigrants

IMMIGRATION ACT OF 1882

- First general immigration law
- Established a system of central control of immigration
- Excluded admission of people likely to become a public charge (paupers, convicts, and mental defectives)

IMMIGRATION ACT OF 1917

- Codified all previously enacted exclusion provisions
- Excluded admission of illiterate persons
- Expanded list of people excluded for mental health and other reasons
- Further restricted admission of Asian immigrants
- Broadened classes of deportable aliens

IMMIGRATION ACT OF 1924

- Established first permanent numerical limitation on immigration
- Established national origins quota system
- Excluded Japanese admissions
- Established a preference system for relatives of U.S. citizens and agricultural immigrants
- Exempted Western Hemisphere immigrants from quota limitations
- Imposed fines on transportation companies that landed illegal immigrants

DISPLACED PERSONS ACT OF 1948

- First expression of U.S. policy for admitting persons fleeing persecution
- Aimed at addressing the problem of over one million displaced people in Europe following World War II
- Admitted displaced people by borrowing from future years' quotas

> **TABLE 2.3** *(continued)*
>
> **IMMIGRATION AND NATIONALITY ACT OF 1952 (INA)**
>
> • Brought into one comprehensive statute the multiple laws that had been enacted previously
> • Eliminated race and gender as barriers to immigration
> • Maintained national origins quota system, with modified formula
> • Introduced four-category preference system based on skills and relationship to U.S. citizens and permanent residents
> • Broadened grounds for deportation, but gave greater procedural safeguards to deportable aliens
> • Established a central registry of all aliens in the U.S.
>
> **REFUGEE RELIEF ACT OF 1953**
>
> • Authorized admission of refugees from war-torn Europe and escapees from Communist countries
>
> **REFUGEE-ESCAPEE ACT OF 1957**
>
> • Removed the requirement, contained in the Displaced Persons Act of 1948, of borrowing from future years' quotas for admission of refugees and escapees
> • Facilitated admission of stepchildren, illegitimate children, and adopted children
> • Gave Attorney General authority to admit certain formerly excludable aliens
>
> *Source:* U.S. Immigration and Naturalization Service, 1997b.

2.2.2 CONTEMPORARY POLICIES

CONTEMPORARY U.S. IMMIGRATION and refugee policies have their roots in 1965 legislation that radically changed prior laws. Contemporary policies are guided by five major goals: "*social*—unifying U.S. citizens and legal residents with their families; *economic*—increasing U.S. productivity and standard of living; *cultural*—encouraging diversity; *moral*—promoting human rights; and *national and economic security*—controlling illegal immigration" (Fix and Passel 1994, p. 13). Social, economic, and cultural goals are embodied in policies pertaining to legal immigration; moral goals are embodied in policies pertaining to refugees; and national and economic security goals are embodied in policies pertaining to illegal immigration.

Like historical policies, contemporary policies have been shaped by shifting public sentiments related to economic concerns, humanitarian concerns, foreign policy, and general public attitudes. As will be seen, contemporary immigration policy "has been subject to many twists and turns—proposals put forth and discarded, compromises reached and abandoned, legislation passed and modified. [It is developed] in an environment that is subject to push and pull factors from a number of directions: Congress, presidents, Supreme Court decisions, interest groups, U.S. domestic and foreign policy concerns, public opinion, intergovernmental organizations, and international and national guidelines" (McBride 1999, p. 23). The major contemporary policies, their causes, and consequences, are reviewed below. The policies and their principal provisions are summarized in table 2.4.

TABLE 2.4 MAJOR CONTEMPORARY UNITED STATES IMMIGRATION AND REFUGEE POLICIES

IMMIGRATION AND NATIONALITY ACT AMENDMENTS OF 1965

- Abolished national origins quota system, eliminating national origin, race, or ancestry as a basis for admission
- Established an admissions preference system based on family reunification and employment skills
- Placed numerical limits on Eastern and Western Hemisphere immigration
- Established per-country numerical limits
- Exempted Western Hemisphere countries from preference system and per-country limits
- Established requirement of demonstrating that employment-based immigrants would not adversely impact U.S. labor force

IMMIGRATION AND NATIONALITY ACT AMENDMENTS OF 1976

- Applied per-country limits and a modified version of preference system to Western Hemisphere
- Subsequent legislation passed in 1978 combined separate total admissions limits for Eastern and Western Hemispheres into one, and applied a single preference system to both hemispheres

REFUGEE ACT OF 1980

- Provided the first permanent and systematic procedure for the admission and effective resettlement of refugees of special humanitarian concern to the U.S.
- Defined the term "refugee" to conform to international refugee law
- Eliminated refugees as a category of the preference system

TABLE 2.4 *(continued)*

- Removed refugees from worldwide numerical limit on immigration
- Established procedures for determining annual numerical limits for refugees, and for responding to emergency refugee situations
- Distinguished between refugees and asylees
- Provided for adjustment to permanent resident status of refugees after one year of U.S. residence, and for asylees one year after asylum is granted
- Established a comprehensive program for domestic resettlement of refugees

IMMIGRATION REFORM AND CONTROL ACT OF 1986 (IRCA)

- First comprehensive legislation addressing illegal immigration
- Established sanctions prohibiting employers from knowingly hiring or recruiting illegal aliens
- Increased border control and enforcement
- Established amnesty program authorizing legalization of certain illegal aliens who had resided continuously in U.S. since 1982
- Created new classification of seasonal agricultural workers and provisions for their legalization

IMMIGRATION ACT OF 1990

- Increased total annual legal immigration limits by 40%
- Tripled the admission limit for employment-based immigration
- Revised preference system of family-sponsored and employment-based admissions
- Created new category of diversity immigrants
- Authorized Attorney General to grant Temporary Protected Status to illegal aliens from countries subject to armed conflict or natural disasters
- Repealed legislation that permitted exclusion or deportation of aliens based on political or ideological grounds
- Increased border patrols
- Revised employer sanction provisions of IRCA
- Revised naturalization requirements

PERSONAL RESPONSIBILITY AND WORK OPPORTUNITY RECONCILIATION ACT OF 1996 (PRWORA)

- Established restrictions on the eligibility of legal immigrants for means-tested public assistance
- Barred legal immigrants (with certain exceptions) from obtaining food stamps and SSI
- Barred legal immigrants (with certain exceptions) entering the U.S. after date of enactment from most federal means-tested programs for five years
- Provided states with broad flexibility in setting public benefit eligibility rules for legal immigrants by allowing states to bar current legal immigrants from both major federal programs and state programs

TABLE 2.4 *(continued)*

- Increased the responsibility of immigrants' sponsors by making the affidavit of support legally enforceable, imposing new requirements on sponsors, and expanding sponsor-deeming requirements to more programs and lengthening the deeming period
- Broadened the restrictions on public benefits for illegal aliens and nonimmigrants
- Barred illegal aliens from most federal, state, and local public benefits
- Required INS to verify immigration status in order for aliens to receive most federal public benefits

ILLEGAL IMMIGRATION REFORM AND IMMIGRANT RESPONSIBILITY ACT OF 1996 (IIRIRA)

- Placed added restrictions on benefits for aliens
- Declared illegal aliens ineligible for Social Security benefits
- Established procedures for requiring proof of citizenship for federal public benefits
- Provided for verification of immigration status for purposes of Social Security and higher educational assistance
- Made the sponsor's affidavit of financial support a legally binding contract
- Provided authority of states to limit general cash assistance to aliens
- Exempted illegal aliens who are victims of domestic violence from denial of public benefits
- Exempted nonprofit organizations from the requirement to verify immigration status of public benefit applicants
- Established measures to control U.S. borders, protect legal workers through worksite enforcement, and remove deportable aliens
- Allowed denial of admission to people deemed likely to become public charges
- Required asylum applications to be filed within one year of entry into the U.S., and expedited procedures for asylum hearing and appeals

ANTITERRORISM AND EFFECTIVE DEATH PENALTY ACT OF 1996 (AEDPA)

- Expedited procedures for removal of alien terrorists.
- Established specific measures to exclude members and representatives of terrorist organizations.
- Modified asylum procedures to improve identification and processing of alien terrorists.
- Provided for criminal alien procedural improvements.

Source: U.S. Immigration and Naturalization Service, 1997b.

IMMIGRATION AND NATIONALITY ACT AMENDMENTS OF 1965 The Immigration and Nationality Act Amendments of 1965 abolished the national origins quota system. In the place of ethnic and national origin admissions criteria, a preference system was established based on family reunification and needed employment skills. This change represented a major policy shift.

This shift was caused in large part by two major factors—the personal influence of President John F. Kennedy, and the civil rights movement (Congressional Research Service 1991; Fix and Passel 1994). John Kennedy had written a book entitled *A Nation of Immigrants* that severely criticized the national origins quota system. Kennedy was also influential in the civil rights movement, which led to massive legislation prohibiting racial and ethnic discrimination. The strong anti-discrimination sentiments of the general public during this period extended to immigration, resulting in the 1965 amendments, which ended admissions discrimination based on ethnicity, race, or national origin.

The amendments established a seven-category admission preference system that placed priority on relatives of U.S. citizens and permanent residents, needed occupationally skilled immigrants, and refugees. An annual limit of 170,000 immigrants from the Eastern Hemisphere, with a 20,000-per-country limit, was established. Immediate relatives (spouses, children, and parents) of U.S. citizens were exempted from the numerical limitations. Additionally, for immigrants entering under the employment preference categories, it was required that the Secretary of Labor issue a finding that the immigrant's admission would not replace a worker in the United States, nor adversely affect the wages and working conditions of similarly employed people in the U.S. Further, for the first time, a numerical limit was placed on Western Hemisphere immigrants at 120,000 annually. However, Western Hemisphere immigrants were not subject to the per-country limits or the preference system.

The 1965 Amendments resulted in a massive shift in the national origin of immigrants. Prior to the 1965 law, most immigrants were from Europe. Since then most immigrants have been from Asia and Latin America. Asians, who had been effectively barred under previous legislation, were now able to enter, mostly under the skills preference categories. Latin Americans entered under both the family reunification and skills preference categories. These post-1965 arrivals are sometimes referred to as "the new immigrants." The preference system established by the 1965 law, with some modifications described below, has remained the basis for admission of legal immigrants.

IMMIGRATION AND NATIONALITY ACT AMENDMENTS OF 1976 This legislation applied the 20,000-per-country limit to the Western Hemisphere, and also applied a slightly modified version of the seven-category preference system to the Western Hemisphere. In 1978, the separate total admissions limits for the Eastern and Western Hemispheres were combined into one, and a single preference system was applied to both hemispheres (Congressional Research Service 1991).

REFUGEE ACT OF 1980 Between 1975 and 1980, the United States was inundated with a large-scale influx of refugees from Southeast Asia. These people fled the region as a result of the end of the Vietnam War and the consequent Communist takeover of South Vietnam. In this five-year period, more than 400,000 of these refugees entered the U.S. (Congressional Research Service 1991). During the same time, the Soviet Union began allowing Jews to emigrate, and large numbers of them came to the United States (Feen 1985). The federal government found it increasingly difficult to effectively cope with these massive influxes under the existing refugee policies. These existing policies had been developed in a piecemeal fashion, in response to refugee crises in various regions of the world over time. However, it had become evident that rather than being occasional crises, refugee outflows were a persistent problem. A general consensus developed that a more comprehensive and coordinated approach to refugee admission and resettlement was needed. Consequently, the Refugee Act of 1980 was developed and enacted.

This legislation provided the first permanent and systematic procedure for the admission and resettlement of refugees. The act entailed major revisions of refugee policy. First, it redefined the term refugee. Previously, refugees had been defined as people fleeing Communist or Middle East countries. The 1980 act replaced this ideologically and geographically based definition with the international definition of refugees contained in the UN Convention and Protocol Relating to the Status of Refugees (i.e., a person who is outside his / her country of origin and is unable or unwilling to return to the country of origin due to a well-founded fear of persecution because of race, religion, nationality, membership in a particular social group, or political opinion). Second, the act removed refugees as a category of the preference system for admissions. Thus refugees were recognized as a special case which should not be subject to the numerical limitations set on legal immigrants. Procedures were established for setting annual numerical limitations on refugee admissions, as well as for responding to emergency refugee situations that were outside of these numerical limitations.

Third, the legislation made a clear distinction between refugees and asylees. Refugees were identified as people who applied for admission to the U.S. from outside of the U.S., usually after having been granted asylum by another country. Asylees were identified as people who applied for asylum after they were already in the U.S., usually having entered illegally. Fourth, the act allowed refugees and asylees to apply for adjustment to permanent resident status after one year of residence in the U.S.

Finally, this act created for the first time a comprehensive and coordinated program for resettlement assistance to refugees after their arrival in the U.S. This resettlement program was established in recognition of the fact that refugees differ fundamentally from immigrants, in that they are fleeing persecution, their departure is involuntary and usually unplanned, they frequently have been traumatized, and they arrive with little if any money and usually no family or business connections. Thus, "there is a strong practical and ethical case for providing them support upon arrival" (Fix and Passel 1994, p. 63). Consequently, refugees are eligible for far more public assistance than immigrants, and such assistance is delivered through a coordinated program, which is also not the case for immigrants.

The Refugee Act of 1980 defined the goal of the refugee resettlement program as helping refugees achieve economic self-sufficiency and social adjustment as rapidly as possible. Economic self-sufficiency was defined as not receiving financial assistance from public welfare programs. In order to achieve this goal, three forms of assistance were established: cash and medical assistance, social services, and preventive health services. Cash and medical assistance are provided to refugees who arrive with no financial resources and who are not eligible for other public welfare programs such as Temporary Assistance to Needy Families (TANF), Supplemental Security Income (SSI), or Medicaid. Under the original legislation, refugees were eligible for this assistance for the first three years after arrival, but since then the eligibility period has been progressively reduced, and is now eight months. Social services are primarily English language training and employment training and placement. Refugees who receive cash and medical assistance are required to participate in employment training and to accept offers of employment. Preventive services are preventive health assessment and treatment for infectious diseases (Office of Refugee Resettlement 1999a).

In addition to these direct services, the Refugee Act also authorized funds for a Voluntary Agency Matching Grant Program and a Targeted Assistance Grant Program. The Voluntary Agency Matching Grant Program matches federal funds to private funds or in-kind donations from private agencies assisting refugees during the first four months after arrival. The Targeted Assistance Grant Program provides additional funds to local communities that have a high concentration of refugees and a high use of public assistance by refugees (Office of Refugee Resettlement 1999a).

A few months after passage of the Refugee Act, the United States experienced a large influx of people from Cuba and Haiti, who arrived by boat. In response, Congress passed the *Refugee Education Assistance Act of 1980*, which provided for services for Cuban and Haitian entrants identical to those for refugees under the Refugee Act.

In the years since the passage of the Refugee Act, several controversial issues have arisen. First, even though the act was intended to eliminate ideological biases in the determination of refugee status, in reality, most refugees that have been admitted since 1980 have continued to be from Communist countries. This was made possible by a clause in the 1980 act that essentially gave preference to the admission of refugees who are "of special humanitarian concern to the United States." Consequently, this allowed the government to continue to apply ideological and foreign policy considerations to decisions about which refugees to admit, and this was manifested in a preference for refugees from Communism. However, since the fall of Communism in the former Soviet Union and Eastern Europe, as well as the resettlement of most Southeast Asian refugees, the proportion of refugees admitted from non-Communist countries has increased somewhat.

Second, the asylum provision of the Refugee Act has been problematic in that large numbers of people have applied for asylum after entering the U.S. illegally, or overstaying their nonimmigrant legal stays. This situation puts humanitarian interests in conflict with the interest of controlling illegal immigration (Fix and Passel 1994). "Most asylum applicants have not only been granted work authorization while they await their hearings, they have also been extended broad procedural safeguards if their petitions are denied. Further, few denied applicants have ever been deported. Thus, despite the fact that most asylum applicants come from countries where human rights abuses have been documented, the process has been viewed skeptically by its critics" (Fix and Passel 1994, p. 15). Another problem with the asylum provision is that it excludes asylum-seekers who are intercepted at sea by U.S. ships. Under the Refugee Act, such people are considered neither asylees, since they are not on U.S. soil, nor refugees, since they have not been granted asylum in another country. Consequently, they are usually returned to their countries of origin. However, this practice is in conflict with the *non-refoulement* principle of international refugee law.

A final controversial issue is the steady and sharp reduction in the eligibility period and funds allocated for the refugee resettlement program. As noted above, the eligibility period for assistance has declined from three years to eight months. And federal funding per refugee dropped from $7300 in 1982 to $2200 in 1993, for example (Fix and Passel 1994). This is seen as an unfavorable development by refugee advocates, and by states and local communities that have had to pick up much of the costs. Despite these controversies, the Refugee Act of 1980 remains the major piece of legislation that guides refugee admission and resettlement to the present.

IMMIGRATION REFORM AND CONTROL ACT OF 1986 (IRCA) Beginning in the early 1970s, the U.S. government considered ways of reforming immigration law to better control illegal immigration. This concern arose from the increasingly large numbers of illegal aliens that were apprehended each year (Congressional Research Service 1991). The increase in illegal immigration was fueled in part by an economic recession in Mexico in the 1970s (McBride 1999). There was concern that the large number of illegal immigrants threatened the economic security of U.S. workers. Consequently, the Immigration Reform and Control Act (IRCA) was passed in 1986.

This act contained three major provisions pertaining to the control of illegal immigration. First, it imposed sanctions, or penalties, on employers who knowingly hired illegal aliens. It also created a national tracking system for aliens and required states to use the system to check the immigration status of aliens who applied for welfare. These measures were intended to decrease illegal immigration by reducing the monetary incentives. Second, IRCA increased border control and enforcement. Finally, the act provided for the legalization of certain illegal aliens. In order to deal humanely with illegal aliens who had already established roots in the U.S., IRCA included an amnesty provision that permitted the legalization of those who had resided in the U.S. continuously since 1982. And in order to address the needs of U.S. agriculture, which depended heavily on seasonal migrant laborers, IRCA created a new classification of seasonal agricultural workers and provisions for their legalization (Congressional Research Service 1991; Fix and Passel 1994; McBride 1999).

The amnesty provision of IRCA led to the legalization of almost 3 million residents. However, the employer sanctions largely failed in controlling illegal immigration. They have been difficult to enforce because of the prevalence of fraudulent documents, which make it difficult for employers to ascertain the real immigration status of job applicants. Additionally, limited government resources were allocated for enforcement of the employer sanctions (Fix and Passel 1994).

IMMIGRATION ACT OF 1990 After addressing illegal immigration with IRCA, Congress turned its attention to legal immigration. There were some concerns about the numerical limits and preference system created in 1965 and subsequently amended. One concern was that more immigrants had been admitted under the family reunification categories than under the employment-based categories. Another concern was that a limited number of admissions were available under the preference system to certain countries. These concerns led to the passage of the Immigration Act of 1990 (Congressional Research Service 1991).

This act entailed a major revision of immigration law. It contained several major revisions. First, it increased total annual legal immigration limits by 40 percent, including almost tripling the admission limit for employment-based immigration. Second, it revised the preference system, creating new family-sponsored preference categories, employment-based preference categories, and two categories of legal immigrants that are outside of the preference system. This system, which is shown in table 2.5, remains in place to the present.

The total annual limit for legal immigration is set at 675,000. Additionally, each admission category has numerical limits associated with it. The annual limits are adjusted each year based on usage in the previous year. There are three major admission categories: family-sponsored, employment-based, and diversity. Refugees are not included in these categories. Their admission is governed by the Refugee Act of 1980. The family-sponsored and employment-based categories each consist of preference categories. The preference categories represent descending order of admission priority. Any unused admissions in a given preference category are reallocated to the next lower category.

Family-sponsored immigrants are required to have a "sponsor" (a U.S. citizen or permanent resident family member) who promises to support them if they are unable to support themselves. There are four preference categories of family-sponsored immigrants. Immediate relatives (spouses, minor children, and parents) of U.S. citizens are outside of the preference system and their admission is unlimited. Thus, total family-sponsored ad-

TABLE 2.5 LEGAL IMMIGRATION ADMISSION PREFERENCE SYSTEM

PREFERENCE	DESCRIPTION	ANNUAL LIMIT (1995 AND AFTER)
FAMILY-SPONSORED IMMIGRANTS		480,000
First	Unmarried adult sons and daughters of U.S. citizens and their minor children	23,400
Second	Spouses, minor children, and unmarried adult sons and daughters of permanent resident aliens	114,200
Third	Married adult sons and daughters of U.S. citizens	23,400
Fourth	Brothers and sisters of adult U.S. citizens	65,000
	Immediate relatives (spouses, minor children, and parents) of adult U.S. citizens and minor children born abroad to alien permanent residents	Not limited; assumed to be 254,000
EMPLOYMENT-BASED PREFERENCES		140,000
First	Priority workers (aliens with extraordinary ability, outstanding professors and researchers, and certain multinational executives and managers)	40,040
Second	Professionals with advanced degrees or aliens with exceptional ability	40,040
Third	Skilled workers, professionals, and needed unskilled workers	40,040
Fourth	Special immigrants (ministers of religion, certain employees / retirees of the U.S. government abroad, Panama Canal or Zone employees, certain doctors, certain international-organizations related aliens, certain members of the U.S. Armed Forces recruited abroad)	9,940
Fifth	Employment creators (investors who will create employment for at least ten U.S. citizens or permanent residents)	9,490
DIVERSITY IMMIGRANTS		55,000
TOTAL		675,000

Sources: Gimpel and Edwards, 1999; Immigration and Nationality Act; U.S. Immigration and Naturalization Service, 1999a.

missions in a given year could exceed the overall allocation of 480,000, if the admissions in the unlimited category exceed the "assumed" number of 254,000.

In the employment-based category, there are five preferences that together have an overall allocation of 140,000. Additionally, the 1990 act created a new category, "diversity immigrants," which was intended to increase admissions from countries from which relatively few immigrants had been admitted since the 1965 act. Because most immigrants since 1965 had been from Latin America and Asia, the diversity category was intended to increase the number of immigrants from Europe. It was also intended to increase the overall skill level of new arrivals, and to promote the ethnic and cultural pluralism of the U.S. (Fix and Passel 1994).

Another major provision of the Immigration Act of 1990 was its authorization of the Attorney General to grant Temporary Protected Status to undocumented aliens from countries that were subject to armed conflict or natural disasters. An additional major provision was the repeal of previous laws that permitted exclusion or deportation of aliens based on political or ideological grounds. Further, the 1990 act revised enforcement activities pertaining to illegal immigration control. This included making some changes in the employer sanction provisions of IRCA and increasing border patrols.

Finally, the Immigration Act of 1990 made some revisions to naturalization requirements. The current requirements for naturalization, as established by this act and subsequently slightly modified, are summarized in table 2.6. The Immigration and Nationality Act as amended by the Immigration Act of 1990, with some minor subsequent revisions, remains the major piece of legislation guiding legal immigration admissions and naturalization to the present.

PERSONAL RESPONSIBILITY AND WORK OPPORTUNITY RECONCILIATION ACT OF 1996 (PRWORA) In the mid-1990s, public sentiment became increasingly anti-immigrant. This national trend was led by California, the state with the largest number of foreign-born residents. California was undergoing a severe economic recession. At the same time, the flow of illegal immigrants into California continued in large numbers, despite the various measures that had recently been enacted to control illegal immigration (Fix and Zimmerman 1999). Many California citizens, including the governor, blamed

TABLE 2.6 GENERAL NATURALIZATION REQUIREMENTS

AGE

Applicant must be at least 18 years old.

RESIDENCY

Applicant must have been lawfully admitted to the U.S. for permanent residence.

RESIDENCE AND PHYSICAL PRESENCE

Applicant has:
• Resided continuously as a lawful permanent resident in the U.S. for at least 5 years prior to filing, with absences from the U.S. totaling no more than one year.
• Been physically present in the U.S. for at least 30 months out of the previous five years (absences of more than six months but less than one year break the continuity of residence unless the applicant can establish that he or she did not abandon his or her residence during such period).
• Resided within a state or district for at least three months.

GOOD MORAL CHARACTER

Applicant must show that he or she has been a person of good moral character for five years prior to filing. Applicant is permanently barred from naturalization if he or she has ever been convicted of murder, or has been convicted of an aggravated felony on or after November 29, 1990. A person cannot be found to be of good moral character if he or she:
• Has been convicted of certain crimes.
• Is or has earned his or her principal income from illegal gambling.
• Is or has been involved in prostitution or commercialized vice.
• Is or has been involved in smuggling illegal aliens into the U.S.
• Is or has been a habitual drunkard.
• Is practicing or has practiced polygamy.
• Has willfully failed or refused to support dependents.
• Has given false testimony under oath in order to receive a benefit under the Immigration and Nationality Act.

ATTACHMENT TO THE CONSITUTION

Applicant must show that he or she is attached to the principles of the U.S. Constitution.

LANGUAGE

Applicant must be able to read, write, speak, and understand words in ordinary usage in the English language. Applicants exempt from this requirement are those who on the date of filing:

TABLE 2.6 *(continued)*

- Have been residing in the U.S. subsequent to a lawful admission for permanent residence for at least 15 years and are over 55 years of age.
- Have been residing in the U.S. subsequent to a lawful admission for permanent residence for at least 20 years and are over 50 years of age; or
- Have a medically determinable physical or mental impairment that affects the applicant's ability to learn English.

U.S. GOVERNMENT AND HISTORY KNOWLEDGE

Applicant must demonstrate a knowledge and understanding of the fundamentals of the history, principles, and form of U.S. government. Applicants exempt from this requirement are those who, on the date of filing, have a medically determinable physical or mental impairment that affects the applicant's ability to learn U.S. history and government. Applicants who have been residing in the U.S. subsequent to a lawful admission for permanent residence for at least 20 years and are over the age of 65 will be afforded special consideration in satisfying this requirement.

OATH OF ALLEGIANCE

To become a citizen, an applicant must take the oath of allegiance. By doing so, an applicant swears to:
- Support the Constitution and obey the laws of the U.S.
- Renounce any foreign allegiance and / or foreign title; and
- Bear arms for the U.S. Armed Forces or perform services for the U.S. government when required.

In certain instances where the applicant establishes that he or she is opposed to any type of service in armed forces based on religious teaching or belief, INS will permit the applicant to take a modified oath.

WAIVERS, EXCEPTIONS, AND SPECIAL CASES

Spouses of U.S. Citizens
Certain lawful permanent residents married to a U.S. citizen may file for naturalization after residing continuously in the U.S. for three years if immediately preceding the filing of the application:
- The applicant has been married to and living in a valid marital union with the same U.S. citizen spouse for all three years
- The U.S. spouse has been a citizen for all three years and meets all physical presence and residence requirements; and
- The applicant meets all other naturalization requirements

There are also exceptions for lawful permanent residents married to U.S. citizens stationed or employed abroad. Some lawful permanent residents may not have to comply with the residence or physical presence requirement.

> **TABLE 2.6** *(continued)*
>
> *Children*
> Children born abroad of U.S. citizen parents derive citizenship from their parents. Adopted children of citizen parents acquire citizenship.
>
> **VETERANS**
>
> Special provisions apply to certain veterans of U.S. Armed Forces, lawful permanent residents with three years U.S. military service, and veterans who have served honorably in certain armed conflicts with hostile foreign forces.
>
> *Source:* U.S. Immigration and Naturalization Service, 1999b.

illegal immigrants for contributing to the state's economic hardship and crime (DeSipio and de la Garza, 1998). Consequently, the public placed a proposition addressing this issue on the state ballot. This was made possible by California's unique initiative process, which allows individuals to organize to place propositions on the ballot. Such propositions, if passed, override state statutes, and can be reversed only by a constitutional amendment or another initiative (DeSipio and de la Garza, 1998).

The illegal immigrant proposition that was placed on the ballot became known as Proposition 187. The proposition contained the following provisions for the treatment of illegal immigrants:

> Enrollment in all public schools, colleges, and universities would be barred; parents or guardians of all school children would have to show legal residence and school administrators would have to report suspected illegal immigrants; non-emergency public health care, including pre-natal and post-natal services, would be denied to those who could not prove legal status; access to many state programs which dealt with troubled youths, the elderly, the blind, and others with special needs would be cut off; law enforcement agencies would be required to cooperate fully with INS officials; and penalties for the sale and use of fraudulent documents were to be increased.
>
> (MCBRIDE 1999, P. 17)

The proposition was passed by the voters, but was immediately challenged in court by its opponents, which included many organizations "including police departments, teachers and school administrators, medical groups, lawyers, human rights bodies, and representatives of minority groups" (McBride 1999, p. 17). A series of court rulings declared most of the provisions of the proposition to be unconstitutional. These rulings were founded on the argument that the regulation of immigration and immigrants was a federal, rather than a state responsibility. An additional basis for the rulings was that the provisions might violate immigrants' constitutional rights to due process since there was no provision for hearings before or after the denial of services (McBride 1999). Consequently, these court rulings blocked the implementation of most of the elements of the proposition (DeSipio and de la Garza 1998; McBride 1999).

However, even though the measures were not implemented, the proposition had a strong influence on public opinion nationwide. It brought to the forefront the general public's negative sentiments toward immigrants, and particularly illegal immigrants (DeSipio and de la Garza 1998; McBride 1999). At the same time, nationwide use of public benefits by noncitizens was rising faster than use by citizens (Zimmerman and Tumlin 1999). Citizens in several other states mounted similar initiatives, but failed because those states did not have initiative procedures such as California's (DeSipio and de la Garza 1998). Additionally, the state of California has strong influence on national politics because of the size of its population. The state has over 10 percent of the nation's population and controls 20 percent of the Electoral College votes needed to elect the U.S. president. Consequently, California interests are extremely important to Congress and the Presidency (DeSipio and de la Garza 1998). These elements combined to lead to the passage of two major pieces of federal immigration legislation in 1996 (DeSipio and de la Garza 1998; Fix and Zimmerman 1999; McBride 1999; Zimmerman and Tumlin 1999).

The first of these was the Personal Responsibility and Work Opportunity Reconciliation Act (PRWORA). This act, commonly known as welfare reform, pertained to the welfare system in general and contained major provisions pertaining specifically to immigrants and refugees. This law represented "an unprecedentedly tough legislative agenda that substantially restricted the legal and social rights of immigrants" (Fix and Zimmerman 1999, p. 7). These laws fundamentally changed the nation's approach toward immigrants following their arrival.

While *immigration policy* is concerned with the admission of immigrants, policy that addresses the social and economic integration of immigrants following their admission is variously referred to as *immigrant policy, immigrant integration policy,* or *settlement policy* (DeSipio and de la Garza 1998; Fix and Passel 1994; Fix and Zimmerman 1995; Zimmerman and Tumlin 1999). In contrast to immigration policies, which have been explicit ever since the passage of the first immigration legislation in 1882, "immigrant integration policies historically have been policies of benign neglect" (Fix and Zimmerman 1995, p. 1). "Immigrant policy—how immigrants should be treated once in the United States—has been implicit and de facto, made up of a variety of rules governing noncitizens' access to education, public benefits, and the like" (Zimmerman and Tumlin 1999, p. 8–9). The one exception to this is the Refugee Act of 1980, which explicitly detailed a resettlement program for refugees. However, no such explicit policy existed for immigrants (nonrefugees) prior to welfare reform. "PRWORA begins to define a U.S. immigrant policy more clearly—establishing an explicit policy of exclusion" (Zimmerman and Tumlin 1999, p. 9).

Before PRWORA, native-born citizens, naturalized citizens, and legal permanent residents generally had equal eligibility for public benefits and services, and few rights and priviliges were denied to legal permanent residents (DeSipio and de la Garza 1998; Fix and Zimmerman 1995, 1999). However, "PRWORA institutionalized the concept of immigrant exceptionalism—treating noncitizens differently from similarly situated citizens—to a new and unprecedented degree in social welfare policy" (Zimmerman and Tumlin 1999, p. 5). On the other hand, even before PRWORA, illegal immigrants were ineligible for most public benefits, and were denied many rights and priviliges (DeSipio and de la Garza 1998; Zimmerman and Tumlin 1999). Therefore, PRWORA did not fundamentally change the eligibility and rights of illegal immigrants, although it did make the denials of rights and benefits more explicit. However, PRWORA broadened ineligibility for certain benefits and programs to include certain groups of legal immigrants (Zimmerman and Tumlin 1999).

Additionally, immigrant policy had previously been the domain of the federal government, as established by several Supreme Court rulings and federal statutes (Zimmerman and Tumlin 1999). Further, in its benign neglect, the federal government essentially left the process of immigrant settlement to private institutions (DeSipio and de la Garza 1998). However, PRWORA "shifts the level of control over immigrant policy to a greater extent than ever before from the federal government to the states" (Zimmerman and Tumlin 1999, p. 9).

PRWORA contained numerous welfare reform provisions that pertained to both citizens and aliens. The act abolished the Aid to Families with Dependent Children (AFDC) program and replaced it with the Temporary Assistance to Needy Families (TANF) program, which consisted of block grants to states to provide time-limited cash assistance to needy families. Adults were limited to a total of 60 months of TANF assistance over their lifetimes. States were given the option to exempt up to 20 percent of their caseloads from this time limit. PRWORA also established work requirements for TANF recipients. Adults receiving assistance (with certain exceptions) were required to begin performing community service within two months of receiving the assistance. After a maximum of two years of assistance, parents and caretakers were required to engage in work activities. Single parents were required to work at least 20 hours per week, and two-parent families were required to work at least 35 hours per week, in order to maintain benefit eligibility. The act also limited food stamp eligibility. Unemployed adults between the ages of 18 and 50 who were not disabled or raising minor children were limited to receiving food stamps for a total of three months out of a 36-month period. Only those who were working or participating in a work or training program could continue to receive food stamps beyond three months (Allen 1997).

The provisions of PRWORA that were specific to aliens included the following:

- Barring most immigrants from food stamps and Supplemental Security Income (SSI)—cash assistance for the poor, elderly, and disabled. Immigrants barred from these programs included "current" immigrants who were already in the United States at the time the law was enacted [August 22, 1996] and new "future" immigrants who had yet to enter.
- Barring new immigrants for five years from "federal means-tested benefits," defined so far to include Temporary Assistance to Needy Families (TANF), Medicaid, and the Child Health Insurance Program (CHIP).
- Giving states the option of barring current immigrants (i.e., those in the United States on or before August 22, 1996) from TANF, Medicaid, and the Social Services Block Grant. The law also gave states the option of barring new immigrants (arriving after August 22, 1996) from TANF and Medicaid following a mandatory five-year bar. In so doing, the Congress overrode set-

tled Supreme Court doctrine by permitting states to discriminate against legal immigrants in determining eligibility for certain federal, state, and locally funded benefit programs.
• Exempting some legal immigrants with strong equities from the benefit restrictions. These include refugees during their first several years in the United States, legal immigrants who have worked for 10 years or whose spouse or parents have done so, and noncitizens who have served in the U.S. military.
• Barring "unqualified immigrants" from all "federal public benefits" and requiring that public agencies that dispense them verify the legal status of applicants. Unqualified immigrants include not only undocumented aliens but also other groups with authority to remain in the United States without permanent residence, some of whom had been determined to be eligible for selected federal benefits by the courts.

(FIX AND ZIMMERMAN 1999, P. 7–8)

Further, PRWORA required that family sponsors of immigrants entering after August 22, 1996 sign a legally enforceable affidavit promising to financially support the immigrant. Further, the sponsor's (and sponsor's spouse's) income was required to be included in determining the immigrant's eligibility for public benefits (Zimmerman and Tumlin 1999).

PRWORA gave authority to states to make the following decisions:

• Whether to provide jointly funded federal and state programs to immigrants (namely, TANF and Medicaid).
• Whether to create new substitute food, cash, and health programs for immigrants losing eligibility for federal assistance.
• Whether to extend their existing safety net programs to immigrants (e.g., General Assistance and health insurance programs).
• Whether to implement new restrictions on eligibility for federal, state, and local public benefits for undocumented and other unqualified immigrants.
• Whether to create or expand programs that promote naturalization.

(ZIMMERMAN AND TUMLIN 1999, P. 10)

PRWORA created a set of extremely complex eligibility rules. These rules were based upon a set of distinctions among different groups of immigrants. The first fundamental distinction was between citizens and noncitizens. Under PRWORA, naturalized citizens have the same rights, priviliges, and benefit eligibility as native-born citizens. Noncitizens do not have the same rights, privileges, and eligibility. Additionally, PRWORA created an entirely new set of distinctions within the noncitizen category (Zimmerman and Tumlin 1999). The first distinction is between pre-enactment and post-enactment immigrants. Different eligibility criteria were established for immigrants who were already in the U.S. at the time of PRWORA's enactment on August 22, 1996, and those who entered after that date:

> States were given the option to bar most pre-enactment immigrants from TANF and nonemergency Medicaid programs. Most post-enactment immigrants, however, were barred from federal means-tested benefits, defined to include SSI, food stamps, TANF, nonemergency Medicaid, and the state Child Health Insurance Program (CHIP) for their first five years in the United States. Part of the rationale for these restrictions on post-enactment immigrants was that they were required by PRWORA to have sponsors who had proven that they could financially support the new entrants and signed a legally enforceable affidavit promising to do so.
> (ZIMMERMAN AND TUMLIN 1999, P. 14)

A SECOND NEW DISTINCTION was between exempt and nonexempt aliens:

> Several groups of immigrants with arguably the strongest claims were totally exempted from PRWORA's various immigrant bars. These groups include refugees and asylees during their first several years in the United States. Refugees and asylees historically have been given greater access to public benefits than have other immigrants and they are generally poorer than other immigrants and do not have sponsors. Immigrants with a strong attachment to the U.S. labor force (i.e., those who have worked for at least 10 years) or who have served in the U.S. military are also exempt from the restrictions.
> (ZIMMERMAN AND TUMLIN 1999, P. 16)

A FINAL NEW DISTINCTION was between qualified and nonqualified aliens:

> Qualified aliens include lawful permanent residents, refugees and other groups admitted for humanitarian reasons, and certain battered spouses and children. All other immigrants are considered unqualified, including those with permission to remain in the United States but without legal permanent resident status. These unqualified immigrants are now barred from a

broader set of benefits than they were before, including federal child care and federal low-income heating assistance. Unqualified immigrants are eligible, however, for emergency services under Medicaid, immunizations, and testing and treatment for symptoms of communicable diseases.

(ZIMMERMAN AND TUMLIN 1999, P. 16)

Definitions of the major terms that are contained in PRWORA and in subsequently developed government guidelines are summarized in table 2.7.

TABLE 2.7 KEY TERMS IN IMMIGRANT WELFARE REFORM

QUALIFIED IMMIGRANTS

- Lawful permanent residents
- Refugees / asylees (defined below)
- Persons paroled into the United States for at least one year
- Battered spouses and children (with a pending or approved spousal visa or a petition for relief under the Violence Against Women Act)

UNQUALIFIED IMMIGRANTS

An immigrant not falling within the qualified immigrant group (see above). This group includes undocumented immigrants, asylum applicants, as well as those with temporary status such as students and tourists.

REFUGEES / ASYLEES

Those admitted for humanitarian reasons. The following groups are subject to the same exemptions as refugees and asylees:
- Persons with deportation / removal withheld
- Cuban-Haitian entrants
- Amerasians

40 QUARTERS EXEMPTION

Lawful permanent residents who have worked at least 40 qualifying quarters as defined by the Social Security Act are exempt from certain bars on immigrants' eligibility. No credit is given for quarters worked after 12/31/96 if the immigrant received a federal means-tested benefit in that quarter. Credit is also given to immigrants for work performed by:
- Their parents (before the immigrant reaches age 18)
- Their spouse during the marriage (unless the marriage ended in divorce or annulment)

TABLE 2.7 *(continued)*

MILITARY EXEMPTION

Noncitizens are exempt from bars on eligibility if they are or were:
- On active duty
- Honorably discharged
- The spouse, unremarried surviving spouse, or unmarried dependent child of a veteran or active-duty service member
- Filipino war veteran who fought under U.S. command in World War II

FEDERAL MEANS-TESTED BENEFITS

Qualified immigrants entering the United States after 8/22/96 are barred from these benefits for their first five years in the country. These benefits have been defined as:
- Federal food stamps
- Medicaid
- Supplemental Security Income (SSI)
- Temporary Assistance for Needy Families (TANF)
- The state Children's Health Insurance Program (CHIP)

FEDERAL PUBLIC BENEFITS

Unqualified immigrants are barred from these programs. These benefits have been defined to include certain services provided under 31 programs, such as:
- Social Services Block Grant (SSBG) services
- Low-Income Home Energy Assistance Program (LIHEAP)
- Child Care and Development Block Grant (CCDBG) services

Exemptions include programs that provide immunizations; testing and treatment of communicable diseases; and short-term noncash disaster relief. Programs delivering in-kind services; programs not targeted to individuals or means-tested; and those necessary to protect life or safety are also exempt.

SPONSOR-DEEMING

The attribution of the income and resources of an immigrant's sponsor or sponsors (and their spouse) to the immigrant for purposes of determining eligibility for public benefits.

Source: Zimmerman and Tumlin, 1999. Copyright © 1999, Urban Institute. Reprinted with permission.

When President Clinton signed PRWORA into law, he specifically objected to many of its immigrant provisions and stated that he would take steps to reverse them (Administration for Children and Families 1999;

DeSipio and de la Garza 1998; Zimmerman and Tumlin 1999). Subsequently, even some Congress members, particularly Republicans, who had voted for the act began to question some of its immigrant provisions (McBride 1999; Zimmerman and Tumlin 1999). There were several reasons for this shift:

> First, the [Republican] party found that it was losing support among Hispanic and Asian-American voters, an issue that became even more important as many legal immigrants sought naturalization (which would also give them the right to vote) to avoid the loss of benefits which had been curtailed by the legislation. Second, one of the major proponents of immigration reform, Alan Simpson, retired from the Senate. His place on the Senate immigration panel was taken by a more moderate Senator.
>
> (MCBRIDE 1999, P. 20)

ADDITIONALLY,

> Well-publicized stories about the anticipated effects of the termination of SSI benefits for elderly and disabled immigrants and the initial impacts of food stamp cuts were major contributors. Growing advocacy efforts at federal and state levels have also had an effect. To a greater extent than ever before, immigrant advocacy organizations teamed up with groups that serve broader low-income constituencies to lobby on behalf of immigrants. In addition, long waits for naturalization—up to two years in some cities, such as Los Angeles—have probably played a part in rising public frustration over the federal restrictions. (ZIMMERMAN AND TUMLIN 1999, P. 12)

Consequently, several pieces of legislation were subsequently passed that eased some of the immigrant restrictions of PRWORA. The Balanced Budget Act of 1997 restored SSI eligibility to most elderly and disabled immigrants who were in the U.S. at the time that PRWORA was passed. The Emergency Supplemental Appropriations Act of 1997 allowed states to purchase federal food stamps for newly ineligible immigrants and delayed the implementation of both food stamp and SSI benefit terminations. The Agriculture Research, Extension, and Education Reform Act of 1998 restored food stamp eligibility to most elderly, disabled, and child-age immigrants who were living in the U.S. when PRWORA was passed. The Noncitizen Benefit Clarification and Other Technical Amendments Act of 1998 allowed certain elderly and disabled unqualified immigrants to maintain their SSI benefits (Zimmerman and Tumlin 1999). Additional benefit restorations have been proposed, but not yet passed, by both Congress and the President (Administration for Children and Families 1999; Zimmerman and Tumlin 1999).

Another way in which the government has limited PRWORA's original broad restrictions is by narrowly defining key terms. For example, federal means-tested benefits have been defined through regulation to include only five programs, rather than the 52 programs that qualified immigrants could have potentially lost under the original legislation. However, the restorations to date have addressed only pre-enactment immigrants (Zimmerman and Tumlin 1999). Table 2.8 shows the current (as of writing) eligibility criteria as established by PRWORA and the subsequent modifications to it.

The implementation of PRWORA has had numerous consequences for immigrants and refugees, as well as for states. One result has been that the social safety net for immigrants and refugees has been weakened (Zimmerman and Tumlin 1999). Because of the discretion granted to states by PRWORA in determining public benefit eligibility, there is considerable variation across states. States that have strong safety nets in general, and states with high per capita incomes, have been more likely to maintain benefits for immigrants. Almost every state has chosen to maintain TANF and Medicaid eligibility for pre-enactment immigrants, and more than half of the states have chosen to provide substitute assistance for some immigrants who became ineligible for federal assistance. Additionally, many states have chosen to maintain immigrants' eligibility for state General Assistance programs. And most states that have a state health insurance for low-income people have chosen to maintain immigrant eligibility, but less than half the states have such a program. These substitute and General Assistance programs fall short of the federal assistance. They usually target children and the elderly, leaving out working-age adults. Additionally, the substitute programs often have sponsor deeming requirements, which disqualifies some immigrants. Further, some programs mandate that recipients apply to naturalize in order to receive benefits. This can disqualify some immigrants that have particular difficulty meeting the English and civics requirements of naturalization (Zimmerman and Tumlin 1999).

TABLE 2.8 ALIEN ELIGIBILITY FOR PUBLIC BENEFITS

IMMIGRANT STATUS	BENEFITS				
	SSI Stamps	Food	Medicaid	TANF Benefits	State/Local
QUALIFIED IMMIGRANTS ARRIVING ON OR BEFORE AUGUST 22, 1996					
Qualified Immigrants	Eligible[1]	Eligible[2]	State option	State option	State option
Exempted Groups					
With 40 quarters of work	Eligible	Eligible	Eligible	Eligible	Eligible
Military personnel	Eligible	Eligible	Eligible	Eligible	Eligible
Refugees/Asylees	Eligible for first 7 years	Eligible for first 7 years	Eligible for first 7 years; state option afterward	Eligible for first 5 years; state option afterward	Eligible for first 5 years; state option afterward
QUALIFIED IMMIGRANTS ARRIVING AFTER AUGUST 22, 1996					
Qualified Immigrants	Ineligible	Ineligible	Barred for first 5 years; state option afterward	Barred for first 5 years; state option afterward	State option

TABLE 2.8 (continued)

IMMIGRANT STATUS	BENEFITS				
	SSI Stamps	Food	Medicaid	TANF Benefits	State/Local
Exempted Groups					
With 40 quarters of work	Barred for first 5 years; eligible afterward	Barred for first 5 years; eligible afterward	Barred for first 5 years; state option afterward	Barred for first 5 years; state option afterward	Eligible
Military personnel Refugees/Asylees	Eligible Eligible for first 7 years	Eligible Eligible for first 7 years	Eligible Eligible for first 7 years; state option afterward	Eligible Eligible for first 5 years; state option afterward	Eligible Eligible for first 5 years; state option afterward

IMMIGRANT STATUS	BENEFITS				
	SSI Stamps	Food	Medicaid	TANF Benefits	State/Local
UNQUALIFIED IMMIGRANTS					
Unqualified Immigrants	Ineligible	Ineligible	Eligible for emergency services only	Ineligible	Ineligible[3]

[1] Qualified immigrants receiving SSI on 8/22/96 are eligible. All qualified immigrants lawfully residing in the U.S. on 8/22/96 who are or become disabled are also eligible. All other qualified immigrants are ineligible unless exempted.

[2] Qualified immigrants who were lawfully residing in the U.S. on 8/22/96 and are under 18 years; disabled or blind; or 65 years or older on 8/22/96 are eligible. All other qualified immigrants are ineligible unless exempted.

[3] States may provide state and local public benefits to unqualified immigrants only if they pass a law after 8/22/96.

Source: Zimmerman and Tumlin, 1999. Copyright © 1999, Urban Institute. Reprinted with permission.

PRWORA has also had major consequences for families in which some members are citizens but others are not (Fix and Zimmerman 1999). This is the case for 85 percent of immigrant families. In most of these cases, one or both parents are not citizens, but their children are citizens because they were born in the United States. One of the consequences of PRWORA for these families is inequitable treatment of family members. For example,

> A legal immigrant child who entered the United States [before PRWORA enactment] would not be eligible for Medicaid but her U.S.-born citizen brother would be, even though both live in the same household and have the same resources available to them. The older child's lack of health insurance will mean that she has less access to preventive and other forms of health care than her sibling. (FIX AND ZIMMERMAN 1999, P. 9)

ANOTHER CONSEQUENCE IS that citizen children's benefits are diminished. For example,

> When Congress barred noncitizens from food stamps, citizen children remained eligible but their noncitizen parents did not. Food stamps, though, are provided on a household, not an individual basis. That is, the amount of food stamps received is based on the number of eligible people in the household. Thus, mixed-family households, along with the citizen children in them, receive fewer food stamps than they did before the cuts and presumably have less to eat [Consequently], it could be argued, for example, that welfare reform has created two classes of citizen children. One class lives in households with noncitizens and suffers the disadvantage of losing benefits and the reduced overall household resources that may result; a second class of citizen children lives in households with only citizens and suffers no comparable disadvantage. The emergence of these two classes of citizen children begs the question whether their differing eligibility for benefits should be viewed as an example of constitutionally acceptable discrimination against aliens or as a more problematic instance of unacceptable discrimination between similarly situated citizens. (FIX AND ZIMMERMAN 1999, P. 3, 9)

Overall, the shifting of responsibility for immigrant policy from the federal government to the states has resulted in greater inequality across state safety nets for immigrants than for citizens. Many immigrants, particularly post-enactment immigrants, remain ineligible for both federal and state benefits. Further, many immigrants who are eligible for benefits have not accessed them. This is likely due to a combination of factors, including confusion caused by the complexity of the eligibility rules (Zimmerman and Tumlin 1999).

Further, the states that have the largest numbers of immigrants now bear an even greater disproportionate share of the financial burden than they did before PRWORA. Additionally, PRWORA has created a sharp discrepancy between immigration policy and immigrant policy:

> States have a bigger role in setting immigrant policy and paying for it. But the federal government retains exclusive authority over immigration policy, determining how many and which immigrants enter each year. As a result, our federally set immigration policy remains fairly liberal and inclusive while our immigrant policy, now largely in the hands of the states, has become more exclusionary and fragmented.
>
> (ZIMMERMAN AND TUMLIN 1999, P. 50)

In regard to the effect of PRWORA on actual utilization of public benefits by immigrants and refugees, a recent study of utilization before and after welfare reform found the following (Fix and Passel 1999):

- Use of public benefits among noncitizen households fell more sharply (35 percent) between 1994 and 1997 than among citizen households (14 percent). These patterns hold for AFDC / TANF, SSI, General Assistance, food stamps, and Medicaid.
- Refugees experienced declines (33 percent) that were at least as steep as those within the noncitizen population—despite the protections for refugees incorporated into welfare reform and the fact that few refugees had lost their eligibility benefits.
- For low-income populations (i.e., with incomes below 200 percent of poverty), program usage also fell faster for noncitizen than citizen households.
- Welfare use in noncitizen households with children also fell faster (36 percent) than in households with children where all adults are citizens (23 percent).
- Noncitizens accounted for a disproportionately large share of the overall decline in welfare caseloads that occurred between 1994 and 1997. While 23 percent of the drop in welfare caseloads can be ascribed to noncitizens, they represented only 9 percent of households receiving welfare in 1994.
- Welfare use among elderly immigrants and naturalized citizens did not appear to change between 1994 and 1997.
- When welfare use among all households is examined, noncitizen partici-

pation levels were higher than citizens' in both 1994 and 1997. But when we look at poor households (i.e., with incomes under 200 percent of poverty), noncitizens' participation rates in 1994 were no different from those of citizens; by 1997, however, levels had declined so that noncitizens had lower participation rates than citizens (14.5 versus 17.9 percent). When we examine poor households with children, noncitizen rates were lower for both 1994 and 1997—falling to almost half of the level of citizens in 1997 (14.0 versus 25.8 percent).
• Neither naturalization nor rising incomes accounted for a significant share of noncitizens' exits from public benefit use.

(FIX AND PASSEL 1999, PP. 2-3)

A certain way for noncitizens to regain their benefit eligibility is to become naturalized. Consequently, some states have required benefit recipients to apply for naturalization, and some have established initiatives to help immigrants naturalize (Zimmerman and Tumlin 1999). Such initiatives usually include public information campaigns about the benefits of naturalization and English and civics classes to help people meet the naturalization requirements. Some critics have expressed concern that the pressures of PRWORA would fundamentally change the reasons for naturalization—that people would naturalize simply in order to retain benefits rather than as an expression of allegiance to the United States (DeSipio and de la Garza 1998; Keigher 1997). However, this does not appear to be happening. Data indicate that few immigrants are naturalizing in order to retain benefits (Fix and Passel 1999). Naturalization rates were already increasing in the years preceding welfare reform, for a variety of other reasons (U.S. Immigration and Naturalization Service 1998).

Thus, welfare reform appears to have achieved its intended effect of reducing noncitizens' welfare utilization. But it has also had undesirable and unintended effects of reducing benefits to some particularly vulnerable subgroups such as refugees and children. Further, the economic well-being of noncitizens does not appear to have improved and has likely worsened as a result of welfare reform.

ILLEGAL IMMIGRATION REFORM AND IMMIGRANT RESPONSIBILITY ACT OF 1996 (IIRIRA) Within a few weeks of passing PRWORA, Congress passed a second major piece of immigration legislation, the Illegal Immigration Reform and Immigrant Responsibility Act (IIRIRA). The impetus for this legislation was the same restrictionist sentiments that had led to PRWORA.

Portions of IIRIRA also addressed public benefit eligibility. IIRIRA imposed for the first time a minimum income requirement on legal immigrants' sponsors. The minimum income requirement was defined as 125 percent of the poverty level. Further, sponsors were required to support the immigrants until they had worked for 10 years or had become citizens; and sponsors were made liable for repayment of certain benefits that the immigrants may have used during that time (Fix and Zimmerman 1999). Additionally, IIRIRA declared aliens not lawfully present ineligible for Social Security benefits; established procedures for requiring proof of citizenship for federal public benefits; required verification of immigration status for Social Security and higher educational assistance; and provided states the authority to limit general cash public assistance to aliens (U.S. Immigration and Naturalization Service 1997b). Further, IIRIRA allowed the denial of admission of people who were deemed likely to become a "public charge," i.e., likely to use public benefits (Gimpel and Edwards 1999).

IIRIRA eased some of PRWORA's restrictions. For example, it allowed illegal aliens who were victims of domestic violence to receive public assistance. Also, it exempted nonprofit organizations from having to verify an applicant's immigration status in order to determine benefit eligibility (Gimpel and Edwards 1999).

IIRIRA also contained provisions for increasing control of illegal immigration. These included increasing border and workplace enforcement personnel; increasing penalties for illegal entry, overstay, alien smuggling, and document fraud; reforming exclusion and deportation procedures in order to expedite removal; and increasing detention space for deportable aliens (U.S. Immigration and Naturalization Service 1997). A final major provision of IIRIRA was requiring asylees to file an asylum application within one year of entry into the U.S., and creating expedited procedures for asylum hearings and appeals (Gimpel and Edwards 1997).

Critics have expressed concerns about some of the anticipated effects of IIRIRA. One concern is that many potential sponsors will be unable to meet the new minimum income requirement, and therefore will not be able to reunite with their family members (Fix and Zimmerman 1999). Other concerns relate to the expedited removal procedures and expedited asylum procedures. Critics fear that deportable aliens and asylum-seekers will not be provided due process in hearings and in judicial review of decisions (Fix and Zimmerman 1999; McBride 1999). Expedited removal is also likely to split up families (Fix and Zimmerman 1999).

Partially in response to some of these concerns, Congress subsequently passed several pieces of legislation intended to correct some of the problems of IIRIRA for some categories of aliens. These laws include the *Nicaraguan Adjustment and Central American Relief Act of 1997 (NACARA); the Haitian Refugee Immigration Fairness Act of 1998 (HRIFA);* and the *Legal Immigration Family Equity Act of 2000 (LIFE).* Nonetheless, significant concerns about the negative consequences of IIRIRA remain (National Immigration Forum, 2000c; 2000d).

ANTITERRORISM AND EFFECTIVE DEATH PENALTY ACT OF 1996 (AEDPA) This third major piece of immigration legislation passed in 1996 was developed to improve procedures for identifying, excluding from entry, and removing alien terrorists from the United States. The law also provided for improvements in dealing with criminal aliens.

OTHER POLICIES AND LAWS AFFECTING IMMIGRANTS AND REFUGEES Immigrants and refugees are affected not only by specific immigration and refugee policies, but also by other more general policies that address people's rights and priviliges. Further, in addition to policies, which form *statutory law*, numerous alien rights and priviliges have been established by *case law*, or judicial rulings on specific cases. Such rulings establish precedents that are then a basis for law.

In general, outside of specific immigration and refugee laws, aliens are subject to the same laws as citizens. Major exceptions to this are in the areas of public benefits (which have been described above), electoral rights, and employment / occupational rights (DeSipio and de la Garza 1998). In regard to electoral rights, in general, noncitizens do not have the right to vote, except in a very few local elections in a few jurisdictions. Clearly, this has implications for the political power and influence of immigrant groups. In regard to employment and occupation, legal immigrants generally have the same rights and priviliges as citizens, except that most government jobs are restricted to citizens. Undocumented aliens, of course, do not have the right to work. However, undocumented alien children have been granted the right to public education (DeSipio and de la Garza 1998).

Additionally, aliens have benefited from laws designed for U.S.-born ethnic minorities such as African Americans, Hispanic Americans, Asian Americans, and Native Americans. These laws, such as civil rights laws, voting rights protections, and affirmative action programs, were not originally designed for aliens, but have nonetheless benefited those aliens who are also members of these ethnic minority groups (DeSipio and de la Garza 1998). This has caused some controversy because these laws were designed to remedy past discrimination experienced by U.S.-born minority groups, but aliens did not experience this past discrimination since they were not in the U.S. at the time. This leads to concerns about the equity and effectiveness of these laws, sets up the potential for backlash by the U.S.-born minority groups against aliens, and puts the two populations in competition for public resources and public sympathy (DeSipio and de la Garza 1998). Consequently, it has been argued that separate explicit policies addressing aliens' needs should be developed, in order to adequately address the different needs of both aliens and native-born minorities (DeSipio and de la Garza 1998).

POLICY IMPLEMENTATION Immigration and refugee policies usually provide broad authority and apply to general situations. Agencies must then apply the general provisions of the statutes to specific, detailed situations. In order to implement immigration and refugee policies, federal agencies such as the Immigration and Naturalization Service (INS) develop regulations that apply the law to daily situations. These regulations are published in the *Federal Register*, a centralized government document that is published daily. The *Federal Register* contains proposed, interim, and final rules. Proposed rules are open to public comment before they become interim or final rules, both of which have the force of law. After publication in the *Federal Register*, the regulations are collected and published in the *Code of Federal Regulations (CFR)*. Title 8 of this code, often referred to as *8 CFR*, pertains to "Aliens and Nationality" and contains most of the immigration and refugee regulations. Other regulations pertaining to immigrants and refugees may also be found under other CFR titles. Further, the INS develops *Operation Instructions* and *Interpretations* to supplement and clarify the provisions of statutes and regulations. These deal specifically with procedural matters. An additional source of legal interpretations of immigration laws and regulation is administrative decisions made by the Federal Board of Immigration Appeals. (U.S. Immigration and Naturalization Service 1999c). Finally, the ultimate implementation of policies is carried out through the daily operations of a variety of federal, state, and private agencies. These are described in the next chapter, as part of the service delivery system.

CHAPTER 3

SERVICE DELIVERY SYSTEMS

A LARGE AND DIVERSE NETWORK of organizations and personnel delivers human services to refugees and immigrants. This network includes international, national, state, and local agencies, both public and private. It also includes professionals and paraprofessionals from a variety of disciplines. This chapter describes these organizations and workers, and the major service delivery strategies that they use.

3.1 SERVICE DELIVERY ORGANIZATIONS

3.1.1 INTERNATIONAL ORGANIZATIONS

INTERNATIONAL ORGANIZATIONS PROVIDE ASSISTANCE during the pre-migration, departure, and transit stages of the migration process. Most immigrants do not require assistance during these stages, and they make their departure and travel arrangements on their own. However, some immigrants and all refugees do require international assistance. International organizations include intergovernmental organizations and private agencies. Specific organizations are discussed below; additional information about them can be obtained from the website addresses that are provided.

INTERGOVERNMENTAL ORGANIZATIONS Intergovernmental organizations are associations such as the United Nations, which consist of member nations. Many intergovernmental bodies are involved with immigrants and refugees, although that is not their exclusive mandate. These include the following United Nations divisions: Center for Human Rights; Department of Humanitarian Affairs (DHA); World Food Program (WFP); Department for Economic and Social Information and Policy Analysis (DESIPA); Department for Policy Coordination and Sustainable Development (DPCSD); Development Program (UNDP); Population Fund (UNFPA); International Labor Organization (ILO); Children's Fund (UNICEF); Educational, Scientific, and Cultural Organization (UNESCO); and the World Bank (http://www.un.org). Additionally, many regional intergovernmental organizations are also involved (Good, et al. 1995).

The two major intergovernmental organizations that are exclusively concerned with international migration are the *International Organization for Migration (IOM)* (http://www.iom.int) and the *United Nations High Commissioner for Refugees (UNHCR)* (http://www.unhcr.ch). Both of these organizations are headquartered in Geneva, Switzerland. IOM's mission is to "assist in meeting the operational challenges of migration; advance understanding of migration issues; encourage social and economic development through migration; and uphold the human dignity and well-being of migrants" (International Organization for Migration, 1998, p. 1). In terms of direct assistance to international migrants, IOM provides numerous services during the pre-migration stage:

> Pre-migration services may include: establishing emigration dossiers, doing pre-screening activities at the request of and in accordance with the criteria of specific governments, obtaining exit permits and safe conduct passes, arranging for medical examinations, arranging interviews and interpretation services, and making all the operational and functional arrangements to ensure movement by the safest, most direct and economical means. Support programs may also provide counseling on immigration procedures, legal requirements, social and economic conditions; language training and cultural orientation; processing of required documentation; and notification of receiving sponsors or entities. (GOOD ET AL. 1995, P. 106).

IOM ALSO PROVIDES ASSISTANCE in the transit phase:

> For those who spend only a short time in transit the primary assistance consists of payment for or provision of direct transportation. Transport arrangements may be straightforward for individual cases but may require contracting or chartering of transportation on short notice for mass emergency evacuations. The technical nature of making these arrangements for

movement usually centers around the logistical aspects of arranging the transport, facilitating exit and entry procedures, maximizing the speed of the operation and minimizing costs. IOM coordinates transport arrangements and supervises relations with the airline industry with respect to negotiating and concluding favorable transport agreements for all persons moved under the auspices of IOM. After transportation is completed, IOM also verifies claims and collects payment from individuals who have been granted travel loans. (GOOD ET AL. 1995, PP. 108–109)

While IOM assists both immigrants and refugees, UNHCR's mandate is concerned exclusively with the latter. UNHCR has two main functions: to protect refugees and to seek durable solutions to their problems (UNHCR 1999c). UNHCR forms the core of what is termed the *international refugee regime*, which refers to the collection of laws, agreements, and institutions that have been established to regulate and resolve refugee problems (UNHCR 1997).

UNHCR's responsibility to protect refugees is referred to as *international protection*. It is aimed at ensuring refugees' basic human rights, particularly the right to *non-refoulement*, that is, the right not to be forcibly returned to a place where they fear persecution. To carry out this function, UNHCR promotes adherence to international refugee law and continuously monitors government compliance. UNHCR staff work in refugee camps and other refugee populated areas to protect refugees from attack or *refoulement*. UNHCR also coordinates the provision of shelter, food, water, sanitation, and medical care in emergency situations, including refugee camps (UNHCR 1999c).

In seeking durable solutions for refugees, UNHCR focuses on three options, in descending order of priority: (1) *repatriation*—helping refugees return home voluntarily, safely, and with dignity; (2) *integration*—helping refugees integrate into a country of first asylum; and (3) *resettlement*—helping refugees permanently resettle in a third country. Since most refugees want to return home pending political stabilization in their countries, and since most governments do not want to accept refugees, repatriation is always the first option sought. If repatriation is achieved, UNHCR continues to monitor the living and working conditions of the returnees to ensure their continued safety. However, if repatriation is not possible, the next option is to integrate the refugees into the country where they have been granted asylum. This is usually a neighboring country and integration would typically involve moving the refugees out of camps and into the society. However, many asylum countries are unwilling to accept refugees on a permanent basis in their society. Thus, the last option is resettlement in a third country. The United States is a major country for third-country resettlement.

PRIVATE ORGANIZATIONS In carrying out their missions, both IOM and UNHCR work closely with private, nonprofit international relief organizations. Such organizations are often referred to in the international arena as *nongovernmental organizations* (NGOs) or *private voluntary organizations* (PVOs). Unlike IOM and UNHCR, which are funded by contributions from the governments of their member countries, PVOs are funded by both government and private donations. Many PVOs are associated with religious organizations and receive funding from them.

> PVOs act primarily as conduits of emergency assistance rather than as major donors themselves.... While governments and international organizations have the money, PVOs have the manpower and the willingness to field individuals to work in the difficult and unpleasant circumstances that usually occur in refugee-impacted areas.... In a typical relief situation PVOs sign tripartite agreements with the UNHCR and host governments to act as implementors of specific relief projects. (GORMAN 1985, PP. 87–88)

Thus, PVOs often carry out many of the assistance tasks during the premigration stage, such as the administration of refugee camps and the provision of food, shelter, and medical care. Many PVOs have a broader orientation toward social and economic development, yet they are also relevant to refugees. This is because 90 percent of the world's refugees are in developing countries, and the successful, long-term resolution of refugee problems depends in part on the larger issue of development (Gorman 1985). PVOs play a critical role in immigrant and refugee assistance at the international level. Because they are not tied to governments, they can remain apolitical. This flexibility frequently allows PVOs to intervene in situations where governments and intergovernmental organizations cannot (Good et al. 1995; Gorman 1985). Some of the major private international relief agencies and their activities are listed in table 3.1.

TABLE 3.1 MAJOR PRIVATE INTERNATIONAL RELIEF ORGANIZATIONS INVOLVED WITH IMMIGRANTS AND REFUGEES

AGENCY	ACTIVITIES
American Friends Service Committee (AFSC) (http://www.afsc.org)	Supports reconciliation and development worldwide, especially in situations of conflict. Provides relief and rehabilitation assistance to refugees. Advocates for resolution of conflicts and for refugee rights throughout the world.
American Jewish Joint Distribution Committee (JDC) (http://www.jdc.org)	Provides for rescue, relief, and rehabilitation of Jewish communities around the world.
American Refugee Committee (ARC) (http://www.archq.org)	Provides health care, self-help training, and related services to refugees in Africa, Europe, and Southeast Asia.
CARE (http://www.care.org)	Aims to mitigate the effects of disasters, launch a quick and effective response to people's immediate need for food, water, shelter, and medical care, and help rebuild communities. Programs include emergency preparedness, relief and recovery, agriculture and natural resources, maternal/child health and family planning, water and sanitation, and basic education.
Catholic Relief Services (CRS) (http://www.catholicrelief.org)	Overseas relief and development agency of the U.S. Catholic Church. Responds to emergencies and helps the poor overcome poverty.
InterAction (http://www.interaction.org)	A coalition of U.S.-based agencies working to promote human dignity and development around the world. Assists and protects refugees. Works to prevent future disasters and to promote sustainable development.
International Catholic Migration Commission (ICMC) (http://www3.itu.ch/MISSIONS/US/bb/icmc.html)	Coordinates assistance to refugees, migrants, and internally displaced persons through a network of local agencies. Assistance includes vocational and language training, processing of refugees and migrants, and resettlement assistance.

TABLE 3.1 *(continued)*

AGENCY	ACTIVITIES
International Committee of the Red Cross (ICRC) (http://www.icrc.org)	Acts as a neutral intermediary during armed conflict. Aims to ensure that victims of war receive protection and assistance and that humanitarian law is respected. Protection activities include visiting prisoners of war and civilian detainees, tracing missing persons, and arranging exchanges of family messages. Assistance activities include providing medical care and material assistance to victims.
International Council of Voluntary Agencies (ICVA) (http://www.icva.ch)	Provides a forum for voluntary agencies engaged in humanitarian and development activities. Does not implement projects but provides support services to member agencies to enable them to cooperate and perform more effectively.
International Federation of Red Cross and Red Crescent Societies (IFRC) (http://www.ifrc.org)	Provides disaster relief operations and development support. Cares for refugees and internally displaced persons outside areas of conflict. Provides health, social welfare, logistics, and managerial staff.
International Rescue Committee (IRC) (http://www.intrescom.org)	Assists refugee and internally displaced persons. Provides medical services, food, public health, and sanitation assistance, training and education, and self-reliance projects.
Jesuit Refugee Service (JRS) (http://www.jesuit.org/refugee)	Provides health, education, legal assistance, research, and advocacy on human rights and humanitarian issues surrounding forced displacement.
Lutheran World Relief (http://www.lwr.org)	Assists with long-term and emergency help and development, especially in Asia, Africa, and Latin America.
Médecins Sans Frontières (MSF) (Doctors Without Borders) (http://www.msf.org)	Provides emergency medical aid to victims of disasters and conflicts. Major programs involve assistance to refugee and displaced populations, surgical and medical programs in war zones, epidemic and famine warning and response programs, rehabilitation of medical infrastructures, and training.

TABLE 3.1 *(continued)*

AGENCY	ACTIVITIES
Mennonite Central Committee (http://www.mcc.org)	Provides material aid and development assistance to victims of human-made and natural disasters in Africa, Middle East, Central America, and South/Southeast Asia.
Partners for Development	Provides long-term development assistance and emergency assistance. Provides services in public health, sanitation, household food and economic security, and infrastructure repair.
Presbyterian Disaster Assistance (http://www.pda.pcusa.org)	Provides disaster, relief, and refugee services around the world.
Salvation Army World Service Office (SAWSO) (http://www.salvationarmy.org)	Provides technical assistance and support in developing countries. Programs include primary health care, micro-enterprise credit, community development, vocational training, leadership development, relief, and reconstruction.
Save the Children (http://www.savethechildren.com)	Provides early childhood programs, emergency relief, and psychosocial rehabilitation for refugee children and families.
World Concern (http://www.worldconcern.org)	Administers long-term development and emergency relief programs. Programs include material assistance, agricultural assistance, micro-enterprise assistance, and management training.
World Council of Churches (WCC), Refugee and Migration Service (http://www.wcc-coe.org)	Works with local churches in support of refugee and migration services, including emergency and long term assistance. Also advocates on behalf of refugees and migrants and provides public information and training.
World Relief (http://www.worldrelief.org)	Provides relief and development assistance worldwide.
World Vision (http://www.worldvision.org)	Provides emergency disaster relief, child sponsorship, primary health care, agricultural development, and community leadership training projects worldwide.

Sources: Good, Jensen, Thompson, and Webster, 1995; U.S. Committee for Refugees 1998a.

As can be seen, the organizational service delivery system for international migrants is large and complex. Consequently, services are not always delivered effectively and efficiently. "In the midst of a relief crisis, confusion, mismanagement, and misguided relief efforts are more common than many would care to admit" (Gorman 1985, p. 88). Several factors contribute to these problems (Good et al. 1995; Gorman 1985). One is the categorization system of various types of migrants, which limits eligibility for assistance. For example, refugees are eligible for different services than are internally displaced people, even though both groups may have been uprooted by the same causes. A second factor is lack of harmony and ineffective enforcement of international and national laws and policies. A third factor is overlap and gaps in services due to insufficient coverage and funds. A final factor is lack of coordination. Often, the different phases of migration are handled by different agencies.

Likewise, different assistance efforts, such as relief and development, may also be handled by different agencies, thereby limiting continuity of assistance. Further, there can be conflict between the aims and approaches of international and local agencies working in the same area. And there can also be conflict between the philosophical or religious orientations of PVOs. Finally, although PVOs may strive to be apolitical, this is not always achieved, since their activities may have political implications for the country they are in. Efforts to improve inter-agency cooperation include expansion of definitions and coverage, coordination of international and national policies, and efforts to prevent gaps and duplication of services (Good et al. 1995).

In addition to international agencies that provide and coordinate direct assistance to immigrants and refugees, there are also agencies that provide indirect assistance through advocacy. These organizations monitor human rights around the world, mount public information campaigns, and lobby for policy changes. The major advocacy organizations and their activities are listed in table 3.2.

TABLE 3.2 MAJOR ADVOCACY ORGANIZATIONS INVOLVED WITH IMMIGRANTS AND REFUGEES IN INTERNATIONAL ARENA

AGENCY	ACTIVITIES
Amnesty International (AI) (http://www.amnesty.org)	Campaigns for freedom for prisoners of conscience, fair and prompt trials for political prisoners, and the abolition of the death penalty and other cruel treatment of prisoners. Opposes abuses by opposition groups, hostage taking, and arbitrary killings. Raises awareness of human rights of refugees and migrants by targeting government officials, military and police, legal groups, the media, and the general public through conferences, lobbying, public protest letters, and information campaigns.
Human Rights Watch (HRW) (http://www.hrw.org)	Monitors human rights practices and violations of humanitarian law by governments and rebel groups. Documents and denounces murders, "disappearances," torture, arbitrary imprisonment, censorship, and other abuses of human rights, including the rights of immigrants and refugees. Engages in publishing, information campaigns, and lobbying directed at governments, ruling bodies, intergovernmental and non-governmental organizations, and the media.
Lawyers Committee for Human Rights (LCHR) (http://www.lchr.org)	Works to apply and enforce international human rights law and refugee law throughout the world.
Refugees International (http://www.refintl.org)	Identifies life-threatening gaps in the international response to refugee emergencies and makes policy recommendations to address them.
U.S. Committee for Refugees (USCR) (http://www.refugees.org)	Defends the rights of refugees, asylum seekers, and displaced persons worldwide. Promotes principle of non-refoulement and rights to fair and impartial hearings, humane treatment, protection, and assistance. Makes refugee needs known to governments, international and non-governmental humanitarian relief organizations, and the general public through public briefings, testimony before U.S. Congress, publications, and media campaigns.

TABLE 3.2 *(continued)*

AGENCY	ACTIVITIES
Women's Commission for Refugee Women and Children (http://www.hypernet.com/wcrwc.html)	Speaks on behalf of refugee women and children worldwide. Serves as a technical advisor on reproductive health, protection and participation of refugee women, protection of refugee children, and detention of women and children asylum seekers. Testifies before U.S. Congress and presents findings to intergovernmental and non-governmental organizations.

Sources: Good et al. 1995; U.S. Committee for Refugees, 1998a.

3.1.2 UNITED STATES NATIONAL ORGANIZATIONS

NATIONAL ORGANIZATIONS serving immigrants and refugees in the United States are concerned primarily with admissions, border control, deportation, and the resettlement stage of migration. Like international organizations, national organizations include both governmental and non-governmental agencies.

U.S. GOVERNMENT AGENCIES Several federal agencies are involved with immigrants and refugees. First is the *Immigration and Naturalization Service* (INS) (http://www.ins.usdoj.gov), which is part of the Department of Justice. The INS is responsible for enforcing the laws regulating the admission of aliens into the U.S., and for administering various immigration benefits, including naturalization. INS's law enforcement functions include border control, port-of-entry inspections, detention and removal of criminal aliens, worksite enforcement, apprehension of illegal aliens, deportation and exclusion, denial of benefits to ineligible applicants, and investigating document fraud. INS's immigration benefit functions include administration of immigrant and nonimmigrant sponsorship, adjustment of status, work authorization and other permits, naturalization, and issues pertaining to refugees and asylees. The INS has offices located throughout the United States, as well as offices outside the U.S. which serve as linkages between INS and U.S.

Foreign Service officers and foreign government officials abroad (U.S. Immigration and Naturalization Service 1999d).

A second major federal government agency is the *Bureau of Population, Refugees, and Migration* (PRM) (http://www.state.gov/www/global/prm), which is part of the State Department. PRM has primary responsibility for formulating policies on population, refugees, and migration, and for administering refugee admissions and refugee assistance programs. PRM administers the admission of refugees who are of special humanitarian concern to the U.S. or who are referred by UNHCR. PRM establishes a worldwide processing priority system that sets the guidelines for the orderly management of refugee applications for admission. Eligibility for refugee status is decided on a case-by-case basis through an interview with an INS officer abroad. Refugees who are determined to be eligible may enter the U.S. along with members of their immediate family. At the port of entry into the U.S., the refugees and their families are officially admitted by the INS, which also authorizes employment.

In terms of assistance to refugees, PRM acts at both the international and domestic levels. At the international level, PRM administers U.S. government contributions to intergovernmental and international nongovernmental refugee assistance organizations, and monitors their operations. For those refugees and family members who have been determined to be eligible for admission into the U.S., PRM coordinates with other agencies to arrange for pre-departure medical examinations and cultural orientation sessions. PRM also arranges for transportation to the U.S., usually through the International Organization for Migration. At the domestic level, PRM contracts with private voluntary agencies in the U.S. which provide initial resettlement assistance to refugees during their first 90 days in the U.S. PRM assigns refugees to private agencies prior to their departure (Bureau of Population, Refugees, and Migration 1997a, 1997b, 1998, 1999).

A final major federal agency is the *Office of Refugee Resettlement* (ORR) (http://www.acf.dhhs.gov/programs/orr), located within the Administration for Children and Families in the Department of Health and Human Services. This agency plans, develops, and directs implementation of the comprehensive domestic refugee resettlement program. This program provides cash, medical, and social service assistance to eligible refugees during their first eight months in the U.S. in order to help them attain self-sufficiency as rapidly as possible. ORR develops, recommends, and issues program policies, procedures, and interpretations to provide program direction. ORR administers grants to state social welfare departments to implement the resettlement program. The states, in turn, typically contract with private agencies to deliver the resettlement services. ORR monitors and evaluates the performance of the states and private agencies in administering the program and supports actions to improve them. ORR also funds technical assistance to states and private agencies and funds demonstration programs designed to increase refugee self-sufficiency (Office of Refugee Resettlement, 1999b).

Several other federal agencies also serve immigrants and refugees, although that is not their exclusive function. The *Bureau of Consular Affairs* (http://www.travel.state.gov) in the State Department issues visas to immigrants and nonimmigrants at its overseas offices (Bureau of Consular Affairs 1999). The *U.S. Agency for International Development* (USAID) (http://www.info.usaid.gov) provides and coordinates humanitarian assistance to victims of natural disasters and complex emergencies in foreign countries, primarily through grants to NGOs (U.S. Committee for Refugees 1998a). The *Labor Department* (http://www.dol.gov) issues work certifications for permanent and temporary aliens. The certifications are designed to assure that alien workers will not adversely affect the job opportunities, wages, and working conditions of U.S. workers (U.S. Department of Labor 1999). Finally, the *Centers for Disease Control and Prevention (CDC)* (http://www.cdc.gov) in the Department of Health and Human Services provide technical assistance and training to organizations involved in immigrant and refugee health care (U.S. Committee for Refugees 1998a).

At the state government level, each state has a refugee coordinator within its social welfare department, who serves as the liaison with the federal Office of Refugee Resettlement and is responsible for all facets of refugee assistance in the state. The state social welfare department also administers all public benefits to immigrants and refugees under the federal and state welfare laws. Some state and local governments may have additional designated departments or employees that deal specifically with immigrants or refugees.

U.S. NATIONAL PRIVATE ORGANIZATIONS At the national level, private organizations in the U.S. are primarily involved with immigrants and refugees in the resettlement stage of migration. Since there is a comprehensive resettlement program for refugees but not for immigrants, most private agencies at the national level coordinate services to refugees. Agencies that provide these refugee services exclusively are known as *resettlement agencies*. These agencies and their local offices contract with federal and state governments to deliver resettlement services.

Agencies contract with the federal State Department's Bureau of Population, Refugees, and Migration to provide pre-departure and initial resettlement assistance. Pre-departure assistance is provided abroad prior to the refugees' departure for the U.S. It includes gathering basic information about family members, determining any medical problems that will require follow-up, determining addresses of any relatives already in the U.S., and determining where in the U.S. refugees and their family members will be resettled. The resettlement agency decides where to resettle refugees based on whether they already have relatives in the U.S. and the availability of jobs and resettlement services (Center for Applied Linguistics 1998a).

Initial resettlement assistance provided for refugees by resettlement agencies includes meeting refugees at the arrival airport and covering all necessary expenses for the first 30 days. For the first 90 days, resettlement agencies arrange for food, housing, furnishings, clothing, employment, medical care, counseling, English-language training, cultural orientation, orientation to the public transportation system, orientation to the U.S. monetary system, school enrollment for children, and any other necessary services (Center for Applied Linguistics 1998a; National Immigration Forum 1999a).

Resettlement agencies also contract with state social welfare departments to deliver services under the resettlement program of the federal Office of Refugee Resettlement. Such services are provided to certain needy refugees who are ineligible for other federal or state assistance programs. These services are aimed at helping refugees become self-sufficient and are available for the refugees' first eight months in the country. The services include cash and medical assistance and social services. The bulk of social services consists of English-language training, employment training, and job placement, and may also include other interventions aimed at enhancing self-sufficiency, such as counseling (National Immigration Forum 1999a; Office of Refugee Resettlement 1999a). The resettlement agency that serves refugees during the first 90 days under a federal State Department contract may or may not be the same agency that provides services under the ORR resettlement program. Resettlement agencies may also provide additional services outside of the scope of their government contracts, such as providing assistance to asylees in the U.S.; participating in national policy development; engaging in advocacy; and mounting public education campaigns to increase awareness of immigrant and refugee issues and to build community between newcomers and established residents.

Most private resettlement agencies are national organizations with local chapters or affiliates. Many are associated with religious institutions and receive part of their funding from them, but they are prohibited from encouraging refugees to join the agencies' affiliated religions or religious activities (Center for Applied Linguistics 1998a). The major national refugee resettlement agencies are listed in table 3.3. They all undertake similar activities as described above.

In addition to these direct service organizations, there are also national organizations that provide indirect service through advocacy. These organizations promote harmonious relations between newcomers and established residents, and lobby for humane, fair, and generous national immigration and refugee policies and procedures. The major advocacy organizations are listed in table 3.4.

TABLE 3.3 MAJOR UNITED STATES NATIONAL REFUGEE RESETTLEMENT AGENCIES

- Church World Service (CWS) (http://www.churchworldservice.org)
- Episcopal Migration Ministries (EMM) (http://www.dfms.org/emm/index.html)
- Ethiopian Community Development Council (ECDC) (http://www.ecdcinternational.org)
- Hebrew Immigrant Aid Society (HIAS) (http://www.hias.org)
- Immigration and Refugee Services of America (IRSA) (http://www.irsa-uscr.org)
- International Rescue Committee (IRC) (http://www.intrescom.org)
- Lutheran Immigration and Refugee Service (LIRS) (http://www.lirs.org)
- Southern Baptist Refugee Resettlement Program (http://www.namb.net/ccm)
- U.S. Catholic Conference/Migration and Refugee Services (USCC/MRS) (http://www.nccbuscc.org/mrs)
- World Relief (WR) (http://www.worldrelief.org)

Source: U.S. Committee for Refugees, 1998a.

TABLE 3.4 MAJOR NATIONAL IMMIGRANT AND REFUGEE ADVOCACY ORGANIZATIONS

- American Immigration Lawyers Association (http://www.aila.org)
- Exodus World Service (http://www.e-w-s.org)
- Lawyers Committee for Human Rights (http://www.lchr.org)
- National Immigration Forum (http://www.immigrationforum.org)
- National Network for Immigrant and Refugee Rights (http://www.nnirr.org/nnirr)
- Refugee Voices (http://www.irsa-uscr.org)
- U.S. Committee for Refugees (http://www.irsa-uscr.org)

Source: U.S. Committee for Refugees 1998a.

LOCAL ORGANIZATIONS As noted above, many national organizations have affiliates that operate at the local level. In addition to these, immigrants and refugees may receive services from other agencies that are essentially local. These agencies may be either public or private, and they may or may not serve immigrants and refugees exclusively or predominantly.

Service delivery systems that are not targeted specifically to immigrants or refugees are referred to as *mainstream* organizations. These include *hospitals, medical clinics, community mental health centers, schools, child welfare agencies, family service agencies,* and others. Sometimes these organizations have a program specifically designed for immigrants and refugees, but often they do not. Frequently, the staff members of these organizations do not have any specialized training to work with immigrants and refugees. When these agencies do not take into account the unique characteristics and needs of immigrants and refugees, they severely limit access to and effectiveness of their services for these populations.

Historically, mainstream social service agencies have presented barriers to service utilization by members of ethnic minority groups, including immigrants and refugees. Minority people may feel distrustful of mainstream services because of a history of oppression of the minority group by the majority group that operates the mainstream services. Minority clients may also feel that they have no input into the operation of the mainstream service delivery system. They may feel that the mainstream system is paternalistic. And the values of many ethnic groups also discourage seeking help from outside the group (Iglehart and Becerra 1995).

Due to these barriers within mainstream agencies, in many communities, private social service agencies have been established specifically to serve certain immigrant or refugee populations, or certain ethnic populations, which might include immigrants and refugees. Such agencies are referred to as *ethnic agencies*. An ethnic agency is defined by the following characteristics:

- it serves primarily ethnic [minority] clients;
- it is staffed by a majority of individuals who are of the same ethnicity as the client group;
- it has an ethnic majority on its board;
- it has ethnic community and/or ethnic power structure support;
- it integrates ethnic content into its program;
- it views strengthening the family as a primary goal; and
- it maintains an ideology that promotes ethnic identity and ethnic participation in the decisionmaking process.

(JENKINS 1981, CITED IN IGLEHART AND BECERRA 1995)

Ethnic agencies may focus on one area of social service, such as mental health, or they may be multi-service agencies. Ethnic agencies are founded upon the belief that access and effectiveness of services for ethnic minority clients will be enhanced as a result of staff-client similarity and client participation in decisionmaking (Iglehart and Becerra 1995).

Another type of ethnic-specific service delivery system, which exists in many refugee and immigrant communities, is the *Mutual Assistance Association* (MAA). These are self-help organizations formed by the community members themselves. They differ from ethnic agencies in that they usually do not have a professional paid staff. These organizations provide services such as community orientation, transportation, clothing, and furniture to newcomers (Center for Applied Linguistics 1998a).

Some advantages and disadvantages of both ethnic agencies and mainstream agencies have been noted (Westermeyer 1991a). Ethnic agencies have the advantage that they are more aware of and responsive to their clients' unique needs. However, a disadvantage of ethnic agencies is that the services they provide may be substandard because the agency is likely to have less access to resources, such as funds and personnel, from the general society. Additionally, ethnic agencies may increase isolation of ethnic groups from the majority society. And workers in ethnic agencies may be less employable in other settings, which may lead them to foster client dependence on the agency as a means of maintaining their own job security.

One advantage of mainstream services is that minimal funding for services to ethnic minority groups can be leveraged with more general funds. Further, the mainstream agency can serve as a model of minority-majority group integration. And job security for agency workers tends to be better. However, a disadvantage is that special minority group funding may get lost in the general funds, so that promises of service delivery to minority populations may not be met. And, as noted above, the major disadvantage of mainstream services is that they frequently present barriers to access by minority clients.

Mainstream organizations, such as hospitals and schools, provide essential services that cannot be provided by ethnic agencies alone. Thus, in order to assure adequate and effective service delivery to immigrants and refugees, it is important for mainstream organizations to decrease their access barriers. Mechanisms for achieving this include addressing the language needs of immigrant and refugee clients by employing well-trained interpreters; addressing the special cultural issues of clients, such as their beliefs about problem causation; using a holistic perspective in assessment; establishing credibility within the immigrant or refugee community; establishing linkages and continuity between different services; and establishing a formal means for clients to provide feedback to the agency (Kinzie 1991). These and other strategies for appropriate service delivery to immigrants and refugees are discussed more fully in the next chapter.

In summary, a vast and complex system of organizations delivers social services to immigrants and refugees. Some social workers are employed in agencies that specifically serve these populations. However, most social workers' contacts with refugees and immigrants will occur in the course of their work in mainstream social service agencies. In either case, it is important for social workers to be familiar with the variety of available organizations and services, in order to help clients navigate a system that can often be confusing and overwhelming to them (Boehnlein 1987).

3.2 SERVICE DELIVERY PERSONNEL

MOST UNITED STATES SOCIAL WORKERS who work with refugees or immigrants will encounter these clients in the resettlement stage of migration, through work in resettlement agencies, ethnic agencies, or mainstream agencies. In these agencies, social services to immigrants and refugees are delivered by professionals and paraprofessionals. *Professionals* include social workers, physicians, nurses, psychologists, teachers, marriage and family therapists, vocational counselors, attorneys, and so forth. Professionals have at least a bachelor's degree in their discipline, and usually have a graduate degree. *Paraprofessionals* are workers who have not completed a course of formal education in the discipline, but who come from the same background as the clients they serve (i.e., they are *indigenous* to the client population). Paraprofessionals often have different job titles in different agencies, such as interpreter, counselor, social adjustment worker, mental health assistant, mental health worker, or outreach worker (Egli 1991).

There are two fundamental distinctions between professionals and paraprofessionals. First, health and social service professionals have the authority to diagnose, treat, and prescribe treatment for health and social problems. Paraprofessionals do not have such authority. Second, professional service delivery is based on technical skills and specialized information, whereas paraprofessional service delivery is based on personal knowledge through experience, background, or culture (Ivry 1992).

Ideally, social services to refugees and immigrants would be delivered by professionals who have good familiarity with the service delivery system and who also share the client's language and have a deep appreciation for the client's social, political, and historical background (Ivry 1992). Thus, the ideal worker would be a member of the client's own refugee or immigrant group, who is a professional in the relevant discipline. However, there is a scarcity of such bilingual, bicultural professionals among many immigrant and refugee groups (Egli 1991; Le-Doux and Stephens 1992; Leiper de Monchy 1991; Musser-Granski and Carrillo 1997). Therefore, the next best option is service delivery by teams of professionals and paraprofessionals working together.

Although professionals have a high degree of training in their particular disciplines, they often do not have special training for working with refugees and immigrants. This is especially true for professionals in mainstream agencies. The specialized knowledge and skills needed by social work professionals in working with these populations are addressed in detail in the forthcoming chapters. The remainder of this section will focus on the functions of paraprofessionals, the challenges that they may present to agencies, and issues of hiring, training, and supervision of paraprofessionals.

Paraprofessionals serve as bridges between immigrant or refugee clients and non-indigenous professional staff (Egli 1991; Leiper de Monchy 1992). Thus, they serve the dual function of representing "the ideals, values, and perspectives of the refugee [or immigrant] community to the agency, and those of the agency to the community" (Egli 1991, pp. 90–91). Paraprofessionals provide numerous benefits to agencies and clients:

> Benefits in employing an indigenous staff include a shared common historical, cultural, and linguistic background with the client population as well as close ties, insights and information which may facilitate rapport and enhance communication between service provider and service recipient. As a member of the client group . . . the indigenous worker can also be a socializing agent, role model and guide to the challenges of assimilating into a new society. Furthermore, the indigenous worker is usually less formal than the professional, more responsive. (IVRY 1992, P. 109).

Paraprofessionals may have several roles within an agency (Egli 1991). One role is that of *translator*, which involves producing a written document in a different language from the original source. A second role is that of *interpreter*, which refers to verbal communication across different languages, such as interpreting between a client and professional staff member during an interview. A third role is *culture broker*, which involves educating staff and clients about each others' cultural norms, beliefs, values, behaviors, and practices. A fourth role is *outreach and community education*, which involves decreasing the agency's access barriers by informing potential clients about available services, and networking with other community agencies. A final role is that of *mental health worker* or *co-therapist*, which entails performing clinical functions in a semi-autonomous fashion.

Without careful training and supervision, the use of paraprofessionals can create problems for clients and agencies. This is particularly a hazard in the interpreter and mental health worker roles.

> Interpreting is extremely demanding because the interpreter does not have time to sit and consider the best translation, or to use a dictionary, and must

try not to interrupt the flow of speech. Interpretation is a highly developed art and skill, with formal education, certification, and licensure requirements in international and business settings. In the mental health context, interpretation requires that the bilingual worker utilizes his or her expertise and sensitivity with respect to the differing languages and cultures, providing messages which conserve as much as possible the language and psychological meaning of the original message. In order to be effective, the interpreter needs to be familiar with both cultures and languages and to some extent also with the specific topic under discussion. (EGLI 1991, P. 95)

Interpreters must be able to communicate both verbatim and elaborated interpretations that take into account cultural subtexts, idioms, affect, and nonverbal cues. There are three major sources of communication distortions by interpreters: deficient linguistic skills, lack of clinical sophistication, and the interpreter's attitudes toward the client or interviewer (Egli 1991). These problems can lead to distortions such as misunderstanding of terms, misleading paraphrasing, omission of details that the interpreter felt uncomfortable repeating or felt were inappropriate to repeat, and distortion of an interviewer's question in order to make it more culturally acceptable to the client (Egli 1991). In order to overcome these potential problems, it is important to hire interpreters with excellent linguistic skills, provide them with training in clinical issues as well as in the technical aspect of interpreting, and develop close, long-term working relationships between the professionals and paraprofessionals (Egli 1991).

Unfortunately, this is not always done. Sometimes, agency staff members such as secretaries or custodians, other clients, or family members are brought into an interview to interpret. This is completely inappropriate, except in a medical emergency. In the case of family members as interpreters, in addition to the normal hazards of interpretation, "existing family loyalties and power differences among members can result in the withholding of sensitive information by both the client and the family member doing the. translating. . . . this may also negatively affect family dynamics after the interviews have been completed" (Amodeo, Grigg-Saito, and Robb 1997, p. 79).

When paraprofessionals take on the role of mental health worker, problems can arise from their lack of training in mental health. Such problems include "overidentification with the patient, unresolved personal grief, and overadherence to traditional or personal value systems when they conflict with norms in the new culture" (Egli 1991, p. 102). As with interpretation problems, the solution to this problem lies in adequate training and close supervision.

In hiring paraprofessionals, several issues need to be considered (Egli 1991; Musser-Granski and Carrillo 1997). First, paraprofessionals must possess excellent language skills, good knowledge of both cultures, and personal qualities such as genuine concern for clients and ability to maintain confidentiality. Additionally, demographic and socioeconomic factors such as gender, age, religion, ethnicity, socioeconomic level, and sociopolitical orientation need to be considered because they can pose barriers between clients and paraprofessionals. For example, in many cultures it is not appropriate for younger people to give advice to older people, or for unrelated men and women to discuss their personal problems with each other. And in refugee situations, two members of the same community may be enemies because of their political orientations.

Training of paraprofessionals should include topics such as interpretation of both words and affect; norms of the new culture; mental health terminology, concepts, and interventions; medications; beginning assessment skills to identify clients in need; interviewing techniques; crisis intervention; family violence; case management; confidentiality, ethics, and the law; advocacy; community organizing, outreach, education, and prevention; personal boundaries, burnout, and overidentification with the client; and community resources and referrals (Musser-Granski and Carrillo 1997). Paraprofessionals should also be given opportunities for formal education and career advancement. There are few formal programs for training of paraprofessionals. Therefore, agencies usually have to undertake their own training. Unfortunately, few agencies have sufficient funds for this function (Egli 1991).

In the supervisory relationship, the supervisor must be attuned to potential conflicts (Egli 1991; Musser-Granski and Carrillo 1997). For example, professionals might find themselves dependent upon paraprofessionals for carrying out their jobs, and this might cause resentment. Likewise, paraprofessionals might feel that they are devalued by professionals, and they might resent working in a subsidiary position when they may have been highly respected professionals in their native country. Supervisors also need to be alert to potential abuses of power by paraprofessionals, such as showing favoritism to family and friends, or conducting after-hours work at home under the auspices of the agency. In some paraprofessionals' native countries, such practices may have been commonplace, but they are unethical in the new culture. Supervisors should also be aware that paraprofessionals are often caught between the demands of their refugee or immigrant community and the agency. Sometimes community members resent paraprofessionals for their apparently privileged position.

Good supervision should include support, trust, and respect. Supervisors may need to help paraprofessionals deal with their own issues related to their immigrant or refugee experience, and their position in the community. Paraprofessionals may need help in setting boundaries and establishing limits as to the help they are able to offer their community. Clinical supervision should include pre- and post-session debriefings.

Finally, effective work with paraprofessionals requires the development of clear job descriptions for all agency employees, training in effective teamwork, and monitoring of the effectiveness of the team approach. It also requires the development of "sound agency policy and programming which encompasses recruitment, training, monitoring, and recognition as essential components" (Le-Doux and Stephens 1992, p. 42).

3.3 SERVICE DELIVERY STRATEGIES AND TECHNIQUES

SERVICE DELIVERY to immigrants or refugees in the resettlement phase entails a wide range of strategies and techniques. Some of these have already been alluded to above in the discussions of organizational functions and professional and paraprofessional worker functions. Murase (1992) has compiled a detailed inventory of strategies and techniques of service delivery to immigrants and refugees in the resettlement phase, based on a study of relevant agencies. This inventory is summarized in table 3.5.

TABLE 3.5 STRATEGIES AND TECHNIQUES OF SERVICE DELIVERY TO REFUGEES AND IMMIGRANTS IN THE RESETTLEMENT PHASE

DIRECT SERVICES

- Information and referral
- Case advocacy, case management, and networking
- Counseling and treatment
- Health services
- Drug abuse services
- Protective services
- Vocational rehabilitation
- Youth services
- Housing services
- Employment services
- Immigration and legal assistance
- Refugee resettlement services

INDIRECT SERVICES

- Planning, coordination, and advocacy
- Consultation and technical assistance

Source: Murase, 1992.

The listing includes direct and indirect services. *Direct services* are those that entail direct contact with clients. *Indirect services* are those that are conducted on behalf of clients through contact with other entities. Under direct services, *information and referral* entail providing information about the agency's services and eligibility criteria, and referring to other agencies when appropriate. *Case advocacy, case management, and networking* "involve matching individual clients with community resources, following up with agencies to which clients are referred, and coordinating or networking with the services of the various agencies involved in an individual case" (Murase

1992, p. 105). *Counseling and treatment* services include "individual and group therapy, marital counseling, crisis intervention, day treatment, and related services" (p. 106). *Health services* include "health screening, primary health care, family planning, nutrition, hot meals, and home health care" (p. 106). *Drug abuse services* include outpatient and residential treatment programs and preventive education. *Protective services* address child abuse and battered women.

Vocational rehabilitation includes counseling, job training, and placement for physically disabled clients. *Youth services* are targeted for "youth from economically disadvantaged backgrounds, as well as recent immigrant youth who encounter problems of discrimination, language barriers, unemployment, and alienation" (p. 107). *Housing services* include activities such as renovation, securing housing for low-income residents, "taking the lead in the enforcement of housing code violations, and generally mobilizing the community to preserve existing housing and develop new housing" (p. 107). *Employment services* include "career counseling, job training and placement, job development, and English as a Second Language classes" (p. 107). *Immigration and legal assistance* includes working with the INS and other government agencies on immigration status issues. Finally, refugee resettlement services include "most of the services described above" (p. 107).

Under indirect services, *planning and coordination* typically entails councils or federations of agencies that work together to enhance service delivery to the community. *Advocacy* includes activities such as conducting policy analyses, public education forums, public information publications, and testifying before legislative bodies in order to improve conditions for clients. *Consultation and technical assistance* includes "grant writing, organizational development, management, economic development, and resource development" (p. 108).

In addition to these direct and indirect services, another important agency and worker function is *research and evaluation*. These are conducted in order to identify client needs, develop appropriate services, and assess service effectiveness. Research and evaluation include activities such as collecting data through surveys or interviews, reviewing the literature to gain understanding of client problems and to identify promising service approaches, and designing studies to assess service effectiveness and efficiency.

In conclusion, social workers serving refugees or immigrants work in and with a variety of organizational structures, with a variety of service delivery personnel, and use a wide array of service delivery strategies and techniques. The following chapters address in detail each of these service delivery and research and evaluation methods, in the context of helping immigrant and refugee clients in various problem domains.

PART II
PROBLEM AREAS AND BEST PRACTICES

CHAPTER 4

CULTURALLY COMPETENT SOCIAL WORK PRACTICE

THIS CHAPTER BEGINS Part II of this book. Whereas Part I focused on establishing the context for social work practice with refugees and immigrants, Part II now turns to the practice itself. The chapters in this part will describe specific problems faced by refugees and immigrants, and best social work practice responses. This book advocates and focuses on using *empirically based practice* in social work with immigrants and refugees. A social worker who uses empirically based practice is one who:

- Makes maximum use of research findings.
- Collects data systematically to monitor the intervention.
- Demonstrates empirically whether or not interventions are effective.
- Specifies problems, interventions, and outcomes in terms that are concrete, observable, and measurable.
- Uses research ways of thinking and research methods in defining clients' problems, formulating questions for practice, collecting assessment data, evaluating the effectiveness of interventions, and using evidence.
- Views research and practice as part of the same problem-solving process.
- Views research as a tool to be used in practice.

(SIEGEL, 1984, P. 329, CITED IN BLYTHE AND TRIPODI, 1989, P. 13)

ACCORDINGLY, *best practices* are defined as practice activities that are grounded in this empirically based practice paradigm.

All work with refugees or immigrants must be based on a foundation of culturally competent practice. That is the focus of this chapter. *Culturally competent practice* is defined as a set of *attitudes and beliefs, knowledge,* and *skills* that a social worker must possess in order to work *effectively* with clients who are from a different culture than the worker (Sue, Arredondo, and McDavis 1992; Lum 1999). It is important to note that the concept of *cultural competence* goes beyond earlier concepts such as *cultural awareness* (Green 1999) and *ethnic sensitivity* (Devore and Schlesinger 1999). These concepts refer to being aware of and being sensitive to cultural differences and adapting practice so that it is congruent with the norms and expectations of the client's culture. The concept of cultural competence includes these elements. However, in addition, the concept of cultural competence is concerned with *practice effectiveness.*

Lum (1999, p. 174) defines *cultural competencies* as "a series of related behaviors that are observable and measurable and demonstrate effective multicultural practice." However, even this definition falls short because it focuses only on measuring worker behaviors, and does not include measuring client outcomes such as accessing services, staying in treatment, satisfaction with treatment, resolution of problems, and achievement of goals. All of the worker attitudes, beliefs, knowledge, and skills that constitute culturally competent practice are intended to enhance these client outcomes. Therefore, another important element of culturally competent practice is measurement of these outcomes in order to determine the extent to which the intervention has been effective. This means that culturally competent social workers must include *program evaluation* and *practice evaluation* activities in their daily practice with clients. Unfortunately, this element has been largely neglected in the social work literature on culturally competent practice. This makes it even more critical for social workers to evaluate their practice with culturally different clients and to disseminate their findings in order to add to the profession's knowledge base about what really works for these clients.

The following discussion of culturally competent practice first provides definitions of some important terms. Then, the specific attitudes and beliefs, knowledge, and skills needed for culturally competent practice are described. This discussion builds upon the work of prior authors in the areas of culturally competent practice and empirically based practice.

4.1 TERMINOLOGY FOR CULTURALLY COMPETENT PRACTICE

DESCRIPTIONS OF CULTURALLY COMPETENT PRACTICE rely on the use of many terms that must first be defined. These include terms regarding characteristics of people, processes that people experience, characteristics of societies, and attitudes and behaviors of people toward other ethnic groups.

4.1.1 CHARACTERISTICS OF PEOPLE

IN DISCUSSING CULTURALLY COMPETENT PRACTICE, reference is made to characteristics of people such as race, culture, and ethnicity. Race refers to genetic differences among people that are manifested in physical characteristics such as skin color. The U.S. government has created four official race categories for use in collecting data: American Indian or Alaskan Native; Asian and Pacific Islander; Black; and White. However, it has been demonstrated that the concept of race has no scientific validity. That is, physical differences between people are not due to genetics, but to environmental influences and the biological process of evolution (Clark and Hofsess 1998; Green 1999). Nonetheless, the fact remains that people do differ in physical appearance, and their appearance affects their life experiences. In most societies, there is a majority of people who look "alike" in basic characteristics such as skin color, and there are minority groups of people who look "different" from the majority in terms of those characteristics. And almost universally, the members of the minority groups have been and are subject to mistreatment by members of the majority group. Thus, the most important implication of the concept of race for social work is understanding of the societal advantages (for majority group members) and disadvantages (for minority group members) that physical appearance bestows upon people. These are discussed further throughout this chapter.

Culture refers to "the way of life of a society and life patterns related to conduct, beliefs, traditions, values, language, art, skills, and social/interpersonal relationships" (Lum 1999, p. 80). Culture is transmitted from generation to generation. *Ethnicity* refers to groupings of people based on shared elements such as physical appearance, culture, religion, and history (Devore and Schlesinger 1999). Often ethnicity is used to refer to national origin or national ancestry, such as the term "Hispanic," which refers to people who have ancestors from Spain. Other times, ethnicity is used in place of race in order to signify that people in a "racial" group may also share other characteristics and experiences besides physical appearance.

People who are members of minority racial or ethnic groups are sometimes referred to as *minorities*, which is intended to convey not just the notion of numerical minority, but also the fact that these people are disadvantaged and receive unequal treatment in society (Lum 1999). In the United States, the term "minorities" commonly refers to African Americans, Asian or Pacific Islander Americans, Native Americans, and Hispanic Americans. Alternately, these people are sometimes referred to as *people of color*.

No one of the above terms is sufficient to describe a person's total and unique reality. Many people do not belong to a distinct racial or ethnic category. Additionally, there are great variations among people within categories. For example, the term "Hispanic" encompasses an extremely diverse group of people, including people from many different countries and all races. People within categories are also further differentiated by socioeconomic status. For example, the reality of a poor Black person may be more similar to that of a poor Hispanic person than to a middle-class Black person. Thus, application of broad categories to describe people may be more harmful than helpful. It is important to remember that the U.S. population is characterized by "diversity within diversity." It is also important to consider not only these static categories, but also the dynamic processes that people undergo in relation to culture and ethnicity.

4.1.2 HUMAN PROCESSES

INDIVIDUALS VARY in the degree to which they feel a sense of belonging to a particular ethnic group. This sense of belonging is referred to as *ethnic identity*. For some people, ethnic identity is not very strong or important. This may be particularly true for White Americans whose ancestors immigrated to the United States two or more generations previously (i.e., grandparents or earlier generations). Often, for these people, the traditions, values, and practices of the original culture have faded over the generations. These people consider themselves simply "Americans" (Devore and Schlesinger 1999; Green 1999; Lum 1999). For other people, particularly immigrants and refugees, ethnic identity tends to be very strong, because their traditions, values, and practices clearly contrast with those of the dominant "American" culture; these contrasts increase the awareness of ethnic identity (Devore and Schlesinger 1999).

Ethnic identity changes over time. It is influenced by factors such as desire for belonging, desire for protection from others who are hostile toward an ethnic group, and by world events that raise awareness of one's sense of identity with others (Devore and Schlesinger 1999). Ethnic identity also tends to change across generations. Identity with the original culture is strongest among immigrants and refugees, and tends to decrease among their children and subsequent generations, although among some groups and individuals, a certain degree of identity with the original culture is maintained even after many generations.

The process of adaptation between two cultures is known as *acculturation*. This process is faced by all immigrants and refugees as their native traditions, values, language, beliefs, and so forth, come into contact with those of the new, dominant culture. In general, it is the newcomers who are faced with adapting to the new culture, rather than members of the dominant culture adapting to the culture of the newcomers. Early theories viewed acculturation as a unidimensional continuum, with complete maintenance of the native culture on one end, and complete adoption of the new culture on the other, with varying degrees of blending the two cultures in between. However, it is now understood that acculturation is much more complex than this (Clark and Hofsess 1998).

One current model of acculturation incorporates two dimensions—the native and the new cultures—with people having varying degrees of identity in relation to both cultures. This results in four possible outcomes of the acculturation process (Berry 1990), which are depicted in table 4.1.

TABLE 4.1 TWO-DIMENSIONAL MODEL OF ACCULTURATION

DEGREE OF IDENTITY WITH NATIVE CULTURE	DEGREE OF IDENTITY WITH NEW CULTURE	
	High	Low
High	Integration (Biculturalism)	Separation
Low	Assimilation	Marginalization

Source: Adapted from Berry, 1990.

When an individual has high identity with the native culture and low identity with the new culture, the outcome is *separation*. These people either choose to completely maintain their native cultural traditions, values, etc., and choose not to participate in the new culture; or, they have not been allowed access to the dominant culture by its members. When an individual has low identity with the native culture and high identity with the new culture, the outcome is *assimilation*. In this case, the individual has completely given up the native ways and adopted the new. When an individual has high identity with both cultures, the outcome is *integration* or *biculturalism*. In this case, the person feels equally comfortable in both cultures. Finally, when a person has low identity with both cultures, the outcome is *marginalization*. These people do not feel at home in either culture. They have either withdrawn from or been excluded by members of both cultures. They feel like "outsiders" regardless of which cultural setting they are in.

Another current model of acculturation posits that acculturation is multidimensional. In this model, individuals maintain their native culture in relation to some traits, such as child-rearing practices, native foods, and music preferences, but adopt the norms of the new culture in relation to other traits, such as language and dress (Clark and Hofsess 1998). People who selectively acculturate in this way are also termed *bicultural* in this model.

Although the United States has one dominant culture (the "White Anglo-Saxon Protestant" culture, sometimes called "Anglo" or "WASP"), there are other well-established cultures, such as African-American and Hispanic-American cultures. The most recent theoretical developments on the concept of acculturation recognize that immigrants and refugees may acculturate not to the dominant culture, but to one of the "native-born minority" cultures. For example, some Black immigrants or refugees may acculturate to African-American culture, whereas others may acculturate to the dominant culture. This is referred to as *segmented assimilation* (Portes and Zhou 1993).

Acculturation is a process, and therefore a person's position on the various acculturation dimensions changes over time. The process is influenced by factors such as personality, family influences, environmental influences, and socioeconomic status (Clark and Hofsess 1998). The acculturation process is stressful for individuals and for families. Further, acculturation status has major implications for service delivery. These issues will be addressed in subsequent chapters.

4.1.3 CHARACTERISTICS OF SOCIETIES

THE ABOVE DISCUSSION of acculturation has referred to the acculturation of individuals, which is termed *psychological and behavioral acculturation*. However, acculturation also takes place at the group level. This is termed *structural acculturation*, and refers to the physical, socioeconomic, and political positions of various ethnic groups in a society in relation to each other. As with psychological acculturation, there are several possible outcomes of structural acculturation.

The worst possible outcome is *genocide*, in which one group almost completely destroys another, as was the case with European settlers and Native Americans in the United States (Green 1999). Another possible outcome is *structural assimilation*, in which the new group completely gives up its native culture and is completely absorbed into the dominant culture. In the United States, this has also sometimes been referred to as *Americanization*, and was viewed as the appropriate outcome for new immigrants throughout much of U.S. history. Some early social work interventions at the beginning of the twentieth century were aimed at Americanizing new immigrants. However, structural assimilation has come to be viewed as harmful and destructive since it means completely taking away a group's native culture. Consequently, other early social work interventions, in particular the settlement house movement, were aimed at helping immigrants maintain their native cultures while also adapting to American culture (Devore and Schlesinger 1999; Potocky 1997a).

In recognition of the harmfulness of structural assimilation, a more benign ideal arose in the 1920s, the *melting pot*. The concept of the melting pot is that people from many cultures come together, and each group contributes equally to the development of a new culture that is a combination of them all. This term is still popular today among lay people, but social scientists have long recognized that the melting pot is a concept that has never been manifested in reality (Devore and Schlesinger 1999; Green 1999; Potocky 1997a).

In place of the melting pot, the newer terms of *tossed salad* or *salad bowl* have arisen. These terms refer to a society that is *multicultural, diverse,* or *pluralistic* (Green 1999; Lum 1999). All of these terms are intended to describe the coexistence of many different and distinct ethnic groups within one society. Like the concept of the melting pot earlier in history, these contemporary terms represent ideals—in this case, a society where everyone can maintain their native ethnic traditions, yet have equal political and economic participation in society as a whole.

Unfortunately, this ideal is also not reality in contemporary U.S. society. The structural acculturation outcomes that most accurately describe the relationships among ethnic groups in the U.S. today are *residential segregation* and *economic and political stratification*. These terms mean that different ethnic groups tend to live apart from each other, and that economic and political power is stratified such that the majority group (native-born Whites) has the most power and minority ethnic groups have less power (and within minority groups, some have more power than others). Although there are some exceptions to this segregation and stratification, it is generally characteristic of most communities in the U.S. This current reality is a result of the negative attitudes and behaviors that people have toward members of other ethnic groups.

4.1.4 ATTITUDES AND BEHAVIORS TOWARD OTHER ETHNIC GROUPS

THERE ARE A VARIETY OF TERMS used to describe people's negative attitudes and behaviors toward members of other ethnic groups (Devore and Schlesinger 1999; Greene et al. 1998; Lum 1999, 2000; Mayadas and Elliott 1992; Van Voorhis 1998). *Ethnocentrism* is an attitude that places one's own ethnic group as the central point of reference. The norms of one's own ethnic group are considered "normal," whereas those of other groups are not even considered. *Prejudice* goes farther than this in that it is a clearly negative attitude, such as hatred, anger, or hostility, toward other ethnic groups. Prejudice is closely related to *stereotyping*, which means making negative generalizations about an ethnic group and attributing perceived negative characteristics to all members of that group. Another related term is *xenophobia*, which means fear and hatred of foreigners. *Racism* goes even farther than prejudice and xenophobia: it is the belief that one racial or ethnic group is inherently superior to others and has the right to dominate them. Finally, *discrimination* is the behavioral manifestation of these negative attitudes and beliefs. It is an action that denies ethnic minority group members equal opportunity in society. In the U.S., this individual-level behavior has become widespread and systematized, resulting in *institutional discrimination* (sometimes called *institutional racism*) or *oppression*, which refers to policies and procedures that lead to denial of equal opportunities in employment, housing, education, political participation, health care, and other areas.

It is likely that all people have some degree of negative attitudes and beliefs about other ethnic groups. A starting point for culturally competent social work practice is examination of one's own attitudes and beliefs in this regard.

4.2 ATTITUDES AND BELIEFS FOR CULTURALLY COMPETENT PRACTICE

TABLE 4.2 LISTS a number of attitudes and beliefs that culturally competent workers possess. Culturally competent practice begins with the awareness that practice cannot be value-free and neutral. All social work practice is influenced by the worker's culture, the client's culture, and the organizational and societal culture. Thus, a first step in developing culturally competent practice is to be aware of one's own racial, cultural, and ethnic backgrounds, and how these have influenced one's life experiences and outlooks. By doing so one also becomes aware that the decisions one makes may be ethnocentric. Cultural self-awareness and security in one's own ethnic identity lead to greater flexibility and openness toward members of other ethnic groups, and lessen negative reactions and judgmental attitudes (Lum 1999). Green (1995) suggests doing the following tasks as a means of increasing awareness of one's own background:

- Identify your family origins as far back as you can trace specific ancestors. Specify the earliest dates, names, and places of which you can be sure. If you are unsure, speculate about probable ancestors and how far back you might be able to trace them.
- Why and how did your ancestors come to this country? Speculate on the conditions they left behind and their possible motives for leaving those conditions.
- Describe both a disadvantage and an advantage your ancestors may have experienced because of their ethnicity. Examples might include matters of religion, racial characteristics, economic background, language, family patterns, and political connections.
- Look at any of the ethnic advantages you have listed. These are often reflected in family strengths. Can you name any specific family strengths that you or your family members can link to your family's ethnic background or identity? List these.
- Look at your list of family strengths. For each one, indicate how that strength has conferred some advantage or [disadvantage] on you or members of your immediate family. How have you or your family members benefited, or suffered, because of something you believe to be an important family characteristic?
- In one or two sentences, name your ethnic background, and describe one specific benefit that you have received or enjoyed as a consequence of your ethnicity.

GREEN (1995, P. 316)

TABLE 4.2 ATTITUDES AND BELIEFS FOR CULTURALLY COMPETENT PRACTICE

Culturally competent social workers:
• Are aware that practice cannot be neutral, value free, or objective.
• Are aware of and sensitive to their own cultural heritage.
• Are aware of how their own cultural backgrounds and experiences, attitudes, values, and biases influence psychological processes.
• Are aware that their decisions may be ethnocentric.
• Are aware of their negative emotional reactions toward other racial and ethnic groups that may prove detrimental to their clients.
• Are aware of stereotypes and preconceived notions that they may hold toward other racial and ethnic groups.
• Are willing to make purposive changes in their feelings, thoughts, and behaviors toward other ethnic groups.
• Value and respect differences that exist between themselves and clients in terms of race, ethnicity, culture, and beliefs, and are willing to contrast their own beliefs and attitudes with those of their culturally different clients in a nonjudgmental fashion.
• Respect clients' religious and/or spiritual beliefs and values about physical and mental functioning.
• Respect indigenous helping practices and respect ethnic community intrinsic help-giving networks.
• Value bilingualism and do not view another language as an impediment to practice.
• Value the social work profession's commitment to social justice.
• Value the importance of empirically based practice.
• Are able to recognize the limits of their competencies and expertise.

Sources: Adapted from Greene, et al., 1998; Sue, Arredondo, and McDavis 1992.

ADDITIONAL QUESTIONS that can be used in order to increase cultural self-awareness include the following (Arredondo et al. 1996; Lum 1999):
• How strong is your sense of ethnic identity?
• How have your individual, family, neighborhood, and community contexts affected your cultural self-awareness?
• Where would you place yourself in Berry's (1990) acculturation framework: assimilated, bicultural, separated, or marginal?
• What are the significant values, beliefs, and cultural traits of your ancestors' ethnic groups that you have incorporated into your own values and beliefs?

- How has your cognitive development and learning style been influenced by your cultural background?
- What cultural factors in your history have influenced your views of social belonging, interpretations of behavior, motivation, problem-solving and decision methods, and thoughts and behaviors in relation to authority and institutions?

After becoming aware of one's ethnic background and how it has shaped one's outlook and experiences, the next step is identifying one's own negative attitudes, beliefs, and behaviors toward other ethnic groups. This is a challenging task because most people, and particularly those who are in the helping professions, do not like to think of themselves as possessing these negative traits. However, the fact is few, if any, people are completely free of these negative characteristics. It may help to realize that these attitudes, beliefs, and behaviors have been acquired through learning—that is, from the messages received from parents, other significant role models, peers, and media, and from interactions (or lack thereof) with members of other ethnic groups. No one was born with prejudiced or racist attitudes and behaviors. Since these are learned attitudes and behaviors, they can also be unlearned. Thus, identifying these negative characteristics in oneself should be viewed as a positive step toward reversing them. It is a necessary prerequisite to effective helping:

> Self-awareness [is] the ability to look at and recognize oneself—not always nice, and sometimes judgmental, prejudiced and noncaring. Self-awareness is the ability to recognize when the judgmental, noncaring self interferes with the ability to reach out, to explore, and to help others.... And it refers to the ability to make use of this type of understanding to attempt to hold in check those narcissistic and destructive impulses that impede service delivery. (DEVORE AND SCHLESINGER 1999, P. 100)

The following are some tasks that can be done to increase awareness of one's own negative attitudes and behaviors toward other ethnic groups (Arredondo et al. 1996; Lum 1999):

- Identify specific attitudes, beliefs, and values from your cultural background that impede or hinder respect and valuing of ethnic differences.

- Describe the level of contact you have had with different ethnic groups throughout your life in neighborhood, social, school, and work settings.
- Describe a positive, a negative, and a mixed experience you have had with people of other ethnic groups.
- Identify stereotypes that you have about other ethnic groups.
- Identify stereotypes that other people might have about you.
- Identify significant people in your life who have transmitted prejudiced or racist messages to you.
- Describe an encounter with a client in which your attitudes, beliefs, and values interfered with providing the best service.
- Identify your common emotional reactions to members of specific ethnic groups. Identify how these reactions could influence your effectiveness in working with clients from those ethnic groups.

In addition to identifying one's negative attitudes toward other ethnic groups, it is also important to realize that one may have negative attitudes toward members of one's own group. For example, workers who are ethnic minorities themselves may have negative feelings toward members of their ethnic group who have been less successful in society—an attitude of "I made it, why can't you?" (Devore and Schlesinger 1999, p. 179). On the other hand, one can also be in denial about negative characteristics of one's own ethnic group or its members (Devore and Schlesinger 1999). These are issues that also need to be identified by the worker.

After identifying one's own negative attitudes and behaviors, one can begin to shift one's feelings and thoughts toward valuing and respecting cultural differences. This is the next step in becoming culturally competent. The culturally competent social worker is nonjudgmental about cultural differences, recognizing that no culture is superior to another. However, there is a limitation to this: when cultural norms lead a person to harm someone else. For example, in the native cultures of some immgrants and refugees, it is acceptable for a man to beat his wife. It would not be acceptable for a social worker to be nonjudgmental of this harmful behavior. The social worker has an ethical obligation in this case to intervene (in many possible ways) to attempt to stop the harm. Thus, being nonjudgmental about cultural differences means "the willingness to accept another person and allow him or her to be what he or she wants to be, as long as the individual does not harm someone else" (Lum 1999, p. 57).

Barring harmful actions, the following are some possible areas of cultural differences that social workers should be aware of and respect:

- Autonomy
- Self-determination or choice
- Intuition
- Group or collective orientation
- Rationality
- Interrelatedness
- Hierarchy
- Role performance
- Trust
- Self-disclosure
- Competitiveness
- Productivity
- Use of time
- Use of space
- Relationship to the earth
- Individuation
- Unique familial obligation
- Family caregiving responsibilities
- Separation
- Timing of life events
- Intimacy
- Interdependence
- Authority
- Power
- Privacy

(GREENE ET AL. 1998, P. 50)

The process of shifting from an ethnocentric and negative perspective to a nonjudgmental one requires a conscious and purposeful effort to change one's attitudes. The process is enhanced by increasing one's contacts with members of other ethnic groups, including social contacts and contacts with clients and co-workers. Such contacts should be purposively sought out and used to enhance one's learning about ethnic differences (Lum 1999). The following exercise is also useful:

> Recall the details of a case from your experiences in a social service agency. The case must be one that, at the time you observed it, seemed to present special difficulties in cross-cultural communication, agreement on the nature of the problem, or compliance with treatment plans, a case where racial and/or cultural differences seemed to be a factor. Recall what was said and who did what. Then critique the case using the following questions:
> • What specific things did the staff seem to misunderstand about the client?
> • What presumptions did the staff hold about the client, the nature of his or her concerns, and what could or couldn't be done about them?
> • What questions were asked to clarify the nature of the client's presenting problem? How thorough was the questioning?

- What was done with the information the client offered?
- What questions were asked to ascertain that the client clearly understood the professional advice offered and was prepared to use it in the ways recommended?
- Propose specific steps that you or others might have taken to address the difficulties described. (GREEN 1995, PP. 320–21)

Valuing and respecting cultural differences also entails value and respect for factors directly related to the helping process. These include the client's religious and/or spiritual beliefs about health and mental health, indigenous helping practices of the client's culture, and ethnic helping networks within the client's community. Respecting these means recognizing that the perspectives and helping approaches developed by social scientists and social service professionals are not the only alternatives, or may not be the best alternatives, for addressing the client's problem situation. Frequently, service effectiveness can be enhanced by incorporating clients' traditional helping approaches with professional ones. Thus, respect for these alternate approaches is demonstrated by learning about them (from co-workers, community members, or clients) and considering whether and how they may be useful in any given case. The client's language must also be respected. This means making efforts to deliver services in the language that the client is most comfortable with, using an interpreter if necessary.

Culturally competent practice also requires valuing the social work profession's commitment to social justice. This means recognizing that ethnic minority clients' problems frequently have their roots in society and not in the client, or in a combination of client and societal causes. The societal causes are those which lead to social injustice, such as institutional discrimination. Thus, valuing a commitment to social justice means implementing interventions aimed at not only changing the client, but also changing society. Stated differently, it means using macro- as well as micro-level interventions.

Further, culturally competent workers must value empirically based practice. Social workers have an ethical obligation to provide clients with the most effective services for their problems (Myers and Thyer 1997). Thus, valuing empirically based practice means using interventions that have previously been evaluated and found to be effective, whenever possible. However, many interventions have not been evaluated specifically for ethnic minority clients, especially immigrants and refugees. Further, while an intervention may be reported as effective in the literature, this does not mean that it will always work for all clients. Thus, valuing empirically based practice also means systematically evaluating one's own practice. Doing so makes workers accountable to their clients, and also can contribute to the knowledge base about what works (Blythe, Tripodi, and Briar 1994).

Finally, culturally competent workers recognize their own limitations. This means that workers are able to identify cases in which their effectiveness is hampered by cultural differences or attitudes that the worker has difficulty dealing with. In these cases, culturally competent workers seek consultation from supervisors or co-workers, seek professional development activities to enhance their cultural competency, or refer the client to more appropriate helping resources (Arredondo, et al. 1996).

4.3 KNOWLEDGE FOR CULTURALLY COMPETENT PRACTICE

THE KNOWLEDGE THAT IS NEEDED for culturally competent practice is listed in table 4.3. In order to be culturally competent, social workers need a broad base of knowledge that includes multiple theories, knowledge of the self, characteristics of different ethnic groups, environmental influences upon people, the cultural basis of social work practice, and knowledge about empirically based practice.

4.3.1 MULTIPLE THEORIES

CULTURALLY COMPETENT SOCIAL WORKERS draw upon a wide range of theories from the social sciences, including the fields of psychology, sociology, anthropology, government, history, ethnic and women's studies, and economics (Lum 1999). Particularly important among these are theories pertaining to ethnicity, ethnic identity, culture, acculturation, prejudice, discrimination, and related concepts. Theories from each of the disciplines provide varied perspectives on these issues. These theories serve as a foundation for the development of interventions. Familiarity with a broad range of theories increases the likelihood of developing interventions that are successful, since the worker is not limited by a narrow perspective.

TABLE 4.3 KNOWLEDGE FOR CULTURALLY COMPETENT PRACTICE

MULTIPLE THEORIES

Culturally competent social workers are knowledgeable about:
- Social science theories.
- Human behavior theories.
- Social work practice theories.
- Critical thinking about theories.

SELF-KNOWLEDGE

Culturally competent social workers are knowledgeable about:
- Their own racial and cultural heritage and how it personally and professionally affects their definitions and biases of normality, abnormality, and the practice process.
- How oppression, racism, discrimination, and stereotyping affect them personally and in their work.
- How their communication style may clash with or facilitate the practice process with ethnic minority clients and how to anticipate the impact it may have on others.

CHARACTERISTICS OF ETHNIC GROUPS

Culturally competent social workers are knowledgeable about:
- Demographic characteristics of ethnic minority populations.
- The life experiences, cultural heritage, and historical backgrounds of different ethnic groups.
- Family structures, hierarchies, values, and beliefs of different ethnic groups.
- The effects of race, culture, ethnicity, and minority status on personality formation, life choices, manifestation of psychological disorders, help-seeking behavior, and the appropriateness or inappropriateness of practice approaches.
- Culture as a source of cohesion, identity, and strength as well as a source of strain and discordance.
- An ethnic group's adaptive strategies.
- Ethnic community characteristics and community resources.

TABLE 4.3 *(continued)*

INFLUENCES UPON PEOPLE

Culturally competent social workers are knowledgeable about:
• How a person's behavior is guided by membership in families, groups, organizations, and communities.
• How sociopolitical influences such as immigration issues, poverty, racism, stereotyping, discrimination, and powerlessness impact the lives of ethnic minority clients and may influence the practice process.

CULTURAL BASIS OF SOCIAL WORK PRACTICE

Culturally competent social workers are knowledgeable about:
• The cultural characteristics of generic social work practice and how they may clash with the cultural values of different ethnic groups.
• Potential bias in assessment instruments and diagnostic systems.
• Institutional barriers that prevent ethnic minorities from using health, mental health, and social services.

EMPIRICALLY BASED PRACTICE

Culturally competent social workers are knowledgeable about:
• Critical evaluation and application of research studies.
• Empirical literature on intervention effectiveness.
• Program and practice evaluation methods.

Sources: Adapted from Greene et al., 1998; Lum 1999; Sue, Arredondo, and McDavis, 1992.

dation for the development of interventions. Familiarity with a broad range Culturally competent social workers also need to be familiar with a broad range of theories of human behavior. These include theories such as the following (Greene et al. 1998; Lum 1999):

• general and social systems theories
• behavioral theories
• cognitive-behavioral theories
• ego-psychodynamic theories

- learning theories
- humanistic theories
- role theory
- family theory
- conflict theory
- stress theory
- symbolic interactionism
- social constructionism
- gestalt theory
- field theory
- attachment theory
- life span development theories

Familiarity with these theories allows the social worker to conduct a holistic assessment of a client's problem, its causes, and resources that can be helpful in resolving it. Such an assessment, in turn, leads to the development or application of interventions that have a greater likelihood of success.

In order to select an appropriate intervention, social workers need to be familiar with multiple theories of social work practice. These include the following models (Devore and Schlesinger 1999):

- psychosocial
- problem solving
- task centered
- structural
- systems
- ecological

Further, social workers need to be familiar with multiple theories of intervention for each of the following levels:

- individuals
- couples
- families
- small groups
- organizations
- communities

For each of these levels, numerous intervention theories are available. For example, for individual counseling interventions, the list includes the following models: psychodynamic, existential, person-centered, crisis intervention, gestalt, transactional analysis, behavioral, rational-emotive, reality, and feminist (Corey 1982; Zastrow 1995). Again, familiarity with a broad range of intervention theories allows the culturally competent social worker to select those that are best suited to the client's problem and therefore have the greatest likelihood of success.

Since there are so many theories of social science, human behavior, and intervention, the culturally competent social worker must apply critical thinking to the process of choosing among them. Critical thinking means systematic, rational consideration of each theory in order to determine its usefulness for understanding or resolving a particular client problem. For this purpose, the following aspects of a theory should be examined:

- Historical perspective, or a discussion of how and why a theory developed in a historical context.
- Assumptions, or a discussion about the explicit and implicit premises of a theory concerning the client, human nature, the roles of the social worker and the client, and the change process.
- Logical flaws, or a discussion about the logic, contradictions among theories, fit with the mission of social work, and errors in reasoning.
- Usefulness in practice, or a discussion about the application of a theory to one's own practice.
- Strengths and weaknesses of a theory and a comparison of theories and their potential benefit to specific problems, clients, or settings.
- Practice dilemmas, or a discussion of how theories apply to specific problems, clients, or settings.

(LUM 1999, P. 84)

Application of this critical thinking process will often reveal the inappropriateness of a given theory for ethnic minority clients. For example:

> Existential-humanistic theories maintain that the quality of the practitioner-client relationship is the substance of the helping process.... This relationship is characterized as nondirective and equalitarian, with an emphasis on self-disclosure. Such an approach may not be appropriate for Asians who adhere to traditional cultural values, such as a belief in hierarchical and role relationships and emotional reticence, and who prefer active direction from the practitioner.
> (MOKUAU AND MATSUOKA 1992, P. 73)

4.3.2 SELF-KNOWLEDGE

EARLIER, the importance of awareness of one's own ethnic background was stressed. Self-knowledge is closely related to self-awareness, but it goes further in that it involves more specific information, the critical analysis of theories in relation to oneself, and the analysis of one's impact in the helping relationship. Social workers' awareness of their own ethnicity may be limited to what they have personally experienced in their lives. Self-knowledge requires workers to actively learn about their ethnic backgrounds. This learing can include such methods as reading about their ethnic group, interviewing family or other ethnic group members, and participating in traditional activities.

One element of self-knowledge is specific knowledge about how one's ethnic background affects one's views of what is normal and abnormal, and of the helping process. The following tasks can be helpful in developing this knowledge :

• Discuss your family's and culture's perspectives of acceptable (normal) and unacceptable (abnormal) codes of conduct and how these may or may not vary from those of other cultures and families.
• Identify five specific features of your culture of origin and explain how these features affect your relationship with culturally different clients.

(ARREDONDO ET AL. 1996, P. 59)

Another element of self-knowledge is knowledge of how oppression, racism, discrimination, and stereotyping affect one personally and professionally. The following tasks can be helpful in developing this knowledge :

• Identify and discuss privileges that you personally receive in society due to your race, socioeconomic background, gender, physical abilities, or other characteristics.
• Discuss a theory of human development and how it relates to your personal experiences.
• Describe a situation in which you have been judged on something other than merit. Describe a situation in which you judged someone on something other than merit.
• Read a recent research article addressing issues of racism, ethnic identity, or related concepts. Discuss its relationship to your personal and professional development.

(ARREDONDO ET AL. 1996, P. 60)

A third element of self-knowledge is knowledge of one's communication style and its effect on clients. Communication styles vary across cultures and individuals in terms of both verbal and nonverbal components. Verbal components include things such as word choices, intonation, speed, affect, and interjections such as jokes, asides, allusions, and topic shifting. Nonverbal components include things such as hand gestures, posture, eye movements, physical proximity, touching, dress, and physical environment (Green 1995). To assess one's style and its impact on others, it can be very helpful to view videotapes of worker-client interactions. It is also helpful to observe the styles of members of one's own and other ethnic groups to identify common patterns. The following tasks are helpful in increasing knowledge in this area:

- Describe your verbal and nonverbal behaviors, your interpretations of others' behaviors, and your expectations.
- Describe the cultural bases of your communication style and the differences between your style and the styles of members of other ethnic groups.
- Describe the behavioral impact of your communication style on culturally different clients.
- Give an example of a situation in which you modified your communication style to complement that of a culturally different client, how you decided on the modification, and the result of that modification.

(ARRENDONDO ET AL. 1996, PP. 60–61)

4.3.3 CHARACTERISTICS OF ETHNIC GROUPS

CULTURALLY COMPETENT SOCIAL WORKERS need to be knowledgeable about the characteristics of the ethnic groups whose members they work with. One facet is knowledge about demographic characteristics, such as those provided in chapter 1. This information is important because it forms the basis for program planning and administration, and enhances understanding of factors such as family structure and economic adaptation patterns (Lum 1999). It is also crucial for social workers to have knowledge about an ethnic group's cultural heritage, historical background, and cultural values, beliefs, and norms. Such knowledge is important because it allows the worker to critically evaluate the relevance and usefulness of theories and practice approaches for a given ethnic group. It also provides the worker guidance in adapting practice to make it compatible with cultural expectations, thereby increasing the probability of success. Additionally, knowledge of cultural stresses and strengths, adaptive strategies, and community resources allows the worker to identify factors that contribute to a client's problem and factors that can be used to help resolve the problem.

Green (1999) delineates three ways for social workers to gain knowledge about ethnic groups: background preparation, use of cultural guides, and participant observation. Background preparation involves reading about the group. Sociological, psychological, and anthropological studies, personal narratives, and fiction all provide valuable insight into the experiences of ethnic group members. It is important to read both general information and information that is specific to one's local community. The latter may be more difficult to access, but can sometimes be found in local government or social service agencies.

Cultural guides are members of the ethnic group who can teach the social worker about that group. They are often referred to as *key informants*. They can include community or religious leaders, co-workers, or former clients. Information is obtained from key informants through interviews. These interviews have the following purposes: "to learn something of the community as community members see it; to better understand why clients from the community have need of specific services; to appreciate how people use community resources to deal with their problems; [and] to discover how people feel about their relations with the larger society in general and with social service institutions and providers in particular" (Green 1995, p. 327). In selecting key informants, the worker should look for people who are knowledgeable and articulate about their community and have the time, interest, and willingness to share information with the worker. It is best to have more than one key informant, in order to obtain varied perspectives. Further, relationships with key informants need to be built over time, and trust needs to develop in order for informants to share sensitive information. Additionally, it is important for the worker to be able to give something back to the key informant in exchange for the information provided. Otherwise, the key informant may feel exploited. Thus, the worker must discern the key informant's motives for participating, and determine what can appropriately be provided in exchange (Green 1999).

The third method of learning about an ethnic community is participant observation. This is a research method developed by cultural anthropologists for the purpose of gaining a detailed "insider's view" about life in a community. It involves entering the community, with the help of a cultural guide, and spending fairly extensive amounts of time participating in community activities. This can include participating in family events, community meetings or celebrations, religious activities, or the activities of an ethnic social service agency. Participant observation is usually combined with key informant interviewing. Together, these two methods should be used to gather the following information:

- Identification and location of an ethnic group in an area.
- Description of the community's social organization.
- Description of the residents' beliefs and ideological characteristics.
- Identification of patterns of wealth, its accumulation, and its distribution.
- Description of the patterns of mobility, both geographical and social.
- Information on access and utilization of available human services.

(GREEN 1999, P. 96)

This information should result in a *social map*, which is "a short document containing one or more physical maps and descriptive information for each of the six items listed above, provided in sufficient detail that a stranger could read it and gain some general sense of who lives in the area, how they live, what they believe and do, and how they use social services" (Green 1999, p. 96). Although the development of a social map is time-consuming, it is an extremely valuable means for enhancing one's cultural competence. After completing background preparation and a social map, culturally competent social workers should be able to do the following:

- Describe differences between themselves and the ethnic group members in nonverbal and verbal behavior.
- Discuss viewpoints of the ethnic group members regarding issues such as gender, aging, and disability.
- Describe the ethnic group's cultural expectations regarding role and responsibility in family, participation of family in life decisions, appropriate family members to be involved when seeking help, and culturally acceptable means of expressing emotions.
- Adequately understand an ethnic group member's religious and spiritual beliefs to know when and what topics are and are not appropriate to discuss regarding those beliefs.
- Describe one theory of personality development and how it does or does not relate to the ethnic group members.
- Give examples of how a social work practice theory may or may not be appropriate for the ethnic group members.

- Identify the role of gender, socioeconomic status, and physical disability as they interact with personality formation for the ethnic group members.
- Be familiar with organizations that provide support and services in the ethnic community.
- Discuss traditional ways of helping within the ethnic group.

(ARREDONDO ET AL. 1996)

4.3.4 ENVIRONMENTAL INFLUENCES UPON PEOPLE

IN ADDITION to knowledge about the cultural characteristics of ethnic groups, it is crucial for culturally competent social workers to have knowledge about how ethnic group members are influenced by forces at the levels of family, group, organization, community, and society. This includes information about the effects of negative attitudes and behaviors of others toward members of the group, such as stereotyping, racism, xenophobia, and individual and institutional discrimination. These issues must be understood from both historical and contemporary perspectives. Thus, it is important to know not only what discriminatory practices ethnic group members face today, but also what they have faced historically. History is important not only because it shapes a person's ethnic identity, experiences, and outlook, but also because it provides lessons about past achievements, mistakes, and failures (Lum 1999). In order to improve societal conditions for ethnic group members, it is important to avoid perpetuating past oppression and not to repeat past mistakes.

Knowledge about these past and present influences can be gained in the same manner as described above, namely, background preparation, use of cultural guides, and participant observation. Through this process the culturally competent social worker should be able to do the following:

- Explain the historical point of contact of the ethnic group with the dominant society and the impact of the type of contact (refugee, immigrant, enslaved, conquered, and so forth) on current issues in society and on potential relationships and trust when seeking help from dominant culture institutions.
- Identify the influences upon ethnic group members of such issues as institutional discrimination, privilege, and the historical and current political climate regarding immigration, poverty, and welfare.

- Explain how factors such as poverty and powerlessness have influenced the current conditions of ethnic group members.
- Describe the economic benefits and contributions gained by the work of ethnic group members to the daily life of the social worker and the country at large.
- Identify current issues in legislation, social climate, and so forth that affect ethnic group members. (ARREDONDO ET AL. 1996)

In learning about other ethnic groups, it is important to remember that there are differences among individuals and families within those groups. These differences are a function of variations in socioeconomic status, level of acculturation, and many other factors. Thus, not all ethnic group members will strictly conform to a generalized description about that group. It is essential to approach each client as an individual. The knowledge that one has about the client's ethnic group should serve as a starting point for working with the client, not as a set of unquestioned assumptions about the client. Often, it is appropriate to check with the client about the validity of ethnic group characteristics for that client. This can be done by asking a question such as, "In many families from your cultural background, [describe a common belief or behavior]. Is this true in your family?" Additionally, it is likely that most immigrant and refugee clients will be happy to share information about their ethnic group characteristics and experiences with the social worker, because their ethnicity is important to them and they welcome an expression of genuine interest and respect.

4.3.5 CULTURAL BASIS OF SOCIAL WORK PRACTICE

CULTURALLY COMPETENT SOCIAL WORKERS must understand that generic social work practice (i.e., practice not developed specifically for ethnic minority clients) is itself culture-bound. This means that social work practice has developed in a specific cultural context and subscribes to specific cultural values. Social work has its most fundamental roots in Western civilization's view of the individual and society, and in Judeo-Christian beliefs (Lum 2000). Further, generic social work practice is greatly influenced by five values or assumptions that characterize mainstream American culture:

- Active self-expression.
- Equality and informality in social relationships.
- Achievement and accomplishment.
- Control of self and one's destiny while in pursuit of a better future.
- Individualism and autonomy experienced in democratic, nonauthoritarian relationships with others. (GREEN 1999, P. 89)

The cultural background and values of social work are manifested in the way that a client's problem is defined and approached. This clearly poses a conflict when the client is from a different culture that defines and approaches problems differently. For example, table 4.4 shows some common contrasts between many United States helping professionals and many immigrant or refugee clients in regard to cultural background and views of mental health and mental health treatment.

The theories that guide social work practice are also culture-bound. For example, it has been noted that "much of the so-called theory that guides pscyhotherapeutic endeavors is an imaginative creation of white, middle-class males to be employed with white, middle-class females" (Wright et al. 1983, p. 7). Clearly, theories developed in this context may not be applicable to most refugees and immigrants.

Similarly, many commonly used assessment instruments were initially developed using white, middle-class respondents. These initial respondents are called the *normative group*, and their responses establish the *norms* for the instrument, i.e., they determine what scores define the "normal" and "abnormal" ranges. When these instruments and norms are applied to people who are different from the normative group, they often result in biased assessments. In other words, the interpretations of these test results for culturally different people are inaccurate. Thus, clients may be assessed as being abnormal when in fact they are normal in relation to their own cultural group. This is because people in different cultures experience and express thoughts and feelings differently. The problem is further compounded when the client's language is different from the original language of the instrument. Simply translating the instrument is an insufficient solution because of linguistic nuances that may change the meanings of statements. Accurate translation and cross-cultural application of instruments requires a lengthy and complex research process (Burnette 1998; Ortega and Richey 1998).

The same issues pertain to the use of diagnostic systems, particularly in the area of mental health. Diagnostic systems such as the *Diagnostic and*

TABLE 4.4 COMMON CONTRASTS BETWEEN HELPING PROFESSIONALS AND REFUGEE OR IMMIGRANT CLIENTS

U.S. HELPING PROFESSIONALS	REFUGEE OR IMMIGRANT CLIENTS
Contrasting Cultural Backgrounds	
Secure societal status	Insecurities in language, vocation, societal position
Autonomy and independence	Interdependence and traditional family values
Relativity in values; situational ethics;	"Correct" social relationships rejection of authority
People versus nature: the need to master or control nature	Holistic cultures: people living in harmony with nature
Contrasting Concepts of Mental Health and Treatment	
Relatively comfortable attitude about	Fear of mental illness handling mental illness and symptoms
View of mental illness as a result of psychological and biological factors	View of mental illness as caused by imbalance of cosmic forces or supernatural events, by an agent such as a ghost, or by a strong emotional experience
Belief that psychotherapy is valuable and promotes growth	No cultural analogy of extended psychological therapy
Awareness that cure will be extended and time consuming with the therapist often passive	Belief that cure should be rapid with the healer active

Source: Jaranson, 1990. Copyright ©1990, Hogg Foundation for Mental Health. Reprinted with permission.

Statistical Manual of Mental Disorders (DSM) (American Psychiatric Association 1994) have developed in a specific historical, cultural, and sociopolitical context. When indiscriminately applied to ethnic minority clients, they frequently result in overdiagnosis, i.e., identifying a problem where one does not exist (Lin 1991). Therefore, culturally competent social workers are knowledgeable about the cultural biases in assessment instruments and diagnostic systems, and use them with caution.

It is also important to understand that organizations themselves are culture-bound. The structures, functions, ideologies, and processes of organizations all reflect the cultural norms of the dominant culture that created the organization. These cultural features often serve as barriers to culturally different clients:

> Bureaucratic jargon, excesses of paperwork, technical complexity, burdensome rules and regulations, and the impersonality of functionaries have all worked to stymie reaching out to potential but culturally different recipients. In addition, ... the demeanor and manner of helpers, the décor and arrangement of organizational fronts, appearances and impressions given off, and the rituals of helping often work to create intercultural tension. Seated behind a desk, dressed in a suit, asking personal questions in order to fill out a form, and using stilted language, the helper becomes an imposing and frightening figure. (WRIGHT ET AL. 1983, P. 15)

THUS, IT IS IMPORTANT for culturally competent social workers to have knowledge about institutional barriers such as these that hamper effective service delivery to ethnic minority clients.

In summary, in regard to the cultural basis of social work practice, culturally competent workers must be able to do the following:

- Articulate the historical, cultural, and racial context in which traditional theories and interventions have been developed.
- Identify, within various theories, the cultural values, beliefs, and assumptions made about individuals and contrast these with values, beliefs, and assumptions of different cultural groups.
- Recognize the predominant theories being used within the worker's organization and educate colleagues regarding the aspects of those theories and interventions that may clash with the cultural values of various cultural groups.
- Describe concrete examples of institutional barriers within their organizations that prevent minorities from using services and share those examples with colleagues and decisionmaking bodies within the institution.
- Recognize and draw attention to patterns of usage (or nonusage) of services by specific populations.
- Identify and communicate possible alternatives that would reduce or

eliminate existing barriers within their institutions and within local, state, and national decisionmaking bodies.
• Demonstrate ability to interpret assessment results including implications of dominant cultural values affecting assessment and interpretation.
• Discuss information regarding the cultural, racial, and gender profile of the normative group used for validity and reliability of any assessment instrument used by the worker.
• Understand the limitations of translating assessment instruments as well as the importance of using language that includes culturally relevant connotations and idioms.
• Use assessment instruments appropriately with clients having limited English skills.
• Give examples, for each assessment instrument used, of the limitations of the instrument in regard to various ethnic groups.
• Recognize possible historical and current sociopolitical biases in diagnostic systems based on racial, cultural, and gender issues.

(ARREDONDO ET AL 1996)

4.3.6 EMPIRICALLY BASED PRACTICE

THE FINAL AREA of necessary knowledge for culturally competent social workers is knowledge about empirically based practice. Such knowledge has several components. First, social workers must be able to critically evaluate research studies that have been conducted by others. This means that social workers must have knowledge of research concepts such as sampling, measurement, research design, data collection, and data analysis. They must apply this knowledge to assess the strengths and weaknesses of a research study and the applicability of its findings to working with a particular client or client population.

Second, culturally competent social workers must have knowledge about what interventions have been demonstrated through rigorous research studies to be effective in resolving particular problems among particular clients. As noted earlier, many interventions have not been specifically evaluated for refugee and immigrant clients. In this case, workers must have knowledge of the existing empirical literature for other populations, and be able to determine what interventions, or modifications of interventions, appear most promising for immigrant or refugee clients based on demonstrated effectiveness for other populations. The remaining chapters of this book focus on this empirically based knowledge for particular refugee and immigrant problem areas.

Finally, because there is still a considerable lack of knowledge about what interventions work for ethnic minority clients, culturally competent social workers need knowledge to evaluate their own practice and programs. In many cases, social workers will adapt existing interventions or programs to make them culturally compatible with the ethnic backgrounds of immigrant or refugee clients. Therefore, they need to know whether these adaptations were successful. Thus, social workers need knowledge of various evaluation methods such as group designs, single-system designs, and qualitative evaluation (Rubin and Babbie 1997).

4.4 SKILLS FOR CULTURALLY COMPETENT PRACTICE

SKILLS ARE THE BEHAVIORS that effective social workers use in the practice process. "Skills represent the practical application of cultural awareness and knowledge" (Lum 1999, p. 112). Regardless of what particular theoretical orientation is used, the social work practice process consists of the following sequential steps (Blythe and Tripodi 1989; Devore and Schlesinger 1999; Hepworth, Rooney, and Larsen 1997; Lum 1999, 2000; Zastrow 1995):

- Engagement.
- Problem identification and assessment.
- Goal setting and contracting.
- Intervention implementation and monitoring.
- Termination and evaluation.
- Follow-up.

Culturally competent social workers need to possess specific skills for each of these phases. The specific skills that are needed in each area are summarized in table 4.5 and discussed below.

4.4.1 ENGAGEMENT SKILLS

THE WORKER'S INITIAL CONTACT with the client marks the beginning of the *engagement* phase of the social work practice process. The major tasks of

TABLE 4.5 SKILLS FOR CULTURALLY COMPETENT PRACTICE

ENGAGEMENT SKILLS

Culturally competent social workers:
- Take responsibility for providing services in the language requested by the client.
- Have a strong ability to develop client trust, mutual respect, acceptance, and positive regard.
- Are able to overcome client feelings of suspicion, distrust, or anger.
- Use a positive and open communication style.
- Use appropriate terms and words, visual clues, tone, facial expressions, and cadence.
- Follow culturally appropriate relationship protocols.
- Sincerely convey signals of respect congruent with the client's cultural beliefs.
- Use appropriate self-disclosure.

PROBLEM IDENTIFICATION AND ASSESSMENT SKILLS

Culturally competent social workers:
- Identify the client's problem in terms of wants or needs, levels, and details.
- Use ethnographic interviewing skills to help identify the problem.
- Assess the problem within the client's total biopsychosocial context.
- Help clients determine whether a problem stems from racism or bias in others so that clients do not inappropriately blame themselves.
- Assess stressors and strengths relevant to the problem and its resolution.
- Use assessment and testing instruments appropriately.

GOAL SETTING AND CONTRACTING SKILLS

Culturally competent social workers:
- Actively involve their clients in goal setting and contracting.
- Help clients prioritize problems.
- Educate their clients about the processes of intervention, such as goals, expectations, legal rights, and the worker's orientation.
- Establish culturally acceptable goals and objectives.
- Formulate multilevel intervention alternatives.
- Identify and use the client's definition of successful coping strategies and problem resolution strategies.
- Select culturally appropriate, empirically based interventions.
- Formulate explicit contracts.

INTERVENTION IMPLEMENTATION AND MONITORING SKILLS

Culturally competent social workers:
- Enhance or restore a client's psychosocial functioning and seek to redress structural inequities at the societal level.

TABLE 4.5 *(continued)*

- Tailor intervention strategies to differences in help-seeking patterns, definition of problems, and selection of solutions.
- Use a blend of formal and informal helping resources.
- Consult with traditional healers or religious and spiritual leaders and practitioners when appropriate.
- Explore issues of authority or equality in the therapeutic relationship.
- Aim to increase personal, interpersonal, or political power of individuals, families, groups, and communities through empowerment techniques.
- Promote a client's sense of self-efficacy and mastery of his or her environment.
- Aim to promote a sense of the collective, increase access to resources, and to co-developed client-worker solutions.
- Exercise institutional intervention skills on behalf of their clients to eliminate biases, prejudices, and discriminatory practices.
- Monitor intervention implementation and client progress.

TERMINATION AND EVALUATION SKILLS

Culturally competent social workers:
- Review progress and growth with their clients.
- Refer clients to other workers or agencies if they believe they are unable to help.
- Evaluate problem change and attainment of objectives.
- Evaluate intervention effectiveness.
- Address the client's and worker's feelings about termination.
- Help clients establish goals and tasks for the future.
- Connect clients with other community resources.
- Establish a follow-up plan.
- Evaluate agency effectiveness.

FOLLOW-UP SKILLS

Culturally competent social workers:
- Facilitate maintenance of client change.
- Implement follow-up contacts.
- Collect client information during follow-up.
- Evaluate follow-up data.
- Reinstate intervention if necessary

Sources: Greene et al., 1998; Lum, 1999; Sue, Arredondo, and McDavis, 1992.

this phase are to build rapport, establish trust, and establish a mutually respectful relationship. These are fundamental prerequisites to work in the subsequent phases. In the absence of these characteristics, the worker cannot help the client. In working with immigrants and refugees, the first step in engagement is to take responsibility for providing services in the language requested by the client. Some clients will be comfortable interacting in English, but others will not. If the worker does not adequately speak the client's language, the worker should either obtain the services of a competent interpreter, or refer the client to a competent bilingual / bicultural worker (Arredondo et al. 1996). The worker should make all such efforts to provide services in the client's language; nonetheless, there will be cases when this is not possible because no trained interpreter or referral source is available. In such cases, the work must proceed in English if the client does have some comprehension; clearly, the worker will need to spend more time overcoming linguistic barriers. If the client has no English comprehension, it will be necessary to use a family member or friend to interpret; however, the worker must be highly sensitive to the inaccuracies and relationship problems that can arise in this circumstance.

After establishing common linguistic ground, the worker must begin to build a relationship with the client that engenders trust, mutual respect, and acceptance. Sometimes, this will require overcoming client feelings of suspicion, distrust, or anger. The client may have such feelings toward the worker as a result of past oppression by members of the worker's ethnic group or by people in authority, which the worker represents. By asking a question such as, "How do you feel about coming here?" (Lum 2000, p. 143), the worker may uncover such negative feelings. The worker then needs to accept these feelings, discuss their causes, and express understanding of their legitimacy.

There are several skills that culturally competent social workers use to overcome clients' negative feelings and build trust (Lum 1999, 2000). First is using a positive and open communication style. This includes body language. "A posture in which the body leans slightly forward, attentive and relaxed, conveys willingness to listen with anticipation and understanding. The worker can exhibit sincerity and concern through facial expression, voice, and open-palm hand gestures" (Lum 2000, p. 170).

Positive and open communication includes five types of verbal responses: supportive, understanding, probing, interpreting, and evaluating (Lum 2000). Supportive responses are restatements of what the client said, in the worker's own words, in order to convey that the worker has accurately received the client's message. Understanding responses demonstrate that the worker has comprehended the meaning and significance of what the client has said. Understanding responses entail rephrasing what the client said, checking with the client about the accuracy of the rephrasing, and adjusting any incorrect worker perceptions. Probing responses seek further information about what a client has said, through the use of open-ended questions, such as asking for examples. Interpreting responses involve providing an initial meaning for what has been happening with the client. After using understanding and probing responses to grasp the issues, "the worker can then develop a hunch or a hypothesis that offers a reasonable explanation of events, places, and people" (Lum 2000, p. 174).

Interpretive responses should be used in later stages of the rapport-building process, and should be phrased tentatively and revised according to the client's feedback. Evaluating responses are assessments of the client's situation in terms of the negative issues that confront the client and the positive potentials for change. Evaluating responses are made toward the end of the engagement phase and set the stage for the next practice phase, problem identification and assessment. "An evaluating response contains several elements: expression of concern, recognition of barriers in life, and expression of positive outcomes" (Lum 2000, p. 176).

In addition to these fundamental skills of open and positive communication, culturally competent workers must adjust their communication styles to be compatible with those of the client's culture. This includes using terms or words appropriate to the client's education and socioeconomic background, and using appropriate visual clues, tone of voice, facial expressions, and so forth. For example, it is well known that steady eye contact is considered a sign of attentiveness in the dominant American culture, but is considered rude or disrespectful in some other cultures. As another example, "for a Japanese person, nodding the head does not necessarily signify agreement. Rather, it conveys attentiveness and assures the communicator that he or she has been heard. Unaware of its meaning, a social worker could totally misinterpret this gesture" (Lum 2000, p. 170). Workers will not always know about all the cultural nuances of communication style of various ethnic groups. But to the extent that workers do have such knowledge, they should adjust their own communication style accordingly. In the absence of such knowledge, the need for the skillful use of the verbal responses described above becomes evident.

Culturally competent social workers also need to follow culturally appropriate relationship protocols:

> A protocol is a code of ceremonial formality and courtesies. In many cultures a relationship protocol is a prelude to conducting business. It may involve a formal greeting, inquiry about the health and well-being of family, and other friendly topics of conversation. It may be considered rude to pro-

ceed directly to the main order of business or to the presenting problem without proper protocol conversation. Following a relationship protocol involves the communication of respect and recognition to the head of household, grandparents, and other adults. It is important to practice a relationship protocol regarding the father and mother in a family situation, which means supporting their authority and roles rather than undermining their family influence. (LUM 1999, P. 116)

USE OF THESE PROTOCOLS conveys sincere respect in a manner congruent with the client's cultural beliefs.

A final crucial skill in building trust and rapport is the appropriate use of self-disclosure. This means sharing information about oneself with the client. Self-disclosure presents the worker as a human being who has some common experiences and feelings with the client, rather than as a remote professional who is superior to the client. Self-disclosure is important in working with culturally different clients because in many cultures discussion of personal problems occurs only in the context of close personal relationships; self-disclosure begins to establish that type of relationship (Lum 2000). Further, given the many cultural barriers that may exist between workers and clients, self-disclosure helps to establish common ground and a basis for mutual understanding. Appropriate topics for self-disclosure are sharing information about one's background and family, work, and helping philosophy; experiences and feelings that the worker has had that are similar in some way to those of the client; and strategies one has successfully used to deal with one's own problems (Lum 2000). It is not appropriate to use self-disclosure to seek help from the client for the worker's problems, thereby reversing the helping roles. It is also important not to overidentify with the client, and to overtly acknowledge the differences in feelings and experiences that do exist.

The use of these skills of body language, verbal responding, adjusting communication style, following relationship protocols, and self-disclosure all help to build rapport and trust with clients. These, in turn, allow clients to begin to discuss their personal problems with the worker.

4.4.2 PROBLEM IDENTIFICATION AND ASSESSMENT SKILLS

PROBLEM IDENTIFICATION is the process of creating a definition of the problem that is mutually agreed upon by the client and the worker. *Assessment* is the analysis of personal and environmental stressors that contribute to the problem, and personal and environmental strengths that can be used to help resolve it. The first step in this phase is to facilitate the client's disclosure of the problem (Lum 1999, 2000). In many cultures, disclosure of personal problems to anyone but immediate family members is strongly discouraged. Clients from such cultural backgrounds may feel hesitation and shame about discussing the problem with the worker. The worker needs to exhibit patience and give the client time. The client may disclose the problem indirectly, by describing a "friend's" problem and seeking advice for the "friend." Or the client may make only vague allusions to the problem:

> Rather than spelling out all the negative details and unburdening one's self in humiliation, one learns to infer and allude to problem issues. In turn, the worker must read between the lines and piece together the inferences. As a result, it may be culturally more appropriate for the worker to figure out the problem, spell out the details, and ask for comments from the client, who is excused from disgracing himself or herself. A culturally competent social worker is able to pick up on this approach and decipher these indirect messages from the client. (LUM 1999, P. 120)

Problem disclosure can also be facilitated by the skillful use of ethnographic interviewing techniques. Ethnographic interviewing is a research technique used by cultural anthropologists to get detailed, in-depth descriptions about respondents' lives, as perceived by the respondents themselves. When used in the helping context, ethnographic interviewing aims to elicit the client's own definition and understanding of the problem (Green 1999). Techniques of ethnographic interviewing include asking open-ended and probing questions; treating the client as the "expert" and the worker as the "learner" in regard to the problem; and allowing for extended silences. Another technique is to limit the worker's use of the word "you," in order to allow the client to depersonalize the problem, which may make disclosure easier. In other words, clients can be encouraged to talk about "people who experience this problem" rather than to talk about themselves directly.

Sometimes a client's problem will appear obvious, for example when a client is referred for a specific service such as employment assistance. However, even when the problem seems to be obvious, it is important to get the client's perspective, since it may well differ from the perspective of the referring agency.

The culturally competent social worker should define the problem in terms of the client's wants or needs. When the problem is defined as an *unsatisfied want* or an *unfulfilled need*, the definition implies a positive opportunity for satisfaction or fulfillment, rather than focusing on client pathology or blaming the client for the problem (Lum 1999). In this way, the worker utilizes a *strengths perspective* (Saleebey 1997), as opposed to a *client deficit perspective*.

Additionally, the problem definition should identify the *levels* of the problem. There are three possible levels where a problem may be located: micro (individual, family, and small group), meso (local communities and organizations), and macro (complex organizations or systems) (Lum 2000). The problem often lies at the boundary between two levels, such as in the interactions between an individual and the local community. For example, for a refugee who is experiencing difficulty finding a job, the problem is located at this micro-meso boundary. Part of the problem may be that the client does not have appropriate work skills needed in the local community, or that the client lacks job-seeking skills. Another part of the problem may be that local employers are unwilling to hire refugees because of xenophobia, fear of high training costs, or other reasons. Thus, identifying the levels of the problem points the way toward appropriate interventions. In this case, appropriate interventions would include both working on skill development with the client and working with potential employers to increase hiring of refugees.

For refugee and immigrant clients, problems often lie in the meso or macro levels in the form of societal discrimination as manifested in factors such as lack of access to health care or employment. Thus, environmental and societal conditions may be responsible for the client's unsatisfied needs and unfulfilled wants (Lum 2000). In such cases, meso and macro level interventions are required, since working only with the client is highly unlikely to resolve the problem. Thus, the culturally competent social worker must avoid the tendency to focus only on micro-level problem definitions, and make a deliberate effort to comprehensively identify the problem levels.

Another essential task in problem definition is to identify the problem *details* (Lum 1999). This means defining the problem in terms of specific feelings, thoughts, behaviors, or events; when and where these occur; and their frequency, duration, or magnitude (Bloom, Fischer, and Orme 1999). The more detailed the problem definition, the easier it is to identify appropriate interventions and the greater the likelihood of successful problem resolution. For example, defining the problem as "acculturation difficulty" is much less useful than defining it as "the client has felt very lonely and has cried every day for the past six months because she wishes she had someone from her home country to talk to."

In arriving at a problem definition in terms of wants or needs, levels, and details, it is critical that the definition be mutually developed by the worker and the client. This is done by continuously verifying the accuracy of tentative definitions with the client until a mutually agreed upon definition is arrived at. Culturally competent social workers do not impose their views of the problem on the client.

After appropriately defining the problem, the next task is problem assessment. As stated above, this means identifying the factors that contribute to the problem and those that can be used to help resolve it. The first step in assessment is to examine the problem within the client's total biopsychosocial context. This means analyzing the problem in the context of factors such as the following:

- Culture
- Sociopolitical life
- History
- Life course or cohort
- Social class
- Community
- Religion
- Gender
- Age
- Sexual orientation
- Physical challenges and abilities
- Mental challenges and abilities

- Legal context
- Nationality
- Citizenship status
- Physical appearance
- Living environment
- Health status
- Immigration status
- Length of U.S. residence
- Economic integration
- Family characteristics
- Educational history

(GREENE ET AL. 1998, P. 53)

Within each of these areas, the worker should assess stresses and strengths that are relevant to the problem. *Stresses* are the factors that contribute to or exacerbate the problem. *Strengths* are factors that keep the problem from being worse, or that can be used to help resolve the problem. Identification of strengths as well as stressors is in keeping with the strengths perspective mentioned above. Stressors and strengths should be systematically identified at the micro, meso, and macro levels. For example, for a refugee client seeking employment, a micro stressor may be lack of job-seeking skills; a meso stressor might be a high local unemployment rate; and a macro stressor might be societal age discrimination in hiring practices. A micro strength might be the refugee having a good educational background; a meso strength might be the local refugee community having a good job-referral network; and a macro strength might be the availability of a federally funded program for refugee job training.

In working with immigrant or refugee clients, it is important to assess cultural strengths:

> Examples of cultural strengths are religious beliefs, historical achievements, ethnic pride, capacities for endurance and hard work in the family, and related areas. . . . The cultural strengths perspective emphasizes the discovery of strengths in the person and the culture, the motivation toward perseverance and change based on inner strength and endurance, and the environment as full of resources at the family, group, and community levels.
>
> (LUM 1999, PP. 122–123)

There are a variety of tools to assist in the assessment process, such as interview guides, questionnaires, and testing instruments. When using the latter, the worker must have the skill to apply and interpret them correctly based on the client's culture versus the normative group's culture, as discussed above. This means not using instruments that appear to be irrelevant to the client's cultural background, and analyzing test results in relation to the norms of the client's culture. Skillful use of these instruments will avoid errors of assessment—i.e., assessing something as a stressor when it is not, or not assessing something as a stressor when it really is. Specific assessment approaches for various problem areas will be presented in subsequent chapters.

The discussion of problem identification and assessment so far has referred to "the problem," as though there were only one. In reality, however, immigrant and refugee clients usually are confronted with a multitude of problems. Thus, culturally competent social workers must identify and assess the totality of the problems that clients are facing. The identification and assessment techniques described above should be applied to each of the problems separately. Additionally, the worker and client must analyze how the problems are related to each other. Often, drawing some type of diagram or map can be helpful in this process. Following this, the work can proceed to the next phase.

4.4.3 GOAL SETTING AND CONTRACTING SKILLS

GOAL SETTING involves determining what the client and practitioner expect the client to experience at the end of their work together. *Contracting* involves developing an agreement between the client and the worker about how the goals will be achieved, including the responsibilities of the worker, the client, and other relevant parties. A fundamental element of culturally competent practice in this phase is actively involving the client in determining goals and intervention approaches. This means that workers should solicit clients' input about desired goals and intervention alternatives and come to a mutual agreement on them. Workers should never impose goals and contracts upon clients.

The first step in this process is to help clients prioritize their problems. As noted above, immigrant and refugee clients are usually faced with a multitude of problems. Since the worker and client usually do not have the time or resources to address all the problems at once, they must decide which one to tackle first. The problem that is selected to work on first should meet as many of the following criteria as possible.

- It is one that the client prefers to start with or about which the client is most concerned.
- It has the greatest likelihood of being changed.
- It is relatively concrete and specific.
- It can be readily worked with by the practitioner given the practitioner's resources.
- It has the greatest chance of producing the most negative consequences if not handled.
- It has to be handled before other problems can be tackled.
- Changes in the problem will result in tangible, observable changes for those involved, thereby perhaps increasing the client's motivation to work on other problems.   (BLOOM, FISCHER, AND ORME 1999, P. 73)

If the client's problems have been appropriately identified and assessed as described above, then it should not be too difficult to select the first problem to be worked on using these criteria. The practitioner should involve the client by asking a question such as "Based on everything you've said, it seems to me that the best place for us to start is to work on problem ___ because ___. After we solve that problem, we can decide which one to work on next. How does that sound to you?"

After deciding together which problem to work on first, the next step is for the worker to educate the client about the intervention process, such as goal setting, expectations, the worker's orientation, and any relevant legal issues. This is necessary because many refugee and immigrant clients come from cultures where formal helping relationships such as social work do not exist, or where such relationships may have actually been used to oppress people rather than help them. Therefore, this helping process will be an entirely new experience for these clients. Explaining the process to clients before it begins will decrease confusion, bewilderment, fear, resistance, or other reactions that could impede effectiveness. Thus, culturally competent social workers should do the following:
• Assess the client's understanding of the services into which the client is entering and provide accurate information regarding the process, limitations, and function of the services.
• Ensure that the client understands client rights, issues, and definitions of confidentiality, and the expectations placed on the client.

(ARREDONDO ET AL. 1996, P. 73)

Following this, the worker and the client together determine the goals and objectives of the work. *Goals* are long-term, ultimate outcomes, whereas *objectives* are shorter-term outcomes, or subgoals, which are steps on the way toward achieving goals. For example, a client's goal may be to obtain work in the same profession that he or she had in the country of origin. The objectives that have to be achieved in order to attain this ultimate goal may include reaching a certain level of English competency, completing necessary educational requirements for professional licensure, and getting licensed. Since goals cannot be attained without attaining their relevant objectives, the social work process is aimed directly at achieving objectives.

There are some rules for formulating appropriate goals and objectives (Bloom, Fischer, and Orme 1999; Blythe and Tripodi 1989). First, as stated above, the client must be actively involved. The worker should involve the client by asking questions such as, "What would you like to achieve at the end of our work together? What do you think are the necessary steps to reach that?" Second, goals and objectives must be stated in terms of what the client will experience, not what the worker will do. For example, "The client will obtain a full-time job paying at least $6.00 per hour, and accessible by public transportation, within three months," is an appropriately stated objective. On the other hand, "The worker will contact potential employers to identify possible job openings for the client," is not an appropriately stated objective; it is an intervention intended to achieve the objective, but it is not the objective itself.

Third, goals and objectives need to specify the degree of change expected, and the time frame in which it is expected to occur. This is evident in the above objective, where the expected degree of change is a change from the client's current work situation to "a full-time job paying at least $6.00 per hour, and accessible by public transportation," and the time frame is "within three months." As another example, an objective might be, "The number of arguments between the mother and her adolescent daughter will decrease from 10 per week to 3 per week within six weeks." As seen from these examples, a fourth rule for appropriate goals and interventions is that they be measurable. In the first example, the objective is measured by whether or not the client has obtained the specified job, and in the second example, the objective is measured by counting the number of arguments. To say that something is measurable does not necessarily mean that it is a behavior that can be easily observed. It can be a thought, a feeling, or some other experience, as long as some means is devised for measuring it, such as a scale.

A fifth rule for appropriate goals and objectives is that they be realistic and attainable. For example, it would not be realistic for a new immigrant with a low educational level to immediately obtain a high paying job; or to expect a mother and her adolescent daughter to have no arguments at all. Establishing such objectives would set the clients up for failure. Finally, goals and objectives need to be culturally acceptable. This means they must fit with the values, beliefs, and norms of the client's culture. For example, if the client is a caretaker of an elderly parent and they are from a culture that highly values respect and duty to elders, then it would not be appropriate to establish a goal such as placing the elderly parent in a nursing home, since this would bring shame to the family.

After establishing appropriate goals and objectives, the next step is to formulate alternative interventions that may be used to attain the objectives.

> An intervention is a set of activities designed to meet client needs and/or ameliorate client problems. Because no single set of activities may be sufficient to address all the problems of a client, more than one intervention may be employed. Interventions may be complex, involving a theory of practice and a number of techniques designed to help clients achieve their goals....
> In contrast, an intervention may be relatively simple, involving a single procedure to accomplish one particular sub-goal in working with a client.
> (BLYTHE, TRIPODI, AND BRIAR 1994, P. 88)

Culturally relevant practice requires that intervention alternatives be multilevel, that is, they target micro, meso, and macro systems. Micro interventions are those that target the individual or family only. Meso interventions involve the local community, such as church and community support systems, with the goal of connecting clients with their ethnic communities, which provide a basis for identity, support, and cultural resources. Macro interventions target the larger society, such as legal advocacy or community organizing (Lum 1999, 2000). Since the problems of immigrant and refugee clients often have a basis in meso and macro systems, as discussed above, then it is logical that culturally competent interventions must target those systems for change. To aim for change in the client when the problem really lies in society would further the client's oppression; it would make the helping relationship a means of oppression rather than a means of help.

In developing intervention alternatives, the worker and client should brainstorm together to come up with numerous possible ways to address the problem. The worker should ask the client for ideas about how to solve the problem. In doing so, the worker should also find out what coping strategies and problem resolution strategies the client has successfully used in the past. These are client strengths that should be built upon for addressing the current problem. All the possible intervention alternatives that the worker and client generate should be written down.

The next step is to choose one or more interventions from the list of alternatives that has been developed. There are several criteria for choosing the most appropriate interventions. First, those which are chosen need to be culturally appropriate. Culturally appropriate interventions fit with the values, beliefs, and norms of the client's culture. Following are two examples:

> Cognitive behavioral therapies bear some striking similarities to many Buddhist teachings. . . . Behavioral techniques such as modeling, stimulus control, reciprocal inhibition, social skills training, and use of specific rewards all have parallels in the early Buddhist writings. Techniques of dealing with intrusive thoughts such as thought stopping, thought switching, distraction, and considering negative effects of thoughts were also elaborated. . . . The similarity of modern cognitive behavioral approaches, especially when recognized by the practitioner, helps make these approaches very acceptable to cultures with Buddhist traditions.

> Hispanic clients [often] expect treatment to be characterized by immediate symptom relief, guidance and advice giving, a concrete focus, and a problem-

centered approach.... Cognitive-behavioral therapy [is] particularly applicable due to its lack of emphasis upon insight or emotional release and the expectations brought to therapy by clients. (EGLI ET AL. 1991, PP. 169–170)

In addition to cultural appropriateness, social workers should also use the following criteria in selecting the best interventions: consistency with the worker's prior experience, feasibility, ethicalness, effectiveness, and efficiency (Tripodi 1994). Consistency with prior experience means workers should choose those interventions that, in their experience, have been successful with similar clients and similar problems. The chosen intervention needs to be feasible given the available time and resources for work with the client. The intervention also needs to be ethical, as perceived by the worker, the client, and society. Finally, the chosen intervention should have support in the research literature for its effectiveness and efficiency. Effectiveness means that the intervention has been shown through rigorous research to be successful in resolving similar problems with similar clients. When an intervention has been shown to be effective for similar problems but different clients, which will often be the case in working with immigrants and refugees, the worker should evaluate the cultural appropriateness of the intervention, and whether it can be adapted to be culturally appropriate. When several equally effective interventions are available the worker should use the criterion of efficiency, which means selecting the one that is least costly in terms of time and resources. Using the criteria of effectiveness and efficiency based on the research literature, as well as the worker's past experience, means that the chosen intervention is empirically based.

A final criterion for intervention selection is that the intervention must be acceptable to the client. The worker should fully involve the client in evaluating each alternative intervention using the above criteria, and the worker should obtain the client's opinions about willingness to participate in that intervention and its perceived likelihood of success (Lum 1999).

After selecting an intervention or set of interventions, the final step in this phase of practice is to formulate an explicit contract. The contract is an agreement that spells out the intervention(s) to be employed; the responsibilities of the worker, the client, community resources, and other relevant parties; the time frame; the frequency of intervention activities; mechanisms for monitoring the process; and practical activities for problem-solving (Lum 2000). The intervention should be specified in terms of who will do what with whom and where (Blythe, Tripodi, and Briar 1994). Contracting is important because it brings focus to the work with the client, and helps prevent meaningless interactions or getting sidetracked with extraneous issues (Devore and Schlesinger 1999; Zastrow 1995). The contract is usually verbal, but can be written.

Some immigrant or refugee clients may be fearful or apprehensive about contracting since it may be perceived as an instrument of authoritarian coercion. Therefore, it is essential for the worker to fully involve clients in the contracting process in order to help them "recognize and believe that they can play a part in determining why and how something is to be done" (Devore and Schlesinger 1999, p. 196). Clients can be involved by asking for their suggestions about elements of the contract, and getting their opinions and approval of the worker's suggestions.

4.4.4 INTERVENTION IMPLEMENTATION AND MONITORING SKILLS

INTERVENTION IMPLEMENTATION is the process of carrying out the intervention. It involves the activities, behaviors, and statements that the worker, client, and relevant others engage in. *Monitoring* consists of two parts: monitoring the intervention implementation, and monitoring client progress. The exact nature of interventions will vary depending on what approach is selected in the preceding practice stage. However, there are some common elements that interventions should have in order to make for culturally competent practice.

Interventions in culturally competent practice have a dual aim: to enhance or restore a client's psychosocial functioning and to change structural inequities at the societal level. This is a logical extension of the issues discussed above in terms of multilevel problem assessment and formulation of multilevel intervention alternatives. Additionally, culturally competent interventions are uniquely tailored to the client's problem definition, help-seeking patterns, and selection of solutions. Again, this is a natural extension of actively involving the client in the preceding practice stages. Further, culturally competent interventions employ both formal help, which is that provided by the social worker or other professionals, and informal help, which is that provided by community resources such as traditional healers, religious or spiritual leaders, mutual aid groups, and volunteers (Greene and Barnes 1998). This follows from the earlier principles of building on community and cultural strengths and choosing culturally appropriate interventions.

In regard to enhancing or restoring clients' psychosocial functioning, there are some general elements of culturally competent intervention, which apply in addition to whatever specific intervention strategies have been selected. First, the worker must explore issues of authority or equality in the therapeutic relationship (Greene et al. 1998). By virtue of the helping situation, the worker is an expert who has access to helping resources, whereas the client is in need of those resources; this establishes a power differential between the worker and the client. Further, workers, by virtue of their education, socioeconomic status, and often, membership in the dominant ethnic group, have greater power in society than do immigrant or refugee clients. These power differences will always be obvious to clients; if the worker fails to acknowledge them, this communicates a lack of respect and understanding of the client's reality. The worker must acknowledge the power differences and work to decrease them by actively involving the client in the intervention implementation phase, just as was done in earlier phases. The client should be involved by undertaking specific intervention tasks, contributing to the monitoring process (described below), and providing feedback about the relevance and effectiveness of intervention activities.

Power differentials are also decreased by using interventions to empower the client. Empowerment increases the client's power not only in relation to the worker, but also to society as a whole. Client empowerment is a fundamental aim of culturally competent interventions. It aims to decrease client *powerlessness*, which is "the inability to control self and others, to alter problem situations, or reduce environmental distress" (Lum 2000, p. 198). *Empowerment* has been defined in the following ways:

- The use of strategies that enable clients to experience themselves as competent, valuable, and worthwhile both as individuals and as members of their cultural group. They no longer feel trapped in the subordinate cultural group status that prevents them from meeting their goals.
(PINDERHUGHES 1989, P. 111, CITED IN LUM 2000, P. 260)

- The development of skills that enable the person . . . to implement interpersonal influence, improve role performance, and develop an effective support system.   (LUM 2000, P. 260)

- A sense of personal power, an ability to affect others, and an ability to work with others to change social institutions.
(GUTIÉRREZ 1990, P. 150, CITED IN LUM 2000, P. 274)

- [The ability] of people and communities . . . to define their own best interests, promote their self-sufficiency, and be free to live out their historical values. (GREEN 1999, P. 5)

- The ability to . . . find and make use of resources. (GREEN 1999, P. 91)

- [The ability of people to] rediscover their own capacities and to modify their environments to conform to rights, needs, and goals.
(SOLOMON 1976, P. 21, CITED IN GREENE ET AL. 1998)

Culturally competent social workers help empower their clients by using *empowerment techniques*, which have been identified by various authors as follows:

- Educating the person regarding the effects of the oppressing system, mobilizing material and interpersonal resources, building support systems, informing people about their societal entitlements and rights, and strengthening a positive self-image. (LUM 2000, PP. 260–261)

- Using [client] self-observation (through things such as diaries, checklists, and the like) and self-monitoring [to help clients] to see themselves as active agents in the solution of the problem, to understand both environmental constraints and possibilities, and to perceive the practitioner as a peer-collaborator or partner in the problem solving effort. (KOPP 1989, P. 277)

- Helping clients define their own needs and clarify their personal goals so they can derive a sense of purposefulness; providing clients with education and access to resources; helping clients see that the direction and ability to change lie within themselves; and focusing on the identification and enhancement of clients' strengths rather than their pathologies.
(ZASTROW 1995, P. 523)

- [Helping] clients define themselves and affirm their identity as a member of one or more marginalized population groups; supporting clients to develop identity pride and synthesize an identity that reflects all aspects of themselves; increasing clients' mutually empathic relationships; aiding clients to overcome alienation from significant others and the [dominant] population; and engaging clients in seeking change in conditions that oppress and violate their freedom. (VAN VOORHIS 1998, P. 105)

EMPOWERMENT TECHNIQUES also aim at four interrelated psychological changes :

- Increasing self-efficacy. [This is] defined as a belief in one's ability to produce and to regulate events in one's life... [This includes] strengthening ego functioning, developing a sense of personal power or strength, developing a sense of mastery, developing client initiative, or increasing the client's ability to act.
- Developing group consciousness. [This] involves the development of an awareness of how political structures affect individual and group experiences. The development of group consciousness... results in a critical perspective on society that redefines individual, group, or community problems as emerging from a lack of power. [This] creates within the individual, or among members of a group or community, a sense of shared fate. This consciousness allows them to focus their energies on the causes of their problems, rather than on changing their internal subjective states.
- Reducing self-blame... By attributing their problems to the existing power arrangements in society, clients are freed from feeling responsible for their negative situation... This shift in focus allows clients to feel less defective or deficient and more capable of changing their situation.
- Assuming personal responsibility for change. [This] counteracts some of the potentially negative results of reducing self-blame. Clients who do not feel responsible for their problems may not invest their efforts in developing solutions unless they assume some personal responsibility for future change.... By taking personal responsibility for the resolution of problems, clients are more apt to make an active effort to improve their lives.

(GUTIERREZ 1990, P. 150, CITED IN LUM 2000, PP. 274–275)

In addition to helping to empower clients, culturally competent social workers must themselves take action at the agency and societal levels to eliminate biases, prejudices, and discriminatory practices. This is part of the dual aim of culturally competent intervention. The agency barriers that hinder ethnic minority clients' access to and effectiveness of services were described in the previous chapter. Agencies that effectively serve ethnic minority clients have the following characteristics:

- Are engaged with the community.
- Reexamine and address issues of community power differentials.

- Provide access to other resources.
- Are consumer oriented.
- Use participatory management techniques.
- Work to bring down barriers between workers and clients.
- Provide in-service training about cultural competence.
- Examine and enhance program development with community members.

(GREENE ET AL. 1998, P. 54)

Culturally competent social workers must recognize cultural barriers when they exist in their own agencies, and work toward decreasing those barriers and developing the above agency characteristics through actions such as the following:

- Designing social service programs for ethnic minority clients and communities.
- Developing accessible, pragmatic, and positive service delivery systems.
- Recruiting bilingual/bicultural workers.
- Participating in community outreach programs.
- Establishing linkages with other social agencies.
- Correcting insensitive services that lead to agency underuse.
- Incorporating cultural information into agency procedures, structures, and services.

(GREENE ET AL. 1998; LUM 1999; SUE, ARREDONDO, AND MCDAVIS 1992)

At the societal level, culturally competent social workers must address structural inequity through macro-level interventions such as social policy development, social planning, social administration, community organizing, political impact, and legal advocacy (Devore and Schlesinger 1999; Lum 2000).

While implementing the intervention, the social worker must simultaneously monitor it. The purpose of monitoring is to determine whether the intervention is being implemented as planned, and whether it is being implemented consistently (Blythe and Tripodi 1989). Intervention monitoring is an important function of evaluation, because when a client problem improves, worsens, or stays the same, it is essential to know exactly what intervention activities were associated with that outcome. In other words, it is of little use to know that a client problem has improved if there is no clear knowledge of the intervention that was associated with that improvement, because then that intervention cannot be replicated with other clients. This is particularly important when working with ethnic minority clients since there is relatively little empirical information about what works for these clients. Also, interventions with ethnic minority clients frequently have to be adapted to be culturally appropriate, so it is important to document these adaptations and their results in order to build knowledge for work with future clients.

Further, implementation monitoring helps the worker stay on course with the planned intervention. If an intervention is known to be effective based on prior research or the worker's prior experience, then staying on course will increase the likelihood of being effective with the current client. In other words, if an intervention is known to be effective, but is not implemented in the way it is supposed to be, then it will probably not be as effective with the current client as it should have been.

Intervention implementation is monitored by developing forms or checklists that very specifically describe the guidelines, prescriptions, and behaviors that are supposed to constitute the intervention (Blythe and Tripodi 1989). The form or checklist is developed before the intervention is implemented; it is a plan for what is to be done. Ideally, there should be a form or checklist for every planned contact with the client, as well as for other planned intervention activities undertaken on the client's behalf. Forms should be developed for worker intervention activities and client intervention activities.

Client intervention activities are things that the client is supposed to undertake. For example, if a client is supposed to practice a certain behavior at home, that is a client intervention activity. The client then needs to maintain a form to record each time he or she practices the behavior. The rationale for this needs to be explained to the client in order to make it meaningful. The worker needs to explain to the client that the worker is monitoring him or herself just as the client is monitoring him or herself. It is also possible for the client to monitor the worker using the form that has been developed for the worker's intervention activities. This is a good means of empowering the client in the working relationship. In addition to forms and checklists, intervention implementation can also be monitored by methods such as live observation, content analysis of tape recordings or case records, and interviewing clients to assess the degree to which they have carried out intervention tasks and what obstacles they may have faced (Blythe, Tripodi, and Briar 1994).

A final element of the implementation stage is monitoring client progress. This is different from monitoring intervention implementation. Monitoring client progress refers to tracking the problem that is being addressed in order to determine whether it is improving, worsening, or staying the same. This means that the problem has to be measured in some way, such as the frequency, magnitude, or duration of problem behaviors, thoughts, feelings, abilities, or events. There are many possible ways to measure and record problems, such as questionnaires, scales, observation, and so forth. The literature on single-systems research provides details of these methods (Bloom, Fischer, and Orme 1999; Tripodi 1994). In addition to these written monitoring methods, progress should also be reviewed verbally by the worker soliciting the client's perceptions as to whether and how the problem is improving, worsening or staying the same.

Monitoring client progress should be an ongoing task throughout the intervention implementation phase. This means that the problem should be measured at regular intervals during the intervention implementation. Further, the client should be actively involved in this monitoring process through such activities as selecting the measurement method, doing the recording, and charting progress on a graph. Such involvement is another means of empowering clients in the working relationship. The results from this monitoring should be used as feedback for possibly changing the intervention. If the results indicate that the problem is improving, then the intervention should probably stay on course. However, if the results indicate that the problem is not changing or is getting worse, then the client and worker need to identify possible reasons for this, and adjust the intervention accordingly. These adjustments then need to be recorded on the intervention implementation monitoring form.

These monitoring activities may seem to be a lot of "extra" work on top of everything else that the worker needs to do in order to be culturally competent. However, after the worker has some experience with these activities, they become much less time-consuming and become a routine part of the practice process; they do not take time away from helping activities, but rather, they are a helping activity. The value of these activities, especially for working with ethnic minority clients has been described above. In summary, these monitoring activities:

- Help you define and structure what you are doing.
- Help you and the client know where you are going and when you get there.

- Provide crucial feedback for you and the client.
- Provide additional flexibility in allowing you to make specific rational decisions about needed changes in your intervention.
- Most likely serve to enhance the quality of your relationship.

(BLOOM, FISCHER, AND ORME 1999)

4.4.5 TERMINATION AND EVALUATION SKILLS

TERMINATION is the end of the working relationship. *Evaluation* is the assessment of the extent to which the client's problems have been resolved and objectives achieved, and the extent to which the intervention may have contributed to the problem resolution. Evaluation also includes an assessment of agency effectiveness overall. Termination can occur for one of three reasons: the client's problems have been resolved and there is no further work to be done; the worker believes he or she cannot help the client or cannot help any further; or the client drops out before the problem has been resolved. The following discussion will first address the first two termination possibilities; client dropout will be addressed subsequently.

Sometimes after identifying and assessing the client problems, workers may believe that they cannot help the client. There may be many reasons for this, such as the worker's professional or personal limitations or agency limitations. In other cases, workers may be implementing an intervention or interventions with a client for some time, but find that the problem is not improving or is getting worse. If the worker and client run out of intervention ideas, then the worker is no longer able to help the client. In yet other cases, the worker and client may have successfully resolved one or more problems, but for various reasons the worker is unable to help with other client problems that still remain. In all these cases, termination is appropriate.

In all these cases, the culturally competent social worker must refer the client to other helping resources that seem more likely to be able to help the client. The referral process involves several tasks:

> The worker must prepare the client for the referral and discuss the need for and importance of the referral. The worker should discuss with the client any hesitations he or she might feel and any doubts and questions the client might have about the new agency. It is crucial that the client and worker examine a range of referral sources. . . . The client should make an appointment at the new agency after clearance has occurred between the two work-

ers. This groundwork involves discussing the client's needs and advocating the new agency's acceptance of the client. The worker should make sure the client accepts the referral, contacts the agency, and becomes involved with its services. (LUM 2000, P. 324)

When termination occurs because all or some client problems have been resolved, there are several tasks that culturally competent workers must undertake (Devore and Schlesinger 1999; Lum 1999, 2000). First, workers should review with clients the progress and growth that clients have made. Workers should provide positive verbal reinforcement for the gains the client has made and the hard work that went into achieving those gains. This review and reinforcement serves to increase the client's sense of mastery, and is therefore an empowering process. Additionally, the review helps clients identify their own strengths and coping strategies, as well as community resources, that they can use when faced with future problems.

In undertaking this review, the worker and client must evaluate the extent to which the client problems have been resolved and the original objectives achieved. This is done by comparing the client's current state to the original objective, by examining the results from the problem monitoring process, and by obtaining verbal feedback from the client. If proper procedures for measuring and monitoring the problem were established in the earlier phases of practice, then this evaluation should easily flow from the information that has been collected. It is often helpful to graph the results from the monitoring procedure. Such a graph shows the change in the problem over time. The literature on single-system designs describes how to create and analyze such graphs (Bloom, Fischer, and Orme 1999; Tripodi 1994). For the client, seeing positive improvement in a graphical form can make the progress seem more "real" and further increase the client's sense of mastery.

In evaluating problem resolution, workers should focus on the *clinical significance* (also called *substantive significance* or *practical significance*) of the problem change. These terms refer to the meaningfulness of the change to the client, and in some cases, to society (Bloom, Fischer, and Orme 1999). The client should be asked whether the improvement in the problem situation was large enough to be meaningful. If so, then the change was clinically significant. If not, then there is still further work to be done, either with the worker, other resources, or by the client alone. If the client problem was a problem to society (such as juvenile delinquent behavior) then the worker needs to make a judgment as to whether the degree of change achieved is meaningful to society.

After evaluating the extent of change achieved, the worker should evaluate the intervention effectiveness, or the extent to which the intervention or interventions contributed to the change in the problem. This requires the application of concepts of research design. Again, the literature on single-system designs provides this information (Bloom, Fischer, and Orme 1999; Tripodi 1994).

In most real life practice situations, it is impossible to prove that an intervention was the cause of an improvement in the client's problem. This requires the use of highly controlled experiments, which are usually not feasible or desirable in practice. However, the worker and client can usually make an informed judgment about the degree to which the intervention led to the improvement. This is done by ruling out other possible explanations for the improvement. There are many possible reasons why a client's problem may improve, other than the application of the intervention. For example, a change in the client's life situation may lead to an improvement in the identified problem; or the client may participate in other activities besides the intervention that are helpful, such as getting advice from friends; or the problem may simply get better over time, even if no intervention had been implemented. Thus, the worker and client should discuss these possibilities and make a judgment about the impact of the intervention.

In this regard, some useful questions that the workers can ask clients include whether the intervention was helpful; what else clients did or experienced that may have been helpful; what specific worker activities were and were not helpful, and so forth. The importance of this is so that workers can add to their knowledge base about what interventions do and do not work for specific problems with specific immigrant and refugee clients. Although definitive information about intervention effectiveness cannot be gained from only one client, if positive results are consistently achieved with the same intervention with similar problems and similar clients, that provides good evidence of intervention effectiveness and is an important addition to the knowledge base.

Another important task of the termination and evaluation phase is to discuss the client's and the worker's feelings about termination. Such feelings are likely to be both positive and negative (Lum 1999). Positive feelings include happiness and pride about the accomplishments that have been made, and a sense of enrichment from participating in the helping relationship. Negative feelings may include sadness about ending the relationship and apprehension about what might happen in the future. Workers should acknowledge clients' feelings of sadness and let clients know that they will be available if needed in the future. They should also reiterate the mastery and new skills that clients have gained in the helping process, so that clients feel more able to face future problems on their own.

To further address clients' apprehensions about the future, workers should help clients establish goals and tasks for the future, connect clients with other community resources, and develop a follow-up plan. Goals and tasks for the future are established in order to help clients maintain or build further upon the gains they have made in the working relationship. It is important that clients be able to maintain their gains after the worker is no longer providing help. If the client's problem is only improved while the worker is involved, then the client has not been empowered. The social work process should aim for long-term change. Thus, at termination, clients should be helped to establish new goals and objectives and identify the necessary tasks they need to undertake in order to accomplish those goals and objectives. Workers should also help clients identify any obstacles or problems they may face in the future, and identify ways that the clients can cope with or address those obstacles or problems. If appropriate, clients can role-play possible coping strategies and responses to anticipated problems (Lum 2000).

Workers should connect clients with other community resources that can help clients maintain their gains or deal with future problems. Such resources can include neighborhood networks, religious institutions, social or recreational organizations, educational institutions, mutual aid groups, and so forth. In some cases it may be appropriate to involve family members in helping clients maintain the gains achieved in the working relationship (Lum 2000).

Culturally competent workers should also develop a follow-up plan. The purpose of this is to find out how clients are doing after termination and to provide additional support or referrals if necessary. Follow-up involves establishing a schedule of less frequent client-worker contact than during the intervention implementation phase. For example, if the intervention implementation phase involved weekly meetings, follow-up may involve two to three monthly meetings. Follow-up can also be done by telephone, either in place of meetings, or following the scheduled reduced-contact meetings. The follow-up plan should include the following elements:

The social worker should involve the client in the planning for follow-up.... The rationale for follow-up (such as checking on client maintenance of gains, or providing an opportunity for the client to discuss her/his experience and future plans) should be provided, and the nature of the follow-up itself should be discussed. The client will want to know when and where the follow-up will occur, the types of data to be gathered, and the length of the interview. The worker and client should discuss a tentative date, noting that it can be changed, if necessary. They should also determine the most convenient place for the client to have a follow-up interview. Clients should be given self-stamped change of address postcards in the event they move, and should be told what the follow-up procedures would be. As an example of possible follow-up procedures, about a month prior to the follow-up date, a letter could be sent to the client explaining again the purpose of follow-up and the procedures to be followed; one or two weeks before the follow-up, a telephone call could be made to serve as a reminder.

(BLYTHE AND TRIPODI 1989, P. 145)

The discussion of termination and evaluation tasks so far has addressed the situation when termination occurs because all or some of the client's problems have been resolved and objectives met. Unfortunately, however, many ethnic minority clients drop out of treatment before problems have been resolved or objectives met. Dropout may occur after only one meeting with the worker. As discussed in the previous chapter, such premature termination is more common among ethnic minority clients than clients who are members of the dominant ethnic group. The reasons for this are often the agency cultural barriers, or worker cultural incompetence. Other reasons may include difficulties with transportation, problems with child care, or inability to pay for the services (Lum 2000). If the worker has followed the principles of culturally competent practice described in this chapter, these premature terminations should be reduced.

However, premature terminations point to a need to evaluate the agency's overall effectiveness in serving clients from particular ethnic minority groups. Thus, in addition to evaluating their own practice effectiveness, culturally competent workers need to evaluate agency effectiveness. Agency effectiveness should be evaluated in five areas:

- Dropout rate, which can be evaluated by identifying the factors that increase the probability of continued treatment.

- Improvement rate by approach, which examines which [interventions] work most effectively with which problems for which clients.
- Time effectiveness, which shows which modality used fewer sessions than another, with similar results than the other.
- Maintenance rates, which demonstrate continued improvement after termination versus the "revolving door" effect.
- Consumer satisfaction with the way [ethnic minority] clients were treated. (MUÑOZ 1982, CITED IN LUM 2000, P. 321)

The above indicators of agency effectiveness can be evaluated by a variety of program evaluation methodologies, such as exit or follow-up surveys or interviews, focus groups, or group research design studies. The literature on social work research and evaluation provides information about these methods (Blythe, Tripodi, and Briar 1994; Rubin and Babbie 1997). Results from these agency evaluations should be used to change agency procedures to increase ethnic minority clients' access to services, staying in treatment, treatment effectiveness, maintenance of gains, and satisfaction with services.

4.4.6 FOLLOW-UP SKILLS

FOLLOW-UP is the final stage of the social work process. As stated above, follow-up involves maintaining decreased contact with the client, either in person or by telephone. The purposes of follow-up are:

- Encouragement of clients to continue progress after termination.
- Brief assistance for residual difficulties during follow-up.
- Assessment of the durability of change.
- Continuance of the worker's interest in the client.

(LUM 2000, PP. 323–324)

During the follow-up period, the worker gathers information from the client and evaluates it. Three types of information can be obtained: continued monitoring of the client problem; information on factors that might be influencing the problem, or the development of new problems; and information about the client's perceptions about the worker and the intervention (Tripodi 1994). The first type of information gathering involves monitoring the problem in the same way that it was monitored during the intervention implementation phase. Thus, the client continues to monitor the problem using the same measurement procedures and the same frequency of measurement that was established during the earlier phase. This information can be graphed and compared with the graph for the intervention phase to determine whether client gains have been maintained, increased, or deteriorated.

The second type of information gathering involves interviewing clients about their experiences since termination. This information can be gathered in person or by telephone. The following types of questions can be asked:

- Have you received help from other resources or persons?
- Have you had any recurrences of the major problem for which you received help?
- Have you changed any of your daily habits?
- Have there been any changes in your living circumstances?
- Have there been any changes in your personal relationships with family and friends?
- Have any other major problems occurred?
- Have there been any unexpected positive or negative changes resulting from the services you received? (TRIPODI 1994, P. 138)

Based on the information obtained from this interview and the problem monitoring during follow-up, the worker and client should decide how to proceed. If there has been no worsening of the problem and no new problems have appeared, then the worker and client will probably decide to have no further planned contact. On the other hand, if the problem has worsened or new problems have appeared, then the worker should either offer to reinstate the intervention, or another intervention, if the worker believes he or she can be helpful, or should refer the client to another helping resource.

The final type of information that can be obtained during follow-up is information on client satisfaction. This information can be obtained by in-person or telephone interview, or by written questionnaire. Someone from the agency other than the client's worker should gather this information, since clients may feel pressured to respond favorably if the worker is collecting the information. Questions such as the following can be asked:

- To what extent has the social worker been sensitive to your needs?
- Did the social worker meet with you on time for your appointments?

- Did the social worker review progress with you?
- Did the social worker provide you with graphic information about your progress?
- Did the social worker help you identify the problems(s) you worked on?
- Did the social worker provide you with good advice that you could use on everyday practical problems?
- Were you comfortable discussing your personal problems with the social worker?
- Was the social worker helpful to you? (TRIPODI 1994, P. 140)

For each response to the above questions, clients should be given the opportunity to elaborate, in order to obtain more detail about what was or was not helpful. Workers should then use this information constructively to improve their performance with future clients, if this is indicated.

4.5 CONCLUSION

CULTURAL COMPETENCY IS NOT something that a social worker acquires overnight. In fact, no one is probably ever completely culturally competent. Rather, cultural competency is a process in which the social worker is continually developing and improving. Cultural competency requires lifelong learning. Culturally competent social workers continually evaluate their practice and the policies and procedures within their agencies to determine how they might better serve, and be more effective with, ethnic minority clients. Culturally competent workers continually examine their attitudes and beliefs, knowledge, and skills in working with culturally different clients. Some specific activities that workers can undertake for this purpose include the following:

- Have a culturally diverse caseload and use this as an opportunity to learn new information about the various ethnic groups.
- Have your culturally diverse clients, as your teachers, help you understand them in terms of commonalities and differences.
- Learn about your agency's culturally diverse clients from senior staff who have had numerous contacts and experiences in the agency setting.
- Establish short-term research projects about characteristics of and issues related to culturally diverse clients, families, groups, and communities.

- Take cultural competence workshops sponsored by public and private agencies and universities in your area.
- Keep up with current books and journal articles on cultural diversity.
- Keep up periodic correspondence with your former professors who have a commitment to culturally competent social work practice.

(LUM 1999, PP. 76–77)

CHAPTER 5
HEALTH

IMMIGRANTS AND REFUGEES have been identified as a vulnerable population that has high risk for poor health (Riedel 1998). Therefore, social work with members of this population must address their health status and health care needs. Whether social workers are employed in health care settings or other settings that serve immigrants and refugees, they should be familiar with the unique health issues of this population, and with appropriate interventions. This chapter will begin by describing the relevant health issues, including the reasons for this population's vulnerability to poor health. The chapter will then discuss best practices for addressing these issues. The chapter will conclude with some case study exercises for contemplation of appropriate social work action.

5.1 HEALTH AND HEALTH CARE PROBLEMS

THE MAJOR CONSIDERATIONS pertaining to the health and health care of immigrants and refugees are health care access problems; differential health status; health beliefs and health practices; psychosocial issues; and subpopulations with unique health issues.

5.1.1 HEALTH CARE ACCESS

ACCESS TO HEALTH CARE is defined as "the timely use of personal health services to achieve the best possible outcomes" (Institute of Medicine 1993, p. 33, cited in Riedel 1998, p. 105). Inadequate access is identified by underutilization and delayed utilization of preventive and treatment services (Ell and Castañeda 1998). Studies have shown that in general, immigrants' use of public health care programs is lower than their eligibility for those programs (National Immigration Law Center 1999).

Additionally, there have been many studies on health care utilization by ethnic and racial minority groups, which often include foreign-born people and their offspring (i.e., first- and second-generation immigrants and refugees). These studies consistently show that ethnic and racial minorities underutilize and delay utilization of health care services (Chung and Lin 1994; Ell and Castañeda 1998; Kass, Weinick, and Monheit 1999; Mayberry et al. 1999; Meadows 1999; Tran, Dhooper, and McInnis-Dittrich 1997; Yamashiro and Matsuoka 1997; U.S. Department of Health and Human Services 1998). For example, compared to other racial/ethnic groups, Hispanics are least likely to have a usual source of care, more likely to have a hospital-based source of care (as opposed to office-based), and most likely to experience difficulty, delay, or failure to receive needed health care (Kass, Weinick, and Monheit 1999). Among Asian Americans, newly arrived immigrants, and refugees from Southeast Asia, have less health care access than other subgroups such as Japanese Americans (Meadows 1999). Another indicator of health care underutilization is that racial and ethnic minority mothers are less likely than White mothers to receive early prenatal care (U.S. Department of Health and Human Services 1998).

Inadequate access to health care affects not only the health of the immigrants and refugees themselves, but also affects society as a whole (National Council of State Legislatures 1997). Delayed health care often results ultimately in higher public expenditures. For example, when a person seeks emergency treatment after a condition has become life threatening, rather than receiving early preventive treatment, the cost is higher. Untreated communicable diseases pose a threat to the public health. Finally, "when newcomers are healthy, they have better prospects for early employment, self-sufficiency, and successful integration into their communities" (National Council of State Legislatures 1997, p. 3).

There are three major factors that contribute to inadequate health care access for immigrants and refugees: structural barriers, financial barriers, and personal and cultural barriers.

STRUCTURAL BARRIERS Structural barriers are "impediments to medical care directly related to the number, type, concentration, location, or organizational configuration of health care providers" (Institute of Medicine 1993, p. 39, cited in Riedel 1998, p. 105). Racial and ethnic minorities are more likely than whites to live in medically underserved areas, and poor urban racial and ethnic minority communities are more likely to have a shortage of physicians (U.S. Department of Health and Human Services 1998). Additionally, racial and ethnic minority physicians are more likely than other physicians to treat racial and ethnic minority patients, but minority students are underrepresented in health professions schools, and their enrollment in medical schools is declining (U.S. Department of Health and Human Services 1998). Additional structural barriers include limited clinic hours, discontinuity in physicians, limited public transportation, and fragmentation of the health care system (Ell and Castañeda 1998; Meadows 1999; National Conference of State Legislatures 1997).

Further, differential treatment of minority patients by health care providers and health care delivery systems also restricts access to certain types of care. For example, it has been found that members of some minority groups are less likely to be referred for cancer screening, less likely to receive aggressive cancer therapy, less likely to receive surgical treatment for heart problems, and less likely to receive the most technologically advanced diagnostic tests and treatment procedures (Ell and Castañeda 1998; Mayberry et al. 1999).

Another critical structural barrier is policies that link health care eligibility to legal status of immigrants and refugees. The major policy in this regard is the Personal Responsibility and Work Opportunity Reconciliation Act of 1996 (PRWORA), which was described in chapter 2. Under this policy, qualified aliens (with the exception of exempt groups such as refugees, as described in chapter 2) who entered the U.S. on or after August 22, 1996 are barred from receiving Medicaid, the Children's Health Insurance Program (CHIP), or any other designated federal means-tested public benefit during their first five years in the country. Further, the immigrant's sponsor's income must be added to the immigrant's income in determining eligibility for Medicaid and CHIP. This makes most recent immigrants ineligible for these programs. Nonqualified aliens, a category that includes undocumented aliens and temporary residents, are barred from receiving Medicaid, CHIP, or any other designated federal means-tested public benefit, regardless of when they entered the country. Both qualified and nonqualified aliens may receive Medicaid coverage of emergency medical services only, provided they meet their state's eligibility criteria (Families USA 1999). Further, because PRWORA largely shifts responsibility for immigrant policy from the federal to the state level, immigrants' and refugees' eligibility for public health programs varies by state.

Although PRWORA severely restricted access to a range of health benefits for immigrants, they do remain eligible for some health benefits. "All aliens, regardless of immigration status, are eligible for public health assistance funded through sources other than the Medicaid program. The public health assistance is limited to immunizations . . . and for testing and treatment of symptoms of communicable diseases [e.g., tuberculosis, HIV/AIDS, and sexually transmitted diseases] whether or not such symptoms are caused by a communicable disease" (Schlosberg 1998, p. 5). Further, all aliens, regardless of immigration status, are eligible for community based programs that are necessary to protect life and safety. These include emergency services, public safety services such as ambulance and sanitation, as well as the following health and health-related services:

- Crisis counseling and intervention programs, services and assistance relating to child protection, adult protective services, violence and abuse prevention, victims of domestic violence or other criminal activity, or treatment of mental illness or substance abuse.
- Short-term shelter or housing assistance for the homeless, for victims of domestic violence, or for runaway, abused, or abandoned children.
- Programs, services, or assistance to help individuals during periods of heat, cold, or other adverse weather conditions.
- Soup kitchens, community food banks, senior nutrition programs such as meals on wheels, and other community nutritional services for persons requiring special assistance.
- Medical and public health services (including treatment and prevention of diseases and injuries) and mental health, disability, or substance abuse assistance necessary to protect life or safety.
- Activities designed to protect the life and safety of workers, children and youths, or community residents.
- Any other programs, services, or assistance necessary for the protection of life and safety. (SCHLOSBERG 1998, P. 6)

Although all aliens, including undocumented aliens, remain eligible for the above services and programs, their access is nonetheless hampered by undocumented aliens' fears of being reported to the Immigration and Naturalization Service (INS), and subsequently being deported, if they apply for these health services. Numerous reports have documented that large numbers of undocumented aliens do not seek needed health care for this reason (Families USA 1999; Schlosberg 1998; Schlosberg and Wiley 1998). These fears arise from lack of knowledge and confusion about verification and reporting requirements, on the part of both the aliens and the service providers.

According to the law, only agencies that administer SSI, housing assistance under the U.S. Housing Act of 1937, or block grants under the TANF program are required to provide the Immigration and Naturalization Service with the names and addresses of anyone that the agency knows is not lawfully present in the U.S. However, the law does not mandate reporting of immigration status when an alien applies for Medicaid or other health benefits. Further, the Social Security Act requires states to protect information regarding Medicaid applicants and recipients, and prohibits disclosure of that information to an outside entity. Although reporting immigration status to INS is not mandated, government agencies are required to verify immigration status for the purpose of determining Medicaid eligibility. However, non-Medicaid programs are explicitly directed by law not to verify an applicant's immigration status, since all aliens, including undocumented aliens, are eligible for non-federal health benefits. Thus, hospitals and other health care providers should not attempt to verify an alien's immigration status as a condition of receipt of any health care services. Although this is the law, there is nonetheless considerable confusion among health care providers about their reporting obligations. Further, some state policy directives about verification and reporting are in contradiction to these federal laws, and are therefore erroneous. A related problem is that many health program application forms request the applicant's Social Security Number, which undocumented aliens do not have. Even though these programs are not required to verify or report immigration status, undocumented aliens fear being reported to INS as a result of leaving the requested information blank. In many cases, undocumented alien parents' fears prevent them from seeking needed health care not only for themselves, but for their U.S.-born citizen children (Schlosberg 1998).

In addition to the fears of undocumented aliens, legal immigrants also have fears that prevent them from accessing health care. These fears arise from the "public charge" provisions of PRWORA and the Illegal Immigration Reform and Immigrant Responsibility Act of 1996 (IIRIRA). Under these laws, aliens who wish to enter the U.S., to obtain permanent residency, or to re-enter the U.S. after traveling abroad for more than six months, must show that they are not likely to become a public charge, i.e., dependent on public benefits for subsistence. If a person is determined likely to become a public charge, "potential consequences include delay or denial of changes in immigration status, delay or denial of re-entry after traveling abroad, rejection of petitions to sponsor a relative seeking to immigrate, or, in rare cases, deportation" (Families USA 1999). The public charge does not apply to applications for citizenship, or to refugees or other exempt groups.

In determining whether a person is likely to become a public charge, factors to be considered include the person's age, health, assets, resources, family status, education, skill, financial status, and past receipt of benefits. This final element, past receipt of benefits, has caused a major health care barrier for legal immigrants because the 1996 laws did not specify what types of benefits could and could not be considered in making a public charge determination. This was not clarified until the INS issued new guidelines in 1999. Consequently, during this time, many legal immigrants did not apply for public benefits, including needed health care, for which they were eligible, for fear that by using these benefits they would be deemed a public charge, and therefore be deported or barred from permanent residency or sponsorship of relatives. In fact, this did happen in some cases (Bowie 1999; Families USA 1999; National Health Law Program 1999; Schlosberg 1998; Schlosberg and Wiley 1998).

The 1999 guidelines (Federal Register, Document 99–13188) specify which public benefits may and which may not be considered in making a public charge determination. The only two benefits that are to be considered are receipt of public cash assistance for income maintenance, including SSI, TANF, and state and local cash assistance programs; and institutionalization for long-term care at public expense, such as Medicaid funds used for nursing home or mental health institutionalization. The benefits that are not to be considered in making a public charge determination include:

- Medicaid and other health insurance and health services (except for long-term care)
- CHIP
- Nutrition programs, including food stamps, the Women, Infants, and Children (WIC) program, and school lunch and breakfast programs
- Housing assistance

- Energy assistance
- Emergency disaster relief
- Foster care and adoption assistance
- Educational assistance
- Job training programs
- In-kind community based programs, services, and assistance

This means that immigrants may use any public health benefits, services, or programs, except long-term institutionalization, with no adverse effect on their immigration status or sponsorship of relatives (Bowie 1999; Families USA 1999; National Health Law Program 1999). Nonetheless, many immigrants remain unaware of these new guidelines, and the fear that has prevented many from seeking health care for themselves and for family members is likely to persist for some time.

Linguistic barriers constitute a final structural barrier to health care for immigrants and refugees. People with limited English proficiency face numerous obstacles to health care access such as getting an appointment, understanding directions to the facility, registering with a health care provider, making sense of parking instructions, navigating the facility, greeting the receptionist, and filling out intake forms at the front desk (Jackson 1998). These obstacles all occur before the person is even seen by the health care provider, when linguistic differences cause further problems such as misunderstanding, misdiagnosis, incorrect treatment, and lack of adherence to treatment recommendations.

> A recent study of public and private teaching hospitals found that more than 11% of patients required the use of interpreter services. In some areas, the number of non-English speaking patients is much higher. [For example], at San Francisco General Hospital, one in four inpatients, and 60–70% of outpatients require interpreters. In some cities, residents speak more than one hundred separate languages and dialects. Despite the growing need for linguistically appropriate health care services, many health care providers have done very little to overcome language barriers to health care.... Health care providers largely rely upon untrained bilingual staff, such as janitors or food service workers, and friends and family members of patients for interpreting. In addition, fewer than one fourth of hospitals provide any training for their staff in interpreting. Patient care has often suffered needlessly as a result. Children have been asked to interpret for parents about sexual

matters and spousal abuse. Non-English speaking patients sometimes wait for hours for treatment due to the lack of available interpreters. Language barriers have caused avoidable delays in diagnosis and treatment, the use of needless and expensive tests and patient failures to comply with doctors' orders.   (DIVERSITY RX 1997A, P. 1).

Three factors have been identified that contribute to linguistic barriers to health care (Perkins et al. 1998). First, the number of languages spoken in the U.S. has increased dramatically over the past thirty years, and the health care system is not equipped to operate in such a linguistically diverse environment. Second, current levels of funding are inadequate to meet the rising demand for interpretive services. Finally, most health care organizations are not aware of federal and state laws that require linguistic access, and those laws are rarely enforced.

A major law that mandates linguistic access to publicly funded health care is *Title VI of the Civil Rights Act of 1964*. It states that "no person in the United States shall, on ground of race, color, or national origin, be excluded from participation in, be denied benefits of, or be subjected to discrimination under any program or activity receiving federal financial assistance." Because federal funding for health care is widespread, almost every health care provider is bound by Title VI. The federal government interprets Title VI as requiring linguistic access to health care, including the provision of qualified interpreter services and translated materials at no cost to patients. Another relevant law is the *Hill-Burton Act of 1946*. This Act funded the construction and modernization of public and nonprofit community hospitals and health centers. Recipients of those funds agreed to comply with community service obligations forever. Again, the government has interpreted this to include providing linguistic access. Additionally, there are a number of other federal and state laws and regulations that mandate linguistic access. Further, accrediting bodies such as the Joint Commision on the Accreditation of Healthcare Organizations (JCAHO) have adopted standards requiring linguistic access (Diversity Rx 1997b; Perkins et al. 1998). Health care providers have used a variety of strategies to increase linguistic access. These will be described in the practice section of this chapter.

FINANCIAL BARRIERS "Financial barriers restrict access by inhibiting patients' ability to pay for or reimburse providers for needed medical services;

financial barriers also discourage physicians and hospitals from treating patients of limited means" (Riedel 1998, p. 105). The financial barriers to health care access are low socioeconomic status and indequate, or total lack of, health insurance. As described in chapter 1, immigrants and refugees as a whole have lower socioeconomic status than the native-born population. "Numerous evidence suggests [that] . . . socioeconomic status is a stronger predictor of health care seeking behavior than racial-ethnic or immigrant status" (Ell and Castañeda 1998, p. 131).

Socioeconomic status is correlated with health insurance. People who have low socioeconomic status are more likely to work in jobs that do not offer health insurance benefits, or to be unable to afford their share of the premiums if health benefits are offered (Meadows 1999; Ross 1999). A recent study showed that nationally, foreign-born people were twice as likely to be uninsured, and less likely to have Medicare coverage, compared to native-born people. Among Hispanics, 40.8% of foreign-born Hispanics were uninsured, compared to 24.8% of U.S.-born Hispanics. The difference in insurance status between foreign-born and native-born Asians and Pacific Islanders was approximately 11% (Riedel 1998). Additionally, among all uninsured but Medicaid-eligible children in the U.S., nine out of ten are U.S. born, but more than one-third live in immigrant families (Schlosberg and Wiley 1998).

Overall, Hispanics and Blacks are less likely than Whites to have employer-sponsored health insurance, and Hispanics, both foreign- and native-born, are less likely to be insured than any other racial / ethnic group (Kass, Weinick, and Monheit 1999; Meadows 1999; Ross 1999; U.S. Department of Health and Human Services 1998). "National data on health insurance coverage of Asian Americans gives the impression that, as a group, they are well insured. [However], relatively small numbers of Asian Americans are included in national surveys, and oftentimes those surveyed are more highly educated and have higher incomes (with a greater potential to afford health insurance or to get it through their employer) than the general population of Asian Americans. . . . Generalizing . . . to all Asian/Pacific Islander groups creates the image, nationally, that Asian Americans are relatively well insured, while state and local data document a different picture" (Takada, Ford, and Lloyd 1998, p. 305). Foreign-born Asian Americans are less likely to have health insurance than native-born Asian Americans (Riedel 1998; Takada, Ford, and Lloyd 1998).

PERSONAL AND CULTURAL BARRIERS Personal and cultural barriers are factors that "may inhibit people who need medical care from seeking it or from following the recommendations of caregivers" (Institute of Medicine 1993, p. 39, cited in Riedel 1998, p. 105). The health-care-seeking behavior of immigrants and refugees is influenced by three sets of personal and cultural factors: demographic and social-relational issues; culturally determined beliefs, perceptions, and expectations; and pathways to care and decision-making processes (Ell and Castañeda 1998).

Demographic and social-relational factors include individual attributes such as age, gender, education level, health status, length of residence in the U.S., and family structure. Immigrants and refugees who have poorer health, are elderly, female, or live alone, are more likely to seek health care. On the other hand, those who have lower education, lower English ability, or have been in the U.S. a shorter period of time are less likely to seek health care (Chung and Lin 1994; Ell and Castañeda 1998; Jang, Lee, and Woo 1998; LeClere, Jensen, and Biddlecom 1994; Portes, Kyle, and Eaton 1992; Tran, Dhooper and McInnis-Dittrich 1997). Knowledge of health care resources is also an important factor. Immigrants and refugees who are not familiar with the U.S. health care system or with health care organizations in their community will not access those resources.

Another important individual attribute that is relevant to the health-care-seeking behavior of immigrants and refugees is level of acculturation. "Acculturation is related to health care utilization in complex and subtle ways, with some studies showing a direct effect of acculturation on increased utilization of health services, and others showing no direct effect and only limited indirect effect of acculturation on utilization" (Clark and Hofsess 1998, p. 48). These inconsistent findings may be due to the different ways in which acculturation is measured in various studies. Various measures have included "whether a particular language is used in a variety of situations and social relations, the consumption of particular ethnic foods, parental heritage, life experiences in one culture or another, cultural identification, exclusivity of association with similar immigrant peers, and even cultural pride" (Ell and Castañeda 1998, p. 132). Probably the most important aspect of acculturation in regard to health-care-seeking behavior is the extent to which a person subscribes to health beliefs of the old and the new culture.

Culturally determined beliefs, perceptions, and expectations that influence health-care-seeking behavior include beliefs about the causes of illness; knowledge about illness, including biomedical explanations of disease; and culturally patterned classification of symptoms into illness categories and symptom expression (Ell and Castañeda 1998). Different cultures have varying health beliefs about the causes and control of health and illness. These various beliefs, which are discussed later in this chapter, contrast with biomedical models of disease and illness causation. Immigrants and refugees who hold strong traditional health beliefs may be more likely to delay or to not seek medical care at all than those who have more knowledge of and belief in biomedical models.

Some cultures also have culturally patterned symptom classifications that are manifested in "culture-bound syndromes" or "folk illnesses." These are situations in which the person feels ill or manifests symptoms of illness, but there is no medically recognized underlying disease. Belief in these folk illnesses can contribute to not seeking formal health care or not following treatment recommendations. Various folk illnesses are discussed further later in the chapter.

Health-care-seeking behavior can be influenced by the way in which members of different cultures perceive, define, and present symptoms.

> In some cultures, for example, even slight symptoms are considered adequate justification for initiating treatment or seeking medical or other professional health care advice, while in others a person is hardly to be defined as truly ill or in need of treatment unless incapacitated or unable to carry out usual duties and activities. Attention and concern may focus more intensely on some body systems or sets of symptoms than on others. For example, blood and its conditions and functions are a focal point in Haitian culture; gastrointestinal symptoms in Mexican culture; *qi* [energy] and its states of flow in traditional Chinese medicine; humoral equilibrium in the Ayurvedic tradition of the Indian subcontinent; ... and symptoms produced by "wind" in the body in Vietnamese tradition.   (O'CONNOR 1998, P. 159)

Health-care-seeking behavior is also influenced by pathways to care, which refers to "the sequence of contacts with individuals and organizations prompted by the distressed person's efforts, and those of his or her significant others, to seek help as well as the help that is supplied in response to such efforts" (Rogler and Cortes 1993, p. 555, cited in Ell and Casteñeda 1998, p. 133). Immigrants' and refugees' pathways to health care are influenced by two factors: "reliance on network member advice, information, actual provision of care, and decision making; and use of folk healers and practices before seeking professional care, in lieu of seeking professional care, or in combination with professional care" (Ell and Casteñeda 1998, p. 133). Ethnic minority people tend to rely on family caregiving more than U.S.-born White people do. Family members and friends also influence the decision-making process in health care seeking, by providing coping resources, advice, and material resources such as medications and transportation. Many immigrant and refugee communities have traditional healers whose healing practices are based on the health beliefs of the culture. The use of traditional healers also influences professional health-care-seeking behavior and treatment adherence. Traditional healers and healing practices are further discussed later in the chapter.

In summary, Table 5.1 lists some of the major personal and cultural factors that influence health care access and treatment adherence.

TABLE 5.1 PERSONAL AND CULTURAL FACTORS INFLUENCING HEALTH CARE ACCESS AND TREATMENT ADHERENCE

Historical distrust: Past injustices may cause ethnic minority patients to mistrust health care providers.

Interpretations of disability: Physicians believe that treatment should include intervention and that biological anomalies should be corrected. However, some cultures believe that the disability is spiritual rather than physical or that the disability itself is a blessing or reward for ancestral tribulations.

Concepts of family structure and family identity: For patients, family often extends beyond the sphere of the traditional nuclear family. Patient decisionmaking may include members of the extended family and the community.

Communication styles and views of professional roles: Westerners tend to separate professional and personal identity. The need for objectivity depersonalizes communication style. However, many cultures value personal relationships that use both roles.

Incompatibility of explanatory models: If patients' and providers' ideas differ about the structure and function of the body, for example, causes of diseases being bacteria, virus, or the environment versus the "evil eye," "loss of soul" or "curses," it will be difficult to get patients to comply with treatment.

Disease without illness: Health care providers are well indoctrinated about the dangers of "invisible" diseases like hypertension, high cholesterol, and HIV infection, but people in other cultures are not as willing to intervene when there are no symptoms.

Illness without disease: The existence of a folk illness, when a patient feels that he or she has an illness that is not defined by biomedicine, may be an area of disagreement between patient and provider.

Source: American Medical Student Association, 1999.

5.1.2 DIFFERENTIAL HEALTH STATUS

DIFFERENT IMMIGRANT AND REFUGEE GROUPS vary widely in their overall health status and in the prevalence and incidence of different diseases and other health problems. It is beyond the scope of this book to describe all of these variations among all the different immigrant and refugee populations. Therefore, only some general facts will be noted. Social workers who work in health care settings should familiarize themselves with the prevalent health problems among specific immigrant and refugee groups that they serve. The literature contains descriptions of common health problems among populations such as immigrants and refugees in general (American Academy of Pediatrics 1997; Gavagan and Brodyaga 1998; Olness 1998); migrant farmworkers (Napolitano and Goldberg 1998); Hispanic immigrants (Guendelman 1998); Asian and Pacific Islander immigrants and refugees (Dhooper and Tran 1998; Takada, Ford, and Lloyd 1998); African immigrants and refugees (Faust, Spilsbury, and Loue 1998); refugees from the former Soviet Union (Duncan and Simmons 1996), and Haitian refugees (Holcomb, et al. 1996; Wilk 1986).

In general, the health status of ethnic minorities, including many immigrants and refugees, tends to be worse than that of White Americans (Kaiser Family Foundation 1999; Kass, Weinick, and Monheit 1999; Office of Minority Health 1999). The federal government has established an initiative to eliminate racial and ethnic disparities in six areas of health status by 2010 (Office of Minority Health 1999). These six areas were selected for emphasis because they reflect areas of disparity that affect multiple racial and ethnic minority groups at all life stages. They are infant mortality, cancer screening and management, cardiovascular disease, diabetes, HIV infection / AIDS, and immunizations. However, it is important to note that although ethnic and racial minorities in general fare worse in these areas than White Americans, there is great variation within minority groups on these and other health indicators. For example, the terms "Hispanic" and "Asian" each encompass an extremely diverse set of ethnic or national-origin subgroups, and health status varies greatly across those subgroups (Guendelman 1998; Takada, Ford, and Lloyd 1998). Additionally, the broad racial/ethnic categorizations typically used in epidemiological studies fail to provide useful information about groups such as African, African-Caribbean, and European immigrants and refugees, since they are lumped together with African Americans and White Americans, even though they constitute only very small proportions of those larger groups.

These multiple disparities in health status across various immigrant and refugee groups are due to a complex combination of socioeconomic, physiological, psychological, societal, and cultural factors (Mayberry et al. 1999). As noted above, socioeconomic factors greatly influence access to health care, which in turn influences health status. Physiological factors include genetic traits that predispose members of particular ethnic groups to particular diseases. Psychological factors include things such as health-care decisionmaking processes, knowledge about health and disease, mental health, risk-taking behaviors such as smoking and alcohol consumption, and healthy habits such as exercise. Societal factors include the health-care-access barriers discussed previously, as well as conditions in the country of origin or in a refugee camp, including endemic infectious diseases, environmental toxins, inadequate nutrition, and experience of violence or torture. Finally, cultural factors include things such as diet, social support networks, social norms such as prohibitions against certain behaviors and acceptance of other risky behaviors, and health beliefs and health practices. It is important to note that these cultural factors also serve as protective factors in some cases. Thus, immigrants and refugees often have better health status in regard to some health conditions, compared to the native born population. When these people adopt the cultural norms of the host society, those health conditions tend to worsen and the rates of those health problems become similar to those in the native-born population (Guendelman 1998; Takada, Ford, and Lloyd 1998).

5.1.3 HEALTH BELIEFS AND HEALTH PRACTICES

"BELIEFS AND PRACTICES relating to health are organized into complex and coherent systems of thought and action that are articulated with larger cultural worldviews" (O'Connor 1998, p. 146). The healing systems of immigrants and refugees can be described in terms of four major elements: common concepts; folk illnesses; common therapeutic practices; and integration of traditional and conventional healing systems (O'Connor 1998).

COMMON CONCEPTS O'Connor (1998) identifies five concepts that are common to many of the healing systems of immigrant and refugee populations. They are the concepts of health as harmony or balance; integration of body, mind, and spirit; vital essence; magical and supernatural elements; and envy and other strong emotions as etiologic factors.

The concept of harmony or balance is applied to internal bodily states, to social relationships, and to relationships with spiritual entities. In regard to internal bodily states, many cultures subscribe to a belief in a hot/cold balance. A healthy body is in a neutral state between hot and cold; if there is an imbalance toward one or the other, an opposite action (such as ingestion of a hot or cold substance) is taken to restore balance. This concept is held in Hispanic, Asian Indian, Haitian, and Middle Eastern cultures. Chinese and some other Asian cultures have an analogous concept of yin / yang, which encompasses not only hot/cold but also other opposites. In many cultures, imbalance in social relationships is believed to be a cause of poor health. Cultural rules regarding communication, emotional expression, and so forth are intended to maintain harmonious relationships. Imbalance in relationships with spiritual beings is also believed to cause poor health. Haitian *voudou* and Hispanic Caribbean *santería* are similar belief systems that combine African religion with Catholicism. These systems include a belief in powerful spiritual entities (*loas* in *voudou* and *orichas* in *santería*) that strongly influence all events in life, including health. In many Asian cultures, deceased ancestors are believed to be in contact with family members, and are worshipped. Disrespect toward deceased ancestors is believed to lead to illness.

Many healing systems include a belief in integration of the body, mind, and spirit. Imbalance or disharmony in one of these areas is believed to cause sickness or symptoms in the other areas. There is not a clear distinction between mental and physical illness. Strong emotions, both positive and negative, are believed to cause bodily sickness. It is believed that emotions should be moderate, not excessive.

The concept of vital essence is a part of many healing systems. It is a belief that life is sustained by a special force, energy, or essence. Good health depends upon proper functioning of the vital essence. This vital essence is known as the soul in Hispanic cultures, the *gros bon ange* ("big good angel") in Haitian culture, and *qi* (or *chi*) in Chinese culture.

In many healing systems, magical or supernatural elements are believed to cause illness. These may include retributions by deities or spirits for dereliction of duty or unintentional slights; possession by demons or other entities; or evil human actions such as curses, hexes, and sorcery. It is believed that these supernatural causes must be addressed in order for healing to occur.

A final concept that is common to many healing systems is that the emotion of envy causes illness in both the envious person and the one who is envied. The latter is affected by a strong or covetous gaze known as the "evil eye." Admiration or compliments can be indicative of envy or the evil eye, and various rituals exist to counteract it. Evil eye beliefs and practices exist in many Hispanic, Mediterranean, Islamic, Anglo-Celtic, African, and Asian cultures (O'Connor 1998).

FOLK ILLNESSES As mentioned earlier, folk illnesses are symptomatic clusters that are not recognized as a disease or syndrome by Western medicine. The related term "culture-bound syndromes" refers to folk illnesses whose primary symptoms are behavioral changes (Baer, Clark, and Peterson 1998). The term "folk illness" is ascribed by Western medical practitioners; for members of the culture, the "folk illness" is very real. "Folk illnesses, like other illnesses, have recognized etiologies, particular constellations of symptoms, identified sequelae, and specified preventive and therapeutic measures" (O'Connor 1998, p. 152). Folk illnesses should not be treated trivially because they can be associated or lead to medically recognized diseases or death (O'Connor 1998).

A folk illness that is common in many different cultures is "soul loss." It is believed that the soul can depart a person who is still living because of shock, fright, trauma, or severe hardship; leaving during sleep and finding a beautiful place to stay, getting lost, trapped, or entering another living being; or being captured by human sorcerers or evil spirits. Some other folk illnesses are listed in table 5.2.

COMMON THERAPEUTIC PRACTICES Cultural healing systems employ herbs and other natural substances, religious and spiritual actions, physical therapies, and traditional healers (O'Connor 1998). Natural substances include botanical, animal, and mineral substances. They are used to produce physical, mental, emotional, or spiritual effects. They are used in a variety of ways including ingestion, inhalation, in baths, or moxibustion, which is burning small amounts of herbs on or near the skin.

"Religious and spiritual actions commonly used to promote health and healing include prayer, meditation, reading or recitation of sacred texts, recitation of verbal charms and brief formulaic utterances to ward off evil

TABLE 5.2 EXAMPLES OF FOLK ILLNESSES

ILLNESS NAME	CAUSE	SYMPTOMS
KOREAN CULTURE		
Hwabyung	Lasting anger, disappointments sadness, miseries, hostility, grudges, unfulfilled dreams or expectations	Gastric, cardiac, respiratory, musculoskeletal, circulatory symptoms; feeling hot; nightmares
HAITIAN CULTURE		
Hot blood	Being overly nervous, physical or mental exertion, giving birth, sleeping	High fever
Thin blood	Fright or hypertension	Pallor
Mother's milk complications	Anger, fright in nursing mother	Headache, depression, psychoses, milk mixed with blood
Wandering womb	Postpartum womb wandering throughout body in search of "lost" fetus	Dizziness, weakness, confusion
VIETNAMESE CULTURE		
Soul loss	Fright, shock, sleep	Thinness, fatigue, pallor
CUBAN CULTURE		
Empacho	Consuming starchy, heavy foods; foods sticking in digestive tract	Abdominal pain and swelling, thirst
Mal aire	Excess heat or cold	Back pain, muscle spasms, paralysis, respiratory symptoms
Susto	Soul loss caused by traumatic event	Anorexia, weight loss, listlessness, pallor
Mal de ojo	Being envied	Headaches, nervousness, rash, weeping, diarrhea, vomiting, fever, disturbed sleep
MEXICAN CULTURE		
Empacho, mal ojo, susto, mal aire	See above	See above
Mal puesto	Witchcraft	Psychological symptoms, infertility, insanity

Source: Adapted from Baer, Clark, and Peterson, 1998; O'Connor, 1998.

influences, laying on of hands, offerings of food and other goods to ancestors and other spiritual entities, visits to holy sites and healing shrines, temporary internment in places of worship or spiritual contemplation, spiritual cleansings, soul callings and restorations, use of amulets and other protective items, and a huge array of additional actions" (O'Connor 1998, p. 154). They may also involve physical exercises such as *tai chi* or *qi gong*, which are intended to control the movement of *qi* in the body.

Physical therapies include massage and rubbing of specific body parts. In Southeast Asian cultures, physical therapies include cupping and dermabrasion. In cupping, small cups, tubes, or jars made of metal, wood, bamboo, or glass are heated and placed on the skin. The heat creates a vacuum and suction, which is supposed to draw impurities out of the body. In dermabrasion, also called coining, a lubricated spoon or coin is rubbed against the skin to remove "wind" from the body. Both of these techniques cause red marks or bruising. Also, moxibustion, mentioned above, can cause small burns or blisters. When seen in a medical setting, these marks are sometimes mistaken for signs of abuse, especially when seen on children.

Most healing systems include traditional healers:

> These commonly include midwives, massagers, bonesetters, blood-stoppers, healers of burns and other skin conditions, spiritual specialists, and herbalists or "leaf doctors." The knowledge and practice of herbalists typically extends to animal and mineral natural substances in addition to botanicals. The *curandero/a* ("healer"), well-known in most Spanish-speaking cultures, is often a general practitioner, using both material and spiritual modalities to treat an array of ills. Some *curanderos* specialize in spiritual problems, or the spiritual aspects of common illnesses. Spiritualist healers and mediums (found in many Latino traditions) carry out their diagnostic and healing activities with the aid of spirit guides who come to them with information, while shamanic healers enter trance states or make ecstatic journeys into the spirit realm to receive diagnostic and etiologic information and to negotiate with supernaturals for the well-being of their patients.
>
> (O'CONNOR 1998, P. 155)

INTEGRATION OF TRADITIONAL AND CONVENTIONAL HEALING SYSTEMS Typically, immigrants and refugees make use of both their traditional healing systems and conventional Western medical systems (O'Connor 1998). This integration may have been common in their country of origin, or may be a new practice adopted after arrival in the new country. Contrary to expectations, it has been found that neither educational level nor acculturation level are associated with preference for Western medicine or with continued use of traditional healing methods. Thus, even highly educated and assimilated immigrants and refugees often use traditional healing systems in combination with Western medicine. Decisions about which approach to use at what time are based on a complex combination of factors including cultural pattern, generation, gender, illness type, illness episode, availability and access, and individual preference (O'Connor 1998). In many cases, some types of illness are considered appropriate for traditional healing, whereas others are considered appropriate for Western medical intervention.

Finally, in regard to the use of traditional healing systems, it is important to remember that such use varies among individuals within cultures (O'Connor 1998). As always, one should never stereotypically assume that common cultural norms, including health beliefs and health practices, apply to all individuals in that group (Horowitz 1998). A recent study of health care providers and ethnic minority health care consumers revealed that some health care providers do hold stereotypes of some ethnic groups, such as "Asians won't discuss symptoms or complain"; "Obtaining medical history information from immigrants is impossible"; "Asians won't complete prescription drug regimens"; and "Hispanics won't lose weight or eat health diets" (Frederick Schneiders Research 1999, p. 4). Such stereotypes can lead to lower quality of care for ethnic minority clients (Frederick Schneiders Research 1999).

5.1.4 PSYCHOSOCIAL ISSUES

IN ADDITION TO health beliefs and health practices, there are a number of other psychosocial issues related to the health and health care of immigrants and refugees. These include treatment adherence, somatization, family involvement, and ethical issues.

TREATMENT ADHERENCE Immigrants and refugees often do not adhere to the recommendations of physicians and other health care professionals.

There are many reasons for this. They include linguistic problems, inadequate explanations by health care providers, or financial problems such as inability to afford recommended prescriptions. Another factor is differences in health beliefs. For example, patients may stop a treatment or a medication as soon as symptoms have disappeared (Holcomb et al. 1996; Jaranson 1991), because they may not understand or believe that the underlying illness may still be present in the absence of symptoms. They may also stop taking medication if they experience side effects (Egli 1991). People whose cultural norms place emphasis on the present rather than the future may not follow recommendations for preventive care, since they do not perceive any benefit for their present health status (Holcomb et al. 1996). Cultural health beliefs that place control over illness in an external force such as God, rather than within the patient's or physician's control, can also lead people to not adhere to treatment recommendations (Ell and Castañeda 1998). Religious practices such as fasting during certain holy days may also prevent people from following treatment recommendations (Horowitz 1998). Finally, the simultaneous use of traditional healing can sometimes mitigate the effects of Western medical treatments. For example, if prescription medications are believed to contribute to hot/cold imbalance, they may not be taken, the dosage may be reduced, they may be prematurely discontinued, or they may be counteracted by other substances (O'Connor 1998).

SOMATIZATION "Somatization refers to anatomical or physiological complaints and bio-medical treatment-seeking that occur as an expression of psychological or psychosocial distress or maladaptation" (Westermeyer 1991b, p. 70). Immigrants, and particularly refugees, have been reported to have a high rate of somatization (Garcia-Peltoniemi 1991a; Gavagan and Brodyaga 1998). Some authors have argued that the rate of somatization among refugees is not necessarily higher than in the general population, but is commonly seen initially as the presenting medical problem (Kinzie 1991; Westermeyer 1991b).

The reasons for somatization among refugees include "the traditional backgrounds of most refugees which discourage direct expression of feelings; culturally shaped health beliefs which favor psychosomatic unity; lack of familiarity with the concepts of mental health and mental health care; and the language barriers which prevent refugees from communicating in a more abstract psychological manner" (Garcia-Peltoniemi 1991a, p. 49).

Somatization, if unrecognized, can lead to unnecessary and costly medical procedures and delay in receiving appropriate psychosocial treatment (Garcia-Peltoniemi 1991a; Kinzie 1991). A person's frequent use of medical services, including hospital and emergency room visits, should alert health care providers and social workers to the possibility of somatization (Garcia-Peltoniemi 1991a).

FAMILY INVOLVEMENT Families have a significant role in health and health care. "Family members can facilitate and provide care, report symptoms, assist in decision making, and help patients adopt healthy lifestyles and cope with illness" (Horowitz 1998, p. 165). Family problems can also contribute to illness. For immigrants and refugees, family involvement in health and health care may be more relevant or more important than it is for the general population. There are several reasons for this (Horowitz 1998). The stress of immigration and of living in a foreign culture may create stronger family ties and family dependence. Conversely, family members may have been separated by immigration and therefore may lack their accustomed sources of social support. Additionally, immigrant families may have different structures than U.S.-born families. "For example, in Asian families, vertical relationships (e.g., parent-child) often take precedence over horizontal relationships (e.g., husband-wife) and in other cultures women may rely most heavily on sisters or close female friends" (Horowitz 1998, p. 166).

Further, immigrants and refugees may rely on family for functions that U.S.-born people typically handle without family involvement. In many cultures, family needs take precedence over individual needs. Thus, illness will be treated as a family matter and health care decisions will be made in the context of their impact on the family.

Families also play an important role in treatment adherence. For example, families may maintain traditional diets as a means of maintaining their cultural identity. If treatment recommendations include dietary changes, then the whole family needs to be involved.

Finally, immigrant and refugees families may also define "family members" differently. "Clinicians may inadvertently leave nontraditional but key 'relatives' out of discussions, decision making, and informed consent . . . If clinicians allow only spouses to participate actively in care, tension and animosity may develop" (Horowitz 1998, p. 166).

ETHICAL ISSUES Health care frequently poses moral dilemmas that must be resolved through the application of ethical principles. The U.S. health care system has developed such a set of principles that are to be applied to resolve ethical problems. However, "the orientation of bioethics reflects the strong emphasis on individualism and autonomy in the United States" (Marshall et al. 1998, p. 204). This orientation conflicts with that of many immigrant and refugee cultures. Consequently, bioethical dilemmas, which are already complex and difficult, become even more so when they pertain to immigrants and refugees. One of the major ethical issues pertaining to immigrants and refugees is the principle of autonomy:

> Current biomedical practices emphasize strongly the importance of self-determination and autonomy in decisions about medical care. Yet, the centrality of patient autonomy and a patient's right to decide represents a decidedly Western philosophical orientation. For example, the application of informed consent for medical treatment, disclosure of medical information, and the implementation of advance directives, which emphasize a patient's "right" to limit or withdraw unwanted therapy, presuppose a particular kind of patient.... This "ideal" patient possesses a clear understanding of the illness, prognosis, and treatment; a belief that it is possible to control the future; the perception of freedom of choice; and a willingness to discuss topics of sickness and death openly.... Immigrants or refugees from non-Western cultures may not share the proclivity for autonomous informed consent, advance care planning, or the disclosure of distressing medical news.
>
> (MARSHALL ET AL. 1998, P. 207)

Therefore, the principle of autonomy must be adjusted to the patient's cultural background. While there are no clear resolutions to these cultural / ethical dilemmas, "three elements are essential in successfully resolving moral problems in cross-cultural patient care: an ability to communicate effectively with patients and their families; sufficient understanding of the patient's cultural background; and identification of culturally relevant value conflicts" (Marshall et al. 1998, p. 204).

5.1.5 SUBPOPULATIONS WITH UNIQUE HEALTH ISSUES

THREE SUBPOPULATIONS of immigrants and refugees have particularly unique health issues that are different from the health issues of the general immigrant and refugee population. These subpopulations are women, gays and lesbians, and elderly people.

WOMEN The unique health issues of women pertain to reproductive health. "Reproductive health is composed of four elements: (a) fertility regulation without adverse side effects; (b) risk-free pregnancy and childbirth; (c) having and raising healthy children; and (d) enjoying sexual relationships without fear of infection, unwanted pregnancy, or social and physical abuse" (DeSantis 1998, p. 449). The aspects of reproductive health that are particularly relevant to immigrant and refugee women are folk concepts of reproductive anatomy and physiology; prenatal care; infectious diseases that impact pregnancy; nutritional deficiencies; pregnancy outcomes; contraception; and female genital mutilation (DeSantis 1998).

The folk concepts that constitute health beliefs and healing systems are applied to all aspects of health, including reproductive anatomy and physiology. Thus, these concepts influence decisionmaking about conception, birth, and prenatal and postnatal behavior (DeSantis 1998). For example, hot / cold beliefs are applied to reproduction. Pregnancy is considered a hot state and menstruation a cold state. In each case, measures are taken to maintain hot / cold balance. "The critical factor in dealing with hot-cold beliefs during pregnancy and postpartum is to ascertain the individual immigrant woman's concept of foods, medicines, activities, and environments that are safe. If they are contradictory to biomedical concepts, methods will need to be found to accommodate them in order to maintain adequate nutrition and other healthful self-care activities" (DeSantis 1998, pp. 450–451).

Immigrant and refugee women are at risk of not receiving adequate prenatal care due to the health care barriers discussed earlier. Additionally, in many cultures prenatal care is not believed to be necessary unless there is some overt problem with the pregnancy. Further, women may be reluctant to seek prenatal care because of cultural concepts of modesty and privacy. Exposure of the pelvic region and discussion of sexual and reproductive matters with strangers, i.e., health care providers, may be culturally unacceptable, particularly if the health care provider is male. Pelvic examinations may be physically and psychologically traumatic for refugee women who may have experienced rape, sexual torture, or other sexual abuses in their countries of origin during war, civil unrest, or ethnic violence.

Immigrant and refugee women are also at risk for infectious diseases and nutritional deficiencies that may affect pregnancy. These problems may be a function of their current living conditions as well as conditions in their country of origin.

Despite their risks for inadequate prenatal care, infectious diseases, and nutritional deficiencies, foreign-born women, compared to U.S.-born women, generally have better birth outcomes in terms of infant mortality, low birth weight, and preterm birth. The reasons for this include fewer births to adolescents, fewer births to single mothers, lower rates of tobacco and alcohol use and tobacco smoke exposure during pregnancy, and lower rates of unwanted or unplanned pregnancies. However, there is variation in birth outcomes across different immigrant and refugee groups, with some having worse outcomes compared to others (DeSantis 1998). Thus, each individual woman's risk factors affecting pregnancy outcomes need to be considered in providing health care.

Immigrant and refugee women may encounter a number of problems with contraception:

> Immigrant women have encountered multiple barriers when desiring to use contraception. Some have faced sanctions from pronatalist governments while others have been forcibly sterilized or coerced into contraception by governments attempting to dramatically impact population growth. Immigrant women have been subjected to spousal or societal abuse for attempting to regulate their fertility. Many have been unable to maintain contraception due to the inability to obtain resupplies or adequate medical care for complications. Others have sustained unintended pregnancies from lack of knowledge about reproductive anatomy and physiology or the mechanism of action of the contraceptive method. Health care providers counseling immigrant women on fertility regulation will need to explore past methods used and results to adequately assess the appropriateness of contraceptive methods requested or advocated. (DESANTIS 1998, P. 460)

Immigrant women from some countries, such as Latin and Central America, the Caribbean, and Africa, may be unaware of the availability of safe and medically sanctioned abortion services in the U.S. and may resort to dangerous illegal or clandestine abortion procedures, including folk-based procedures. Conversely, women from other countries, such as China and the former Soviet Union, may routinely use legal abortion as a birth control method instead of using contraceptive techniques that are available in the U.S.

The final major reproductive health issue pertaining to immigrant and refugee women is female genital mutilation, sometimes referred to as female circumcision. This is a surgical procedure that involves removal of parts or all of the female external genitalia, and sometimes sewing together the remaining portions of the outer labia to leave only a very small opening. This procedure is practiced in 26 African countries, in the southern region of the Arabian Peninsula, portions of the Persian Gulf, and among Muslim groups in Malaysia, Indonesia, the Philippines, Pakistan, Brazil, Peru, and Mexico. It also continues to be practiced by immigrants from those countries after arrival in the new country (DeSantis 1998).

The procedure is typically performed on girls when they are seven or eight years old, although it may be done during infancy or early adulthood. The procedure is performed by medically untrained women with limited knowledge of surgery. It is performed without anesthesia and using non-sterile instruments such as razor blades, broken glass, sharpened stones, and thorns. The reasons for performing female genital mutilation are to preserve and provide proof of virginity prior to marriage, to serve as a rite of passage, to provide income for those who perform it, to reduce female sexual desire, and the belief that it is necessary for the hygiene or health of the male partner or newborn infant (DeSantis 1998; Lightfoot-Klein 1993).

Female genital mutilation causes numerous short-term and long-term health problems, including pain, infection, uncontrolled bleeding, death, urinary and menstrual problems, sexual problems, psychological problems, increased risk of HIV infection, and problems in childbirth (DeSantis 1998). The procedure is illegal in the United States and other Western countries, and fear of undergoing the procedure in one's country of origin has been recognized as a legitimate basis for granting asylum (DeSantis 1998; Faust, Spilsbury, and Loue 1998).

GAYS AND LESBIANS In most immigrant and refugee cultures, homosexuality is strongly disapproved and stigmatized. Thus, immigrants and refugees who are gay or lesbian must cope with multiple stresses: the stress of immigration and adaptation, the stress of being gay or lesbian in U.S. society, and the additional stress of being stigmatized and possibly ostracized within one's own ethnic group. These multiple stresses can place these people at increased risk of developing health problems. Immigrant or refugee gay men may be at greater risk of HIV infection than U.S.-born White gay men due to their reluctance to participate in HIV-prevention programs because they fear having their sexual orientation revealed to their family or community, because those programs are not culturally relevant, or because they do not think of themselves as homosexual (Roffman et al. 1998)

However, HIV/AIDS is not the only health issue relevant to gays and lesbians (Murguía 1999). As mentioned, these individuals may have greater risk for stress-related illnesses. Further, patients usually do not discuss their sexual orientation with health care providers, nor do health care providers usually ask. For these reasons, there is "a lack of data about the specific health care needs of gays and lesbians, and whether being gay or lesbian increases one's risk for certain diseases or health conditions" (Murguía 1998, p. 10). Social workers need to be aware of the increased potential for health problems among immigrant and refugee gays and lesbians.

ELDERLY PEOPLE Elderly people are more likely than younger people to experience chronic or terminal illness, disability, and the need for long-term care (Ikels 1998). Elderly immigrants and refugees, particularly those who came to the U.S. when they were already elderly, are likely to be socially isolated, have low English ability, have much greater identification and familiarity with their culture of origin than with the host culture, and have a high degree of dependence upon their adult children (Ikels 1998; Weeks and Cuellar 1983). Therefore, all of the issues discussed above, such as health care access, traditional health beliefs and health practices, family issues, and ethical issues, become even more salient in the provision of health care for elderly immigrants and refugees. Further, immigrants and refugees facing the end of their lives often have unique psychosocial needs, such as coming to terms with the loss of their homeland and the likelihood that they will never return (Feinberg 1996; Ikels 1998). All of these issues must be considered in the context of providing health care for this population.

5.2 BEST PRACTICES

SOCIAL WORK IN HEALTH CARE to immigrants and refugees takes place within the broader context of health care social work in general. Thus, it is first necessary to have a basic understanding of this context before addressing the specific needs of immigrants and refugees. The following discussion will primarily address social work in the health care setting, but it is also relevant to social workers who encounter immigrants and refugees in other settings and who will need to work cooperatively with the health care system to meet their clients' needs.

Social work in health care is defined as "a form of practice that occurs in hospitals and other health care settings that facilitates good health, prevention of illness, and aids physically ill clients and their families to resolve the social and psychological problems related to disease and illness" (Dziegielewski 1998, p. 28). Social work in health care is based upon five premises that have been empirically supported (Bracht 1978):

• Social, cultural, and economic conditions have a significant and measurable effect on both health status and illness prevention.
• Illness-related behaviors, whether perceived or actual, frequently disrupt personal or family equilibrium and coping abilities. Illness conditions, whether acute, chronic, or terminal, can be exacerbated by the effects of institutionalization.
• Medical treatment alone is often incomplete and occasionally impossible to render, without accompanying social support and counseling services.
• Problems of access to and appropriate utilization of health services are sufficiently endemic to our health care delivery system to require concerted community and institutional innovation.
• Multiprofessional health team collaboration on selected individual and community health problems is an effective approach to solving complex sociomedical problems.   (BRACHT 1978, PP. 24–31)

Social work in health care entails a broad range of roles, functions, and tasks at the macro, meso, and micro levels. These are summarized in table 5.3.

TABLE 5.3 SOCIAL WORK SERVICES IN HEALTH CARE

SERVICE	DESCRIPTION
MACRO LEVEL	
Service outreach	Identify unmet needs and services that are not available to clients; advocate for programs and services.
At-risk service outreach	Identify clients who are at risk of decreased health or illness; advocate to secure services for them.
Community consultation	Provide consultation services to communities to assist with the development of community-based services.
Health education	Participate and instruct communities on developing and implementing health education programs.
Policy and program advocacy	Assist in formulation and implementation of health care planning policies and programs that will help to meet client need.
Liaison to the community	Serve as a contact or connection person between the client and his or her family and the community.
MESO LEVEL	
Agency consultation	Provide consultation to agency administrators on how to enhance service delivery to clients and organizations.
Program development	Assist the agency to refine and develop new and improved programs to service client needs.
Quality improvement	Assist the agency to be sure that continuous quality services are provided that meet professional and efficient standards.
Service advocacy	Assist the agency in recognizing the needs of clients, helping to develop new or needed services.
Agency liaison	Serve as liaison to the agency on behalf of the client, ensuring connections are made between the client, the agency, and the community.
MICRO LEVEL	
Case finding and outreach	Identify and assist clients to secure services they need
Preservice and planning	Identify and subsequently help client/family to plan and gain access to health care services.
Assessment	Identify clients in need of service, screening to identify health and wellness issues.

TABLE 5.3 *(continued)*

SERVICE	DESCRIPTION
MICRO LEVEL	
Concrete service provision	Assist client/family to secure concrete services to assist with current and posthealth service needs, such as admission, discharge, and after-care planning and services.
Psychosocial evaluation	Gather information on client biopsychosocial, cultural, financial, and situational factors for a formal psychosocial assessment plan or report.
Identification of goals and objectives	Establish mutually negotiated goals with specific objectives to address client health and wellness issues.
Direct clinical counseling	Help client/family to deal with situation and problems related to health intervention needed or received.
Assistance with short- or long-term planning	Help client understand, anticipate, and plan for services needed based on current or expected health status.
Access to remedial or rehabilitative services	Help to identify service needs in those areas and assist client/family to overcome potential barriers to service access.
Information and health education	Direct provision of knowledge through instruction on areas of concern regarding client/family health and wellness.
Assistance with wellness training	Help clients to establish a plan to secure continued or improved health status based on a holistic prevention model.
Referral services	Provide information regarding services available and direct connection when warranted.
Continuity of care	Assist client/family to be sure proper connections are made with the linking of all services needed considering the issue of multiple health care providers.
Client advocacy	Teach and assist clients how to obtain needed resources, or, on a large scale, advocate for changes in policy or procedure that can have the direct or indirect benefit of assisting the client.

Source: Dziegielewski, 1998. Copyright 1998, Springer Publishing Company, Inc. Reprinted with permission.

In recent years, the health care environment has undergone major changes that have affected social work practice (Dziegielewski 1998; Volland et al. 1999). The following have been identified as current and future trends in health care delivery:

- Move from acute care to chronic illness and diseases of aging
- Increased emphasis on market forces and cost control
- Increased recognition of social and environmental determinants of diseases
- Increasing role of families, broadly defined, in provision of home care
- Increased patient participation in health care decisions

IN TURN, these trends have the following implications for health care professionals in general:

- Long-term management of chronic illness as a primary focus
- Shift from acute care setting to ambulatory settings
- Use of population focused interventions to improve health status
- Increased focus on disease prevention and health promotion

AND THE ABOVE TRENDS have the following implications for health care social workers specifically:

- A move away from hierarchical practice and toward a team-based approach
- New attention to brief interventions and solution focused therapy
- Increased need for and importance of case management
- Greater emphasis on patient outcomes research and evaluation of social work services
- Increased need for patient education about health care coverage and financing
- Increased emphasis on health promotion and preventive interventions

(VOLLAND ET AL. 1999, PP. 1–2)

The following discussion will integrate the above issues of the health care social work context with the previously identified health and health care issues of immigrants and refugees. Best social work practices will be addressed at the macro, meso, and micro levels.

5.2.1 MACRO PRACTICE

THE DISCUSSION of the health and health care issues of immigrants and refugees began with the problems of health care access and differential health status. These are macro level issues; consequently, they require macro level social work interventions. As seen in table 5.3, macro level health care social work practice includes community-needs assessment, policy and program advocacy, community consultation and policy and program planning, and community health education.

COMMUNITY NEEDS ASSESSMENT As the first step in macro practice, social workers need to identify the specific health care access problems and differential health status issues that impact the immigrants and refugees in the local community. The community needs assessment is developed to answer questions such as the following:

- What health problems are prevalent among immigrants and refugees in the local community?
- What health care resources are available in the community to address the above-identified problems?
- What are the existing service gaps and service duplications?
- To what extent do immigrants and refugees utilize the available health care services?
- What are the specific barriers to immigrants' and refugees' health care service utilization?
- What community resources can be mobilized to enhance health care utilization?

Various community needs assessment methods can be employed, such as surveys, key informant interviews, observations, structured groups such as focus groups, public forums, archival research (i.e., using existing sources of public data such as vital statistics), and rates-under-treatment (e.g., using hospital or clinic records to assess treatment rates for various health problems) (Candelaria et al. 1998; McKillip 1987). The needs assessment should result in a written report that serves as the basis for intervention planning.

POLICY AND PROGRAM ADVOCACY Having identified the health and health care needs of immigrants and refugees in the local community, interventions are planned and implemented to address those needs. One critical macro-level intervention is policy and program advocacy to change policies and to change or develop programs to better serve the health care needs of immigrants and refugees. Clearly, policy advocacy is needed at the national level to address the problems in health care access and differential health status identified earlier in this chapter. Social workers concerned with immigrant and refugee health should undertake such national-level advocacy, as well as local- and state-level advocacy to address the unique needs of their communities. A best practice model for effective health care policy advocacy is presented in table 5.4.

TABLE 5.4 BEST PRACTICES FOR EFFECTIVE HEALTH CARE POLICY ADVOCACY

STEP 1: ANALYSIS

Analysis is the first step to effective advocacy, just as it is the first step to any effective action. Activities or advocacy efforts designed to have an impact on public policy start with accurate information and in-depth understanding of the problem, the people involved, the policies, the implementation or non-implementation of those policies, the organizations, and the channels of access to influential people and decision-makers. The stronger the foundation of knowledge of these elements, the more persuasive the policy advocacy can be. Key questions are:
- What are the problems?
- What are the existing policies that cause or relate to these problems and how are they implemented?
- How would changes in policy help resolve the problems?
- What type of policy change is needed (legislation, proclamation, regulation, legal decision, committee action, institutional practice, or other)?
- What are the financial implications of the proposed policy change?
- Who are the stakeholders associated with the desired policy change?
  - Who are the advocates and supporters?
  - Who are the opponents?
  - Who are the decision-makers?
  - Who are the undecided or swing voters?
- How are changes in policies made at different levels?
- Who and what influences the key decision-makers?
  - Whom do they believe?
  - Who are their influential constituents and co-workers?

TABLE 5.4 *(continued)*

- What arguments are they most likely to respond to?
- What are their priorities—rational, emotional, personal?
- What is the communication structure related to policy-making?
  - What are the channels that reach policy-makers?
  - What is a credible message for policy-makers?

STEP 2: STRATEGY

Every advocacy effort needs a strategy. The strategy phase builds upon the analysis phase to direct, plan, and focus on specific goals and to position the advocacy effort with clear paths to achieve those goals and objectives.
- Establish a working group to develop a strategy and plan activities.
- Identify your primary and secondary audiences (pro, undecided, and your competition).
- Develop SMART objectives (specific, measurable, appropriate, realistic, and timebound).
- Position your issue to offer key decision-makers a unique and compelling benefit or advantage.
- Follow a model for policy change that suits the situation and advocacy objectives.
- Identify your resources and plan to build coalitions and mobilize support. Seek out and work with appropriate partners, coalition advocates, spokespeople, and the media. Identify your competition.
- Plan the activities that are the most appropriate for your intended audience.
- Refine positions to achieve a broader consensus. Minimize the opposition or find areas of common interest as often as possible.
- Prepare an implementation plan and budget.
- Plan for and combine multiple channels of communication, including personal contacts, community media, mass media (print, radio, TV), e-mail, and the Internet.
- Develop intermediate and final indicators to monitor the process and evaluate the impact.
- Give the proposed policies or policy change an appealing name, easily understood and designed to mobilize support.

STEP 3: MOBILIZATION

Coalition-building strengthens advocacy. Events, activities, messages, and materials must be designed with your objectives, audiences, partnerships, and resources clearly in mind. They should have maximum positive impact on the policy-makers and maximum participation by all coalition members, while minimizing responses from the opposition.
- Develop an action plan describing the situation, intended audience, the audience impacted by change, advocacy objectives, key activities and timelines, and indicators to evaluate each activity.
  - Encourage all coalition partners to participate actively.
  - Plan events incorporating credible spokespersons from different partner organizations.
  - Develop schedule and sequence of activities for maximum positive impact.

TABLE 5.4 *(continued)*

- Delegate responsibilities clearly to coalition members to implement and monitor specific events and activities.
- Network to enlarge coalitions and keep them together.
- Organize training and practice in advocacy.
- Identify, verify, and incorporate key facts and data to support your position. Compile data/documentation which supports your position and which shows importance of taking action.
- Link your position to the interests of policy makers.
- Present information in a brief, dramatic, and memorable fashion.
- Incorporate human interest and anecdotes into your messages.
- Specify desired actions clearly.
- Emphasize urgency and priority of recommended action.
- Plan for and organize news media coverage to publicize appropriate events, present new data, and credit key players.
- Rally visible grassroots support.

STEP 4: ACTION

Keeping all partners together and persisting in making the case are both essential in carrying out advocacy. Repeating the message and using the credible materials developed over and over helps to keep attention and concern on the issue.

- Monitor and respond rapidly to other views and opposition moves. Be flexible.
- Carry out planned activities continuously and on schedule.
- Establish a means to keep all coalition members informed of activities and the results.
- Develop and maintain media support with personal contacts, press releases, press conferences, and professional assistance.
- Do not fear controversy and try to turn it to your advantage.
- Avoid any illegal or unethical activities.
- Hold policy-makers accountable for commitments.
- Keep a record of successes and failures.
- Monitor public opinion and publicize positive changes.
- Acknowledge and credit the role of policy-makers and coalition partners.

STEP 5: EVALUATION

Advocacy efforts must be evaluated as carefully as any other communication campaign. Since advocacy often provides partial results, an advocacy team needs to measure regularly and objectively what has been accomplished and what more remains to be done. Process evaluation may be more important and more difficult than impact evaluation.

- Establish and measure intermediate and process indicators.
- Evaluate specific events and activities.
- Document changes based on initial SMART objectives.

> **TABLE 5.4** *(continued)*
>
> - Compare final results with indicators to measure change.
> - Identify key factors contributing to policy changes.
> - Document unintended changes.
> - Share results. Publicize successes in a clear and understandable manner to stakeholders.
>
> **STEP 6: CONTINUITY**
>
> Advocacy like communication is an ongoing process rather than a single policy or piece of legislation. Planning for continuity means articulating long-term goals, keeping coalitions together, and keeping data and arguments in tune with changing situations.
> - Evaluate resulting situations.
> - If desired policy changes occur, monitor implementation.
> - If desired policy changes do not occur, review previous strategy and action, revise, repeat advocacy process or identify other actions to be taken.
> - Develop plans to sustain/reinforce change.
> - Persevere.
>
> *Source:* Center for Communication Programs, Johns Hopkins School of Public Health 1999. Copyright 1999, Johns Hopkins University Center for Communication Programs. Reprinted with permission.

COMMUNITY CONSULTATION AND POLICY AND PROGRAM PLANNING In addition to advocacy, social workers should engage in consultation with community members and policy and program planning to develop services to meet the health and health care needs of immigrants and refugees in their community. Community-level policy and program planning should address preventive, screening, treatment, and support programs (American Public Health Association 1999a). Collaboration among different segments of the community enhances service effectiveness by:

- Facilitating strategic planning
- Helping prevent duplication of cost and effort
- Maximizing scarce resources
- Integrating diverse perspectives to create a better appreciation and understanding of the community
- Providing comprehensive services based on clients' needs
- Increasing client accessibility to health services

- Improving communication between agencies
- Providing liaison for clients unwilling to seek services from government organizations (CENTERS FOR DISEASE CONTROL 1995, P. 14)

THE FOLLOWING SEGMENTS of the community should work cooperatively to address the health needs of immigrants and refugees in the community (American Public Health Association 1999b; Horowitz 1998):

- Immigrant and refugee community leaders
- Traditional healers
- Medical interpreters
- Public health agency
- Medical community
- Community organizations
- Religious institutions
- Community employers and labor organizations
- Media
- Academia

A BEST PRACTICE MODEL for effective community-level policy and program planning is presented in table 5.5.

TABLE 5.5 BEST PRACTICES FOR EFFECTIVE COMMUNITY HEALTH POLICY AND PROGRAM PLANNING

STEP 1: ASSESS AND DETERMINE THE ROLE OF THE LEAD AGENCY

The lead agency develops a mission statement and agrees on a long-range vision that provides employees and the community with a clear description of the agency's role and serves as a guide for the steps that follow.

STEP 2: ASSESS THE LEAD AGENCY'S ORGANIZATIONAL CAPACITY

The director and staff of the agency should assess the organization's readiness to exercise leadership. Such an assessment can be accomplished by conducting a review of the agency's structure and capacity to determine if it has the skills, community support, and staff capacity to lead the community.

TABLE 5.5 *(continued)*

STEP 3: DEVELOP AN AGENCY PLAN TO BUILD THE NECESSARY ORGANIZATIONAL CAPACITY

Once an agency has conducted an assessment of its organizational capacity, it should develop a plan to build on its internal strengths, overcome its weaknesses, and enhance its organizational effectiveness for carrying out community wide efforts.

STEP 4: ASSESS THE COMMUNITY'S ORGANIZATIONAL AND POWER STRUCTURES

The lead agency should work in partnership with key community agencies, community leaders, interest groups, and community members. Identifying key people and organizations to involve in this effort is fundamental to success and is an essential part of community leadership. The agency should conduct an assessment of the community's organizational and power structures either on a formal or informal basis as part of its strategy to develop such partnerships.

STEP 5: ORGANIZE THE COMMUNITY TO BUILD A STRONGER CONSTITUENCY FOR PUBLIC HEALTH AND ESTABLISH A PARTNERSHIP FOR PUBLIC HEALTH

The lead agency should convene community groups to assess health needs, to address health problems, and to assist in the coordination of responsibilities. Agency staff should develop a focus on health outcomes and strategies.

STEP 6: ASSESS HEALTH NEEDS AND AVAILABLE COMMUNITY RESOURCES

A community assessment provides the information needed to identify a community's most critical health problems. Community assessment should include both formal and informal information collection. It should identify the perceptions and values of community leaders, groups, agencies, individuals, and health care providers about health priorities for the community. The effort should also examine pertinent health data and/or survey information to identify and verify the extent of major health problems and the level of risk for subpopulations.

TABLE 5.5 *(continued)*

STEP 7: DETERMINE LOCAL PRIORITIES

Establishing local priorities should involve major health agencies, community organizations, and key interest groups and individuals. Information gathered from a community assessment is intended to aid in determining local priorities. Selection of priorities is usually the result of negotiation among community groups resulting in a selected set of priority health problems to be targeted for community action.

STEP 8: SELECT OUTCOME AND PROCESS OBJECTIVES THAT ARE COMPATIBLE WITH LOCAL PRIORITIES

Community members should negotiate and select appropriate goals and outcome and process objectives for resolving community health problems. Goals and objectives should establish measurable health status outcomes. After establishing these objectives, the community coalition can develop process objectives for meeting them.

STEP 9: DEVELOP COMMUNITY-WIDE INTERVENTION STRATEGIES

Developing community-wide interventions provides the means to achieve selected community goals and objectives. Once interventions have been selected, responsibilities should be assigned so that activities can be distributed and coordinated among agencies and organizations.

STEP 10: DEVELOP AND IMPLEMENT A PLAN OF ACTION

Establishing goals, objectives, and community-wide intervention strategies is an important step, but success depends on developing and executing a plan of action that implements intervention activities and services. Establishing timelines and the assignment of responsibilities for activities and services is an essential part of this process.

STEP 11: MONITOR AND EVALUATE THE EFFORT ON A CONTINUING BASIS

The achievement of improved health status will attest to the effectiveness of community efforts. In the short term, achievement of local process objectives will show movement toward improved health status, if effective interventions have been selected. New services, improved community linkages for coordinating efforts, and enhanced staff skills and morale are evidence of process effectiveness.

Source: American Public Health Association, 1999c.

In order for community members to work together successfully in the planning effort as outlined in table 5.5, the following factors must be present:

- The group must develop a sense of mutual respect, trust, purpose, and understanding.
- There must be an appropriate representation of groups from all segments of the community for whom the activities will have an impact.
- All members must "buy into" and develop ownership in the development and outcome of the process.
- Effective communication among members must be constant and ongoing.
- The group must position itself as a leader in the community, eager to work with persons from all communities in developing effective strategies.
- The group must be willing to try nontraditional strategies.

(CENTERS FOR DISEASE CONTROL 1995, P. 14)

A recent demonstration project paired county public health agencies with ethnic community organizations in an effort to improve health care access for Hispanic and Asian and Pacific Islanders, including immigrants and refugees, in local communities. As a result of the experience, the project administrators made the following recommendations for achieving the above elements of effective collaboration:

- Meet frequently and be willing to invest time and energy in developing relationships.
- Identify a staff person to act as a liaison with the collaborating agencies.
- Find the right people at the other agencies to build a relationship with and persist in trying to build a relationship if the first efforts fail.
- Establish trust by following through on commitments.
- Be patient.
- Make an effort to formalize the relationship in order to maintain a long-term commitment.
- Alert community based organizations about the limits and constraints of bureaucracy in government organizations.
- Develop multicultural workshops. (DIVERSITY RX 1997C, P. 2)

COMMUNITY HEALTH EDUCATION The final macro-level social work practice strategy that social workers should employ is community health education. Community-level health education aims to improve health status by promoting healthy behaviors and changing those factors that negatively affect the health of a community's residents (Centers for Disease Control 1995). Community-level interventions are directed at populations rather than individuals (Centers for Disease Control 1995). Community-level education programs can be used to increase immigrants' and refugees' awareness of health problems for which the specific population is at high risk; increase awareness of available health care resources and eligibility requirements; increase awareness and use of preventive, screening, and treatment services; and modify health-related behaviors such as diet, exercise, tobacco use, and safe sex practices.

Community education interventions, or public information programs, may include working with print and broadcast media, producing educational materials, hotlines, and special events. "Public information programs craft and deliver data-driven and consumer-based messages and strategies to target audiences" (Centers for Disease Control 1995, p. 27). They are intended to:

- Raise awareness
- Increase knowledge
- Refute myths and misconceptions
- Influence attitudes and social norms
- Reinforce knowledge, attitudes, and behaviors
- Suggest and enable action
- Show the benefits of a behavior
- Increase support and/or demand for services
- Help coalesce organizational relationships

(CENTERS FOR DISEASE CONTROL 1995, P. 27)

EFFECTIVE PUBLIC INFORMATION PROGRAMS have the following characteristics:

- A person in charge who manages the program well.
- Activities planned to fit what the community and target audience need and want.
- A variety of activities, including mass media, that can be directed over a period of time to the target audience.
- A measurable program objective or purpose.
- A commitment to evaluation—tracking and measuring progress toward objectives.

TABLE 5.6 STANDARDS FOR EFFECTIVE PUBLIC HEALTH INFORMATION PROGRAMS

- Public information activities must support other components of health education and risk reduction activities.
- Target audiences for public information activities must be selected, based on needs identified through the community-needs assessment.
- Objectives for public information must be based on a realistic assessment of what communications can be expected to contribute to prevention.
- Messages must be based on the target audience's values, needs, and interests.
- Messages and materials must be pretested with the target audience to assure understanding and relevance to their needs and interests.
- Community representatives must be involved in planning and developing public information activities to ensure community "buy in."

Source: Centers for Disease Control, 1995.

- A time schedule
- Efficient use of people and other resources.

(CENTERS FOR DISEASE CONTROL 1995, P. 27)

IN PLANNING A PUBLIC INFORMATION PROGRAM, the following questions should be addressed:

- What are the media preferences and habits of the target audience? What information sources (such as social networks, religious institutions) do they consider credible?
- What are the media and other organizations that provide information in the targeted area?
- What program goals and objectives can public information support (e.g., increased knowledge, change in attitudes, motivation to act, increased skills, other behaviors)?
- What services/program activities should be promoted?
- What measurable objectives can be established? How can progress be tracked?
- What are the broad message concepts for the target audience? What should they be told? What do they want to know? Whom will they believe and trust?
- What communication channels are most appropriate for reaching target audiences (e.g., radio, TV, print media, worksite, face-to-face, voluntary organizations, or the health care sector)?

TABLE 5.7 BEST PRACTICES FOR EFFECTIVE PUBLIC HEALTH INFORMATION PROGRAMS

- Commit adequate time, effort, and resources to communication planning and pretesting.
- Review existing market research on the target audience to understand what will motivate them. Conduct new research only when necessary.
- Make sure that messages and materials appear where the target audience will pay attention to them.
- Produce/tag existing public service announcements (PSAs) that are of high production quality, community-specific, marketed to stations, and targeted to audiences likely to see them when public service air time is available.
- Combine PSAs with news and other uses of the mass media to increase exposure to prevention issues.
- Use a combination of the mass media and community channels that will reach the target audience.
- Work collaboratively with other organizations and/or community sectors that have complementary strengths. Begin to coordinate as early as possible in program planning.
- Use a two-pronged communication strategy to focus both on what an individual should do and on factors that help enable individual change such as peer approval and community support.
- Track progress and identify when and what kind of changes are needed in public information activities.
- Set reasonable, short-term public information objectives to reach the long-term goals. Then, commit to public information as one program component over the long term. Remember that one-shot public information campaigns are unlikely to leave a lasting effect, and that progress toward prevention goals is incremental.

Source: Centers for Disease Control, 1995.

- What materials/formats will best suit these channels and messages? Are there any existing materials than can be used or adapted?
- How can the resources be used most effectively and for what combination of activities? (CENTERS FOR DISEASE CONTROL 1995, P. 28)

TABLES 5.6 AND 5.7 list standards and best practices for effective public information programs.

In developing public information programs, the appropriate communication channels need to be selected. Communication channels include the mass media, such as ethnic radio and television stations and ethnic newspapers and magazines; community channels such as schools, employers, community meetings and organizations, religious institutions, and special events; and interpersonal channels such as hotline counselors, parents, health care providers, religious leaders, traditional healers, and educators (Centers for Disease Control 1995). Each channel has relative advantages and disadvantages. The appropriate channel or channels for a specific project can be selected by assessing whether the channel is:

- Likely to reach a significant portion of the target audience.
- Likely to reach them often enough to provide adequate exposure for the message.
- Credible for the target audience.
- Appropriate and accessible for the selected message.
- Appropriate for the program purpose (e.g., provide new information versus motivate action).
- Feasible, given available resources.

(CENTERS FOR DISEASE CONTROL 1995, P. 30)

After selecting appropriate communication channels, effective educational materials need to be developed. Table 5.8 lists possible formats for educational materials. Table 5.9 lists best practices for effective educational materials.

Public information programs can also include telephone hotlines. Hotlines can serve the following functions:

- Provide easy and immediate access for persons or populations who may not be reached by other methods.
- Provide an opportunity for a person to frame a question and have anonymous human contact.
- Provide information in a confidential manner.
- Provide information in appropriate language level and style and permit discussion of issues caller does not understand.
- Provide up-to-date, accurate information.
- Provide referrals for prevention, screening, treatment, and support services.
- Serve as a monitoring mechanism for impact of public information activities (e.g., public service announcements that publicize the hotline number). (CENTERS FOR DISEASE CONTROL 1995, P. 37)

TABLE 5.8 FORMATS FOR COMMUNITY HEALTH EDUCATIONAL MATERIALS

TELEVISION

- Public service announcements
- Paid advertisements
- Editorials
- News releases
- Question and answer for public affairs programs

RADIO

- Live announcer public service announcements
- Taped public service announcements
- Topic ideas for call-in shows

NEWSPAPER

- News releases
- Editorials
- Letters to the editor

OUTDOORS

- Transit ads
- Billboards
- Ads/posters at bus stops

COMMUNITY

- Posters for pharmacies, grocery stores, worksites, etc.
- Shopping bag inserts
- Paycheck inserts
- Special event giveaways (calendars, fact cards, pencils, balloons, key chains)
- Table top displays for health fairs, waiting rooms, libraries, schools
- Newsletter articles for community, employer, business newsletters, flyers, pamphlets

INTERPERSONAL

- Posters for physicians' offices and clinic waiting and examination rooms
- Talking points for patient counseling, presentations at schools, organizations, religious institutions
- Videos for classroom use

Source: Centers for Disease Control, 1995.

TABLE 5.9 BEST PRACTICES FOR EFFECTIVE HEALTH EDUCATION MATERIALS

- Material is clearly introduced and states the purpose of the text.
- Major points of text are summarized at the end.
- Materials are brief, concise, and in the language or dialect of the target audience.
- Materials are written at the educational and reading level of the target audience. Jargon and technical phrases are avoided.
- Use active verbs and short, simple sentences, with one concept per sentence in short paragraphs.
- Use terms consistently.
- Materials are straightforward and clear (do no use abbreviations, acronyms, euphemisms, symbolism, or statistics)
- Text uses lists, bullets, or illustrations instead of long discussions.
- Text is underlined, boldfaced, or "boxed" for reinforcement.
- The text dispels myths, refers to value systems for reasons to change behavior or adopt a new perspective.
- Materials provide a call for action.
- The text illustrates manual skills from audience perspective.
- The text provides reasons for changing behavior.
- Materials provide current and accurate medical information.
- Text offers alternative behaviors to the one(s) that put a person at risk.
- Realistic and relevant examples are given.
- The format of the text is not visually distracting.
- Graphics are immediately identifiable, relevant, and simple. They reinforce the text.

Source: Centers for Disease Control, 1995.

Lastly, community health education can be delivered through special events such as street fairs, job fairs, health fairs, and local celebrations. Table 5.10 lists best practices for effective special events.

In keeping with the principles of empirically based practice, all community health education programs need to be evaluated. The following are best practices for effective evaluation:

- Include process evaluation, such as monitoring the quantity and type of literature or materials distributed.
- Require consistent and accurate data collection procedures. A description of the tools used and definitions of various measurements should be outlined.

> **TABLE 5.10** BEST PRACTICES FOR EFFECTIVE HEALTH PROMOTION THROUGH SPECIAL EVENTS
>
> - Identify persons and organizations in the community interested in planning an observance or event.
> - Consider what types of activities will draw the target audience to an event (e.g., different people may be drawn to music, dance, art, sports, celebrity events).
> - Agree to sponsor an activity or a group of activities making sure that each will contribute to public information objectives with the designated target audience.
> - Discuss resources needed, such as a guest speaker, financial sponsors, and publicity materials.
> - Get members of the target audience involved in planning.
> - Create a planning schedule and set a date for the activity.
> - Delegate responsibilities for work by assigning persons to be in charge of specific aspects of the planned activity; put people in charge of location, special attractions, hospitality, publicity, and media according to their skills and interests.
> - Develop a publicity plan to assure attendance.
> - Decide on the most effective way to publicize events; e.g., announcements in the media and at meetings, flyers, public service announcements, posters, or mass mailings.
> - Track planning progress. Use the planning schedule and publicity plan as a guide to make sure that the event is a success.
> - Evaluate the success of the event by comparing the number of attendees expected with actual attendance; identify how many of the target audience attended and what they thought of the event; review media coverage and other publicity that supported prevention objectives; identify increased awareness of the program as a result of publicity (e.g., through pre- and post-event surveys); compare effort involved in developing the event with the value of the outcome.
>
> *Source:* Centers for Disease Control, 1995.

- Include staff supervision, observation, evaluation, and feedback on a regular basis.
- Include feedback from persons served.
- Designate staff who are responsible for evaluation and quality assurance activities, for compiling and analyzing data, and for documenting and reviewing findings.
- Define methods for assessing progress toward stated process and outcome goals and objectives.
- Include mechanisms for measuring the use of referral services.
- Provide findings for program modifications.

(CENTERS FOR DISEASE CONTROL 1995, P. 10)

5.2.2 MESO PRACTICE

MESO-LEVEL SOCIAL WORK PRACTICE in health care for immigrants and refugees involves organizational activities within the worker's health care agency to improve the agency's effectiveness in serving the immigrants and refugees in the local community. As seen in table 5.3, these organizational activities include providing consultation to agency administrators on how to enhance service delivery; assisting the agency in recognizing client needs and developing new or improved services and programs; assisting the agency in continuous quality improvement to effectively meet client needs; and serving as a liaison to the agency on behalf of the client.

A set of best practices for culturally competent health care service delivery has been developed, based on an analytical review of key laws, regulations, contracts, and standards currently in use by federal and state agencies and other national organizations, and with input from a national advisory committee (Fortier and Shaw-Taylor 1999a). These best practices are listed in table 5.11. The purpose of meso-level social work practice for immigrant and refugee health care should be to assist organizations to implement these best practices. There are two ways in which social workers can do this: through interdisciplinary collaboration, and through organizational development.

TABLE 5.11 BEST PRACTICES FOR CULTURALLY AND LINGUISTICALLY APPROPRIATE HEALTH CARE SERVICES

Culture and language have considerable impact on how patients access and respond to health care services. To ensure equal access to quality health care by diverse populations, health care organizations and providers should:
- Promote and support the attitudes, behaviors, knowledge, and skills necessary for staff to work respectfully and effectively with patients and each other in a culturally diverse work environment.
- Have a comprehensive management strategy to address culturally and linguistically appropriate services, including strategic goals, plans, policies, procedures, and designated staff responsible for implementation.
- Utilize formal mechanisms for community and consumer involvement in the design and execution of service delivery, including planning, policymaking, operations, evaluation, training, and, as appropriate, treatment planning.
- Develop and implement a strategy to recruit, retain, and promote qualified, diverse, and culturally competent administrative, clinical, and support staff that are trained and qualified to address the needs of the racial and ethnic communities being served.

TABLE 5.11 *(continued)*

- Require and arrange for ongoing education and training for administrative, clinical, and support staff in culturally and linguistically competent service delivery.
- Provide all clients with limited English proficiency access to bilingual staff or interpretation services.
- Provide oral and written notices, including translated signage at key points of contact, to clients in their primary language informing them of their right to receive interpreter services free of charge.
- Translate and make available signage and commonly used written patient educational material and other materials for members of the predominant language groups in service areas.
- Ensure that interpreters and bilingual staff can demonstrate bilingual proficiency and receive training that includes the skills and ethics of interpreting, and knowledge in both languages of the terms and concepts relevant to clinical or nonclinical encounters. Family or friends are not considered adequate substitutes because they usually lack these abilities.
- Ensure that the clients' primary spoken language and self-identified race/ethnicity are included in the health care organization's management information system as well as any patient records used by provider staff.
- Use a variety of methods to collect and utilize accurate demographic, cultural, epidemiological, and clinical outcome data for racial and ethnic groups in the service area, and become informed about the ethnic/cultural needs, resources, and assets of the surrounding community.
- Undertake ongoing organizational self-assessments of cultural and linguistic competence, and integrate measures of access, satisfaction, quality, and outcomes for culturally and linguistically appropriate services into other organizational internal audits and performance improvement programs.
- Develop structures and procedures to address cross cultural ethical and legal conflicts in health care delivery and complaints or grievances by patients and staff about unfair, culturally insensitive, or discriminatory treatment, or difficulty in accessing services, or denial of services.
- Prepare an annual progress report documenting the organization's progress with implementing culturally and linguistically appropriate service standards, including information on programs, staffing, and resources.

Source: Fortier and Shaw-Taylor, 1999a.

INTERDISCIPLINARY COLLABORATION It was noted earlier that team-based practice is an emerging trend in social work in health care. Team-based practice entails interdisciplinary collaboration. There are several forms of collaborative practice: case-by-case collaboration, consultation, and education (Dziegielewski 1998). Using these methods, social workers can assist physicians, nurses, and other health care providers to develop culturally competent practice.

Culturally competent health care practice entails being able to recognize and respond to health beliefs and cultural values, population-specific disease incidence and prevalence, and treatment efficacy (Fortier and Shaw-Taylor 1999a). It also includes the active participation of community members and consumers (U.S. Department of Health and Human Services 1998). Research has shown that culturally competent care improves diagnostic accuracy, increases adherence to recommended treatment, reduces delays in seeking care, and allows for more service use (Center for Cross-Cultural Health 1999, U.S. Department of Health and Human Services 1998).

Culturally competent health care providers integrate traditional healing approaches into their treatment plan when appropriate (American Medical Student Association 1999; Boehnlein 1990; Fortier and Shaw-Taylor 1999a; Gavagan and Brodyaga 1998). For example, a Mexican mother "might believe that her child is suffering from *empacho*, a folk illness caused by food 'sticking' to the inside of the stomach and causing pain. The physician diagnoses viral gastroenteritis and prescribes medication, but also tells the mother to rub her child's stomach. This is not harmful and it fits the cultural beliefs of the patient, possibly increasing compliance" (American Medical Student Association 1999, p. 7).

Most folk medical beliefs and practices are not harmful and do not interfere with biomedical treatment, and therefore can be integrated with Western medicine. However, health care providers cannot ethically support cultural practices that are harmful or illegal (American Medical Student Association 1999). For example, one Southeast Asian healing practice involves burning the abdomen with a lit cigarette to treat abdominal pain; this practice should be discouraged by health care providers (Boehnlein 1990). Likewise, health care providers should not support female genital mutilation or other practices that are reportable as child abuse (American Academy of Pediatrics 1997). These and other best practices for culturally competent health care practice are summarized in table 5.12.

TABLE 5.12 BEST PRACTICES FOR CULTURALLY COMPETENT HEALTH CARE WITH IMMIGRANTS AND REFUGEES

- Health care providers should oppose denying needed services to anyone residing within the borders of the United States.
- Health care providers should take advantage of educational opportunities and resources to achieve a better understanding of immigrant and refugee cultures and the health care needs of immigrant and refugee families. Important in the care of immigrants and refugees is an awareness of the family's culture, health beliefs, and the possible use of traditional or folk medicines. Health care providers may need to ask families to describe or explain their beliefs, values, attitudes, and practices to educate patients and families on health in a way that will complement, rather than replace, existing beliefs and practices. Health care providers should also explore their own attitudes toward patients' use of English; eating habits; health practices; folk remedies; understanding and perceptions of illness; use of health care services and medication; and family structure and roles.
- To provide culturally effective health care, health care providers should tolerate and respect differences in attitudes and approaches to child-rearing. However, this does not include any traditional practices that are clearly injurious to children and reportable under the Child Abuse Prevention and Treatment Act.
- Health care providers should be aware of the special health problems for which immigrants and refugees are at risk.
- Health care providers in training and in practice should be educated about the unique stresses that immigration may place on individuals and families. Education should include information on the availability of local resources that provide services in the language spoken at home.
- Health care providers should recognize and support the extended family in health care activities. In many cases it is useful to identify and communicate with key authority figures in the extended family. It also is important to be aware of whether the extended family resides nearby or in the country of origin and whether family support still exists. Health care providers also should be aware of whether patients are receiving medical care in the country of origin on a part-time basis.
- Any health screening that immigrants or refugees receive before U.S. entry should be followed up with continuing health supervision and, in many cases, mental health and social services. Health care providers should be familiar with linkages between public health and the private sector to ensure comprehensive health supervision.
- In communities where immigrant or refugee families reside, health care providers should develop linguistically and culturally appropriate services in concert with public health, social services, and school systems.
- Professional health organizations' local chapters should identify the health care needs of immigrants and refugees in their areas. In addition, chapters should work with state legislatures and agencies to assess the local impact of welfare and immigration reform measures and advocate responses that assure unimpeded access to all medically necessary services for all immigrants and refugees, as well as assure care for catastrophic illness or injury.

> **TABLE 5.12** *(continued)*
>
> • Health care providers should be encouraged to support and participate in locally developed, community-based activities that increase access to health care for immigrants and refugees.
>
> *Source:* Adapted from American Academy of Pediatrics, 1997.

Social workers can assist physicians and other health care providers to incorporate these general principles of cultural competence into their practice. Through the collaborative processes of case-by-case collaboration, consultation, and education, the following components of culturally competent health care can be addressed:

• Cultural awareness: Appreciating and accepting differences.
• Cultural knowledge: Deliberately seeking out various worldviews and explanatory models of disease.
• Cultural skill: Learning how to culturally assess a patient to avoid relying only on written "facts;" explaining an issue from another's perspective; reducing resistance and defensiveness; and acknowledging interactive mistakes that may hinder the desire to communicate.
• Cultural encounters: Meeting and working with people of a different culture to help dispel stereotypes and to remain open to the individuality of each patient. (AMERICAN MEDICAL STUDENT ASSOCIATION 1999, PP. 4–5)

THE FOLLOWING "LEARN" MODEL for developing cultural competence has also been suggested for physicians and other health care providers:

• Listen with sympathy and understanding to the patient's perception of the problem
• Explain your perceptions of the problem and your strategy for treatment.
• Acknowledge and discuss the differences and similarities between these perceptions.
• Recommend treatment while remembering the patient's cultural parameters.

- Negotiate agreement. It is important to understand the patient's explanatory model so that medical treatment fits in their cultural framework.

(BERLIN AND FOWKES 1983,
CITED IN AMERICAN MEDICAL STUDENTS ASSOCIATION 1999, PP. 7–8)

ORGANIZATIONAL DEVELOPMENT In addition to helping individual health care providers develop cultural competence, social workers can also help enhance the cultural competence of the organization as a whole. This entails implementing the best practices listed in table 5.11. Extensive discussions of issues related to the implementation of these best practices are provided by their authors (Fortier 1999; Fortier and Shaw-Taylor 1999a, 1999b).

In general, social workers should be familiar with several models that have been used by health care organizations to overcome linguistic and cultural barriers. These include using bilingual/bicultural providers; bilingual/bicultural community health workers; employee language banks; professional interpreters; and written translation materials (Diversity Rx 1997d).

Using bilingual/bicultural physicians, nurses, and other direct health care personnel is an ideal solution to overcoming linguistic and cultural barriers. However, there is an inadequate supply of such personnel. Three methods have been suggested for overcoming this problem: retraining foreign-trained health care workers for certification or licensing in professional or paraprofessional roles; working with traditional healers as partners with professional health care providers; and encouraging health sciences students to study another language while in training (Diversity Rx 1997d). In all cases, it is important to make an assessment of the providers' linguistic skills in both languages, particularly in regard to such issues as medical terminology and dialects.

Since there are insufficient numbers of bilingual/bicultural health care professionals, bilingual/bicultural community health workers, or paraprofessionals, are often used. Such workers can have several functions: outreach and health promotion activities; facilitating community participation in the health care system; educating providers about cultural relevance; and contributing to the continuity, coordination, and overall quality of care. Effective training and ongoing support for such staff is essential (Diversity Rx 1997d).

Many health care organizations, particularly hospitals, use employee language banks in an effort to overcome linguistic barriers. These consist of bilingual employees who volunteer to serve as interpreters when needed. While this is a low-cost and convenient option, it has numerous problems from the perspective of effective health care delivery. There is usually no formal evaluation of the volunteers' linguistic skills, and they often have little or no training in medical interpretation skills, ethics, or vocabulary. Also, job conflicts can arise when volunteers are called away from their regular duties to interpret (Diversity Rx 1997d).

A much better strategy is the use of professional interpreters. There are several options for this: hiring interpreters as full-time or part-time regular employees; hiring hourly, on-call employees or independent contractors; using an outside agency; and using telephone interpretation. Using interpreters who are regular employees is a good option when there is a high demand for a particular language. Using on-call interpreters or outside agency services is best when there is intermittent demand for one or more languages. Telephone interpretation involves a service through an outside company such as AT&T, which operates a language line with interpreters for more than 140 different languages (American Medical Student Association 1999). Such a service may be used for emergencies, for rare languages for which a local interpreter is not available, or for simple communications such as setting up appointments. However, telephone interpreters generally do not have training in medical interpretation and therefore should not be used for more complex communications (Diversity Rx 1997d). Medical interpretation requires an advanced level of training in order to prevent "miscommunication, misdiagnosis, inappropriate treatment, reduced patient comprehension and compliance, clinical inefficiency, decreased patient and provider satisfaction, malpractice, injury, or death" (Fortier and Shaw-Taylor 1999a, p. 30). Several resources are available that provide detailed discussion of medical interpretation and appropriate training, standards, and licensing (DiversityRx 1997d; Fortier 1999; Jackson 1998).

A final strategy often used for overcoming cultural and linguistic barriers is the use of translated written materials. This can include bilingual written phrases that clients and providers can point to in order to communicate. This is clearly a limited method that should only be used if there is no other option. Written materials can also include translated forms, documents, and health education materials (Diversity Rx 1997d). Like interpretation, medical translation is a complex process. At a minimum, the material should be translated, back translated, and reviewed by the target audience groups (Fortier and Shaw-Taylor 1999a).

Social workers can help their organizations implement these strategies as well as the other elements of organizational cultural competence listed in table 5.11 by engaging in the process of continuous quality improvement. Continuous quality improvement (CQI) is a methodology adopted by many health care organizations (Dziegielewski 1998; Joint Commission on Accreditation of Healthcare Organizations 1991; Rehr et al. 1998). It is "a system of continuous self-examination of institutional and provider practice in defined areas. . . . CQI is an expectation held by consumers, providers, institutions, payers, and regulators, and those in the community-at-large. The CQI process focuses on improving outcomes for patients and populations while incorporating patients' views of those outcomes" (Rehr et al. 1998, p. 65). Given all that has been said up to this point about the need to develop effective health care services for immigrants and refugees, and the need to involve members of immigrant and refugee communities into service development, it is logical to apply CQI to organizational cultural competence. The basic principles of CQI are summarized in table 5.13.

5.2.3 MICRO PRACTICE

MICRO SOCIAL WORK PRACTICE ENTAILS direct service delivery to clients. It may involve working with individuals, families, or small groups. As seen in table 5.3, micro practice entails many separate tasks. These can be summarized into three categories: case management, health education and counseling, and psychosocial treatment. Each of these will be addressed below, following a discussion of general principles for micro social work practice in health care for immigrants and refugees.

GENERAL PRINCIPLES As discussed in the previous chapter, the first steps of the social work practice process involve engagement, problem identification and assessment, and goal setting and contracting. In general, the principles for culturally competent practice in each of these steps, as discussed in the previous chapter, should be followed in the health care practice setting. There are also some additional considerations.

In the engagement stage, social workers may need to develop criteria for identifying immigrants and refugees in the health care setting who may be in need of micro social work services. For example, in hospitals, not all

TABLE 5.13 PRINCIPLES OF CONTINUOUS QUALITY IMPROVEMENT FOR HEALTH CARE ORGANIZATIONS

- Create constancy of purpose for improvement of products and services.
- Adopt the philosophy of doing things right the first time.
- Cease dependence on inspection to achieve quality.
- End the practice of awarding business on the basis of price tag.
- Improve constantly and forever every process for planning, production, and service.
- Institute training on the job.
- Adapt and institute leadership for system improvement.
- Encourage risk-taking.
- Break down barriers between disciplines.
- Remove barriers that rob people of pride of workmanship.
- Institute a vigorous program of education and self-improvement for everyone.
- Put everyone in the organization to work to accomplish the transformation.

Source: Adapted from Joint Commission for Accreditation of Health Care Organizations, 1991.

patients are referred to the social work department. Many hospitals have-screening protocols to identify and refer for social work services those patients who may be at high risk of experiencing psychosocial difficulties related to their presenting health problem (Rosenberg 1983). For example, referral criteria may include cases of suspected child abuse, or cases involving financial problems. However, the screening protocols may not include any criteria specifically pertaining to immigrants and refugees. Thus, social workers may need to develop such criteria. For example, it may be logical to refer all clients who have limited English proficiency or who are recent arrivals in the U.S. In developing screening criteria, social workers will need to collaborate with other members of the health care team to determine what factors related to immigrant or refugee status (e.g., legal issues, family conflicts, treatment noncompliance) seem to pose particular problems. These identified factors then need to be developed into screening criteria. Additionally, since many immigrants and refugees do not access health care services in the first place, engagement with this population also needs to include outreach. This is discussed further below under health education and counseling.

In the problem identification and assessment stage, the principles per-

TABLE 5.14 BEST PRACTICE PRINCIPLES FOR IMPROVING THE HEALTH CARE PROVIDER/CLIENT RELATIONSHIP ACROSS CULTURES

- Do not treat the client in the same manner you would want to be treated. Culture determines the rules for polite, caring behavior and will formulate the client's concept of a satisfactory relationship.
- Begin by being more formal with clients who were born in another culture. In most countries, a greater distance between caregiver and patient is maintained through the relationship. Except when treating children or very young adults, it is best to use the client's last name when addressing him or her.
- Do not be insulted if the client fails to look you in the eye or ask questions about treatment. In many cultures, it is disrespectful to look directly at another person (especially one in authority) or to make someone "lose face" by asking him or her questions.
- Do not make any assumptions about the client's ideas about the ways to maintain health, the cause of illness or the means to prevent or cure it. Adopt a line of questioning that will help determine some of the client's central beliefs about health/illness/illness prevention.
- Allow the client to be open and honest. Do not discount beliefs that are not held by Western medicine. Often, clients are afraid to tell Western caregivers that they are visiting a folk healer or are taking an alternative medicine concurrently with Western treatment because in the past they have experienced ridicule.
- Do not discount the possible effects of beliefs in the supernatural on the client's health. If the client believes that the illness has been caused by *embrujado* (bewitchment), the evil eye, or punishment, the client is not likely to take any responsibility for his or her cure. Belief in the supernatural may result in his or her failure to either follow medical advice or comply with the treatment plan.
- Inquire indirectly about the client's belief in the supernatural or use of nontraditional cures. Say something like, "Many of my clients from ____ believe, do, or visit ____. Do you?"
- Ascertain the value of involving the entire family in the treatment. In many cultures, medical decisions are made by the immediate family or the extended family. If the family can be involved in the decision-making process and the treatment plan, there is a greater likelihood of gaining the client's compliance with the course of treatment.
- Be restricted in relating bad news or explaining in detail complications that may result from a particular course of treatment. "The need to know" is a unique American trait. In many cultures, placing oneself in the doctor's hands represents an act of trust and a desire to transfer the responsibility for treatment to the physician. Watch for and respect signs that the client has learned as much as he or she is able to deal with.
- Whenever possible, incorporate into the treatment plan the client's folk medication and folk beliefs that are not specifically contraindicated. This will encourage the patient to develop trust in the treatment and will help assure that the treatment plan is followed.

Source: American Medical Student Association, 1999.

taining to defining the problem and conducting a comprehensive assessment, as discussed in the previous chapter, should be followed. Additionally, the following assessment questions are particularly useful for eliciting clients' health beliefs and expectations of treatment (American Medical Students Association 1999; Kleinman 1980):

- What do you call your problem? What name does it have?
- What do you think caused your problem?
- Why do you think it started when it did?
- What does your sickness do to you? How does it work?
- How severe is your sickness? How long do you expect it to last?
- What problems has your sickness caused you?
- What do you fear about your sickness?
- What kind of treatment do you think you should receive?
- What are the most important results you hope to receive from this treatment?

In the remaining stages of the social work process (i.e., intervention implementation and monitoring, termination and evaluation, and follow-up), the principles discussed in the last chapter should be followed. Table 5.14 lists some additional best practice principles that are useful for social workers as well as other providers in the health care setting.

CASE MANAGEMENT It was stated earlier that there is an increased need for and importance of case management in the contemporary health care system. "Case management is defined as the process of planning, organizing, coordinating, and monitoring the services and resources needed to respond to an individual's health care needs" (Rose 1992, p. 151). In table 5.3, the micro-level services of concrete service provision, assistance with short- or long-term planning, access to remedial or rehabilitative services, referral services, continuity of care, and client advocacy are functions that are specific to case management. In case management, the engagement, problem identification and assessment, goal setting and contracting, intervention monitoring, termination and evaluation, and follow-up phases are all essentially the same as in other forms of micro social work practice. What distinguishes case management is the intervention itself, which entails referral, linkage, and brokering functions (Raiff and Shore 1993).

Case management is particularly important in social work with immigrants and refugees since they are often unfamiliar with available services and programs, and may not have the necessary skills or resources to access them. Effective case management requires social workers to have knowledge of community services and programs, to have good working relationships with workers in the referral agencies, and to be assertive in following through on referrals. Since it can sometimes be difficult to find services and programs that provide a perfect fit to a client's needs, effective case managers also need skills in compromise and conflict resolution. Effective case managers also have the capacity to deal with emergency situations and to connect clients to needed services quickly (Raiff and Shore 1993).

Effective case management is enhanced by effective service coordination. Service coordination involves "ensuring that the different providers continue to view the client holistically and understand the contribution of their program to the client's overall functioning; reconnecting to community support services in anticipation of discharge from more restrictive treatment settings and vice versa; and making sure all the elements of the service plan have been implemented in a timely fashion and that service duplication is avoided" (Raiff and Shore 1993, pp. 47–48). Table 5.15 lists best practices for ensuring quality service coordination.

Effective case management may require case advocacy when there is difficulty in securing a needed service, resource, or entitlement for the client (Raiff and Shore 1993). Case advocacy differs from policy advocacy, which was discussed earlier, in that case advocacy concerns the service access of an individual client or family, whereas policy advocacy concerns the service access of an entire population. Case advocacy may be necessary both within one's agency and with outside agencies. Case advocacy is likely to be more necessary in work with immigrants and refugees than with other clients, due to the health care access barriers that were discussed earlier. "Effective advocacy requires at a minimum that staff be thoroughly familiar with eligibility criteria, application processes, and appeals procedures for each needed service and program" (Raiff and Shore 1993, p. 55). Additional best practices for effective case advocacy are listed in table 5.16.

Finally, case management with immigrants and refugees requires cultural competence and effectiveness in working with interpreters. Best practices for these qualities are listed in tables 5.17 and 5.18.

TABLE 5.15 BEST PRACTICES FOR ENSURING QUALITY SERVICE COORDINATION

BUILD IN SUFFICIENT LEAD TIME

- Establish a joint task force to identify problems in coordination and the most common shared issues.
- Conduct needs assessment to determine the scope of need.
- Explore solutions and their costs.
- Allow staff to voice concern about any perceived loss of professional control and barriers to sharing.
- Plan what is needed.

EDUCATE PROGRAM STAFF ABOUT CASE MANAGEMENT

- Define the case manager's role and the role of the agency.
- Identify what case management can do to facilitate the process or to assist staff.
- Explain the lines of accountability.

DEVELOP FORMAL WORKING AGREEMENTS THAT DESCRIBE:

- Who is the joint client.
- What are the service elements.
- Who can initiate the coordinating process.
- Under what conditions program functions will be performed, either jointly or separately.
- Who is responsible for seeing that records can be physically shared (e.g., who is responsible for ordering, copying, and coordinating the record exchanges)
- Where the elements of the case management record will be kept and what components can be shared.
- Who can institute closure of the arrangement.

DEVELOP ADVANCED METHODS OF COORDINATING SERVICES

- Cross train to develop a common knowledge base.
- Develop methods for joint review and decision making.
- Develop procedures for conflict resolution.
- Explore the use of shared forms (e.g., joint referral form for a "single point of contact" inquiry no matter where the client enters the system)
- Explore joint information system, share computerized tracking.

Source: Raiff and Shore, 1993. Copyright © 1993, Sage Publications, Inc. Reprinted with permission.

TABLE 5.16 BEST PRACTICES FOR EFFECTIVE CASE ADVOCACY

- Explore the client's or provider's understanding of the situation's causes and what they want to see changed. Explore their preferred solution and what they will settle for. Encourage them to ask for everything on their priority list, rather than just the minimum they think they can get.
- Develop a plan and decide on the advocacy strategies necessary to achieve the goals. Define how pervasive the problem or issue is.
- Do your homework; know the issues, the services, and the people in the system. Be able to speak knowledgeably about the chances for success.
- Review what roles the client or provider will play in the intervention beforehand. Discuss whether a neutral third party (e.g., an ombudsman, friend, or family advocate) should be present to provide the client with needed, additional support. This party can also raise pointed questions or offer statements of fact without having the case manager risk further alienating "the system."
- Plan a formal or informal meeting with the most appropriate level of staff.
- Begin by clarifying the meeting's objectives, stating the problems clearly and allowing all interested parties to discuss the problem.
- Separate the person from the problem; recognize that staff need to be part of the solution and are also frustrated by a situation.
- Go "hard on problems, easy on the person." Reinforce your support for the other and identify the real or perceived barriers. Focus on the big picture; appeal to underlying ethical values.
- Jointly develop a definition of needed changes and negotiate for these changes.
- Develop a written statement (e.g., a draft memorandum that is circulated for approval, a change in the service plan, or a file note) outlining what has been agreed.
- If agreement is not achieved and change is not accomplished:
- Reinforce that the client is not being abandoned.
- Assure the client that the matter will continue to be worked on or that the next supervisory or administrative levels will be activated.
- Document the meeting and prepare a clear presentation to the supervisor or administrator in anticipation of further action.
- Continue to keep good records of all subsequent meetings, conversations, site visits, and surveys.

Source: Raiff and Shore, 1993. Copyright © 1993, Sage Publications, Inc. Reprinted with permission.

TABLE 5.17 BEST PRACTICES FOR CULTURALLY COMPETENT CASE MANAGEMENT

- Concentrate on what the client sees as "real life" problems.
- Do a complete current environmental analysis; assess financial and social needs; back this with action.
- Prepare clients for services by offering role rehearsal and information; help clients complete forms; provide information on neighborhood resources using materials (e.g., graphics, translated materials) the client can understand.
- Call clients by their correct name and with the degree of formality expected in their culture; if in doubt, ask the client about pronunciation and cultural protocols related to the first and last name and other honorifics.
- Be prepared to disclose about yourself, your home, your family, and your ideas so that the client can get to know you as a person.
- Be prepared to involve the family.
- Accompany clients and family members to clients' appointments.
- Be supportive of clients and family members who want to use indigenous healers/helpers.
- Be alert to clues about intergenerational conflict.
- Be sensitive to indirect issues that are raised.
- Make advance calls to service providers to confirm they are ready to receive the family.
- Coordinate service appointments and locations.
- Provide transportation and coaching in the use of mass transit.
- Explore reimbursement mechanisms for neighbors or other supports who could provide transportation or other short-term assistance.
- Have staff available after hours, evenings and weekends, at places where community members congregate; attend cultural immersion activities (e.g., festivals, ceremonies)
- Develop relationships with the community's most trusted helpers and gatekeepers.
- Develop relationships with cultural informants.
- Teach/encourage self-advocacy.
- Link to the community's agency supports and volunteer assistance.
- Be patient.

Source: Raiff and Shore, 1993. Copyright © 1993, Sage Publications, Inc. Reprinted with permission.

TABLE 5.18 BEST PRACTICES FOR PROVIDING CASE MANAGEMENT SERVICES WITH AN INTERPRETER

PRE-CONTACT TELEPHONE CALL

• Check if the interpreter will be available. Will this be on a one-time or on a continuing basis?
• Explain what you are trying to accomplish.
• Explore the client's and the interpreter's backgrounds: How good is the match (e.g., in terms of gender, age, rural-urban differences in experience, competence in dialects, whether the interpreter is related to the family).
• Negotiate and schedule a pre-session face-to-face discussion. How much extra time is anticipated for interpretation and clarification, and for a short post-session debriefing?

AT THE PRE-SESSION DISCUSSION

• Review confidentiality.
• Explain and reinforce the meeting's goals.
• Build a relationship with the interpreter.
• Learn how to pronounce the client's name.
• Request information about proxemics—norms of eye and physical contact—and culturally sensitive topics (e.g., personal finances).
• Decide if the interpretation will be word for word or paraphrased.
• Establish norms about timing and clarification: How long will each speak? When are interruptions permitted?
• Discuss technical terms (e.g., medications, providers, entitlement programs) that are likely to be used in the upcoming contact.
• Decide how each person will be introduced to the client.
• Establish ground rules for interpreter feedback: Will this be provided during or after the session? Will it include nonverbal cues, speech pattern observations, and volunteered cultural information?

THE CLIENT CONTACT

• Introduce everyone present at the beginning.
• Establish the client's agreement to the ground rules for communication.
• Try to establish how much English the client knows; do not assume that the client does not understand what you and the interpreter are discussing.
• Be sensitive to indications that the client is attempting to "split" your relationship with the interpreter.
• Use simple English; avoid technical terms and slang.
• Monitor nonverbal and process dynamics while the interpreter and the client are speaking.

TABLE 5.18 *(continued)*

POST-SESSION DISCUSSION

- Debrief issues that were not adequately discussed during the session.
- Exchange impressions of the client.
- Discuss problems or misunderstandings.
- Schedule follow-up sessions, if needed.

Source: Raiff and Shore, 1993. Copyright © 1993, Sage Publications, Inc. Reprinted with permission.

HEALTH EDUCATION AND COUNSELING Social work in the contemporary health care environment involves an increased emphasis on health promotion and preventive intervention, as stated earlier. This is achieved in part through the macro-level intervention of community education as discussed above, and in part through micro-level health education and counseling. Health education and counseling is a service delivered directly to individuals, families, and small groups. Its purpose is to assist "individuals to become cognizant of what factors are important to maintaining their own health and wellness . . . ; to help communicate needed information that will assist the individual in making needed changes; assist individuals in using this information to develop self-help skills that can empower them to address health needs; and assist individuals to gain access to the techniques or technology that can help them in meeting their needs" (Dziegielewski 1998, p. 194).

> An underlying principle of patient education and counseling is that knowledge is necessary but not sufficient to change health behaviors. . . . Patient education involves more than simply telling people what to do or giving them an instructional pamphlet. . . . A growing body of evidence suggests that when people have confidence that they can affect their health, they are more likely to do so than those without such confidence. This confidence has been termed 'perceived self-efficacy.' Self-efficacy can be enhanced through skills mastery, modeling, reinterpreting the meaning of symptoms, and persuasion. (U.S. PREVENTIVE SERVICES TASK FORCE 1996, P. 2)

Research has shown that health education and counseling is effective in changing many health-related behaviors such as smoking, problem drinking, weight control, exercise, contraceptive use, and compliance with medication and with other preventive or therapeutic regimens (U.S. Preventive Services Task Force 1996). In turn, these behavioral changes have been shown to lead to improved health outcomes in areas such as high blood pressure, cancer, pain and disability, low birth weight, and diabetes (U.S. Preventive Services Task Force 1996). Since immigrants and refugees tend to have higher than average rates of preventable illness and treatment noncompliance, health education and counseling is a logical intervention for this population.

Health education and counseling can be delivered in several forms: community outreach using presentations and workshops; use of peer educators; and individual, family, and small group counseling (Centers for Disease Control 1995). Community outreach through workshops and presentations typically involves providing health information in a lecture format to a small group. Effective health education workshops and presentations need to be carefully planned, have clear goals and objectives, be tailored to the characteristics and knowledge level of the audience, follow a detailed outline, and encourage audience participation (Centers for Disease Control 1995). Effective presenters have the following characteristics:

- Possess organizational and public speaking skills.
- Are well informed and comfortable talking about the subject.
- Ensure that the presentation is linguistically appropriate for the audience.
- Elicit and encourage audience participation.
- Are adaptable to logistics and audience needs.
- Are nonjudgmental.
- Assess the nature of questions and make appropriate responses.
- Seek accurate answers to difficult questions and provide information in a timely manner.   (CENTERS FOR DISEASE CONTROL 1995, P. 19)

Many community outreach programs for immigrants and refugees use peer educators, also known as lay health advisors, community health advisors, or *promotores/as* or *consejeros/as* in Spanish. Community health advisors are paraprofessionals who are indigenous members of the community and are natural leaders to whom community members often turn for help (Candelaria et al. 1998).

Peer education implies a role-model method of education in which trained, self-identified members of the client population provide [health] education to their peers. This method provides an opportunity for individuals to perceive themselves as empowered by helping persons in their communities and social networks, thus supporting their own health enhancing practices. . . . Peer education can be very powerful, if it is applied appropriately. The peer educator not only teaches a desired risk reduction practice but s/he also models it. Peer educators demonstrate behaviors that can influence the community norms in order to promote . . . risk reduction within their networks. They are better able to inspire and encourage their peers to adopt health seeking behaviors because they are able to share common weaknesses, strengths, and experiences. (CENTERS FOR DISEASE CONTROL 1995, P. 19–20)

EFFECTIVE PEER EDUCATORS must possess the following characteristics:

- Have a shared identity with the targeted community or group.
- Are within the same age range as the targeted community or group.
- Speak the same language as the community or group.
- Are familiar with the group's cultural nuances and are able to convey these norms and values to the agency.
- Act as an advocate, serving as a liaison between the agency and the targeted community or group. (CENTERS FOR DISEASE CONTROL 1995, P. 20)

In addition to the use of community outreach and peer educators, social workers themselves can deliver health education and counseling to individuals, families, or small groups. As noted earlier, involving family members when working with immigrants and refugees will likely enhance effectiveness. Small groups have the additional advantage that they "provide access to social networks that enable and reinforce health enhancing behavior change through peer modeling and peer support" (Centers for Disease Control 1995, p. 21). Health education and counseling may be delivered in a single session or in a series of sessions. Best practices for effective health education and counseling are listed in table 5.19.

TABLE 5.19 BEST PRACTICES FOR EFFECTIVE HEALTH EDUCATION AND COUNSELING

- Frame the teaching to match the client's expectations. Consider and incorporate the beliefs and concerns of the client, including ethnic and religious beliefs and practices. To persuade clients to change their behavior, it is first necessary to identify their beliefs relevant to the behavior and to provide information based on this foundation. A fixed message will not be effective for all patients.
- Fully inform clients of the purpose and expected effects of interventions and when to expect these effects. This may avoid discouragement when immediate benefits are not forthcoming, and might increase the likelihood of long-term compliance. If side effects are common, the client should be told what to expect, and under what circumstances the intervention should be stopped or the provider consulted.
- Suggest small changes rather than large ones. By achieving a small goal, the client has initiated positive change. Successful persuasion involves not only increasing a client's faith in his or her capabilities, but also structuring interventions so that people are likely to experience success.
- Be specific. Specific and informational instructions will generally lead to better compliance. Behavior change is enhanced if the regimen and its rationale are explained, demonstrated to the client (if appropriate), and written down for clients to take home.
- It is sometimes easier to add new behaviors rather than to eliminate established behaviors.
- Link new behaviors to old behaviors. Suggest that the client add new behaviors to established routines.
- Get explicit commitments from the client. Ask clients to describe what specifically they plan to achieve this week (i.e., what, when, and how often). The more specific the commitment from the client, the more likely it is to be followed. After getting the commitment, ask the client how sure he or she is that he or she will carry out the commitment. If a client expresses uncertainty, explore the problems that might be encountered in carrying out the regimen and seek solutions for those problems.
- Use a combination of strategies. Educational efforts that integrate individual counseling, group classes, audiovisual aids, written materials, and community resources are more likely to be effective than those employing a single technique.
- Involve other team members. A team approach facilitates patient education. The receptionist can encourage patients to read educational materials in the reception area. Staff members and the agency environment can communicate consistent positive health messages. Forming a patient education committee can help to generate program ideas and promote staff commitment.
- Monitor progress through follow-up contact. Scheduling a follow-up appointment or telephone call within the next few weeks to evaluate progress, reinforce success, and identify and respond to problems improves the effectiveness of counseling.

Source: Adapted from U.S. Preventive Services Task Force, 1996.

PSYCHOSOCIAL TREATMENT The final micro social work intervention in health care is psychosocial treatment, or direct clinical counseling. The purpose of such treatment is to help clients and families cope with and adapt to illness, and to address psychosocial issues that impact on health, such as "interpersonal conflicts, psychological and behavior problems, dissatisfaction with social relations, difficulties in role performance, problems of social transition, problems in decision making, problems with formal organizations, and cultural conflicts" (Dziegielewski 1998, p. 83). It was noted earlier that contemporary social work in health care is characterized by an emphasis on brief treatment. Most social work interventions in health care consist of only one or two sessions (Dziegielewski 1998). Brief interventions are designed for this short time frame, or for periods up to six or eight weeks (Dziegielewski 1998).

Research over several years has established that brief treatment is an effective intervention for certain problems (Dziegielewski 1998). Brief interventions have seven major characteristics (Dziegielewski 1998):

- The client is viewed as basically having healthy psychosocial functioning, with an interest in increasing personal or social changes.
- Brief interventions are most helpful when administered during critical periods in a person's life.
- The goals and objectives of the intervention are mutually defined by the client and the worker.
- Goals and objectives are concretely defined and intervention activities extend outside the client-worker encounter.
- There is little emphasis on insight.
- The therapist is seen as active and directive.
- Termination is discussed early in the process.

These characteristics of brief treatment are highly congruent with the cultural expectations of many immigrants and refugees, who view the helping professional as an expert and expect rapid and active treatment (Jaranson 1990). Lengthy, insight-oriented therapy is a concept that is unfamiliar to most immigrants and refugees. Thus, brief treatment often may be appropriate for refugees and immigrants in an acute health care setting such as a hospital. However, due to the complex psychosocial issues of immigrants and refugees, it must be recognized that brief treatment alone is insufficient to address the totality of their needs. Brief treatment should be viewed as part of a comprehensive social work approach that includes all the other interventions discussed in this chapter and throughout the rest of this book.

Brief treatment includes all of the elements of engagement, problem identification and assessment, goal setting and contracting, intervention implementation and monitoring, termination and evaluation, and follow-up that were discussed in the previous chapter. In brief treatment, these tasks must be compressed into a short time frame. Thus, the need for specific, concrete, and measurable problem definitions and goals, as discussed in the previous chapter, becomes particularly evident in brief treatment. Once the problem is identified, goals are established, and contracting is done, the intervention phase begins. "Guidelines that can assist in this stage ... include planning each session in advance, summarization of each session, and maintaining flexibility if re-negotiation needs to occur in regard to the problem-solving process" (Dziegielewski 1998, p. 107). Each session should include restatement of objectives and summarization:

> Initiation of each formal encounter is dedicated to the client actually stating the agreed upon objectives that are to be addressed. This will allow both client and social worker to quickly focus on the task at hand. Summarization should also be practiced at the end of each session. This will allow the client to recapitulate what she or he believes has transpired in the session, and how it relates to the stated objectives. Clients should use their own words to summarize what has transpired. In acknowledging and summarizing the content and objectives of the session (a) the client takes responsibility for his or her own actions; (b) repetition allows the session accomplishments to be highlighted and reinforced; (c) the client and the social worker ascertain that they are working together on the same objectives; and (d) the therapeutic environment remains flexible and open for renegotiation of contracted objectives. (DZIEGIELEWSKI 1998, P. 108)

There are four specific methods of brief treatment that are commonly used in social work in health care: interpersonal psychotherapy, solution-focused intervention, cognitive-behavioral interventions, and crisis intervention (Dziegielewski 1998).

Interpersonal psychotherapy focuses on reducing symptoms and dealing with interpersonal problems such as grief, role disputes, or role transitions. It focuses strictly on the present.

Treatment strategy is directly related to the identified interpersonal problem. For example, if there is a role conflict between a client and his or her family member regarding limitations of a particular medical condition, treatment would begin with clarifying the nature of the dispute. Discussion of the medical condition would result with an explanation of usual limitations that oftentimes are beyond the control of the client. Limitations that are causing the greatest problem would be identified, and options to resolve the dispute are considered. If resolution does not appear possible, strategies or alternatives to replace it are contemplated. (DZIEGIELEWSKI 1998, P. 118)

Interpersonal psychotherapy also addresses applying what has been learned in the sessions to problems that may arise in the future. Further, this method often involves "helping the client to learn how to recognize the need for continued intervention" (Dziegielewski 1998, p. 119). This is particularly likely to be true for immigrants and refugees, due to the complexity of the problems they encounter. In this case, social workers need to use their case management function to arrange for ongoing interventions.

Solution-focused intervention focuses on identifying alternative solutions to problems using the client's strengths. There is little attention to the cause of the problem.

Simply stated, in "solution-focused" interventions, the emphasis in practice is placed on constructing probable solutions to a problem. The idea that it is easier to construct solutions than it is to actually attempt to change problem behaviors prevails. By not spending a great deal of time on the cause of the problem, the emphasis on the intervention is switched away from the past toward present and future survival. There is often more than one solution, and it becomes the role of the health care social worker and the client together to help construct alternative and possible scenarios of assistance. (DZIEGIELEWSKI 1998, P. 120)

Cognitive-behavioral interventions address the thought processes that influence emotions and behavior.

The literature supports that individuals develop different styles or patterns of information processing based on their life experiences. These schemas may influence an individual's reaction, resulting in cognitive distortion when interpreting a current situation or event. Cognitive-behavioral therapies focus on the present and seek to replace distorted thoughts or unwanted behaviors with clearly established goals.... A cognitive-behavioral approach can be helpful to the health care social worker who must deal with clients who are suffering from medical problems. Medical problems often happen quickly, and individuals may be frustrated with their inability to perform in areas in which they previously were proficient. When faced with a medical situation, clients may develop negative schemas or ways of dealing with the situation that can clearly cause conflicts in their physical, interpersonal, and social relationships. Specific techniques, such as identifying irrational beliefs, and using cognitive restructuring, behavioral role rehearsal, and systematic desensitization, can assist the client to adjust and accommodate to the new life status that will result.... Cognitive and behavioral techniques can help the client to not only recognize the need for change but assist with a plan to provide the behavior change needed for continued health and functioning. (DZIEGIELEWSKI 1998, P. 122)

The final method of brief treatment in health care social work is crisis intervention. A crisis "is defined as a temporary state of upset and disequilibrium, characterized chiefly by an individual's inability to cope with a particular situtation" (Dziegielweski 1998, p. 123). Crisis intervention consists of several stages:

The first stage refers to assessing the nature and extent of the ... illness or ... emergency that is overwhelming the client at the time. The second stage involves helping the person in crisis prioritize his or her concerns. In the middle phase, the crisis intervention approach should focus on encouraging the person in crisis to talk to the counselor about the event; understand and conceptualize the meaning of the event; and integrate the cognitive, affective, and behavioral components of the crisis. The third stage of crisis intervention consists of helping the person in crisis to problem solve and find effective coping methods.... This active crisis state provides an important turning point and energy for the change effort. The client's individual personal resources, problem-solving skills, adaptability to withstand sudden intensely stressful life events, and social support networks need to be assessed. In the final phase of intervention, ... the client needs to be prepared to deal with recurring problems stemming from the original crisis event.... It would be useful to help the client decide on the best person to turn to for support in dealing with delayed or post-traumatic reactions if they should develop....

Emphasis is placed on the ability of an individual to adapt or restore himself or herself to a balanced state—preferably one that exhibits restored or enhanced levels of confidence and coping. (DZIEGIELEWSKI 1998, PP. 124–125)

As with all other social work interventions discussed in this chapter, outcome evaluation needs to be a component of these brief interventions. The importance of outcome evaluation was discussed in the previous chapter, and is also a major focus of the contemporary health care environment, as mentioned earlier.

In working with immigrants and refugees, all of these methods of brief intervention may need to be adapted to be culturally congruent. The specific application of these methods, as well as other psychosocial interventions, to immigrants and refugees will be discussed in much more detail in the next two chapters, which address mental health and family dynamics.

5.3 CASE STUDY EXERCISES

FOLLOWING ARE SEVERAL case study exercises. For each one, describe the course of action you would take if you were the social worker assigned to the case.

5.3.1 CASE 1

Lia was a three-month-old Hmong child with epilepsy. Her doctors prescribed a complex regimen of medication designed to control her seizures. However, her parents felt that the epilepsy was a result of Lia's "losing her soul" and did not give her medication as indicated because of the complexity of the drug therapy and the adverse side effects. Instead, they did everything logical in terms of their Hmong beliefs to help her. They took her to a clan leader and shaman, sacrificed animals and bought expensive amulets to guide her soul's return. Lia's doctors felt her parents were endangering her life by not giving her the medication so they called Child Protective Services.

(AMERICAN MEDICAL STUDENT ASSOCIATION 1999)

5.3.2 CASE 2

Mrs. Lee was a 49-year-old Cantonese-speaking woman who had immigrated years ago from China to the U.S. She lived with her husband and youngest son, Arnold, 22. Mrs. Lee suffered from lung cancer that had spread to her lymph nodes and adrenal glands. Arnold did not want Mrs. Lee's diagnosis known to her. Eventually, the cancer spread to her brain. Her physician, knowing her poor prognosis, suggested a "do not resuscitate" order to her son, who refused to even discuss the possibility with his mother. Arnold felt that his role as son and family member meant he must protect his mother from "bad news" and loss of hope. He believed telling her the dim prognosis would be cruel and cause unnecessary stress. Though futile, the son insisted that all heroic methods be used, including a ventilator, to save his mother's life. He accused the hospital staff and physician of racism and threatened litigation.

(AMERICAN MEDICAL STUDENT ASSOCIATION 1999)

5.3.3 CASE 3

Flora M., an 84-year-old Russian speaking woman with end-stage renal disease was referred to the hospital social worker for a nursing home placement following a two-week hospitalization. Such placement became necessary when it was established that Flora's 54-year old daughter, Bronya, was unable, because of her own poor health, to take the patient into her home. While the patient's only request was that the home be a kosher one, Bronya insisted that it be a particular nursing home. She explained that the home had a good reputation in the Russian community and was near her home, which would make it possible for her to visit daily. When Flora was asked to comment on Bronya's stipulations, she said, angrily, "That's nonsense. She does not need to visit me daily. Once every two weeks would suffice." She would not repeat that in her daughter's presence, however, fearing her daughter's anger. Bronya's comment on her mother's statement was, "She does not know what she is talking about. She is helpless as a babe and needs me to be around her all the time." Several weeks later, following an intensive search for a skilled nursing facility, the patient was offered a bed at a kosher nursing home some 25 miles away, which the patient, unbeknownst to her daughter, willingly accepted. However, when the time of the departure arrived, the patient adamantly refused to go "without the permission of my daughter."

(ALTHAUSEN 1993)

CHAPTER 6

MENTAL HEALTH

"**M**IGRATION IS A CONDITION of risk for developing mental disorder. If one migrates as a refugee, the jeopardy to emotional well-being is even greater. . . . But risk is not destiny. The social and historical contingencies surrounding resettlement as well as personal strengths which individuals bring to the situation determine whether exposure to risk results in break-down or in personal fulfillment" (Beiser 1990, p. 52).

Refugees and immigrants are at risk of developing mental health problems due to the unique stressors experienced during the pre-migration and departure, transit, and resettlement stages of the migration process. This chapter will begin with a brief review of these stressors. It will then examine the role of cultural factors in mental health. Next, it will dicuss the common manifestations of mental health problems among refugee and immigrant populations and then address best practices in this area. Finally, some case study exercises will be presented for consideration of appropriate social work action.

This chapter focuses primarily on individuals, and primarily on adults. However, mental health is intricately intertwined with family dynamics, which is the subject of the next chapter. Issues unique to particular family members, such as children, women, and the elderly, are also addressed in the next chapter. The purpose of addressing individual mental health in this chapter is not to separate the individual from the family context, but rather to provide a full treatment of both topics. The close links between this chapter and the next should be kept in mind. Additionally, many of the issues discussed in the previous chapter on health are also directly applicable to mental health, and this should be kept in mind also.

6.1 MENTAL HEALTH AND MENTAL HEALTH CARE PROBLEMS

THE MAJOR ISSUES related to the mental health of refugees and immigrants are migration stressors, cultural factors, and the common manifestations of mental health problems among this population. Each of these issues is addressed below.

6.1.1 MIGRATION STRESSORS

AS DISCUSSED IN CHAPTER 1, each stage of the migration process entails unique stressors. The pre-migration and departure stage entails the loss of family members, friends, home, and the familiar environment. Additionally, for refugees, this stage often involves traumatic experiences such as war, famine, violence, rape, imprisonment, torture, witnessing violent death of family members, as well as discrimination, ostracization, and other forms of persecution within their homeland (Beiser 1990; Berry 1991; Drachman 1992; Gonsalves 1992; Nicholson, 1999). For refugees, departure is often unplanned, hasty, chaotic, and dangerous.

The transit stage is usually not overly stressful for legal immigrants, but is for refugees and illegal immigrants. Refugees frequently face dangerous conditions during transit such as being victims or witnesses of violence, or physical deprivation such as starvation, dehydration, hypothermia, sun exposure, or risk of death such as by drowning. Refugees may also spend lengthy periods in refugee camps that are often overcrowded with poor sanitary conditions, and where the refugees' future is uncertain (Beiser 1990; Berry 1991; Drachman, 1992). For illegal immigrants, as discussed in chapter 1, transit often entails dangerous border crossings by land or water, and exploitation or violence by smugglers.

The resettlement stage entails a host of new stressors as migrants attempt to come to terms with their losses and to adapt to life in the new country (Aroian 1990, 1993; Beiser 1990; Ben-Porath 1991; Berry 1991; Drachman 1992; Nicholson 1999; Rodriguez & DeWolfe, 1990). The losses that must be faced include the loss of family, friends, possessions, and familiar surroundings, as noted above, as well as loss of status in society. Loss of status refers to the fact that immigrants and refugees often have a lower social and occupational status in the new country than they did in the country of origin. The stresses of adaptation include language problems, employment problems, social isolation, stress of modernization and industrialization, stress related to legal status, family conflict, role changes, and discrimination, racism, and xenophobia from members of the host society.

Another adaptation stressor is acculturative stress. "The concept of acculturative stress refers to one kind of stress, that in which the stressors are identified as having their source in the process of acculturation, often resulting in a particular set of stress behaviors that include anxiety, depression, feelings of marginality and alienation, heightened psychosomatic symptoms, and identity confusion" (Williams and Berry 1991, p. 634). Acculturative stress is commonly known by the lay term of "culture shock." It arises from the societal disintegration due to migration, where "the old social order and cultural norms often disappear . . . [and] previous patterns of authority, civility, and welfare no longer operate" (Williams and Berry 1991, p. 634).

A number of theorists and researchers have divided the resettlement stage itself into distinct phases (Ben-Porath 1991; Beiser 1990; Gonsalves 1992). For example, early models suggested that resettlement is characterized by an initial stage of euphoria, followed by disillusionment, which is then followed by resolution (Tyhurst 1951). More recently, Gonsalves (1992) developed a five-stage model of refugee resettlement that identifies particular refugee tasks and mental health treatment issues relevant to each stage (table 6.1). Although developed specifically in relation to refugees, the model is also applicable to immigrants to a large extent.

A framework such as this is useful for understanding the issues that immigrants and refugees face at various times during the resettlement phase. However, it is important to realize that the time periods and experiences identified in this framework and others are neither rigid, nor applicable to all immigrants and refugees. For example, only a small proportion of refugees actually experience complete decompensation (Gonsalves 1992). Certainly, not all immigrants and refugees will follow the same time-related pattern of adaptation (Beiser 1990), and the process is not linear (Espin 1987). Further, although Gonsalves's model is limited to seven years after initial resettlement, research shows that migration stressors and their effects on mental health may persist for many decades (Nicholson 1999; Westermeyer 1987).

In terms of the relative importance of the pre-migration, transit, and resettlement stressors in their effects on mental health, research suggests that "although current [resettlement] stressors more strongly predict mental health outcome, past [pre-migration and transit] traumatic experiences are

TABLE 6.1 RESETTLEMENT STAGES, REFUGEE TASKS, AND TREATMENT ISSUES

STAGE	REFUGEE TASKS	TREATMENT ISSUES
Early arrival (1 week to 6 months)	Learn surroundings, remain involved with homeland, meet fellow refugees	Disorientation, sadness, anger, guilt
Destabilization (6 months to 3 years)	Acquire survival tools, learn the language, learn new customs and roles, develop support group	Hostility, resistance to new culture, denial
Experimentation and stabilization (3–5 years)	Develop flexible culture learning, continue role adjustment, remain linked to other refugees	Fear of failure, isolation, premature culture or identity foreclosure
Return to normal life (5–7 years)	Maintain flexible cultural accommodation, develop realistic expectations of new generations, develop a positive identity, expect lasting personality changes	Rigidity, intergenerational conflict
Decompensation (1 week to 7 years)	Meet survival needs; modify identity; reentry into new culture; continue commitments; connect past, present, and future	Psychosis, identity disorders, depression, continuity of family crisis

Source: Gonsalves, 1992. Copyright © 1992, American Psychological Association. Reprinted with permission.

primary determinants of how individuals deal with these current stressors and, therefore, how this affects mental health status" (Nicholson 1999, p. 649). Thus, the stressors in each stage of migration may be seen as having a cumulative effect upon mental health.

Not all immigrants and refugees develop mental health problems as a result of these migration stressors. Many other factors play a role. These include demographic "characteristics such as age, education, ethnicity, gender, rural or urban locality of origin, and marital status" (Nicholson 1999, p. 637). Past mental health history is another factor. "On general grounds one would expect that prior history of psychiatric illness, social maladjustment, or behavior difficulties would increase the likelihood of subsequent difficulties following migration" (Garcia-Peltoniemi 1991b, p. 39).

Conversely, immigrants' and refugees' personal resources, coping behaviors, and social resources can serve as protective factors against the development of mental health problems (Beiser 1990; Nicassio 1985; van der Veer 1998). Personal resources refer to personality characteristics that enable individuals to overcome obstacles, such as internal locus of control, personal mastery and self-esteem, hardiness, and learned resourcefulness. Coping responses refer to cognitive, affective, and behavioral processes that individuals use in coping with stressors. Finally, social resources refer to characteristics of the social environment that provide help to individuals in times of crisis, such as social support, the social network, and social service programs (Nicassio 1985). These conceptions of personal resources, coping processes, and social resources are consistent with recent theoretical frameworks of mental health that stress the importance of protective factors and resiliency. Although these concepts have been identified as promising for research on refugee and immigrant mental health (Ahearn 2000; van der Veer 1998), much of the research in this area continues to be based on a "pathology" perspective rather than a "strengths" perspective (Witmer and Culver, in press).

6.1.2 CULTURAL FACTORS AND MENTAL HEALTH

IN ADDITION TO THE STRESSES OF MIGRATION, the mental health of immigrants and refugees, and its assessment and treatment, are influenced by cultural factors. Culture impacts the following areas: conceptualizations of mental health; diagnosis and symptom expression; communication styles; and service utilization. Each of these is addressed below.

CONCEPTUALIZATIONS OF MENTAL HEALTH Cultural beliefs influence how people conceptualize what is normal and abnormal behavior, the etiology and symptomatology of mental health problems, what is considered appropriate treatment, help-seeking behavior, and responses to mental health services (Butcher 1991; Gaines 1998; Lin 1991; Surgeon General 2000). For example, loud, boisterous behavior may be considered normal in U.S. mainstream society, but may be considered cause for concern in cultures where reticence and restraint of emotional expression are the norm. Conversely, individuals from such cultures might be viewed as abnormally shy or unsociable in the U.S. mainstream culture.

In regard to etiology and symptomatology, as discussed in the preceding chapter on health, many cultures do not distinguish between physical health and mental health. Consequently, the very idea of mental health problems is foreign to many immigrants and refugees. Thus, symptoms are often expressed in other ways, such as somatic complaints, or expressed problems in areas such as language difficulties or employment difficulties (Butcher 1991). The concept that psychological difficulties such as depression or anxiety may underlie or accompany these expressed complaints or difficulties is not within many cultural belief systems. Also, as described in the previous chapter, in many cultures health problems are commonly attributed to spiritual, supernatural, or magical forces. Accordingly, appropriate treatment would be viewed as being provided by spiritual healers or medical doctors, rather than by mental health professionals. "The idea that a troubled person might receive help by talking over problems with a stranger is an alien idea to many refugees [and immigrants]" (Butcher 1991, p. 114). Thus, immigrants and refugees may not be responsive to mainstream mental health services and are likely to discontinue such treatment.

DIAGNOSIS AND SYMPTOM EXPRESSION Symptoms and signs are unique expressions or indicators of underlying health or mental health problems. Symptoms are subjective experiences reported by an individual, such as worry. Signs are behaviors or physical indicators that can be observed by others, such as agitated behavior or high blood pressure. On the other hand, diagnoses are medical constructions of the underlying problems based on the presentations and patterns of symptoms and signs. In regard to symptoms, signs, and diagnoses in mental health, it is important to distinguish between the concepts of *universality* and *cultural relativity* (Lin 1991). In general, symptoms and signs are universal across cultures, meaning people from all cultures sometimes experience certain symptoms and signs. For example, "patients everywhere complain of insomnia, worry, crying spells, anorexia, weakness, anergy, anhedonia, suicidal ideation, and ego-dystonic hallucinations and delusions; and their families and communities report social withdrawal, inappropriate or purposeless behavior, incomprehensible speech, damage to property, and assaultiveness" (Westermeyer 1991b, p. 60).

On the other hand, in general, diagnoses are culturally relative, or what is also referred to as *culture-bound*, meaning that they are recurrent patterns of behavior and experience that are specific to certain cultures (American Psychiatric Association 1994). Although the term *culture-bound syndrome* is most frequently applied to folk illnesses outside of mainstream American culture, it is important to realize that the diagnostic categories developed by the American Psychiatric Association (APA) in its *Diagnostic and Statistical Manual of Mental Disorders (DSM-IV)* (APA, 1994) are also culture-bound (Gaines 1998). That is, these diagnostic categories have been developed in a certain place and time. Consequently, "seemingly universal psychiatric disorders found commonly in the West such as schizophrenia, depression, but also anorexia and Posttraumatic Stress Disorder are absent from other cultures. . . . Indeed, there are dramatic differences even among Western nations' nosologies and we find that disorders present in one nosology may be absent in others. . . . As paradigms shift, diseases appear, disappear, and sometimes, reappear in the standard nosologies" (Gaines 1998, p. 410). This does not mean that people from non-American cultures do not suffer *symptoms* commonly associated with schizophrenia, depression, etc., but that the presentations and patterns of those symptoms do not necessarily correspond to the American psychiatric diagnostic categories.

Thus, most cultures have culture-bound syndromes or *idioms of distress*, which refers to characteristic modes of expressing suffering:

> Idioms of distress often reflect values and themes found in the societies in which they originate. One of the most common idioms of distress is somatization, the expression of mental distress in terms of physical suffering. Somatization occurs widely and is believed to be especially prevalent among persons from a number of ethnic minority backgrounds. . . . A number of idioms of distress are well recognized as culture-bound syndromes. . . . Among culture-bound syndromes found among some Latino psychiatric patients is *ataque de nervios*, a syndrome of uncontrollable shouting, crying, trembling, and aggression typically triggered by a stressful event involving family. . . . A Japanese culture-bound syndrome . . . *taijin kyofusho*, is an intense fear that one's body or bodily functions give offense to others. Culture-bound syndromes sometimes reflect comprehensive systems of belief, typically emphasizing a need for a balance between opposing forces (e.g., ying/yang, "hot-cold" theory) or the power of supernatural forces.
>
> (SURGEON GENERAL 2000, P. 6)

A number of these culture-bound syndromes, or folk illnesses, were listed in table 5.2; others are listed in the *DSM-IV*. The main point regarding symptoms, signs, diagnoses, and culture-bound syndromes is that practitioners must keep both concepts of universality and cultural relativity in mind when conducting assessments in order to avoid misdiagnosis:

> Overinterpretation of symptoms leading to "overdiagnosis" is a frequently encountered problem in cross-cultural psychiatric evaluation. Close adherence to the tenet of "cultural relativity," together with efforts in obtaining relevant information regarding the meaning and consequence of the "symptoms" in the patient's cultural context, is essential in correcting this kind of mistake. On the other hand, an excessive preoccupation with cultural influences in psychiatric symptom presentation will tend to lead to underestimation of psychopathology, which can also result in therapeutic failures. Adequate attention to the universal aspect of psychopathology is essential in counterbalancing such a tendency. (LIN 1991, PP. 124–125)

These issues will be addressed in more detail in a subsequent section of this chapter on assessment.

COMMUNICATION STYLES In general, the communication style that is favored in mainstream American society consists of elements such as assertiveness, forthrightness, and open expression of emotions. In contrast, the communication styles of many other cultures do not include these elements. For example, many Asian persons may avoid expressing their emotions, and mask personal suffering with politeness and smiles; and people from Middle Eastern countries may talk about trivial matters first before broaching a distressing subject (van der Veer 1998). In general, people from many different cultures do not readily communicate their feelings and personal matters with non-family members. These differences in communication styles can lead to misunderstandings, misdiagnoses, and ineffectiveness in service provision.

SERVICE UTILIZATION As is the case with physical health services, refugees and immigrants in general underutilize, delay utilization, and prematurely terminate utilization of mental health services (Surgeon General 2000; Western Interstate Coalition on Mental Health [WICHE] 1998). All of the reasons for this that were extensively discussed in the preceding chapter apply here as well. These include the various structural, financial, personal, and cultural barriers to service access.

Underutilization of mental health services is probably even greater than underutilization of physical health services, due to the lack of familiarity with the concepts of mental health and mental health treatment within many cultures, as well as the fact that many cultures stigmatize mental problems, thereby discouraging help-seeking (Jaranson 1990; Surgeon General 2000). For example, among Asian populations in the U.S., "studies have linked [mental health service] underuse to the shame, stigma, and other cultural factors that influence symptom expression and conceptions of illness, as well as to limited knowledge about the availability of local mental health services, and a tendency to seek more culturally congruent care. The latter may include herbalists, accupuncturists, and other forms of indigenous healing. . . . Latinos often perceive historic U.S. mental health models as unnecessary, unwelcoming, or not useful" (WICHE, 1998, pp. 6–7).

Additionally, for some refugees, the concept of mental illness has political connotations. For example, in Communist regimes, which many refugees come from, mental illness was cast as a problem of capitalist societies that had been solved by Communism; and further, psychiatric and psychological "helping" were used as a tool to "reform" political dissidents, rather than to treat true mental health problems (Brodsky 1988). Consequently, refugees from such regimes may not have an understanding of mental health as such, nor do they trust mental health service providers.

6.1.3 MANIFESTATIONS OF MENTAL HEALTH PROBLEMS

DUE IN PART to the cultural factors discussed above, it is difficult to estimate accurately the incidence and prevalence of mental health problems among immigrant and refugee populations. In addition, there is no systematic epidemiological data collection specifically for foreign-born persons. Therefore, the available data are limited to local studies of particular immigrant or refugee groups. This results in yet another difficulty: the problem of nonrandom sampling. Most studies of incidence and prevalence rates of mental health problems among immigrants and refugees are based on clinical populations, i.e., people who are in treatment of some type (Nicholson 1999; WICHE 1998). This possibly results in overestimates of incidence and prevalence. On the other hand, since immigrants and refugees underutilize mental health care systems, it is also possible that studies based on clinical samples underestimate true incidence and prevalence rates (WICHE 1998).

Few studies have assessed incidence and prevalence rates in nonclinical populations, and these studies also suffer from methodological problems. Further, reported rates are influenced by other factors such as "the circumstances under which the migration took place, the immigration and emigration policies of the time, the presence of coexisting disorders such as alcoholism which may mask other diagnostic entities, the diagnostic biases of clinicians, and the availability of treatment for a particular condition" (Garcia-Peltoniemi 1991b, p. 25).

Despite these difficulties in arriving at accurate estimates of rates of mental health problems among immigrant and refugee populations, the accumulation of data from many studies over time does indicate that in general, refugees and immigrants have higher rates of mental health problems compared to the native-born population. "It appears that the relationship between migration and psychopathology is both real and stable" (Garcia-Peltoniemi 1991b, p. 24). The most commonly observed mental health problems of immigrants, and particularly refugees, include grief, alienation and loneliness, decreased self-esteem, depression, anxiety, somatization, paranoia, guilt, post-traumatic stress disorder, and substance abuse (Arredondo-Dowd 1981; Espin 1987; Garcia-Peltoniemi 1991a; Rebhun 1998). Each of these is discussed below. Intervention approaches for each of these problems are addressed in a subsequent section.

It should be noted from this list of mental health problems that not all of them are diagnosable psychiatric disorders. For example, loneliness is not a psychiatric disorder, but is certainly a painful emotional problem. Further, as discussed above, symptom expressions may not match the American psychiatric diagnostic categories. Thus, for example, an immigrant or refugee with depression may not meet the DSM-IV diagnostic criteria, but clearly this does not mean that the person is not suffering from depressive symptoms. Therefore, the following discussion makes no reference to diagnostic criteria, but instead focuses on the general features and manifestations of these mental health problems among immigrants and refugees.

GRIEF Grief is a common reaction among immigrants and refugees in response to the multiple losses they have experienced. This is true even for those who migrated voluntarily. Despite their motivations for coming to the new country in order to have a better life, the stresses of resettlement lead to feelings of grief for what was left behind. Arredondo-Dowd (1981) has applied a three-phase model of grief to immigrants and refugees, which she describes as follows (p. 377):

> In the first phase of the grieving process, persons experience numbness, shock, and disbelief. The immigrants cannot comprehend that they actually left, that they are no longer going to see familiar faces and sites. This sense of estrangement is heightened by the foreignness of the new environment. The move has caused them to assume a minority status in a majority culture. They feel out of place and overwhelmed. . . . The enthusiasm with which they came has slowly been tempered by hardships and disappointments. . . . These reactions may then develop into feelings of pain, despair, and disorganization, which are symptomatic of phase two. Homesickness sets in as persons experience their emotional losses. More and more, references to the homeland are filled with sentiments of idealization and longing. . . . Defense mechanisms such as displacement, projection, and reaction formation may be used more frequently as stress mounts. Anger over feeling confused, upset, and lonely may be directed toward another family member or internalized. . . . In phase three, feelings are more hopeful and positive. There is a resolution to reorganize one's life, to start anew and to build new relationships. New successes such as employment, friends, and the new home and car may be the stimuli. There is an acceptance of the new life and a greater sense of identification with [the new country]. . . . In essence, the immigrant ceases to grieve over her or his losses, so it seems. . . . It is unclear . . . how long the grieving process will take and whether, in fact, it ever completely ceases. There is empirical evidence that suggests that sadness and other feelings around loss of homeland may recur many years after the departure. Not being there when a loved one dies and never reestablishing contact with siblings who moved to other parts of the world or were left behind are hidden pains an immigrant may live and die with.

THUS, SOCIAL WORKERS NEED to be alert to the possibility of grief arising at any time in the resettlement phase, and also to the possibility that some overt reactions such as anger may have their roots in grief.

ALIENATION AND LONELINESS Refugees and immigrants have left behind all or part of their natural support system, i.e., family members and friends. Even when family members migrate together, the family system as a whole is stressed by the migration process and the members are not likely to be able to provide each other with support in the same way they did prior to migration. This is further compounded by the fact that the immigrants and refugees are now in a land of strangers, who may be hostile toward them. Even in the absence of hostility, language and cultural differences are significant barriers to establishing new friendships. More subtle barriers may exist as well:

> For example, in tropical countries people spend much of their time outdoors. The chances of being involuntarily alone are therefore limited. In . . . Europe and North America things are different, and a refugee [or immigrant] who comes from a tropical country has to acquire a new set of social skills in order to find company, and learn to deal with being alone more often than he [or she] was used to. (VAN DER VEER 1998, P. 19)

Even when immigrants and refugees live or work in a community with others from the same country, social support does not necessarily follow. Sometimes the only commonality that individuals may have with each other is the fact of their migration. They may have personality differences, socioeconomic background differences, and political differences that would have prevented them from being friends, even in the country of origin. Further, individuals' differing reactions to the process of adaptation in resettlement can form barriers to friendship. For example, an individual who is highly adaptable and copes well with change and loss may have difficulty empathizing with one who experiences substantial distress in the adaptation process, and may in fact blame that person for not coping better.

Additionally, many immigrants and refugees come from cultures in which friendship formation is a lifelong process that often begins in childhood. New relationships in adulthood are characterized by formal interaction, and intimate sharing of feelings or family issues is not considered appropriate until a lengthy relationship has been established, perhaps extending over many years. All of these factors contribute to an increased likelihood of alienation and loneliness.

DECREASED SELF-ESTEEM Immigrants and refugees are at risk of decreased self-esteem for several reasons. One is downward occupational mobility. Many immigrants, and particularly refugees, must take jobs that are of lower occupational status than they had in their country of origin. For example, highly educated individuals who may have been physicians or engineers may be able only to obtain jobs as manual laborers. The major reason for this is language difficulty; other reasons include barriers to obtaining professional licensure, lack of familiarity with competitive capitalistic practices, and employer biases against hiring foreigners (Ben-Porath 1991). The lowered occupational status frequently leads to lowered self-esteem.

A second reason for lowered self-esteem is changing gender and generation roles. Most immigrant and refugee cultures are male-dominated; however, upon migration, women adopt egalitarian perspectives more quickly than men do (Ben-Porath 1991; Espin 1987). Women may also obtain jobs more quickly, may be working outside the home for the first time, and may be the sole financial providers for the family (Ben-Porath 1991). Thus, in many cases, men lose their traditionally dominant position, leading to lowered self-esteem. Additionally, children assimilate into the mainstream culture and acquire language skills more quickly than their parents. Thus, children often become translators and culture brokers for their parents; this is a role reversal that leads to lowered self-esteem of the parents (Ben-Porath 1991).

A third reason for lowered self-esteem is that, due to their unfamiliarity with cultural norms, immigrants and refugees may experience embarrassment or feelings of being ridiculed (Westermeyer 1991b). A final reason is the acquisition of minority status within society. Persons who were not minorities in their country of origin become minorities by definition upon migration, and this is even more so for "visible" minorities who have darker skin color (Espin 1987). Because minority status and the discrimination that accompanies it are new experiences for many immigrants and refugees, lowered self-esteem often results.

DEPRESSION Depression has been extensively documented among refugee and immigrant populations (Garcia-Peltoniemi 1991a; Vega et al. 1986). It is the most frequent mental health problem leading to psychiatric treatment among many different refugee groups (Garcia-Peltoniemi 1991a). All of the risk factors and emotional reactions identified above, including grief, loneliness, and decreased self-esteem, are associated with depression. Depression among immigrants and refugees may manifest itself in a large variety of symptoms. Frequently, somatic symptoms rather than emotional or psychological complaints are presented (Garcia-Peltoniemi 1991a). Consequently, medical personnel are often the first source of professional treatment (Vega et al. 1986), and therefore they need to be alert to the possibility of depression underlying the somatic problems. Depression in turn may lead to further adaptation problems. Additionally, it is of substantial concern due to its strong association with suicide and suicide attempts (Garcia-Peltoniemi 1991a).

ANXIETY Symptoms of anxiety are frequent in refugee populations (Garcia-Peltoniemi 1991a; Nicholson 1999). Traumatized refugees sometimes develop panic attacks or phobias to stimuli that remind them of the traumatic experience, such as people in uniform (Garcia-Peltoniemi 1991a). Among illegal immigrants, anxiety about being apprehended and deported is quite common (Aroian 1993). As with depression, symptoms of anxiety may often appear in somatic forms.

SOMATIZATION As described above and in the preceding chapter, psychological symptoms are often expressed as somatic complaints among refugees and immigrants. As discussed in the previous chapter, reasons for this include cultural norms that discourage expression of feelings; health beliefs that do not distinguish between mind and body; unfamiliarity with Western concepts of mental health and mental health care; and language barriers which inhibit the expression of feelings (Garcia-Peltoniemi 1991a). Additional explanations are the shame and stigma associated with mental problems, and, in some cases as noted above, the political connotations associated with mental health and mental health providers. In all these cases, psychological problems are more likely to be expressed in somatic form.

Somatic symptoms appear in many forms that are widely distributed anatomically, may have a multisystemic physiological effect, and can lead to severe impairment (Westermeyer 1991b). Common somatic symptoms are arthritis, gastrointestinal problems, headaches, allergies, respiratory disorders, and sexual dysfunctions (Barudy 1989; Garcia-Peltoniemi 1991a). Somatic symptoms usually resolve as clients begin to respond to mental health treatment (Garcia-Peltoniemi 1991a).

PARANOIA Refugees, who have been subject to various forms of persecution in their homelands, are vulnerable to developing symptoms of paranoia in relation to social systems, institutions, or authority figures (Garcia-Peltoniemi 1991a; Westermeyer 1991b). The stresses in the resettlement stage, particularly hostile actions by members of the host society, also increase the vulnerability to paranoia for both refugees and immigrants (Westermeyer 1991b). Additionally, due to the numerous resettlement stressors such as social isolation, and associated factors such decreased self-esteem, "pathological jealousy and delusions about spouse infidelity are common and can lead to physical abuse and family violence" (Garcia-Peltoniemi 1991a, p. 51).

Paranoid reactions may range from transient feelings to psychotic delusions. There is a danger of misdiagnosing paranoid symptoms as schizophrenia among refugees (Garcia-Peltoniemi 1991a). Therefore, the origins of the paranoid thoughts need to be carefully explored, as they often have a well-founded basis in reality. In fact, a certain level of mistrust can serve as a positive adaptive function for newcomers; it is only when paranoia is severe and prolonged that it becomes problematic (Westermeyer 1991b).

GUILT Refugees and immigrants are at high risk for feelings of guilt for several reasons. Refugees who have come from situations of war or violence may suffer from survivor guilt. This means that they repeatedly ask themselves the unanswerable question of why they survived when so many others did not (Baker 1992). They feel guilty about their survival, and ruminate about what they did to maintain their survival and what they did or did not do to help those who did not survive (Miller 1992). Refugees who have been tortured may experience guilt about information or names they were forced to divulge under torture, violent acts they were forced to carry out by their torturers or in order to escape, or having been forced to sign papers stating they were well-treated (van der Veer 1998; Vesti and Kastrup 1995). War combatants or torture victims may also feel guilty about what they did to the enemy, or about pleasant excitement they may have had while committing violence themselves or even, occasionally, while being violated (van der Veer 1998).

In addition to these traumatic sources of guilt in the pre-migration and departure stage, the resettlement stage may also engender guilt. Both refugees and immigrants are likely to feel guilty about having left family members behind. This may be compounded by the reactions of those left behind:

At least part of the difficulties stem from misapprehensions on the part of those who stayed behind who think that their newly Americanized relatives, having reached "the promised land," should be doing more to help them. They are frequently unaware of the difficulties encountered by refugee [or immigrant] relatives and make unrealistic demands for economic support. Thus, while having to deal with the harsh realities of becoming and being a refugee [or immigrant], some are riddled with guilt and frustration over the possibility that they are not doing enough for those who stayed behind. These feelings may then be reinforced by harsh and demanding letters from home. (BEN-PORATH 1991, P. 12)

POST-TRAUMATIC STRESS DISORDER The multiple pre-migration, departure, and transit traumas experienced by refugees in particular place them at risk of developing symptoms of post-traumatic stress disorder (PTSD). "Both the disorder and, perhaps to an even greater extent, the isolated symptoms ... of this condition, are very prevalent among refugees" (Garcia-Peltoniemi 1991a, p. 50). "The symptoms include re-experiencing of a traumatic event, for example through recollections, dreams, and acting or feeling as if the event were recurring, in combination with persistent avoiding of stimuli associated with the trauma and symptoms of increased arousal such as difficulty in falling asleep, concentration problems, or outbursts of aggression" (van der Veer 1998, p. 28). The symptoms of PTSD may appear soon after the traumatic experience, or they may be delayed for substantial periods of time (McNally 1992; van der Veer 1998). The PTSD problems may persist for decades, and may even be transmitted multigenerationally to the trauma survivor's children (Mollica 2000). Additionally, PTSD in refugees is very commonly accompanied by depression (Baker 1992; Garcia-Peltoniemi 1991a; van der Veer 1998).

SUBSTANCE ABUSE Substance abuse among refugees and immigrants varies widely by country of origin, gender, age, socioeconomic status, and many other factors. In general, however, immigrants and refugees are considered to be at risk for substance abuse for at least two reasons: the process of assimilation, which includes the adoption of the substance use norms of the new country; and the stresses of the migration process, which may lead people to use substances for relief of symptoms. Research shows that in general, substance use increases with increased assimilation, and is also higher among subsequent generations of immigrants and refugees than among the first generation. Research also suggests that patterns of and reasons for involvement in substance abuse are different for immigrants and refugees than for the native-born, nonminority population. These differences are related to cultural influences, family structures, social networks, and economic situations, among other factors. Immigrant and refugee youth are considered to be at particularly high risk for substance abuse. Substance abuse prevention and treatment with immigrants and refugees needs to consider the cultural norms related to substance use, as well as the unique stressors faced by these populations. Additionally, the high likelihood of comorbidity (i.e., substance abuse co-existing with another mental health problem) among these populations needs to be considered (Garcia-Peltoniemi 1991a; Rebhun 1998).

6.1.4 SUMMARY OF MENTAL HEALTH PROBLEMS

THE ABOVE EXTENSIVE LISTING AND DESCRIPTION of potential mental health problems among immigrants and refugees has the danger of giving the erroneous impression that all members of these populations suffer from such problems. It is critical to remember that in reality most immigrants and refugees do not develop significant mental health problems. Although all immigrants and refugees experience the various migration stressors, in most cases significant mental health problems are prevented by the personal and social protective factors described above. Nonetheless, the high risk remains. Given this, prevention and intervention efforts are warranted. "Decades of research have increased our understanding of the forces which can help prevent emotional disorder among new settlers and the factors which promote healthy adaptation. It is both moral and expedient to put this knowledge to work in resettling refugees [and immigrants]" (Beiser 1990, p. 63). The remaining sections of this chapter will address this knowledge related to assessment, prevention, and intervention.

6.2 BEST PRACTICES

SOCIAL WORK PRACTICE in mental health care for immigrants and refugees should fundamentally be based upon a set of best practice principles that are shown in table 6.2.

TABLE 6.2 BEST PRACTICE PRINCIPLES OF MENTAL HEALTH CARE FOR IMMIGRANTS AND REFUGEES

PRINCIPLE OF CULTURAL COMPETENCE

Cultural competence includes attaining the knowledge, skills, and attitudes to enable administrators and practitioners within systems of care to provide effective care for diverse populations, i.e., to work within the person's values and reality conditions. Recovery and rehabilitation are more likely to occur where service delivery systems, services, and providers have and utilize knowledge and skills that are culturally competent and compatible with the backgrounds of consumers from diverse ethnic groups, their families, and communities. Cultural competence acknowledges and incorporates variance in normative acceptable behaviors, beliefs, and values in determining an individual's mental wellness/illness, and incorporating those variables into assessment and treatment.

PRINCIPLE OF CONSUMER-DRIVEN SYSTEM OF CARE

A consumer-driven system of care promotes consumer and family as the most important participants in the service-providing process. Whenever possible and appropriate, the services adapt self-help concepts from the ethnic culture, taking into account the significant role that families play in the lives of many immigrants and refugees.

PRINCIPLE OF COMMUNITY-BASED SYSTEM OF CARE

A community-based system of care includes a full continuum of care. The focus is on including familiar and valued community resources from the ethnic culture; investing in early intervention and preventive efforts; and treating the consumer in the least restrictive environment possible.

PRINCIPLE OF MANAGED CARE

The costs of a mental health care delivery system are best contained through the delivery of effective, quality services, not by cutting or limiting services. Effective systems provide individualized and tailor-made services that emphasize outcome-driven systems and positive results. Such systems acknowledge the added value of including immigrants and refugees as treatment partners. The system includes an emphasis on managing care, not dollars. It recognizes that dollars will manage themselves if overall care is well managed. It recognizes ethnic group-specific variables that have significant implications for individualized treatment and assessment.

TABLE 6.2 *(continued)*

PRINCIPLE OF NATURAL SUPPORT

Natural community support and culturally competent practices are viewed as an integral part of a system of care that contributes to desired outcomes. Traditional healing practices are used when relevant or possible, and family is defined by function rather than by bloodlines, as immigrants and refugees generally conceive of family much more broadly than mainstream individuals.

PRINCIPLE OF COLLABORATION AND EMPOWERMENT

Immigrants and refugees and their families have the capacity to collaborate with mental health systems and providers in determining the course of treatment. The greater the extent of this collaboration, the better the chances that recovery and long-term functioning will occur and be sustained. Empowerment of consumers and families enhances their self-esteem and ability to manage their own health.

PRINCIPLE OF HOLISM

Immigrants and refugees are more likely to respond to service delivery systems, organizations, and providers who recognize the value of holistic approaches to health care and implement these in their clinical work, policies, and standards.

PRINCIPLE OF FEEDBACK

Service delivery systems, organizations, and providers shall improve the quality of their services and enhance desired outcomes of their service delivery to immigrants and refugees through legitimate opportunities for feedback and exchange. Where such opportunities for feedback are absent, there is a greater likelihood that the system of services and policies will not be congruent with the needs of immigrants and refugees and will not result in high levels of consumer satisfaction. Service delivery systems that lack opportunities for this feedback limit their chances of making culturally specific corrections in their approaches to services while simultaneously increasing their risks.

PRINCIPLE OF ACCESS

In order for immigrants and refugees to seek, utilize, and gain from mental health care, service, facilities, and providers shall be accessible. Where services and facilities are geographically, psychologically, and culturally accessible, the chances are increased that immigrants and refugees will respond positively to treatment. Inadequate access to services will result in increased costs, limited benefit to the consumer, and a greater probability that services will not result in the outcomes desired.

TABLE 6.2 *(continued)*

PRINCIPLE OF UNIVERSAL COVERAGE

Where health care coverage, benefits, and access are based on employment or ability to pay, immigrants and refugees are more likely to be underserved. The greater the extent to which health care is universally available without regard to income, the greater the likelihood that the health status of immigrants and refugees will be enhanced.

PRINCIPLE OF INTEGRATION

Immigrants and refugees have higher than expected rates of physical health problems. Integrating primary care medicine, mental health, and substance abuse services in a service delivery system increases the potential that immigrants and refugees will receive comprehensive treatment services and recover more rapidly, with fewer disruptions due to a fragmented system of care.

PRINCIPLE OF QUALITY

The more emphasis that is placed on ensuring continuous quality culturally competent service to immigrants and refugees, the greater the likelihood that relapse will be prevented, with sickness treated appropriately and costs lowered.

PRINCIPLE OF DATA DRIVEN SYSTEMS

The quality of decisionmaking, service design, and clinical intervention for immigrants and refugees in mental health care is increased where data on prevalence, incidence, service utilization, and treatment outcomes are used to inform and guide decisions.

PRINCIPLE OF OUTCOMES

Immigrants and refugees and their families evaluate services on the basis of actual outcomes relative to the problems that stimulated help seeking. The greater the extent to which mental health care systems, organizations, and providers emphasize and measure these outcomes in comparison to the expectations of immigrant and refugees consumers, the higher the degree of consumer satisfaction.

TABLE 6.2 *(continued)*

PRINCIPLE OF PREVENTION

States, mental health care organizations, and provider organizations should provide community education programs about mental illness and the risk factors associated with specific disorders. The goal should be to increase the capacity of families to provide a healthy environment and to identify the early warning signs when mental health problems do exist. Early problem identification and intervention can prevent the exacerbation and reduce the disabling effects of mental illness.

Source: Adapted from Western Interstate Commission for Higher Education, 1998.

It will be noted that these guiding principles echo to a large extent the various practice recommendations in chapter 4 on culturally competent practice and chapter 5 on social work practice in health care. Accordingly, all of the recommendations made in those chapters apply as well to the current topic of mental health practice. Additionally, mental health requires specialized practice approaches at the micro level. Therefore, the bulk of this section on social work practice in mental health will be devoted to these micro level approaches. First, however, macro and meso level practice will be briefly addressed.

6.2.1 MACRO PRACTICE

THE MACRO PRACTICE APPROACHES—community needs assessment, policy and program advocacy, community consultation and policy and program planning, and community health education—that were discussed in the preceding chapter on health are directly relevant and applicable to mental health as well. As with physical health, these approaches are aimed at increasing immigrants' and refugees' access to mental health services and preventing mental health problems through community education.

In regard to the latter goal, there is less empirical knowledge thus far about prevention of mental health problems than prevention of health problems, particularly in regard to community-based prevention (Hirayama, Hirayama, and Cetingok 1993; Surgeon General 2000; Williams and Berry 1991). Nonetheless, some empirically derived recommendations can be made. Prevention models "use risk status to identify populations for intervention, and then . . . target risk factors that are thought to be causal and malleable and target protective factors that are to be enhanced" (Surgeon General 2000, p. 4). In the case of immigrants and refugees, the risk factors for mental health problems are well established empirically, as documented above. Consequently, macro interventions should be targeted at reducing those risk factors during each stage of the migration process. For example, to reduce the risk of mental health problems among refugees in the premigration and departure stage, social workers should engage in advocacy and activism at the international level to pressure governments to respect human rights (Barclay 1998). In the transit stage, for example, various services should be provided in refugee camps both to improve living conditions in the camps and to prepare refugees for the stressors of the resettlement stage (Williams and Berry 1991).

However, not all of the stressors during each migration stage are equally malleable. Most social workers will encounter refugees and immigrants during the resettlement stage, when the stressors of the earlier stages have already occurred and therefore can no longer be changed. In that case, the logical preventive strategy is to change the risks that are most easily and quickly amenable to intervention (Surgeon General 2000). For example, the following recommendations have been made for macro-level prevention of mental health problems among immigrants and refugees during the resettlement stage:

- Broadening the definition of "family" for purposes of admission in order to increase the available social support system
- Improving core or basic funding for ethnocultural settlement service agencies
- Developing school curricula that promote multicultural and multiracial understanding and tolerance
- Public education to increase the knowledge and acceptance of the benefits of pluralism to a society, and of the contribution of newcomers to the cultural and economic life of the country
- Increasing public awareness of the possible difficulties faced by newcomers, and the effects of prejudice on both victim and perpetrator

- Improving access to language courses and to trades and professions for those educated outside the resettlement country
- Establishing research and teaching centers dealing with immigrant and refugee mental health
- Creating a national information center to collect, coordinate, and disseminate information about research, evaluation, and application in the area of immigrant and refugee mental health. (WILLIAMS AND BERRY 1991, P. 637)

THESE GOALS SHOULD BE PURSUED using the various macro practice strategies previously discussed.

6.2.2 MESO PRACTICE

AS WITH MACRO PRACTICE, the meso practice strategies discussed in the previous chapter on health are also directly relevant and applicable to mental health. As previously described, these strategies of interdisciplinary collaboration and organizational development are aimed at enhancing agencies' effectiveness in serving refugees and immigrants. The Western Interstate Commission on Higher Education (WICHE 1998) has developed a set of system/organizational best practice standards for culturally competent mental health services. These are listed in Table 6.3, with the language modified slightly to refer specifically to immigrants and refugees.

TABLE 6.3 OVERALL SYSTEM BEST PRACTICE STANDARDS FOR MENTAL HEALTH CARE FOR IMMIGRANTS AND REFUGEES

CULTURAL COMPETENCE PLANNING

A Cultural Competence Plan for both public and private sectors shall be developed and integrated within the overall mental health system and/or provider network, using an incremental strategic approach for its achievement, to assure attainment of cultural competence within manageable but concrete timelines.

TABLE 6.3 *(continued)*

GOVERNANCE

Each mental health organization's governing entity shall incorporate a board, advisory committee, or policy-making and policy-influencing group which shall be proportionally representative of the consumer populations to be served and the community at large, including age and ethnicity. In this manner, the community served will guide policy formulation and decision making, including Request for Proposals development and vendor selection. The governing entity shall be accountable for the successful implementation of cultural competence standards.

BENEFIT DESIGN

Mental health systems and organizations shall ensure equitable access and comparability of benefits across population and age groups. Coverage shall provide for access to a full continuum of care (including prevention programs) from most to least restrictive in ways which are comparable, though not identical, acknowledging that culturally competent practice provides for variance in individualized care.

PREVENTION, EDUCATION, AND OUTREACH

Each mental health system shall have a prevention, education, and outreach program which is an integral part of the system's operations and which is guided in its development and implementation by consumers, families, and community-based organizations.

QUALITY MONITORING AND IMPROVEMENT

Mental health systems and organizations shall have a regular quality and improvement program that ensures (1) access to a full array of culturally competent treatment modalities, (2) comparability of benefits, and (3) comparable successful outcomes for all service recipients.

DECISION SUPPORT AND MANAGEMENT INFORMATION SYSTEMS

Mental health systems and organizations shall develop and maintain a database which will track utilization and outcomes for immigrants and refugees across all levels of care, ensuring comparability of benefits, access, and outcomes. Mental health systems and organizations shall also develop and manage databases of social and mental health indicators on the covered population of immigrants and refugees and the community at large.

TABLE 6.3 *(continued)*

HUMAN RESOURCE DEVELOPMENT

Staff training and development in the areas of cultural competence and immigrant and refugee mental health shall be implemented at all levels and across disciplines, for leadership and governing entities, as well as for management and support staff. The strengths brought by cultural competence form the foundation for system performance rather than detract or formulate separate agendas.

Source: Adapted from Western Interstate Commission on Higher Education, 1998.

Again, it will be noted that these recommendations echo much of what has been discussed in preceding chapters. Further, the emphasis within these standards on outcomes-based evaluation is also notable, and the importance of this has also been emphasized in preceding chapters. The original document containing these standards provides very extensive and detailed guidelines for implementing the standards, recommended performance indicators, and recommended outcomes, including measurable benchmarks (i.e., criteria for successful organizational performance). It is highly recommended that this document, which is available on the World Wide Web, be consulted for the development of effective, culturally competent agencies and systems providing mental health services to refugees and immigrants.

6.2.3 MICRO PRACTICE

MICRO PRACTICE IN MENTAL HEALTH entails the provision of direct clinical services. A set of clinical best practice standards for culturally competent mental health services has also been developed by WICHE (1998), and is shown in table 6.4, again with slight adaptations in wording. The recurrence of earlier themes will again be noted. As with the overall system standards discussed above, the original document contains extensive and detailed implementation guidelines, recommended performance standards, and recommended outcomes with measurable benchmarks for success. Again it is highly recommended that the full document be consulted for the development of effective, culturally competent clinical services.

TABLE 6.4 CLINICAL BEST PRACTICE STANDARDS FOR MENTAL HEALTH CARE FOR IMMIGRANTS AND REFUGEES

ACCESS AND SERVICE AUTHORIZATION

Services shall be provided irrespective of immigration status, insurance coverage, and language. Access to services shall be individually- and family-oriented (including client-defined family) in the context of cultural values. Access criteria for different levels of care shall include health, behavior, and functioning in addition to diagnosis. Criteria shall be multidimensional in six domains: psychiatric, medical, spiritual, social functioning, behavior, and community support.

TRIAGE AND ASSESSMENT

Assessment shall be multidimensional including individual, family, and community strengths, functional, psychiatric, medical, and social status, as well as family support.

CARE PLANNING

Care plans for immigrants and refugees shall be compatible with the cultural framework and community environment of consumers and family members. When appropriate, care plans shall involve culturally indicated family leaders and decisionmakers.

PLAN OF TREATMENT

The treatment plan for immigrants and refugees shall be relevant to their culture and life experiences. It shall be developed by or under the guidance of a culturally competent provider in conjunction with the consumer, and, where appropriate, family.

TREATMENT SERVICES

Mental health systems shall assure that the full array of generally available treatment modalities are tailored such that they are culturally acceptable and effective with immigrant and refugee populations (e.g., education, psychiatric rehabilitation, family therapy, specialized group therapy, behavioral approaches, use of traditional healers, and outreach).

TABLE 6.4 *(continued)*

DISCHARGE PLANNING

Discharge planning for immigrants and refugees and their families shall include involvement of the consumer and family in the development and implementation of the plan and evaluation of outcomes. Discharge planning shall be done within a culturally competent framework and in a communication style congruent with the consumer's values. The plan shall allow for transfer to less restrictive levels of care in addition to termination of treatment based on accomplishment of mutually agreed upon goals in the treatment plan.

CASE MANAGEMENT

Case management shall be central to the operation of the interdisciplinary treatment team and shall be based on the level of care needed by the primary consumer. Case managers for immigrants and refugees shall have special skills in advocacy, access of community-based services and systems, and interagency coordination. Case management shall also be consumer- and family-driven. Case managers shall be accountable for the cost and appropriateness of the services they coordinate. The mental health system or organization shall maintain responsibility for the successful and appropriate implementation of the case management plan and provision of adequate administrative resources and endorsement.

COMMUNICATION STYLES AND CROSS-CULTURAL LINGUISTIC AND COMMUNICATION SUPPORT

Cross-cultural communication support across all levels of care shall be provided at the option of consumers and families at no additional cost to them. Access to these services shall be available at the point of entry into the system and throughout the course of services.

SELF HELP

Culturally competent self help groups shall be created to provide services to immigrants and refugees and their families. The self help groups shall function as part of a continuum of care. Self help groups for immigrants and refugees shall incorporate consumer-driven goals and objectives that are functionally defined and oriented toward rehabilitative and recovery outcomes. Equal consideration and support shall be given to family and primary consumer self help groups.

Source: Adapted from Western Interstate Commission on Higher Education, 1998.

Micro practice in mental health with immigrants and refugees should adhere to these best practice standards and to the elements of culturally competent practice discussed in chapter 4, i.e. the skills related to engagement, problem identification and assessment, goal setting and contracting, intervention implementation and monitoring, termination and evaluation, and follow-up. Additionally, there are particular approaches for the assessment and treatment of mental health problems. The following sections will address these approaches in the areas of assessment, general clinical considerations, and interventions specifically for acculturative stress, depression and anxiety, post-traumatic stress disorder, and substance abuse. The other common manifestations of mental health problems discussed above, i.e., grief, alienation and loneliness, decreased self-esteem, somatization, paranoia, and guilt, will be considered to be symptoms subsumed under the above diagnostic categories, or symptom clusters. This chapter will address individual and group interventions primarily for adults. Marital interventions, family interventions, and children's interventions will be addressed in the next chapter on family dynamics.

ASSESSMENT Fundamentally, assessment in mental health should follow the principles of culturally competent assessment described in chapter 4. This includes assessing the problem within the client's total bioposychosocial context, identifying stressors and strengths relevant to the problem and its resolution, and using assessment and testing instruments appropriately. There are also some additional considerations specific to mental health assessment.

First, practitioners need to allow more time for the assessment process with immigrants and refugees than with mainstream clients. This is necessary due to the linguistic and cultural differences and the need to obtain a full history of the pre-migration and departure, transit, and resettlement stages of the client's life (Lin 1990). Second, practitioners should obtain a clear understanding of the client's expectations of treatment (Butcher 1991). As noted earlier, many immigrants and refugees are not familiar with mental health concepts or mental health services. Thus, the worker needs to determine "the kind of help the refugee [or immigrant] expects and wants from the therapist, the way in which the therapist could, and is, willing to help, and what the refugee [or immigrant] ... can do to contribute to the solution of ... problems " (van der Veer 1998, p. 72).

Third, the worker should ask particular types of questions (van der Veer

1998). Usually, short statements and simple questions are more productive than just sitting back and listening. Open-ended questions usually elicit more information about feelings than closed-ended questions. The latter are better for eliciting information about facts, such as past experiences. "Sometimes suggestive additions to open-ended questions (e.g., 'How did you feel when this happened? Didn't you become very angry?') can be stimulating, at least if they are empathetic and allow alternative responses" (van der Veer 1998, p. 70). It is helpful to ask questions about what brought the client to treatment. Usually there is a precipitating incident that "often shows in a nutshell where the problem lies, and is in a sense representative of the way in which the [client] experiences [the] present situation" (van der Veer 1998, p. 71). Exploration of the precipitating incident should be aimed at getting details about what happened and the feelings, behaviors, and cognitions of the client during and after the incident.

Additionally, in the case of refugees, the worker should "carefully ask some questions about possible traumatic experiences in order to obtain relevant information, to make it clear to the refugee that [the worker] has knowledge about the kinds of things that happen [to refugees], and that [the worker] is prepared to discuss these kinds of topics if the refugee wants to" (van der Veer 1998, p. 71). The following kinds of questions may be asked:

- Were you ever affected by violence, combat, or other threats? If so, please tell me what occurred.
- Were you subjected to threats of harm? If so, did you have to do things that you did not want to do to avoid harm?
- Have you ever experienced purposeful physical mistreatment or torture?
- What was the source of the violence or threat against you?
- Did you harm anyone else, or do you feel responsible for harm that befell others?
- Tell me about your life since the violence. Were there any troublesome events recently that caused your symptoms to become worse?

(WESTERMEYER AND WAHMENHOLM 1989, PP. 246–248)

Fourth, the assessment interview should focus on facilitation and clarification; statements of interpretation should be used with extreme care, if at all (Lin 1990). Fifth, the practitioner should carefully observe the client's body language and general appearance for indications of emotional state (Lin 1990; van der Veer 1998). Sixth, assessment should use a multi-method approach that includes interview, observation, and the administration of written instruments (Aroian and Patsdaughter 1989).

Seventh, psychological and psychiatric tests and instruments must be used appropriately in regard to the cross-cultural context. The following issues need to be addressed:

- Assurance of test translation adequacy.
- Assurance of test equivalence with the target population.
- Determination of test reliability in the new testing situation. That is, assuring that the test is measuring the personality characteristics in the same way in the target population.
- Determination of test validity. One must insure that the test is predicting the same behaviors in the target population as it did in the developmental culture.
- Assuring that the test is relevant for the target population.

(BUTCHER 1991, P. 121)

The above test properties cannot be determined without extensive research undertakings. Therefore, it is generally preferable to use "symptom checklists, significant life event forms, and specific face valid health questionnaires [that are] fairly straightforward and require little theoretical discussion" (Butcher 1991, p. 118), as opposed to personality tests that only indirectly reflect the characteristics being measured and that require substantial interpretation. This is also preferable since many immigrants and refugees are unfamiliar with mental health concepts and will view the latter types of tests as irrelevant to their problems.

Standardized symptom checklists such as the SCL-90 (Derogatis, Lipman, and Covi 1973), the Brief Symptom Inventory (BSI; Derogatis and Melisaratos 1983), the Hopkins Symptom Checklist (HSCL; Derogatis, 1974), the Hamilton Rating Scale for Depression (HDS; Hamilton 1960), the Hamilton Rating Scale for Anxiety (HAS, Hamilton 1959), and the Harvard Trauma Questionnaire (Mollica et al. 1992) require little alteration and have been used with immigrants and refugees (Aroian and Patsdaughter 1989; Butcher 1991; Roskin 1986; Vesti and Kastrup 1995). The use of such symptom checklists with these populations generally provides more valid data than the use of personality tests requiring interpretation (Butcher 1991). Furthermore, given the culture-bound nature of diagnosis that was discussed earlier in this chapter, it is preferable to focus on symptoms rather than on DSM-IV diagnostic criteria.

Eighth, assessment of mental health must be placed within the context of the client's total situation. As extensively documented earlier, immigrants' and refugees' problems are "multi-dimensional and intricately interrelated" (Lin 1991, p. 127), and clearly not limited to the mental health dimension. Furthermore, most immigrants and refugees do not compartmentalize their problems into different categories as practitioners might, and therefore the holistic perspective must be considered (Lin 1991).

Finally, all assessments must be considered to be hypotheses subject to further verification. The practitioner's provisional assessments should be continually reevaluated. There should be a reevaluative cycle that includes "the complaints, the diagnostic hypotheses, the questions aimed at obtaining more information or other therapeutic interventions made on the bases of the diagnostic hypotheses, decisions made on the basis of new information, an evaluation of their effects, and reappraisal of the original hypotheses" (van der Veer 1998, p. 66).

GENERAL CLINICAL CONSIDERATIONS In providing clinical intervention to immigrants and refugees, there are several general issues to be considered: the use of traditional healers, cultural differences and role preparation, language problems and the use of interpreters, the use of psychotropic medications, and empirical knowledge about treatment effectiveness.

Traditional Healers. In general, clinical treatment should be combined with the use of traditional or spiritual healers whenever appropriate, as this is likely to increase effectiveness (Berthold 1989; Gong-Guy, Cravens, and Patterson 1991; Hiegel 1984).

Cultural Differences and Role Preparation. To overcome cultural differences, the worker must employ the numerous attitudes, knowledge, and skills of culturally competent practice as discussed in chapter 4. Additionally, since many immigrants and refugees are unfamiliar with psychotherapy, it is important for the worker to conduct role preparation. The purposes of this are to:

- Clarify the role of the client and the therapist in the course of treatment.
- Provide a rational basis for the patient to accept psychotherapy as a means of helping him/her deal with problems, recognizing that talking is not seen by most patients as a helping modality.
- Provide a general outline of the course of therapy with its changes, with

particular emphasis on the clarification of the client's hostile and negative feelings.
• Convey information designed to create more positive and realistic attitudes concerning the psychotherapeutic enterprise.

(LAMBERT AND LAMBERT 1984, PP. 263–264)

Research has shown that such role preparation for immigrant clients reduces premature termination, reduces dependence upon the therapist, increases perceptions of the therapist as a peer rather than a parent, increases perceptions of the therapist as respectful and accepting, and increases treatment satisfaction and perceptions of improvement (Lambert and Lambert 1984).

Language Problems and Use of Interpreters. Workers need to be aware of the role of language in the clinical encounter:

> In the case of refugees [or immigrants] who do speak the therapist's language it is necessary to realize that they are likely to have only a limited vocabulary of common terms. They do not know or understand many of the terms which they need to describe or express their emotions. This means they are limited in their ability to articulate their problems. The therapist must take care that what he [or she] says comes across in the intended manner. He [or she] must be constantly alert for misunderstandings stemming from the use of an unfamiliar language. In such cases therapeutic sessions will be slower than usual. . . . The therapist can check whether the refugee has understood abstract concepts by asking him [or her] to give examples. The refugee can be taught concepts which facilitate communication in the same way. (VAN DER VEER 1998, P. 80).

Interestingly, language differences can sometimes facilitate therapy, because "sometimes it is easier to discuss a private matter or a taboo in a second language rather than in one's native tongue" (van der Veer 1998, p. 80). This is in part because when people switch languages, they also tend to switch roles to some extent, adopting the cultural expectations of the context in which they acquired each language.

When neither the worker nor the client have sufficient fluency in each other's language, it is necessary to use an interpreter. The many potential difficulties arising from this have been described in previous chapters. They include inaccurate communication, omitting portions of what was said or adding things that were not said, power struggles, alliances, transference and countertransference, inhibition on the part of the clients in honestly expressing themselves, and other problems (Egli 1991; Egli et al. 1991; van der Veer 1998). As has previously been emphasized, interpreters must have extensive training in the languages, in mental health, and in interpretation itself. Untrained personnel and family members should never be used except in medical emergencies. General recommendations for working with interpreters include the following:

> The therapist will have to build a working relationship with the interpreter. It can be helpful to take time to inform the interpreter about the basic principles of the therapist's approach: for example, that he [or she] assumes the client has to make decisions himself [or herself], that the topics discussed during sessions are confidential, that silence during sessions may be meaningful, and so on. Also, the counselor can instruct the interpreter to translate as literally as possible: by using the first person whenever the person speaking does so; by not trying to translate an incoherent sentence as more coherent than it originally was, and by translating short phrases one after the other instead of translating a group of statements by giving a summary. It can be very useful also for the therapist to have a preparatory conversation with the interpreter before a session, in which the objective of the session is discussed. It can be very enlightening to check whether certain questions (e.g., about sexual behavior) can be expressed at all by this interpreter in the client's language. An evaluation after the session can be aimed at discussing the interpreter's emotions and the difficulties encountered with regard to the translation. (VAN DER VEER 1998, P. 83)

Psychotropic Medication. Psychotropic medication has been found to be effective in treating a number of mental health problems such as depression and anxiety in the general population (Surgeon General 2000). However, when considering psychotropic medication for refugees and immigrants, there are some unique issues to be considered. One important issue is the fact that people from different ethnic backgrounds respond differently to drugs. For example, persons of Asian and African descent tend to metabolize certain drugs, such as antidepressants, more slowly than persons of European descent, and this may also be true for some Hispanics. This means that persons of Asian, African, and possibly Hispanic descent tend to respond favorably to lower doses and have more adverse side effects with higher doses, compared to persons of European descent. There are many possible explanations for these differences, including genetics, environmental factors, diet, and psychological, social, and cultural factors (Jaranson 1991; Lin and Shen, 1991, Surgeon General 2000). Essentially, the study of ethnic variations in drug response, known as *ethnopsychopharmacology* or *pharmacoanthropology*, is complex. Therefore, clinicians who prescribe psychotropic medications to immigrants and refugees should familiarize themselves with this field and with the specific variations among particular subpopulations.

In addition to ethnic differences in dose response, there are several other relevant issues in the use of psychotropic medication with immigrants and refugees (Jaranson 1991; Lin and Shen, 1991, Surgeon General 2000; van der Veer 1998). One issue is that of noncompliance, which was discussed in the previous chapter. Another is clients' expectations about drug effects. For example, clients may expect medications to have immediate therapeutic effects, but this is generally not true for psychotropic medications. Additionally, since many immigrants and refugees use traditional and mainstream healing systems concurrently, they may be taking herbal medications together with the prescribed psychotropic medications, which can cause harmful interactions. Also, clients may not be able to read or understand the instructions that come with the medication. Finally, refugees who had been in combat or experienced torture may have been forcibly administered psychotropic medication or other drugs in the process of torture or before combat. Therefore, they may have an aversion to the prospect of such medication. Also, they may be aversive to such medication due to a desire to remain alert at all times, which has developed as a survival response to their past situation.

In view of all these issues, the following are best practices for the use of psychotropic medications with immigrants and refugees:

- Diagnostic assessment and evaluation should ideally be completed prior to starting treatment with psychotherapeutic medication. However, it is often necessary to treat target symptoms ... in order to provide distressed patients some relief, develop a trust level, and enable greater participation in other forms of therapy.
- Maximizing compliance is critically important. [There should be] careful instructions about medication, frequent follow-up visits, and monitoring blood levels of medication, especially antidepressants, on a monthly basis. It

might also be useful to ask the patient at each visit exactly how the medication has been taken rather than assume that the patient has been compliant with instructions.

- The clinician should be alerted to concurrent use of abusable drugs such as opium or alcohol, herbal medicine, over-the-counter medicines, or prescriptions provided by other physicians. The patient should be asked to bring in bottles of all pills at the next clinic visit.
- The clinician should be aware that variation among individuals within any given culture is greater than variation from one culture to another, and that the major variations in response are quantitative rather than qualitative.
- Clinicians should consider other therapies in conjunction with medication, including other somatic treatment such as acupuncture, hypnosis, relaxation, as well as counseling. In addition, the clinician needs to know when not to treat with medication and when to rely only on these other therapies. In general, if the patient's symptoms are of relatively recent onset or are not disabling, then non-medical intervention may be more appropriate. Other therapies should also be considered for patients who refuse to take increased dosages of medication.
- Medication treatment for persons of non-European descent should generally be initiated at lower doses than those recommended for persons of European descent. (JARANSON 1991, PP. 141–142)

Empirical Knowledge About Treatment Effectiveness. The final issue to be considered in providing clinical mental health services to immigrants and refugees is the state of empirical knowledge about treatment effectiveness with these populations. Although there has been some accumulation of knowledge in recent years, there is still not a wealth of knowledge derived from well-designed studies on treatment effectiveness for immigrant and refugee mental health. Therefore, many of the existing recommendations for mental health intervention with immigrants and refugees are based on logical deductions and inferences and on clinical experience, rather than proven evidence of effectiveness.

In regard to ethnic minorities in general, "inferior treatment outcomes are widely assumed but are difficult to prove, especially because of sampling, questionnaire, and other design issues, as well as problems in studying patients who drop out of treatment after one session or who otherwise terminate prematurely" (Surgeon General 2000). However, it is important not to assume that certain approaches will not work for immigrants and refugees. For example, numerous articles on immigrant and refugee mental health make conceptual contrasts between "Western" therapy and non-Western cultural beliefs and suggest that the former will not be effective due to the conceptual disparities (Egli, et al. 1991). However, the empirical evidence may not support this assumption. For example, it has often been argued that the American value of individualism, which underlies many therapeutic approaches, would reduce treatment effectiveness for Asian clients, who place a greater value on collectivism. However, this assumption was not supported when subjected to empirical testing (Lee and Kelly 1996).

Therefore, mental health treatment with immigrants and refugees must be approached as a knowledge-building enterprise, consistent with the principles of empirically based practice as described throughout this book. Workers should choose and adapt their approaches based on existing knowledge and logic, and should continually evaluate the effectiveness of their own practice using various methodologies described in earlier chapters. The following sections will address best practices for particular problem areas, based on the existing empirical knowledge, logic, and clinical experience as described above. The interventions discussed below pertain primarily to the resettlement stage, since that is when most social workers will work with these populations.

INTERVENTIONS FOR ACCULTURATIVE STRESS Interventions for acculturative stress are primary prevention methods aimed at decreasing this source of stress, thereby reducing the risk of developing the various mental health problems such as depression and anxiety. These interventions are usually implemented during the resettlement stage, but they could also be used during the pre-migration stage for people who know they will emigrate, or during the transit stage, such as in a refugee camp while people are awaiting resettlement. There are four main interventions for acculturative stress: case management, supportive counseling, information and skills training, and crisis intervention.

Case Management. Case management is essential early in the resettlement phase to connect newcomers to the resources they need to survive. The case manager makes and follows up on referrals for housing, education, language training, job training and employment, health care, and other needed resources. Provision of these basic needs is a necessary foundation for the other interventions for acculturative stress; i.e., if these needs are not met, stress cannot be reduced (Gonsalves 1992; Hirayama, Hirayama, and Cetingok 1993; Lin 1991). Strategies for effective, culturally competent case management were described in the preceding chapter.

Supportive Counseling. Supportive counseling aims to promote more adequate daily functioning and to reduce symptoms of distress (van der Veer 1998). It includes provision of empathetic understanding; problem solving and resolving target issues through giving advice, suggestions, and encouragement; and improving social relationships within the family, the immigrant/refugee community, and the host community (Egli et al. 1991). Some examples of supportive counseling techniques are the following:

- Discussing overpowering negative feelings and making them understandable for the refugee [or immigrant] by relating them to everyday occurrences.
- Discussing the refugee's [or immigrant's] ideas about the development of his [or her] mental problems in order to contextualize feelings of helplessness and powerlessness.
- Explaining the development of refugees' [or immigrants'] mental problems in general, in order to reduce the possibility of the client developing a negative self-image, and to contextualize the fear of being or going mad.
- Discussing the positive side of his [or her] functioning, to strengthen adequate coping skills.
- Analyzing recent, everyday experiences of associating with other people, so that the refugee [or immigrant] gains more insight into the way in which people socialize, and how to avoid unpleasant situations and create pleasant ones.
- Stimulating orderly thinking about the political and social aspects of human existence, so that the refugee realizes his [or her] special position, both in relation to his [or her] native country from which he [or she] has fled and in relation to the country in which he [or she] has gone into exile.

(VAN DER VEER 1998, P. 99)

Supportive counseling may also include the technique of cognitive restructuring, which is aimed at changing maladaptive thoughts (Edleson and Roskin 1985; Hirayama, Hirayama, and Cetingok, 1993):

> Several types of thoughts can create difficulties for new immigrants. These include inaccurate interpretations about the meaning of an event, ignoring possible long-term consequences, inaccurate estimation of one's impact on a

situation, and telling oneself that "people should behave" this or that way....
Teaching an immigrant how to change such cognitions, once identified, may
follow one of several approaches. In general, these approaches lead an individual to analyze and change internal dialogues as well as the thinking patterns and beliefs underlying those dialogues. After identifying the internal
dialogues (self-talk) that are causing problems, the individual develops disputational or more positive alternatives.

(EDLESON AND ROSKIN 1985, PP. 222–223)

CHANGING ONE'S MALADAPTIVE THOUGHTS in this way is intended to result in more effective coping in intercultural situations.

Information and Skills Training. These interventions are aimed at helping newcomers learn about the customs and everyday life of the new culture, and acquiring skills to effectively deal with those customs and everyday experiences. These interventions are usually delivered in a group modality. The groups should be held in places where the immigrants or refugees naturally gather, such as language classes, job training centers, or religious institutions (Gonsalves 1992). These interventions may be delivered by professionals or indigenous paraprofessionals; the latter can serve as models of successful adaptation (Gonsalves 1992).

Typically, the format of the group sessions is didactic and follows a structured curriculum. The length typically ranges from one session (Bohon et al. 1994; Chan, 1991) to several weekly sessions (Roskin 1986). Informational topics that are covered may include the following (Chan 1991; Roskin 1986).

- How to survive the cold winter
- How to understand the way people relate (or don't) with each other in the host society
- How to find good and inexpensive entertainment
- Relationships between support systems, community involvement, and personal health
- How others in the same situations have felt and reacted
- Local geography
- Community life, various types of social services and facilities, e.g. postal and police service, art center activities
- Transportation, e.g., different types, passenger classes, bus routes, road safety
- Shopping and money

- How to save money
- Social atmosphere, i.e., the general feelings and attitudes of members of the host society toward newcomers
- Customs and taboos
- Gender roles and parenting
- Local and national laws
- Legal rights
- Personal hygiene and medical care
- Banking
- Education and communication systems

IN ADDITION TO DISCUSSION, these groups may include action in the form of visits to various public sites to further familiarize the newcomers with these various activities (Gonsalves 1992; Hirayama, Hirayama, and Cetingok 1993).

In addition to didactic information sharing, these groups also typically entail social skills training. Research has demonstrated that social skills are positively correlated with mental well-being (Bohon et al. 1994). Immigrants who have participated in social skills training have shown improved knowledge about social skills and relationship attitudes (Bohon et al. 1994), and have reported increased social support networks and greater satisfaction with interactions in the new culture (Edleson and Roskin 1985).

Social skills training is based on discussion or modeling of culturally sanctioned behavior. For example, one discussion technique is the cultural simulator method:

> First, participants are presented with a short vignette of an intercultural encounter. Second, they are asked to choose between one of several possible interpretations of the encounter. Only one of the interpretations is "correct" for the society in which the interaction occurred. The other possible choices represent variations of misinterpretations based upon meanings of similar events in a different culture. In the third step, participants are supplied feedback on their choice and, if incorrect, asked to repeat the exercise.
> (EDLESON AND ROSKIN, 1985, P. 220)

MODELING MAY BE DONE *in vivo*, or by video, for example:

> The video begins with some vignettes in which . . . actors illustrate poor communication practices. At this point, [a clinician] speaks directly to the

audience. He reviews the vignettes, outlines the problems, and suggests ways to improve communication. He focuses specifically on the following topics: showing respect . . . ; communication skills such as expressing emotions, expressing attitudes; rules of conversation and argument, for example, listening, not interrupting, keeping one's voice modulated . . . ; and exhibiting proper nonverbal behavior indicating concern, for example, maintaining eye contact and open posture. . . . The same vignettes are shown again, only this time the suggestions are incorporated and the vignettes have a happy ending. (BOHON ET AL. 1994)

To be maximally effective, social skills training should consist of modeling, behavioral rehearsal, and corrective feedback. For example:

First, specific situations in which an immigrant has experienced difficulties are identified. . . . Using skills training, the group worker helps the immigrants to analyze this situation in terms of a "critical moment" at which the immigrant could have intervened to alter this situation. . . . The group worker helps the immigrants identify and choose critical moments that present the best chance for positive outcomes. After identifying a critical moment, the group discusses various ways of achieving a more positive outcome. The leader and others can help this immigrant by sifting through the various possible courses of action she [or he] might have taken in the given situation. Eventually, through the group interactions, the immigrant selects one course of action that is most likely to increase her [or his] chances of a positive outcome. This alternative is then demonstrated by others in a role-played enactment. After observing the demonstration, the immigrant rehearses the new skills in a role play. Others act the part of significant persons in the situation. Afterward, the immigrant receives feedback on her [or his] performance and she [or he] is offered the option of rehearsing the new skills a second time to incorporate ideas provided in the feedback. To increase the effectiveness of demonstrations and rehearsals, role plays often include members of the new culture or former immigrants as models and antagonists. After rehearsals are completed, the skill-training process culminates with an agreement by the immigrant to apply the new skills in an upcoming situation and to report back on the effect.
(EDLESON AND ROSKIN 1985)

For some immigrants or refugees, it may be important to acquire skills in assertiveness, since this is not a behavior that is part of their culture yet is important for survival in American culture (Hirayama and Cetingok 1988; Hirayama, Hirayama, and Cetingok 1993). Assertiveness training consists of discussion, modeling, and rehearsal of the assertive communication sequence, which entails describing another person's behavior, expressing one's feelings about it, requesting a specific change, and identifying a positive consequence (Hirayama, Hirayama, and Cetingok 1993).

In conducting social skills training as well as the cognitive restructuring described above, workers must be careful to strike a delicate balance between helping immigrants and refugees cope with their new environment yet maintain their own cultural heritage. There is a danger of promoting an assimilationist agenda that pressures the newcomers to adopt all the new behaviors and attitudes and devalue and drop all the old behaviors and attitudes. Workers must help clients to identify those situations in which using the new behaviors and attitudes would be adaptive, rather than adopting them wholesale. The assimilationist tendency can also be countered by including activities in the group sessions that celebrate the newcomers' cultural heritage.

Crisis Intervention. Ideally, provision of the above services would prevent the occurrence of crises during the resettlement stage. However, these services are often not available. Although there is a service system in place in the U.S. for newly arrived refugees, there is not a comparable system for immigrants. Further, even when these services are available, immigrants and refugees most often do not use mental health services until a crisis occurs (Egli et al. 1991; van der Veer 1998). Therefore, crisis intervention is often an appropriate method for dealing with acculturative stress.

A crisis occurs when a person is unable to cope with a situation using previously learned coping mechanisms. Feelings of tension and anxiety increase, and if continued efforts to resolve the problem fail, extensive personality disorganization and emotional breakdown may occur (Egli et al. 1991). Immigrants and refugees are particularly vulnerable to crises since they are faced with new situations in which their prior coping strategies may be ineffective, particularly given the absence of their former support systems (Egli et al. 1991).

Crisis intervention aims to reduce stress, relieve symptoms, and prevent further breakdown by restoring self-esteem and avoiding further maladjustment. Crisis intervention bears the hallmarks of brief intervention that were described in the preceding chapter. These include a limited time frame, often just one session; limited goals; development of a working alliance; maintenance of focus; high therapist activity; rapid, early assessment; therapeutic flexibility; promptness of intervention; and encouragement of ventilation (Egli et al. 1991). As described in the preceding chapter, crisis intervention follows a sequence of steps: assessing the nature of the crisis, helping the client prioritize concerns, helping the client ventilate feelings, helping the client solve the problem by marshalling effective personal and social coping resources, and determining ways to deal with similar problems in the future. Crisis intervention also contains many elements of supportive counseling as described above. It also involves case management, since the crisis can often be resolved by connecting the client to needed resources. Specific tactics used in crisis intervention may include the following:

- Offering emotional support
- Providing opportunities for catharsis
- Communicating hope and optimism
- Being interested and actively involved
- Listening selectively for key problems and issues
- Providing factual information
- Formulating the problem situation
- Being empathetic and open to the client
- Predicting future consequences
- Giving advice and making direct suggestions
- Setting limits to minimize destructive behavior
- Clarifying and reinforcing adaptive coping mechanisms
- Confronting the client when he or she is resisting
- Making concrete demands
- Working out a contract
- Enlisting the aid and cooperation of others   (EGLI ET AL. 1991, P. 166)

IT IS ALSO VERY HELPFUL to teach clients the sequential steps of the problem-solving process: delay immediate action; formulate and define problems; develop strategies to deal with the problem; evaluate strategies; and select and carry out specific actions (Hirayama, Hirayama, and Cetingok 1993).

In summary, all of the interventions for acculturative stress discussed above are fundamentally aimed at empowering immigrants and refugees by supplying them with the following "power" resources:

- Knowledge or information about where and how to secure needed resources such as money, job, house, health care, and education.

- Knowledge about civil, political, and legal systems as well as American methods of problem solving.
- A set of attitudes and behaviors or interpersonal skills that are effective in dealing with social systems or organizations.
- Clients' support systems, that is, building networks of friends and acquaintances within and outside of one's own ethnic community.

(HIRAYAMA AND CETINGOK 1988, P. 44)

IN THIS PROCESS, the social worker takes on the empowerment roles of resource consultant, sensitizer, and teacher/trainer (Hirayama and Cetingok 1988).

INTERVENTIONS FOR DEPRESSION AND ANXIETY When migration stressors overwhelm an individual's resiliency and protective factors, or when primary prevention is ineffective, depression and/or anxiety may result. Both depression and anxiety may be manifested in somatic symptoms. Therefore, the therapist will first have to discuss the mind-body connection with the client and provide a rationale for using psychotherapy. Psychotherapy may be used in conjunction with somatic therapies, including psychotropic medication or traditional healing methods.

Research has demonstrated that among the general population, the most effective psychotherapeutic approaches for both depression and anxiety are cognitive and behavioral therapies (Dulmus and Wodarski 1998; Egli et al. 1991; McLellarn and Rosenzweig 1998; Surgeon General 2000). Additionally, for depression, interpersonal psychotherapy is as effective as cognitive and behavioral therapies (Dulmus and Wodarski 1998; Surgeon General 2000). Cognitive, behavioral, and interpersonal therapies may be delivered in both individual and group modalities (Dulmus and Wodarski 1998).

Cognitive and Behavioral Therapies. The underlying premise of cognitive approaches is "the view that how a person thinks affects how they feel and function, and that recovery from emotional disorder can be achieved and maintained by correcting erroneous, unproductive and dysfunctional thinking" (Egli et al. 1998, p. 168). The underlying premise of behavioral approaches is that depression and anxiety are "the by-product of living in a particularly aversive environment, or one in which meaningful reinforcers are absent or have been lost" (Dulmus and Wodarski 1998, p. 279). Both cognitive and behavioral approaches are time-limited, have a here-and-now focus, emphasize client education and active collaboration, use evaluation of apparent cause and effect relationships between thoughts, feelings, and behaviors, and use straightforward strategies to lessen symptoms (Surgeon General 2000).

Specific techniques of behavioral therapies include *in vivo* exposure, desensitization, modeling, covert and overt rehearsal, thought stopping, social skills training, relaxation, and biofeedback. Behavioral therapies "generally involve close monitoring of target behaviors, thoughts, antecedents, and consequences as ways of monitoring progress and of generating clinical information necessary in designing treatment strategies" (Egli et al 1991, p. 168). Specific techniques of cognitive therapies include educating, challenging and testing assumptions about the self and the world, adopting the perspectives of others, role playing, cognitive restructuring, and rational persuasion. There are various systems of both behavioral and cognitive therapies that use combinations of these techniques, such as Beck's therapy for depression, Lewinsohn's therapy for depression, Ellis's rational-emotive therapy, and Meichenbaum's stress inoculation training (Egli et al. 1991). Cognitive and behavioral techniques are frequently combined. Treatment of both depression and anxiety uses many of the same techniques. One difference is that successful treatment of anxiety must include *in vivo* exposure to the feared stimulus or situation (Egli 1991; Surgeon General 1998).

There have been very few reports of cognitive and behavioral therapies specifically with immigrants and refugees. However, "it is likely that similar effectiveness [to that of the general population] could be obtained with refugees [and immigrants] if the linguistic and cultural issues are resolved" (Egli et al. 1991, p. 167). Cognitive and behavioral therapies are considered to be appropriate for immigrants and refugees for several reasons: they use a targeted approach to symptoms; they are active and directive; they address concrete aspects of life; they are based upon a mind-body holism, and they are more culturally neutral and responsive to individual needs, and less language-bound, than insight-oriented therapy (Egli et al. 1991). Further support for the likely effectiveness of these approaches with immigrants and refugees is the fact that they have been successfully used in a variety of cultural contexts such as in Latin America, Asia, and Africa (Egli et al. 1991), as well as Europe and North America. Cognitive and behavioral approaches are compatible with several religious belief systems, such as Buddhism and Hinduism, and with health belief systems such as those of many Hispanics (Egli et al. 1991). In using cognitive and behavioral approaches with immigrants and refugees, the following general guidelines should be followed:

- Behavioral analyses should be conducted within the cultural context, with the meaning of significant events, disabilities, and social disruptions considered accordingly.
- Challenges to existing dysfunctional belief systems should be handled delicately, frequently enlisting cooperative family members.
- Dysfunctional global beliefs and assumptions should be dealt with after successfully applying behavioral treatments and establishing a trusting therapeutic relationship. (EGLI ET AL. 1991, P. 171)

Interpersonal Psychotherapy. As stated above, interpersonal psychotherapy (Klerman et al. 1984) has been found to be equally effective as cognitive and behavioral therapies for the treatment of depression. This approach is based on the recognition that depression occurs in the context of interpersonal relationships. Like cognitive and behavioral approaches, interpersonal psychotherapy is time-limited, present-oriented, active, and collaborative.

> Interpersonal psychotherapy is aimed at improving the depressed individual's interpersonal functioning and social adjustment by focusing on current interpersonal functioning. Past behaviors are examined only as a means of gaining understanding into the patterns of present relationships. The difficulties faced by the client are not regarded as related to intrapsychic conflict, rather they are conceptualized in terms of interpersonal relationships. When cognitive distortions are uncovered, the interpersonal therapist makes no attempt to work on them systematically, as occurs in the cognitive behavioral approach. Rather, these distortions are examined in terms of the effect they may have on interpersonal relationships. The interpersonal therapist typically addresses problems from four major areas: (1) grief, (2) interpersonal disputes with family members, friends, or co-workers, (3) role transitions, and (4) interpersonal deficits, such as loneliness and social isolation.
> (EGLI ET AL. 1991, P. 176)

There have been no reports of the use of interpersonal psychotherapy specifically with immigrants or refugees. However, given the four areas of focus identified above, interpersonal psychotherapy appears to be highly appropriate for depressed immigrants and refugees, since these are the very stressors that they experience. The action orientation is also compatible with the treatment expectations of many refugees and immigrants.

INTERVENTIONS FOR POST-TRAUMATIC STRESS DISORDER Post-traumatic stress disorder is a form of anxiety disorder; consequently, the most effective treatments are fundamentally the same ones that are effective for anxiety (Basoglu 1992). Thus, the psychotherapeutic interventions that have been demonstrated to be most effective for PTSD are those that contain behavioral components (Basoglu 1992; Freedy and Hobfoll 1995; Keane, Albano, and Blake 1992; Vonk and Yegidis 1998).

As with other forms of anxiety, the critical element of successful treatment of PTSD is exposure to anxiety-provoking situations (Basoglu 1992). Additionally, "effective treatments of PTSD maintain a focus on the trauma and related memories, thoughts, and feelings; avoid blaming or stigmatizing the victim; provide information about responses to trauma; attempt to strengthen the client's internal resources, such as ability to manage anxiety, along with external resources, such as work, family, and social support; and instill hope about the chances for improvement" (Vonk and Yegidis 1998, p. 371). Fundamental goals of PTSD treatment are to reduce symptoms, establish a more satisfactory lifestyle, help clients better understand their condition, and have clients develop a broader support system (Freedy and Hobfoll 1995).

The exposure element of treatment always involves imagined exposure through discussion of the memories of the traumatic event or events (Basoglu 1992). It also almost always includes *in vivo* exposure to external cues that provoke anxiety (Vonk and Yegidis 1998). Specific treatment approaches that have been found to be effective for PTSD include direct therapeutic exposure, which may include systematic desensitization, flooding, implosive therapy, and other variations of imagined and *in vivo* exposure; cognitive-behavior therapy; stress inoculation training; and cognitive processing therapy (Basoglu 1992; Keane, Albano, and Blake 1992; Vonk and Yegidis 1998). Successful treatment may be delivered in individual or group formats (Keane, Albano, and Blake 1992; Vonk and Yegidis 1998). One model that combines various elements of the above approaches is the following:

Initial interview:
1. Identification of problem areas: presenting complaints, most distressing / disabling symptoms, impact of problems on social functioning
2. Assessment of suitability and motivation for treatment
3. Re-education concerning the nature of the symptoms
4. Discussion of treatment, its method, rationale and aims
5. Setting of treatment goals

Treatment phase:
1. Implosive therapy (imaginal exposure to anxiety-evoking imagery and thoughts)
2. Exposure in vivo: behavioral exposure to anxiety-evoking/avoided situations
3. Cognitive therapy (BASOGLU 1992, P. 405)

If interventions are delivered soon after the occurrence of the trauma, they may prevent the development of chronic PTSD symptoms. Therefore, as with preventive interventions addressing acculturative stress, it is logical to provide preventive interventions in the transit stage or early in the resettlement phase to traumatized refugees. Three interventions are considered to be appropriate for prevention: provision of social support; trauma debriefing, which entails discussion of the traumatic event; and stress inoculation training (Keane, Albano, and Blake 1992).

The literature contains numerous reports of PTSD treatment among refugees, but none of these studies have used controlled research designs (Weine et al. 1998). However, the controlled studies that have resulted in the findings of effectiveness described above have been conducted with survivors of combat and rape, which are among the major causes of pre-migration trauma of refugees. Therefore, the effectiveness of these treatments is extremely likely to be generalizable to refugees (Keane, Albano, and Blake 1992).

However, in contrast to the behavioral approaches described above, much of the literature on PTSD treatment for refugees addresses two other approaches: psychodynamic and testimonial psychotherapy. It is important to note that there is no empirical evidence for the effectiveness of these approaches. In fact, in regard to psychodynamic approaches, the evidence from its use with survivors of the Holocaust strongly indicates that it is not effective in alleviating the suffering produced by their traumatic experiences (Basoglu 1992). Therefore, the use of this method with refugees should be strongly discouraged, despite its preponderance in the literature.

The second method, testimonial psychotherapy, also referred to as *testimonio* or oral history therapy, was originally developed in Chile in the 1970s for survivors of political violence (Cienfuegos and Monelli 1983). The method entails having the survivors provide detailed accounts of their traumatic experiences. The accounts are recorded for posterity, as documentary evidence (Aron 1992; Basoglu 1992; Herbst 1992; Weine et al. 1998). Although there have been some reports of beneficial therapeutic effects with this method, again it is important to note that there have been no controlled studies (Weine 1998). It is also important to note that this method essentially constitutes the imagined exposure element of the behavioral approaches described above (Basoglu 1992).

Consequently, if the testimonial method is used, it should be used as only one part of the more complete behavioral treatment approach. Aron (1992, p. 186) states, "The Testimonio is far from a final solution to the psychological damage wrought by political oppression. It holds open wounds that, if not properly cared for, may continue causing pain." Furthermore, Basoglu (1992, p. 421) warns:

> Care has to be taken that exposure is complete and sufficiently long to enable habituation to all aspects of the traumatic experience. Partial and brief exposures are usually ineffective. . . . This implies that . . . treatments without due emphasis on complete and prolonged exposure may be less than effective. Incomplete exposure may also explain the worsening of symptoms observed for some survivors following a review of the trauma story.

A final issue to be considered in the treatment of PTSD is what is referred to as *countertransference* (Bustos 1992; Vesti and Kastrup 1992; van der Veer, 1998) *vicarious traumatization,* or *secondary traumatic stress syndrome* (Vonk and Yegidis 1998). These terms refer to the therapist's reactions to the client's stories of horror and inhumanity. The therapist may experience "rage, sadistic gratification, dread and horror, shame, viewing the survivior as a hero, and privileged voyeurism" (Vesti and Kastrup 1992, p. 356), among many other possible reactions. The therapist may find the accounts of horror too overwhelming and engage in a "conspiracy of silence" with the client, avoiding discussing the traumatic events (Bustos 1992). The therapist may also experience symptoms of traumatic stress (van der Veer 1998; Vonk and Yegidis 1998). In order to cope with these reactions, therapists should take time off in between working with traumatized clients, not take on too many such clients, discuss their reactions with colleagues and supervisors, and practice the same techniques of anxiety management and cognitive restructuring that they teach the clients (van der Veer 1998; Vonk and Yegidis 1998).

INTERVENTIONS FOR SUBSTANCE ABUSE As with all clients, assessment with immigrants and refugees should routinely include assessment of alcohol and other drug use (Amodeo et al. 1997; Smyth 1998a). Some suggestions for such assessment with immigrants and refugees are as follows:

> Questions can be asked about methods used by the client to reduce the level of physical and emotional pain during the process of being uprooted, and whether anything currently brings relief (e.g., religious beliefs, visiting with friends, keeping busy with activities) or helps the person forget painful memories (e.g., visiting with a doctor, taking prescribed medications, sleeping long hours, drinking alcohol or using other drugs, borrowing medications from other family members or neighbors). . . . Interviewers should avoid asking about problems caused by or related to alcohol and/or other drugs. Such an approach is likely to yield little information since many clients do not see the connection between drinking and drug use and problems. Exploring the positive role played by drinking and/or drug use (for example, physical, psychological, social benefits) is a useful approach. As a stronger bond is established with the client, the clinician can do a more intensive alcohol and drug history covering typical questions such as quantity, frequency, and duration of use, precipitants of use, efforts to cut down or control use, periods of abstinence, and withdrawal symptoms.
>
> (AMODEO ET AL. 1997, PP. 73–74)

Accurate assessment, as well as treatment, of substance abuse among immigrants and refugees also requires knowledge about the client's cultural norms regarding alcohol and other drug use (Gilbert 1991; Rebhun 1998). Since excessive use may be sanctioned for some members (e.g., males) of some cultures, the client may need to be educated about the harmful effects of such use (Amodeo 1997; Gilbert 1991). Since substance abuse among immigrants and refugees is frequently associated with other mental health problems such as anxiety, depression, or PTSD, accurate assessment also needs to make an effort to distinguish which symptoms may be due to substance use and which may be due to the other problems (Amodeo et al. 1997). However, such differentiation can be very difficult to make; ideally, psychiatric diagnoses should be made only after the client has been free of substances for some time (Smyth 1998b).

If a substance abuse problem has been confirmed, it is then necessary to assess the client's readiness to change (Smyth 1998a). There are five stages of readiness to change addictive behaviors: precontemplation, contemplation, preparation or determination, action, and maintenance (Prochaska and DiClemente 1984). The client's stage has implications for choosing the appropriate course of treatment. "Studies have confirmed that clients with the best outcomes are those who are in the preparation or action stages during intervention. Clients in the earlier stages of precontemplation and contemplation should receive interventions designed to move them from one stage to the next" (Smyth 1998a).

Following assessment of the stage of change and, if appropriate, the use of motivational interventions, appropriate treatment goals then need to be determined. Although in the case of illegal substances, the goal must be complete abstinence, in the case of alcohol, research has shown that moderate drinking is a realistic goal for problem drinkers whose use is of low to moderate severity (Smyth 1998a).

As with the other mental health problems discussed above, the most effective treatments for substance abuse have been shown to be cognitive and behavioral approaches (Smyth 1998a, 1998b; O'Hare and Tran 1998). Also as with the other mental health problems, there is a dearth of research on substance abuse treatment specifically for immigrants and refugees (Rebhun 1998). However, for the reasons described above, cognitive and behavioral approaches appear to be highly appropriate for these populations. For example, O'Hare and Tran (1998) advocate the use of cognitive and behavioral approaches for substance abuse treatment among Asian refugees, due to the complementarity between these methods and Asian cultural values, such as:

- Respect for the teaching modality inherent in psychoeducation and skill-based approaches.
- The relative structure and emphasis on personal initiative and responsibility in treatment.
- The ability to examine cognitive schemas relevant to the problem without being unnecessarily intrusive.
- The use of stress management techniques based on Asian philosophies which clients may find familiar.
- The ease of incorporating cognitive-behavioral methods into family and community-based interventions. (O'HARE AND TRAN 1998, P. 75)

These commonalities appear to be relevant not only for Asians but for immigrants and refugees from many other cultures as well.

Cognitive-behavioral treatments for substance abuse typically include the following components:

- Self-monitoring thoughts, feelings, and situations which are likely to "trigger" an impulse to abuse alcohol or drugs.
- Teaching more effective social skills to deal with situations in which the client may be pressured to use drugs.
- Teaching stress management skills to lower anxiety, deal with somatic complaints, and covertly rehearse new behavioral skills.

(O'HARE AND TRAN 1998, PP. 74–75)

As with the other mental health problems discussed above, these interventions may be applied in individual or group formats, both of which are equally effective (Smyth 1998b). Effective treatment must also include relapse prevention, which entails "self-monitoring drinking or drug use or urges to use, identifying high-risk situations, assessing the client's current coping skills and resources and self-efficacy, developing coping strategies and a plan to manage high-risk situations, and developing or strengthening lifestyle balance" (Smyth 1998b, p. 136).

Also as with the other mental health problems, psychodynamic, insight-oriented approaches should be avoided (O'Hare and Tran 1998). Further, the particular spiritual orientation underlying 12-step self-help programs such as Alcoholics Anonymous and Narcotics Anonymous may be incompatible with the spiritual beliefs of some immigrants and refugees (O'Hare and Tran 1998). Also, there is no empirical evidence for the effectiveness of 12-step self-help groups as interventions themselves (Smyth 1998b).

Due to the high coexistence of substance abuse with other mental health problems among immigrants and refugees, treatment with these populations must address the dual disorders. Research indicates that integrated treatment, wherein both the substance abuse and the mental health problems are assessed and treated together within one treatment program, is the most effective approach to dual disorders (Smyth 1998b). Additionally, case management improves treatment outcome in dual diagnoses (Smyth 1998b).

Finally, substance abuse treatment among immigrants and refugees, like all other mental health treatments, must incorporate the role of the family. Also in this vein, prevention among adolescents is critical, and this by definition entails consideration of the family and the conflicting expectations frequently faced by immigrant and refugee youth (Gilbert 1991; Rebhun

1998). Substance abuse as related to the roles of women and the elderly within immigrant and refugee families must also be considered. These general issues related to families, youth, women, and the elderly are the subject of the next chapter.

6.3 CASE STUDY EXERCISES

THIS CHAPTER HAS CONSIDERED numerous issues in the etiology, assessment, and treatment of mental health problems among immigrants and refugees. Using the knowledge you have obtained from this chapter, consider how you would proceed with the following cases.

6.3.1 CASE 1

A new immigrant reported considerable frustration in her interactions with a clerk at [a government agency]. As part of a job application process, she was required to obtain a certificate from [the agency]. She appeared at the [agency] office several hours before the job interview at which she would be required to show the certificate. She took a number and sat down. The office would close in two hours, which, she thought, would allow her plenty of time to get to the interview with the necessary certificate. She still had not been called 20 minutes before closing time and noticed a clerk carrying on a social conversation with another person at the counter. She was becoming increasingly frustrated and angry at the casual pace of the office worker. Just before closing time the clerk called her number but informed her that she would have to return the next day for processing of her request. At this, the immigrant exploded and gave the clerk a "piece of her mind."

(EDLESON AND ROSKIN 1985, P. 221)

6.3.2 CASE 2

Mr. Binh was a 55 year old Vietnamese who had lived in the United States for the past ten years. He was married and had four children. He was employed in a high tech field. Recently, he visited a doctor at the local health center, complaining of chronic abdominal pain and insomnia. His ability to speak English was limited and an interpreter was needed during his appointments. When questioned further, he reported that he had lost ten pounds in the last two months. A full battery of medical tests was done but all findings were negative. The medical staff suggested that he return within a week and meet with a staff member from the mental health program. He was encouraged to bring his wife so she could add her perspective on the problem. On the return visit, the mental health worker learned from Mrs. Binh that Mr. Binh had many recent worries that were difficult for him to discuss with anyone. As the mental health worker talked further with Mr. Binh, she learned that his mother, who had remained in Vietnam, was seriously ill. Mr. Binh wanted to see her before she died but was understandably afraid that if he returned to Vietnam, he might be imprisoned. His wife reported that he had become distant from the family and no longer showed his usual interest in the children's activities and school achievements. He was also finding it more difficult to get up for work in the morning.

(AMODEO ET AL. 1997, PP. 72–73)

6.3.3 CASE 3

Miss A was in her 20s when she was picked up by the police [in her country of origin]. She was a schoolteacher and was head of a small school when arrested, not because of her own behavior, but because the police authorities wanted to arrest her brother, who was accused of terrorism. She was taken to the local police station and kept in isolation for 6 weeks. During this time she was regularly interrogated in a small room by two or three police officers. She was kicked and beaten all over, stripped naked, and abused verbally, all while being blindfolded. Allegedly she was not raped. On five occasions she was suspended [by] a stick [that] was put between her flexed knees and elbows and then lifted to rest on two chairs, and in this position she was beaten on the soles of her feet. She was burned repeatedly with cigarette butts and her head was pushed towards a wall, to be jerked back just before impact. Her back was hyperextended, and she reported excruciating pain. Her cell was next to the interrogation room, and she had to listen to the screams and cries from the victims under torture. After release from prison [after four years], she managed to come to [a resettlement country]. She was bedridden, with some atrophy of both legs, and it became obvious that the initial trauma to the back had developed into a functional paralysis. She still had scars from the cigarette burns and suffered headaches and insomnia. She was also full of guilt because she had given some names of innocent friends who had eventually been arrested, and she felt that she had changed as a person and "that the world could never be the same again."

(VESTI AND KASTRUP 1995, P. 360)

CHAPTER 7

FAMILY DYNAMICS

IT HAS BEEN OBSERVED that "migration is one of the most obvious instances of complete disorganization in the individual's role system" (Bar-Yosef 1980, p. 20). The stressors of the migration process typically lead to changes in family roles and family dynamics, or the ways in which family members relate to one another. These role changes in turn place additional stress on the family members. As in the case of individual response to stress, family response to stress is affected by the family's coping resources and protective factors. If families are highly adaptable, meaning they are able to change their power structure, role relationships, and relationship rules in response to stress, and if supportive community resources are adequate, then families will be able to re-establish balance in their family functioning (Ben-David 1995). However, if families lack these internal and external strengths, or if migration stressors overwhelm these strengths, then family conflict will result.

Marital and intergenerational conflict have been extensively reported in immigrant and refugee families (Ben-David and Lavee 1994; Carlin 1990; De Santis and Ugarriza 1995; Egli et al. 1991; Ying 1999). In severe cases, such conflicts may lead to domestic violence, including intimate partner violence, child abuse, and elder abuse (Ben-David 1995; Chang and Moon 1997; Friedman 1992; Ho 1990; Loue and Faust 1998; Rhee 1997). The cultural norms of some refugee and immigrant groups also predispose those families to domestic violence.

In addition to family conflicts, family members experience unique life cycle issues that are affected by migration (Pettys and Balgopal 1998). For example, children and adolescents in immigrant and refugee families face particular individual issues apart from the issues facing the family as a whole, and the same is true for elderly family members (Carlin 1990).

This chapter will discuss these various family dynamics issues commonly faced by immigrant and refugee families. As in preceding chapters, the focus again will be primarily on the resettlement stage. Following the discussion of these issues, best practices for assessment and intervention will be described. It should be noted that "family" in this context is defined as however the clients themselves define it. Therefore, it is not necessarily defined by blood ties or legal ties, or by particular structures such as the "nuclear" family.

7.1 FAMILY DYNAMICS ISSUES

AS STATED ABOVE, the common issues faced by immigrant and refugee families are marital conflict, including intimate partner violence; intergenerational conflict, including child abuse and elder abuse; and life cycle issues. Each of these is addressed below.

7.1.1 MARITAL CONFLICT AND VIOLENCE

THE MOST COMMONLY REPORTED SOURCE of marital conflict among immigrant and refugee couples is gender role reversals, which are accompanied by shifts in status and power (Ben-David and Lavee 1994; Ben-Porath 1991; Egli et al. 1991; Friedman 1992; Gopaul-McNicol 1993). As noted in the previous chapter, most immigrants and refugees come from male-dominated cultures in which men hold most of the power in family decisionmaking. Such cultures also typically have clearly defined gender roles in which men are responsible for supporting the family by paid work outside the home, and women are responsible for supporting the family by unpaid work inside the home. Since men hold the power, they maintain the status quo of gender roles; even though some women may desire to work for pay outside the home, or to have help from the men inside the home, the men often do not permit such crossing of the gender lines. Even in countries where there has been a high participation of women in the paid labor force, such as the former Soviet Union and Eastern Europe, traditional gender roles were still maintained inside the home. Thus, typically women were responsible for both outside and inside work, while men remained responsible for outside work only.

Upon migration to a Western country such as the United States, these gender roles frequently reverse. It is usually necessary for both partners to work outside the home in order to financially support the family. Further, women are often able to obtain work faster than their spouses. This may be because there are more jobs available for women, women may be more willing to take low-status jobs, women may acquire language skills more rapidly, or other reasons (Ben-Porath 1991; Ben-David and Lavee 1994; Gopaul-McNicol 1993; Song-Kim 1992). Because the women are working outside the home, they require assistance with the work inside the home. Therefore, gender role reversals result and men lose their traditional positions of power and status. The men may become frustrated; they may be depressed or angry about their lowered status in society due to their unemployment or underemployment; they may believe that they have lost the respect of their family members; or they may refuse to assist their wives with work inside the home; all of which leads to marital conflict (Ben-Porath 1991; Friedman 1992; Santos, Bohon, and Sanchez-Sosa 1998).

Besides gender role reversals, several other factors can contribute to marital conflict (Ben-David and Lavee 1994). One is a difference in the desire to migrate. Frequently, one partner had a stronger desire to leave the country of origin, and the other partner, who may have preferred to remain in the country of origin, followed due to the stronger power of the other partner, or due to a desire to keep the family together. When faced with the stressors of migration and resettlement, the reluctant follower may blame the partner for the difficulties encountered. Similarly, the partners may have differing desires to return to the native country. One partner may strongly desire to return while the other wishes to remain in the new country. For refugees, this difference can reach a crisis point when political changes occur in the native country that make return a real possibility (van der Veer 1998).

Another cause of marital conflict may be differential acculturation between the marital partners. One spouse may adopt the new cultural norms or adjust to changes more quickly than the other. This most often becomes problematic when the woman adapts faster than the man, leading to the power shifts described above. Even if the more rapid adaptation does not necessarily lead to more rapid or better employment, it will lead to the woman having to take the responsibility for interaction with the outside world in regard to the family's needs, thereby also shifting the power away from the man.

Cultural differences can also be a cause of marital conflict if the partners are from different cultural backgrounds. Intermarriage among different cultural groups is not uncommon among immigrants and refugees. For example, an immigrant or refugee may marry a member of the host culture. Frequently, it is the very cultural differences that attract the couple to each other in the first place. However, as time passes, these cultural differences tend to become a source of discord rather than a source of attraction. Often, however, the couple does not recognize the cultural nature of the problem and tends to view it in personal rather than cultural terms (Gopaul-McNicol 1993).

Another source of marital conflict may be increased physical closeness between the spouses. Immigrant and refugee families frequently live in crowded conditions during early resettlement, often with multiple generations under one roof. Additionally, if both spouses are unemployed or employed only part-time, they are likely to be spending more time together than they are accustomed to. This enforced physical closeness and togetherness, as well as a lack of privacy from other family members, may lead to short tempers.

Marital conflict may also increase because previously established methods of conflict resolution may no longer be effective in the new situation. For example, previous support systems that were helpful in resolving conflicts in the past are likely to be absent. A final cause of marital conflict is simply that spouses are convenient targets on whom to displace anger arising from the stressors of the migration process (Egli et al. 1991). Also, it is important to realize that some couples would have experienced marital conflict even if they had not migrated; thus, not all conflicts may be attributable to the migration stressors.

As noted earlier, severe marital conflict, as well as cultural norms, may lead to intimate partner violence (also referred to as domestic violence). "Some examples of domestic violence include: beatings, rape, incest, murder or threats to life, male control and dominance over a woman's access to food, water, shelter, and fertility (forced pregnancies and abortions)" (Women's Commission for Refugee Women and Children 2000, p. 1). Although intimate partner violence may be perpetrated by both men and women (Loue and Faust 1998), because of the male-dominated cultures of most immigrants and refugees, it is far more likely that such violence is perpetrated by males against female partners. The actual prevalence of intimate partner violence among immigrants and refugees is not known because it has not been studied systematically; however it is known that intimate partner violence is widespread throughout the world, across societies, cultures, religions, ethnic groups, and socioeconomic strata (Loue and Faust 1998).

All of the above factors that lead to marital conflict also lead to marital violence (Ho 1990; Rhee 1997; Song-Kim 1992). Men may resort to spouse abuse in an effort to regain the power and control that they lost in the migration process (Friedman 1992). Past victimization of both men and women in the country of origin may also be a risk factor for subsequent domestic violence. For example, men whose wives or daughters had been raped in their presence may feel a sense of failure at not having been able to protect their family members, which may lead them to use domestic violence in an effort to re-establish their position of power. Also, men may be more likely to abuse women who have been raped, because those women have lost status in the community and the men may feel that those women have brought shame to the family (Friedman 1992).

Additionally, in many cultures, wife beating is an accepted norm (Ho 1990; Loue and Faust 1998; Rhee 1997; Song-Kim 1992). Thus, women may have few resources to turn to for help within such cultures. The women may also blame themselves for the abuse or feel that they do not have the right to oppose such treatment (Friedman 1992). Thus, "although the problem is widespread, it is often kept a secret as a result of the social, political, and religious customs in which refugees [and immigrants] have been raised" (Friedman 1992, p. 73). Therefore, most immigrant and refugee women will not readily seek help for intimate partner violence.

However, even though intimate partner violence may be acceptable within some cultures, it is not acceptable to use culture as an excuse for such violence. "Violence against women is oppressive and intolerable regardless of a woman's cultural and social background" (Ho 1990, p. 130). Intimate partner violence is a violation of internationally recognized human rights. Therefore, social workers and other human service providers cannot sanction intimate partner violence under the guise of being culturally sensitive.

7.1.2 INTERGENERATIONAL CONFLICT AND ABUSE

INTERGENERATIONAL CONFLICT, i.e., conflict between parents and children, between parents and grandparents, and between children and grandparents, is very common in immigrant and refugee families (Ben-Porath 1991; Carlin

1990). In fact, it has been suggested that such conflict in immigrant and refugee families may be the norm rather than the exception (Ying 1999). Intergenerational conflict is due in large part to differential acculturation between the generations, meaning that the different generations tend to adopt the norms of the new culture at different rates, resulting in differing expectations of behavior (Matsuoka 1990).

An overview of conflicts across three generations is provided by Pettys and Balgopal (1998), based on a study of immigrant families from India. This study was unusual and important in that the researchers interviewed not only the immigrant families (parents and adolescent children) in the United States, but also traveled to India to interview the grandparents who had remained there, to determine the effects of their descendants' emigration upon them. This is important because today many immigrant and refugee families maintain close ties with family members remaining in the homeland. "Advances in telecommunication, personal and internet computing, video production and dissemination, and even travel have shrunk the world and made access to one's homeland and culture not only more accessible but more affordable" (Pettys and Balgopal 1998, p. 412). Thus, for many immigrants and refugees, the concept of family extends across international borders in a very real sense, in that physically distant family members may have significant influence upon each other.

Pettys and Balgopal's (1998) overview of intergenerational conflicts is shown in table 7.1. Although developed with data on immigrants from India, the framework also appears to be highly applicable to other immigrant and refugee families, based on literature that will be described below. Therefore, some of the language in the original table has been modified slightly so that it generalizes beyond Indian immigrants. Further, although the grandparents in this study had remained in the country of origin, the framework also appears to be highly applicable to grandparents who migrate, again based on the literature on elderly immigrants to be described below.

Clearly, not all immigrant and refugee families will experience all of the conflicts shown in table 7.1. For example, for many refugee families, returning to the country of origin (under "Sojourner vs. Immigrant") is not an option; likewise, for some families in the country of origin, having relatives in the U.S. may be a source of political oppression rather than a source of prestige (under "Power Shifts"). Nonetheless, this framework is useful for providing a general understanding of the range of intergenerational conflicts faced by most immigrant and refugee families.

TABLE 7.1 CONFLICTS ACROSS THREE GENERATIONS OF IMMIGRANT AND REFUGEE FAMILIES

ADOLESCENTS	PARENTS	GRANDPARENTS
	Gender Roles	
Expectations regarding education, work, chores, dating, discriminating rules	Decision making, careers, roles for children, who cares for grandparents?	Expectations of education and careers for children; who will care for them as they age?
	Respect	
How much assertiveness is tolerated by parents? How do I respect parents and grandparents and still disagree with them? Am I viewed as aggressive by other members of the immigrant culture?	How do I encourage assertiveness without losing respect of children? How do I be assertive in my career and with Americans? How do I deal with Americans who do not show respect?	How much assertiveness should be tolerated of children and grandchildren? How do I maintain respect of both my children in America and in the country of origin?
	Power Shifts	
How much influence do aunts and uncles have over me? What role does tradition and religion have in guiding my future? How much say do I have in my own future?	How much influence do my parents have over me? What is my role with my siblings? How do I empower my children without losing them to American culture?	How can I set different expectations for children in the U.S. and in the country of origin? What is my role with the grandchildren? What kind of prestige comes form having family in the U.S.?

ADOLESCENTS	PARENTS	GRANDPARENTS
	Life Cycle	
How does identity change across the life cycle? How do I incorporate the best of both worlds as I mature? How much of the old culture do I want? How much of the new culture do I want? What models do I have to learn from? How can I fit in with my peers without showing disrespect to my parents?	How does identity change over the life cycle for me and my children? Have I prepared my children to be ethnic Americans? How do I prove to my parents that leaving the country of origin was a good idea? How do I prove that I will remember my culture and heritage? What role should I play in choosing a spouse for my children? What is my role in helping them find career? How do I maintain discipline?	How does identity change over the life cycle? How will aging children and grandchildren maintain their identity? Have I prepared them and taught them enough?
	Triangulation	
In what way am I caught in the middle between my parents and grandparents and their conflicts?	In what way am I in the middle between middle between children and grandparents? What must I do to maintain their relationship?	In what way am I caught in the middle between children and grandchildren and their conflicts?

ADOLESCENTS	PARENTS	GRANDPARENTS
	Americanization	
What does it mean to be American? How much Americanism do I want to incorporate into my identity? How do I avoid aspects of American culture while living in the culture?	How much Americanism is unavoidable among children? How do I avoid negative American values while living in America?	How much American culture should be adopted by family living in the country of origin?
	Social Context of Immigration	
	What was the culture like in the country of origin when I left? How has it changed? What was the cultural climate of the U.S when I immigrated? How does that affect my identity?	
	Sojourner vs. Immigrant	
	Will I return to the country of origin? When? Will my children return with me? If I stay how will I care for my family?	

Source: Adapted from Pettys & Balgopal, 1998.

In addition to these intergenerational conflicts which arise primarily from differential acculturation, refugee families in particular may also experience intergenerational conflicts arising from the traumatic experiences of family members (van der Veer 1998). The following discussion will elaborate on intergenerational conflicts specifically in relation to children and youth, the elderly, and refugee families. A subsequent section will address the life cycle issues, which are also identified in the above framework, that are unique to each generation.

INTERGENERATIONAL CONFLICT AND ABUSE RELATED TO CHILDREN AND YOUTH
As noted above, the major source of intergenerational conflict is differential acculturation. This is particularly true in relation to children and youth:

> Refugee and immigrant children usually learn the new language and customs before their parents and grandparents learn. Thus, the child may be placed in the role of translator or culture-broker in relation to welfare assistance workers, doctors, schools, and others. This role-reversal may lead to lack of respect of parents and grandparents by these children. Also the children will try to follow the example of their peers in school and in the neighborhood, behavior that their parents and grandparents may see as bad, upsetting the elders. (CARLIN 1990, P. 228)

Sometimes the intergenerational role reversal extends beyond translation and culture brokering to emotional support. Parents may be so emotionally overwhelmed by the stressors of the migration process that they are unable to provide emotional support to their children, and may in fact turn to the children for emotional support for themselves (Athey and Ahearn 1991).

Another source of conflict between children and parents may be gender roles. Parents may have gender-role expectations for their children that are incompatible with behaviors the children need in order to function effectively in the new society. For example, parents may expect girls to be quiet, obedient, and subservient, whereas in order to achieve in school, initiative, independence, and competitiveness are needed (DeSantis and Ugarriza 1995). When faced with these contradictions, the girls may rebel at home. Furthermore, parents may place more restrictions on the behavior of girls than on boys within the family, leading to resentment on the part of the girls when they see that this often does not happen in non-immigrant families (Pettys and Balgopal 1998).

Intergenerational conflicts are also influenced by the social context of immigration. This means that the parents' understanding of the culture of their country of origin is in relation to how that culture was at the time they emigrated. However, as time passes, the cultural norms in the country of origin change, but the immigrants' frame of reference does not. Thus, the parents place cultural expectations upon their children that are outdated even in the country of origin. If the children have some knowledge about the country of origin, such as through return visits or knowledge acquired through the media, they can see this contradiction and it can be a further cause of resentment, disregard for parents, or rebellion (Pettys and Balgopal 1998).

Alliances between generations, referred to as triangulation, are not uncommon. Parents may triangulate by attempting to form alliances with children in regard to the parents' marital conflicts. Parents may also engage in triangulation by pressuring their children to maintain the customs of the old culture in order to demonstrate to grandparents that the old culture is not being lost and to thereby assuage the parents' own guilt about leaving the country of origin (Pettys and Balgopal 1998).

Parental discipline of children is often problematic. The long hours that both parents often must spend working in order to meet the family's basic survival needs may lead to children being left unattended, thereby lacking in adequate oversight and discipline (Matsuoka 1990). Further, the intergenerational role reversals result in a loss of parental authority over the children (Ben-Porath 1991; Gopaul-McNicol 1993). Children tend to become more assertive than is the norm in their cultures of origin, and they rebel against their parents' efforts to discipline them, viewing their parents as too rigid and autocratic. Further, "children soon learn that some kinds of discipline are considered abusive in the new culture. Some children use this knowledge against their parents, and when they do not get their ways, they threaten to report the parents to teachers and to the police for child abuse" (Carlin 1990, pp. 228–229).

While the actual prevalence of child abuse among immigrant and refugee families is not known (Korbin 1991), it is clear that some cultures do sanction child discipline practices, such as severe beating, that are considered abusive in the United States and other Western cultures (Faust, Spilsbury, and Loue 1998; Korbin 1991). Further, the stressors of the migration process and the intergenerational conflicts place immigrant and refugee children at increased risk of child abuse (Korbin 1991). As in the case of intimate partner violence, it is not acceptable to use culture as an excuse for child abuse. On the other hand, it is important not to label some cultural practices as abusive when in fact they are not. For example, the practice of coin rubbing among Southeast Asians was described in the chapter on health. This practice is intended to be a healing method for certain illness. The practice produces bruises, but cannot be considered to be abusive (Korbin 1991). In general, social workers should be alert to the increased risk of child abuse in immigrant and refugee families and parents should be educated about the social and legal norms regarding child discipline in the new country.

INTERGENERATIONAL CONFLICT AND ABUSE RELATED TO THE ELDERLY Immigrants and refugees who are of advanced age when they arrive in the new country generally experience substantial difficulty in adjusting to the norms of the new culture. It is harder for them to acquire language skills and to adopt new beliefs and behaviors. Thus, they generally try to maintain the ways of the old culture, whereas their children, and even more so their grandchildren, tend to adopt the ways of the new culture. Consequently, the elderly may come to feel like "strangers in their own family" (Yee 1992a, p. 27). Again, this differential acculturation leads to intergenerational conflict (Ben-Porath 1991; Gusovsky 1995). Conflicts are likely to arise between grandparents and grandchildren, and also between grandparents and parents, because grandparents may disapprove of the parents' new child-rearing practices (Carlin 1990; Gusovsky 1995). For example, conflicts about what language should be used in the home are common. Further, the elderly's lack of language ability and cultural knowledge also makes them highly dependent upon younger family members, adding to the other migration stressors and again increasing the likelihood of conflict (Carlin 1990).

Additionally, the cultures from which most immigrants and refugees come place a high value on *filial piety*, which refers to children treating parents with high respect and taking care of them in their old age (Aday and Kano 1991; Althausen 1993; Chang and Moon 1997; Tsai and Lopez 1997). In such cultures, the elderly are viewed as wise advisors. However, upon immigration, the elderly lose their advisor role, since their life experiences are seen as largely irrelevant to life in the new culture (Gusovsky 1995; Yee 1992a). Consequently, the younger generations may lose respect for the elderly (Ben-Porath 1991; Carlin 1990). Thus, conflicts may arise, such as those between parents and children when the parents disapprove of the children's disrespectful treatment of the grandparents. It is interesting to note that these issues, which have been widely reported among elderly immigrants and refugees, also arise for those elderly who are left behind in the country of origin, as indicated in the Pettys and Balgopal (1998) study presented above.

Additionally, as the adult children adopt the norms of the new culture that place less value on children caring for aging parents, or as economic demands on the family make such caretaking difficult, more conflicts regarding appropriate family roles arise (Sakauye 1992; Tsai and Lopez 1997). Sometimes, such conflicts remain dormant until a health crisis arises for the elderly parent, which forces the cultural conflict to the forefront and may impede effective service delivery in the health care setting (Althausen 1993).

As with the other family conflicts described above, conflicts with the elderly have the potential to lead to abuse. Again, as with the other kinds of abuse, the extent of elderly abuse within immigrant and refugee families is not known, but it is a phenomenon that is known to exist across many cultures and nations (Kosberg et al., in press). Elder abuse may include passive and active neglect, physical abuse, sexual abuse, theft or misappropriation of finances or possessions, and denial of rights (Kosberg et al., in press). However, definitions of elder abuse have been found to vary widely across cultures and across nations (Anetzberger, Korbin, and Tomita 1996; Chang and Moon 1997; Kosberg et al., in press). For example:

> Elder abuse in Norway includes "family disharmony," in Hong Kong includes "elder dumping," and in India includes "disrespect" by a daughter-in-law, [and in France includes] "moral cruelty" in the home. Given strong values for filial piety in the Far East, and elsewhere, the possible placement of an elderly relative into an institutional setting . . . might be considered an example of elderly abuse. On the other hand, given a tradition of public responsibility for the care of the elderly in Sweden, it has been suggested that turning to family caregiving (seen as an economically attractive alternative by the government) can be perceived to be abusive by both the elderly and their families.   (KOSBERG ET AL., IN PRESS)

Therefore, immigrants and refugees can be expected to have varying definitions of what constitutes elder abuse. As with the other types of familial abuse, this may pose a moral dilemma to social workers in trying to balance respect for cultural values with the obligation to intervene in abuse cases (Kosberg et al., in press). However, based on the above examples, it seems that the definitional problems arise primarily in the area of psychological abuse. The other types of elder abuse—physical, financial, etc.—should be treated as unacceptable regardless of the family's cultural background.

INTERGENERATIONAL CONFLICT IN REFUGEE FAMILIES Refugee families are subject to all of the intergenerational conflicts described above and, as already noted, may face additional conflicts arising from the traumatic experiences of family members. van der Veer (1998) has identified seven sources of such conflict: dysfunctional circular interaction; disturbances in communication; family secrets; overprotectiveness; parentification; a hierarchy of suffering; and trans-generational phenomena.

Dysfunctional circular interaction refers to the assumption that interactions between people are circular, such that they build upon one another. Thus, a family member who is suffering from symptoms of post-traumatic distress disorder brings the distress into the family; however, rather than alleviating the individual's distress, the family may in fact reinforce it due to dysfunctional interaction patterns; the individual and family distress then continues to build. Related to this is disturbances in communication, in which family members do not accurately decode the emotional messages behind verbal expressions. Since most traumatized individuals do not readily discuss their emotions about the trauma in a straightforward manner, such communication disturbances can readily occur. Family members may misidentify the emotions underlying verbal messages, leading to continued conflict.

Family members may also keep their traumatic experiences secret from each other. Often parents keep such secrets from their children in an effort to protect them, believing that the children would not be able emotionally to handle the knowledge. However, this usually causes problems in itself because the children do sense that something is wrong, but they don't know what. Further, overprotectiveness can cause family members to act in rigid ways in which they adopt stereotypical roles such as protector and victim. "Because they [were] unable to protect each other from external violence a form of overprotection develops which impedes communication and emotional support. It seems as though the family is falling apart. In reality, it is an artificial distancing stemming from a mutual concern" (van der Veer 1998, p. 43).

Parentification refers to the role reversal between parents and children that was described above. In refugee families this has the additional aspect that the children may take on the role of emotional caretaker for a traumatized parent. Hierarchy of suffering refers to the following phenomenon:

> In some families where one or more members have suffered from traumatic experiences, the members who have had no traumatic experiences, or less spectacular ones, may feel their traumatized relatives think they have not suffered seriously and therefore should not whine. The members of the family who have low standing in the hierarchy of suffering then have the feeling they are merely putting it on when they feel depressed, or under stress, and avoid communication about their problems with other members of the family. (VAN DER VEER 1998, P. 45)

A final phenomenon affecting refugee families is that the effects of traumatic experiences may be transmitted trans-generationally. This means that children may experience symptoms of post-traumatic stress even though they were not the ones who experienced the original trauma. Children may also adopt certain attitudes or feelings toward life or toward people that their parents have developed as a result of their traumatic experiences. And parents may place great expectations on their children with the idea that their children's achievements will redeem their own suffering. All of these family phenomena are likely to lead to additional intergenerational conflict in refugee families in addition to those conflicts arising from differential acculturation.

7.1.3 LIFE CYCLE ISSUES

IN ADDITION TO INTERGENERATIONAL CONFLICTS, table 7.1 also identified unique life cycle issues for each generation. These issues are considered separately here because they are less about the actual interactions between family members and more about the individuals' psychological reactions to family and societal interactions. These reactions primarily concern issues of identity and meaning. These issues are most acute for children, particularly adolescents, and the elderly. Although adult immigrants and refugees may also face these issues, they are usually less acute for them; the major psychological issues for adults are those that were discussed in the preceding chapter on mental health. The specific life cycle issues of adolescents and the elderly are described below.

LIFE CYCLE ISSUES OF ADOLESCENT REFUGEES AND IMMIGRANTS A major developmental task of adolescence is identity formation. Immigrant and refugee adolescents frequently experience substantial conflict regarding their ethnic identity. Essentially, they are caught between two worlds:

> Trying to integrate new customs with old customs, and living and thinking in two languages—one for home and one for school—create many problems and much identity confusion for refugee [and immigrant] children. Most of them want to respect the past, but they do not know how. Some want to forget the past and embrace the new culture totally, denying their origins. This denial causes problems for them and for their families. . . . Refugee [and immigrant] adolescents have to find their identities as, for example, being both American and Vietnamese. This double identity is not easy to accomplish. Adolescents have few, if any, role models for this identity. Their parents are Vietnamese but living in America. Their peers are Americans. With such dual identities, these children may try to deny one part or the other.
> (CARLIN 1990, PP. 228–229)

The task of forging an ethnic identity is compounded by competing demands from the two worlds. "Whereas at school and with their peers they are rewarded for 'Americanizing' as quickly as possible, at home their newly acquired habits are often discouraged" (Ben-Porath 1991, p. 11). Immigrant and refugee parents may not have an understanding of the identity conflicts confronting their children, because the psychological impacts of migration on the two generations are essentially different. Referring specifically to refugee families, Rumbaut (1991, pp. 60–61) clearly articulates this difference:

> To the parent generation, as the protagonists (from the Greek *protos* and *agonistes*, meaning "first actors") in the decision to leave, exile represents a profound loss and a profound commitment. Their adaptive response typically demands a prolonged mourning of that loss and a vigorous justification of

that decision; a lingering sense of the provisionality of their exile and a wish to return to the homeland under new political circumstances; ... and a bitter resistance to any alternative interpretations that may denigrate the meaning of their exile and thus threaten ego integrity. For adults, going into exile is a crucial act of self-definition, and the events [that spurred the exodus] constitute the decisive crisis defining the parent generation of ... refugees. But to the generation of their children, the deuteragonists (from *deuteros*, meaning "second") in this drama, exile carries a different relevance and represents less of a vividly felt personal loss than an opaque discontinuity with one's origins, less of a personal commitment than an inherited circumstance. . . . In many ways they are marginal to both the old and the new worlds, and are fully part of neither of them. Still they need to search for an identity and define themselves with respect both to their society of origin, to which they may never return, and to the adoptive society where they are being formed, which is itself rapidly changing.

Adolescents' reactions to this ethnic identity conflict vary. Some may reject one culture or the other, effectively removing themselves from interaction with members of that culture. Some may develop a heightened sense of ethnic pride, often in reaction to experiencing discrimination or hostility from the host society (Rumbaut 1991). Some may experience alternating periods of identifying more with one culture or the other. Some may develop a bicultural identity, in which they selectively choose those elements from each culture that best fit their circumstances (Gopaul-McNicol 1993). This is considered to be the ideal outcome. On the other hand, the ethnic identity conflict may persist into young adulthood, leading to the marginalized outcome of the acculturation process, in which the person feels that he or she does not fit in with either ethnic group.

Another life cycle issue that many immigrant and refugee adolescents face is high expectations from parents for school success (Carlin 1990; Fuligni 1998; Rumbaut 1999):

> Many refugee [and immigrant] families see their children as their tickets to a better future. They claim that they escaped [or left] in order to find a better life for their children. The children do know that much is expected of them. Some are very intelligent and do very well. Others are of average ability and feel they are failing their parents. . . . Some children may become suicidal or get into trouble because of the intense pressure to succeed.
>
> (CARLIN 1990, P. 229)

THE ISSUE OF EDUCATION with immigrant and refugee children and adolescents will be extensively addressed in the next chapter; it is raised here to point out its importance as a life cycle issue.

It must be remembered that in addition to these unique life cycle issues, immigrant and refugee adolescents also experience the other stressors of the migration process, as well as the developmental tasks of adolescence not related to migration (Athey and Ahearn 1991; Ben-Porath 1991). Yet, despite the ethnic identity conflicts, pressure to succeed, and other migration stressors, most immigrant and refugee adolescents adapt well to resettlement (Westermeyer 1991c). A comprehensive synthesis of the research on the health and adjustment of immigrant and refugee adolescents reveals the following findings:

> Among adolescents overall and for most specific countries of origin studied, immigrants are less likely than U.S.-born adolescents with immigrant and U.S.-born parents to consider themselves in poor health or to have school absences due to health or emotional problems. First-generation immigrant adolescents are also less likely to report that they engage in risky behaviors, such as first sexual intercourse at an early age, delinquent or violent behaviors, and use of cigarettes or substance abuse. . . . Adolescents in immigrant families also appear to experience overall levels of psychological well-being and self-esteem that are similar to, if not better than, adolescents in U.S.-born families. . . . Several studies have reported that educational aspirations, grade point averages, and math test scores for adolescents in immigrant families are comparable to or higher than those for adolescents in U.S.-born families. (HERNANDEZ AND CHARNEY 1998, P. 10)

However, all of these positive outcomes deteriorate the longer that the adolescents live in the U.S., and also with successive generations (Hernandez and Charney 1998). Additionally, "care must be taken not to overgeneralize these findings, in light of the diversity that characterizes children from different countries of origin with different histories of migration, family circumstances, and experiences at school and in their neighborhoods" (Hernandez and Charney 1998, p. 11). Thus, some refugee and immigrant children and adolescents are at risk of developing mental health problems arising from these multiple stressors. Those most at risk "include those without their families, children with brain damage from trauma or malnutrition, those in partial families, and those whose parents are psychiatrically or socially disabled" (Westermeyer 1991c, p. 127).

LIFE CYCLE ISSUES OF ELDERLY REFUGEES AND IMMIGRANTS The major developmental task of old age is to find integrity, or meaning in and acceptance of the life one has lived. If this is not achieved, despair may result. For elderly immigrants and refugees, a major element of this task is coming to terms with leaving their homeland. The immigration experience produces a "discontinuity in the sense of self or identity" (Feinberg 1996, p. 42). Consequently, the elderly find themselves revisiting the task of identity formation that characterizes adolescence. For refugees or immigrants who migrated when they were already elderly, the migration often represents an end rather than a new beginning. They have no further opportunity to live the life they had known, nor any reminders of that life or that self (Feinberg 1996). They sense a profound loss of the homeland to a greater degree than younger emigrants (Feinberg 1996, Gusovsky 1995).

The longing for the homeland frequently manifests itself as a longing for its physical surroundings, where a lifetime of memories resides. For example, one elderly refugee in Feinberg's study stated, "My parents are buried there. Memories of playing are there. My grandchildren never ask" (Feinberg 1996, p. 43). These elderly frequently spend time reminiscing about the homeland. As a means of reconciling these losses and identity issues, as well as coming to terms with their life in the new land, which often did not meet their expectations and dreams of success, the elderly often transfer their hopes for a better life onto their children and grandchildren (Feinberg 1996; Yee 1992b). This is helpful in decreasing or preventing their despair.

Elderly immigrants and refugees must often face the fact that they will never return to their homeland, not even to be buried there. This can be extremely difficult to come to terms with. For members of some religions, this has spiritual implications as well, as they believe they will be prevented from reuniting with their deceased ancestors if they do not receive a proper burial in the homeland; thus they believe their spirits may wander forever in the afterlife (Carlin 1990).

Elderly immigrants and refugees also frequently experience social isolation (Carlin 1990; Weeks and Cuellar 1983). Also, due to the intergenerational role reversals described earlier, the elderly may feel useless, unneeded, and unappreciated (Carlin 1990; Yee 1992b). These factors compound the sense of despair arising from the identity and meaning issues.

Finally, it is important to be aware that identity and meaning issues are not unlikely to arise even for those elderly immigrants and refugees who were young when they emigrated, and who have resided in the new country for decades. Such issues are particularly likely to arise when the elderly person experiences other life transitions. A refugee from the Holocaust describes this phenomenon:

> Fifty years after finding a refuge on these shores from the unspeakable threat of total Jewish annihilation, my subconscious still brings up feelings of not really belonging, being a guest not quite sure of her welcome, a foreigner uncertain of the social or linguistic subtleties of the new world. These feelings tend to get reactivated when I have been exposed to a more than usual dose of incidents that can occur when I am a woman in a man's world, an old woman in a youth-oriented culture, a Jew among non-Jews, and now a widow in a world of couples. . . . Often I feel 'other,' 'alien,' 'ignored,' 'left out,' and those feelings reverberate with memories of my childhood as a wandering Jew without a country. Such immigrant memories, dreams, feeling states, or flashbacks also occur when I am in a learning situation that requires the acquisition of a new language, or in situations in which what I know and what others know is not the same. This can happen, for instance, when Jewish friends speak of their childhood in the Bronx as if I too must surely have played softball in an empty lot. At such times I feel as if their words and mine have different connotations, different associations that are not being acknowledged. I retreat into silence, or I try harder to make myself understood, while they, more likely than not, stare at me with incomprehension or try to convince me that we have more in common than I think. It feels as if the burden of fitting in is on me. (SIEGEL 1992, PP. 108–9)

7.2 BEST PRACTICES

THIS CHAPTER WILL NOW TURN to best practices for the various family issues described above. The macro- and meso-level interventions described in preceding chapters are also largely applicable to the family dynamics issues addressed here. Therefore, macro and meso interventions will be only briefly discussed, followed by discussion of micro-level interventions.

7.2.1 MACRO INTERVENTIONS

AS DESCRIBED IN PRECEDING CHAPTERS, macro interventions are aimed at increasing immigrants' and refugees' access to services and at prevention of problems. In the context of families, macro interventions would include developing policies and programs to serve the needs of families. For example, the federal Office of Refugee Resettlement (ORR) has developed a program for "Community and Family Strengthening and Integration" (ORR 2000a). This program was developed specifically in recognition of the issues faced by refugee families, and by women, youth, and the elderly in particular. The program has its policy basis in the Refugee Act of 1980. The program intends to "promote a local planning process where service providers and community members come together to assess how the existing services are serving refugees and what additional activities might be funded. . . . [The program] seeks to strengthen cooperation among local service providers, community leaders, Mutual Assistance Associations, voluntary agencies, churches, and other public and private organizations involved in refugee resettlement [and] family, youth, and child welfare" (ORR 2000a, p. 2).

Examples of specific activities for family strengthening that fall within the scope of this program include the following:

- Promotion of access to family service agencies that support families.
- Classes and activities to support parenting skills, including information about U.S. cultural and legal issues, e.g., parental interaction with schools, family recreation, discipline practices, practices of corporal punishment, intergenerational conflict, child abuse, child protective services.
- Development of refugee families as foster parents for refugee children.
- Cross-cultural training for child protective service agencies, courts, county agencies, private businesses, and other organizations that work in this area.
- Orientation and information regarding U.S. family structure, roles of men and women, divorce practices, intra-family violence intervention, sexual harassment and coercion, techniques for protection and agencies for refuge and support.
- Training for staff and/or bilingual staff development for domestic violence or runaway youth shelters, etc. (ORR 2000A, PP. 7–8)

IT WILL BE NOTED THAT this federal program entails some of the primary macro interventions described in preceding chapters, including community consultation, program planning, and community education.

Another example of macro-level intervention is the development of federal policy pertaining to spouse abuse and child abuse within immigrant and refugee families:

Prior to recent changes in the law, immigrant spouses were particularly vulnerable to intimate partner violence. They were often dependent on the U.S. citizen or lawful permanent resident spouse for the filing of a petition with the INS that would initiate the process of obtaining permanent residence.... Undocumented spouses who challenged the violence in their households or threatened to report it were not infrequently threatened by their citizen or legally resident spouse with being turned over to the INS for deportation proceedings.... The Violence Against Women Act of 1994 attempted to address this situation by permitting both self-petitioning and a special form of cancellation of removal (a remedy to deportation) to abused spouses and children of U.S. citizens and lawful permanent residents. (LOUE AND FAUST 1998, P. 536)

Social workers can contribute to the continued development of policies and programs such as these through the specific strategies of community needs assessment, policy and program advocacy, interagency collaboration, and community education that were discussed in preceding chapters. As part of this process, social workers should advocate for stable funding for refugee assistance programs, since the need persists over decades (Westermeyer 1991c).

7.2.2 MESO INTERVENTIONS

AS DESCRIBED IN PRECEDING CHAPTERS, meso-level interventions are aimed at enhancing agencies' and systems' effectiveness in serving immigrant and refugee clients. The techniques for doing this that were described in preceding chapters are equally relevant to the present topic of family dynamics. In this context, it is especially important to develop agency policies and procedures that aim to empower women. As described above, most of the cultures of immigrants and refugees are male-dominated, and the unique family issues that women, as well as men, face in the resettlement stage are related to changing gender roles. In order to serve effectively families that are struggling with these issues, agencies must explicitly include women from the community in their program planning. The following checklist of questions has been developed for assessing agency effectiveness in this regard:

- How many refugee/immigrant women serve on program planning and implementation committees?
- Do women community leaders comprise 50% of all program committees?
- How many refugee/immigrant women monitor program effectiveness?

- Do the refugee/immigrant women involved represent a cross-section of the community?
- How many refugee/immigrant women work in the agency in decision-making and leadership positions?
- How many programs are targeted specifically to women and offered at times and places readily accessible to all women?
- How many female interviewers and interpreters are available?
- Is outreach to women being conducted to increase their participation?
- Are agency staff trained on gender sensitivity, gender equity, and human rights?
- Are refugee/immigrant women being informed directly of their human rights and legal rights?
- Are mechanisms in place by which women can report physical or sexual abuse confidentially?

(WOMEN'S COMMISSION FOR REFUGEE WOMEN AND CHILDREN 1997, P. 6–7)

7.2.3 MICRO ASSESSMENT AND INTERVENTIONS

THIS SECTION WILL ADDRESS clinical assessment and interventions specifically for marital conflict and violence, intergenerational conflict and abuse, and for adolescents and the elderly.

ASSESSMENT AND INTERVENTIONS FOR MARITAL CONFLICT AND VIOLENCE
Assessment of marital conflict and violence should follow all the general principles for assessment described in chapter 4. Additionally, social workers should assess the language ability of each member of the couple. Frequently, one member is more fluent in the new language than the other; workers need to be careful not to be overly influenced by the more fluent member's version of the marital situation (Egli et al. 1991). Standardized instruments or structured interview questions may be helpful in assessing the degree of marital conflict or violence. As with individual mental health assessment, such instruments should be fairly short and straightforward. A number of such instruments and screening tools exist (Garrison and Keresman 1998; Loue and Faust 1998), but they have not been translated and validated specifically for refugees and immigrants; therefore, they should be used with caution pending extensive research.

Marital Therapy. "The goal of marital therapy is to help both spouses formulate appropriate expectations for each other and to teach them ways to mutually achieve their goals" (Egli et al. 1991, p. 179). There have been few, if any, empirical reports of marital therapy specifically with immigrants and refugees. However, some forms of marital therapy have been suggested as holding promise for these populations; these include behavioral marital therapy, cognitive marital therapy, and structural-strategic marital therapy (Egli et al. 1991, p. 179):

> Behavioral marital therapy is highly structured and goal-directed. It focuses on specific behavioral goals, overt behavioral change, and maintenance of newly learned behaviors.... Couples are taught communication and problem solving skills in order to experience a more positive exchange. Short-term, time-limited therapy is recommended with this treatment approach.... Some writers within this orientation are moving away from the traditional ... model to include cognitive and affective components. Because of this shift in thinking, the evolved version of behavioral marital therapy may now be called a social learning-cognitive approach to marital therapy. Structural-strategic marital therapy applies the systems theory of both structural and strategic family therapy models [described below] to the treatment of couples.... The therapist tries to establish a healthy and self-sufficient marital system in a goal-oriented and pragmatic manner. This is achieved by active participation on the part of the therapist to encourage any positive skills already possessed by the couple and to develop new and desired skills. Strategic techniques are also devised and implemented to help produce change.

BOTH BEHAVIORAL AND COGNITIVE MARITAL THERAPY have been found to be effective for distressed couples in the general population (Egli et al 1991; Garrison and Keresman 1998).

Interventions for Intimate Partner Violence. There have been no empirical reports on interventions for intimate partner violence specifically for refugees and immigrants. Only general recommendations have been made (Friedman 1992; Ho 1990; Rhee 1997; Song-Kim 1992). These include:

- Establishing a telephone hotline targeted for a specific immigrant or refugee group to provide crisis intervention in an anonymous manner.
- Educating immigrant and refugee women about the problem, prevention

strategies, legal aspects and helping resources through educational articles in ethnic newspapers.
• Enlisting an ethnic community's elders in helping to intervene in the problem.
• Establishing consciousness raising discussion groups
• Empowering women through leadership and organizational training.

Numerous interventions have been developed for intimate partner abuse in the general population, but well-designed empirical evaluations of the effectiveness of these programs have been rare (Corcoran 2000; Garrison and Keresman 1998; Loue and Faust 1998). In general, effective programs have been found to include the following components:

• Services to victims.
• Services to batterers.
• Teamwork with prosecutorial units and law enforcement.
• Coordination of or participation in community response.
• Advocacy to change laws and procedures affecting victims of domestic violence and their children and abusers.

(GARRISON AND KERESMAN 1998, P. 234)

The dominant approach to the treatment of intimate partner violence is separate treatment for the abuser and for the victim (Corcoran 2000). Such treatment is usually delivered in a group format. Groups for the abusers (most often men) focus on anger management or anger control, using cognitive-behavioral techniques to develop skills for successful communication and nonviolent conflict resolution (Corcoran 2000; Garrison and Kereson 1998). Additionally, "men are educated about sex-role socialization and their beliefs about entitlement to power and control in relationships" (Corcoran 2000, p. 396). The victim's (usually women) groups focus on support and empowerment to leave the relationship (Corcoran 2000).

In most cases, treatment for the abuser is court-ordered (Loue and Faust 1998). Ho (1990) argues that this is a culturally consistent approach for Asian abusers due to the high value Asians place on authority and hierarchy. For the same reason, the psychoeducational anger management approach used in batterers' treatment groups is also thought to be appropriate for Asians (Ho 1990). Similar inferences can probably be made regarding other immigrant and refugee groups.

In contrast to the dominant separate-gender treatment approach, some writers advocate couples treatment. There are several rationales advanced for this, including the fact that women often desire to stay in their relationships (Corcoran 2000). This may be particularly true for immigrant and refugee women, who may face cultural, economic, and linguistic constraints on their ability to leave. However, the couples approach is highly controversial because it is feared that the battered woman will be at high risk for further violence due to both revealing the violent nature of the relationship, and not being encouraged to leave (Corcoran 2000; Garrison and Kereson 1998). Another shortcoming of this approach is that "while the systemic nature of relationships is emphasized, larger systemic influences are ignored for their impact on interpersonal relationships, such as sex-role socialization and cultural and social sanctions for domestic violence (Corcoran 2000, p. 397). On the other hand, this approach's focus on family factors may make it more effective for immigrant and refugee groups due to the high cultural value they place on family (Corcoran 2000).

Corcoran (2000, p. 398) indicates that the couples approach should be used only when "the victim and perpetrator desire conjoint treatment; the victim has a safety plan in case of potential danger; a lethality evaluation suggests a low probability of danger; the perpetrator does not display obsessional thoughts or behaviors toward the victim; no psychotic behavior is present on either part of the couple; neither are abusing substances; and therapists are trained in both family therapy and domestic violence." A primary consideration in this approach is the need to develop safeguards for the victim, such as continuous monitoring for violent incidents and provision of emergency contact numbers. Couple therapy for intimate partner violence may occur in a couple-only or a couples group setting. Typically, a cognitive-behavioral approach is used:

> Through instruction, behavioral rehearsal (during class exercises and as assignments for homework), and feedback, several interventions are used. First, couples are taught that violence does not erupt suddenly or happen at random or in isolation. Instead, violence is the end result of a coercive process that builds in a sequence of small steps. Couples are taught to become aware of this process and recognize cues, such as bodily symptoms, cognitions, and feelings that signal the need for a time-out. Time-out involves separating at signs of rising conflict for a brief designated time period, which allows anger to subside and cognitive evaluation to occur be-

fore the couple comes together again. Couples are also trained in stress-management techniques, such as relaxation and visual imagery, and to apply these techniques to identified anger cues and stressors that may trigger conflict and abuse. Another major intervention is cognitive restructuring with an emphasis on self-talk . . . , with the identification of automatic thoughts and irrational assumptions that may underlie anger. Assertiveness and communication skills training emphasize reflective listening, validation of feelings, and the use of "I" messages to express emotions and convey requests.

(CORCORAN 2000, P. 399)

Strong empirical evidence for the effectiveness of the couples approach is still lacking (Corcoran 2000). As with all interventions for intimate partner abuse, and particularly in the case of immigrants and refugees, much more research is needed (Loue and Faust 1998).

ASSESSMENT AND INTERVENTIONS FOR INTERGENERATIONAL CONFLICT AND ABUSE In addition to general principles of assessment described earlier, assessment with immigrant and refugee families should address issues such as the following (Gopaul-McNicol 1993, p. 132; Pettys and Balgopal 1998, p. 421):

- What does being [of the native ethnicity] mean to family members? How traditional [abiding by native cultural values] are they?
- What is the role and status of women in the family?
- What is the social context of immigration?
- Where is the family in respect to the progression of cultural identity conflicts?
- What is the seating arrangement of family members—who sits next to whom?
- Who is the powerful figure in the family?
- Who speaks on behalf of the family?
- Are the children allowed to speak?
- What significant family members are missing?

In addition to questions such as these, family assessment tools such as the genogram and the eco-map may be useful with immigrant and refugee families (Gopaul-McNicol 1993; Kelley 1994):

The genogram, which highlights family generational patterns, is especially useful in understanding families from other cultures by highlighting past and current relationship patterns. Eco-maps assess the family system's connections in the community, noting sources of strength and stress in the social network. . . . Eco-maps and genograms help therapists understand family structure, encourage cooperation, require fewer language skills, and view the family's current situation in context.   (KELLEY 1994, P. 543)

Kelley (1992) argues that the genogram is a culturally compatible tool for Asian clients, due to its focus on family ancestors, which is an important element of Asian culture. The same is true for many other immigrant and refugee groups. Another advantage of the genogram and ecomap is their visual nature, which can get the family involved in the drawing, does not require sophisticated language skills, and helps the worker to see the family structure and social networks from the family's own point of view (Kelley 1992). On the other hand, this method may not be useful for all clients. For example, "West Indians, because of the nature of their countries' educational systems, use auditory learning modes better than visual ones. Therefore the use of drawings and maps, such as the genogram, may not necessarily result in engaging the family" (Gopaul-McNicol 1992, p. 133). Again, the same may be true for other refugee and immigrant groups as well.

General Principles of Family Therapy. In working with immigrant and refugee families, there are some general principles that should be followed regardless of what specific therapeutic approach is used. First, therapists should be aware of and acknowledge the traditional family hierarchy, which is typically male-dominated and elder-dominated (Gopaul-McNicol 1993; Matsuoka 1990). Thus, in a two-parent family, the father should be addressed first, followed by the mother, and then the children in descending order of age (Gopaul-McNicol 1993). Because of the male's strong position in the family, significant efforts should be made to involve him in the therapeutic process (Gopaul-McNicol 1993).

Also because of the male-dominated and elder-dominated nature of many cultures, female therapists and young therapists may need to take special steps to establish their credibility (Baptiste, Hardy, and Lewis 1997; Gopaul-McNicol 1993). They may enlist the aid of male or older cotherapists, or of elder family members who can serve as intermediaries between the therapist and the family (Gopaul-McNicol 1993). If this is not possible, it is a good idea to openly address gender or age bias early in the therapeutic process before it has a negative effect (Baptiste, Hardy, and Lewis 1997).

In accordance with many cultural protocols, workers should typically address adult family members in a formal manner, using titles and surnames rather than first names. Children should be addressed by their first names (Gopaul-McNicol 1993).

Another general principle is that workers need to be flexible in scheduling appointments around the family's work and school schedules. Since education and work are of critical importance to most immigrant and refugee families, "if treatment results in the loss of wages, the family or individual may become resistant and resentful" (Gopaul-McNicol 1993, p. 120). Finally, workers should follow all the principles described in previous chapters for establishing trust, rapport, and preparation for the therapeutic process.

Family Therapy. There are numerous approaches to family therapy that have been advocated for use with immigrant and refugee families and that have at least some degree of support for effectiveness with these populations. These include psychoeducational approaches, behavioral approaches, family systems approaches, and combinations thereof.

Psychoeducational approaches aim to increase family members' understanding of the migration-related and culture-related causes of their intergenerational conflicts. This method also entails a behavioral element aimed at increasing family members' coping skills, effective communication skills, and problem solving skills. For example, Gopaul-McNicol (1993) reports on a psychoeducational component of a comprehensive therapy program for West Indian families. Parents are taught the following:

• The causes of childhood misbehavior, and the principles and concepts underlying the social learning of such behavior.
• The cultural differences in values and discipline as they affect their child's adjustment.
• The emotional stress and fears that emerge in a child as a result of migration and adjustment to a new family, and the difference between an emotional disturbance and cultural adjustment.
• The differences in the school structure and school expectations.
• The criteria used by the school system in placing children in special programs, and their parental rights in such a case.
• How the parents can build positive self-esteem and self-discipline in their

child via a home study program, so that the child will be empowered to maintain a positive self-image in this race-conscious society.
- How to communicate more effectively with their child, and how to be critical without affecting their child's self-esteem.
- The impact of peer pressure and how it can be monitored.

(GOPAUL-MCNICOL 1993, PP. 135–136)

Children are taught the following:

- To understand the sociocultural differences between their native country and the United States.
- To cope with peer taunts about accent, mode of dressing, foods, family, and so forth.
- To communicate more effectively with their families.
- To acquire the social skills and assertiveness skills needed.
- To improve study skills and to understand cultural differences in test taking, school structure, school expectations, and language factors.
- To cope with the emotional stress and fears that come with migration.
- To understand the psychology of being black in American society.
- To understand the concept of self-esteem; its relation to performance and success; and the sources, institutions, and images that affect self-esteem.

(GOPAUL-MCNICOL 1993, P. 136)

Another example of the psychoeducational approach is the "Program for Strengthening of Intergenerational/Intercultural Ties in Immigrant Chinese American Families" (Ying 1999). This program consists of eight weekly two-hour classes for immigrant parents of school-age children. The class sessions address the following topics:

- Class 1. Simulation of a Cross-Cultural Encounter: Migrant parents often prefer to remain in a social world inhabited by members of their own cultural group, while their children are actively engaged in cross-cultural encounters. In order to help parents better empathize with and assist with the challenges of these encounters, a cultural simulation game is used to simulate a cross-cultural encounter and its accompanying cultural dissonance and conflict. This exercise often engenders feelings of dismay, helplessness, and anger. Parents are debriefed afterwards, and its relevance to the class is discussed.

- Class 2. Learning about Cultural Differences: This class provides an overview of current theories and knowledge about ethnic identity formation, and underlines potential variation between migrant parents and their children. In addition, to highlight and illustrate cultural differences in general, and their application to the parent-child relationship in particular, popular fairy tales from each culture are used to demonstrate fundamental differences in the nature of Chinese and mainstream American parent-child relationships and definitions of adulthood. Parents are invited to ponder the dissonance of the two cultures and how they may help their children negotiate them.
- Class 3. Understanding Your Child: The third class provides an overview of the major developmental milestones from birth to adolescence, and the concomitant challenges for parenting. Parents are invited to reflect on potential differences in the standards they uphold to their children and what is normative in mainstream American culture. This more theoretical presentation is followed by an autobiographical account of a parent-child relationship by an American-born Chinese young adult, which provides a child's view of the intergenerational relationship. The presenter discusses the challenges of relating to his/her immigrant Chinese parents, and offers suggestions about maintaining a close intergenerational relationship in the larger American context.
- Classes 4–6. Promoting Parenting Effectiveness: Parenting methods, such as active listening, conveying parents' messages, setting structure and limits, rewarding the child, and Special Time are presented. Each parenting technique is presented with a rationale, followed by an explanation of its use, a demonstration, in-class practice, and home practice. These parenting methods are grounded in mainstream American culture. Immigrant parents are asked to assess their merits and try then in appropriate situations. It is not suggested that the traditional perspective be abandoned; instead, it is proposed that at different times and contexts, one may be more appropriate than the other.
- Class 7. Coping With Stress: The stresses of parenting, particularly in a culturally different context, are discussed. Parents are taught to recognize signs of distress, which may range from physical (loss of appetite and sleep disturbance) to psychological (irritability, depression, anxiety) manifestations. They are taught three methods of dealing with the distress: relaxation, doing pleasant activities, and developing and strengthening social networks.
- Class 8. Review and Integration: In the review, it is emphasized that intergenerational relationships are likely to be strengthened when, *affectively*, parents care about their child's view and feelings; *cognitively*, they under-

stand the context in which their child is growing up as different from that of their own childhood and are open to learning about this new context; and, *behaviorally*, they seek to reach out to their child and his/her world.

(YING 1999, PP. 91–92)

A PILOT STUDY of this program suggested that it improved the parents' perceptions of the quality of their relationships with their children (Ying 1999).

Behavioral approaches to family therapy aim to change dysfunctional patterns of reinforcement within the family:

> In order to achieve the desired behavioral change, a functional analysis of behavior is undertaken so that antecedents and consequences of the target behavior can be identified. Appropriate treatment programs in which the therapist directly manipulates contingencies and reinforcement are then implemented. Once the desired behavior changes are achieved, family members are taught to modify their own contingencies of reinforcement so that the changes are maintained. The goals of therapy are to increase the rate of rewarding and positive interactions between family members by fostering positive behavioral change, to decrease the frequency of undesired behavior and the rate of aversive control, and to teach more effective communication and problem solving. This approach gives little attention to the bidirectionality of family interactions and it typically focuses on the subsystem within the family which is considered central to the targeted behavior.

(EGLI ET AL. 1991, P. 183)

Although this method is suggested by Egli et al. (1991) as one possible approach for refugee families, there have been no empirical reports of its use alone specifically with immigrant or refugee families. The cultural compatibility of behavioral approaches in general, as discussed in the preceding chapter, suggests that this may be an appropriate method for such families. However, given this method's lack of attention to cultural factors in the intergenerational relationship, it would probably be best to combine it with other approaches that give recognition to these factors.

Family systems approaches are derived from family systems theory:

> Family systems theory is a way of explaining human behavior as that which makes sense in context; that is, the context of the family system as well as the community and larger social systems. Biological, psychological, and social factors are all taken into account, but the focus is more on interpersonal and

interactive factors than on intra-psychic factors, and on problem resolution or reduction over uncovering unconscious motives. Interventions are aimed at interrupting negative interactive patterns more than restructuring an individual's personality or mental process. Key concepts in systems practice include the search for strengths in the system and the positive connotation of the intent behind behavior, including symptomatic behavior.

(KELLEY 1992, P. 4)

Family systems approaches have been advocated as being particularly useful for refugee and immigrant families for the following reasons:

- The focus is on problems arising from interaction between systems rather than on problems situated within a person.
- The interventions are goal-oriented and concrete.
- Family systems theory explains behavior as a logical part of family and community systems, which is consistent with the cultural beliefs of many refugee and immigrant groups.
- The problem-focused approach is not intrusive.
- The approach is parsimonious. Too much change, too fast, is stressful for persons who are already coping with rapid change. Maintaining stability while acclimating to change is important. Ideally, a change in one part of the system ripples out to other areas at a rate that allows members to adapt.
- Most family systems approaches emphasize hierarchical structure, which is consistent with the beliefs and values of many cultures. The therapist stays in charge of the sessions, and the parents are expected to be in charge of the children.
- The systemic concepts of equifinality and equipotentiality—that same beginnings can have different endings and that same endings can have different beginnings—are important ideas for persons beginning a new life in a new place. (KELLEY 1992, P. 4; 1994, PP. 542–545):

Four specific types of family systems therapy have been advocated for use with refugee and immigrant families: Bowen's systems therapy, structural family therapy, strategic family therapy, and Milan systems therapy (Egli et al. 1991; Gopaul-McNicol 1992; Kelley 1992).

Bowen's systems therapy (Bowen 1978) is based on identifying transgenerational patterns:

What has occurred in the past and what the older generation feels about it are important in Bowenian therapy. One goal of therapy is to increase differentiation of individuals within their families. Another goal is to decrease individual anxiety and emotional reactivity by diverting the focus from the "identified patient" to past and present family members. Doing this permits the individual to think clearly and avoids the need for triangulation and emotional cutoff, which Bowen believes occurs when anxiety is high. . . . Therapy constitutes a cognitive re-encounter with one's past as it is represented in one's present life. The focus is on facts and patterns, not feelings. Bowen also establishes leverage within the family system by discovering the most likely entry point (the person most capable of change, i.e., the least resistant family member). He then uses this least resistant, most motivated member to deal with the resistance of other family members.

(GOPAUL-MCNICOL 1993, P. 124)

Structural family therapy (Minuchin 1974) aims to change the structures underlying family interactions:

The focus is mainly on boundaries, the patterns of the family, and the relationship between the family system and its wider ecological environment. An individual's symptoms are perceived as stemming from a family's failure to accommodate its structure to the changing developmental and environmental requirements. These dysfunctional reactions to stress create problems that manifest themselves in family interrelations. The responsibility for change rests primarily on the therapist, who utilizes three strategies—challenging the symptom, challenging the family structure, and challenging the family reality. The therapist must negotiate the family boundaries in such a manner as to be given the power to be therapeutic. These boundary issues incorporate the concepts of "enmeshment" (in which some or all of the family boundaries are relatively undifferentiated or permeable) and "disengagement" (in which family members behave in a nonchalant manner since they have little to do with one another, because family boundaries are very rigid and impermeable). (GOPAUL-MCNICOL 1993, PP. 124–125)

The structural approach appears to be particularly appropriate for immigrant and refugee families:

The structural family therapy approach, which emphasizes hierarchies within the family, is very relevant to [many immigrant and refugee cultures].

Parents and grandparents are usually in favor of Minuchin's emphasis on generational boundaries, instead of approaches that emphasize equal rights for all family members. By actively restructuring the family interactions, rather than relying on expressions of feelings to create change, the therapist helps to realign the family's boundaries. This approach is particularly helpful in aiding in the process of acculturation, since Minuchin emphasizes that the individual's symptoms can be traced to the family's failure to accommodate its structure to the changing environmental requirements. Many first-generation immigrants often have difficulty "letting go" and endorsing the concept of biculturalism. Minuchin's approach helps the parents recognize that the children need to become involved in American society in order to assimilate with minimal difficulty. Therefore, when therapy challenges the family structure, the family is moved to examine the enmeshment syndrome . . . that may be impeding cultural adjustment. In addition, Minuchin's use of the extended family as an integral component of therapy is very effective with [many immigrant and refugee families], since the extended family plays a pivotal role in [their] family life.

(GOPAUL-MCNICOL 1993, PP. 142–143)

A modification of structural family therapy, the ecological structural approach (Aponte 1991), which was initially developed for work with poor and minority populations, has been identified as being especially relevant to refugee and immigrant families (Kelley 1994). "Aponte stresses that this therapy must deal with the immediacy and concreteness of the problems, the family's structural organization, the values of the family and its community, the family's community resources, and the links between the family and the community" (Kelley 1994, p. 544).

Szapocznik et al. (1978) have applied the ecological structural approach to work with Cuban families:

According to the ecological structural family therapy approach, family problems in [refugee and immigrant families] are primarily acculturation-related dysfunctions that are manifested within the family system. Thus it is important to examine the effects of acculturation in terms of a family systems model and to treat the family system rather than the individual. An ecological model of etiology and treatment is suggested since a shift in the person's position vis-à-vis his or her environment may also shift his or her experience. Therefore, an effective therapeutic approach must promote new interactions within the family and the extrafamilial environment so that each individual person in the family can experience more effective ways of dealing with the environment. Ecological structural family therapy attempts to help family members facilitate interaction within the family and also with their extrafamilial roles.... One of the major sources of family disruption is intergenerational differences between traditional parents and the acculturated adolescents. Parental authority is often questioned and the parents face marital tension that impedes effective parenting. Szapocznik et al. (1978) suggest that the therapist accept this organization and blend in with the family first, and then establish a strong alliance with the parents in order to reinforce their authority and clarify generational boundaries. Community agencies can then be enlisted to assist in setting limits on the adolescent's problem behaviors. This strategy often helps lessen the gap between the family and the host community. In addition, the therapist assists in working out a more functional interaction pattern within the family and in reestablishing the parental role, in providing new peer relationships for the adolescent with the goal of discouraging antisocial behaviors, and in working out the marital conflict. (EGLI ET AL. 1991, P. 186)

Strategic family therapy (Watzlawick, Weakland, and Fisch 1974) operates as follows:

The therapist treats the presenting problem instead of addressing hypothesized interaction patterns. Problems are believed to be the result of faulty life adjustments and continue due to the use of inappropriate solutions.... The basic goal of strategic therapy is to devise tactics that will outwit resistance and force people to behave differently. The solution is often, paradoxically, found in intensifying the problem through the technique of "prescribing the symptom." That is, clients are asked to maintain their symptoms in ways that will exacerbate them. In this way the symptoms come under the control of the therapist and are no longer controlled by the client. This enables the therapist to work more directly with the presenting symptoms in trying to change the problem behavior of the client. (EGLI ET AL. 1991, P. 182)

Kelley (1994) noted that in working with refugee families, useful elements drawn from strategic family therapy include obtaining a clear and solvable problem definition and using minimal intervention aimed at interrupting the problem sequence. This is consistent with the expectations of many cultural groups in regard to concrete, goal-oriented treatment that focuses on symptom relief, rather than on "talking therapy."

The final family therapy approach advocated for use with refugee and immigrant families is the *Milan systemic approach* (Boscolo et al 1987):

> Three key concepts of this school are neutrality, circularity, and hypothesizing, which are also the interventions used to help create change in the system. Hypothesizing is an assessment procedure, where the [therapist] engages in a research process with the family about the problem. After gathering information, a systemic hypothesis is formed which accounts for the behaviors of all of the persons in the system, and which forms the basis for an intervention. The "truth" of the hypothesis is not as important as its usefulness. Circular questioning is an interviewing technique based on the idea that the [therapist] conducts his or her research on the basis of feedback from the family in response to information obtained about relationships and differences. Family members are asked to comment on their beliefs about differences in degree or in perceptions with each other, ... giving the interviewer a picture of this family's belief system, the meaning they attach to events, and how they want things to be. Thus, the therapist understands the situation from the family's perspective, rather than trying to fit behaviors and events into a preconceived framework, which may not be culturally sensitive and which actually blocks the therapist's understanding. Neutrality is the basic therapeutic stance of the systemic therapist. Neutrality refers to the therapist's attempts to see and understand all sides of the issues as presented by various system members, which translates into non-induction into the system. When there are sticky coalitions escalating against each other, this multi-positional view helps the therapist move in between the conflicting sets.
>
> Rather than saying that the system creates the problem, these theorists view the problem as creating the system. Thus, ... the existing situation is viewed as a creation of the family's attempt to solve a problem. The intervention is not intended to give a new blueprint for action but to help the system get unstuck. An intervention is often organized around helping system members view the situation differently, thus seeing new options. This may involve positive connotation of intent; for example, if the parents or school personnel view the intent behind a youth's behavior more positively, the youth may see the attempts of others to stop his behavior in a different light, too. (KELLEY 1992, PP. 6–7)

Many authors recommend a combination of the above family therapy approaches in working with refugee and immigrant families. For example, Kelley (1992) recommends a combination of structural, strategic, and Milan systemic approaches; and Gopaul-McNicol (1993) presents a highly detailed "multicultural/multimodal/multi-systems" approach that combines psychoeducation, behavioral therapy, cognitive therapy, Bowen's systems therapy, structural therapy, and empowerment techniques. Support for the effectiveness of these combined approaches is provided by their authors' clinical experience; however, empirical research is needed to substantiate this.

Interventions for Child Abuse and Elder Abuse. There have been no reports in the literature on interventions for child abuse or elder abuse specifically with immigrant and refugee families. Therefore, only interventions pertaining to the general population are available to guide social workers in this area. The first step must be to report all suspected cases of abuse to the state child protective services or adult protective services departments. Social workers are mandated to report such cases, and cultural sensitivity cannot be used as an excuse for not reporting.

In regard to specific interventions for child abuse, the most promising interventions are behavioral, cognitive, and family preservation approaches (Corcoran 2000). Behavioral and cognitive approaches include methods such as relaxation training, cognitive restructuring, problem-solving skills training, communication skills training, and training in effective discipline methods such as positive reinforcement and time out (Corcoran 2000). Family preservation approaches are effective in preventing out-of-home placements of abused or neglected children (Corcoran 2000; Surgeon General 2000). "The success of these family preservation programs is based on the following: services are delivered in a home and community setting; family members are viewed as colleagues in defining a service plan; back-up services are available 24 hours a day; skills are built according to the individual needs of family members; marital and family interventions are offered; community services are efficiently coordinated; and assistance with basic needs such as food, housing, and clothing is given" (Surgeon General 2000, p. 15–16). This comprehensive approach is consistent with the multiple needs of refugee and immigrant families, suggesting that this may be an appropriate method for such families experiencing problems with child abuse and neglect; however, culturally compatible adaptations will likely have to be made.

In regard to elder abuse, "there have been no rigorous studies evaluating the outcome of interventions for elder abuse. In case series where outcome has been reported, the results have generally been disappointing" (Patterson 1994, p. 925). Some general suggestions for the prevention of elder abuse include:

- Sufficient income, health care, and social services for all older adults.
- Public awareness and professional training in relation to elder abuse.
- Coalition building.
- Mental health services, family counseling, and substance abuse treatment available to all in need of such services.
- Assertiveness training, promotion of elder rights, and self-advocacy training for all older adults.
- Adequate caregiver training and services.
- Adequate and available financial management and planning services.
- Violence reduction, conflict resolution, and mediation services available to all in need of such services.
- Awareness and facilitation of positive and productive aging.

(WOOLF 1998, PP. 8–9)

These suggestions can be readily adapted to immigrant and refugee communities. Additionally, the use of the above-described methods of intervention for intergenerational conflict, as well as interventions to mitigate the many other stressors of migration, may prevent child and elder abuse. However, empirical research is needed on the effectiveness of prevention and intervention with these problems for both the general population and immigrant and refugee families specifically.

ASSESSMENT AND INTERVENTIONS FOR CHILDREN AND ADOLESCENTS Assessment with refugee and immigrant children should include the following issues (Kopala, Esquivel, and Baptiste 1994):

- The child or adolescent's state of acculturation (assimilation, separation, marginalization, or biculturalism).
- Communication, coping, and social skills.
- Amount of family and external support.
- Willingness and ability to ask for help, express feelings openly, and to resist the demands of others.

Additionally, children may be assessed for mental health problems by a thorough evaluation that includes interviews with the parents, teachers, and other service providers, as well as interview and observation of the child (Surgeon General 2000). The same problems and caveats that exist regarding mental health diagnosis in immigrant and refugee adults apply to children as well. The problem of diagnosis is even more compounded in children due to their rapidly changing developmental process and the fact that many behaviors that may be indicative of mental health problems are normal at certain ages and in certain circumstances (Surgeon General 2000). As with adults, mental health assessment may be aided by brief symptom inventories such as the Children's Depression Inventory (Kovacs 1985) or the Child Behavior Checklist (Achenbach and Edelbrock 1983). Again, however, such instruments have not been validated for refugee and immigrant populations, so caution is warranted.

Interventions for Identity Conflict. The most commonly reported interventions specifically for immigrant and refugee children and adolescents are group interventions aimed at helping resolve ethnic identity conflicts and facilitating the acculturation process. Such interventions primarily have a preventive and educational aim and are often delivered in the school setting. One element that is commonly recommended is activities aimed at increasing participants' cultural pride about their native culture. This includes teaching about the history, traditions, and values of the native culture, and the differences between the culture in the homeland and the culture of immigrants. As part of this process, it may be useful to have the students give a presentation about their native culture in the school in a setting that ensures respect and attention (Salvador, Omizo, and Kim 1997; Mazzetti 1997).

Additionally, participants should be helped to understand what is happening to them in terms of cultural conflict. Thus, they need to be taught about the competing demands of their two cultural worlds. In this regard, Mazzetti (1997, p. 222) notes that "more than real cultures, [adolescents' understandings] are often caricatures of cultures, the result of superficial family, social, and mass media messages, expressions of "insensitivity" of Western culture, on the one hand, and of the "backwardness" of the culture of origin on the other. Thus it may be useful to help the teenager understand the true, important aspects of the two cultures." The goal of this cultural education is to help the participants to become bicultural, "to feel that they belong to both cultures rather than to neither and to feel OK in this condition, to begin discovering their identity as an individual who lives and shares in both, and to find effective means of negotiating this 'double citizenship'" (Mazzetti 1997, p. 222).

Another element commonly used in interventions for immigrant and refugee children and adolescents is social skills training, in which participants are helped to acquire new skills, such as assertiveness, that are functional for the new environment. This may also extend to areas such as dating practices (Tsui and Sammons 1988).

Some authors suggest the use of peer counselors in intervention programs for immigrant and refugee youth (Kopala, Esquivel, and Baptiste 1994; Tsui and Sammons 1988). The peers are immigrant and refugee youth who have been in the new country longer and are able to serve as a bridge between the old and new cultures. Tsui and Sammons (1988) state that the use of peer counselors facilitates open discussion and better learning, and also gives the peer counselors the opportunity to practice assertiveness skills with group participants. Alternatively, intervention programs may use a "buddy system" in which the immigrant or refugee student is paired with a student from the host culture (Kim, Omizo, and Salvador 1996; Kopala, Esquivel, and Baptiste 1994). This has the goal of helping the new arrival adjust to the new culture, as well as helping members of the host culture understand the new arrivals, thereby decreasing negative interactions.

While these are all logical suggestions for intervention with immigrant and refugee youth, it must be noted that none of these interventions have been empirically evaluated. Therefore, research is needed to determine their effectiveness in helping these youth resolve their identity conflicts.

Interventions for Mental Health Problems. As noted earlier, in addition to identity conflicts, immigrant and refugee children and adolescents also experience the other stressors of the migration process. Consequently, they are at risk of developing some of the same mental health problems as adults, such as depression, anxiety (including post-traumatic stress disorder), and substance abuse, as well as problems unique to children and adolescents, such as disruptive disorders characterized by antisocial behavior (e.g., conduct disorder and oppositional defiant disorder). There have been no empirical reports in the literature on interventions for mental health problems specifically among immigrant and refugee children and adolescents. Therefore, again, social workers must be guided by the empirical literature on interventions for the general population of children and adolescents.

In general, the empirical evidence base for the effectiveness of mental health interventions for children is not as strong as that for adults. Most of the interventions used were originally developed for adults and then adapted for children; there has been little research conducted to determine which interventions are most effective for which problems; and few of the interventions have been tested in real-world settings (Surgeon General 2000).

For the treatment of depression and anxiety, various forms of behavioral and cognitive therapy are considered to be "probably effective" (Surgeon General 2000, p. 11). These essentially entail the same elements described in the preceding chapter for treatment of these problems in adults. For the treatment of antisocial behaviors in disruptive disorders, behavioral treatments directed at the parents that teach them to reward desirable behaviors and to ignore or punish deviant behaviors have been found to be effective. However, it is noted the degree to which these interventions may be effective with ethnic minority populations is not known, since these groups have not been sufficiently represented in the research (Surgeon General 2000). For the treatment of both disruptive disorders and substance abuse among youth, multisystemic therapy (Henggeler et al. 1998) has strong empirical support for effectiveness (Corcoran 2000; Surgeon General 2000).

> Multisystemic therapy (MST) is an intensive, short-term, home- and family-focused treatment approach for youth with severe emotional disturbances. . . . MST intervenes directly in the youth's family, peer group, school, and neighborhood by identifying and targeting factors that contribute to the youth's problem behaviors. The main goal of MST is to develop skills in both parents and community organizations affecting the youth that will endure after brief (3 to 4 months) and intensive treatment. MST was constructed around a set of principles that were put into practice and then expanded upon in a manual (Henggeler et al. 1998). (SURGEON GENERAL 2000, P. 16)

The comprehensive nature of this approach, its focus on family and community, and its short-term, goal-directed nature are all highly consistent with general recommendations for intervention with refugees and immigrants. Thus, it appears to be a promising intervention for this population; again, however, cultural adaptations are likely to be necessary.

In addition to these approaches, other mental health interventions may also be effective for immigrant and refugee youth, but as yet there are no outcome data on these. For example, Miller and Billings (1994) report on the use of expressive arts therapy, including play therapy, picture drawing, and sociodrama, with traumatized refugee children. Although the authors report success based on their own clinical observations, empirical data are lacking.

ASSESSMENT AND INTERVENTIONS FOR ELDERLY REFUGEES AND IMMIGRANTS

As with adults and children, mental health assessment in elderly refugees and immigrants is complicated by the multiple factors previously discussed.

Assessment with the elderly in general is further complicated by a higher rate of somatization, a high comorbidity with physical disorders, cognitive decline, and erroneous stereotypes about aging. Consequently, mental health problems among the elderly are often unidentified and there is a large unmet need for treatment (Surgeon General 2000). Therefore, social workers must take extra time in assessing elderly immigrants and refugees and must be knowledgeable about gerontology in general.

As described earlier, a primary task facing elderly immigrants and refugees is that of coming to terms with their migration experiences. If this task is not successfully negotiated, these individuals are at risk of falling into despair, or depression. For the general population, "several forms of psychotherapy are effective for the treatment of late-life depression, including cognitive-behavioral therapy, interpersonal psychotherapy, problem-solving therapy, brief psychodynamic psychotherapy, and reminiscence therapy, an intervention developed specifically for older adults on the premise that reflection upon positive and negative past life experiences enables the individual to overcome feelings of depression and despair. Group and individual formats have been used successfully" (Surgeon General 2000, pp. 18–19).

Reminiscence therapy in particular has been used with elderly refugees. It is considered particularly suitable, inasmuch as it focuses on reminiscing about the migration experience. Feinberg (1996) reports on the use of this method with a small group of elderly Russian refugees; and Szapocznik et al. (1981) used reminiscence therapy in combination with an ecological approach with elderly Cuban refugees. Feinberg (1996) reported success based on clinical observation, and Szapocznik et al. (1981) provided empirical evidence of the effectiveness of this approach.

SUMMARY OF MICRO ASSESSMENT AND INTERVENTIONS The above discussion indicates that a large range of interventions are potentially applicable to resolving the myriad challenges faced by refugee and immigrant families. However, as noted repeatedly, application and evaluation of these approaches specifically to these populations is needed in many instances.

7.3 CASE STUDY EXERCISES

BASED ON WHAT HAS BEEN DISCUSSED in this chapter, describe how you would intervene in the following cases.

7.3.1 CASE 1

I. E. was referred to the therapist because he had difficulty in sleeping. He was a refugee from Africa. He and his wife arrived in [the resettlement country] together. I. E. had trouble learning the language because of his concentration problems, while his wife mastered it in a year and went on to university. She made friends with other female students, and embraced some of their ideas about the position of women in society. I. E. felt threatened by these ideas. The couple started to have serious disagreements.

(VAN DER VEER 1998, P. 46)

7.3.2 CASE 2

The Matthews family was referred for therapy by the school psychologist because of the academic and behavioral problems of their two sons, Michael and Kendall, ages 7 and 9, respectively. The eldest child, Taiesha, age 13, was also having academic difficulties; she was failing all courses except gym. Mr. Matthews was originally from Jamaica, and Mrs. Matthews from Trinidad and Tobago. They had met in Jamaica, where Mrs. Matthews spent two years after completing high school in Trinidad. They had been married for 14 years, although eight years after they married Mrs. Matthews migrated to the United States "for a better life and to give my children the chance to get a good education." The children lived in Jamaica with their father and paternal grandparents. Michael was 1 year old when his mother left home, Kendall was 3, and Taiesha was 7. Since Mrs. Matthews had come to the United States on a holiday visa but had decided to stay on doing domestic work, she had lived for three years illegally in this country. In that time, she was unable to visit her children in Jamaica because she would not have been allowed reentry into the United States. She was later sponsored by her employer and obtained permanent residency (approximately five years after leaving home). She immediately sponsored the other members of her family, who were now here. Although they were not legal permanent residents yet, she expected them to become so within the next few months. When the family joined Mrs. Matthews, the children were then 6, 8, and 12. Currently the household was comprised of the nuclear family, a maternal aunt and uncle, and the maternal grandmother. The children had not seen the paternal grandparents with whom they lived in Jamaica since they left the island.

These background data were sent by the school psychologist along with the referring information. In addition, there were allegations of possible child abuse and educational neglect because of the children's excessive absences from school. School officials were strongly considering placing both boys in special education because of their emotional disturbances, and Taiesha in special education because of a learning disability. However, they agreed to withhold special education placement until psychotherapeutic intervention occurred. (GOPAUL-MCNICOL 1993, PP. 144–145)

7.3.3 CASE 3

Mrs. V., a 71-year-old Russian woman, developed severe abdominal pain shortly after her arrival in the United States and was admitted to a general hospital. Physical examination did not reveal any significant findings that could account for her symptoms. Despite this, she continued to complain of severe pain. Her hospital social worker noticed that she refused to eat food served her, but ate off her roommate's tray. It became apparent that Mrs. V. suspected secretly that her food had been poisoned. When referred for outpatient psychotherapy she was highly resistant, suspicious about her therapist, and focused mostly on somatic issues. She repeatedly questioned her therapist's ethnic and cultural identity and expressed mistrust both of the therapist and the method of treatment. She maintained that the reason for her depressed mood was her poor physical health and denied any intrapsychic conflicts. She also rejected the idea of psychotropic medications, citing her fear of side effects. . . . In time, Mrs. V. was able to develop a more trusting relationship with the therapist and began to discuss her family history and her life in Russia, full of deprivation, loss, and trauma. She described a typical life story for her generation, revealing that during the Stalinist purges her husband, a prominent historian, had been denounced as an "enemy of the people" in an anonymous letter to authorities. He was imprisoned (there was no investigation, no trial), and subsequently exiled to Siberia, where he eventually perished. Mrs. V. and her two young children struggled to survive on their own. . . . As the treatment progressed, Mrs. V. began to express resentment toward her family, feeling that they had left her no choice but to follow them to the United States. (GUSOVSKY 1995, PP. 223–224)

CHAPTER 8

LANGUAGE, EDUCATION, AND ECONOMIC WELL-BEING

IMMIGRANTS' AND REFUGEES' ENGLISH LANGUAGE ABILITY, educational attainment, and economic well-being are closely interrelated. These issues form the major area of concern with regard to immigration among policymakers and the general public. They are also most often the primary concern among immigrants and refugees themselves. Therefore, social workers working with immigrants and refugees need to be well-prepared to address these issues. This chapter will first summarize research findings in this area. Then, best practices for enhancing language ability, educational attainment, and economic well-being of refugees and immigrants will be presented. The chapter will conclude with several case study exercises for consideration of social work action.

8.1 RESEARCH FINDINGS ON LANGUAGE, EDUCATION, AND ECONOMIC WELL-BEING

IMMIGRANTS' AND REFUGEES' LANGUAGE ABILITY, educational attainment, and, in particular, economic status, are areas that have been extensively studied, particularly within the discipline of sociology. The following discussion will summarize the most recent research findings for each of these topics, including an examination of the factors that influence each one and the interrelationships among them.

8.1.1 LANGUAGE

ENGLISH-LANGUAGE ABILITY is frequently regarded as an important indicator of immigrants' and refugees' integration or adaptation to the new society

(Fix and Passel 1994; National Immigration Forum [NIF] 2000a). Therefore, numerous studies have examined the English language abilities of refugee and immigrant adults and children. Studies have also examined the concept of bilingualism. Each of these issues is addressed below.

LANGUAGE ABILITY OF ADULTS Among all foreign-born persons residing in the U.S., approximately one-half do not speak English well (U.S. Bureau of the Census 1993). This rate varies substantially by country of origin; excluding English-speaking countries, the rate of not speaking English well ranges from a high of more than 70 percent for persons from Mexico, China, El Salvador, and Guatemala, to a low of less than 15 percent for persons from Germany.

People who speak English "less than very well" are referred to as having "limited English proficiency (LEP)" (Fix and Passel 1994). This population has grown during the past two decades. This growth, however, is due to an overall growth in the number of immigrants and refugees; it is not due to an increase in the proportion of the foreign-born that are LEP, which has remained steady at approximately 60 percent (Fix and Passel 1994). In other words, the increase in the LEP population "is because the total level of immigration to the U.S. has grown, not because immigrants are refusing to speak English" (NIF 2000a, p. 2).

On the contrary, immigrants and refugees appear to be highly motivated to learn English (NIF 2000a). The demand for English-as-a-Second-Language (ESL) classes far exceeds their availability (National Clearinghouse on ESL Literacy Education [NCLE] 2000; NIF 2000a). Nationwide, ESL classes for adults serve almost 2 million people annually; however, these classes consistently report long waiting lists, with some programs actually having stopped keeping waiting lists because they were too long (NCLE 2000; NIF 2000a). Although no nationwide system exists to keep track of waiting lists, a recent study estimated that almost 3 million people expressed interest in ESL classes but were not participating for a variety of reasons (NCLE 2000).

For most immigrants and refugees, English ability improves with length of residence (NCLE 2000; NIF 2000a). For adults, "it is generally accepted that it takes from 5–7 years to go from not knowing any English at all to being able to accomplish most communication tasks including academic tasks" (NCLE, 2000, p. 3). However, the actual rate of English language acquisition by a given individual depends on many factors, including age, education, time available for language learning, level of literacy in the native language, opportunities to interact with native English speakers, and the value that the individual places on being bilingual (Langdon 1996; NCLE 2000; NIF 2000a).

LANGUAGE ABILITY OF CHILDREN Across generations, the rate of English language acquisition appears to be increasing:

> It appears that between generations, immigrants are becoming completely dominant in English, and losing their native language at a faster pace than immigrants early in this century. Previously, it had taken three generations for an immigrant family to completely lose its native tongue: immigrants would learn enough English to get by while remaining dominant in their native language; their children would be bilingual, gradually losing their ethnic language as they grew older; and their children—the grandchildren of the immigrants—would be largely monolingual English speakers. In recent decades, there appears to be a trend toward monolingual English speaking in the children of immigrants. (NIF 2000A P. 1)

Nationally, more than 2 million public school students are identified as Limited English Proficient (Center for Applied Linguistics 2000). However, once exposure to the new language begins, immigrant and refugee children acquire English much faster than their parents, due to the rapid cognitive learning of children as compared to adults, and to the children's greater exposure to English outside the home. This can sometimes cause problems in immigrant and refugee families. When children become largely monolingual in English, they may lose the ability to effectively communicate with their parents who are less proficient in English (Langdon 1996; Mouw and Xie 1997). Such communication problems can then persist throughout the family members' lives (Hinton 1999).

Children's language use is also associated with both family conflict and ethnic identity:

> The majority of immigrant parents want their children to retain proficiency in their native language in addition to learning English, and a preference by immigrant children to speak English significantly increases the incidence of

parent-child conflict. There is evidence that native language use is associated with the maintenance of ethnic identity among immigrants. It has been argued, for example, that the preference among some immigrant children to speak only English may entail abandoning not only a mother tongue but also a personal identity. . . . Because of this close connection between language and ethnic identity, bilingualism is . . . an indicator of the maintenance of ethnicity. In this sense, bilingualism provides an important means through which immigrants can accommodate without assimilating, by adapting to the functional demands of American society without giving up their linguistic and ethnic identity. (MOUW AND XIE 1997, PP. 2–3)

BILINGUALISM It is generally accepted that bilingualism is the desired outcome for immigrant and refugee children. Not only does it enhance family communication, reduce the probability of family conflict, and help maintain ethnic identity, it also may provide the children a competitive advantage in the workforce once they become adults (Marcos 1999; McLaughlin 1995), particularly as the economy becomes increasingly global. Similarly, for adults, bilingualism is desirable because it facilitates adaptation and integration into the new society without giving up one's ethnic identity.

However, for both children and adults, it is important to recognize that being bilingual does not necessarily mean equal proficiency in both languages. Immigrants and refugees who learn English as children and whose educational experiences are in English generally become more proficient in and have a preference for English rather than their native language (Hinton 1999; Langdon 1996; Rumbaut 1999); conversely, those who learn English as adults generally remain more proficient in and have a preference for their native language. From a developmental perspective, in general, people who acquire a new language before puberty do not have a foreign accent in the new language, whereas those who acquire the new language after puberty have a foreign accent (Marcos 1999). "At times an accent may prevent a second language learner of English to be fully accepted by certain members of the mainstream" (Langdon 1996, p. 44).

Bilingual individuals tend to use the two languages in different situations. They may use the native language with family and close friends, and English in other situations. Bilingual speakers also commonly engage in "code switching" in which two different languages are used within the same conversation (Langdon 1996; McLaughlin 1995). This may occur at the level of single words, phrases, or sentences (McLaughlin 1995). Code switching may occur because the speaker knows the appropriate expression in one language but not the other, or an equivalent expression does not exist in one of the languages. Code switching may be accompanied by a switching of affect that reflects the person's background experiences in the acquisition of each language, or the cultural norms of behavior that accompany each language. Thus, "studies of code switching in adults show it to be a sophisticated, rule-governed communicative device used to achieve goals such as conveying emphasis or establishing cultural identity" (McLaughlin 1995, p. 2).

When code switching occurs due to unequal proficiency in the two languages, it frequently leads to the invention of new words or expressions that are a combination of the two languages. For example, the amalgamation of Spanish and English in this way is called "Spanglish," mixed Korean and English is called "Konglish," and mixed Hindi and English is called "Hinglish" (Hinton 1999). Such mixed-language use is not uncommon, particularly among second-generation immigrants and refugees.

Thus, social workers should be aware of the role of language in cultural identity, in family dynamics, and in the way immigrants and refugees interact in various aspects of their lives. Additionally, English-language ability is important because it is a strong determinant of both educational attainment in the new country and economic well-being, as is discussed below.

8.1.2 EDUCATION

THE FOLLOWING DISCUSSION will address the educational attainment of adult immigrants and refugees, followed by the academic achievement of immigrant and refugee children and the factors that influence it.

EDUCATIONAL ATTAINMENT OF ADULTS National data on the educational attainment of adult immigrants and refugees have been summarized by Fix and Passel (1994, pp. 32–34):

> Immigrants are concentrated at the extremes of the educational spectrum in comparison with natives. They are much more likely than natives to have

very low educational attainment. But they are also more likely than natives to have advanced degrees. In 1990, 26 percent of the foreign-born over age 25 had less than nine years of education compared to only 9 percent of the native population. But 20 percent of both natives and immigrants have a college degree and recent immigrants (24 percent) are more likely than natives to have a college degree....

Country of origin makes a difference in educational attainment. At the low end of the range, 40 percent of immigrants from Latin America have less than nine years of education compared with 20 percent of European and Canadian and 15 percent of Asian immigrants. At the high end, 15 percent of Asian immigrants have advanced degrees versus 9 percent for European immigrants, 4 percent for Latin American immigrants, and 7 percent for natives....

The educational disparities [between foreign-born persons with differing legal status] are striking. Over 75 percent of recent immigrants from the major source countries for illegal immigrants have less than a high school diploma. This contrasts with the 46 percent of immigrants from refugee sending countries and only 26 percent from [the major source countries for legal immigrants]. At the same time, recent legal immigrants are much more likely to hold college degrees (33 percent) than natives (20 percent) or the other [foreign-born] groups.

Beyond descriptive statistics such as these, there have been very few studies about the educational attainment of immigrant and refugee adults. There have been almost no studies on changes in the educational attainment of adults after arrival in the new country, the factors that influence such changes, nor programs or strategies specifically targeted toward enhancing the educational attainment of immigrant and refugee adults. One exception to this is an annual survey conducted by the Office of Refugee Resettlement (ORR), which, among other things, collects data on school and university attendance of adult refugees who entered the U.S. during the prior five years. Recent survey results showed that approximately 24 percent of the refugees in the sample had attended a school or university since arrival in the U.S., and approximately 18 percent had attended a school or university for a degree or certificate, most commonly a high school diploma or a bachelor's degree (ORR 1998a). However, the report did not examine what factors had influenced these refugees to seek to advance their education.

ACADEMIC ACHIEVEMENT OF CHILDREN In contrast to the dearth of research on adults, there has been a wealth of research on the educational attainment of immigrant and refugee children and adolescents, and the factors that influence their academic achievement. This research interest is due in part to the increasing number of immigrant and refugee students in public schools. Currently, children from immigrant families comprise 19 percent of all schoolchildren, and half of the growth in school-age children in the next decade will be attributable to children from immigrant families (Grantmakers Concerned with Immigrants and Refugees [GCIR] 2000). The research interest is also spurred by the widespread belief that "the long-term effects of contemporary immigration will hinge more on the trajectories of [the children of immigrants] than the fate of their parents. Children of today's immigrants . . . represent the most consequential and lasting legacy of the U.S.'s new mass immigration" (Rumbaut 1999, p. 4).

Despite the linguistic and other challenges that immigrant and refugee children face, numerous studies have demonstrated that their academic achievement overall is quite high, in some cases better than that of native-born students (Caplan, Choy, and Whitmore 1991; Fuligni 1997; Kao 1999; Kao and Tienda 1995; Rumbaut 1999; Vernez, Abrahamse, and Quigley 1996; Zhou and Bankston 1994). For example, "first- and second-generation adolescents in immigrant families nationally have slightly higher grades and math test scores than adolescents in native-born families" (Hernandez 1999, p. 11). Additionally:

• Immigrant high school students are as likely as natives to graduate from high school within four years of their sophomore year.
• Immigrants are more likely than native-born youth to make choices, beginning early in school, consistent with eventual college-going, regardless of race or ethnicity. They follow an academic track, take advanced courses in mathematics and science, take the SAT or ACT, and work hard to achieve their expectations.
• Overall, immigrants are more likely than natives to enroll in postsecondary education, attend college, and stay continuously through four years of college. Asian immigrants are more likely to go continuously to college than any other racial/ethnic immigrant group.
• Variations among immigrant ethnic groups generally parallel variations among native-born groups: Asian immigrants perform better on indicators of college preparation, followed by white and black immigrants.

(SCHWARTZ 1996, PP. 1–2)

Although academic achievement of immigrant and refugee children overall is good, it does differ by country of origin and generation. For example:

> First-, second-, and higher-generation Mexican adolescents are similar in grades and math scores, although there is a tendency, especially for reading test scores, toward improvement across generations. Mexican adolescents of all generations have substantially lower educational achievements than non-Hispanic white adolescents in native-born families. . . . Chinese adolescents in immigrant families, especially the second generation, exceed Chinese adolescents in native-born families in grades and math test scores. However, only the second generation exceeds the third and higher generations in reading test scores. Chinese first- and second-generation adolescents also exceed non-Hispanic white adolescents in native-born families in grades and math test scores. The second generation has higher reading scores as well. . . . Among Filipino adolescents, the second generation also achieves better grades and math and reading scores than the first or third and higher generations. Compared to non-Hispanic white adolescents in native-born families, first- and second-generation Filipino adolescents achieve higher grades.
> (HERNANDEZ 1999, PP. 11–12)

Additional research findings regarding academic achievement include the following, from a large-scale study of first- and second-generation immigrant and refugee adolescents in the Miami-Fort Lauderdale and San Diego school districts (Rumbaut 1999, pp. 13–16):

- Children of immigrants are ambitious. Two-thirds aspire to advanced degrees and one-fourth would be dissatisfied with less than a college degree. While most of these youths aim high, the least ambitious expectations are exhibited by Mexicans, Cambodians, and Laotians.
- Even more ambitious are their parents. While 44 percent of the students "realistically" expected to attain an advanced degree, 65 percent of their parents did; and while 18 percent of the children expected to stop short of a college degree, only 7 percent of the parents held such low expectations.
- In contrast to the perceived parental pressure to achieve are the plans of the students' close friends. The peer groups in which they are embedded vary. The sharpest contrast is between the Jamaicans, Filipinos, and other Asians, most of whose friends intended to attend four-year institutions, and

Mexican students, only a quarter of whom had friends planning to attend four-year colleges and about 8 percent of whom reported most of their close friends had already dropped out.
- The children of immigrants almost universally value the importance of a good education. 90 percent regarded a good education as "very important," and another 85 percent deemed becoming an expert in one's field "very important."
- The majority of these children invest a substantial amount of time on daily homework. Although wide variations are seen among the different groups, about 80 percent of the sample spent more than an hour each day on homework, and over 40 percent spent about two hours daily, well above the national average of less than an hour a day. Asian-origin groups invested the most time on homework, while the Latin Americans invested the least.
- In both school districts, a significantly greater proportion of students district-wide drop out of school than do the youth from immigrant families. In Miami, the multi-year dropout rate for grades 9–12 was about double the rate for the immigrant youth; in San Diego, the multi-year dropout rate was about triple the rate for the immigrant youth. The immigrant youth dropout rates were also noticeably lower than the district-wide rates for predominantly native non-Hispanic white high school students. Lower dropout rates for children of immigrants were seen for both genders and every racial-ethnic category.
- At every grade level, the children of immigrants outperformed the district norms in grade point average, although the gap narrowed over time and grade level.
- The Chinese finished high school with the highest GPAs and the lowest dropout rates, as well as ambitious educational goals matching those of other Asian-origin immigrant groups, especially those from India, Japan, and Korea. Exhibiting above-average performance were the Vietnamese and the Filipinos, followed by the Laotians and Cambodians. The latter two groups also exhibited the lowest educational expectations. Jamaicans and other West Indians had lower GPAs, yet they still reported above-average ambitions. Overall, the worst performance was registered by Latin American youth, with the lowest GPAs found among the Dominicans, and the highest dropout rates among Cubans, followed by Mexicans. Among the Latin Americans, Mexican, Dominican, and Central American children showed the lowest educational expectations, while Cubans and South Americans were the most ambitious in their expressed educational aspirations.

FACTORS AFFECTING ACADEMIC ACHIEVEMENT OF CHILDREN Research has shown that the academic achievement of immigrant and refugee children is influenced by many factors at the levels of the individual, the family, the peer group, the school, and the community. Most of the differences in academic achievement across the various national-origin groups are explained by these factors; in other words, there is nothing inherent about national origin itself that causes some groups to perform better or worse. To a large extent the factors that influence the academic achievement of refugee and immigrant children are the same ones that influence non-immigrant children, although a few factors are unique (Rumbaut 1999; Schwartz 1996).

Individual factors. These include the child's motivation, aspirations, and expectations; English proficiency; self-esteem; sense of belonging to the school; time spent studying, doing homework, seeking extra help, and watching television; gender; age at immigration and length of residence in the new country; and bilingualism, level of acculturation and ethnic identity (Fuligni 1997; Gibson 1987; Gonzalez and Padilla 1997; Portes and MacLeod 1996; Rivera-Batiz 1996; Rumbaut 1999; Schwartz 1996). Academic achievement is positively influenced by having higher motivation, aspirations, and expectations; by having better English proficiency; by having higher self-esteem; and by having a sense of belonging to the school, as indicated by having a positive attitude toward school and teachers and feeling accepted by peers (Fuligni 1997; Gonzalez and Padilla 1997; Rivera-Batiz 1996; Rumbaut 1999). Academic performance is positively influenced by spending more time studying, doing homework, and seeking extra help; and is negatively influenced by spending more time watching television (Fuligni 1997; Rumbaut 1999).

In regard to demographic variables such as gender, age at immigration, and length of residence, "while gender makes only a small difference in terms of dropping out . . . , it strongly affects grades and ambitions, with females exhibiting superior performance compared to male students, as well as having a significant edge in educational expectations" (Rumbaut 1999, p. 16). Children who arrive in the new country at younger ages, particularly by age 6 or 7, do better academically than those who arrive later, particularly after age 15; and the shorter time that youth have been in the U.S., the lower are their college-going and continuing rates (Gibson 1987; Schwartz 1996).

The relationships between bilingualism, acculturation, ethnic identity, and academic achievement are complex and somewhat controversial. Several studies have shown that bilingual students have better academic achievement than both Limited English Proficient and English-only monolingual students (Marcos 1999; McLaughlin 1995; Rumbaut 1999). This finding has been used by advocates of bilingual education as an argument in its favor. However, it is important to recognize that the association between bilingualism and academic achievement does not mean that bilingualism leads to better academic achievement; it may be a spurious correlation, meaning that both bilingualism and academic achievement are influenced by a common cause. "In other words, for immigrant children, rapid acquisition of English and retention of native language ability are affected by unobserved factors such as intelligence and motivation, which also have a positive effect on academic achievement. Thus, part of the apparent association between bilingualism and school performance may be due to these unobserved factors as common causes" (Mouw and Xie 1997, p. 6). Rather than bilingualism having a direct effect on academic achievement, Mouw and Xie (1997) demonstrated that its importance lies in preventing a language gap within the immigrant family; this, in turn, leads to improved academic achievement. Thus, bilingualism has a positive effect on academic achievement only if the parents do not speak English well, once the parents become moderately proficient in English, the apparent positive effect of the children's bilingualism upon academic achievement disappears.

In general, research suggests that as immigrant and refugee children become more assimilated into the mainstream culture, their academic achievement declines (Rivera-Batiz 1996). However, the actual relationship between acculturation and academic achievement is more complex than this. Portes and Zhou (1993) have proposed a theory of "segmented assimilation" that is specific to immigrant and refugee youth who are also minorities of color (i. e., Blacks, Hispanics, and Asians). The theory suggests that these youth have three options for acculturation: assimilation into the white middle class; assimilation into the urban "underclass," that is, native-born ethnic minority groups; or deliberate preservation of the national origin identity. Portes and Zhou (1993) argue that assimilation into the urban "underclass" is associated with decreased academic achievement and downward mobility, due to the racial discrimination and reduced economic opportunities for minorities of color. These theorists and others (Gibson and Ogbu 1991) also suggest that the adoption of minority ethnic identities "may disparage doing well in school as 'acting White' and a betrayal of ethnic loyalty, with counterproductive consequences for educational achievement" (Rumbaut 1999, p. 18).

On the other hand, deliberate preservation of the national origin identity is said to be associated with increased academic achievement and upward mobility. "The basic idea is that certain cultural values and practices, which are carried on mostly within immigrant families but further reinforced by the larger ethnic community, . . . may be mobilized for the educational success of immigrant children" (Mouw and Xie 1997, p. 6).

However, recent research only partially supports the theory of segmented assimilation. Rumbaut (1999) examined the academic achievement of immigrant and refugee youth in relation to four types of ethnic identity, based on how the youth defined themselves: a plain "American" identity; a hyphenated-American identity; a national-origin identity (e. g., Filipino, Cuban, Jamaican); and a pan-ethnic minority group identity (e. g., Hispanic, Asian, Black). He found that those with a pan-ethnic identity had lower grade point averages, somewhat higher dropout rates, and lower aspirations than the other three ethnic identity groups, which did not differ from each other on these indicators of academic achievement. This supports the theoretical prediction regarding downward mobility associated with assimilation into native-born ethnic minority groups, but it does not support the prediction regarding upward mobility associated with preservation of the national origin identity. Similarly, Gonzalez and Padilla (1997) found that cultural loyalty, as indicated by nonassimilation and cultural pride, was not predictive of academic achievement among Mexican-American students. Furthermore, "an important but largely unexplored question raised by the literature on segmented assimilation . . . is whether the academic success of upwardly mobile immigrants really is due to the preservation of a distinct ethnic identity or due instead to a more general set of practices such as hard work, high aspirations, and parental involvement which are easily transferred across different ethnic cultures" (Mouw and Xiu 1997, p. 2).

Family factors. The family factors that influence academic achievement include family socioeconomic status, family structure, parent-child conflict, parental expectations for children's achievement, and parental involvement in educational activities (Duran and Weffer 1992; Fuligni 1997; Gonzalez and Padilla 1997; Hernandez 1999; Rivera-Batiz 1996; Portes and MacLeod 1996; Rumbaut 1999; Schwartz 1996). Academic achievement is positively influenced by higher socioeconomic status, as indicated by family income and parents' educational levels and occupations (Fuligni 1997; Hernandez 1999; Portes and MacLeod 1996; Rivera-Batiz 1996; Rumbaut 1999; Schwartz 1996). "More [socioeconomically] advantaged students have educational supports such as encyclopedias and computers. They are also likely to have better educated parents who can help them with homework, and can set an example of academic achievement" (Rivera-Batiz 1996, p. 2). Much of the variation in academic achievement across national origin groups is due to variations in socioeconomic status (Hernandez 1999; Schwartz 1996).

Children from families in which both parents are present in the home perform better than children in single-parent families or stepfamilies (Rumbaut 1999). Additionally, "immigrant college-going is positively affected by a mother working outside the home, and negatively affected by the presence of three or more siblings" (Schwartz 1996, p. 2). Also, lower levels of parent-child conflict are associated with higher academic achievement (Rumbaut 1999). Finally, academic achievement is positively influenced by greater parental expectations and greater parental involvement in educational activities (Fuligni 1997; Gonzalez and Padilla 1997; Hernandez 1999; Rumbaut 1999; Schwartz 1996). Research on parental involvement reveals the following findings:

> Family members can foster school success by engaging in various activities with their young children, including teaching them letters and numbers, reading to them, and working on projects with them. . . . Children in immigrant families [are] equally or only somewhat less likely than non-Hispanic white children in native-born families to have parents who engage in . . . different activities of this type. . . . Parents can also foster school achievement by taking their children on a variety of educational outings. Estimates of the proportion of immigrant and native-born children whose parents took them on . . . different types of outings . . . [do] not vary systematically. The involvement of parents in their children's schools is a third set of activities that foster successful school achievement. Children in immigrant families [are] about as likely as children in native-born Hispanic and black families to have parents who report themselves as being highly involved in their children's schools. Although children in immigrant families [are] somewhat less likely than children in non-Hispanic white families to have parents who [are] highly involved in school, most of the difference [is] accounted for by the higher proportion with a moderate level of parental involvement.
>
> (HERNANDEZ 1999, PP. 8–9)

Peer Factors. Peer factors that influence academic achievement include peers' educational expectations and experiences, and involvement of peers in educational activities (Fuligni 1997; Gonzalez and Padilla 1997; Rumbaut

1999). "[Peer] social circles are a powerful influence in reinforcing or undercutting [students'] aspirations as well as their confidence.... The worst outcomes [are] associated with having close friends who [have] dropped out or [have] no plans for college while, conversely, the best outcomes [are] attained by students whose circle of friends [consists] largely of college-bound peers" (Rumbaut 1999, p. 14, p. 23). Students who have a network of friends that help each other with homework, study together for tests, and encourage each other to do well perform better than students without such a peer network (Fuligni 1997).

School Factors. School factors that influence academic achievement include the ethnic composition of the school, school curriculum, and the wealth of the school as reflected by its neighborhood location (Duran and Weffer 1992; Gonzalez and Padilla 1997; Portes and MacLeod 1997). Schools that have a high concentration of students from a particular ethnic group may foster a greater sense of school belonging among those students, which in turn leads to greater academic achievement (Gonzalez and Padilla 1997). Enhanced school curricula designed to reinforce student learning for students who are disadvantaged by low family socioeconomic status have a positive effect on students' academic achievement (Duran and Weffer 1992). Lastly, the relationship between school wealth, as reflected by location, and student achievement is complex:

> The gain [in academic achievement] attributable to relatively successful and well-integrated immigrant groups appears to be impervious to changes in school contexts: It is as strong in the impoverished inner-city schools as in suburban schools. On the other hand, the negative effects associated with disadvantaged ethnicity are most apparent when second-generation students face the stiffer academic competition of schools outside the central city. (PORTES AND MACLEOD 1997, P. 270)

Community Factors. This is the final set of factors that influence academic achievement. The most relevant community factor for immigrant and refugee children is the community's "mode of incorporation," or the context in which the foreign-born are received (Portes and Rumbaut 1990):

> The context that receives immigrants plays a decisive role in their process of adaptation.... Immigrants who are granted legal status, receive resettlement assistance, and are not subject to widespread discrimination are expected to experience both faster economic progress and a smoother process of social

and psychological integration.... There is evidence that a favorable governmental and societal reception leads to faster socioeconomic mobility, a more positive self-image, and better integrated immigrant communities.... [This] should have positive effects on children's attainment even after parents' socioeconomic status is controlled. Conversely, offspring of disadvantaged immigrants would be caught in the double bind of slower socioeconomic mobility and weaker and more unstable community bonds.... Modes of incorporation . . . are eventually reflected in the confident optimism with which some parents look at the future and point proudly to their group's achievements and the insecurity and collective despair of others.... Inequalities in the objective situations and subjective outlooks of parents converge with the . . . academic performance of children, indicating that both class and ethnic privilege are transmitted from one generation to the next.

(PORTES AND MACLEOD 1996, P. 257, P. 271)

Summary. While many children in immigrant and refugee families perform well in school, many are also disadvantaged by low family socioeconomic status, limited English proficiency, late entry into the U. S. school system, assimilation into societally disadvantaged minority groups, and the many other factors described above. In the context of the educational system, it is these children who are of particular concern to social workers and for whom specialized interventions need to be targeted. This is critical because educational attainment is a crucial factor in economic well-being later in life, as is discussed below.

8.1.3 ECONOMIC WELL-BEING

THE ECONOMIC STATUS of immigrants and refugees is the issue that is of greatest concern to the general public and policymakers in immigration debates. This concern focuses less on the economic well-being of the immigrants and refugees themselves, and more on their impact on the economic well-being of the native-born population. However, from the perspective of the social work profession, which has its roots in helping poor people, the concern is more with the economic well-being of the immigrants and refugees themselves. Nonetheless, these are two sides of the same coin, since the economic well-being of immigrants and refugees in turn influences the economic well-being of society as a whole.

The following discussion will first address the research findings on the economic impact of immigrants and refugees. This will be followed by a discussion of the findings related to the economic well-being of immigrant and refugee individuals and families, and the factors that influence it.

ECONOMIC IMPACT OF IMMIGRANTS AND REFUGEES Contrary to prevailing public perceptions, immigrants are net economic contributors to the U. S. economy. A synthesis of data from the most recent and methodologically best studies reveals the following findings:

- Immigrants add about $10 billion each year to the U. S. economy. This estimate does not include the impact of immigrant-owned businesses or the impact of highly skilled immigrants in overall productivity.
- By conservative estimates, immigrants paid an estimated $133 billion in direct taxes to federal, state, and local governments in 1997. The typical immigrant and his or her children pay an estimated $80,000 more in taxes than they will receive in local, state, and federal benefits over their lifetimes.
- Immigrants who become U. S. citizens typically pay more in taxes than do native-born Americans. Adult, foreign-born, naturalized citizens have higher adjusted gross incomes (averaging $40,502) than families with U. S.-born citizens only ($35,249). Federal taxes paid by families with a naturalized citizen average $6,580 per year compared with $5,070 for U. S.-born-only families.
- Immigrant businesses add at least another $29 billion to the total amount of taxes paid by immigrants.
- Immigrants' earnings rise over time. In their first years in the United States, immigrants typically are net drains on the public coffers, but over time—usually after 10 to 15 years—they turn into net contributors.
- More than 70 percent of immigrants are over the age of 18 when they arrive in the United States. That means there are roughly 17.5 million immigrants in the United States today whose education and upbringing were paid for by the citizens of the sending country, not American taxpayers. The benefit to the United States of obtaining this human capital at no expense is roughly $1.43 trillion.
- The total net benefit (taxes paid over benefits received) to the Social Security system in today's dollars from continuing current levels of immigration is nearly $500 billion for the 1998–2022 period and nearly $2 trillion through 2072.
- Like natives, immigrants use more state and local services than they pay

for in state and local taxes. The average immigrant imposes a net lifetime fiscal cost on state and local governments of $25,000. Their overall net tax contribution, when considering all levels of government is explained by the fact that most of the taxes immigrants pay—income and social security tax—go to the federal government, while many of the services used—schools, hospitals, and roads—are provided by local governments. Despite this imbalance, there is no evidence that states or cities with large immigrant populations perform worse economically than those with small immigrant populations. In fact, the opposite is generally true.

• Working-age immigrants who have been in the United States for more than ten years are less likely to receive welfare than the native-born. With their special needs, refugees and elderly immigrants are more likely to receive welfare than the native-born. However, given that recent welfare rules enacted in 1996 make newly arriving immigrants ineligible for most welfare benefits, the net fiscal benefit of future immigrants will be higher than it is today. (NATIONAL IMMIGRATION FORUM 1999B, PP. 1–2)

In addition to these data on the net economic contribution of immigrants, many studies have been conducted on the impact of immigrants upon the labor market. A comprehensive synthesis of these studies reveals the following findings:

> There is no strong evidence that immigration reduces overall availability of jobs or wages. Immigrants may reduce the employment opportunities of low-skill workers, however, especially in areas where the local economy is weak and immigrants are concentrated. Immigration does not hurt the job prospects of African Americans as a whole, but it reduces their economic opportunities in areas of high immigration during recessionary periods. New immigrants appear to hurt the overall labor market chances of one population group—the immigrants who immediately preceded them. Immigration may also be altering the movement of native workers into and out of high-immigration areas. (FIX AND PASSEL 1994, P. 47)

In contrast to these facts indicating that in general, immigrants do not have a negative impact on either the labor force prospects of native-born workers or on the economy as a whole, a number of highly publicized studies have reported that immigrants are a net drain on the economy. It has been demonstrated that these studies used flawed analyses. These flaws include the following:

- Tax collections from immigrants are understated.
- Service costs for immigrants are overstated.
- Benefits of immigrant-owned businesses as well as the economic benefits generated by consumer spending from immigrants are ignored.
- Job displacement impacts and costs are overstated.
- Parallel computations for natives, which would show that natives are also net tax users [at the local and state levels], are not done.
- The size of the immigrant population—particularly the undocumented population—is overstated. (FIX AND PASSEL 1994, P. 59)

CONSEQUENTLY, ANTI-IMMIGRANT ARGUMENTS based on these flawed studies are without merit.

ECONOMIC WELL-BEING OF IMMIGRANTS AND REFUGEES Despite the overall net positive economic contribution as described above, it is important to understand that the economic well-being of immigrants and refugees themselves varies considerably, particularly in relation to legal status (i. e., legal immigrants, refugees, undocumented immigrants, naturalized citizens). The economic well-being of immigrants and refugees may be assessed by a variety of indicators, including labor force participation, income, occupation, poverty rates, welfare utilization, and home ownership (Potocky 1996a). Some data on these indicators were presented in chapter 1 (see tables 1.20, 1.21, 1.23). These data are reviewed below, along with additional research findings. Data separated by the legal status of the foreign-born are presented where available; comparable data by legal status are not available for all the indicators.

Labor Force Participation. Immigrants and refugees participate in three labor markets: the primary labor market, the secondary labor market, and the enclave economy labor market. The primary market is the legal employment market of the general society. Most immigrants and refugees are employed in this market. The secondary labor market is the illegal, "unofficial" market where labor laws regarding such things as minimum wage, working hours, and taxes are ignored. This includes occupations such as housekeepers in private households, garment workers in some large factories, and many other types of employment. This secondary market is the major market for illegal immigrants. Finally, the enclave economy refers to geographic areas with high concentrations of immigrant- or refugee-owned businesses, which in turn employ members of their own ethnic groups (Portes and

Rumbaut 1990). Official statistics on labor force participation do not include data on the secondary labor market. Additionally, these statistics typically reflect only a worker's main job; thus, it is not known how many such workers also hold second or third jobs, which may be in any of the three labor markets.

According to official statistics, the foreign-born population accounts for 12 percent of the U. S. labor force, and 20 percent of new entrants into the labor force are immigrants and refugees (Grantmakers Concerned with Immigrants and Refugees [GCIR] 2000). Employment rates are very similar across various categories of foreign-born and native-born persons: approximately 63 percent each for all native-born citizens and all naturalized citizens, approximately 61 percent for all noncitizens, and approximately 56 percent for refugees who arrived during the past five years (Office of Refugee Resettlement 1998b; U. S. Bureau of the Census 1998).

Income. As was seen in table 1.20, annual earnings are similar for native-born citizens and naturalized citizens: 21 percent and 23 percent, respectively, have earnings below $20,000. In contrast, 46 percent of noncitizens have earnings below $20,000. However, at the highest income level, over $50,000, the proportion of naturalized citizens exceeds that of native-born citizens. Additional data indicate that "notwithstanding individual earning differences, households headed by immigrants have virtually the same average income as native-headed households, because immigrant-headed households are larger and have more earners" (Fix and Passel 1994, p. 36). As expected, household income varies considerably by legal status:

> Households headed by [recent] immigrants ... from the major source countries for illegal immigration have average incomes of 36 percent less than natives. Even [longer-term illegal immigrants] fall 23 percent below natives. But recent immigrants from the major source countries for legal immigration have incomes falling only slightly below those of natives. . . . [Longer-term legal immigrants] have incomes 16 percent above those of natives. The entrants from refugee countries tend to fall between the other two groups. Here again, average household incomes of [longer-term entrants] from refugee countries exceed those of natives. (FIX AND PASSEL 1994, P. 37).

Occupation. "The two largest occupational groups for immigrants . . . are operators/laborers/fabricators and service workers—40 percent of all foreign-born work in those two occupation groups, compared with 30 percent for natives" (Fix and Passel 1994, p. 36). The service sector alone, which includes occupations such as food preparation, child care, and janitorial services, employs 19 percent of recent immigrants, versus 9 percent of natives (GCIR 2000). And "immigrants are less likely than natives to have clerical, professional, and managerial jobs—25% of the foreign-born hold such jobs compared with 30% for natives" (Fix and Passel 1994, p. 36). In two of the nation's major immigrant areas, New York City and Los Angeles, "it is the traditional immigrant industries that comprise the leading immigrant employers of today: restaurants (number one in both cities), apparel (number two in both cities), private household (number three in both cities), and then a variety of personal service and manufacturing industries, with services to buildings, laundries, hotels, and auto repair among the top ten in both places" (Waldinger 1995, p. 2).

A portion of the sociological literature on immigrant economic adaptation is devoted to immigrant entrepreneurship, or self-employment (e. g., Portes and Rumbaut 1990; Aronson 1997a). Overall, however, only 6.8 percent of the foreign-born are self-employed, a proportion which is small and similar to the proportion for the native-born, 7 percent (U.S. Bureau of the Census 1993). Further, although entrepreneurship is conceivably an important element in job creation and wealth generation for both the foreign-born and natives, there are almost no data available on the extent to which this is true empirically (Aronson 1997a). What evidence is available indicates that immigrant-owned businesses neither help nor hinder the economic well-being of other immigrants from the same ethnic group, and their role in the economic advancement of the owners themselves is questionable (Aronson 1997a). Thus, immigrant entrepreneurship appears to have minimal importance to the economic well-being of the vast majority of immigrants.

Finally, some immigrants and refugees, particularly in the early years after arrival, experience underemployment or "status inconsistency." This refers to having a job that is below one's level of education or abilities. This situation may be due to many factors, such as poor English proficiency, the nonrecognition of education, training, or licensure obtained in the country or origin, or employment discrimination. Status inconsistency frequently leads to poor psychological well-being and overall difficulty in the adaptation process (Aycan and Berry 1996; Tang and O'Brien 1990; Vinokurov, Birman, and Trickett 2000; Westwood and Ishiyama 1991).

Poverty. As was shown in table 1.20, the rates for people living below the poverty level are higher for noncitizens (21%) but lower for naturalized citizens (9%), compared to the native-born (11%). More recent foreign-born arrivals have higher poverty rates (25%) than longer-term foreign-born residents (13%; Fix and Passel 1994). It is notable that nearly 30 percent of all children of foreign-born parents live in poverty (GCIR 2000).

Welfare Utilization. As was shown in table 1.23, utilization of welfare benefits (i. e., Temporary Aid to Needy Families, Supplemental Security Income, and General Assistance), is approximately the same between the native-born and naturalized citizens (7% each), is slightly higher for noncitizen immigrants (9%), and much higher for refugees (25%). Also as seen in table 1.23, utilization rates for food stamps and Medicaid follow similar patterns to that for welfare benefits. As was explained in preceding chapters, the high utilization rate by refugees is due to their greater eligibility for these benefits, which in turn is based on the recognition of their greater need as involuntary migrants.

Home Ownership. Home ownership is an important indicator of economic well-being since it helps individuals and families to increase their net worth through the accumulation of equity, it is a financial investment that yields gains, and it contributes to a community's growth and stability (Cheney and Cheney 1997; Johnston, Katimin, and Milczarski 1997). As was shown in table 1.20, rates of home ownership are similar for native-born and naturalized citizens (70% and 67% respectively), and are lower for noncitizens (34%). Comparable data are not readily available specifically for refugees, but other data indicate that 14% of refugees purchase a home within their first five years in the U. S. (Office of Refugee Resettlement 1998b).

Overall Economic Well-Being. In view of all the above indicators, an overall assessment of the economic well-being of the foreign-born has been summarized by Fix and Passel (1994, p. 39):

> In the aggregate, immigrants are less well off than natives on virtually all measures of socioeconomic status. However, data for immigrants who have been in the country for at least 10 years suggest that over time immigrants increasingly resemble natives. Furthermore, the recent immigrant group contains a substantial fraction of illegal immigrants, formerly illegal immigrants [who have been granted legal amnesty], and refugees—all groups with low average socioeconomic attainment. Immigrants admitted legally through employment and family preferences resemble natives much more. . . .

And those legal immigrants who have been here [for at least 10 years] are better off than natives on a variety of measures.

Since refugees have the lowest socioeconomic status among all legally admitted groups, they are of the greatest concern and in need of the most help. As was described in chapters 2 and 3, this fact is well recognized both in policy and in program funding. The federal refugee resettlement program is specifically targeted at helping refugees enhance their economic well-being; comparable programs do not exist for legal immigrants.

FACTORS AFFECTING ECONOMIC WELL-BEING An extensive body of research identifies several factors that influence refugees' and immigrants' economic well-being: financial capital, human capital, household composition, social capital, and community contexts of reception. Similar to what was stated in regard to educational attainment, observed differences in economic well-being across different national origin groups are largely explained by these factors, as well as by legal status, as described above. Again, there is nothing inherent about national origin that has an influence on economic well-being. Each of the explanatory factors is examined below.

Financial Capital. It is self-evident that having financial capital, i. e., monetary assets, generates further capital. For example, some amount of capital is necessary to establish a bank account, finance higher education, make a down payment on a house, or start a business, all of which are intended to ultimately produce further capital. However, most immigrants and refugees arrive with none or very little financial capital. Therefore, their asset accumulation must begin after arrival. This, in turn, is dependent upon the other factors that influence economic well-being.

Human Capital. Human capital refers to the personal characteristics that enhance individuals' economic well-being. These include education, skills, work experience in both the country of origin and the new country, English proficiency, and familiarity with capitalistic systems and processes such as job search strategies, business practices, financing and purchasing practices, and so forth. Extensive research on refugees and immigrants has clearly demonstrated that the greater these human capital resources, the greater is their economic well-being; conversely, the lack of or low levels of these resources is associated with worse economic well-being (e. g., Fix and Passel 1994; Meisenheimer 1992; Office of Refugee Resettlement 1998a; Portes and

Rumbaut 1990; Potocky and McDonald 1995; Potocky 1997b; Potocky-Tripodi in press).

One of the single most important human capital variables is education. It is a stronger predictor of economic well-being than English proficiency or length of residence—which is typically used as an indicator of work experience in the new country (Meisenheimer 1992; Haines 1988; McCarthy and Vernez 1997; Potocky and McDonald 1995; Potocky 1997b; Potocky-Tripodi in press). Clearly, English proficiency is a necessary prerequisite for attainment of higher education after arrival in the U. S.; however, it is the education itself and not the English proficiency that yields the most economic returns. Furthermore, higher education is crucial for economic advancement in the contemporary labor market, which is focused on high-skill service and technology industries. Most new jobs require workers with at least some college education; however, as noted earlier, a large proportion of immigrants and refugees do not possess such educational levels (McCarthy and Vernez 1997; Mitra 2000).

A substantial proportion of immigrants and refugees with little or no English proficiency is able to obtain employment by working in the enclave economy or in jobs in the primary labor market that do not require English skills (Meisenheimer 1992; ORR 1998a). However, these are low-wage jobs with little opportunity for enhancement of economic well-being (GCIR, 2000; ORR 1998a).

As mentioned, familiarity with work and business practices in the new country is also an important human capital factor. Such practices are often different in the country of origin than in the new country. Thus, persons who are new to the United States are likely to be unfamiliar with such issues as what career choices and opportunities are available, how to access them, what qualifications are needed, or how to find, obtain, and keep a job (Westwood and Ishiyama 1991). In the area of home buying, it has been found that immigrants and refugees are commonly hindered by barriers such as lack of a bank account, which may be due to unfamiliarity with or distrust of financial institutions; poor understanding of America's "credit culture"; and lack of knowledge of financing and purchasing practices (Cheney and Cheney 1997; Johnston, Katimin, and Milczarski 1997).

Two final human capital factors that are less frequently mentioned in the literature, but are important nonetheless, are health and mental health. Poor health and mental health negatively affect economic well-being (Uba and Chung 1991; Westermeyer, Callies, and Neider 1990; Westwood and Ishiyama

1991). For example, refugees who are disabled due to a health or mental health condition are much more likely to have poor economic well-being than those that are not disabled (Potocky and McDonald 1995; Potocky 1997b; Potocky-Tripodi in press). Among recently-arrived refugees who are not working or seeking work, 15 percent report that poor health or a handicap is the reason (ORR 1998b). Conversely, good health and mental health positively affect economic well-being; and economic well-being, in turn, has a positive influence on health and mental health, as discussed in preceding chapters.

Household Composition. Immigrant and refugee households that are headed by married couples, households that have more workers, and households without children or elderly persons have better economic well-being than their counterparts (Office of Refugee Resettlement 1998a; Potocky and McDonald 1995; Potocky 1997b; Potocky-Tripodi in press). For immigrant and refugee women with children, a lack of childcare is a major impediment to working (GCIR 2000; ORR 1998b). A common strategy used by immigrants and refugees to enhance economic well-being is to live in large households with multiple wage-earners (Fix and Passel 1994).

Social Capital. Social capital refers to social support provided by the ethnic community that helps enhance economic well-being. Such social capital is posited to derive from two sources. The first is cultural values and practices that positively affect economic well-being, such as motivation and hard work (Mouw and Xie 1997; Portes and McLeod 1996). The second is the ethnic enclave economy, which is posited to provide economic opportunities to co-ethnic group members that would not be available in the primary labor market due to factors such as low English proficiency of job-seekers or discriminatory practices of employers (Aronson 1997a; Portes and Bach 1985; Portes and Sensenbrenner 1993). Thus, the fundamental concept of social capital is that "as distinctive 'outsiders,' immigrants manifest a tendency to affiliate with others of their own ethnicity or national origin, creating a community of buyers, sellers, laborers, employers, and financiers, as well as tightly meshed networks of information [regarding economic matters]" (Aronson 1997a, p. 5).

Although the theory of social capital has been quite prominent in the sociological literature on immigrant and refugee economic adaptation, the theory has not been empirically tested until recently (Aronson 1997a). An accumulation of recent studies does not support the theory that social capital, as defined above, enhances immigrants' and refugees' economic well-being (Aronson 1997a; Bates 1994; Pessar 1995; Potocky-Tripodi 2000; Sanders and Nee 1996). In other words, in general, the presence of an ethnic enclave does not appear to affect the economic well-being of the community's immigrants or refugees either positively or negatively. Furthermore, factors such as motivation and hard work appear to have far more influence at the level of the family than the ethnic community, and as was described above, these values are not specific to particular ethnic groups. It appears that human capital and household composition are far more important determinants of refugees' and immigrants' economic well-being than social capital.

Nonetheless, social capital likely has importance in terms of the information networks that enhance people's knowledge about employment and business opportunities and practices, thereby enhancing their human capital. For example, immigrant information networks have a positive influence on home buying (Cheney and Cheney 1997; Johnston, Katimin, and Milczarski 1997). Likewise, most jobs are found through informal network referrals, rather than any other means (Burke 1998; Parker 1991).

Community Contexts of Reception. Social capital theory has not been supported by recent findings, perhaps because the theory was based on observation of certain ethnic enclaves that were simultaneously affected by larger community factors that could also account for part of the enclaves' economic well-being. Such factors include federal refugee assistance provided to enclave members, or enclave members simply being "in the right place at the right time" in regard to the fit between what the immigrants and refugees could provide and what the local economy needed (Aronson 1997a; Perez-Stable and Uriarte 1997). Such factors are part of what is referred to as the community contexts of reception (Portes and Rumbaut 1990). Specifically, this refers to the policies of the receiving government and the conditions of the labor market (Portes and Rumbaut [1990] also include the ethnic enclave under this umbrella, but this has been addressed separately above).

As stated earlier, policymakers are primarily concerned about the economic impact of immigrants and refugees upon society as a whole. Consequently, immigrant and refugee policies are aimed at minimizing immigrants' and refugees' costs to society. Specifically, as described in chapter 2, both the Personal Responsibility and Work Opportunity Reconciliation Act (PRWORA) of 1996 and the Refugee Act of 1980 are aimed at reducing the welfare utilization of legal immigrants and refugees, respectively. However, while PRWORA does not contain any provisions for helping legal immigrants reduce welfare usage, the Refugee Act specifically authorizes a large, multi-service refugee resettlement program to help refugees become economically "self sufficient" (i. e., not receiving welfare). As was described in earlier chapters, the reason for this difference is based on the fundamental distinctions between immigrants and refugees, namely, that immigrants are voluntary migrants whereas refugees are involuntary migrants, and accordingly, refugees are expected to encounter much more difficulty in the resettlement process.

Accordingly, these varying policies influence immigrants' and refugees' economic well-being. For example, empirical data have demonstrated that legal immigrants' welfare utilization did decrease sharply following the enactment of PRWORA, and this had a negative effect on their economic well-being overall (Fix and Passel 1999). However, it has been more difficult to evaluate the effects of the refugee resettlement program upon the economic well-being of refugees. The literature does not contain any pre-post evaluations of refugee welfare utilization from the time of the enactment of the legislation in 1980, such as Fix and Passel's (1999) pre-post evaluation of the 1996 legislation. Now that the policy has been in place for more than two decades, such a pre-post evaluation is no longer possible. Additionally, the multi-service nature of the resettlement program makes it difficult to attribute any changes in refugees' welfare utilization to specific program components (Haines 1988). Finally, and more importantly, no analyses have been conducted to determine the extent to which changes in refugees' economic well-being are attributable to the refugee resettlement program or to the myriad other factors discussed above that influence economic well-being. The Office of Refugee Resettlement does report on the employment status, earnings, and welfare utilization rates of recently admitted refugees (ORR 1998b). However, it does not link those outcomes to measures of refugees' participation in the various services provided by the program, except in a few cases where limited evaluations of particular services have been done (which are discussed later in this chapter). Thus, this is an important area for future research.

The conditions of the labor market also presumably affect the economic well-being of refugees and immigrants. Such conditions include the stage of the business cycle, demand for specific kinds of labor, regional wage differentials, and employment discrimination (Portes and Rumbaut 1990). Other community conditions such as the local prevalence of labor unions may also be a factor (Milkman and Wong 1999; Waldinger 1995). Again, however, there have been few empirical studies on the effects of these labor market factors, particularly in relation to the other factors that influence economic well-being. The results of existing studies are inconclusive. For example, the findings of one study on a national sample of refugees suggested that their economic well-being is not greatly influenced by regional variations in economic conditions, such as wage differentials, local unemployment rates, or local variations in economic opportunity (Potocky-Tripodi in press). On the other hand, other studies have suggested that immigrants' and refugees' economic well-being is affected by changes in economic conditions over time, such as economic recessions (Aycan and Berry 1996; Haines 1988). Anecdotal evidence also suggests that immigrants and refugees fare better in times of economic prosperity (Temple-Raston 2000).

As noted earlier, another labor market condition is employment discrimination. Various forms of discrimination may include "biased job interview and employee assessment, exploitation of ethnic workers, racial remarks, social alienation, and misattribution of technical and social problems to racial or cultural traits" (Westwood and Ishiyama 1991) Various sources of evidence have demonstrated the existence of employment discrimination against immigrants and refugees (Armour 2000; Aycan and Berry 1996; Portes and Rumbaut 1990). Nationwide, between 1986 and 1999 complaints of workplace harassment based on national origin increased tenfold, with more than 15,000 such complaints filed with the Equal Employment Opportunity Commission in the 1990s (Armour 2000). Apart from overt discrimination, generally poor relations between managers and immigrant and refugee workers, such as lack of recognition or respect, inadequate representation, and poor communication also negatively affect refugees' and immigrants' economic well-being (Gouveia and Stull 1997).

Another type of labor market discrimination is gender discrimination. For example, among refugees, women consistently have lower economic well-being than men, even after controlling for human capital, household composition, social capital, and community economic factors (Potocky and McDonald 1995; Potocky 1997b; Potocky-Tripodi in press). Although this fact is not unique to immigrants and refugees, since it holds for native-born women as well, immigrant and refugee women may be particularly vulnerable to gender discrimination due to their less powerful position in society (Armour 2000). These women are also more vulnerable to sexual harassment on the job. "The number of employees filing sexual harassment complaints based on national origin (comprised mostly of immigrants) has jumped 143% from 1990 to 1999, despite a recent drop in overall sexual harassment complaints" (Armour 2000, p. 9A).

Overall, immigrant and refugee workers, and particularly women, are vulnerable to exploitation (Armour 2000; Aronson 1997b). One example of this is the garment industry, which predominantly employs foreign-born women:

> The large profit margins the major retailers insist upon—and their ability to farm out work abroad—means that contractors are squeezed to the bone. Because start-up costs are so low, new firms are constantly undercutting older ones. The result is that pay in non-union shops is often below minimum wage for all but the fastest piece-workers, working conditions are harsh, and hours are long. The real wages for the garment industry's work force—once as high as the auto industry's—have been in decline for years, and more and more work is done by the "self-employed," for whom benefits needn't be paid. With the increasing laxity of labor regulation enforcement and the declining influence of unions, the U.S. has seen the reemergence of sweatshops. Women fare worst of all. Though they are often highly skilled, moving up the vocational ladder is particularly hard. Women who attempt to become contractors or factory owners face grave problems in enforcing contracts or disciplining their labor force. For them, entering the needle trade can mean a lifetime of Dickensian labor. (ARONSON 1997B, P. 2)

MOST OF THESE SWEATSHOPS ARE OWNED by immigrants exploiting other immigrants, often from the same country of origin (Aronson 1997b).

Summary. The economic well-being of immigrants and refugees is influenced by many factors. Based on existing research, the most important factors appear to be human capital and household composition. However, fairly little research has been conducted on the relative effects of social capital and community contexts of reception, including the effects of social program participation and labor market conditions. These are important areas for future research. Based on the knowledge base established thus far, this chapter will now turn to best practices for enhancing refugees' and immigrants' English proficiency, education, and economic well-being.

8.2 BEST PRACTICES

CLEARLY, ECONOMIC WELL BEING is strongly dependent upon education. In turn, the acquisition of higher education after arrival in the new country, or recertification for education acquired in the country of origin, are strongly dependent on English proficiency. Consequently, consistent with the order in which they were introduced in this chapter, strategies for enhancing English proficiency will be discussed first, followed by education, and then economic well-being. As in preceding chapters, macro, meso, and micro strategies for each area will be discussed.

8.2.1 ENHANCING ENGLISH PROFICIENCY

THIS SECTION WILL ADDRESS best practice strategies for enhancing the English proficiency of adult immigrants and refugees. Strategies directed to children are integrated within the educational system, and consequently will be addressed in the next section, on education.

MACRO INTERVENTIONS The major macro intervention that social workers should undertake to enhance immigrant and refugee adults' English proficiency is to advocate for increased funding for ESL programs. As was indicated above, there is a very large documented unmet demand for ESL instruction. There are far more people wanting ESL instruction than there are available programs. Additionally, research has demonstrated that program participants' English literacy skills improve with increasing amounts of ESL instruction and with increasing financial investment in ESL programs (Fitzgerald 1995).

The major policies that authorize federal funding for ESL programs are the Adult Education Act (AEA) and the National Literacy Act, which amended the AEA in 1990 (Fitzgerald 1995). Additional policies exist at the federal, state, and local levels (Center for Applied Linguistics [CAL] 1998b). The government appears to be responding to the need for increased funding. For example, the federal English Literacy and Civics Education Initiative of the Department of Education allocates $75 million for fiscal year 2001 to fund community development of English literacy projects tailored to the unique needs and populations of the local community (ORR 2000b). Thus, social workers should advocate for continued enhanced funding such as this. Best practices for effective policy advocacy have been described in previous chapters.

MESO INTERVENTIONS Meso interventions, i. e., those at the program or organizational level, should be targeted at two areas: ESL program staffing and program design. ESL program staffing appears to be inadequate:

> Most adult ESL teachers have a college degree, but rarely with a specialization in adult education, literacy, or second language learning. The majority of teaching jobs in adult ESL programs are part time, without contracts or benefits. Some programs are staffed almost entirely by volunteers. Many teachers work in several different programs or function as both teachers and administrators within one program. Staff turnover is high, and many teachers and administrators leave the field within a few years. Teacher and tutor training opportunities are limited. Voluntary, unpaid attendance at in-service workshops, conferences, or seminars once or twice a year is the norm. Teachers and tutors may receive 15–20 hours of instruction when they first start working in a program, but little thereafter. (CAL 1998B, P. 1)

ESL instruction should be a professional activity similar to other human-service professions. Thus, ESL instructors should be full-time professionals with education specifically in this topic. Several universities offer degrees or certificates in teaching ESL (NCLE 2000). Therefore, social workers should advocate for appropriate program staffing by such trained professionals. To a large extent, this will overlap with policy advocacy.

In regard to program design, "most adult ESL practitioners agree that adults learn best when they are actively involved with all aspects of their instruction, including identifying content, choosing activities, and assessing progress" (CAL 1998b, p. 1). Research suggests that the following innovative program design components help enhance adult ESL learning:

• Providing a social context for literacy education. Literacy education is most effective if it is tied to the lives of the learners and reflects their experiences as community members, parents, and participants in the workforce.
• Learning through hands-on experience. Linking verbal and non-verbal communication is an effective way of introducing English to non-literate adults.

- Using learner-generated materials. Stories written by students can bring learners together around the shared opportunities of reading, talking, and writing about personal experiences or community concerns.
- Using the native language as a bridge to English. Introducing literacy in the native language can serve as a bridge to ESL literacy.
- Linking communicative competence and language awareness. Most innovative programs put a primary focus on communication and a secondary focus on error correction.
- Using technology. Video applications show great promise in literacy education; by providing a visual context for ideas, video communicates ideas independent of print. (WRIGLEY 1993, PP. 1–4)

Specific instructional approaches used in ESL programs are varied:

Current instructional approaches include competency-based, whole-language, participatory, and more traditional approaches such as grammar-based, the direct and the oral/aural method. Programs often combine approaches and may implement the same approach with a variety of techniques. In fact, many practitioners and academics maintain that, because no single approach is suitable for all ESL populations and contexts, multiple approaches may be required to meet the needs of individual learners.

(CAL 1998B, P. 1)

Generally speaking, social workers themselves will not be providing ESL instruction, but they may work as part of a team with other professionals in designing programs. Thus, social workers should be advocates for the types of innovative and multi-method approaches described above.

MICRO INTERVENTIONS Research suggests that ESL programs are effective in improving basic English skills and reading skills; in developing English skills to a degree that is sufficient for participating in job training or for holding a job requiring the comprehension of simple English text information; and in increasing employability (Fitzgerald 1995). Therefore, the major way in which most social workers will be able to impact their clients' English proficiency is at the micro level, by encouraging limited English proficiency clients to participate in ESL programs, referring them to such programs, engaging in case advocacy to ensure enrollment, and maintaining follow-up with clients to assist with continued attendance. ESL "services are provided by a wide variety of institutions that include local educational agencies, community colleges, libraries, community-based and volunteer organizations, churches, businesses and unions, small for-profit language schools, and some four-year colleges and universities" (CAL 1998b, p. 1). Additionally, "adult ESL program types include survival or life skills, pre-employment ESL, workplace ESL, pre-academic ESL, vocational ESL, ESL for citizenship, and ESL family literacy" (CAL 1998b, p. 1). Consequently, social workers should be familiar with the various programs available in their communities in order to be able to refer clients accordingly.

8.2.2 ENHANCING EDUCATIONAL ATTAINMENT AND ACADEMIC ACHIEVEMENT

ENHANCING EDUCATIONAL ATTAINMENT OF ADULTS Despite the clearly established importance of education to economic well-being, there is virtually no literature on enhancing the educational attainment of immigrant and refugee adults. Therefore, social work interventions in this area will have to begin at a grassroots level. At the macro level, social workers should advocate for universal benefits designed to help people advance their education, such as tax credits for educational expenses; employer flex-time; and on-site child care at adult educational institutions. Such policies should not be targeted only toward immigrants and refugees, but to all adults with limited educational attainment. Although policy and program initiatives such as these entail costs, research indicates that the benefits to be gained by increasing the educational attainment of immigrants would outweigh the costs, in the form of savings in public health and welfare expenditures and increased tax revenues from higher incomes (Sorensen, et al. 1995; Vernez, Krop, and Rydell 1999)

At the meso level, social workers should collaborate with institutions of higher learning to enhance access and retention of immigrant and refugee students. In general, immigrants and refugees are not an identified population within institutions of higher learning, and there is opposition by administrators to the introduction of special support programs or offices for immigrant and refugee students (Gray, Vernez, and Rolph 1997). Thus, a starting point for improvement in this area would be to conduct research to determine the relative benefits and costs of developing targeted support programs for these populations.

The greatest immediate impact can be made at the micro level. Social workers should encourage all adult immigrants and refugees who have limited education to advance their education. Social workers should facilitate this through referral and brokerage activities such as helping clients obtain information about various educational options; assisting them with admissions applications and financial aid applications; and assisting with related issues such as scheduling, transportation, and child care. For assistance with educational expenses, one strategy is individual development accounts, which will be described in the section on enhancing economic well-being. In sum, immigrant and refugee adults, as well as society as a whole, have a great deal to gain through increasing their educational attainment, and they should be provided with opportunity and help to do so.

ENHANCING ACADEMIC ACHIEVEMENT OF CHILDREN AND ADOLESCENTS As was noted earlier, although many immigrant and refugee children perform well academically, a substantial proportion are at risk of poor academic achievement due to limited English proficiency, low socioeconomic status, late entry into the school system, and other factors. It is a school social worker's function to enhance the academic achievement and overall well-being of such at-risk children. School social workers serve as a link between the school, home, and community. They function as members of the educational team, which also includes teachers, administrators, counselors, psychologists, nurses and parents. Integrating information from all these sources, school social workers conduct psychosocial assessments, counseling, consultation, and coordination of services in order to enhance students' academic, social, emotional, behavioral, and adaptive functioning (Indiana Department of Education 2000; National Association of Social Workers 1999). Numerous strategies may be employed by school social workers at the macro, meso, and micro levels to promote academic achievement among immigrant and refugee students. These strategies are targeted at the multiple factors—individual, family, peer group, school, and community—that have been identified as being influential in students' academic achievement.

Macro Interventions. Macro interventions involve action at the level of national, state, and local decisionmaking bodies. London (1990) has suggested a number of such actions aimed at enhancing the academic achievement of immigrant and refugee students (table 8.1.). School social workers should collaborate with representatives of the relevant bodies to implement best practice actions such as these.

TABLE 8.1 BEST PRACTICE MACRO INTERVENTIONS TO ENHANCE ACADEMIC ACHIEVEMENT OF IMMIGRANT AND REFUGEE STUDENTS

- At the national level, the U. S. Immigration and Naturalization Service (INS) could prepare and distribute to immigrant and refugee families information in the languages of the sending countries explaining their educational rights and responsibilities. The federal government, working in tandem with INS, could likewise inform school officials of these rights and responsibilities and of its determination to ensure their execution, once established and disseminated.
- State and local agencies should ensure that their personnel also understand these relevant rights and responsibilities of their recent immigrants and refugees and thus, should prepare in their own language and distribute to the families such information.
- Because most immigrant and refugee families usually settle in inner-city neighborhoods, the public schools they attend are often short of resources, poorly staffed, badly maintained, and overcrowded. State education agencies should work assiduously to ensure a more equitable distribution of funds to ensure equal educational opportunities.
- State and local education agencies should implement plans for recruiting and training bilingual teachers. Teacher education programs at colleges and universities must expand their efforts to prepare qualified graduates to meet the demands of easing the transition to life in the U.S. for immigrant and refugee students.
- At the school district level, there should be the provision of comprehensive information sent out to immigrant and refugee parents about the schools. Such information should also be disseminated through print and electronic media in native language publications; radio and television programs broadcast to local immigrant and refugee communities; through bilingual/bicultural workers; and through community-based self-help and resettlement organizations.
- School districts can help by conducting evaluations on immigrant and refugee children. Such evaluations should include speaking, reading, writing, and comprehension in English and the native language. School districts should evaluate student progress by using broadly-based assessment techniques; they should act on research evidence demonstrating the need for heterogeneous grouping; they should help frontline personnel such as school secretaries to gain cultural sensitivity and to understand the legal rights and responsibilities of immigrant and refugee children and their families.
- School districts should modify their curricula to reflect an accommodation of immigrant and refugee children. Specifically, they should perform the following functions:
    - Provide supplementary services to students with limited proficiency in English.
    - Provide multicultural education for all students, even if no immigrant or refugee students are enrolled.
    - Advise teachers that they ought to supplement, not replace, immigrant and refugee children's first language and culture.
    - Hire bilingual/bicultural staff in order to provide appropriate role models for immigrant and refugee children.
    - Require administrators and teachers to demonstrate respect for all children and adults, regardless of color, race, ethnicity, or the languages they speak.

> **TABLE 8.1** *(continued)*
>
> • At both the district and building levels policy positions should be developed, expressing a strong commitment to the success of immigrant and refugee children, and school districts should establish links with community-based advocacy groups and self-help organizations to ensure the availability of physical and mental health services for immigrant and refugee families.
>
> *Source:* London, 1990.

Additionally, social workers should be familiar with government policies that may provide funding for specialized programs for immigrant and refugee children. At the federal level, such policies include the Emergency Immigrant Education Act and Title VII of the Elementary and Secondary Education Act, which funds programs for limited English proficiency students (Rivera-Batiz 1996).

Social workers also need to be aware of federal law regarding admission of undocumented immigrant children to schools. This law is embodied in the 1982 U. S. Supreme Court Ruling Plyler v. Doe (457 U. S. 202), which guarantees undocumented children the right to a free public education (Morse and Ludovina 1999). Consequently, schools may not:

- Deny admission to a student on the basis of undocumented status.
- Treat a student fundamentally differently from others to determine residency.
- Engage in practices that create fear among undocumented students or their families and thereby restrict access to school.
- Require students or parents to disclose or document immigration status.
- Make inquiries of students or parents that may expose their undocumented status.
- Require Social Security numbers from all students.

(MORSE AND LUDOVINA 1999, P. 3)

SCHOOL SOCIAL WORKERS SHOULD WORK with other members of the educational team to ensure that school policies and procedures are in compliance with this law.

Meso Interventions. At the level of the school, a number of program elements have been identified as being effective in promoting the academic achievement of immigrant and refugee students (table 8.2). Again as part of their teamwork function, social workers should promote the establishment and maintenance of these program components.

TABLE 8.2 COMPONENTS OF EFFECTIVE SCHOOL PROGRAMS FOR IMMIGRANT AND REFUGEE STUDENTS

AFFECTIVE FACTORS

School staff are committed to the educational success of immigrant and refugee students, have high expectations for them, and publicly recognize their achievements. Student's native languages and cultures are valued throughout the school, and some of the staff have backgrounds similar to those of the students.

INSTRUCTION

A wide variety of courses are offered in the students' native languages and in English. This includes advanced content courses made available through instruction in the native language or through sheltered content instruction in English. Teachers are proficient in bilingual and ESL teaching strategies.

COMPREHENSIVE SERVICES

Staff speak the students' native languages, have the same or similar cultural backgrounds, and are knowledgeable about post-secondary educational opportunities for immigrant and refugee students. There is effective assessment of academic needs and language proficiency; appropriate class and course placement; and instruction geared to students' prior knowledge and experience. Academic services are coordinated with social services, counseling, tutoring, mentoring, enrichment actitivities, and health service referrals. In addition, school staff work well with parents and involve them in decisions about their children's education.

MULTICULTURAL EDUCATION

The curriculum reflects concern about the different national backgrounds and cultural experiences of immigrant and refugee students in the school; it features content and processes dealing with hostility, ridicule, prejudice, and school climate. Programs are developed to address conflict resolution, human relations, and multicultural education.

TABLE 8.2 *(continued)*

PROFESSIONAL DEVELOPMENT

School administrators provide leadership by being knowledgeable about recent research and practice in bilingual and ESL education and by developing structures to strengthen curriculum and instruction. High priority is placed on professional development for all school staff, and training is designed to help teachers and counselors serve immigrant and refugee students more effectively.

INTAKE CENTERS OR PARENT INFORMATION CENTERS

These centers are located in schools or district offices and are staffed with bilingual professionals. The centers register, assess, and place students in programs and provide oral and written information to their parents in their native languages. Such centers may also convene ongoing parent meetings.

WORKSHOPS AND SEMINARS

These inform families about school rules, procedures, grading, extracurricular activities, and special support services; expectations regarding attendance, homework, and family involvement; and college preparation and career guidance.

SCHOOL DOCUMENTS AND ORIENTATION MATERIALS

These are translated into the home languages of immigrant and refugee students. However, because some students and their parents may not be literate in their native language, schools do not rely solely on written documents. One option is development of a video in several languages about school procedures, expectations, and opportunities, for parents to view while their children are being enrolled at the intake center.

STRUCTURED RELATIONSHIPS WITH SCHOOL STAFF

Teams, clusters, student buddies, and counselors are key for providing information to immigrant and refugee students and helping them get involved in school activities.

COLLABORATION

Meetings are held in the community, not just in the school. Leaders are chosen who are at ease in both the school and the community. Parents are informed about substantive and realistic contributions they can make to their children's education.

TABLE 8.2 *(continued)*

TRANSITION TO POST-SECONDARY EDUCATION AND WORK

All students are encouraged to pursue higher education. Whether or not students are immediately college bound, all need a secondary education that is academically challenging and develops the required knowledge and skills for success in the labor market. Effective pathways to the world of work include career exploration, career guidance, career academies, cooperative education, youth apprenticeship, school-based enterprises, entrepreneurship education, internships, youth service, service learning, and work-based mentoring.

Sources: Adger, 1996; ERIC Clearinghouse on Languages and Linguistics, 1998; London, 1990; Lucas, 1996; Morse and Ludovina, 1999; Romo, 1993; Vaznaugh, 1995.

For limited English proficiency students, several programmatic alternatives are available. All these alternatives share several core features, which are listed in table 8.3. Specific descriptions of the programmatic alternatives are provided in table 8.4.

TABLE 8.3 CORE FEATURES OF PROGRAMS FOR LIMITED ENGLISH PROFICIENCY STUDENTS

- Extensive and ongoing parental involvement.
- Ongoing, appropriate, and state-of-the-art professional development for teachers in specially designed programs and for mainstream teachers who work with English language learners.
- Instructional personnel who can implement:
  - Strategies that integrate language acquisition and academic achievement at the same time.
  - Strategies that promote proficiency in English (and the primary language, where applicable) for academic purposes, including literacy.
  - Strategies such as sheltered instruction that ensure academic instruction through the second language is meaningful and comprehensible to second language learners.
  - Assessment methods that are linked to instructional objectives and that inform instructional planning and delivery.
- Developmentally appropriate curriculum and instructional materials and aids.
- High standards with respect to both language acquisition and academic achievement
- Strong and knowledgeable leadership among classroom, school, and district personnel.
- Human resources to coordinate communication between parents and schools.

Source: Genessee, 1999.

TABLE 8.4 PROGRAM ALTERNATIVES FOR LIMITED ENGLISH PROFICIENCY STUDENTS

NEWCOMER SCHOOLS

These are special schools for recent immigrant students. A major purpose of these schools is to support the adjustment of recent immigrants into their new society and school. This includes, but is not limited to, English language development, and, in some cases, continued native language development. In many newcomer schools, students attend classes for half a day and then a regular school for the other half; in others, students attend all day for 6 months before they are enrolled in mainstream schools.

ENGLISH AS A SECOND LANGUAGE (ESL) PROGRAMS

These usually consist of a series of courses designed for students with varying levels of English proficiency—beginning, intermediate, and advanced. They may also include special courses for low literate students, students with limited prior schooling, and those who are beyond the advanced level but are not ready for mainstream classes. Students may take a combination of ESL, sheltered content, and mainstream classes, depending on English proficiency, native language literacy, and academic background.

SHELTERED ENGLISH CONTENT PROGRAMS

These programs teach challenging content (e. g., math, science, social studies) in English. Instructional materials, teacher presentations, and classroom interaction are adapted so that learners can understand them and participate. The quality and effectiveness of these programs depend on the ability of teachers to provide instruction in English that is accessible to English learners without oversimplifying the academic content.

BILINGUAL EDUCATION PROGRAMS

These programs acknowledge and build upon students' ability to speak, read, and write in languages other than English. These programs usually consist of content courses in the students' native languages, enabling them to study academic content at their appropriate grade level. Some programs emphasize continued development of the native language, but most are designed to promote the transition to English.

TABLE 8.4 *(continued)*

TWO-WAY IMMERSION PROGRAMS

These programs provide integrated instruction for native English speakers and native speakers of another language, with the goal of promoting high academic achievement, first and second language development, and cross-cultural understanding for all students. Language learning takes place primarily through content instruction. Academic subjects are taught to all students through both English and the non-English language. The student populations are balanced, with approximately 50% native English speakers and 50% native speakers of the non-English language.

Sources: Howard, 1999; Lucas, 1996.

Evaluations of the effectiveness of the various programmatic options in promoting English acquisition and academic achievement are scarce. In some cases, the findings of outcome evaluations are contradictory. For example, in regard to bilingual education programs, some evaluations have found positive effects for LEP students enrolled in bilingual education in comparison to monolingual education, whereas other evaluations have found no difference. These evaluations are complicated by difficulties in formulating a strong research design, in part due to great variations in the types of programs that fall within a particular category (Rennie and Marcos 1998).

In general, educators believe that "one size does not fit all and that different approaches can be successful if implemented well. Local choice and innovation are critical ingredients of educational success" (Genessee 1999). Again, social workers should function as team members in helping to select approaches based on a school district's goals, resources, and the needs and characteristics of its students (Genessee 1999). Once an approach is selected or if one or more are already in place, social workers should participate in conducting an evaluation in order to contribute to the knowledge base about what works best for whom under what conditions.

A problem that has been encountered with these programs is in the transition from these specialized programs into mainstream education. Students can become stigmatized by being separated in these special programs. In order to have equal access to services available to other students, and to get advanced education, they must exit the specialized programs (Rivera-Batiz 1996). However, the programs' exit policies are not always clear or well implemented, with the resulting danger that students may exit these programs too late or never, and they may not receive appropriate support or monitoring after entering the mainstream program (ERIC Clearinghouse on Languages and Linguistics 1998; Rivera-Batiz 1996). Additionally, LEP students are frequently "tracked" into unchallenging vocational courses and away from academic or college-preparatory courses (Harris 1993; Lucas 1996; Romo 1993). Thus, social workers should work with other school personnel on establishing and maintaining appropriate exit and "tracking" procedures.

Apart from work at the programmatic level, social workers can serve as consultants to teachers in developing and implementing specific instructional approaches for immigrant and refugee students. This may be particularly important in schools that do not have a large population of such students and that therefore do not have the types of specialized programs described above and where teachers are less prepared for working with these populations. Research has identified certain principles for instructional practice that best facilitate academic achievement of immigrant and refugee students (table 8.5). Social workers may work collaboratively with teachers in developing and implementing such best practices.

TABLE 8.5 BEST PRACTICE PRINCIPLES FOR INSTRUCTIONAL PRACTICE WITH REFUGEE AND IMMIGRANT STUDENTS

PRINCIPLE 1: FACILITATE LEARNING THROUGH JOINT PRODUCTIVE ACTIVITY AMONG TEACHERS AND STUDENTS

Work that is carried out collaboratively for a common objective and the discourse that accompanies the process contribute to the highest level of academic achievement. "Schooled" or "scientific" ideas are used to solve practical problems presented by the real world. The constant connection of schooled concepts and everyday concepts is basic to the process by which mature schooled thinkers understand the world. Discourse that builds basic schooled competencies can take place only if the teacher shares in these experiences. Joint productive activity between teacher and students helps to create a common context of experience within the school itself, which is especially important when the teacher and the student are not of the same background.

TABLE 8.5 *(continued)*

PRINCIPLE 2: DEVELOP STUDENTS' COMPETENCE IN THE LANGUAGE AND LITERACY OF INSTRUCTION THROUGHOUT ALL INSTRUCTIONAL ACTIVITIES

Whether in bilingual or monolingual programs, language development in the language or languages of instruction is the first goal of teaching and learning. Language and literacy development should be fostered through meaningful use and purposive conversation between teachers and students, not through drills and decontextualized rules. Reading and writing must be taught both as specific curricula and within subject matters. The teaching of language expression and comprehension should also be integrated into each content area. The development of language and literacy also applies to the specialized language genres required for the study of science, mathematics, history, art, and literature. The ways of using language that prevail in school discourse, such as ways of asking and answering questions, challenging claims, and using representations are frequently unfamiliar to English language learners and other at-risk students. However, their own culturally based ways of talking can be effectively linked to the language used for academic disciplines by building learning contexts that will evoke children's language strengths.

PRINCIPLE 3: CONTEXTUALIZE TEACHING AND CURRICULUM IN THE EXPERIENCES AND SKILLS OF HOME AND COMMUNITY

Schools need to assist students by providing experiences that show how rules, abstractions, and verbal descriptions are drawn from and applied to the everyday world. Teachers should try to establish patterns of classroom participation and speech that are drawn from conversational styles of family and community life, yet help students develop the academic style of talk suited for schools. This contextualization utilizes students' funds of knowledge and skills as a sound foundation for new knowledge. This approach fosters pride and confidence as well as greater school achievement.

PRINCIPLE 4: CHALLENGE STUDENTS TOWARD COGNITIVE COMPLEXITY

At-risk students, particularly those of limited English proficiency, are often forgiven any academic challenges on the assumption that they are of limited ability; or they are forgiven any genuine assessment of progress, because the assessment tools do not ft. As a result, both standards and feedback are weakened, with the predictable end that achievement is handicapped. At-risk students require instruction that is cognitively challenging, that is, instruction

TABLE 8.5 *(continued)*

that requires thinking and analysis, not only rote, repetitive, detail-level drills. Working with a cognitively challenging curriculum requires careful leveling of tasks, so students are stretched to reach within their zones of proximal development, where they can perform with teacher guidance.

PRINCIPLE 5: ENGAGE STUDENTS THROUGH DIALOGUE, ESPECIALLY THE INSTRUCTIONAL CONVERSATION

Basic thinking skills are most effectively developed through dialogue, that is, through the process of questioning and sharing ideas and knowledge. The instructional conversation is the means by which teachers and students relate formal, schooled knowledge to the student's individual, community, and family knowledge. The adult listens carefully, makes guesses about the student's intended meaning as needed, and adjusts responses to assist the student's efforts. Such conversation reveals the knowledge, skills, and values—the culture—of the learner, and enables the teacher to contextualize teaching to fit the learner's experience base.

Source: ERIC Clearinghouse on Languages and Linguistics, 1997.

Because many immigrant and refugee students perform very well academically, they may qualify for programs for "gifted" students. However, immigrant and refugee students are frequently not identified as "gifted" due to the linguistic and cultural barriers to valid assessment. Additionally, immigrant and refugee parents may distrust any "special" classes, including classes for gifted students (Harris 1993). A number of best practices have been suggested for identifying and serving gifted immigrant and refugee children (table 8.6). Although these strategies were developed specifically for gifted children, they are also good practices for all immigrant and refugee children, based on the strengths perspective. Again, social workers should collaborate with other team members to promote such best practices.

TABLE 8.6 BEST PRACTICES FOR IDENTIFYING AND SERVING GIFTED IMMIGRANT AND REFUGEE STUDENTS

LINGUISTIC

- Provide enrichment activities to students perceived "not ready" for gifted programs.
- Institute independent or small group research projects using native language references and resources.
- Help staff members become aware of different language structures.

CULTURAL

- Explain the concept of gifted programs to parents in their native language.
- Talk to parents in their native language to learn about aspects of giftedness valued by their culture.
- Develop program services that are culturally sensitive and responsive.

ECONOMIC

- Consider aspirations of the immigrant or refugee group; pay attention to variables such as the parents' occupation and education.
- Work only from facts; assume nothing about economic status or educational background of the family.

ATTITUDINAL

- Transmit a sense of self-reliance; use a biographical approach concentrating on positive aspects of problem-solving, task commitment, and decision making.
- Encourage student involvement in publications or community programs.
- Encourage journal writing and writing of stories and poems.
- Provide opportunities for a peer support counseling group.

SOCIOCULTURAL AND PEER GROUP EXPECTATIONS

- Use narratives, role playing, and bibliotherapy to model conflict resolution.
- Identify conflicting expectations, determine the causes, and provide intervention.
- Use intra/intercultural peer referral as a source of identification.

CROSS-CULTURAL

- Increase motivation for children to identify themselves as candidates for gifted programs by referring to the gifted program as an opportunity for students to work harder and learn more.
- Use care in selecting staff responsible for identification. If possible, select staff members who are familiar with the child's culture, country, or region.

INTERGENERATIONAL

- Use nonverbal expressive arts to involve the family.

TABLE 8.6 *(continued)*

- Involve outreach workers for parents and other family members.
- Use media services in the native language.

SCHOOL SYSTEM

- Identify or place students according to educational background and potential.
- Interpret the child's behavior in the context of the child's experiences.
- Use extracurricular activities as part of the identification process; incorporate successful activities and areas of interest into learning goals.
- Ensure that the screening and selection committee has knowledge of creative production or performance in the respective culture. Include representative community members on selection committees. Avoid using standard identification instruments.
- Assess from the perspective of individual learning styles.
- Place the child in a minimal stress, culturally congruent environment and observe for a period of time.
- Periodically, discuss attitudes and possible biases with teachers. Hold informal sessions to air problems and exchange ideas.
- Use a developmental rather than crisis-oriented model

Source: Harris, 1993.

Micro Interventions. School social workers will often engage with immigrant and refugee students in direct practice. Such micro intervention must begin with appropriate assessment of the student. Immigrant and refugee students are frequently incorrectly assessed, misdiagnosed, or not reassessed at appropriate intervals (Dao 1991; Harris 1993; Rivera-Batiz 1996). Consistent with the principles of holistic, strengths-based assessment as described in earlier chapters, specific best practices for assessment of immigrant and refugee students are presented in table 8.7.

TABLE 8.7 BEST PRACTICES FOR ASSESSMENT OF IMMIGRANT AND REFUGEE STUDENTS

- Short-range prediction of achievement; measurements of growth over time.
- Focus on observed learning and problem solving, either immediate or over time.
- Account for cultural, linguistic, and conceptual foundations, including cognitive learning styles.
- Frequent contact with significant persons in the student's life.
- Observation in various settings (home and school).
- Work-sample analyses.
- Norm-referenced and criterion-referenced tests.
- Physical examination.
- Health, developmental history, and current status.
- Speech and language/communication disorders.
- Evaluation of gross- and fine-motor skills, neurological functioning.
- Evaluation of proficiency levels of English and primary languages.
- Participation in decision making of professionals from the student's culture.
- Evaluation of adaptive behavior; interpretation of maladaptive behavior from the perspective of the acculturation process.
- Determination of prior educational experiences, including evaluation of literacy and basic skills, and current instructional program in the United States.
- Identification of emotional difficulties (e. g., trauma, lack of family support).

Source: Dao, 1991. Copyright © 1991, PRO-ED, Inc. Reprinted with permission.

Micro interventions delivered by school social workers are aimed at enhancing the student's psychosocial functioning in order to enhance academic achievement. In this context, the social worker will typically target the mental health and family dynamics issues that are commonly faced by immigrant and refugee children and adolescents, as described in preceding chapters. Individual, family, and group interventions, as described in preceding chapters, may be used. Peer support groups are frequently used (Cárdenas, Taylor, and Adelman 1993; Làpez 1991; Tannenbaum 1990).

One unique peer group approach reported by Tannenbaum (1990) was an English Conversation Group. The students were averse to psychotherapy due to their cultural background, and were also averse to the idea of a recreational activity group, which they thought would detract from time they needed to spend on academic activities, due to the high demands and academic pressures placed upon them. Consequently, the English Conversation

Group was developed to appeal to the students' high regard for education and their desire to enhance their skills. The group was presented as an opportunity for them to practice their English skills in a non-academic setting. Initially, the group focused on acquiring new English vocabulary. Throughout the group sessions, the members frequently also communicated in their native language. The group leader supported this and did not pressure them to speak English:

> Miscommunications between the worker and group members, once acknowledged, were discussed. This helped the members to be clearer about their own cultural assumptions, and helped them to view their interactions with Americans in light of cultural understanding or misunderstanding. While the members were able to share their anxieties and frustrations over expressing themselves in English, conversing in English also helped them to increase their confidence. (TANNENBAUM 1990, P. 48)

ULTIMATELY, AS TRUST WAS ESTABLISHED, the group addressed other topics:

> The issues which were addressed by the group included contending with acculturation demands (learning English, understanding American culture, reconciling conflicts between old and new cultures); learning to be more assertive in order to function well; meeting the demands placed upon them as primary caretakers of their younger siblings and cousins; dealing with the psychological trauma of the past (loss of family members, friends, and country; the experience of war and flight); and coping in general with feelings of loneliness and alienation. (TANNENBAUM 1990, P. 46)

THIS APPROACH DEMONSTRATES one way in which students' strengths, such as their motivation to learn, can be leveraged to further help them in their adjustment and, in turn, their academic achievement.

In summary, as was stated earlier, academic achievement is critical in promoting immigrant and refugee children's economic success later in life. School social workers, as well as other social workers who encounter immigrant and refugee children and adolescents, should employ the multiple macro, meso, and micro interventions presented here in order to achieve this goal.

8.2.3 ENHANCING ECONOMIC WELL-BEING

NUMEROUS STRATEGIES ARE AVAILABLE to enhance people's economic well-being. These are described below in relation to the major factors that were identified above as influencing economic well-being: human capital, household composition, financial capital, social capital, and community contexts of reception. In many cases, specific strategies target more than one of these factors. However, for purposes of clarity, they are presented separately here based on the major factor that is targeted. Within each factor, macro, meso, and micro strategies are described where applicable.

ENHANCING HUMAN CAPITAL Since human capital has been identified as likely the most important factor in economic well-being, then enhancing human capital is likely the most effective way to enhance economic well-being. And, probably the two most important ways to enhance immigrants' and refugees' human capital are to enhance English proficiency and educational attainment, using the strategies described in the preceding sections. As was stated earlier, education is one of the single most important predictors of economic well-being; and advancing educational attainment after arrival in the new country is, in turn, highly dependent upon English proficiency.

Beyond this, the most widely used strategies for enhancing human capital are employment-related services. These are interventions that aim to enhance clients' skills in job searching, job attainment, and job retention (Westwood and Ishiyama 1991). The fundamental goal of federal refugee resettlement policy is to help refugees obtain employment and become economically self-sufficient as soon as possible after arrival through the provision of employment-related services (Office of Refugee Resettlement 1998a). All newly arrived refugees are eligible for this program. No comparable program exists specifically for legal immigrants. However, they may be eligible for similar programs targeted more broadly at low-income people.

Unfortunately, even though these employment-related services are a focal point of the refugee resettlement program, there is almost no literature available that describes the process and outcomes of such services specifically for refugees or immigrants. Only limited outcome data are available from the Office of Refugee Resettlement (1998a). According to those data, among refugee clients nationally who received employment-related services during a one-year period, approximately 54 percent entered employment, and of those, 74 percent retained their employment for at least 90 days. However, it is not possible to determine how much of this employment and retention was actually due to the services provided. Because of this lack of process and outcome data, the following discussion of specific interventions is based on the literature for the general population. Specific programmatic elements of employment-related services include job search assistance, job coaching, mentoring, self-employment assistance, vocational education and career counseling, and recertification (Burke 1998; Office of Refugee Resettlement 1998a, 2000c).

Job Search Assistance. Job search assistance is a set of short-term, highly focused activities aimed at helping clients find and get jobs. It is a form of behavioral counseling that teaches clients skills for job searching. Specific components of job search assistance may include the following (Burke 1998):

- Résumé preparation, stressing the identification and presentation of behaviorally specific marketable skills.
- Preparation of cover letters, reference letters, and thank-you letters.
- Practice in completing application forms.
- Skills for directly contacting potential employers; scripts for making telephone contact.
- Setting up information interviews with employers for the client to learn more about the business or type of job that the client wants to work in.
- Formulating and practicing making inquiries about job leads to friends, relatives, and acquaintances.
- Development of interviewing skills using role-play and videotape.
- Role playing to anticipate and respond to employer concerns about employability or performance.
- Support and monitoring of search behaviors; positive reinforcement.
- Development of coping skills to deal with setbacks and rejections.
- Arrangement for resources such as telephone, answering machine, word processing, copying, postage, transportation to interviews.

FOR THE GENERAL POPULATION, "some evidence suggests that job search assistance can increase placement rates, decrease the length of time needed to find a job, and result in higher quality employment as indicated by hours worked per week, earnings, and wage rate" (Burke 1998, p. 209).

Job Coaching. Job coaching involves monitoring and supporting client performance in the workplace. It may include assessment of work habits and behaviors, and "issues as diverse as notification of an employer about an absence or tardiness, management of conflicts between clients and coworkers or supervisors, and resolution of problems with child care or transportation" (Burke 1998, p. 213).

Mentoring. This entails matching the client with a volunteer who has a job such as the one the client would like to obtain. The mentor works with the client in modeling the necessary skills for the job (Burke 1998).

Self-Employment Assistance. This consists of workshops that teach about starting and operating small businesses (Burke 1998). They may provide instruction in such aspects as getting licenses, conducting feasibility studies, writing business plans, and keeping account books (Aronson 1997a). They may also facilitate networking and mentoring through public/private partnerships with established business associations (Aronson 1997a; Burke 1998). For the general population, research suggests that such programs increase "the percentage of unemployed individuals who actually start their own businesses, among those who expressed such an intention" (Burke 1998, p. 214).

Vocational Education and Career Counseling. The aim of vocational education and career counseling is the remediation, retooling, or upgrading of job skills. Specific activities include providing clients with:

- Greater clarity about their aptitudes and interests.
- Information about training requirements for specific occupations or jobs.
- Eligibility and admission criteria for various programs.
- Availability of financial assistance during the education or training period;
- Estimates of the commitment (e. g., time, money, effort) required to participate in one program or another.
- Information about logistics such as scheduling, child care, or transportation.
- Supportive counseling to manage stress, stay motivated, and overcome anxiety about their capacity to perform in classroom settings.
- Skills to organize learning into smaller, more manageable steps, and to recognize and reward accomplishments.
- Skills in time management, studying, and test taking.

(BURKE 1998, P. 214)

Research indicates that for the general population, long-term vocational training programs improve clients' employment outcomes, but short-term programs do not (Burke 1998). The Office of Refugee Resettlement has recently begun to stress the importance of job upgrading and interventions to improve refugees' economic well-being over the long term (ORR 2000d). Previously, there had been a short-term focus on getting clients employed as quickly as possible, with no attention to long term enhancement; and research showed that refugees' economic well-being did not improve substantially over the long term (Potocky and McDonald 1995; Potocky 1996b 1997b; Potocky-Tripodi in press). With the new long term focus, vocational education and career counseling should become more important elements of refugee employment services.

Recertification. This option is specifically for refugees and immigrants who had education or training for a specific occupation in their country of origin and who need to be recertified or licensed in order to practice the occupation in the new country. Recertification typically entails further education and taking examinations in order to obtain licensure. Social workers who help clients with recertification engage in tasks such as contacting the relevant licensing boards and educational institutions to determine the requirements for recertification. Additionally, transcripts from the country of origin need to be translated and evaluated. Recertification is typically a long-term process that requires multiple contacts with relevant agencies and institutions, and support for the client (Office of Refugee Resettlement 2000c).

General Considerations. In applying these various employment-related interventions with clients, certain issues must be taken into consideration. The process must begin with an assessment of the client's work history, educational and vocational preparation, and work attitudes and values (Burke 1998). Many standardized instruments are available to assess educational level, preparation for employment, intelligence, aptitude, interests, skills, and so forth (Burke 1998; Westwood and Ishiyama 1991). However, as with all such instruments, these may not be appropriate for immigrants and refugees due to cultural bias; thus caution is warranted (Westwood and Ishiyama 1991).

Immigrant and refugee clients are likely to be unfamiliar with employment-related services (Parker 1991). Because they may be unfamiliar with freedom of choice in employment options and with making decisions, they may expect the social worker to do all the work in obtaining a job for them. Thus, the nature of the social worker's role has to be clearly explained. Significant effort will need to be devoted to determining how their prior work experiences, if any, fit into the current labor market in the new country. The interventions should be concrete and directive, assigning specific tasks to the client. Clients should be urged to consider their interests and motivations in seeking specific occupations, and to be realistic in considering the feasibility of particular options. Additionally, clients should be helped to understand that the first job they obtain will not necessarily last for the rest of their working lifetime (Parker 1991). Particularly if it is a low-level job, clients should be urged to look toward advancement in the future.

Finally, social workers must consider the interrelationships between employment status, health, mental health, and family dynamics (Burke 1998). This is particularly important in the case of immigrants and refugees (Westwood and Ishiyama 1991). As has been previously described, unemployment and underemployment negatively affect people's psychological well-being, health, and family relationships, which in turn may negatively affect their employability, thereby creating a vicious cycle. Thus, as has been stressed repeatedly, it is essential to provide refugees and immigrants with holistic services that address the complexity of their situations. Case management, crisis intervention, mental health treatment, and marital and family therapy should be applied as needed (Burke 1998).

TARGETING HOUSEHOLD COMPOSITION As was described earlier, household composition is an important factor in economic well-being. Unlike the other factors, household composition is not subject to change through social work intervention. However, certain types of households may be targeted for certain interventions, in particular, households with children. As was noted earlier, lack of child care is a major impediment to employment, particularly for women. Further, most immigrant and refugee families have children (Fix and Zimmerman 1999). Thus, a logical and necessary intervention is the provision of child care to these families:

> Quality child care is often critical to ensuring that low-income immigrant families can achieve and maintain self-sufficiency. As welfare reform has increased efforts to move welfare recipients into the workforce, the cost, availability, quality, and accessibility of child care have become major issues among many populations, including immigrants and refugees. Child care

can play a key role in facilitating the adjustment of new immigrant families to the U.S. For many new immigrants, child care serves as the primary point of extrafamilial contact and can help ease the introduction to a new culture and alleviate problems of social isolation.

(GRANTMAKERS CONCERNED WITH IMMIGRANTS AND REFUGEES 2000)

At the policy level, social workers should be familiar with and advocate for subsidized child care and tax incentives that make child care more cost-effective for families (McInnis-Dittrich 1992). At the meso level, social workers should be familiar with child care options in their communities and link clients to them accordingly. In some cases, social workers may advocate for on-site child care at companies that employ large numbers of immigrants or refugees. However, in order to be utilized, such on-site care needs to be affordable to the workers (Gouveia and Stull 1997).

One option that has been advocated by some is home-based child care (Hein, Allen, and Else 1999; Schnur, et al. 1995). It has been argued that this has four advantages. First, if the home-based child care is provided by non-immigrant providers to immigrant or refugee families, it serves as a bridge that connects the immigrants or refugees to the new culture. A study of this type of child care found that the immigrant mothers developed close relationships with the child care providers, valued the relationships of their children with the providers, and believed that the child care had helped their children relate to their peers and eased their transition into the public schools (Schnur et al. 1995).

Second, if the home-based child care is provided by immigrant and refugee families themselves to other families from the same immigrant or refugee group, then the child care is intrinsically culturally congruent and linguistically appropriate (Hein, Allen, and Else 1999; Schnur et al. 1995). This creates a familiar, accessible point of entry for the immigrant parents, and may increase their willingness to use child care services. For both the children and parents, culturally congruent child care may ease acculturative stress and decrease social isolation. Third, if the child care is provided by refugee or immigrant providers to non-immigrant families, it increases cross-cultural experiences of both (Hein, Allen, and Else 1999).

Finally, home-based child care provided by immigrant or refugee families can serve as a source of income to the providers, thereby serving as an option to outside employment (Hein, Allen, and Else 1999). Several publicly funded grant and loan programs are available for families who wish to start such a home-based child care business. However, numerous factors have to be taken into consideration to assess the self-sufficiency potential of such an enterprise, as well as the feasibility and ability of the provider to deliver quality child care (Hein, Allen, and Else 1999).

ENHANCING FINANCIAL CAPITAL There are at least three policy/program initiatives available for enhancing immigrants' and refugees' financial capital: Individual Development Accounts, Microenterprise Development, and home ownership programs. Each of these is described below.

Individual Development Accounts. These are defined as follows:

> Individual Development Accounts (IDAs) are special savings accounts that are designed to help people build assets for increased self-sufficiency and long-term economic security. Account holders receive matching funds as they save for purposes such as buying a first home, job training, going to college, or starting or expanding a small business. IDAs can begin as early as birth and they are progressive (that is, low-wealth individuals and families receive greater matching funds). Funding for IDAs can come from public, non-profit, and/or private sources (funding partnerships are common).
>
> (SHERRADEN ET AL. 2000)

Since the first IDAs were initiated in the early 1990s, IDA programs have expanded greatly (Sherraden et al. 2000). In recent years, the Office of Refugee Resettlement has begun funding IDAs for refugees:

> The Refugee IDA Program represents an anti-poverty strategy built on asset accumulation for low-income refugee individuals and families with the goal of promoting refugee economic independence. In particular, the objectives of this program are to: increase the ability of low-income refugees to save; promote their participation in the financial institutions of this country; assist refugees in advancing their education; increase home ownership; and assist refugees in gaining access to capital.   (ORR 2000E, P. 2)

Eligible refugees may use IDAs for any or all of the following savings goals: home purchase or renovation; post-secondary education, vocational training or recertification; microenterprise capitalization; purchase of an automobile; or purchase of a computer (ORR 2000e). ORR grants IDA funds to public or private agencies that then establish a Savings Plan Agreement with refugee participants. The Savings Plan Agreement includes a proposed schedule of savings deposits by the participant; the rate at which the participant's savings will be matched; the savings goal for which the account is maintained; any training or counseling which the participant agrees to attend; and agreement that the participant will not withdraw funds except for the specified savings goal or for an emergency and only after consultation with the grantee (ORR 2000e). Participating agencies are encouraged to provide financial training for refugee participants, such as budgeting, cash management, savings, investment, and credit counseling (ORR 2000e). Although no comparable program exists specifically for immigrants, immigrants may be eligible for IDA programs targeted for the general population of low-income people.

Since ORR only recently initiated the Refugee IDA Program, no outcome data are yet available. However, outcome data are available from a nationwide evaluation of IDA programs for the general population (Sherraden et al. 2000). These data indicate that the savings performance of most participants was strong, with most participants making regular monthly deposits, and on average saving $0.71 for every dollar that they could save and have matched. A portion of the participants did withdraw their funds and used them for the intended purposes of microenterprise, home purchase, home repair, or education. Thus, these initial data indicate that IDAs appear to be effective in helping low-income people to accumulate assets.

Microenterprise Development. This program entails funds and activities to help low-income people start or expand small businesses. ORR began funding microenterprise development for refugees in 1991, in recognition of the fact that most refugees have neither financial assets nor American business experience, and thus do not qualify for commercial loans (ORR 2000f). The program is described as follows:

> The purpose of microenterprise development is to assist refugees in becoming economically self-sufficient and to help refugee communities in developing employment and capital resources. . . . Project components may include one-on-one business consultation and training, training in classroom settings, access to business credit, individual or peer group lending, and follow-up technical assistance to help stabilize or expand refugee businesses. Microloans consist of small amounts of credit, generally in sums less than $15,000, extended to low-income entrepreneurs for start-up or very small

microenterprises. . . . ORR supports the use of commercial lending institutions for refugee borrowers to leverage the limited amount of ORR funds available for this purpose. (ORR 2000F, PP. 3–4)

OUTCOME DATA INDICATE that the program is successful:

During the last eight years, refugees have started or expanded over 800 micro-businesses, and over 89% of these businesses have survived. ORR grantees have provided over $3 million in financing to these entrepreneurs, and the loan repayment rate is close to 100 percent. By commonly accepted measures of performance (business survival rates, loan default rates, etc.), the ORR programs have excelled, frequently leading the field in achievement. More importantly, over 4000 refugees have gained new entrepreneurial skills and knowledge, and the additional business income is helping refugee families to achieve self-sufficiency. (ORR 2000F, P. 2)

The success of refugee microenterprise programs depends on a combination of many factors, including the program's mission and market; staff; business development focus; business training and technical assistance; partnerships; business financing; administrative capacities and practices; the target population; types of businesses developed; flexibility and adaptability; start-up time; and technical assistance to the programs (Else and Clay-Thompson 1998). All of these must be carefully considered in the development of these programs.

Home Ownership Programs. The following policy and program initiatives have been suggested for helping immigrants and refugees become homeowners:

- Consumer education about homebuying through homebuying clubs, counseling, and seminars to increase home purchase knowledge and comfort level of potential immigrant homebuyers. Such buyer-support programs can be provided (or at least supported) by a number of organizations, such as lenders, public agencies, and community-based organizations.
- Banks, mortgage institutions, and real estate brokerage firms can aid immigrants' entry into, and completion of, the homebuying process by advertising in their native languages, employing staff who speak those languages, and educating the staff about relevant issues and barriers for specific immigrant populations.

- Community-based organizations, social groups, and religious organizations can aid immigrant homebuying by educating and counseling immigrants about the American system of credit and homebuying and by working with banks, mortgage lenders, and realtors to establish first-time and low- to moderate-income homeowner programs that meet the needs of various immigrant populations. One promising way of meeting the needs of newly-arrived, low-income immigrants is through the "full-cycle" approach of providing support for new homeowners from preliminary planning to final payment. With their extensive knowledge about—and credibility with—ethnic populations, community-based organizations provide a useful entry point for interested lenders or public agencies.

(JOHNSTON, KATIMIN, AND MILCZARSKI 1997, P. 88)

ENHANCING SOCIAL CAPITAL Social capital can be enhanced by supporting networking within immigrant and refugee communities for purposes of job search and other economic information, such as information about home buying. Such networking has become increasingly important in the job search process (Burke 1998; Parker 1991). Mentoring of recently arrived immigrants and refugees by more-established residents from the same country is one option. Another option is job clubs or support groups:

> The group context provides more opportunities for members to practice skill building and acts as a source of additional social support and contacts that can generate job leads.... Mutual support from job search assistance groups may include instrumental support such as carpooling or exchange of child care. These groups can also provide clients with companionship, encouragement, and acknowledgement for success in performing search-related behaviors. Contact with others experiencing unemployment can assist in reducing stigma and other negative feelings associated with unemployment.... Job search support groups also provide clients with many of the material resources needed to develop search materials and carry out search activities. (BURKE 1998, PP. 215–216)

Although there have been no reports of such groups specifically for immigrants or refugees, for the general population, Burke (1998, p. 215) reports that "job search assistance programs that combine targeted search behavior training with small-group interactions have been phenomenally successful in helping clients find work." Given the social isolation that endangers many immigrants and refugees, this seems like a very relevant approach for these populations.

ENHANCING COMMUNITY CONTEXTS OF RECEPTION The final way in which the economic well-being of immigrants and refugees may be enhanced is by enhancing the community contexts of reception. By definition this entails macro interventions aimed at society as a whole and the institutions, primarily employers, within it. Potential strategies include community economic development and planning; job development; union organizing; and anti-discrimination strategies.

Community Economic Development and Planning. Community economic development entails broad-based coordinated efforts aimed at creating jobs within a diversified economic base to diminish the risk of economic stagnation and social instability (Gouveia and Stull 1997). An example is providing tax incentives to corporations to locate in a community. Economic development should be supported by better community planning that integrates educational and training programs and social services with the local labor market (Burke 1998).

Job Development. Job development involves contacting potential employers on behalf of clients. It requires extensive knowledge about the local labor market and close relationships with employers (Burke 1998). Job development is a central component of many employment-related services for refugees. Job developers establish close ties with potential employers and may place large numbers of refugees with particular companies. They contact employers on a regular basis in an effort to match refugees with available jobs. The following best practices have been recommended for successful job development for refugees:

- Use every marketing tool at your disposal. For instance, pass out your business cards and notepads with your agency's logo often. These are good and inexpensive visual aids. Advertise your agency and your clients on a website. Put job orders out in the community in appropriate languages. Flyers are another inexpensive and easy form of advertising. Use alternative publications (newspapers) for needs, leads, and advertisement. Speak publicly and advocate readily for refugee services. Civic groups, chambers of commerce, and church groups all may be valuable places to promote word of mouth advertising and may create job orders down the line.
- Build a resource library. Use the telephone book to "cold-call" companies

about job leads. Thirty calls each morning will produce at least one job order.
- Develop strong relationships with your customers and clients. Get to know the human resource managers and production managers to understand their needs and make sure you are working to satisfy their needs.
- Pursue excellence. Always go the extra mile to make sure your client has all the necessary tools and information to be successful in his/her new position. For instance, meet him/her at the work site on the first day to facilitate his/her transition. Make sure there is understanding about expectations, scheduling, and basic needs. Educate the employer about cultural issues of the new American. If a problem arises later, meet with your client to handle the situation and prevent further difficulties. (DUNN 1999, PP. 1–2)

Union Organizing. A third option for enhancing community contexts of reception in areas with high concentrations of immigrants or refugees is to attempt to organize labor unions in order to improve wages and working conditions. However, this is a very lengthy process that may extend over several years, and is not always successful (Milkman and Wong 1999).

Anti-Discrimination Interventions. Finally, social workers need to implement interventions aimed at decreasing discrimination against immigrants and refugees, both in the workplace and in society as a whole. This is so important that the following chapter is devoted entirely to this topic.

8.3 CASE STUDY EXERCISES

BASED ON WHAT HAS BEEN DISCUSSED in this chapter, consider how you would intervene with the following cases.

8.3.1 CASE 1

Maribel and Claudia are two 8-year-old girls who were born in the United States to parents who are originally from Central America. In both families Spanish remains the primary language. Both girls are experiencing difficulties in learning to read. Maribel has been in a school where bilingualism has been regarded as an asset and she has received reading instruction in Spanish only. Claudia has been in a school where bilingualism is accepted but not encouraged. There are almost no staff members who speak Spanish, and all instruction is conducted in English. (LANGDON 1996, P. 43)

8.3.2 CASE 2

A ninth-grade Filipina girl who immigrated with her parents declares: "Our parents don't come [to school functions] because they don't know any English. I don't even tell them when they are supposed to come. They dress so different and I don't want our parents to come because the others will laugh at them and tease us. We are ashamed."
(PORTES AND RUMBAUT 1990, P. 181)

8.3.3 CASE 3

Sergey, a refugee from the former Soviet Union, is a plastics engineer with a master's degree in chemical engineering and 6 years of experience. He has been referred for job search counseling. He arrived feeling that because community volunteers had not been able to help him, this experience would be no different. He explained that he had sent out over 50 letters and résumés per week in response to advertisements and that he understood the job search process. Sergey's résumé had been looked at by American volunteers. His English was passable. However, Sergey had never met an American professional in his area of expertise, nor had he had an interview in his two months of looking for a job. (PARKER 1991, PP. 164–165)

CHAPTER 9

INTERETHNIC RELATIONS

THROUGHOUT THIS BOOK there has been discussion of the negative impacts of prejudice, racism, and discrimination upon immigrants and refugees. It has been demonstrated how discriminatory behaviors, practices, and policies adversely affect immigrants' and refugees' health, mental health, family dynamics, and educational and economic status. Preceding chapters have addressed macro- and meso-level strategies for reducing institutional discrimination (i.e., discriminatory policies and practices) in these specific problem areas. Such strategies are aimed at changing social policies and social service delivery systems. This chapter addresses these issues at a broader and more fundamental level—that is, prejudice, racism, and discrimination among individuals and within society as a whole.

Social work interventions that identify prejudice, racism, and discrimination as the direct targets for change constitute an antiracist model of social work, as opposed to a cultural sensitivity model (McMahon and Allen-Meares 1992; Potocky 1997a; Spencer 1998). "The antiracist model overtly identifies the source of ethnic minority problems as being the prejudiced and racist attitudes [and discriminatory behaviors] of members of the larger society. Thus, this model moves beyond a focus on a small segment of society (i.e., social workers and agencies) to the society as a whole. Interventions stemming from this model attempt to reduce and prevent such attitudes [and behaviors] through strategies aimed at the individual, small group, and community levels" (Potocky 1997a, p. 320).

Prior to examining specific anti-racist social work practice approaches, this chapter will begin with a discussion of key issues in interethnic relations. Best practices at the macro-, meso-, and micro-levels will then be presented. The chapter will close with case study exercises for further consideration.

9.1 KEY ISSUES IN INTERETHNIC RELATIONS

FOLLOWING A BRIEF REVIEW of key concepts, the causes of prejudice, racism, and discrimination will be examined. Then, available evidence about the contemporary state of interethnic relations will be presented.

9.1.1 REVIEW OF KEY CONCEPTS

INTERETHNIC RELATIONS REFERS TO "the ways in which the various groups of a multiethnic society come together and interact over extended periods" (Marger 1997, p. 10). When different ethnic groups come together, an adaptive process at the societal level must occur. As was described in chapter 4, this adaptive process may be referred to as *structural acculturation*, and it has several possible outcomes. These include *genocide*, in which one group is annihilated by another; *structural assimilation*, in which the minority group completely gives up its culture and is completely absorbed into the majority culture; the *melting pot*, in which different groups contribute equally to a new culture; *pluralism*, in which different ethnic groups maintain their distinct cultures yet have equal political and economic participation in the society as a whole; *segregation*, in which the groups maintain largely separate systems in all aspects of social life; and *stratification*, in which the society's resources are distributed unequally across the different groups.

As was also described in chapter 4, the outcomes that characterize contemporary U.S. society are *residential segregation* and *economic and political stratification*. Residential segregation refers to the fact that different ethnic groups tend to live apart from each other. Foreign-born and native-born persons generally reside in separate communities (Bach 1993; Frey and Liaw 1998). This is due partly to immigrants' and refugees' desire to settle in areas with existing concentrations of people from similar ethnic or national backgrounds, and partly to the native-born population's migration away from areas with such high foreign-born concentrations (Frey and Liaw 1998). These residential patterns are more pronounced among people with low educational levels, i.e., high school education or less. Among people with higher educational levels, the foreign-born and native-born are more integrated residentially (Frey and Liaw 1998).

Economic and political stratification refers to the fact that different socioeconomic and ethnic groups are arranged hierarchically in society in such a way that they receive different amounts of society's wealth, power, and prestige (Marger 1997). "The dominant group maintains maximum power to determine the nature of interethnic relations. Minority, or subordinate, groups rank in different places below the dominant group, depending on their cultural and physical distance from it. . . . The power of the dominant group is based on its control of the society's political and economic resources and its ability to shape the society's major norms and values" (Marger 1997, p. 68). In general, ethnic groups in the U.S. are stratified in the following rank order, from greatest to least power and prestige: English origin people; other white European people and white Latino people; Jewish people; Asian people; African American people; Native American people; and Puerto Rican and Mexican people (Devore and Schlesinger 1999). Within each ethnic group, people are further stratified by socioeconomic status; additionally, socioeconomic status and ethnicity are highly correlated, so that on average, the people at the top of the ethnic hierarchy are also the wealthiest, and those on the bottom are the poorest (Devore and Schlesinger 1999; Marger 1997).

As was further discussed in chapter 4, the segregation and stratification in U.S. society are the result of *prejudice, racism,* and *discrimination*. "Prejudices are categorical, inflexible, and negative attitudes toward ethnic groups, based on simplistic and exaggerated group images called stereotypes" (Marger 1997, p. 105). When applied specifically to foreigners, prejudice may be termed *xenophobia, anti-immigrant sentiment,* or *nativism*. "Racism is an ideology, or belief system, designed to justify and rationalize racial and ethnic inequality. The members of socially defined racial categories are believed to differ innately not only in physical traits but also in social behavior, personality, and intelligence. Some 'races,' therefore, are viewed as superior to others" (Marger 1997, p. 35). It should be noted that the term racism applies to ethnic and cultural groups in general, not just to specific "races." For example, anti-Semitism, i.e., the belief that Jews are inferior, is a form of racism.

Finally, "discrimination is the behavioral dimension and involves actions designed to sustain ethnic inequality. Discrimination takes various forms, ranging from derogation to physical attack and even extermination. Two types of discrimination are *individual* and *institutional*, the former carried out by single persons or small groups, usually in a deliberate manner, the latter rendered as a result of the norms and structures of organizations and institutions, often in an unwitting and unintentional manner" (Marger 1997, p. 105). An example of institutional discrimination is the access barriers and reduced effectiveness of social services for ethnic minority populations, as described in preceding chapters. Other examples are policies and procedures that result in inadequate housing, education, federal programs, or municipal services for ethnic minorities; discriminatory administration of justice; discriminatory consumer and credit practices; and ineffectiveness of the political structure and grievance mechanisms (Axelson 1993).

Clearly, prejudice, racism, and discrimination are interrelated, although the causal directions of the relationships can vary. While it is logical that prejudice and racism would lead to discrimination, it is also possible for discrimination to lead to prejudice or racism (Marger 1997; Simpson and Yinger 1985). That is, prejudice or racism may be "used to rationalize discriminatory behavior *after* the fact. This is an important observation, for it seriously challenges the idea that eliminating discrimination requires a change in attitude, that is, the elimination of prejudice" (Marger 1997, p. 97).

9.1.2 CAUSES OF PREJUDICE, RACISM, AND DISCRIMINATION

THE CAUSES OF PREJUDICE, RACISM, AND DISCRIMINATION may be examined from theoretical and empirical perspectives.

THEORETICAL PERSPECTIVES Marger (1997) presents three theoretical frameworks for explaining the causes of prejudice, racism, and discrimination: psychological theories, normative theories, and power-conflict theories. All three are grounded in the empirical fact that these attitudes, beliefs, and behaviors are learned, rather than innate.

"*Psychological* theories focus on the ways in which group hostility satisfies certain personality needs; prejudice and discrimination, in this view, are traced to individual factors" (Marger 1997, p. 106). Two such psychological theories are the theory of frustration-aggression and the theory of the authoritarian personality. The theory of frustration-aggression holds that when people are frustrated in meeting highly desired goals, they become aggressive. If the source of the frustration is unknown or is too powerful to confront directly, people displace their aggression onto "scapegoats," which are convenient, relatively powerless targets. Minority groups often serve as such scapegoats. The theory of the authoritarian personality holds that prejudice, racism, and discrimination are but one aspect of a general personality type, one that is "highly conformist, disciplinarian, cynical, intolerant, and preoccupied with power. . . . Such people strongly support conservative values and resist social change. They are thus more likely to display prejudicial thought and to discriminate" (Marger 1997, p. 91).

"*Normative* theories explain that ethnic hostilities are conforming responses to social situations in which people find themselves" (Marger 1997, p. 106). These theories hold that people become prejudiced, racist, and discriminatory because they receive messages from their own reference groups that these attitudes, beliefs, and behaviors are the norm and are expected; thus they conform to these expectations. By conforming, they are rewarded with a sense of belonging and a sense of self-identity as a member of the reference group. Thus, normative theories hold that prejudice and discrimination are products of the social environment, rather than the psyche. As such, prejudice, racism, and discrimination may change when the social situation changes.

"*Power-conflict* theories see prejudice and discrimination as products of group interests and as tools used to protect and enhance those interests. Focus is placed not on the individual or even the immediate group but on the dynamics of political, economic, and social competition among a society's ethnic groups" (Marger 1997, p. 106). These theories view prejudice and discrimination as serving to maintain the dominant group's position of power and privilege by injuring or neutralizing minority groups who are perceived as threatening to that position. There are five power-conflict theories: the theory of economic gain; Marxian theory; the split labor market theory; the theory of status gain; and the theory of political gain.

The theory of economic gain holds that prejudice, racism, and discrimination yield economic profits for those who engage in them. Minority groups become targets of prejudice, racism, and discrimination when they threaten the economic position of the dominant group. Marxian theory holds that prejudice, racism, and discrimination serve the interests of the capitalist class "by keeping the working class sufficiently fragmented and thus easier to control. The basic idea is 'divide and rule.' One ethnic element of the working class is pitted against another, and as long as this internal discord can be maintained, the chances of the working class's uniting into opposition to the interests of the capitalists are reduced" (Marger 1997, p. 99).

In contrast, the split labor market theory holds that it is the workers themselves, not the capitalists, that benefit from prejudice, racism, and discrimination. According to this theory, the working class itself is split into two classes, the higher paid and the lower paid. "Employers seek to hire workers at the cheapest possible wage and therefore turn to the lower-paid sector when possible.... Recent immigrants... in search of industrial jobs ordinarily make up this source of cheap labor.... Because these groups represent a collective threat to their jobs and wages, workers of the dominant ethnic group become the force behind hostile and exclusionary movements aimed at curtailing the source of cheap labor" (Marger 1997, p. 100).

The theory of status gain holds that people gain prestige from being members of the dominant group, regardless of their social class. Thus, members of the lower socioeconomic class may perpetuate prejudice, racism, and discrimination because it enhances their self-esteem, even though their socioeconomic situation may be similar to that of the ethnic minority groups who are their targets. Finally, the theory of political gain holds that prejudice and discrimination may arise from domestic or foreign political interests. Negative feelings toward political adversaries are thus applied to all members of that ethnic group, and are extended beyond the political issues.

EMPIRICAL EVIDENCE In regard to prejudice, racism, and discrimination specifically directed at immigrants and refugees, the empirical evidence provides the strongest support for the power-conflict theories, and also supports the psychological and normative theories. Historical evidence clearly demonstrates that anti-immigrant sentiments among the public, and anti-immigrant policies, rise and fall in cycles that are linked to changing economic and political conditions (Gimpel and Edwards 1999; National Immigration Forum, 2000b). At times when the economy is performing poorly, anti-immigrant sentiment rises. Such sentiment is manifested in beliefs that the foreign-born take jobs away from native-born workers and drive down wages; that they come to the U.S. to take advantage of welfare policies; that they are an economic drain because they use more in social services than they contribute through taxes; that they commit a high rate of crimes; that they refuse to assimilate and present a threat to "traditional" American culture, values, and language; and that they cause too large an increase in population size and thus threaten the natural environment (Frendreis and Tatalovich 1997; Gimpel and Edwards 1999; Palmer 1996; Suárez-Orozco 1996).

All of these beliefs essentially represent the idea that the foreign-born pose a threat to the wealth, power, and prestige of the native-born. Research indicates that the perception of economic threat is a greater factor in anti-immigrant sentiment than are prejudice and racism (Gimpel and Edwards 1999; Lee 1998; Palmer 1996). Further, empirical evidence indicates that people who are more likely to have anti-immigrant sentiments are those who are less educated, have lower occupational status, and lower income, because they perceive the foreign-born to pose a greater economic threat to them (Cummings and Lambert 1997; Gimpel and Edwards 1999; Hood and Morris 1998; Lee 1998). All of these factors lend support to the power-conflict theories.

However, the above beliefs about the foreign-born are not grounded in reality, as empirical evidence disputes these beliefs (Gimpel and Edwards 1999; Suárez-Orozco 1996). As was discussed in the preceding chapter, immigrants and refugees contribute more to the economy than they consume (National Immigration Forum, 1999b). Additionally, immigrants and refugees do not reduce the overall availability of jobs or wages, although they may reduce the employment opportunities of low-skill workers in areas where the economy is weak and there is a large concentration of immigrants (Fix and Passel 1994). Further, empirical evidence indicates that immigrants do not come to the U.S. in order to receive welfare, nor are their cultural values incompatible with the norms of the dominant culture (Suárez-Orozco 1996). Additionally, empirical data show that the foreign-born are no more likely to commit crimes than the native-born (Alaniz, Cartmill, and Parker 1998; Hagan and Palloni 1998). Thus, the irrational nature of anti-immigrant beliefs provides support to the psychological theory of frustration-aggression, whereby anger is displaced onto inappropriate targets, or scapegoats (National Immigration Forum 2000b; Suárez-Orozco 1996).

Finally, normative theories of prejudice are also supported by empirical findings indicating that people form attitudes toward new immigrant groups based on consensus information from their own reference groups, without having had any direct contact with members of the new immigrant groups themselves (Maio, Esses, and Bell 1994). In sum, in regard to anti-immigrant sentiment, all three major sets of theories about the causes of prejudice, racism, and discrimination have empirical support, with the strongest support for the power-conflict theories.

9.1.3 CONTEMPORARY STATE OF INTERETHNIC RELATIONS

IMMIGRANTS AND REFUGEES CONSTITUTE one segment of the multi-ethnic population as a whole. Therefore, interethnic relations need to be considered from the larger perspective that includes all ethnic groups in the U.S., including native-born and foreign-born. A recent survey of a random national sample of more than 2,500 people examined the public's perceptions and experiences of interethnic relations (National Conference for Community and Justice, 2000a). Some key findings of this survey are summarized in table 9.1. Although not specifically addressing immigrants and refugees, the findings of this study in relation to ethnic minorities are clearly relevant to the full understanding of interethnic relations. Also, since most immigrants and refugees are also members of ethnic minority groups, the findings in relation to those groups are directly relevant to them.

TABLE 9.1 KEY FINDINGS OF NATIONAL SURVEY ON INTERETHNIC RELATIONS

STATE OF INTERGROUP RELATIONS

- People are troubled by the state of intergroup relations in America. Only 29% are satisfied with "how well different groups in society get along with each other" and when looking at the "country as a whole" 79% consider "racial, religious, or ethnic tension" a very serious or somewhat serious problem.
- When considered along a spectrum of other issues, intergroup relations are in the middle of the public's list of priorities for governmental action.
- Among three intergroup relations topics, the public gives greatest priority to dealing with overt crimes, second priority to reducing inequality, and lowest emphasis to the goal of promoting respect and understanding.

DISCRIMINATION

- A majority of Americans perceive that a great deal or some discrimination occurs for all ethnic groups except Whites. The greatest discrimination is thought to be against Blacks (34%), immigrants (26%), Hispanics (22%), American Indians (19%), Asians (11%), and Whites (7%).
- During the last month, 4% of Whites experienced racial discrimination while shopping, 3% at work, 4% in a restaurant, bar, theater, or other entertainment place, less than 1% at one's place of worship, and 3% in some other situation. Altogether in these five circumstances 13% of Whites were discriminated against during the last month.
- For Blacks, the proportion treated unfairly during the last month was 20% while shopping, 14% at work, 12% at a restaurant, etc., 1% at one's place of worship, and 9% elsewhere. 42% of Blacks experienced at least one episode of discrimination during the last month.
- For Hispanics, 8% were discriminated against at a store, 6% at work, 3% at a restaurant, less than 1% at their place of worship, and 3% at some other place. 16% of Hispanics experienced at least one occurrence of ethnic discrimination during the last month.

TABLE 9.1 *(continued)*

- For Asians, 14% suffered discrimination at a store, 11% at a restaurant, 8% at work, none at their place of worship, and 10% in other circumstances. Altogether 31% of Asians were discriminated against during the last month.

INFLUENCE

- The public believes that most groups have less influence than they should have. Whites are the only group that people clearly see as having an excess of influence.

INTERETHNIC CONTACT

- 97% of Americans have personal contact with Whites, 84% with Blacks, 69% with Hispanics, 54% with Asians, 49% with immigrants, and 42% with American Indians.
- 87% of those who are minorities have contact with Whites, 82% of non-Blacks personally know a Black person, 66% of non-Hispanics know a Hispanic person, 52% of non-Asians know an Asian person, and 41% of non-American Indians know a person who is an American Indian.
- The most frequent form of interethnic contact is friendship. The next most frequent contact is as neighbors, co-workers, and co-congregants. Less frequent contact comes with teachers or principals at a child's school, police officers, and with supervisors and subordinates at work.

INTERETHNIC HARMONY

- Most people feel that their race or ethnicity generally gets along with members of other races and ethnicities.
- From the White perspective the ethnic divide between Whites and Blacks remains the greatest with better relations seen with Asians, American Indians, and Hispanics than with Blacks.
- From the viewpoint of the minorities the widest gulf is not between themselves and the White majority, but between various minorities. Blacks and Hispanics see the least harmony with Asians, and Asians and American Indians find their lowest level of getting along with Blacks. Blacks and Hispanics rate Whites as third in getting along with, American Indians view them as second, and Asians put them first, above relations with each of the other minorities.

OPPORTUNITY

- In regard to education, housing, promotions to managerial jobs, access to equal justice, treatment by police, and media attention, most people think that ethnic minorities do not have equal opportunity with Whites. Across these six domains Blacks, Hispanics, and American Indians are seen as about equally disadvantaged. Asians, however, are believed to be better off although still disadvantaged in relation to Whites.

LIFE SATISFACTION

- Whites and Asians have about equal satisfaction with their income, housing, job, education, and access to health care, followed by Hispanics, and finally Blacks.

TABLE 9.1 *(continued)*

ATTITUDES ABOUT INTERETHNIC RELATIONS

- 36% of the public believe that racial segregation is acceptable as long as the races have equal opportunity.
- 51% think that increasing the standard of living of minorities is the best way to improve interethnic relations.
- 54% believe that ethnic minorities must "shape up and realize they can't get a free ride" before interethnic relations can improve.

TRENDS IN INTERETHNIC RELATIONS

Over the last decade:
- People see more tensions, less opportunity for Blacks and Hispanics, more discrimination against Blacks, and a widening satisfaction gap between Whites and Blacks.
- People feel closer to all groups, are less concerned about minorities having too much influence, have more intergroup contact, see less discrimination against minorities besides Blacks, and Blacks report fewer actual incidents of discrimination.
- There is a greater concern about intergroup relations and more acceptance of others, but a worry that things are getting worse, especially for Blacks.

Source: National Conference for Community and Justice, 2000a.

Additional data about the contemporary state of interethnic relations come from incidents of open conflict and violence. Specifically, hate crimes are one overt indicator of interethnic conflict. Hate crimes are defined as "a crime which in whole or part is motivated by the offender's bias toward the victim's status. . . . Hate crimes are intended to hurt and intimidate individuals because they are perceived to be different with respect to their race, color, religion, national origin, sexual orientation, gender, or disability. The purveyors of hate use physical violence, verbal threats of violence, vandalism, and in some cases weapons, explosives, and arson, to instill fear in their victims, leaving them vulnerable to subsequent attacks and feeling alienated, helpless, suspicious, and fearful" (Community Relations Service 2000a, p. 1). In 1996, more than 10,000 hate crimes were reported to the FBI, of which 72 percent were motivated by the victim's race, color, or national origin (Community Relations Service, 2000b). The actual incidence is higher because hate crimes are underreported (American Psychological Association 1998).

Another observable indicator of the state of contemporary interethnic relations is the proliferation of World Wide Web sites that promote hatred of racial, ethnic, and religious minorities. Since the first such site was created in 1995, hundreds more have appeared. Many such sites specifically target children and adolescents as recruits into their racist ideology (Anti-Defamation League 1999).

In regard to interethnic relations specific to immigrants and refugees, in-depth qualitative research has shown that relations between immigrant and refugee newcomers and established residents are commonly characterized by competition, tension, and opposition (Bach 1993). Accurate quantitative data are difficult to obtain. The research on public opinions toward immigrants and refugees is quite limited (Gimpel and Edwards 1999; Hood and Morris 1998). Public opinion polls on this topic are conducted only sporadically, and particularly in those times and places when anti-immigrant sentiment is high. Polls conducted during the 1990s indicated that approximately 50 to 65 percent of the general population favored decreases in legal immigration, between 5 and 8 percent favored increases, and the remainder thought the immigration level should remain the same. The polls also showed that anti-immigrant sentiment peaked in 1994 and had subsided by 1996 (Gimpel and Edwards 1999). Paradoxically, although most people favor decreasing immigration, most also have positive opinions about immigrants themselves, viewing them as honest, hardworking, and as contributing to the national culture, and most also express pride in the U.S. as a nation of immigrants. Overall, data also indicate that immigration is not a top-priority concern for most U.S. residents, but only for those living in areas with high concentrations of foreign-born people (Gimpel and Edwards 1999; Lee 1998).

The extent of discrimination against immigrants and refugees is also difficult to quantify accurately because discrimination is difficult to measure directly. Nonetheless, the available data and anecdotal reports provide evidence for the existence of anti-immigrant discrimination in areas such as employment, housing, and other domains of daily life (Fix and Turner 1999). For example, as was stated in the preceding chapter, between 1986 and 1999 complaints of workplace harassment based on national origin increased tenfold, with more than 15,000 such complaints filed in the 1990s (Armour 2000).

Recent discourse on interethnic relations has focused more attention on relations between different minority groups. As the survey results presented above demonstrated, there is considerable tension between the various ethnic minority groups themselves. Data also clearly indicate that majority group members are not the only perpetrators of prejudice, racism, and discrimination. For example, among the known perpetrators of hate crimes in 1996, one-third were ethnic minorities (Community Relations Service, 2000b).

There is also a perception that African Americans have become increasingly hostile toward Asian, Hispanic, and Black immigrants (Cummings and Lambert 1997; Fuchs 1990). This concern has been spurred by several highly publicized incidents of conflict and violence between African-Americans and immigrants during the 1980s and 1990s (Cummings and Lambert 1997; Fuchs 1990; Rodríguez 1999). Such inter-minority conflicts are consistent with the split labor market theory, which suggests that these minority groups are in competition with each other for jobs which leads to resentment.

At the same time, however, other evidence suggests that perceptions about anti-immigrant sentiment among African Americans are exaggerated (Cummings and Lambert 1997; Fuchs 1990). Numerous authors have identified instances of positive attitudes and actions by African Americans toward immigrant groups (Cummings and Lambert 1997; Fuchs 1990; Rodríguez 1999). Fuchs (1990) has identified four distinct perspectives that characterize African American attitudes toward immigrants. One is the negative *displacement perspective* in which immigrants are seen as displacing African Americans from jobs, housing, health, and other services. However, the other three perspectives are more positive. One is the *human rights perspective*, most prominently espoused by the Rev. Martin Luther King, Jr. and his followers, whereby refugees and immigrants are viewed with compassion, as fellow human beings in the struggle for human rights. Another perspective is the *black immigrant perspective*, in which black immigrants are viewed positively because they represent potential political constituents who may lend strength to the advancement of black interests. A final perspective is the *coalition perspective*, in which African Americans align with native-born Hispanic Americans in the pursuit of a common political agenda, which in turn leads blacks to be more sympathetic to immigration. These varying perspectives indicate that as with all ethnic groups, African American attitudes toward foreigners are not uniform or monolithic.

Finally, prejudice, racism, and discrimination also exist between members of the broad classifications of ethnic groups. For example, there may be tensions between different Hispanic ethnic groups, between different Asian ethnic groups, between different Black immigrant groups, and between different White ethnic groups. Even within the same ethnic group from the same country of origin, there may be prejudice and discrimination based on social class or political differences. Again, members of various ethnic groups are not uniform or monolithic in their attitudes and behaviors toward others.

9.1.4 SUMMARY OF KEY ISSUES

IN SUMMARY, contemporary interethnic relations in the U.S. are complex and cannot be adequately described through simplistic frameworks. Anti-immigrant sentiments and discrimination rise and fall over time and have multiple causes including psychological factors, social factors, and power-conflict factors.

The negative consequences of prejudice, racism, and discrimination for immigrants and refugees have been extensively described in preceding chapters. Being subjected to individual discrimination such as hostile remarks, inequitable treatment, or physical attacks, and to institutional discrimination that limits access to opportunities and limits effectiveness of social services, has adverse impacts upon health, mental health, family dynamics, and educational and economic attainment. Prejudice, racism, and discrimination also have negative psychological, economic, and political impacts upon their perpetrators and society as a whole (Simpson and Yinger 1985). These facts alone should provide sufficient reason for combating prejudice, racism, and discrimination.

However, apart from these empirical facts, the primary reason for combating prejudice, racism, and discrimination lies in moral grounds. Based on the fundamental premise that all human beings are created equal, and on the principles expressed in the Universal Declaration of Human Rights (see chapter 2), as well as the professional code of ethics, social workers have an ethical obligation to act for social justice. Clearly, social work interventions should aim to decrease conflict and competition and increase cooperation and accommodation between ethnic groups. The chapter will now turn to strategies for achieving this.

9.2 BEST PRACTICES

THIS SECTION WILL PRESENT STRATEGIES aimed at reducing prejudice, racism, and discrimination, and at achieving a pluralist society—one in which all members are able to maintain their ethnic heritage yet have equal political and economic power. This is the best possible outcome of interethnic relations, because it is the least harmful of all the outcome options (e.g., genocide, assimilation, stratification, etc.). Further, pluralism is clearly the outcome toward which the United States is already moving, in contrast to assimilation or other patterns in the past (Marger 1997). Relevant strategies directed toward this goal exist at the macro, meso, and micro levels. Following a discussion of assessment and goal-setting issues, each of these will be addressed.

9.2.1 ASSESSMENT AND GOAL-SETTING

SOCIAL WORK PRACTICE in the area of interethnic relations follows the same problem-solving process as practice in other areas, beginning with problem identification, assessment, and goal setting. In order for interethnic relations strategies to be effective, the following issues must first be assessed:

- Types of goals for which different groups are striving.
- Types of persons to be affected, in terms of their relation to prejudice and discrimination.
- Types of situations, in time and place, to which strategy must adjust.

(SIMPSON AND YINGER 1985, P. 379)

CLEARLY, DIFFERENT INDIVIDUALS OR GROUPS may have different goals. Some possibilities are the following:

- To improve the neighborhood by building bridges across racial lines.
- To build new relationships.
- To bring people together who do not typically talk to one another.
- To bring children together to reduce the chance of violence.
- To influence attitudes of local law enforcement.
- To better understand other cultures.
- To open up new economic possibilities.
- To create bonds between organizations that do not usually work together.
- To work on a community project together, such as building a playground.
- To build partnerships across jurisdictional lines.

(COMMUNITY RELATIONS SERVICE 1998)

THUS, EACH INTERESTED PARTY'S GOALS must be articulated and consensus reached on which one, or which combination, to pursue.

In regard to the types of persons affected, Merton (1949) developed a classification of four types in relation to prejudice and discrimination:

- The *unprejudiced nondiscriminator*: These are people who accept the idea of social equality and refrain from discriminating against ethnic minorities.
- The *unprejudiced discriminator*: These are people who adjust their behavior to meet the demands of particular circumstances. When discrimination is normative in the group or community, such people abide by those patterns even though they may harbor no prejudicial feelings toward members of the targeted group. To do otherwise would jeopardize their social standing.
- The *prejudiced nondiscriminator*: These people maintain negative beliefs and stereotypes toward ethnic minorities but are precluded from acting out those beliefs by situational norms. If a situation requires fair treatment toward ethnic groups who are viewed negatively by such people, fair treatment will mark their behavior.
- The *prejudiced discriminator*: These people do not hesitate to turn their prejudicial beliefs into discriminatory behavior when the opportunity arises. Members of organizations such as the Ku Klux Klan or neo-Nazi parties exemplify such people. (MARGER 1997, PP. 382–383)

Simpson and Yinger (1985) note that different strategies will be effective for the different types of people. They argue that the unprejudiced nondiscriminator "must be the spearhead of any effective campaign to reduce prejudice and discrimination" (p. 382), but they believe such people's effectiveness is sometimes limited because they primarily engage in mutually supportive discussions with each other and fail to take action. Suggested strategies for overcoming this problem are to engage such people with the other three types, and to impress upon them the necessity of action. In regard to unprejudiced discriminators, Simpson and Yinger (1985) argue that such people suffer from some degree of guilt for their actions, which are inconsistent with their beliefs, and that this is the strategic leverage point on which to work. They advise engaging these people with groups of unprejudiced nondiscriminators, where they will be rewarded for abiding by their beliefs.

For the prejudiced discriminator, effective strategies should focus on the behavior rather than the beliefs. If discrimination is made illegal, costly, or unpleasant, while tolerance is rewarded, these people will decrease their discriminatory behavior, even though their beliefs may not change. Finally, in regard to the prejudiced discriminator, Simpson and Yinger (1985) argue that strategies must vary depending on the situation. For example, in some cases these people are supported by group norms; in such cases appropriate strategies are "legal and administrative controls and large-scale changes in the economic supports to prejudice" (p. 383). In other cases, such people are isolated and "a change in [their] attitudes and behavior would help to bring integration with people significant to [them]" (p. 383).

Thus, it is essential to assess the distribution of these various types of people within the groups that are targeted for change, in order to choose the strategies with the greatest likelihood of effectiveness. "To try to appeal to all of them in the same way . . . is to make serious strategic errors" (Simpson and Yinger 1985, p. 383).

In assessing situations, questions such as the following should be addressed:

- What is the legal pattern? Does it support discrimination or condemn it? Does the law condemn it ideologically but fail to provide enforcement techniques?
- Is the situation one that requires immediate action, or is there time for more deliberate analysis?
- Is the discrimination supported mainly by lower-class members of the dominant group? Or is the pattern primarily set by powerful groups who are exploiting prejudice to maintain their authority?
- Who makes the key decisions? Whose support is vital?
- What is the level of unemployment, the degree of tension and frustration, the extent of status dissatisfaction?
- What subtle cues are people receiving on issues wholly unrelated to intergroup relations that influence their readiness for various kinds of intergroup behavior? (SIMPSON AND YINGER 1985, PP. 383–384)

Again, different strategies will be optimally effective for different situations. The assessment of goals, persons, and situations lays the foundation for the choice of strategies at the macro, meso, and micro levels.

9.2.2 MACRO PRACTICE

MACRO-LEVEL BEST PRACTICES include policy advocacy, community development, community education, and nonviolent resistance. Each of these is addressed below.

POLICY ADVOCACY Social workers should advocate for the development, adoption, and implementation of federal, state, and local policies that address equal treatment and equal opportunity for immigrants and refugees and harmonious interethnic relations. Table 9.2 presents some general principles to guide policy development in this area.

TABLE 9.2 GENERAL PRINCIPLES FOR POLICY DEVELOPMENT RELATED TO IMMIGRANTS AND REFUGEES

Federal, state, or local policies or regulations regarding immigration or immigrants should meet the following principles and standards:
- Children should not be punished by the immigration status of their family. Basic needs such as food, education, housing, and health care should not be denied. Children should not be required to provide information on the immigration status of their parents.
- Maintaining the family unit should be a fundamental principle and goal.
- Policies should foster an environment of cooperation and trust between persons in the helping professions including doctors, nurses, social workers, teachers, clergy, and others and those who seek their services. This trust necessitates leaving investigative work to immigration authorities rather than those in helping professions.
- Government actions should contribute to increased cooperation and collaboration among communities, and should insure that harassment of or discrimination against individuals of particular ethnicities based on name, accent, skin color, religious affiliation, or national origin does not occur.
- Over-representation of undocumented persons from any country should not lead to governmental powers that intrude on the rights and privileges of others from that country who are United States citizens or legal residents. No racial, ethnic, or religious group should be explicitly or implicitly targeted for enforcement. All groups having undocumented persons should be addressed similarly.
- Any abusive behavior by law enforcement agencies toward undocumented immigrants is intolerable and should be addressed through adequate training, supervision, and effective accountability measures. Similarly, enforcement personnel should be treated with respect and dignity, and sanctions should be given for abusive behavior.
- Immigrants and refugees who are in the United States legally but do not have citizenship status have long been contributors to the great communities of our nation. Sanctions should not be imposed and benefits should not be denied to those who continue to be builders of our collective dream.

Source: National Conference for Community and Justice, 2000b. Copyright © 2000, National Conference for Community and Justice. Reprinted with permission.

In order to be effective advocates, social workers first need to be familiar with existing anti-discrimination policies. For example, one major piece of legislation is Title VII of the Civil Rights Act of 1964, which protects individuals against employment discrimination. Some major provisions of this legislation in regard to national origin are summarized in table 9.3. Social workers should be able to inform their immigrant and refugee clients of their rights under such laws, advocate for them when they believe their rights have been violated, and refer them to appropriate resources, such as the federal Equal Employment Opportunity Commission, which enforces anti-employment discrimination legislation.

TABLE 9.3 LEGISLATION REGARDING EMPLOYMENT DISCRIMINATION BASED ON NATIONAL ORIGIN

Title VII of the Civil Rights Act of 1964 protects individuals against employment discrimination on the basis of national origin as well as race, color, religion, and sex.

GENERAL PROVISIONS

It is unlawful to discriminate against any employee or applicant because of the individual's national origin. No one can be denied equal employment opportunity because of birthplace, ancestry, culture, or linguistic characteristics common to a specific ethnic group. Equal employment opportunity cannot be denied because of marriage or association with persons of a national origin group; membership or association with specific ethnic promotion groups; attendance or participation in schools, churches, temples or mosques generally associated with a national origin group; or a surname associated with a national origin group.

SPEAK-ENGLISH-ONLY RULE

A rule requiring employees to speak only English at all times on the job may violate Title VII, unless an employer shows it is necessary for conducting business. If an employer believes the English-only rule is critical for business purposes, employees have to be told when they must speak English and the consequences for violating the rule. Any negative employment decision based on breaking the English-only rule will be considered evidence of discrimination if the employer did not tell employees of the rule.

ACCENT

An employer must show a legitimate nondiscriminatory reason for the denial of employment opportunity because of an individual's accent or manner of speaking. Investigations will focus on the qualifications of the person and whether his or her accent or manner of speaking had a detrimental effect on job performance. Requiring employees or applicants to be fluent in English may violate Title VII if the rule is adopted to exclude individuals of a particular national origin and is not related to job performance.

TABLE 9.3 *(continued)*

HARASSMENT

Harassment on the basis of national origin is a violation of Title VII. An ethnic slur or other verbal or physical conduct because of an individual's nationality constitute harassment by their agents and supervisory employees, regardless of whether the acts were authorized or specifically forbidden by the employer. Under certain circumstances, an employer may be responsible for the acts of non-employees who harass their employees at work.

Source: U.S. Equal Employment Opportunity Commission, 1997.

Although there are existing federal and state local laws prohibiting discrimination in areas including employment, housing, education, and access to public accommodations, such policies are often lacking at the local government level. This reduces the effectiveness and efficiency of preventing or resolving ethnic conflicts in the community (Community Relations Service, 2000c). In such cases, social workers should advocate for the development of local anti-discrimination policies. Table 9.4 lists relevant policies that should be adopted at the local level.

TABLE 9.4 LOCAL ORDINANCES AND POLICIES TO PREVENT ETHNIC CONFLICT

The commitment of local governments to protect civil rights and promote harmonious ethnic relations can be manifested in the enactment of ordinances and the promulgation of policies. Local governments should consider enacting the following types of ordinances if they do not currently exist. In addition, each municipal department may wish to promulgate policies, procedures, and programs to implement the commitment of the municipality to ensure a comprehensive management system for the enforcement and protection of civil rights.

CIVIL RIGHTS ORDINANCE

This is a general ordinance outlining the local government's commitment to positive ethnic relations. This ordinance might include:

TABLE 9.4 *(continued)*

- The requirement that each municipal department develop its own policy and program regarding positive ethnic relations.
- A section on sanctions, both monetary and disciplinary, that will be enacted against violators.
- An outline of the various measures the municipality will take to assure positive ethnic relations.
- A provision of performance incentive awards to municipal department heads for fostering harmonious ethnic relations.
- A provision for municipal awards ceremonies to honor public and private achievements in ethnic relations.

HUMAN RELATIONS COMMISSION ORDINANCE

This commission (HRC) may be established as the central instrumentality to monitor the local government's commitment to equal rights and assure its conformity with the Constitution and federal and state civil rights laws while at the same time promoting the goals of equality, justice, and harmony. Several factors have been identified as important for the success of such a commission:

- *Mission*: The HRC is the principal municipal instrumentality to protect and safeguard civil rights and to promote harmonious ethnic relations.
- *Mission Statement*: The HRC ordinance should spell out in specific terms the policy, responsibility, powers, and duties of the HRC including sanctions and other penalties for violation of the ordinance.
- *Budget*: The HRC should have adequate funding from either local government appropriations or from an assured source of nongovernmental support, to enable it to accomplish its mission.
- *Professionalism of the Staff*: The executive direction should have strong leadership, management, interpersonal, and communication skills. Staff should have good organizational, interpersonal, and communications skills in addition to the expertise or knowledge required for carrying out their specific duties.
- *Interaction with Community and Political Leaders*: To be effective, the HRC must work closely with local community activists, political leaders, and elected officials.
- *Support from the Aggrieved Community*: The HRC must be seen as a resource and as a partner in addressing the civil rights problems of the aggrieved community.
- *Problem Identification*: The HRC must conduct ongoing outreach to the entire community, including both the minority and nonminority communities, to identify accurately and examine effectively the major problems and issues of discrimination.
- *Mission Workplan*: The HRC workplan is the creative, functional process that carries out the mission of the HRC in a task-oriented manner and that ensures accountability between the HRC and the community.
- *Support from the Community at Large*: Various sectors of the community can be helpful to the HRC in carrying out its mission, including: academic, civic, religious, business, labor, and philanthropic.

TABLE 9.4 *(continued)*

• *Publicity*: The HRC should inform the public about positive human relations developments and its own proactive efforts within the community. This can be done through newsletters, public service announcements on local radio and television, regular interaction with local and regional media, co-sponsorship of forums or seminars within the community, and other means.
• *Avoidance of Internal Disputes*: Too often internal contentiousness or disagreement destroys the effectiveness of HRCs and similar bodies; a work agenda that conforms to the HRC mission and to the accomplishment of the workplan can avoid this.

HATE ACTIVITY ORDINANCE

A local government can further demonstrate its concern about the security and safety of its citizens by establishing an ordinance against hate crime activity. A municipality may:
• Establish an ordinance against hate activity modeled on any existing hate crime law which may be in effect in that state.
• Develop public service announcements and local information campaigns to inform community residents about hate crime.
• Develop a local coalition to counter hate activity involving all segments of the community such as police, educators, clergy, business people, human relations specialists, adults, and young people.
• Establish a local hotline for reporting hate or bias activity. Data collected by such units can aid local officials in measuring trends and in enforcing civil rights protections for all members of the community.

FAIR HOUSING ORDINANCE

These ordinances prohibit discrimination in the following activities:
• The marketing of housing, including publicly assisted housing.
• The sale, purchase, or rental of housing.
• The financing of housing.
• The provision of brokerage services.

BUSINESS ORDINANCE

Policies and procedures may be developed and prominently displayed in all appropriate offices, ensuring that all entities doing business with the local government will be required to comply with all aspects of the municipality's commitment to fairness and equal opportunity. Each entity doing business with the local government could be required by ordinance to do the following:
• Promote nondiscrimination in the workplace.
• Promulgate and post equal opportunity notices.
• Require all subcontractors to comply with the same requirements as primary contractors.

TABLE 9.4 *(continued)*

VOTING RIGHTS ORDINANCE

Local governments should ensure that all citizens eligible to vote are given equal opportunity to exercise that right. The ordinance in this area could:
- State the municipality's commitment to fairness.
- Be posted prominently at all polling places.
- Require those polling places be located at sites convenient to all citizens.
- Require efforts to remove voting barriers that may exist due to language differences.
- Require that municipal voting districts be consistent with federal laws, especially when redistricting is required.

REPRESENTATION ON BOARDS AND COMMISSIONS

Local governments should assure that all members of the community have access to full participation in the life of the municipality, including equal opportunity for minorities and nonminorities to be represented on appointed boards and commissions. To do this, an ordinance may require:
- The listing of all municipal boards and commissions to which appointments are made.
- An outreach effort to all racial and ethnic groups seeking nominations for board or commission appointments.
- Assignment of coordination and oversight responsibility to a particular municipal official or agency to ensure compliance.

MUNICIPAL DEPARTMENTS' POLICIES AND PROGRAMS

Each municipal department, such as the police department and the public schools, should develop its own policy, procedures, and programs related to civil rights protection and promotion. It may be helpful to have each department's policy, procedures, and programs reviewed by the HRC in regard to adequacy and conformity with the municipal policy.

Source: Community Relations Service, 2000c.

In advocating for the development, adoption, and implementation of policies such as these, social workers should use the principles of effective policy advocacy presented in an earlier chapter. Workers may use a variety of tactics such as organizing a coalition to lobby for the policy; generating and gathering signatures on a petition; challenging existing practices in court; providing expert testimony; writing speeches for influential people who support the cause; using publicity to embarrass inactive authorities; and activating existing enforcement agencies. Workers can also empower community members to advocate for themselves by helping to establish social networks among activist groups and by providing training in how to be cohesive, how to know the opponents, how to deal with bureaucratic systems, and how to utilize the courts. The effectiveness of policy advocacy is also enhanced by gaining the support of prestigious advocacy organizations (Chetkow-Yanoov 1999).

COMMUNITY DEVELOPMENT Community development aims to bring citizens and organizations together to address common concerns and improve the communities in which they reside. It is focused on community integration, participation, cooperation, and collaboration to promote consensus among institutions and community groups. Social workers engaged in community development function as agents in helping diverse organizations and citizen groups to work together to achieve common goals.

Recently two large-scale, in-depth ethnographic research projects were undertaken to identify the actions and strategies that promote communication, understanding, accommodation, and accord between immigrant and refugee newcomers and established residents in local communities (Bach 1993; National Immigration Forum 1995). The projects concluded that community development efforts must focus on participation and membership, on opportunities to pursue shared concrete tasks, and on building organizations in local neighborhoods (Bach 1993). Such initiatives also should have concrete goals; should invest substantial time in the process of talking with participants, pulling them together, and keeping them informed; and should complement, rather than replace, organizations that represent the people of one race, ethnic, or national origin (National Immigration Forum 1995). Specific best practice recommendations of these projects for community development activities to enhance relations between immigrant and refugee newcomers and established residents are summarized in tables 9.5 and 9.6. Other groups have also developed additional best practice recommendations for community development activities specifically aimed at preventing and responding to hate crimes and activities by hate groups. These are summarized in tables 9.7 and 9.8.

TABLE 9.5 BEST PRACTICES FOR FOSTERING POSITIVE INTERACTIONS AMONG IMMIGRANT AND REFUGEE NEWCOMERS AND ESTABLISHED RESIDENTS

- A primary rule of policy should be to avoid actions that worsen relations among newcomers and established residents. Anti-immigrant reactions exacerbate community problems. Aggressive "get-tough" policies on immigration seldom work. Increasingly, federal policy that draws legal distinctions among groups of newcomers is part of the problem. Policies should foster inclusion and participation of newcomers.
- Newcomers with permanent residency status should be enabled and encouraged to participate in local elections, reinforcing efforts of coalition-building through local electoral participation.
- Federal budgetary problems and the uniqueness of local combinations of groups require a renewed focus on community building. Grass-roots organizing is a useful approach in promoting opportunities for interaction among groups at the local level. "Bottom-up" processes often work better than "top-down" ones. Leadership training for community members should be encouraged, particularly for teenagers and women, who have already forged interpersonal and intergroup relations in many communities.
- Local activities should encourage participation and mobilization across group lines. Attention should be focused on producing unified activities that require the energy of diverse people to reach a shared goal. It is not enough to simply try to negotiate group differences. These common projects should address community conditions, such as housing, education, and recreation.
- Existing organizations are not necessarily responsive to the new demographic, social, and economic diversity in today's communities. They should consciously seek ways to cross group boundaries and identify common projects. Re-examination of and innovation in membership and approach in all organizations are needed to build cooperation and encourage inclusion of diverse participants.
- Efforts should be expanded to provide newcomers with access to English-language programs, and established residents should be encouraged to learn other languages. Although language differences cause major divisions, development of language skills can be a focal point around which people can rally and seek accommodation.
- Established residents need more and better information about newcomers. Such information could be provided through creative use of community newspapers, library resources, and outreach programs. In schools, efforts to promote better understanding and cooperation among newcomers and established residents should be expanded to include the whole family.
- Media reporting often misrepresents the range of interactions and complexities of relations, especially in crises. Coverage should be continued until such incidents are resolved. There is currently too little media follow-up. Positive intergroup activities should be examined and reported as well.
- Special events and public festivals can create a more tolerant tone in communities and are particularly effective when they involve face-to-face collaboration among groups in planning the events. Such efforts must lead to continued opportunities for inclusion and full participation. One-time efforts often exacerbate rather than resolve tensions.

Source: Bach, 1993.

TABLE 9.6 BEST PRACTICES FOR COMMUNITY INITIATIVES TO IMPROVE RELATIONS AMONG IMMIGRANT AND REFUGEE NEWCOMERS AND ESTABLISHED RESIDENTS

CONNECT HUMAN RELATIONS AND OTHER COMMUNITY GOALS

• Funders and policy makers should seek ways to incorporate the goal of improved relations into existing funding categories, programs, and policies. As long as ethnic relations remain ghettoized in an isolated funding category, intergroup relations will lack the community context that gives them meaning. Work in other areas, such as economic development, housing and community organizing, will also suffer from the lack of a strategic understanding of intergroup relations.
• Community organizations should explore ways in which their mission, goals, and objectives would complement or benefit from an intergroup initiative.

ENSURE ADEQUATE AND APPROPRIATE FUNDING

• Funders and policy makers should provide general funding to support existing intergroup efforts. Care should be taken not to create competition for funding between single-group and intergroup efforts.
• Funders and policy makers should provide funds to help informal intergroup efforts make the transition into permanent initiatives. Without funding, such efforts have little chance of long-term survival.
• Funders and policy makers should provide core support funding for single-group efforts and encourage their interaction with other groups by providing them with additional funds specifically targeted for intergroup work. Single-group organizations should not be forced to sacrifice their core work in order to do intergroup work.

PROVIDE SPECIAL TRAINING AND TECHNICAL ASSISTANCE

• Funders and policy makers should provide funding to create and support training and technical assistance programs that help communities develop newcomer/established resident initiatives that address both human relations and other community goals. Funders and policy makers should also provide community organizations with funding to secure such training and technical assistance.

DEVELOP NEW WAYS TO DOCUMENT SUCCESS

• Funders and policy makers must find ways to measure the effectiveness of human relations work. These measures should assess how an organization works through and with others, as well as how many people an organization serves. For example, such an assessment could measure evidence of strong community participation, such as meeting attendance and volunteer hours contributed.
• Community organizations can influence funders and policy makers by designing programs and funding proposals with measurable intergroup objectives. Community organizations can help redefine effectiveness by introducing practical measures for themselves and those assessing them.
• Community organizations can help change community expectations by speaking out against policies and programs that have a negative impact on intergroup relations.

TABLE 9.6 *(continued)*

DEVELOP INCLUSIVE COMMUNITY PLANNING AND DECISION MAKING

- Funders should develop innovative funding strategies that draw in new and underrepresented populations and help them define what their communities need.
- Policy makers should examine ways to include representatives of marginalized groups—both newcomers and established residents—when deciding what kinds of programs and policies are needed, and by whom.
- Community organizations should find ways to get input from different community members. This could mean seeking new representatives for their boards, establishing advisory committees that include new players in the development of an innovative project, or developing research efforts, such as focus group discussions.
- Funders and policy makers should support studies that examine how specific policies and programs hurt or help relations between newcomers and established residents. They should also support studies of how some employers, landlords, and others may deliberately foster intergroup hostilities to their advantage, and how public policies could be crafted to stop such practices. One goal of these studies should be to demonstrate how much more the costs of responding to intergroup crises are compared with the benefits of investing in proactive community-building strategies.
- Community organizations should examine ways to work with funders and policy makers in gathering information, perhaps seeking funds to conduct local surveys or focus groups, or collaborating with a nearby university.
- Policy makers should draw public attention to the need for newcomer/established resident collaboration by holding hearings on related issues and community and public policy responses.

DEVELOP NEW NETWORK OPPORTUNITIES

- Funders should convene forums and meetings in which representatives of different race, ethnic, and national origin groups discuss overarching concerns. Philanthropists should introduce different leaders and organizations who are addressing similar concerns in different groups.
- Community organizations should commit to identifying and meeting with at least one community leader or program director from a race, ethnic, or national origin group with which they are not yet familiar.

ENSURE ACCESS TO HIGH-QUALITY INTERPRETATION

- Funders and policy makers should provide funding to make interpretation and translation services and equipment available to community organizations and to improve the quality and availability of interpretation services.
- Community organizations should seek ways to provide language interpretation and translation or examine ways to improve the quality of current services.

Source: National Immigration Forum, 1995.

TABLE 9.7 BEST PRACTICES TO PREVENT HATE CRIMES FROM ESCALATING ETHNIC TENSIONS

HATE CRIME ORDINANCES ARE A DETERRENT

A local government may establish an ordinance against hate activity modeled on existing hate crime law in effect in that state. A local government may also establish boards or commissions to review and analyze hate crime activity, create public service announcements, and recommend measures to counter hate activity.

LOCAL ACTIONS TO IMPROVE COMMUNICATION

A Human Relations Commission (HRC) can facilitate and coordinate discussions, training, and events for the benefit of everyone. An HRC can create a forum for talking about ethnic relations and encourage citizens to discuss their differences, commonalities, and hopes. Forums could focus on the common features of community life, including economic development, education, transportation, environment, cultural and recreational opportunities, leadership, community attitudes, and ethnic diversity. The Commission can use multicultural training and special events to promote harmony and stability.

COALITIONS CREATE A POSITIVE IMAGE

Coalitions of representatives from political, business, civic, religious, and community organizations help create a positive climate in the community and encourage constructive dialogue. Coalitions can recommend initiatives to help ethnic communities affected by the loss of jobs, including programs and plans to help local government ensure an equitable disbursement of public and private funds, resources, and services.

INCLUSION INCREASES CONFIDENCE IN GOVERNMENT

Local governments can assure that everyone has access to full participation in the municipality's decision-making processes, including equal opportunity for minorities to be represented on appointed boards and commissions. Local governments might institute a policy of inclusion for appointments on boards and commissions. The policy could require listing all appointive positions, and notifying ethnic groups of open seats through the minority media.

TABLE 9.7 *(continued)*

SCHOOLS AND POLICE MUST WORK TOGETHER

School and police officials should work together to develop a plan to handle hate crimes and defuse ethnic tensions. Officials should consider prevention and response roles, identify potential trouble sites, and plan for phased police intervention. Tension can be eased by regular communication with parents, students, media, and other community organizations. Mediation and conflict resolution classes develop the capacity of young people to peacefully settle disputes and conflicts.

RUMORS FUEL ETHNIC TENSIONS AND CONFLICT

A temporary rumor control and verification center should be operated 24 hours a day during a crisis period by a local government agency. It should be staffed by professionals and trained volunteers. The media and others should publicize the telephone number.

THE MEDIA CAN BE A HELPFUL ALLY

The media can play an important role in preventing hate crimes from increasing community tensions. Local officials should designate an informed single-point-of-contact for hate crime information. Accurate, thorough, and responsible reporting significantly improves the likelihood of regaining stability, and helps alleviate fear, suspicion, and anger.

HATE CRIMES MUST BE INVESTIGATED AND REPORTED

A municipality should assure that its law enforcement agencies adopt a policy for investigating and reporting hate crimes.

HATE CRIMES AND MULTI-JURISDICTIONAL TASK FORCES

Some local governments have institutionalized sharing of expertise and agency resources through memoranda of understanding. Creating a coalition of public and private agencies and community organizations will give cities in the county or region a complete and thorough range of resources and information to promote ethnic relations and counter hate crimes. This network or consortium can also work with coalitions created specifically to investigate and prosecute hate crimes. Such a coalition might include the district attorney, the city attorney, law enforcement agencies, and civil rights, community, and educational organizations.

TABLE 9.7 *(continued)*

VICTIMS, WITNESSES, AND OFFENDERS NEED HELP

Educational counseling programs for young perpetrators of hate crime can dispel stereotypes, prejudice, fears, and other motivators of hate crime. Counseling may include sessions with members of minority groups and visits to local correctional facilities. In addition, "restorative justice," the concept of healing both the victim and the offender while regaining the trust of the community, may be appropriate. The offenders are held accountable and are required to repair both the physical and emotional damage caused by their actions.

Source: Community Relations Service, 2000b.

TABLE 9.8 BEST PRACTICES FOR CREATING POSITIVE COMMUNITY RESPONSES TO HATE

PREPARE IN ADVANCE FOR HATE GROUPS

Hate groups are well organized, well funded, and dedicated to their mission of hate. To counter these groups, people of goodwill and unity must create strategic alliances with other like minded groups to effectively prepare for hate group activity. This entails interfaith dialogue, civic cooperation, and strong leadership from the entire community.

AVOID THE HATE GROUP'S EVENT AND COUNTER-PROTESTS

When hate groups announce plans for an event in a community, confrontational counter-rallies are often planned in the same location. These counter-rallies have proven to be both dangerous and counter-productive, given the increasing amount of violence that occurs when the groups clash. Hate groups have perfected the art of inciting violence and then claiming that the violence came from the protesters, rather than the hate group. Counter-protesters often give hate groups exactly what they need to spread their message of hate: media coverage, large crowds, and an opportunity to claim that their rights under the First Amendment have been violated. In many instances, the media cannot distinguish between the hate groups' sympathizers and curious on-lookers. This can result in inflated estimations of support at rallies and marches. All of this can be avoided by staying away from the proximity of the event.

TABLE 9.8 *(continued)*

ORGANIZE AN ALTERNATIVE EVENT IN ANOTHER PART OF TOWN

To discourage attendance at hate group events, communities should plan a multicultural event that encourages family participation. This event should be in a different part of the town and be held near the time of the hate group's event. By giving the community a positive outlet for their concerns and feelings, the hate group's presence can be turned into an event that strengthens the community in the long run.

DO NOT TRY TO STOP THE HATE GROUP'S EVENT

It is not uncommon for concerned citizens to pressure city officials to deny parade or rally permits to the hate group to prevent their event, but this is rarely effective because of the protections afforded by the First Amendment. Hate groups have won scores of cases against communities that have attempted to block their events. The event is usually held and efforts undertaken by the community result in more publicity for the hate group.

FORM COMMUNITY ANTI-RACISM GROUPS

A very effective way to oppose hate groups is to form a Citizen's Anti-Racism Group. The group should reflect the local community in that it should have people of every race, religion, sexual orientation, and culture. The group's mission should stress cooperation and harmony and discourage confrontational tactics.

MAKE USE OF THE LOCAL NEWSPAPER BY PLACING POSITIVE ADS AND EDITORIALS

When hate groups come to a local community, citizens should consider the option of buying an advertisement in the local newspaper or writing a thoughtful editorial that emphasizes unity and support in the community. Making use of the editorial page or a purchased ad will allow concerned citizens to convey a message of intolerance when it comes to bias, bigotry, and racism. Ultimately, these pieces should denounce the hate group's bigoted views and should run on or before the day of the hate group's event.

RESPOND QUICKLY WITH A SHOW OF UNITY

Concerned citizens should quickly put aside racial, cultural, and religious differences and band together to fight the effects of hate groups in the community. Treating an attack on one group as an attack on the community sends the clear message to the panderers of hate that bias, bigotry, and racism will not be tolerated against any member of the community. Hate groups are quick to point out differences and will capitalize upon them, if they sense that these differences can be exploited to their own advantage.

> **TABLE 9.8** *(continued)*
>
> **KNOW THE LAWS IN THE COMMUNITY AND STATE**
>
> Several states and communities have broad hate crime laws that cover a wide range of incidents regarding racial and religious criminal activity. Others have limitations that allow only the collection of data on specific occurrences such as acts of vandalism. If a particular community does not have a hate crime law or the existing law is weak, citizens should try to organize an effort to push for strong bias crime legislation.
>
> **FOCUS ON THE GROUPS BEING SINGLED OUT BY THE HATE GROUP**
>
> The victims of verbal assaults by hate groups often feel isolated, so that it is most important to let them know their community cares about their well being. The harsh rhetoric used by bigots leaves the victims in need of support and help in dealing with their anger.
>
> **FIND UNIQUE WAYS TO SHOW OPPOSITION**
>
> There is no single way to combat hate, nor is there any one list, including this one, that will work in every community. Individual local needs must be considered and methods must be adapted accordingly. Constantly evolving and new efforts and approaches are key to winning the battle against these groups.
>
> *Source:* National Conference for Community and Justice, 2000c. Copyright 2000, National Conference for Community and Justice. Reprinted with permission.

COMMUNITY EDUCATION Community education entails public information campaigns aimed at reducing prejudice, racism, and discrimination among the general public. It aims to change people's attitudes, behaviors, or both. The education effort may use a variety of approaches, such as the following (Simpson and Yinger 1985):

- Increasing awareness of anti-discrimination legislation.
- Increasing understanding of the harmful effects of prejudice, racism, and discrimination.
- Providing normative information regarding the ethnic harmony views of most people or of prominent figures.
- Appealing to people's morality.
- Emphasizing the absurdity of prejudice, racism, and discrimination.

- Exposing, embarrassing, and discrediting leaders of hate groups.
- Providing accurate information about specific populations, such as immigrants or refugees, to counter misconceptions.

SPECIFIC MEDIA for community education include the following (Anti-Defamation League, 1999; Chetkow-Yanoov 1999; Simpson and Yinger 1985):

- Billboards
- Posters
- Leaflets
- Pamphlets
- Web sites
- Internet e-mail lists
- Cartoons
- Comic books
- Articles
- Public service announcements on radio and television
- Advertisements
- Movies
- Plays
- Television programs
- Performing arts exhibits
- Songs
- Slogans and symbols of interethnic harmony

Empirical evidence indicates that such community education has some effectiveness, although by itself it cannot produce extensive changes (Simpson and Yinger 1985). In order to increase effectiveness, the following conditions must be met: the message must be received under favorable conditions, so that it will be looked at or heard; it must attract and hold the attention of the target audience; it must be enjoyable and not bring pain; and it must be understood, not evaded by misunderstanding (Simpson and Yinger 1985). Many of the best practices for effective community health education presented in an earlier chapter are also applicable to increasing the effectiveness of anti-prejudice, anti-racism, and anti-discrimination community education.

NONVIOLENT RESISTANCE If the various strategies discussed thus far fail to achieve the desired degree of change, it may be appropriate or expedient for social workers to participate in or help organize nonviolent resistance. Nonviolent resistance is a philosophy and set of tactics embodied in the works of Henry David Thoreau, Leo Tolstoy, Mahatma Gandhi, and Martin Luther King, Jr. It is a method for relatively powerless groups to maximize their strength in dealing with an opponent who has some respect for law and a conscience (Simpson and Yinger 1985). This approach rests on two underlying principles. One is Gandhi's concept of *satyagraha*, or "truth force," which holds that people achieve insight into the real nature of an evil situation by seeking truth in a spirit of peace and love, and that non-cooperation with evil is a moral obligation (Martin 2000). This principle prohibits both physical and psychological violence and promotes active caring for the opponent (Shepard 1998). The second underlying principle is Thoreau's concept of *civil disobedience*, which is the refusal to obey laws that are unjust, and the willingness to accept any penalty for such disobedience, such as imprisonment (Simpson and Yinger 1985).

An advantage of nonviolent resistance is that it does not unify the force and aggression of the opponent, as a violent act would (Simpson and Yinger 1985). It is most likely to be effective when members of the opposition are not unified and some are ambivalent, sharing values and goals with the protesters as well as with the opposition. Such people are more likely to be persuaded by nonviolent resistance when it provides them with an effective argument to disidentify with the dominant position of their own group (Simpson and Yinger 1985).

Specific tactics of nonviolent resistance include marches, rallies, demonstrations, boycotts, fasts, sit-ins, pickets, strikes, disruption of services, or causing a work slowdown (Kahn 1991; Chetkow-Yaanov 1999; Simpson and Yinger 1985). In selecting which tactic or series of tactics to use, the following issues should be considered (Kahn 1991):

- How does the tactic convey to the opposition the real power that the protest group has in the situation?
- What does the protest group have that the opposition needs (e.g., votes, spending power, labor)?
- What does the protest group have that the opposition does not want to be used (e.g., power to disrupt the orderly functioning of society)?
- What is the decision that the protest group wants to be made?

- Who is in a position to make that decision?
- Who is in a position to influence the decisionmaker?
- What tactics do the members of the protest group have experience with and are comfortable with?

The answers to these questions will help to identify what is the best tactic and at whom it should be targeted. In addition to these considerations, protest groups should begin with those tactics that require the least resources and thus apply the least pressure, and thereby leave room for escalation (Kahn 1991). Although the approach of nonviolent resistance has sometimes been criticized, particularly by those in favor of violent methods, it has unquestionably been effective in some instances, notably the U. S. civil rights movement of the 1960s (Martin 2000; Simpson and Yinger 1985).

9.2.3 MESO PRACTICE

WITHIN THE CONTEXT OF INTERETHNIC RELATIONS, meso-level practice may be conceived of as those activities in which the social worker functions as a bridge between the diverse segments of the society. As such, the worker functions at the boundaries between different systems. In this capacity, the worker may take on various roles such as facilitator, broker, mediator, enabler, consultant, or cultural interpreter. Two specific methods of meso practice in this context are structured interethnic contact and conflict resolution.

STRUCTURED INTERETHNIC CONTACT Structured interethnic contact refers to planned, facilitated activities that bring together people from different ethnic groups in order to increase mutual understanding and decrease prejudice, racism, and conflict. Such contact must be carefully structured because contact in and of itself does not necessarily lead to these desired goals. Theory and empirical evidence indicate that some types of interethnic contact reduce prejudice, racism, and discrimination, whereas other types of contact increase them (Hood and Morris 1998; Simpson and Yinger 1985). A synthesis of empirical evidence on the effects of interethnic contact indicates the following:

- Incidental, involuntary, tension-laden contact is likely to increase prejudice.
- Pleasant, equal-status contact that makes it unnecessary for the individuals to cross barriers of class, occupational, and educational differences as well as differences in ethnicity is likely to reduce prejudice.
- Stereotype-breaking contacts that show ethnic group members in roles and having characteristics not usually associated with them reduce prejudice.
- Contacts that bring people of different ethnic groups together in functionally important activities reduce prejudice. This is particularly true when those activities involve goals that cannot be achieved without the active cooperation of members of all the groups.

(SIMPSON AND YINGER 1985, P. 396)

RESEARCH ALSO INDICATES that the development of positive interethnic attitudes depends upon the existence of significant, long-term, and high-quality interaction, and the absence of active opposition by powerful authorities (Hood and Morris 1998).

Structured interethnic contact most commonly takes the form of guided workshops consisting of several sessions in which the different ethnic groups engage in structured dialogue. "A dialogue is a forum that draws participants from as many parts of the community as possible to exchange information face-to-face, share personal stories and experiences, honestly express perspectives, clarify viewpoints, and develop solutions to community concerns" (Community Relations Service 1998). Such group dialogues have been found to be effective in reducing interethnic conflict in various settings (Chetkow-Yanoov 1999; Norman 1994).

The U.S. President's Initiative on Race and the federal Community Relations Service have developed best practices for conducting a community dialogue on race and ethnicity (Community Relations Service 1998). These best practice guidelines address the characteristics of effective dialogues; steps in organizing a dialogue; best practices for conducting an effective dialogue; and best practices for the dialogue leader. These issues are summarized in tables 9.9 to 9.12.

TABLE 9.9 CHARACTERISTICS OF EFFECTIVE INTERETHNIC DIALOGUE

MOVE TOWARDS SOLUTIONS RATHER THAN CONTINUE TO EXPRESS OR ANALYZE THE PROBLEM

An emphasis on personal responsibility moves the discussion away from finger-pointing or naming enemies and towards constructive common action.

REACH BEYOND THE USUAL BOUNDARIES

When fully developed, dialogues can involve the entire community, offering opportunities for new, unexpected partnerships. New partnerships can develop when participants listen carefully and respectfully to each other. A search for solutions focuses on the common good as participants are encouraged to broaden their horizons and build relationships outside their comfort zones.

UNITE DIVIDED COMMUNITIES THROUGH A RESPECTFUL, INFORMED SHARING OF LOCAL ETHNIC HISTORY AND ITS CONSEQUENCES FOR PEOPLE IN TODAY'S SOCIETY

The experience of "walking through history" together can lead to healing.

AIM FOR A CHANGE OF HEART, NOT JUST A CHANGE OF MIND

Dialogues go beyond sharing and understanding to transforming participants. While the process begins with the individual, it eventually involves groups and institutions. Ultimately, dialogues affect how policies are made.

Source: Community Relations Service, 1998.

TABLE 9.10 STEPS IN ORGANIZING AN INTERETHNIC DIALOGUE

STEP 1: WHO SHOULD BE INVOLVED?

FORM A PLANNING GROUP

Convene a planning group of six or eight people who represent different backgrounds, professions, and viewpoints. Once you've assembled the group, discuss your approach. You will need to spend enough time together to build a level of trust. This group will be the nucleus that drives the process and should "model" the kind of relationships and openness that you hope to see in the overall effort.

TABLE 9.10 *(continued)*

Look for Other Groups with Which to Partner

Having good partners is important for long-term success. Look for people who are already working to improve ethnic relations and who have experiences to share. Good partners may be able to provide useful information, organizational resources, and greatly increase outreach to the community. Establish partnerships with groups from different racial, ethnic, or religious communities, including religious leaders, law enforcement, small business owners, elected officials, and nonprofit organizations.

STEP 2: WHAT'S HAPPENING IN MY COMMUNITY?

THINK ABOUT THE NEEDS OF YOUR COMMUNITY

Take an inventory. What problems do you see in the community that are related to ethnicity? What are the critical issues? If things are really going to change, who needs to be part of the dialogue? Who are the individuals or groups not talking to each other? What role do language barriers play in groups not talking to each other? Are there people who should be allies, who may be doing similar work, but who are competing rather than working together? What are some of the consequences of ethnic divisions?

STEP 3: WHAT DO YOU WANT TO ACCOMPLISH?

DEVELOP A VISION FOR YOUR COMMUNITY

What is special about your community? What do the different neighborhoods or groups offer that is unique? Are there particular issues that need to be heard?

ESTABLISH SHORT-, MEDIUM-, AND LONG-TERM GOALS

Set attainable goals that the group can work towards together. Look for "hinge issues" around which coalitions may form—education, housing, public transportation, and safety, for example. Where possible, create task forces to study specific needs and to work on concrete action plans. This approach will keep key business and civic leaders at the table.

STEP 4: HOW MANY DIALOGUES SHOULD TAKE PLACE AND FOR HOW LONG?

The answer to this question depends on what you want to accomplish. Dialogues can go from one session of two hours to a series of sessions lasting indefinitely. If your goal is simply to get people you know to come together and have a conversation about ethnicity, you may only want to do one session. If your goal is to create institutional change in your community, you may want to launch a series of dialogues involving broad community representation. Such an effort will require partnering with other groups in the community and seeking out support services.

STEP 5: WHAT ADDITIONAL PLANNING ISSUES MIGHT YOU CONSIDER?

RECRUIT PARTICIPANTS

To ensure the right balance for your group(s), you may need to consider the following: First, "which voices need to be included?" Answering that question will ensure the ethnic

TABLE 9.10 *(continued)*

and religious diversity necessary for successful dialogues. Then, "who is missing?" That answer will steer you towards others who need to be involved. Other people to contact are those in uninvolved or unaffiliated groups who, while a visible part of the community, may be harder to reach through traditional means. Generate interest by doing the following:
- Ask civic leaders and other influential community members to help rally the public.
- Identify the appropriate media for the audience you are trying to reach—consider placing an announcement in a small weekly or monthly newspaper, on a community board, or on an electronic community board.
- Use bilingual communications.
- Post an announcement in grocery stores in the community.
- Invite yourself to various group meetings in the community to get the word out.
- Approach local chapters of national organizations.

CONSIDER LOGISTICS ISSUES

These may include where to have the dialogue, whether any funds need to be raised, and use of mailings lists—often obtainable from other groups

STEP 6: HOW DO WE CONDUCT THE DIALOGUE?

The critical components include welcoming participants and having them introduce themselves; setting out the dialogue's purpose; establishing ground rules; promoting discussion through thoughtful questions, visual media, or other materials; and periodically summarizing and evaluating the dialogue (see Table 9.11).

STEP 7: HOW WELL DID WE DO?

DOCUMENT AND EVALUATE THE PROJECT

Keep a record of the individuals who take part in the dialogues and of how well the discussions go. Include such things as number of participants, group composition, main topics discussed, how productive the discussions were, how they might have been improved, and other thoughts. This will allow you to see how attitudes and perceptions have changed and whether changes need to be made in the dialogue format. Emphasize that what participants share during the dialogue will not be attributed to them in any official record or document.

HAVE PARTICIPANTS EVALUATE THE DIALOGUE

Each group should evaluate the dialogue, whether a single session or a series, after it is over. You may wish to distribute a short evaluation form to elicit participant feedback and to measure the impact of the dialogue. Such a form might include questions such as:
- Why did you join the group?
- What were your expectations?
- Were you comfortable participating in the discussion?
- Did the dialogue give you new insights about how to improve ethnic relations?
- Was the dialogue climate positive and respectful?

TABLE 9.10 *(continued)*

- Did you find the dialogue to be a valuable experience overall?
- How might it have been improved?
- Would you like to participate in a future session?
- Did the experience motivate you to act differently?
- What additional comments do you have?

STEP 8: WHAT'S THE NEXT STEP?

HOLD AN ANNUAL PUBLIC EVENT

This is to celebrate achievements, evaluate effectiveness, and invite new participants.

EXPAND THE TEAM

As the dialogues develop, include representatives of all major areas (politics, different faiths, education, business, media, etc.). With them, you may want to create a statement about your community, its history, the challenges it faces today, and your collective vision for the future.

Source: Community Relations Service, 1998.

TABLE 9.11 BEST PRACTICES FOR CONDUCTING AN EFFECTIVE INTERETHNIC DIALOGUE

The dialogue design presented here contains four phases that have proven useful in moving participants through a natural process from sharing individual experiences to gaining a deeper understanding of those experiences to committing to collective action. Whether meeting for one dialogue session or a series of sessions, participants move through all four phases, exploring and building on shared experiences.

PHASE I: WHO ARE WE?

This phase sets the tone and context for the dialogue, which begins with sharing of personal stories and experiences. In addition to serving an ice-breaking function, this kind of personal sharing helps to level the playing field among participants and improve their understanding by hearing each other's experiences.

Welcome, Introduction, and Overview

- Explain the purpose of the dialogue and the several phases involved.

TABLE 9.11 *(continued)*

- Discuss, clarify, and set ground rules. Some basic ground rules might include the following:
  - We will respect confidentiality.
  - We will share time equitably to ensure the participation of all.
  - We will listen carefully and not interrupt.
  - We will keep an open mind and be open to learning.
  - We will not be disrespectful of the speaker even when we do not respect the views.
- Ask people to briefly introduce themselves.
- Give an overview of the session.
- Describe your role as dialogue leader (see Table 9.12).

Starting the Dialogue

Often the most difficult part of talking about interethnic relations is getting started. People may feel uncomfortable at first and hesitant about expressing their personal beliefs. To get people talking, it may help to relate personal stories or anecdotes, or to bring up an interethnic relations incident that has occurred within the community.
- Begin with questions that allow people to talk about their own lives and what is important to them. Don't focus on ethnicity at first. Give people a chance just to get to know each other and to find out what they have in common. For groups of 15 people or fewer, keep everyone together. Groups of more than 15 people should be separated into smaller groups (3 to 5 people) for a few minutes, then brought back together. Examples of questions to use include:
  - How long have you lived in this community?
  - Where did you live before moving here?
  - What are some of your personal interests?
  - What things in life are most important to you?
- Explore how ethnicity affects us on a day-to-day basis. Examples of questions include:
  - What is your ethnic and/or cultural background?
  - Did you grow up mostly around people similar to you?
  - What are some of your earliest memories of coming in contact with people different from you?
- Summarize the session at meeting's end.
- Evaluate the meeting. Ask such questions as:
  - How did you feel about this meeting?
  - Is there anything you would like to change?
- Bring the meeting to an end and defuse any tensions. In preparation for the next meeting, ask participants to think about the following questions:
  - When it comes to interethnic relations, what problems are we facing?
  - What are the most serious challenges facing our community, and what are the community's greatest strengths for dealing with those challenges?

PHASE II: WHERE ARE WE?

This phase explores questions that highlight our different experiences and different perceptions about the kinds of problems our society is facing with regard to interethnic rela-

TABLE 9.11 *(continued)*

tions. This phase is about people expressing their different understandings about interethnic relations, then exploring the underlying conditions producing them. By the end of this phase, participants should have identified themes, issues, and problems in their community.
• Begin with questions that get people to talk about their current experiences with interethnic relations. Be prepared for the level of conversation to intensify during this phase. Remember to reassure participants that it is okay to feel agitated or uncomfortable, reminding them of the ground rules when necessary. Examples of questions include:
  • How much and what type of contact do you have with people from other ethnic groups?
  • Is it easier or harder than it was a few years ago to make friends from other ethnic groups? Why is that so?
• Focus the dialogue on the state of interethnic relations in the community. Questions to help get started include:
  • How would you describe the overall state of interethnic relations in our community?
  • What are some of the underlying conditions affecting interethnic relations in our community?
  • In what ways do we agree and/or disagree about the nature of our interethnic problems, what caused them, and how serious they are?
• Summarize the session, evaluate it, and bring the meeting to an end. In preparation for the next session, have participants think about the following questions:
  • What can we do to make progress in our community?
  • When it comes to strategies to improve interethnic relations and to eliminate racism, what sorts of proposals do you know about?
  • What are the pros and cons of the various approaches?
  • When it comes to ethnicity, what direction should our public policies take?
  • What goals and values should shape our policies?

PHASE III: WHERE DO WE WANT TO GO?

The goal of this phase is to move away from the "me" and get people to think and talk about possible directions for change. In this segment, participants begin to build their collective vision. They first identify what would be a part of that vision and then brainstorm about how they could all help to build it. By the end of this session, participants should have identified accomplishments, barriers to overcome, and opportunities for further action.
• Have participants talk about their vision of what they would like to see in the community. You could ask questions such as:
  • How would you answer the question of where we want to go in interethnic relations?
  • If we had excellent interethnic relations, what kinds of things would we see in the community? Hear in the community? Feel?
• Help participants to build their future vision. Ask questions like:
  • What are the main changes that need to happen to increase understanding and cooperative action across ethnic lines?

TABLE 9.11 *(continued)*

- What are some of the helping/hindering forces in our community?
- Turn the dialogue to what individuals can do towards improving interethnic relations. Ask questions like:
  - What things have you seen that give you hope for improved interethnic relations?
  - What are some steps we could take to improve interethnic relations in our neighborhood, workplace, organizations, schools, and/or community?
- Explore the roles that the community's institutions and government play in helping interethnic relations. How could they do a better job?
- Summarize the session, evaluate it, and bring the meeting to an end. For the next session, have participants think about these questions:
  - What kinds of concrete steps can you take in your everyday life—by yourself and with others—to improve interethnic relations in the community?
  - What do you think is most needed in this community?

PHASE IV: WHAT WILL WE DO, AS INDIVIDUALS AND WITH OTHERS, TO MAKE A DIFFERENCE?

The purpose of this session is to begin a productive conversation on specific actions that individuals will take, by themselves or with others, to make a difference in their communities. This session presents a range of concrete actions for change.

- Try to get participants to move from words to actions. Ask questions like:
  - What is each of us personally willing to do to make a difference?
  - How can we connect with others who share our concerns?
  - Should we continue and expand this dialogue, get more people involved? How?
  - Are there other issues and concerns that we should address using dialogues?
  - What will we do to ensure follow-up?
- Brainstorm action ideas with participants. Share any follow-up plans.
- Summarize the session, evaluate it, and bring the meeting to an end. Pass out an evaluation form.

Source: Community Relations Service, 1998.

TABLE 9.12 BEST PRACTICES FOR THE INTERETHNIC DIALOGUE LEADER

SET A RELAXED AND OPEN TONE

Welcome everyone and create a friendly and relaxed atmosphere. Well-placed humor is usually appreciated.

STAY NEUTRAL

This may be the most important point to remember as the leader of a dialogue. You should not share your personal views or try to advance your agenda on the issue. You are there to serve the discussion, not to join it.

STRESS THE IMPORTANCE OF CONFIDENTIALITY

Make sure participants understand that what they say during the dialogue session is to be kept completely confidential. Define for them what confidential means. For instance, it is not all right to speak outside of the dialogue about what someone else said or did. It is all right to share one's own personal insights about the issue of interethnic relations as a result of the process.

ENCOURAGE OPENNESS ABOUT LANGUAGE

Dialogue leaders should encourage participants to offer preferred terms if a biased or offensive word or phrase should come up during the dialogue.

PROVIDE BILINGUAL TRANSLATION IF NECESSARY

Also, ensure that provided material is translated into the participants' first languages, or recruit bilingual discussion leaders.

KEEP TRACK OF WHO IS CONTRIBUTING AND WHO IS NOT

You should not only help to keep the group focused on the content of the discussion, but also monitor how well the participants are communicating with each other—who has spoken, who has not, and whose points have not yet received a fair hearing. A dialogue leader must constantly weigh group needs against the requirements of individual members.

FOLLOW AND FOCUS THE CONVERSATION FLOW

A dialogue leader who listens carefully will select topics raised in the initial sharing. To help keep the group on the topic, it is helpful to occasionally restate the key question or insight under discussion. It is important to guide gently, yet persistently. Keep careful track of time.

DO NOT FEAR SILENCE

It is all right if people are quiet for a while. When deciding when to intervene, err on the side of nonintervention. The group will work its way out of a difficult situation. Sometimes

> **TABLE 9.12** *(continued)*
>
> group members only need more time to think through alternatives or to consider what has just been said.
>
> **ACCEPT AND SUMMARIZE EXPRESSED OPINIONS**
>
> "Accepting" shows respect for each participant in the group. It is important for the dialogue leader to make it clear that dialogue discussions involve no right or wrong responses. One way to show acceptance and respect is to briefly summarize what is heard and to convey the feeling with which it was shared. Once in a while, ask participants to sum up the most important points that have come out in the discussion. This gives the group a sense of accomplishment and a point of reference for more sharing.
>
> **ANTICIPATE CONFLICT AND TEND TO THE GROUND RULES**
>
> When conflict arises, explain that disagreement over ideas is to be expected. Remind participants that conflict must stay on the issue. Do not allow it to become personal. Appeal to the group to help resolve the conflict and abide by the ground rules. You may have to stop and reference the ground rules several times throughout the discussion.
>
> **CLOSE THE DIALOGUE**
>
> Give participants a chance to talk about the most important thing they gained from the discussion. You may ask them to share any new ideas or thoughts they've had as a result of the discussion. Ask them to think about what worked and what didn't. You may want to encourage the group to design a closing activity for use at each session. Provide some time for the group to evaluate the process in writing. Remember to thank everyone for their participation.
>
> *Source:* Community Relations Service, 1998.

CONFLICT RESOLUTION Conflict resolution is "a spectrum of processes that all utilize communication skills and creative thinking to develop voluntary solutions that are acceptable to those concerned in a dispute" (Crawford and Bodine 1996, p. D-2). Conflict resolution is frequently used as an intervention in interethnic conflicts between individuals, groups, warring factions within nations, or between nations. Social workers may engage in conflict resolution in either a "contractual" or "emergent" capacity (Barsky 2000). In contractual conflict resolution, the worker is specifically hired to conduct conflict resolution, and a written contract between the practitioner, the disputants, and any other interested parties is established. In emergent conflict resolution, the worker uses the skills and strategies of conflict resolution, but is not specifically hired for that purpose. Thus, the conflict resolution methods are used within the context of an existing relationship between the worker and the interested party or parties. For example, a school social worker might use emergent conflict resolution when an interethnic conflict arises in the school.

In general, all conflict resolution processes follow a series of problem-solving steps consisting of setting the stage; gathering perspectives; identifying interests; creating options; evaluating options; and generating agreement (Crawford and Bodine 1996). Additionally, all conflict resolution processes are based on a set of underlying principles, which are shown in table 9.13. Two major conflict resolution processes are negotiation and mediation (Barsky 2000; Crawford and Bodine 1996). Each of these is addressed below.

TABLE 9.13 PRINCIPLES OF CONFLICT RESOLUTION

SEPARATE PEOPLE FROM THE PROBLEM

Every problem involves both substantive issues and relationship issues. By separating these issues, individuals come to see themselves as working side by side, attacking the problem, not each other. Where perceptions are inaccurate, the conflict resolution practitioner can look for ways to educate. If emotions run high, the conflict resolution practitioner can find ways for each person involved to let off steam. Where misunderstanding exists, the practitioner can work to improve communication.

FOCUS ON INTERESTS, NOT POSITIONS

Understanding the difference between positions and interests is crucial to problem solving. Interests, not positions, define the problem. Positions are something that individuals decide they want; interests are the underlying motivations behind the positions they take. Compromising between positions is not likely to produce an agreement which will effectively take care of the human needs that led individuals to adopt those positions. Where such interests are not identified, temporary agreements may be reached, but typically do not last because the real interests have not been addressed.

INVENT OPTIONS FOR MUTUAL GAIN

Disputants focus on identifying options for resolving the conflict without the pressure of reaching a decision. A brainstorming process is used to invent a wide range of options that advance shared interests and creatively reconcile differing interests. The key ground rule to

> **TABLE 9.13** *(continued)*
>
> brainstorming is to postpone criticism and evaluation of the ideas being generated. To broaden their options, those in a dispute think about the problem in different ways and build upon the ideas presented.
>
> **USE OBJECTIVE CRITERIA**
>
> Using objective criteria ensures that the agreement reflects some fair standard instead of the arbitrary will of either side. Using objective criteria means that neither party needs to give in to the other; rather, they can defer to a fair solution. Objective criteria are determined by disputants based on fair standards and fair procedures.
>
> *Source:* Crawford and Bodine, 1996.

Negotiation. "Negotiation is a problem-solving process in which either the . . . parties in the dispute or their representatives meet face to face to work together unassisted to resolve the dispute between the parties" (Crawford and Bodine 1996, p. 10). Social workers may be involved in negotiation pertaining to interethnic conflict in two ways: by teaching clients the skills and process of negotiation so that they can engage in it themselves; or by directly engaging in negotiation as advocates on behalf of clients (either individual clients or a group). Fundamental negotiation skills, or abilities, that workers can teach clients are shown in table 9.14. The process of interest-based negotiation is shown in table 9.15.

> **TABLE 9.14** FUNDAMENTAL NEGOTIATION ABILITIES
>
> **ORIENTATION ABILITIES**
>
> These encompass values, beliefs, attitudes, and propensities that are compatible with effective conflict resolution. Orientation abilities include:
> - Nonviolence
> - Compassion and empathy
> - Fairness

TABLE 9.14 *(continued)*

- Trust
- Justice
- Tolerance
- Self-respect
- Respect for others
- Celebration of diversity
- Appreciation for controversy

PERCEPTION ABILITIES

These encompass the understanding that conflict lies not in objective reality, but in how individuals perceive that reality. Perception abilities include:
- Empathizing in order to see the situation as the other side sees it.
- Self-evaluating to recognize personal fears.
- Suspending judgment and blame to facilitate a free exchange of views.

EMOTION ABILITIES

These encompass behaviors to manage anger, frustration, fear, and other emotions effectively. Emotion abilities include:
- Learning language for communicating emotions effectively.
- Expressing emotions in nonaggressive, noninflammatory ways.
- Exercising self-control in order not to react to the emotional outbursts of others.

COMMUNICATION ABILITIES

These encompass behaviors of listening and speaking that allow for the effective exchange of facts and feelings. Communication abilities include:
- Listening to understand by using active listening behaviors.
- Speaking to be understood.
- Reframing emotionally charged statements into neutral, less emotional terms.

CREATIVE THINKING ABILITIES

These encompass behaviors that enable individuals to be innovative in defining problems and making decisions. Creative thinking abilities include:
- Contemplating the problem from a variety of perspectives.
- Approaching the problem-solving task as a mutual pursuit of possibilities.
- Brainstorming to create, elaborate, and enhance a variety of options.

CRITICAL THINKING ABILITIES

These encompass the behaviors of analyzing, hypothesizing, predicting, strategizing, comparing, contrasting, and evaluating. Critical thinking abilities include:
- Recognizing existing criteria and making them explicit.
- Establishing objective criteria.

TABLE 9.14 *(continued)*

- Applying criteria as the basis of choosing options.
- Planning future behaviors.

Source: Crawford and Bodine, 1996.

TABLE 9.15 INTEREST-BASED NEGOTIATION PROCESS

FOCUS ON INTERESTS, NOT POSITIONS

- What are your interests?
- What are the other's interests?
- Which interests do you have in common?
- Which interests conflict?
- Are these conflicting interests based on any deeper interests that you do share (e.g., underlying desires, values, or needs)?

INVENT OPTIONS FOR MUTUAL GAIN

- Identify all possible options for solution.
- Is it better to brainstorm individually or together?
- What other sources of information can you access to help you invent options?
- Do not evaluate the options until you have finished identifying them.

APPLY OBJECTIVE CRITERIA

- What standards can be used to assess the options?
- What sources can you explore that might help you identify objective criteria (e.g., experts in the field, literature, precedents)?

IMPROVE COMMUNICATION

- What problems, if any, stem from miscommunication?
- How can you rectify these problems? (e.g., if the conflict is caused by the parties' relying on different information, then sharing information is important; if the parties have different interpretations of the information, then they can explain these differences to one another; if the parties cannot understand one another, consider the use of a linguistic or cultural interpreter).

TABLE 9.15 *(continued)*

- What communication problems do you foresee in upcoming negotiations? How can you preempt these?
- What is your purpose for communication (e.g., to demonstrate that you hear and understand the other party, to persuade, to build trust, to share information, to reach an agreement)?
- How can you tailor the forum for negotiation so that it promotes constructive communication (e.g., sufficient time, good working space, low stress, few distractions)?
- If direct communication is problematic, what type of facilitator might help the process (e.g., representatives for each party, mediator, supervisor)?

BUILD A POSITIVE NEGOTIATING RELATIONSHIP

- Consider use of unconditionally constructive strategies: rationality, understanding, consultation, reliability, noncoercive modes of influence, and acceptance.
- What makes employing these strategies difficult in the present conflict?
- How can you try to overcome these challenges?
- How can you encourage collaboration?

CONSIDER ALTERNATIVES

- What are your alternatives to a negotiated agreement?
- Which of these is your best alternative?
- What are the other party's alternatives?
- Which one is the other's best alternative?
- How will you know when it is best to terminate negotiation and move to another alternative?
- What are the advantages and risks of your best alternative?
- If the other party has a strong best alternative, what incentives can you use to encourage that party to negotiate?
- Rather than negotiate for a specific solution, would it be useful to negotiate a process designed to produce a fair result?

OBTAIN COMMITMENTS

- What commitments do you need in order to make an agreement work?
- What commitments are you prepared to make?
- What commitments is the other party prepared to make?
- Are these commitments feasible?
- How can you solidify the commitments?
- How can you help the other party make commitments?
- What strategies can you use to ensure that commitments are followed by all parties?

Source: Barsky, 2000. Copyright © 2000, Wadsworth. Reprinted with permission.

It has been suggested that this negotiation process works best when "the parties are flexible; they are able to suspend their individual ambitions; they have faith in their own abilities to negotiate; and they have had prior success in resolving some issues" (Barsky 2000, p. 84). Such interest-based negotiation may not be a useful strategy when there is a high degree of mistrust or anger; when the parties cannot perceive the benefits of negotiation; when the conflict is grounded in a strong difference of values or principles; or when a quick decision is needed. Additionally, the approach may not work well within cultures in which "face-saving and conflict avoidance are valued over disclosure and confrontation" (Barsky 2000, p. 84). In such cases, it may be preferable for the social worker to engage in the negotiation on behalf of the clients rather than for the clients to act as negotiators themselves. Additionally, if the goal is not to reach a mutually satisfying agreement, but to advance one party's position or agenda over another's, then negotiation is not appropriate and a more adversarial stance is necessary (Barsky 2000).

It is possible that the goal of negotiation may be not to necessarily reach an agreement, but to increase empowerment and recognition between the parties (Barsky 2000). Negotiating parties are empowered when:

- They realize more clearly what their goals and interests are and why they are important.
- They become more aware of the options available to them (what choices are available and that they have control over them).
- They improve their conflict resolution skills, including their ability to listen, communicate, organize and analyze issues, present arguments, brainstorm, and evaluate alternative solutions.
- They gain awareness of resources already in their possession or available to them to achieve their goals and objectives.
- They reflect, deliberate, and make conscious decisions for themselves about what they want, and are able to analyze the strengths and weaknesses of various choices before making decisions.

(BUSH AND FOLGER 1994, PP. 85–87, CITED IN BARSKY 2000)

Negotiating parties can provide recognition to others by:

- Reflecting on the others' situation out of a general concern for their predicament.
- Consciously letting go of one's own viewpoint in order to open up to seeing the others in a different, more positive light.

- Trying to understand how, what seemed to be a hurtful or irrational act by the others might be the product of the other parties' reasonable response to stresses they have been enduring.
- Openly acknowledging one's changed understanding of others.
- Apologizing for having "thought the worst" about the other party or for past "retaliatory conduct."
- Changing one's behavior to accommodate the other's interests, in light of the new understanding.

(BUSH AND FOLGER 1994, PP. 89–91, CITED IN BARSKY 2000)

Such "transformative" negotiation (Barsky 2000) aimed at increasing empowerment and recognition appears to be particularly relevant to interethnic conflict. In such cases, social workers can act as consultants to the negotiating parties to help them achieve the goals of empowerment and recognition. For example, as already mentioned, social workers can teach clients the skills of negotiation in order to empower them. In the consultant role, social workers could also act as cultural interpreters to help the parties enhance their recognition of each other's viewpoints.

Mediation. "Mediation is a problem-solving process in which the . . . parties in the dispute or their representatives meet face to face to work together to resolve the dispute assisted by a neutral third party called the mediator" (Crawford and Bodine 1996, p. 10). The parties in mediation may be individuals or groups (Barsky 2000). Mediation has been found to be effective in resolving disputes in a variety of contexts. It has been suggested that mediation may be particularly valuable for resolving conflicts in new immigrant and refugee communities (Chetkow-Yanoov 1999). Mediation is a culturally congruent approach because traditional forms of mediation have existed in many cultures throughout history (Barsky 2000).

In cases of interethnic conflict, social workers may act as mediators themselves or may train community members to be volunteer mediators. When social workers act as mediators themselves, one of the most difficult tasks they face is to become neutral and impartial, since they are accustomed to an explicit value stance that advocates for the oppressed parties (Barsky 2000). Thus, mediation requires a reorientation from focusing on the interests of the immigrant or refugee client, to focusing on the interests of all parties in the dispute. The best practices for mediation are shown in table 9.16.

TABLE 9.16 BEST PRACTICES FOR MEDIATION

PREPARATION

- Receive referral.
- Make contact with the parties.
- Screen for safety issues and appropriateness for mediation.
- If situation not appropriate for mediation, explore alternatives and develop safety plan, if needed.
- Decide whether to meet individually with parties first (for further screening, to allow parties to ventilate in privacy, to help prepare them for negotiation, etc.)
- Arrange for interaction between the parties (together, shuttle mediation, or use of telephone)
- Choose and arrange the meeting space/environment conducive to mediation (quiet, impartial, comfortable, soothing).
- Ensure parties have access to legal advice, particularly where the decisions to be made have significant legal consequences.
- Speak with lawyers or other parties who may have an influence over decision making, with permission of the parties.
- Obtain agreement about who will participate in the mediation.

ORIENTATION TO MEDIATION

- Put clients at ease during introductions to parties.
- Explain the mediation process—structure of the communication; purposes; distinguish from other forms of intervention; role of mediator; credentials; role of the parties; what happens if a tentative agreement is reached or not reached.
- Assert control over process.
- Emphasize parties' responsibility for decision making.
- Identify the timing (beginning; duration; finishing; possibility of future meetings).
- Assess cultural factors that may affect the process: values, preferred ways of dealing with conflict, traditions related to the subject of the conflict.
- Determine need for further premediation interventions.
- Obtain parties' agreement about ground rules for communication and process (e.g., one person speaking at a time, use of notes, use of respectful language, smoking, protocol for calling breaks, and other terms that the parties agree upon).
- Describe standards of practice in terms understandable to the parties:
  - Neutrality or impartiality.
  - Confidentiality.
  - Communication with parties, their lawyers, or other parties.
  - Use of caucusing (meeting individually with parties during mediation).
  - Safety issues.
  - Voluntary involvement, ability to withdraw or terminate.
- Establish rapport and trust of clients (by demonstrating genuineness, unconditional positive regard, empathic understanding, impartiality, active listening skills).

TABLE 9.16 *(continued)*

- Clarify the terms of the agreement to mediate (the contract for the mediator's services).
- Encourage informed commitment to the process.
- Reach agreement to mediate (written or oral agreement).
- Obtain preliminary information about the presenting problem.
- Identify motivations of parties for mediating.
- Assess the nature of the conflict (e.g., difference of understandings, ideologies, or interests).
- Congratulate or thank the parties on their decision to commit to the process.
- Encourage positive expectations of the mediation process.
- Invite feedback and criticism from the parties.
- If a party expresses a reluctance to mediate, explore why (in joint session or in caucus).
- If parties do not agree to mediate, explore alternatives with parties and reinforce that the parties are in the best position to decide upon how to proceed.
- Empower clients (e.g., supporting their negotiating skills, giving each a fair opportunity to speak, reinforcing their strengths).

ISSUE DEFINITION

- Provide rationale for "who goes first."
- Allow each party the opportunity to identify their concerns.
- Allow parties to ventilate feelings.
- Put appropriate limits on storytelling and expression of feelings.
- Assure each party hears and understands the others (e.g., encourage each party to use active listening skills to reflect back or summarize what the other has said).
- If a party seems surprised about information provided by another party, explore how this new information changes the first party's understanding of past events.
- Identify key interests of each party (summarized/clarified), including relationship issues.
- Identify areas of agreement and mutual interest.
- Develop a list of concerns that is balanced, exhaustive, and clear.
- Obtain consensus about how to proceed (priorities of parties; order of issues to be addressed: e.g., by most important, least important first; most urgent, easiest, or most difficult first).
- Respond appropriately to different conflict styles.
- Validate identity and role of each party.
- Avoid taking sides (e.g., use neutral statements to demonstrate active listening).
- Conduct own analysis of underlying concerns.

EXPLORE INTERESTS AND NEEDS

- Ask parties to identify their feelings around their own issues.
- Ask parties to identify their perceptions of the other's feelings around the issues in conflict.
- Help parties explore underlying interests and needs.

TABLE 9.16 *(continued)*

- Help parties explore their self-images and how these contribute to the conflict and its possible resolution.
- Ask clear and relevant questions.
- Encourage parties to share information.
- Maintain safe environment for clients.
- Maintain appropriate level of control over emotional climate (e.g., exhibiting relaxation through body language, calling for a breather, exploring immediacy, using humor).
- Keep parties focused on one issue at a time.
- Maintain control over disruptive behavior.
- Partialize issues.
- Establish priorities with parties.
- Achieve understanding or closure on relevant feelings.
- Use interventions as appropriate for balancing power, maintaining problem-solving focus, responding to emotional needs, and resolving impasses.

NEGOTIATION AND PROBLEM SOLVING

- Clarify the goal or purpose of coming to an agreement.
- Help parties develop objective criteria.
- Move from broad principles to more specific topics.
- Encourage cooperative problem solving.
- Encourage generation of options for each issue.
- Make substantive suggestions and proposals.
- Avoid imposing mediator solutions.
- Avoid moving to solutions prematurely.
- Provide a structure for problem solving.
- Narrow issues in dispute (if full agreement not reached).
- Use preemptive strategies.
- Reframe parties' statements to be positive, mutually acceptable, future focused, nonjudgmental and interest-based.
- Maintain appropriate control over process—may turn over more control to the parties as they begin to work more collaboratively.
- Use decision trees, charts, notes, or other visual aids.
- Use caucusing, meeting individually with both parties, where appropriate.
- Encourage parties to use lateral thinking (viewing problems from different angles to try to come up with innovative solutions).
- Propose possible concessions (as options rather than as advice).
- Reward party concessions.
- Link the parties with outside experts or resources to help enlarge their perceived option set.
- Identify information that needs to be produced.
- Supply and filter missing information, or obtain agreement on how parties will obtain it.
- Preempt or correct counterproductive negotiation behavior.

TABLE 9.16 *(continued)*

- Praise constructive negotiation behavior.
- Identify the function or effect of parties' behaviors or attitudes on negotiation.
- Allow all interests of the parties to be discussed.
- Recognize or legitimize the rights of others to be involved in the process.
- Explore cultural differences and misunderstandings.
- Adapt language and behaviors to fit with the cultures of the parties.
- Explore power dynamics and concerns for fairness.
- Encourage parties to remain at the table.
- Help parties save face or undo a commitment.
- Educate the parties about constructive negotiation skills and principled negotiation strategies.
- Change the parties' expectations (e.g., through reality testing questions, role reversals, metaphoric storytelling, looking at hypothetical situations).
- Focus the parties on the future, rather than on the past.
- Focus on one issue at a time (or a manageable number of issues).
- Explore relationship issues.
- If parties express judgmental statements, help them see one another in a more positive frame of reference.
- Ask parties to consider possible changes in future circumstances.
- Help parties separate personality issues from the substance of the negotiations.
- Take responsibility for concessions.
- Prescribe homework tasks for parties to carry out between sessions.
- Ask parties to consider the interests of parties affected who may not be at the mediation table.
- Bring others into the mediation process to contribute to agreement.
- Use constructive confrontation (e.g., help a party to identify incongruencies between two pieces of information the party has given, or between a statement and the party's behavior).
- Draw parties' awareness to the cost of nonagreement (e.g., what is the best alternative to a mediated agreement).
- If parties have forgotten issues raised earlier, give parties an opportunity to put them back on the table.

FINALIZING AN AGREEMENT

- Use appropriate language in the agreement: oral/written, plain language/legal language, impartial/mutual, clear and concise.
- Test agreement with parties to ensure it is realistic.
- Deal with contingencies.
- Clarify the roles and obligations of each party.
- Ensure commitment.
- Explore doubts expressed by either party.
- Ensure access to independent legal advice.

TABLE 9.16 *(continued)*

- Deal with how the tentative agreement will be finalized (drafted by lawyers, court order on consent of parties, informal letter rather than legally binding agreement).
- Help devise ways to monitor and enforce the agreements (defining terms of implementation, evaluation, follow-up and review; including sanctions or other provisions that take effect if certain of the terms are broken).
- Summarize the process that has taken place.
- Reinforce the parties' efforts and decisions (end on a positive note; shake hands, have a meal together, have a drink, or some other ritual).
- Arrange for follow up (date, time, place, who responsible).
- If no agreement is reached:
  - Summarize areas of agreement and disagreement.
  - Explore possible alternatives for resolution of outstanding issues.
  - Explore parties' feelings and frustrations.
  - Link parties to desired resources.
  - Reinforce parties' efforts and successes (including empowerment and recognition).
  - Offer opportunity to return to mediation at future date.

FOLLOW-UP

- Contact the parties (by mediator or other person; set up face-to-face meeting, conduct the interview by telephone, or ask for written feedback by mail).
- Solicit feedback (research, evaluation forms; informal feedback).
- Provide mediation reviews at specific time intervals (e.g., to look at short-term or trial agreements, to consider longer-term arrangements, to consider progress and problems since finalizing the agreement).
- Reinforce positive outcomes.
- Offer further services.

Source: Barsky, 2000. Copyright © 2000, Wadsworth. Reprinted with permission.

In using mediation specifically in interethnic conflicts, the following strategies are suggested, in addition to general best practice principles for culturally competent practice:

- Determine how each culture views what constitutes a conflict, how conflict should be approached, which process is most appropriate for intervention, and what constitutes resolution.
- Use recognition strategies from the transformative paradigm to facilitate understanding and to reconcile past miscommunications.

- Emphasize dialogue as a means to understand one another and gain mutual respect.
- Validate different cultural beliefs, values, and ways of doing things, since many conflicts do not have a right and a wrong; reinforce that conflict is a part of diversity.
- Separate interests and values; help the parties understand the conflict between their values and focus the problem-solving component of mediation on satisfying interests that exist regardless of their difference in values.
- Use cultural interpreters to help each party gain better understandings of one another. If clients have lived most of their lives in a homogeneous culture, they may have difficulty explaining cultural norms to others in language that they can understand. Cultural interpreters have had experience with more than one culture, so they have learned how to translate cultural norms from one culture to another. (BARSKY 2000, PP. 164–166)

9.2.4 MICRO PRACTICE

MICRO PRACTICE IN INTERETHNIC RELATIONS refers to direct practice with individuals or small groups aimed at preventing or reducing prejudice, racism, and individual discrimination, and increasing tolerance toward different ethnic groups. Two major strategies in this regard are education and psychotherapy.

EDUCATION Numerous educational interventions have been developed to counter prejudice, racism, and discrimination at the micro level. Most of these interventions are designed to be delivered to children and youth in the primary and secondary schools. As such, these interventions have a preventive or early intervention focus. Social workers may play a role in these school-based programs by providing the actual educational interventions to students and teachers, or by acting as consultants in this regard.

School-based interventions differ in their underlying philosophy and in the relative emphasis they place on specific goals (Schwartz 1994). In regard to philosophy, programs differ in whether they directly address change in behavior or change in attitudes:

Some projects take the practical position that people in a diverse society must learn how to live with one another peaceably. Using a behavior modification model, they train people how to refrain from acting on their prejudices, assuming that once people become accustomed to controlling their public expression of biases, their attitudes will naturally begin to soften. Projects with the reverse perspective—that changes in behavior commonly follow changes in attitude—may be based on various philosophies: secular morality, religion, or politics. These projects have the potential of engendering fundamental reforms in people's belief systems, but their appeal can be limited, because trainees must first accept the validity of the project's philosophy. (SCHWARTZ 1994, P. 2)

In terms of specific goals, programs differ in whether they emphasize prejudice, bias, and discrimination reduction; conflict resolution; or violence prevention (Schwartz 1994).

Prejudice, Bias, and Discrimination Reduction. Programs that emphasize this goal aim to help students overcome a need to victimize others, and in some cases, to take social action to decrease institutional discrimination (Schwartz 1994). Such programs may use a variety of intervention methods such as teaching about different cultural and ethnic groups, teaching about the nature of prejudice, racism, and discrimination; and using structured interethnic contacts between students (Romo 1997; Spencer 1998).

Educational approaches may include providing direct, accurate information about different ethnic groups and about discrimination. This approach is based on the assumption that as students "gain knowledge about other groups and their histories, they will be more likely to respect members of those groups and cooperate with them" (Romo 1997, p. 3). Educational approaches may also include vicarious experiences, such as films, plays, biographies, novels, and other media that portray the experiences of different ethnic groups. This is based on the assumption that such exposure will help students recognize the commonalities between different groups and reduce a "them vs. us" perspective (Romo 1997). "The effectiveness of a vicarious experience approach depends on how the message of tolerance is presented. Poor presentations, in which the presenter does not know the material well, uses biased materials, or has little rapport with the audience, may actually increase prejudices instead of decreasing them" (Romo 1997, p. 3).

Programs using structured interethnic contacts between students are analogous to the dialogue strategy described earlier (Spencer 1998). They "provide a unique forum for students from different backgrounds and cultural identities to discuss commonalities, learn about differences, and address issues of conflict. Students learn about each other's histories and experiences, challenge stereotypes and misinformation, explore the sources of intergroup conflict, and identify ways of addressing institutional and individual forms of racism and discrimination" (Spencer 1998, pp. 159–160). This strategy may also entail having students from different ethnic groups work together on joint projects (Romo 1997). "These contacts are most successful if the people involved are of equal social status, are working cooperatively on something, if their activity is supported by people in positions of authority, and if the activity involves a high level of intimacy. If the activities are organized inappropriately, students involved in interethnic programs may become more prejudiced" (Romo 1997, p. 3).

Conflict Resolution. Programs whose primary emphasis is on conflict resolution focus on teaching students the skills and processes of negotiation and mediation (Crawford and Bodine 1996; Schwartz 1994). These programs address conflict in general, including interethnic conflict. There are four basic approaches used by such programs: the process curriculum, the mediation program, the peaceable classroom, and the peaceable school (Crawford and Bodine 1996). In the process curriculum approach, a specific amount of class time is devoted to teaching the basic elements of conflict resolution. In the mediation program approach, selected students, and sometimes adults in the school, are trained to act as mediators in school conflicts. In the peaceable classroom approach, "conflict resolution education is incorporated into the core subjects of the curriculum and into classroom management strategies" (Crawford and Bodine 1996, p. 12). Finally, in the peaceable school approach, "conflict resolution principles and processes are learned and utilized by every member of the school community—librarians, teachers, counselors, students, principals, and parents" (Crawford and Bodine 1996, p. 12). Available research to date shows that in general these programs produce positive effects (Crawford and Bodine 1996).

Violence Prevention. Programs that emphasize this goal "take the position that learning to channel negative emotions into positive action will diffuse hatred and lead automatically to less conflict and violence. These emphasize management of emotions, especially anger" (Schwartz 1994, p. 3). Other programs with this goal may aim to change attitudes toward violence in general and teach students to avoid violent confrontations without attempting to settle the conflict (Schwartz 1994). Programs may also take a comprehensive approach to preventing youth hate crime (Community Relations Service, 2000d).

In contrast to the fairly large body of literature on school-based programs, there is much less literature on educational approaches to reducing prejudice, racism, and discrimination among adults. Sandhu and Brown (1996) suggest several approaches including information gathering, attribution training, cultural awareness, cross-cultural training, and experiential training. Information gathering involves group activities aimed at dispelling misperceptions about various ethnic groups by providing accurate information about cultural systems, worldviews, values, and experiences. Attribution training "explains behavior from the point of view of persons in other cultures" (Sandhu and Brown 1996, p. 209). Cultural awareness "emphasizes the distinctiveness of different cultures and cross-cultural relations [with a focus on] reeducating individuals to help reshape society and promote people living together as equals" (Sandhu and Brown 1996, p. 209). Cross-cultural training uses the strategies of behaviorism to help people unlearn the learned attitudes and behaviors of prejudice, racism, and discrimination, and to learn empowering behaviors instead. Finally, in experiential learning, clients participate in cultural simulation activities. Although programs and workshops using these various approaches abound in many settings such as universities, workplaces, and community-based settings, research on their effectiveness in reducing prejudice, racism, and individual discrimination appears to be quite limited.

PSYCHOTHERAPY A few authors have suggested individual and group psychotherapy as possible interventions to reduce prejudice, racism, and discrimination, as part of a comprehensive array of interventions including macro- and meso-level strategies (Sandhu and Brown 1996; Simpson and Yinger 1985; Dobbins and Skillings 2000). This approach is based on the theory that prejudice, racism, and discrimination are due at least in part to personality factors. Sandhu and Brown (1996) suggest several possible therapeutic approaches in this regard. One is the *psychodynamic* approach, which is based on the assumption that prejudiced and racist attitudes function as defense mechanisms. One defense mechanism is projection, in which the prejudiced person denies his or her own prejudice and attributes it to others instead. Another defense mechanism is displacement, in which people who are frustrated but cannot address the true source of their frustration displace their anger onto an innocent scapegoat. In both cases, the therapist's role is to help the client understand these defense mechanisms in order to stop using them.

Another suggested therapeutic approach is the *Adlerian* approach, in which the therapist aims to change the client's motivations from self-interest to social interest. A third suggested approach is the *rational emotive* approach, in which the therapist helps the client see the irrational nature of prejudiced or racist beliefs by having the client test the beliefs against objective facts. Another suggested approach is the *reality therapy* approach, in which the therapist helps the client face the realities of living and working in a multicultural society and to view getting along with others as an acquired skill. Finally, Dobbins and Skillings (2000) suggest a *12-step* approach based on the Alcoholics Anonymous approach, in which racism is treated as an addiction.

It is important to note that there is essentially no evidence to support the use of these therapeutic approaches. This does not necessarily mean, however, that they are ineffective, only that there are virtually no reports of their use. However, it has also been argued that such therapeutic approaches, which are essentially based on a view of racism as an illness or dysfunction, may actually perpetuate the problem rather than reduce it, by failing to address its root causes in social structures (Wellman 2000).

9.2.5 SUMMARY OF BEST PRACTICES

IN SUMMARY, comprehensive intervention is needed at the macro, meso, and micro levels in order to effectively reduce racism, prejudice, and discrimination and to enhance interethnic harmony. As stated earlier, it is essential for social workers to adopt a proactive, antiracist model of practice that directly addresses these causes of social inequity. It is insufficient to focus solely on enhancing the cultural sensitivity of social workers themselves and social agencies and systems. Finally, much work remains to be done in evaluating the effectiveness of all of these various antiracist strategies (Chetkow-Yanoov 1999; Fix and Turner 1999; Simpson and Yinger 1985; Spencer 1998).

9.3 CASE STUDY EXERCISES

BASED ON THE INFORMATION PRESENTED in this chapter, consider how you would intervene with the following cases.

9.3.1 CASE 1

A middle-class suburb of Los Angeles that historically housed the residentially and economically mobile, Monterey Park is feeding off rapid growth throughout the region. It combines White Americans, Latinos, and Asian Americans, and is particularly a magnet for large-scale immigration from Taiwan, Hong Kong, and China. Rapid commercial and residential development, much of it owned and fueled by elite Chinese newcomers, coincided with problems of inflation and congestion. The immigration of Chinese capital and power brought a dramatic response from established residents in the form of an organized political challenge to rapid growth. For some established residents, issues of immigration and Americanization became part of a political campaign against unplanned development. The drama of these rapid changes in Monterey Park obscures the full nature of dominant ethnic relations in the community. The media focus on relations between wealthy, established white residents and the Chinese newcomers, especially the commercial elite. They omit established residents of Mexican origin and new immigrants from Mexico and Central America who now make up, after the Chinese, the second largest population in the city. (BACH 1993, PP. 15–16, 25, 28)

9.3.2 CASE 2

In Miami, a meeting held to improve interethnic relations was undermined by incomprehension. A Latino man representing an immigrant association was the first to speak. He had a heavy Spanish accent. After a couple of minutes an elderly black woman, a grassroots leader, got up and stormed out, saying in an angry tone, "I can't understand him! I can't understand him!"
(BACH 1993, P. 36)

9.3.3 CASE 3

[A local high school] recently suspended Raphael Florez [a student from a Hispanic immigrant family], for acting violently in the schoolyard. The Florez family believes that Raphael, subjected to racist taunting, was justified in defending himself. (BARSKY 2000, P. 166)

CHAPTER 10

SUMMARY AND CONCLUSIONS

THIS FINAL CHAPTER WILL summarize and synthesize the material presented in preceding chapters. The chapter will conclude with recommendations for future practice and research with refugees and immigrants.

10.1 THE CONTEXT OF SOCIAL WORK PRACTICE WITH REFUGEES AND IMMIGRANTS

THE FIRST PART OF THIS BOOK presented background context and knowledge that is necessary as a foundation for practice with refugees and immigrants. This includes an overview of refugees and immigrants; immigration and refugee policies; and service delivery systems. Each of these topics is summarized below.

10.1.1 OVERVIEW OF REFUGEES AND IMMIGRANTS

THE POPULATION OF IMMIGRANTS AND REFUGEES in the United States is growing rapidly. Within the next four to five decades, immigrants and refugees will account for 65 percent of the country's population growth, and first- and second-generation immigrants and refugees will make up more than 25 percent of the population. Thus, all social workers are likely to encounter refugee and immigrant clients in their practice.

Effective service to these populations must begin with an understanding of the distinct categories of foreign-born people; the causes of migration; the process of migration; and the demographic and socioeconomic characteristics and service utilization patterns of refugees and immigrants.

A fundamental categorical distinction is that between immigrants, who leave their countries voluntarily, usually in search of better economic opportunities; and refugees, who are forced out of their countries because of human rights violations against them. An additional distinction is between legal and illegal aliens. Many other subcategories also exist. Definitions of vari-ous categories may be based in law, in social science, or in self-definitions. Such definitions are frequently inconsistent with each other. For example, a person may define him or herself as a refugee, and be so defined by social science definitions, but may not have that legal designation. Thus, social workers need to be familiar with all three types of definitions. These definitions have implications for a person's psychosocial experiences, eligibility for social service assistance, and help-seeking behavior.

Many theories have been developed to explain why people migrate from one country to another. The more comprehensive theories recognize that migration is a result of factors operating at three levels: the macro or structural level, which entails political, economic, cultural, and geographic forces in the international arena, the country of origin, and the country of destination; the meso or relational level, which entails the relationships between potential movers and stayers in both the country of origin and the country of destination; and the micro or individual level, which entails personal characteristics and the individual's freedom to make autonomous decisions about moving or staying.

The process of migration consists of three major stages: premigration and departure, transit, and resettlement. Each stage entails various psychosocial experiences that influence other experiences in the later stages. While some experiences are nearly universal to all immigrants and refugees, others are unique to particular individuals or groups.

The majority of recent immigrants to the U.S. are from Asian and Latin American countries. The majority of refugees to the U.S. are from Communist or formerly Communist countries. In the United States, immigrants and refugees tend to be concentrated in certain metropolitan areas. There are substantial variations in demographic and socioeconomic characteristics among immigrants and refugees based on country of origin and legal status, as well as across individuals within each such grouping. In general, foreign-born people utilize more public welfare benefits but less health and mental health services than the native-born population. Again, however, there are substantial variations in service utilization, depending on numerous factors.

10.1.2 IMMIGRATION AND REFUGEE POLICIES

THE LIVES OF REFUGEES AND IMMIGRANTS are influenced by international and national laws. International laws address the fundamental rights of all immigrants and refugees. The branches of international law that are pertinent are international human rights law, international humanitarian law, international refugee law, and international migrant worker law. These are codified in a number of international conventions.

National laws address admissions and assistance to immigrants and refugees within a particular country. In the United States, historically, immigration and refugee policies have evolved from open admissions to more restricted admissions. At different points in time, different groups of immigrants have been effectively denied admission. These shifts in immigration and refugee policy have been influenced by a combination of factors including the domestic economy, humanitarian concerns, foreign policy, and general public attitudes. The major contemporary policies that influence admission of and assistance to immigrants and refugees are the Immigration and Nationality Act Amendments of 1965, 1976, and 1990; the Refugee Act of 1980; the Immigration Reform and Control Act of 1986; the Personal Responsibility and Work Opportunity Reconciliation Act of 1996; and the Illegal Immigration Reform and Immigrant Responsibility Act of 1996. Contemporary policies are guided by social, economic, cultural, moral, and security goals.

10.1.3 SERVICE DELIVERY SYSTEMS

HUMAN SERVICES FOR REFUGEES AND IMMIGRANTS are delivered by a large and diverse network of organizations and personnel. Social workers need to be familiar with the variety of available organizations and services in order to help clients navigate a system that is often confusing and overwhelming. The network includes public and private agencies at the international, national, state, and local levels. These organizations are staffed by professionals and paraprofessionals from a variety of disciplines.

At the international level, two major intergovernmental organizations are the International Organization for Migration, which provides assistance with the migration process and encourages social and economic development through migration; and the United Nations High Commissioner for

Refugees, which aims to protect refugees and to seek durable solutions for refugee problems. In carrying out their missions, both of these agencies work closely with a number of private, nonprofit international relief organizations. Other private organizations provide indirect assistance through advocacy.

At the national level in the United States, major government agencies are the Immigration and Naturalization Service; the Bureau of Population, Refugees, and Migration; and the Office of Refugee Resettlement. These agencies are concerned with admissions, border control, deportation, and resettlement. Private organizations at the national level are primarily concerned with resettlement assistance and advocacy.

At the local level, services are provided by mainstream agencies, such as hospitals, medical clinics, mental health centers, schools, child welfare agencies, and family service agencies; and by ethnic agencies that provide one or more services to specific ethnic groups. Specific strategies and techniques of service delivery include information and referral; case advocacy, case management, and networking; counseling and treatment; health services; substance abuse services; protective services; vocational rehabilitation; youth services; housing services; immigration and legal assistance; refugee resettlement services; planning, coordination, and advocacy; consultation and technical assistance; and research and evaluation.

10.2 PROBLEM AREAS AND BEST PRACTICES

THE SECOND HALF OF THIS BOOK addressed best practices for social work with refugees and immigrants, as grounded in empirically based practice. This section began with an overview of culturally competent social work practice. This was followed by descriptions of relevant issues and best practices in the areas of health; mental health; family dynamics; language, education, and economic well-being; and interethnic relations. Each of these topics is summarized below.

10.2.1 CULTURALLY COMPETENT SOCIAL WORK PRACTICE

CULTURALLY COMPETENT PRACTICE is a set of attitudes and beliefs, knowledge, and skills that a social worker must possess in order to work effectively with clients who are from a different culture than the worker. The principles of culturally competent practice are generic in that they underlie all specific practice approaches in particular problem areas. Culturally competent practice first requires understanding of basic concepts such as race; culture; ethnicity; ethnic identity; psychological, behavioral, and structural acculturation; prejudice; stereotyping; xenophobia; racism; and discrimination.

The attitudes and beliefs that underlie culturally competent practice include awareness of the worker's own ethnic heritage; awareness of how one's background and biases influence practice; value and respect for client differences in race, ethnicity, culture, beliefs, and religion; nonjudgmentalness; a commitment to social justice; and valuing the importance of empirically based practice. The knowledge that is needed for culturally competent practice includes knowledge of multiple theories; the self; characteristics of different ethnic groups; environmental influences upon people; the cultural basis of social work practice; and empirically based practice. Finally, specific skills for culturally competent practice are necessary in each of the phases of the practice process. These phases include engagement; problem identification and assessment; goal setting and contracting; intervention implementation and monitoring; termination and evaluation; and follow-up.

10.2.2 HEALTH

IMMIGRANTS AND REFUGEES have been identified as a vulnerable population that has high risk for poor health. The major issues influencing the health of immigrants and refugees are health care access problems; differential health status; health beliefs and health practices; psychosocial issues; and subpopulations with unique health issues. Inadequate health care access is caused by structural, financial, and personal and cultural barriers. Different immigrant and refugee groups vary widely in their overall health status and in the prevalence and incidence of different diseases and other health problems. In general, the health status of ethnic minorities, including many immigrants and refugees, tends to be worse than that of White Americans. These disparities are due to a complex combination of socioeconomic, physiological, psychological, societal, and cultural factors.

Relevant cultural factors include health beliefs and health practices, which encompass cultural concepts of health and illness; folk illness; traditional therapeutic practices; and the integration of traditional and conventional healing systems. Psychosocial issues that are related to the health and health care of immigrants and refugees include treatment adherence, somatization, family involvement, and ethical issues. Subpopulations with unique health issues include women, gays and lesbians, and elderly people.

Best practices at the macro level include community needs assessment, policy and program advocacy, community consultation, policy and program planning, and community health education. At the meso level, best practices include interdisciplinary collaboration and organizational development to enhance the effectiveness of organizations and health care providers in serving refugees and immigrants. Finally, best practices at the micro level include appropriate case identification, assessment of health beliefs and expectations of treatment, case management, health education and counseling, and psychosocial treatment.

10.2.3 MENTAL HEALTH

REFUGEES AND IMMIGRANTS ARE at risk of developing mental health problems due to the unique stressors experienced during the various stages of the migration process. These stressors may include loss of family members, friends, home, and the familiar environment; traumatic experiences such as war, famine, violence, rape, imprisonment, and torture; a hasty and dangerous departure; dangerous transit experiences; loss of status; language problems; employment problems; legal problems; social isolation; family conflict; role changes; discrimination, racism, and xenophobia; and acculturative stress. Some of these experiences are common to almost all immigrants and refugees, whereas others, such as traumatic experiences, are experienced only by some, particularly by refugees.

In addition to the stresses of migration, the mental health of immigrants and refugees, and its assessment and treatment, are influenced by cultural factors. These include conceptualizations of mental health; diagnosis and symptom expression; communication styles; and service utilization. The most commonly observed mental health problems of immigrants, and particularly refugees, include grief, alienation and loneliness, decreased self-esteem, depression, anxiety, somatization, paranoia, guilt, post-traumatic stress disorder, and substance abuse.

Best practices for addressing mental health at the macro and meso levels are the same as those for addressing health. At the micro level, best practices include appropriate assessment techniques and consideration of relevant issues, including the use of traditional healers; cultural differences and role preparation; language problems and the use of interpreters; the use of psychotropic medications; and empirical knowledge about treatment effectiveness. Best practice interventions for acculturative stress are case management, supportive counseling, information and skills training, and crisis intervention. Best practice interventions for depression, anxiety, post-traumatic stress disorder, and substance abuse are cognitive and behavioral therapies, and interpersonal psychotherapy in the case of depression.

10.2.4 FAMILY DYNAMICS

THE STRESSORS OF THE MIGRATION PROCESS typically lead to changes in family roles and family dynamics. In some cases, these stressors may overcome the family's ability to cope and adapt, resulting in family conflict. Among the family problems observed in immigrant and refugee families are marital conflict, including domestic violence; and intergenerational conflict, including child abuse and elder abuse. In addition to family conflicts, family members, particularly adolescents and the elderly, experience unique life cycle issues that are affected by migration. These issues center around identity, meaning, and family expectations.

Best practices at the macro level include developing policies and programs to strengthen families. Specific macro strategies for achieving this are the same ones discussed previously. At the meso level, best practices are also the same ones discussed previously for enhancing agencies' and systems' effectiveness in serving immigrant and refugee populations. In the context of family dynamics, it is especially important to develop agency policies and procedures that empower women. At the micro level, best practices to address marital and intergenerational conflict include appropriate assessment techniques; behavioral, cognitive, and structural-strategic marital therapies; domestic violence interventions; psychoeducational, behavioral, family systems, structural, and strategic family therapies; and behavioral, cognitive, and family preservation approaches to address child abuse. Best practice interventions for addressing the life cycle issues of children and adolescents include interventions aimed at helping resolve ethnic identity problems and facilitating the acculturation process. For the life cycle issues of elderly refugees and immigrants, best practice interventions include cognitive-behavioral therapy, interpersonal psychotherapy, problem-solving therapy, brief psychodynamic therapy, and reminiscence therapy.

10.2.5 LANGUAGE, EDUCATION, AND ECONOMIC WELL-BEING

IMMIGRANTS' AND REFUGEES' ENGLISH LANGUAGE ABILITY, educational attainment, and economic well-being are closely interrelated and are a major area of concern among policymakers, the general public, and immigrants and refugees themselves. English-language ability varies substantially across individuals, but in general immigrants and refugees appear to be highly motivated to learn English, as evidenced by high demand for English as a Second Language (ESL) classes. For most immigrants and refugees, English ability improves with length of residence. However, the rate of language acquisition depends on many factors, including age, education, time available for language learning, level of literacy in the native language, opportunities to interact with native English speakers, and the value that the individual places on being bilingual. Across generations, the level of English-language acquisition appears to be increasing, and immigrant and refugee children acquire English much faster than their parents. It is generally accepted that bilingualism is the desired outcome for both children and adults. However, it is important to recognize that being bilingual does not necessarily mean equal proficiency in both languages.

The educational attainment of immigrant and refugee adults is clustered at the low and high ends of the educational spectrum. Educational attainment varies substantially across country of origin and legal status groupings. The academic achievement of immigrant and refugee children overall is high, in some cases better than that of native-born students. Again, it varies by country of origin, and is influenced by numerous factors at the levels of the individual, family, peer group, school, and community. While many children in immigrant and refugee families perform well in school, many are also disadvantaged by low family socioeconomic status, limited English proficiency, late entry into the U.S. school system, assimilation into societally disadvantaged minority groups, and other factors.

As a whole, immigrants and refugees are net contributors to the U.S. economy, although their economic well-being on average is worse that that of the native-born population, as evidenced by numerous indicators. Again, economic well-being varies considerably, particularly in relation to legal status. Economic well-being is influenced by numerous factors including financial capital, human capital, social capital, household composition, and the community contexts of reception.

For enhancing English proficiency, best practice interventions are advocacy for increased ESL program funding at the macro level; improvement of ESL program staffing and program design at the meso level; and referral to ESL programs, case advocacy, and follow-up at the micro level. For enhancing the educational attainment of adult immigrants and refugees, best practices include macro-level advocacy for universal benefits designed to help people advance their education; meso-level collaboration with institutions of higher learning to enhance access and retention of immigrant and refugee students; and micro-level actions to encourage, facilitate, and support immigrants and refugees in advancing their education.

For enhancing the academic achievement of children and adolescents, best practices at the macro level include actions targeting national, state, and local decisionmaking bodies. At the meso level, best practices include teamwork with school personnel to implement various program elements and instructional approaches that have been identified as effective in promoting the academic achievement of immigrant and refugee students. At the micro level, best practices include appropriate assessment, and interventions aimed at enhancing students' psychosocial functioning in order to enhance academic achievement.

For enhancing economic well-being, best practice interventions include those that enhance human capital, address household composition, and enhance financial capital, social capital, and community contexts of reception. Best practices for enhancing human capital are those that enhance English proficiency and educational attainment; and employment-related services including job search assistance, job coaching, mentoring, self-employment assistance, vocational education and career counseling, and recertification. For addressing household composition, best practices are advocacy for and provision of child care. For enhancing financial capital, best practices include policy and program initiatives such as individual development accounts, microenterprise development, and home ownership programs. For enhancing social capital, best practices include supporting networking within immigrant and refugee communities, mentoring programs, and job clubs. Best practices for enhancing community contexts of reception include community economic development and planning, job development, union organizing, and anti-discrimination strategies.

10.2.6 INTERETHNIC RELATIONS

IMMIGRANTS AND REFUGEES CONSTITUTE one segment of the multi-ethnic population in the United States. Contemporary interethnic relations in the U.S. are complex. Relations between immigrants and refugees and the native-born population tend to be characterized by separation, conflict, and competition. Anti-immigrant sentiments and policies rise and fall in cycles that are linked to changing economic and political conditions. Anti-immigrant sentiments are also linked to prejudice, racism, and discrimination. These attitudes, beliefs, and behaviors have multiple causes, including psychological factors, social factors, and power-conflict factors.

Best practices for improving interethnic relations are those aimed at reducing prejudice, racism, and discrimination, and at achieving a pluralist society, one in which all members are able to maintain their ethnic heritage yet have equal political and economic power. Such practices are grounded in a proactive, antiracist model of social work practice. Following appropriate assessment and goal-setting, best practices at the macro level include advocacy for the development, adoption, and implementation of federal, state, and local policies that address equal treatment and equal opportunity and harmonious interethnic relations; community development to foster community integration, participation, cooperation, and collaboration; community education to reduce prejudice, racism, and discrimination among the general public; and nonviolent resistance to promote social justice. At the meso-level, best practices are those activities in which the social worker functions as a bridge between the diverse segments of society. Such interventions include structured interethnic contact and conflict resolution. Finally, at the micro level, best practices include education and psychotherapy aimed at decreasing prejudice, racism, and discrimination among individuals.

10.3 SYNTHESIS OF BEST PRACTICE APPROACHES

THE PRECEDING SUMMARIZATION has been cast within a framework of examining various "problem areas" because the ultimate function of social work is to solve human problems at the micro, meso, and macro levels. It should be clear, however, that this does not mean that immigrants and refugees themselves should be viewed as "problems." As has been repeatedly empha-

Summary and Conclusions **489**

sized throughout the book, most immigrants and refugees adapt well to the new country, and overall, immigrants and refugees are an asset to the new country in terms of their cultural and economic contributions. Fundamental humanitarian values, and the historical tradition of the United States, dictate that immigrants and refugees should be welcomed and should receive equal treatment and equal opportunity along with all members of the society. The unique difficulties faced by these populations also clearly dictate compassionate, and effective, social work intervention.

Thus, social work best practices for these populations are ultimately values-based, strengths-based, and empirically-based. Further, it should be evident from the preceding discussions that best practices must be holistic. They must address the multiple problem areas that are often encountered by refugees and immigrants, and they must address them at multiple levels—micro, meso, and macro.

10.4 RECOMMENDATIONS FOR FUTURE PRACTICE AND RESEARCH

CLEARLY, the most logical and fundamental recommendation for future practice is that the numerous best practices described throughout this book should be implemented, monitored, evaluated, and the findings disseminated to promote further best practice. Additional, related recommendations for culturally competent practice in the twenty-first century include the following (Lecca, et al. 1998):

- Educate consumers and do community outreach.
- Be politically active.
- Educate service providers and organizations.
- Preserve culturally relevant neighborhood agencies.
- Promote ethnic diversity in social agency administration.
- Diminish barriers to care.
- Conduct needs assessment and treatment outcome research.
- Build demonstration projects.

Finally, Ahearn (2000) has articulated a clear agenda for future research on the psychosocial wellness of refugees, which appears to be applicable to research on immigrants as well. The points of this agenda are shown in table 10.1.

TABLE 10.1 FUTURE AGENDA FOR RESEARCH ON THE PSYCHOSOCIAL WELLNESS OF REFUGEES AND IMMIGRANTS

LONG-TERM EFFECTS

There are very few examples of studies of the long-term adjustment of refugees [and immigrants] as most existing studies are short-term comparisons that have little relevance or applicability to other situations. Longitudinal investigations and/or long-term case studies would contribute to our understanding of [refugee and immigrant adaptation].

COMMUNITY FOCUS

The preponderence of existing research . . . examines the individual, his/her reactions, and interventions useful at this level. As a person's support system is a crucial factor in psychosocial adjustment, the family and community should also become the foci for investigation. The social and cultural system of refugees [and immigrants], the supports of extended family, employment, religion, and spirituality, and governmental and nongovernmental services and benefits are areas for understanding the protective factors of a refugee's [or immigrant's] wellness.

PREVENTION AS WELL AS REMEDIATION

The factors that promote and/or prevent . . . trauma and stress are probably those that also will heal quickly the wounds of . . . migration. . . . Researchers could evaluate the early elements that seem to be associated with health, such as increased safety and protection, re-establishment of trust, ability to make decisions that control one's life, participation, self-identity, and esteem.

EVALUATION OF PSYCHOSOCIAL PROGRAMS AND INTERVENTIONS

Governmental and non-governmental organizations have a responsibility to measure their outcomes in order to assess effectiveness of their programmatic strategies and also to be accountable to their funders and the refugees [and immigrants] themselves. Program evaluations, follow-up case histories, process assessments, organizational case analyses, and studies of interventions within the context of local culture would add greatly to our understanding of what services are and are not beneficial.

TABLE 10.1 *(continued)*

REPLICATION OF STUDIES

In order to test the reliability and improve the usefulness of studies, it is necessary to replicate these under similar and different conditions. If measures are utilized to assess psychosocial factors, they must be reliable in the culture in which they are utilized. By replication, we can confirm certain findings, increase our knowledge base, and plan with greater certainty psychosocial interventions for individuals, families, and communities of refugees [and immigrants].

Source: Ahearn, 2000.

REFERENCES

TO THE READER: References to Internet sites were accurate at the time of publication. Some links, of course, may since have expired or moved.

Achenbach, T. M., and Edelbrock, C. S. 1983. *Manual of child behavior checklist and revised child behavior profile.* Burlington, VT: University of Vermont, Department of Psychiatry.

Aday, R. H., and Kano, Z. M. 1997. Attitudes toward caring for aging parents: A comparison of Laotian and U. S. students. *Educational Gerontology* 23:151–167.

Adger, C. T. 1996. Language minority students in school reform: The role of collaboration. *ERIC Digest.* http://www.ed.gov/databases/ERIC_Digests/ed400681.html.

Agriculture Research, Extension, and Education Reform Act of 1998, P. L. 105–185, 112 Stat. 523.

Ahearn, F. L., Jr. 2000. Conclusions and implications for future research. In F. L. Ahearn, Jr. ed., *Psychosocial wellness of refugees: Issues in qualitative and quantitative research.* New York: Berghahn Books, pp. 234–238.

Alaniz, M. L., Cartmill, R. S., Parker, R. N. 1998. Immigrants and violence: The importance of neighborhood context. *Hispanic Journal of Behavioral Sciences* 20:155–174.

Allen, R. I. 1997. Summary of welfare and immigration legislation. Iowa City: Institute for Social and Economic Development. http://www.ised.org/rwirp/summary.html.

Althausen, L. 1993. Journey of separation: Elderly Russian immigrants and their adult children in the health care setting. *Social Work in Health Care* 19:61–75.

American Academy of Pediatrics 1997. Policy statement: Health care for children of immigrant families. *Pediatrics, 100.* http://www.aap.org/policy/970702.html.

American Medical Student Association 1999. Cultural competency in medicine. http://www.amsa.org/programs/gpit/cultural.htm.

American Psychiatric Association 1994. *Diagnostic and statistical manual of mental disorders* (4th ed.). Washington, DC: Author.

American Psychological Association 1998. Hate crimes today: An age-old foe in modern dress. http://www.apa.org/pubinfo/hate/.

American Public Health Association 1999a. The essential services of public health. http://www.apha.org/ppp/science/10ES.htm.

American Public Health Association 1999b. Community strategies for health: Fitting in the pieces. http://www.apha.org/ppp/science/csh.htm.

American Public Health Association 1999c. The guide to implementing model standards. http://www.apha.org/ppp/science/theguide.htm.

Amodeo, J., Grigg-Saito, D., and Robb, N. 1997. Working with foreign language interpreters: Guidelines for substance abuse clinicians and human service practitioners. *Alcoholism Treatment Quarterly* 15:75–87.

Amodeo, M., Robb, N., Peou, S., and Tran, H. 1997. Alcohol and other drug problems among Southeast Asians: Patterns of use and approaches to assessment and intervention. *Alcoholism Treatment Quarterly* 15:63–77.

Anetzberger, G., Korbin, J. E., and Tomita, S. K. 1996. Defining elder mistreatment in four ethnic groups across two generations. *Journal of Cross-Cultural Gerontology* 11:187–212.

Anti-Defamation League 1999. Poisoning the Web: Hatred online. http://www.adl.org/poisoning_web.

Aponte, H. J. 1991. Training on the person of the therapist for work with the poor and minorities. In K. G. Lewis ed., *Family systems application to social work: Training and clinical practice*. New York: Haworth, pp. 23–39.

Armour, S. 2000. Immigrants become easy target for sex harassment on the job. *USA Today*, July 27, 9A-10A.

Aroian, K. J. 1990. A model of psychological adaptation to migration and resettlement. *Nursing Research* 39:5–10.

Aroian, K. J. 1993. Mental health risks and problems encountered by illegal immigrants. *Issues in Mental Health Nursing* 14:379–397.

Aroian, K. J., and Patsdaughter, C. A. 1989. Multiple-method, cross-cultural assessment of psychological distress. *IMAGE: Journal of Nursing Scholarship* 21:90–93.

Aron, A. 1992. Testimonio, a bridge between psychotherapy and sociotherapy. In E. Cole, O. M. Espin, and E. D. Rothblum, eds., *Refugee women and their mental health*. Binghamton, NY: Haworth, pp. 173–190.

Aronson, D., ed. 1997a. Immigrant entrepreneurs. *Research Perspectives on Migration* 1(2): 1–7. http://www.ceip.org/programs/migrat/rpm2main.htm.

Aronson, D., ed. 1997b. From rags to rags. *Research Perspectives on Migration* 1(2): 1–2. http://www.ceip.org/programs/migrat/rpm2rags.htm.

Arredondo, P., Toporek, R., Brown, S. P., Jones, J., Locke, C. C., Sanchez, J., and Stadler, H. 1996. Operationalizion of the multicultural counseling competencies. *Journal of Multicultural Counseling and Development* 24:42–78.

Arredondo-Dowd, P. M. 1981. Personal loss and grief as a result of immigration. *Personnel and Guidance Journal* 59:376–378.

Athey, J. L., and Ahearn, F. L., Jr. 1991. The mental health of refugee children: An overview. In F. L. Ahearn and J. L. Athey, eds., *Refugee children: Theory, research, and services*. Baltimore: Johns Hopkins University Press, pp. 3–19.

Axelson, J. A. 1993. *Counseling and development in a multicultural society.* Pacific Grove, CA: Brooks/Cole.
Aycan, Z., and Berry, J. W. 1996. Impact of employment-related experiences on immigrants' psychological well-being and adaptation to Canada. *Canadian Journal of Behavioural Sciences* 28:240–251. http://www.cpa.ca/cjbsnew/1996/ful_aycan.html.
Bach, R. L. 1993. *Changing relations: Newcomers and established residents in U.S. communities.* New York: Ford Foundation.
Baer, R. D., Clark, L., and Peterson, C. 1998. Folk illnesses. In S. Loue, ed., *Handbook of immigrant health.* New York: Plenum, pp. 183–202.
Baker, R. 1992. Psychosocial consequences for tortured refugees seeking asylum and refugee status in Europe. In M. Basoglu, ed., *Torture and its consequences: Current treatment approaches.* Cambridge: Cambridge University Press, pp. 83–106.
Balanced Budget Act of 1997, P. L. 105–33, 111 Stat. 251.
Baptiste, D. A., Jr., Hardy, K. V., and Lewis, L. 1997. Family therapy with English Caribbean immigrant families in the United States: Issues of emigration, immigration, culture, and race. *Contemporary Family Therapy* 19:337–359.
Barclay, H. H. 1998. Validating tortured refugees: Reconnection in social work policy and practice. *International Social Work* 41:211–226.
Barsky, A. E. 2000. *Conflict resolution for the helping professions.* Belmont, CA: Wadsworth.
Barudy, J. 1989. A programme of mental health for political refugees: Dealing with the invisible pain of political exile. *Social Science and Medicine* 28:715–727.
Barutciski, M. 1998. Tensions between the refugee concept and the IDP debate. *Forced Migration Review* 3:1–5.
Bar-Yosef, R. 1980. Desocialization and resocialization: The adjustment process of immigrants. In E. Krausz, ed., *Studies of Israeli society: Migration, ethnicity, and community.* New Brunswick, NJ: Transaction Books.
Basch, L., Schiller, N. G., and Blanc, C. S. 1994. *Nations unbound: Transnational projects, postcolonial predicaments, and deterritorialized nation-states.* Langhorne, PA: Gordon and Breach Science Publishers.
Basoglu, M. 1992. Behavioural and cognitive approach in the treatment of torture-related psychological problems. In M. Basoglu, ed., *Torture and its consequences: Current treatment approaches.* Cambridge: Cambridge University Press, pp. 402–432.
Bates, T. 1994. An analysis of Korean immigrant owned small business start-ups with comparisons to African-American and nonminority owned firms. *Urban Affairs Quarterly* 30:227–248.
Beiser, M. 1990. Mental health of refugees in resettlement countries. In W. H. Holtzman and T. H. Bornemann, eds., *Mental health of immigrants and refugees.* Austin, TX: Hogg Foundation for Mental Health, pp. 51–65.

Ben-David, A. 1995. Family functioning and migration: Considerations for practice. *Journal of Sociology and Social Welfare* 22:121–137.

Ben-David, A., and Lavee, Y. 1994. Migration and marital distress: The case of Soviet immigrants. *Journal of Divorce and Remarriage* 21:133–146.

Ben-Porath, Y. S. 1991. The psychosocial adjustment. In J. Westermeyer, C. L. Williams, and A. N. Nguyen, eds., *Mental health services for refugees* (DHHS Publication No. [ADM] 91–1824). Washington, DC: U.S. Government Printing Office, pp. 1–23.

Berlin, E. A., and Fowkes, W. C. 1983. Teaching framework for cross-cultural care: Application to family practice. *Western Journal of Medicine, 139,* 934–938.

Berry, J. W. 1990. Acculturation and adaptation: A general framework. In W. H. Holtzman and T. H. Bornemann, eds., *Mental health of immigrants and refugees.* Austin, TX: Hogg Foundation for Mental Health, pp. 90–102.

Berry, J. W. 1991. Managing the process of acculturation for problem prevention. In J. Westermeyer, C. L. Williams, and A. N. Nguyen, eds., *Mental health services for refugees* (DHHS Publication No. [ADM] 91–1824). Washington, DC: U.S. Government Printing Office, pp. 189–204.

Berthold, S. M. 1989. Spiritism as a form of psychotherapy: Implications for social work practice. *Social Casework* 70:502–509.

Bloom, M., Fischer, J., and Orme, J. G. 1999. *Evaluating practice: Guidelines for the accountable professional (3rd ed.).* Boston: Allyn and Bacon.

Blythe, B., and Tripodi, T. 1989. *Measurement in direct practice.* Newbury Park, CA: Sage.

Blythe, B., Tripodi, T., and Briar, S. 1994. *Direct practice research in the human services.* New York: Columbia University Press.

Boehnlein, J. K. 1987. A review of mental health services for refugees between 1975 and 1985 and a proposal for future services. *Hospital and Community Psychiatry* 38:764–768.

Boehnlein, J. K. 1990. The integration of scientific medicine into diverse cultural practices. *International Journal of Mental Health* 19:37–39.

Bohon, L. M., Santos, S. J., Sanchez-Sosa, and Singer, R D. 1994. The effects of a mental health video on the social skills knowledge and attitudes of Mexican immigrants. *Journal of Applied Social Psychology* 24:1794–1805.

Boscolo, L., Cecchin, G., Hoffman, L., and Penn, P. 1987. *Milan systemic family therapy.* New York: Basic Books.

Bowen, D. J., Carscadden, L., Beighle, K., and Fleming, I. 1992. Post-traumatic stress disorder among Salvadoran women: Empirical evidence and description of treatment. In E. Cole, O. M. Espin, and E. D. Rothblum, eds., *Refugee women and their mental health: Shattered societies, shattered lives.* Binghamton, NY: Haworth Press, pp. 267–280.

Bowen, M. 1978. *Family therapy in clinical practice.* New York: Aronson.

Bowie, S. 1999. INS guidelines clarify public charge issue. *Closing the Gap*, August/September 1999, 14. http://www.omhrc.gov.

Bracht, N. 1978. Health care: Issues and trends. In N. Bracht, ed., *Social work in health care: A guide to professional practice*. New York: Haworth, pp. 24–31.

Brodsky, B. 1988. Mental health attitudes and practices of Soviet Jewish immigrants. *Health and Social Work* 13:130–136.

Bureau of Consular Affairs 1999. Mission. http://travel.state.gov/mission.html.

Bureau of Population, Refugees, and Migration 1997a. U.S. Refugee Admissions Program. http://www.state.gov/www/global/prm.

Bureau of Population, Refugees, and Migration 1997b. U.S. Refugee Assistance. http://www.state.gov/www/global/prm/fs_us_refugee_asst.html.

Bureau of Population, Refugees, and Migration 1998. U.S. Refugee Admissions and Resettlement Program Overview. http://www.state.gov/www/global/prm/fs_refugee_adm_9807.html.

Burke, A. C. 1998. Unemployment. In J. S. Wodarski and B. A. Thyer, eds., *Handbook of empirical social work practice, Vol. II*. New York: Wiley, pp. 199–223.

Burnette, D. 1998. Conceptual and methodological considerations in research with non-White ethnic elders. In M. Potocky and A. Y. Rodgers-Farmer, eds., *Social work research with minority and oppressed populations: Methodological issues and innovations*. Binghamton, NY: Haworth, pp. 71–92.

Bush, R. A. B., and Folger, J. P. 1994. *The promise of mediation: Responding to conflict through empowerment and recognition*. San Francisco: Jossey-Bass.

Bustos, E. 1992. Psychodynamic approaches in the treatment of torture survivors. In M. Basoglu, ed., *Torture and its consequences: Current treatment approaches*. Cambridge: Cambridge University Press, pp. 333–347.

Butcher, J. N. 1991. Psychological evaluation. In J. Westermeyer, C. L. Williams, and A. N. Nguyen, eds., *Mental health services for refugees* (DHHS Publication No. [ADM] 91–1824). Washington, DC: U.S. Government Printing Office, pp. 111–122.

Candelaria, J., Campbell, N., Lyons, G., Elder, J. P., and Villaseñor, A. 1998. Strategies for health education: Community-based methods. In S. Loue, ed., *Handbook of immigrant health*. New York: Plenum, pp. 587–606.

Caplan, N., Choy, M. H., and Whitmore, J. K. 1991. *Children of the boat people: A study of educational success*. Ann Arbor, MI: University of Michigan Press.

Cárdenas, J., Taylor, L., and Adelman, H. S. 1993. Transition support for immigrant students. *Journal of Multicultural Counseling and Development* 21:203–210.

Carlin, J. 1990. Refugee and immigrant populations at special risk: Women, children, and the elderly. In W. H. Holtzman and T. H. Bornemann, eds., *Mental health of immigrants and refugees*. Austin, TX: Hogg Foundation for Mental Health, University of Texas, pp. 224–233.

Castex, G. M. 1994. Providing services to Hispanic/Latino populations: Profiles in diversity. *Social Work* 39:288–296.

Center for Applied Linguistics 1998a. Welcome to the United States: A guidebook for refugees. http://www.cal.org/rsc.
Center for Applied Linguistics 1998b. *Research agenda for adult ESL*. http://www.cal.org/ncle/agenda/intro.html.
Center for Applied Linguistics 2000. *Immigrant Education*. http://www.cal.org/public/topics/immigrnt.htm.
Center for Communication Programs 1999. "A" frame for advocacy. Supplement to *Population Reports*, Series J, No. 49, Vol. XVIII, No. 2. Baltimore: Johns Hopkins School of Public Health.
Center for Cross-Cultural Health 1999. Index for six steps toward cultural competence. http://www1.umn.edu/ccch/Six_Steps_2.html.
Centers for Disease Control 1995. *Guidelines for health education and risk reduction activities*. Atlanta: Centers for Disease Control, National Center for Prevention Activities. http://wonder.cdc.gov/wonder/prevguid/p0000389/p0000389.htm.
Chamberlain, G. 1997. Haiti. In Europa Publications, Ltd., eds., *South America, Central America, and the Caribbean* (6th ed.). London: Author.
Chan, L. M. 1991. Application of single-session groups in working with Vietnamese refugees in Hong Kong. *Social Work with Groups* 13:103–120.
Chang, J., and Moon, A. 1997. Korean American elderly's knowledge and perceptions of elder abuse: A qualitative analysis of cultural factors. *Journal of Multicultural Social Work* 6:139–154.
Cheney, S. A., and Cheney, C. C. 1997. Adaptation and homebuying approaches of Latin American and Indian immigrants in Montgomery County, Maryland. *Cityscape* 3:39–61. http://www.huduser.org/periodicals/cityscape/vol3num1/cs3–1_2.pdf.
Chetkow-Yanoov, B. 1999. *Celebrating diversity: Coexisting in a multicultural society*. Binghamton, NY: Haworth.
Chinese Exclusion Act of 1882, 22 Stat. 58.
Chung, D. K. 1992. Asian cultural commonalities: A comparison with mainstream American culture. In S. M. Furuto, R. Biswas, D. K. Chung, K. Murase, F. Ross-Sheriff, eds., *Social work practice with Asian Americans*. Newbury Park, CA: Sage, pp. 27–44.
Chung, R. C., and Lin, K. 1994. Help-seeking behavior among Southeast Asian refugees. *Journal of Community Psychology* 22:109–120.
Cienfuegos, A. J., and Monelli, C. 1983. The Testimony of political repression as a therapeutic instrument. *American Journal of Orthopsychiatry* 53:43–51.
Clark, L., and Hofsess, L. 1998. Acculturation. In S. Loue, ed., *Handbook of immigrant health*. New York: Plenum, pp. 37–60.
Community Relations Service 1998. One America dialogue. http://www.usdoj.gov/crs/pubs/oneamerica.htm.
Community Relations Service 2000a. Responding to hate crimes and bias-motivated

incidents on college/university campuses. http://www.usdoj.gov/crs/pubs/campus.htm.
Community Relations Service 2000b. Hate crime: The violence of intolerance. http://www.usdoj.gov/crs/pubs/htecrm.htm.
Community Relations Service 2000c. Avoiding racial conflict: A guide for municipalities. http://www.usdoj.gov/crs/pubs/avoidracial.htm.
Community Relations Service 2000d. Preventing youth hate crime. http://www.usdoj.gov/crs/pubs/prevyouhatecrim.htm.
Congressional Research Service 1991. Brief history of United States immigration policy. In *Immigration and Nationality Act* (9th Edition). Washington, DC: U.S. Government Printing Office, pp. 548–562.
Corcoran, J. 2000. *Evidence-based social work practice with families: A lifespan approach.* New York: Springer.
Corey, G. 1982. *Theory and practice of counseling and psychotherapy* (2nd ed.). Pacific Grove, CA: Brooks/Cole.
Crawford, D., and Bodine, R. 1996. *Conflict resolution education: A guide to implementing programs in schools, youth-serving organizations, and community juvenile justice settings.* Washington, DC: U.S. Department of Justice. http://www.ncjrs.org/pdffiles/conflic.pdf.
Cummings, S., and Lambert, T. 1997. Anti-Hispanic and Anti-Asian sentiments among African Americans. *Social Science Quarterly* 78:338–353.
Dao, M. 1991. Designing assessment procedures for educationally at-risk Southeast Asian-American students. *Journal of Learning Disabilities* 24:594–601.
Das, A.K., and Kemp, S. F. 1997. Between two worlds: Counseling South Asian Americans. *Journal of Multicultural Counseling and Development* 25:23–33.
Derogatis, L. R. 1974. The Hopkins Symptom Checklist (HSCL): A self-report symptom inventory. *Behavioral Science* 19:1–15.
Derogatis, L. R., and Melisaratos, N., 1983. The Brief Symptom Inventory: An introductory report. *Psychological Medicine* 13:595–605.
Derogatis, L. R., Lipman, R., and Covi, L. 1973. SCL-90, an outpatient psychiatric rating scale. *Psychopharmacology Bulletin* 9:13–28.
DeSantis, L. 1998. Reproductive health. In S. Loue, ed., *Handbook of immigrant health.* New York: Plenum, pp. 449–476.
DeSantis, L., and Ugarizza, D. N. 1995. Potential for intergenerational conflict in Cuban and Haitian immigrant families. *Archives of Psychiatric Nursing* 9:354–364.
DeSipio, L., and de la Garza, R. 1998. *Making Americans, remaking America: Immigration and immigrant policy.* Boulder, CO: Westview Press.
Devore, W., and Schlesinger, E. G. 1999. *Ethnic-sensitive social work practice* (5th ed.). Boston: Allyn and Bacon.
Dhooper, S. S., and Tran, T. V. 1998. Understanding and responding to the health and mental health needs of Asian refugees. *Social Work in Health Care* 27:65–82.

Displaced Persons Act of 1948, 62 Stat. 1009.
Diversity Rx 1997a. Overview: The impact of language barriers on health care and legal protections for limited English speaking patients. http://diversityrx.org/HTML/LEOVER.htm.
Diversity Rx 1997b. Laws. http://www.diversityrx.org/HTML/LELAWS.htm.
Diversity Rx 1997c. Providing culturally appropriate services: Local health department and community-based organizations working together. http://www.diversityrx.org/HTML/PORP01.htm.
Diversity Rx 1997d. Overview of models and strategies for overcoming linguistic and cultural barriers to health care. http://www.diversityrx.org/HTML/MOVERA.htm.
Dobbins, J. E., and Skillings, J. H. 2000. Racism as a clinical syndrome. *American Journal of Orthopsychiatry* 70:14–27.
Doyle, R. 1999. U. S. Immigration. *Scientific American,* 281(3), 28–29.
Drachman, D. 1992. A stage-of-migration framework for service to immigrant populations. *Social Work* 37:68–72.
Drachman, D. 1995. Immigration statuses and their influence on service provision, access, and use. *Social Work* 40:188–197.
Dulmus, C. N., and Wodarski, J. S. 1998. Major depressive disorder and dysthymic disorder. In B. A. Thyer and J. S. Wodarski, eds., *Handbook of empirical social work practice (Vol. I): Mental disorders.* New York: Wiley, pp. 273–285.
Duncan, L., and Simmons, M. 1996. Health practices among Russian and Ukrainian immigrants. *Journal of Community Health Nursing* 13:129–137.
Dunn, D. K. 1999. Guerrilla job development. In Office of Refugee Resettlement, ed., *Proceedings of 1998 National Conference: Employment Services* (p. 1–2). http://www.acf.dhhs.gov/programs/orr/WKS-EMPL.htm.
Duran, B. J., and Weffer, R. E. 1992. Immigrants' aspirations, high school process, and academic outcomes. *American Educational Research Journal* 29:163–181.
Dziegielewski, S. F. 1998. *The changing face of health care social work: Professional practice in the era of managed care.* New York: Springer.
Edleson, J. L., and Roskin, M. 1985. Prevention groups: A model for improving immigrant adjustment. *Journal for Specialists in Group Work* 10:217–224.
Egli, E. 1991. Bilingual workers. In J. Westermeyer, C. L. Williams, and A. N. Nguyen, eds., *Mental health services for refugees (DHHS Publication No. [ADM] 91–1824).* Washington, DC: U.S. Government Printing Office, pp. 90–110.
Egli, E. A., Shiota, N. K., Ben-Porath, Y. S., and Butcher, J. N. 1991. Psychological interventions. In J. Westermeyer, C. L. Williams, and A. N. Nguyen, eds., *Mental health services for refugees* (DHHS Publication No. [ADM] 91–1824). Washington, DC: U. S. Government Printing Office, pp. 157–188.
Ell, K., and Castañeda, I. 1998. Health care seeking behavior. In S. Loue, ed., *Handbook of immigrant health.* New York: Plenum Press, pp. 125–144.
Else, J. F., and Clay-Thompson, C. 1998. *Refugee microenterprise development:*

Achievements and lessons learned. Iowa City: Institute for Social and Economic Development. http://www.ised.org/rande/pdfs/lessonslearned.pdf.

Emergency Supplemental Appropriations Act of 1997, P. L. 105–18, 111 Stat. 158.

ERIC Clearinghouse on Languages and Linguistics 1997. From at-risk to excellence: Principles for practice. *ERIC Digest*. http://www.ed.gov/databases/ERIC_Digests/ed413765.html.

ERIC Clearinghouse on Languages and Linguistics 1998. Qualities of effective programs for immigrant adolescents with limited schooling. *ERIC Digest*. http://www.ed.gov/databases/ERIC_Digests/ed423667.html.

Espin, O. M. 1987. Psychological impact of migration on Latinas. *Psychology of Women Quarterly* 11:489–503.

Faist, T. 1997. The crucial meso-level. In T. Hammar, G. Brochmann, K. Tamas, and T. Faist, eds., *International migration, immobility, and development: Multidisciplinary perspectives*. New York: Berg, pp. 187–218.

Families USA 1999. Fact sheet: Immigrants' eligibility for Medicaid and CHIP and the "public charge" issue. http:www/familiesusa.org/imm.htm.

Faust, M., Spilsbury, J. C., and Loue, S. 1998. African health. In S. Loue, ed., *Handbook of immigrant health*. New York: Plenum, pp. 329–348.

Federal Register 1999. Immigration: Aliens—Inadmissibility and deportability on public charge grounds; public charge definition (FR Doc. 99–13188), May 26, 1999, 28675–28688.

Feen, R. H. 1985. Domestic and foreign policy dilemmas in contemporary U.S. refugee policy. In E. G. Ferris, ed., *Refugees and world politics*. New York: Praeger, pp. 105–119.

Feinberg, R. I. 1996. Use of reminiscence groups to facilitate the telling of life stories by elderly Russian Jewish immigrants. *Smith College Studies in Social Work* 67:39–51.

Fischer, P. A., Martin, R., and Straubhaar, T. 1997. Should I stay or should I go? In T. Hammar, G. Brochmann, K. Tamas, and T. Faist, eds., *International migration, immobility, and development: Multidisciplinary perspectives*. New York: Berg, pp. 49–90.

Fitzgerald, N. B. 1995. ESL instruction in adult education: Findings from a national evaluation. *ERIC Digest*. http://www.cal.org/ncle/DIGESTS/FITZGERA.HTM.

Fix, M., and Passel, J. S. 1994. *Immigration and immigrants: Setting the record straight*. Washington, DC: Urban Institute. http://www.urban.org/pubs/immig/immig.htm.

Fix, M., and Passel, J. S. 1999. *Trends in noncitizens' and citizens' use of public benefits following welfare reform: 1994–1997*. Washington, DC: Urban Institute. http://www.urban.org/immigr/trends.html.

Fix, M., and Turner, M. A. 1999. *A national report card on discrimination in America: The role of testing*. Washington, DC: Urban Institute. http://www.urban.org/civil/report_card.html.

Fix, M., and Zimmerman, W. 1995. Immigrant families and public policy: A deepening divide. Washington, DC: Urban Institute. http://www.urban.org/periodcl/prr25_3p.htm.

Fix, M., and Zimmerman, W. 1999. All under one roof: Mixed-status families in an era of reform. Washington, DC: Urban Institute. http://www.urban.org/immig/all_under.html.

Fortier, J. P. 1999. *Multicultural health best practices overview*. Silver Spring, MD: Resources for Cross Cultural Health Care. http:www/diversityrx.org/BEST/index.html.

Fortier, J. P., and Shaw-Taylor, Y. 1999a. *Cultural and linguistic competence standards and research agenda project*. Silver Spring, MD: Resources for Cross Cultural Health Care. http://www.omhrc.gov/WhatsNew/culturalı.htm.

Fortier, J. P., and Shaw-Taylor, Y. (1999b). *Measuring cultural competence in health care*. Silver Spring, MD: Resources for Cross Cultural Health Care. http://www.healthlaw.org/pubs/199909LingStandards.html.

Frederick Schneiders Research 1999. *Perceptions of how race and ethnic background affect medical care: Highlights from focus groups*. Menlo Park, CA: Kaiser Family Foundation. http://www.kff.org.

Freedy, J. R., and Hobfoll, S. E. 1995. Traumatic stress: A blueprint for the future. In J. R. Freedy and Stevan E. Hobfoll, eds., *Traumatic stress: From theory to practice* New York: Plenum Press, pp. 365–378.

Frendreis, J., and Tatalovich, R. 1997. Who supports English-only laws? Evidence from the 1992 National Election Study. *Social Science Quarterly* 78:354–368.

Frey, W. H., and Liaw, K. L. 1998. The impact of recent immigration on population redistribution within the United States. In J. P. Smith and B. Edmonston, eds., *The immigration debate: Studies on the economic, demographic, and fiscal effects of immigration*. Washington, DC: National Academy Press, pp. 388–448.

Friedman, A. 1992. Rape and domestic violence: The experience of refugee women. In E. Cole, O. M. Espin, and E. D. Rothblum, eds., *Refugee women and their mental health: Shattered societies, shattered lives*. Binghamton, NY: Haworth, pp. 65–78

Fuchs, L. H. 1990. The reactions of Black Americans to immigration. In V. Yans-McLaughlin, ed., *Immigration reconsidered: History, sociology, and politics*. New York: Oxford University Press, pp. 293–314.

Fuligni, A. J. 1997. The academic achievement of adolescents from immigrant families: The roles of family background, attitudes, and behavior. *Child Development* 68:351–363.

Fuligni, A. J. 1998. Adolescents from immigrant families. In V. C. McLoyd and L. Steinberg, eds., *Studying minority adolescents: Conceptual, methodological, and theoretical issues*. Mahwah, NJ: Lawrence Erlbaum, pp. 127–143.

Gaines, A. D. 1998. Mental illness and immigration. In S. Loue, ed., *Handbook of immigrant health*. New York: Plenum, pp. 407–422.

Garcia-Peltoniemi, R. E. 1991a. Clinical manifestations of psychopathology. In J. Westermeyer, C. L. Williams, and A. N. Nguyen, eds., *Mental health services for refugees* (DHHS Publication No. [ADM] 91–1824). Washington, DC: U.S. Government Printing Office, pp. 42–55.

Garcia-Peltoniemi, R. E. 1991b. Epidemiological perspectives. In J. Westermeyer, C. L. Williams, and A. N. Nguyen, eds., *Mental health services for refugees* (DHHS Publication No. [ADM] 91–1824). Washington, DC: U.S. Government Printing Office, pp. 24–41.

Garrison, M. E. B., and Keresman, M. A. 1998. Marital conflict, domestic violence, and family preservation. In B. A. Thyer and J. S. Wodarski, eds., *Handbook of empirical social work practice* (Vol. II). New York: Wiley, pp. 225–240.

Gavagan, T., and Brodyaga, L. 1998. Medical care for immigrants and refugees. *American Family Physician, March 1, 1998*. http://www.aafp.org/afp/980301ap/gavagan.html.

Genessee, F., ed. 1999. *Program alternatives for linguistically diverse students*. Santa Cruz, CA: Center for Research on Education, Diversity, and Excellence, University of California. http://www.cal.org/crede/pubs/edpractice/EPR1.pdf.

Gibson, M. A. 1987. The school performance of immigrant minorities: A comparative view. *Anthropology and Education Quarterly* 18:262–275.

Gibson, M. A., and Ogbu, J. U., eds. 1991. *Minority status and schooling: A comparative study of immigrant and involuntary minorities*. New York: Garland.

Gilbert, M. J. 1991. Acculturation and changes in drinking patterns among Mexican-American women: Implications for prevention. *Alcohol Health and Research World* 15:234–238.

Gimpel, J. G., and Edwards, J. R., Jr. 1999. *The Congressional politics of immigration reform*. Needham Heights, MA: Allyn and Bacon.

Gong-Guy, E., Cravens, R. B., and Patterson, T. E. 1991. Clinical issues in mental health service delivery to refugees. *American Psychologist* 46:642–648.

Gonsalves, C. J. 1992. Psychological stages of the refugee process: A model for therapeutic interventions. *Professional Psychology: Research and Practice* 23:382–389.

Gonzalez, R., and Padilla, A. M. 1997. The academic resilience of Mexican American high school students. *Hispanic Journal of Behavioral Sciences* 19:301–317.

Good, J., Jensen, E., Thompson, P., and Webster, S. 1995. *Overview of international migration*. Geneva: International Organization for Migration. http://www.iom.int/Publications/entry.htm.

Gopaul-McNicol, S. 1993. *Working with West Indian families*. New York: Guilford Press.

Gorman, R. F. 1985. Private voluntary organizations in refugee relief. In E. G. Ferris, ed., *Refugees and world politics*. New York: Praeger, pp. 82–103.

Gouveia, L., and Stull, D. D. 1997. Latino immigrants, meatpacking, and rural communities: A case study of Lexington, Nebraska. *JSRI Research Report #26*. East

Lansing, MI: The Julian Samora Research Institute, Michigan State University. http://www.jsri.msu.edu/RandS/research/irr/rr26abs.html.
Grantmakers Concerned with Immigrants and Refugees 2000. *Fast facts about immigrants and refugees.* http://www.gcir.org/updates.html.
Gray, M. J., Vernez, G., and Rolph, E. S. 1997. Student access and the "new" immigrants: Assessing their impact on institutions. Santa Monica, CA: RAND Corp. http://www.rand.org/Abstracts/.
Green, J. W. 1995. *Cultural awareness in the human services: A multi-ethnic approach* (2nd ed.). Boston: Allyn and Bacon.
Green, J. W. 1999. *Cultural awareness in the human services: A multi-ethnic approach* (3rd ed.). Boston: Allyn and Bacon.
Greene, R. R., and Barnes, G. 1998. The ecological perspective, diversity, and culturally competent social work practice.In R. R. Greene and M. Watkins, eds., *Serving diverse constituencies: Applying the ecological perspective.* New York: Aldine de Gruyter, pp. 63–96.
Greene, R. R., Watkins, M., McNutt, J., and Lopez, L. 1998. Diversity defined. In R. R. Greene and M. Watkins, eds., *Serving diverse constituencies: Applying the ecological perspective.* New York: Aldine de Gruyter, pp. 29–62.
Guendelman, S. 1998. Health and disease among Hispanics. In S. Loue, ed., *Handbook of immigrant health.* New York: Plenum, pp. 277–302.
Gusovsky, T. 1995. New beginnings: Older Russian immigrants in the United States. *Journal of Geriatric Psychiatry* 28:219–233.
Gutiérrez, L. M. 1990. Working with women of color: An empowerment perspective. *Social Work* 35:149–153.
Hagan, J., and Palloni, A. 1998. Immigration and crime in the United States. In J. P. Smith and B. Edmonston, eds., *The immigration debate: Studies on the economic, demographic, and fiscal effects of immigration.* Washington, DC: National Academy Press, pp. 367–387.
Haines, D. W. 1988. The pursuit of English and self-sufficiency: Dilemmas in assessing refugee programme effects. *Journal of Refugee Studies* 1:195–213.
Hamilton, M. 1959. The assessment of anxiety states by rating. *British Journal of Medical Psychology* 32:50–55.
Hamilton, M. 1960. A rating scale for depression. *Journal of Neurology, Neurosurgery and Psychiatry* 12:56–62.
Harper, K. V., and Lantz, J. 1996. *Cross-cultural practice: Social work with diverse populations.* Chicago: Lyceum Books.
Harris, C. R. 1993. Identifying and serving recent immigrant children who are gifted. *ERIC Digest.* http://www.ed.gov/databases/ERIC_Digests/ed358676.html.
Heer, D. M. 1996. *Immigration in America's future: Social science findings and the policy debate.* Boulder, CO: Westview Press.
Hein, M. L., Allen, R. I., and Else, J. F. 1999. *Home-based child care: Assessing the*

self-sufficiency potential (with special reference to refugees). Iowa City: Institute for Social and Economic Development. http://www.ised.org/rwirp/Homebased ChildCare.pdf

Henggeler, S. W., Schoenwald, S. K., Borduin, C. M., Rowland, M. D., and Cunningham, P. B. 1998. *Multisystemic therapy of antisocial behavior in children and adolescents*. New York: Guilford.

Hepworth, D. H., Rooney, R. H., and Larsen, J. A. 1997. *Direct social work practice: Theory and skills*. Pacific Grove, CA: Brooks/Cole.

Herbst, P. K. R. 1992. From helpless victim to empowered survivor: Oral history as a treatment for survivors of torture. In E. Cole, O. M. Espin, and E. D. Rothblum, eds., *Refugee women and their mental health*. Binghamton, NY: Haworth, pp. 141–154.

Hernandez, D. J., ed. 1999. *Children of immigrants: Health, adjustment, and public assistance*. Washington, DC: National Academy Press. http://www.nap.edu/openbook/0309065453/html/R1.html.

Hernandez, D. J., and Charney, E., eds. 1998. *From generation to generation: The health and well-being of children in immigrant families*. Washington, DC: National Academy Press. http://www.stills.nap.edu/html/generation.

Hiegel, J. P. 1984. Collaboration with traditional healers: Experience in refugees' mental care. *International Journal of Mental Health* 12:30–43.

Hinton, L. 1999. Involuntary language loss among immigrants: Asian-American linguistic autobiographies. *ERIC Digest*. http://www.cal.org/ericcll/digest/involuntary.html.

Hirayama, H., and Cetingok, M. 1988. Empowerment: A social work approach for Asian immigrants. *Social Casework* 13:41–47.

Hirayama, K. K., Hirayama, H., and Cetingok, M. 1993. Mental health promotion for South East Asian refugees in the USA. *International Social Work* 36:119–129.

Ho, C. K. 1990. An analysis of domestic violence in Asian American communities: A multicultural approach to counseling. *Women and Therapy* 9:129–150.

Holcomb, L. O., Parsons, L. C., Giger, J. N., and Davidhizar, R. 1996. Haitian Americans: Implications for nursing care. *Journal of Community Health Nursing* 13:249–260.

Hood, M. V. III, and Morris, I. L. 1998. Give us your tired, your poor, . . . but make sure they have a green card: The effects of documented and undocumented migrant context on Anglo opinion toward immigration. *Political Behavior* 20:1–15.

Horowitz, C. R. 1998. The role of the family and the community in the clinical setting. In S. Loue, ed., *Handbook of immigrant health*. New York: Plenum, pp. 163–182.

Howard, E. 1999. *Two-way (dual) immersion*. Washington, DC: Center for Applied Linguistics. http://www.cal.org/ericcll/faqs/rgos/2way.htm.

Iglehart, A. P., and Becerra, R. M. 1995. *Social services and the ethnic community*. Boston: Allyn and Bacon.

Ikels, C. 1998. Aging. In S. Loue, ed., *Handbook of immigrant health*. New York: Plenum, pp. 477–492.
Illegal Immigration Reform and Immigrant Responsibility Act of 1996, P. L.104–208, 110 Stat. 3009.
Immigration Act of 1882, 22 Stat. 214.
Immigration Act of 1917, 39 Stat. 874.
Immigration Act of 1924, 43 Stat. 153.
Immigration Act of 1990, P. L. 101–649, 104 Stat. 4978.
Immigration and Nationality Act Amendments of 1965, P. L. 89–236, 79 Stat. 911.
Immigration and Nationality Act Amendments of 1976, P. L., 94–571, 90 Stat. 2703.
Immigration and Nationality Act of 1952, 66 Stat. 163.
Immigration Reform and Control Act of 1986, P. L., 99–603, 100 Stat. 3359.
Indiana Department of Education 2000. *School social work home page.* http://www.doe.state.in.us/sservices/socwork.htm.
Institute of Medicine 1993. *Access to health care in America.* Washington, DC: National Academy Press.
International Organization for Migration 1998. IOM Mission Statement. http://www.iom.int/iom/Mandat_and_Structure/mission_statement_eng.htm.
Ivry, J. 1992. Paraprofessionals in refugee resettlement. In A. S. Ryan, ed., *Social work with immigrants and refugees.* Binghamton, NY: Haworth Press, pp. 99–118.
Ivry, J. 1992. Paraprofessionals in refugee resettlement. In A. S. Ryan, ed., *Social work with immigrants and refugees.* Binghamton, NY: Haworth, pp. 99–117.
Jackson, C. 1998. Medical interpretation: An essential clinical service for non-English-speaking immigrants. In S. Loue, ed., *Handbook of immigrant health.* New York: Plenum, pp. 61–80.
Jang, M. H., Lee, E., and Woo, K. 1998. Income, language, and citizenship status: Factors affecting the health care access and utilization of Chinese Americans. *Health and Social Work* 23:136–145.
Jaranson, J. 1990. Mental health treatment of refugees and immigrants. In W. H. Holtzman and T. H. Bornemann, eds., *Mental health of immigrants and refugees.* Austin, TX: Hogg Foundation for Mental Health, pp. 207–215.
Jaranson, J. 1991. Psychotherapeutic medication. In J. Westermeyer, C. L. Williams, and A. N. Nguyen, eds., *Mental health services for refugees* (DHHS Publication No. [ADM] 91–1824). Washington, DC: U.S. Government Printing Office, pp. 132–145.
Jenkins, S. 1981. *The ethnic dilemma in social services.* New York: Free Press.
Johnston, S. J., Katimin, M., and Milczarski, W. J. 1997. Homeownership aspirations and experiences: Immigrant Koreans and Dominicans in northern Queens, New York City. *Cityscape* 3:63–90. http://www.huduser.org/periodicals/cityscape/vol3num1/cs3-1_3.pdf.
Joint Commission on Accreditation of Healthcare Organizations 1991. *How to achieve*

quality and accreditation in a hospital social work program. Oakbrook Terrace, IL: Author.

Kahn, S. 1991. *Organizing: A guide for grassroots leaders.* Washington, DC: NASW Press.

Kaiser Family Foundation 1999. *Key facts: Race, ethnicity, and medical care.* Menlo Park, CA: Author. http://www.kff.org.

Kamya, H. A. 1997. African immigrants in the United States: The challenge for research and practice. *Social Work* 42:154–165.

Kao, G. 1999. Psychological well-being and educational achievement among immigrant youth. In D. J. Hernandez, ed., *Children of immigrants: Health, adjustment, and public assistance.* Washington, DC: National Academy Press. http://www.nap.edu/openbook/0309065453/html/R1.html.

Kao, G., and Tienda, M. 1995. Optimism and achievement: The educational performance of immigrant youth. *Social Science Quarterly* 76:1–19.

Kass, B. L., Weinick, R. M., and Monheit, A. C. 1999. Racial and ethnic differences in health, 1996 (MEPS Chartbook No. 2, AHCPR Pub. No. 99–0001). Rockville, MD: Agency for Health Care Policy and Research. http:www.meps.ahcpr.gov/papers/chartbk2/chrtbk2b.htm.

Keane, T. M., Albano, A. M., and Blake, D. D. 1992. Current trends in the treatment of post-traumatic stress symptoms. In M. Basoglu, ed., *Torture and its consequences: Current treatment approaches.* Cambridge: Cambridge University Press, pp. 363–401.

Keigher, S. M. 1997. America's most cruel xenophobia. *Health and Social Work* 22:232–237.

Kelley, P. 1992. The application of family systems theory to mental health services for Southeast Asian refugees. *Journal of Multicultural Social Work* 2:1–13.

Kelley, P. 1994. Integrating systemic and postsystemic approaches to social work practice with refugee families. *Families in Society* 75:541–549.

Kim, B. S. K., Omizo, M. M., and Salvador, D. S. 1996. Culturally relevant counseling services for Korean American children: A systematic approach. *Elementary School Guidance and Counseling* 31:64–73.

Kim, P. K., and Kim, J. S. 1992. Korean elderly: Policy, program, and practice implications. In S. M. Furuto, R. Biswas, D. K. Chung, K. Murase, F. Ross-Sheriff, eds., *Social work practice with Asian Americans.* Newbury Park, CA: Sage, pp. 227–239.

Kinzie, J. D. 1991. Development, staffing, and structure of psychiatric clinics. In J. Westermeyer, C. L. Williams, and A. N. Nguyen, eds., *Mental health services for refugees (DHHS Publication No. [ADM] 91–1824).* Washington, DC: U.S. Government Printing Office, pp. 146–156.

Kleinman, A. 1980. *Patients and healers in the context of culture.* Berkeley: University of California Press.

Klerman, G. L., Weissman, M. M., Rounsaville, B., and Chevron, E. 1984. *Interpersonal psychotherapy of depression.* New York: Basic Books.

Kopala, M., Esquivel, G., and Baptiste, L. 1994. Counseling approaches for immigrant children: Facilitating the acculturative process. *The School Counselor* 41:352–359.

Kopp, J. 1989. Self-observation: An empowerment strategy in assessment. *Social Casework* 70:276–284.

Korbin, J. E. 1991. Child maltreatment and the study of child refugees. In F. L. Ahearn and J. L. Athey, eds., *Refugee children: Theory, research, and services*. Baltimore: Johns Hopkins University Press, pp. 39–50.

Kosberg, J. I., Lowenstein, A., Garcia, J. L., and Biggs, S. (in press). Challenges to the cross-cultural and cross-national study of elder abuse. *Journal of Social Work Research and Evaluation: An International Publication*.

Kovacs, M. 1985. The children's depression inventory. *Pscychopharmacology Bulletin* 21:995–998.

Krumm, D. 1998. No exit: Staying the course in Afghanistan. In U.S. Committee for Refugees, ed., *World refugee survey 1998*. Washington, DC: Immigration and Refugee Services of America, pp. 124–127.

Lambert, R. G., and Lambert, M. J. 1984. The effects of role preparation for psychotherapy on immigrant clients seeking mental health services in Hawaii. *Journal of Community Psychology* 12:263–275.

Langdon, H. W. 1996. English language learning by immigrant Spanish speakers: A United States perspective. *Topics in Language Disorders* 16:38–53.

Lecca, P. J., Quervalé, I., Nunes, J. V., and Gonzales, H. F. 1998. *Cultural competency in health, social, and human services: Directions for the twenty-first century*. New York: Garland Publishing.

LeClere, F. B., Jensen, L., and Biddlecom, A. E. 1994. Health care utilization, family context, and adaptation among immigrants to the United States. *Journal of Health and Social Behavior* 35:370–384.

Le-Doux, C., and Stephens, K. S. 1992. Refugee and immigrant social service delivery: Critical management issues. In A. S. Ryan, ed., *Social work with immigrants and refugees*. Binghamton, NY: Haworth, pp. 31–45.

Lee, E. 1966. A theory of migration. *Demography* 3:47–57.

Lee, I. J., and Kelly, E. W. 1996. Individualistic and collective group counseling: Effects with Korean clients. *Journal of Multicultural Counseling and Development*, 1996, 254–266.

Lee, K. K. 1998. *Huddled masses, muddled laws: Why contemporary immigration policy fails to reflect public opinion*. Westport, CT: Praeger.

Legal Information Institute 1999. International law: An overview. http://www.law.cornell.edu/topics/international.html.

Leiper de Monchy, M. 1991. Recovery and rebuilding: The challenge for refugee children and service providers. In F. L. Ahearn and J. L. Athey, eds., *Refugee children: Theory, research, and services*. Baltimore: Johns Hopkins University Press, pp. 163–180.

Light, D. 1992. Healing their wounds: Guatemalan refugee women as political activists. In E. Cole, O. M. Espin, and E. D. Rothblum, eds., *Refugee women and their mental health: Shattered societies, shattered lives*. Binghamton, NY: Haworth Press, pp. 297–308.

Lightfoot-Klein, H. 1993. Disability in female immigrants with ritually inflicted genital mutilation. *Women and Therapy* 14:187–194.

Lin, K. M. 1990. Assessment and diagnostic issues in the psychiatric care of refugee patients. In W. H. Holtzman and T. H. Bornemann, eds., *Mental health of immigrants and refugees*. Austin, TX: Hogg Foundation for Mental Health, pp. 198–206.

Lin, K. M. 1991. Psychiatric diagnosis and treatment. In J. Westermeyer, C. L. Williams, and A. N. Nguyen, eds., *Mental health services for refugees* (DHHS Publication No. [ADM] 91–1824). Washington, DC:, pp. 123–131

Lin, K. M., and Shen, W. W. 1991. Pharmacotherapy for Southeast Asian psychiatric patients. *Journal of Nervous and Mental Disease*, 179, 346–350.

Loescher, G. 1993. *Beyond charity: International cooperation and the global refugee crisis*. New York: Oxford University Press.

London, C. B. G. 1990. Educating young new immigrants: How can the United States cope? *International Journal of Adolescence and Youth* 2:81–100.

Làpez, J. 1991. Group work as a protective factor for immigrant youth. *Social Work with Groups* 14:29–40.

Loue, S. 1998. Defining the immigrant. In S. Loue, ed., *Handbook of immigrant health*. New York: Plenum Press, pp. 19–36.

Loue, S., and Faust, M. 1998. Intimate partner violence among immigrants. In S. Loue, ed., *Handbook of immigrant health*. New York: Plenum, pp. 521–544.

Lucas, T. 1996. Promoting secondary school transitions for immigrant adolescents. *ERIC Digest*. http://www.ed.gov/databases/ERIC_Digests/ed402786.html.

Lum, D. 1999. *Culturally competent practice: A framework for growth and action*. Pacific Grove, CA: Brooks/Cole.

Lum, D. 2000. *Social work practice and people of color: A process-stage approach* (4th ed.). Pacific Grove, CA: Brooks/Cole.

Maio, G. R., Esses, V. M., and Bell, D. W. 1994. The formation of attitudes toward new immigrant groups. *Journal of Applied Social Psychology* 24:1762–1776.

Malmberg, G. 1997. Time and space in international migration. In T. Hammar, G. Brochmann, K. Tamas, and T. Faist, eds., *International migration, immobility, and development: Multidisciplinary perspectives*. New York: Berg, pp. 21–48.

Marcos, K. 1999. *Why, how, and when should my child learn a second language?* Washington, DC: Center for Applied Linguistics. http://www.accesseric.org/

Marger, M. N. 1997. *Race and ethnic relations: American and global perspectives* (4th ed.). Belmont, CA: Wadsworth.

Marshall, P. A., Koenig, B. A., Grifhorst, P., and van Ewijk, M. 1998. Ethical issues in immigrant health care and clinical research. In S. Loue, ed., *Handbook of immigrant health*. New York: Plenum, pp. 203–226.

Martin, A. 2000. Martin Luther King Jr.'s philosophy of nonviolence to change the status quo. http://www.ncs.pvt.k12.va.us/ryerbury/king-12/king-12.htm.

Matsuoka, J. K. 1990. Differential acculturation among Vietnamese refugees. *Social Work* 35:341–345.

Mayadas, N. S., and Elliott, D. 1992. Integration and xenophobia: An inherent conflict in international migration. In A. S. Ryan, ed., *Social work with immigrants and refugees*. New York: Haworth, pp. 47–62.

Mayberry, R. M., Mili, F., Vaid, I. G. M., Samadi, A., Ofili, E., McNeal, M. S., Griffith, P. A., LaBrie, G. 1999. *Racial and ethnic differences in access to medical care: A synthesis of the literature*. Menlo Park, CA: Kaiser Family Foundation. http://www.kff.org.

Mazzetti, M. 1997. A transactional analysis approach to adjustment problems of adolescents from immigrant families. *Transactional Analysis Journal* 27:220–223.

McBride, M. J. 1999. The evolution of U.S. immigration and refugee policy: Public opinion, domestic politics and UNHCR [New Issues in Refugee Research, Working Paper No. 3]. Geneva: United Nations High Commissioner for Refugees. http://www.unhcr.ch/refworld/pub/wpapers/wpno3.htm.

McCarthy, K. F., and Vernez, G. 1997. *New immigrants, new needs: The California experience*. Santa Monica, CA: RAND Corp. http://www.rand.org/publications/RB/RB8015/.

McInnis-Dittrich, K. M. 1992. The economic well-being of Asian/Pacific Islander female-headed households: Implications for social welfare policy. In S. M. Furuto, R. Biswas, D. K. Chung, K. Murase, and F. Ross-Sheriff, eds., *Social work practice with Asian Americans*. Newbury Park, CA: Sage, pp. 143–166.

McKillip, J. 1987. *Need analysis: Tools for the human services and education*. Newbury Park, CA: Sage.

McLaughlin, B. 1995. *Fostering second language development in young children*. Washington, DC: Center for Applied Linguistics. http://www.cal.org/ericcll/digest/ncrcds04.htm.

McLellarn, R. W., and Rosenzweig, J. 1998. Generalized anxiety disorder. In B. A. Thyer and J. S. Wodarski, eds., *Handbook of empirical social work practice (Vol. I): Mental disorders*. New York: Wiley, pp. 385–397.

McMahon, A., and Allen-Meares, P. 1992. Is social work racist? A content analysis of recent literature. *Social Work* 37:533–538.

McNally, R. 1992. Psychopathology of post-traumatic stress disorder (PTSD): Boundaries of the syndrome. In M. Basoglu, ed., *Torture and its consequences: Current treatment approaches*. Cambridge: Cambridge University Press, pp. 229–252.

Meadows, M. 1999. The problem of accessing health care. *Closing the Gap*, August/September 1999, 1–2. http://www.omhrc.gov.

Meisenheimer, J. R. 1992. How do immigrants fare in the U.S. labor market? *Monthly Labor Review* 115 (12),3–19.

Merton, R. K. 1949. *Discrimination and the American creed*. In R. H. MacIver, ed., *Discrimination and National Welfare*. New York: Harper and Row, pp. 99–126.

Milkman, R., and Wong, K. 1999. *Organizing immigrant workers: Case studies from Southern California*. Los Angeles: Department of Sociology, University of California. http://www.sscnet.ucla.edu/soc/groups/ccsa/milkma1.htm.

Miller, K.E., and Billings, D. L. 1994. Playing to grow: A primary mental health intervention for Guatemalan refugee children. *American Journal of Orthopsychiatry* 64:346–356.

Miller, T. W. 1992. Long-term effects of torture in former prisoners of war. In M. Basoglu, ed., *Torture and its consequences: Current treatment approaches*. Cambridge: Cambridge University Press, pp. 107–135.

Minuchin, S. 1974. *Families and family therapy*. Cambridge, MA: Harvard University Press.

Mitra, S. 2000. *Immigration and New York City's Economy*. New York: Taub Urban Research Center. http://urban.nyu.edu/ny-affairs/immigrants-economy/.

Mokuau, N., and Matsuoka, J. 1992. The appropriateness of personality theories for social work with Asian Americans. In S. M. Furuto, R. Biswas, D. K. Chung, K. Murase, and F. Ross-Sheriff, eds., *Social work practice with Asian Americans*. Newbury Park, CA: Sage, pp. 67–84.

Mollica, R. F. 2000. Invisible wounds. *Scientific American* 282(6):54–57).

Mollica, R. F., Caspi-Yavin, Y., Bollini, P., Truong, T., Tor, S., and Lavelle, J. 1992. The Harvard Trauma Questionnaire: Validating a cross-cultural instrument for measuring torture, trauma, and posttraumatic stress disorder in Indochinese refugees. *Journal of Nervous and Mental Disease* 180:111–116.

Morse, S. C., and Ludovina, F. S. 1999. Responding to undocumented children in the schools. *ERIC Digest*. http://www.ed.gov/databases/ERIC_Digests/ed433172.html.

Mouw, T., and Xie, Y. 1997. *Accommodation with or without assimilation: Bilingualism and the academic achievement of Asian immigrants*. Ann Arbor, MI: Population Studies Center, University of Michigan. http://www.psc.lsa.umich.edu/pubs/papers/rr97-402.pdf.

Muñoz, R. F. 1982. The Spanish-speaking consumer and the community mental health center. In E. E. Jones and S. J. Korchin, eds., *Minority mental health*. New York: Praeger, pp. 362–398.

Murase, K. 1992. Models of service delivery in Asian American communities. In S. M. Furuto, R. Biswas, D. K. Chung, K. Murase, and F. Ross-Sheriff, eds., *Social work practice with Asian Americans*. Newbury Park, CA: Sage, pp. 101–120.

Murguía, M. 1999. Addressing the health needs of gay and lesbian patients. *Closing the Gap*, August/September 1999:10–11. http://www.omhrc.gov.

Musser-Granski, J., and Carrillo, D. F. 1997. The use of bilingual, bicultural paraprofessionals in mental health services: Issues for hiring, training, and supervision. *Community Mental Health Journal* 33:51–60.

Myers, L. L., and Thyer, B. A. 1997. Should social work clients have the right to effective treatment? *Social Work* 42:288–298.

Napolitano, M., and Goldberg, B. W. 1998. Migrant health. In S. Loue, ed., *Handbook of immigrant health*. New York: Plenum, pp. 261–276.

National Association of Social Workers 1999. *NASW School Social Workers*. http://www.naswdc.org/sections/SSW/default.htm.

National Clearinghouse on ESL Literacy Education 2000. *Frequently asked questions in adult ESL literacy*. http://www.cal.org/ncle/FAQS.HTM.

National Conference for Community and Justice 2000a. Taking America's pulse II. http://www.nccj.org.

National Conference for Community and Justice 2000b. Principles and policy statement: Immigration. http://www.nccj.org/htmlmedia/organize.htm.

National Conference for Community and Justice 2000c. Responding to hate groups: A brief overview. http://www.nccj.org/htmlmedia/organize.htm.

National Conference of State Legislatures 1997. America's newcomers: An immigrant policy handbook: Executive summary. http://www.ncsl.org/public/catalog/9366ex.htm.

National Health Law Program 1999. Alert: INS issues long-anticipated public charge guidance. http://www.healthlaw.org/pubs/Alert990525.html.

National Immigration Forum 1995. Together in our differences: How newcomers and established residents are rebuilding American communities (Executive Summary). http://www.immigrationforum.org/Race/default.htm.

National Immigration Forum 1999a. Facts on refugees and asylees. http://www.immigrationforum.org/Refugees&Asylees.htm.

National Immigration Forum 1999b. *Facts on immigrants and the economy*. http://www.immigrationforum.org/Facts/ImmigrantsEconomy99.htm.

National Immigration Forum 2000a. *Learning English: Some basic facts on immigrants and acquisition of the English language*. http://www.immigrationforum.org/Facts/english.htm.

National Immigration Forum 2000b. Cycles of nativism in U.S. history. http://www.immigrationforum.org/Facts/cyclesofnativism.htm.

National Immigration Forum 2000c. *Immigration Policy Handbook 2000*. Washington, DC: Author.

National Immigration Forum 2000d. 106th Congress Leaves Much of Immigration policy agenda undone. http://www.immigrationforum.org/Current Issues/targetgroups/LIFAwrapup.htm.

National Immigration Law Center 1999. Administration clarifies public charge policy for immigrants who use health care and other safety net programs. http://www.healthlaw.org/pubs/Alert990525.html.

Nicassio, P. M. 1985. The psychosocial adjustment of the Southeast Asian refugee: An overview of empirical findings and theoretical models. *Journal of Cross-Cultural Psychology* 16:153–173.

Nicholson, B. L. 1999. The influence of pre-emigration and postemigration stressors on mental health: A study of Southeast Asian refugees. In P. L. Ewalt, E. M. Freeman, A. E. Fortune, D. L. Poole, and S. L. Witkin, eds., *Multicultural issues in social work: Practice and research*. Washington, DC: NASW Press, pp. 635–653.

Noncitizen Benefit Clarification and Other Technical Amendments Act of 1998, P. L. 105–306, 112 Stat. 2926.

Norman, A. J. 1994. Black-Korean relations: From desperation to dialogue, or from shouting and shooting to sitting and talking. *Journal of Multicultural Social Work* 3:87–99.

O'Connor, B. B. 1998. Healing practices. In S. Loue, ed., *Handbook of immigrant health*. New York: Plenum, pp. 145–162.

O'Hare, T., and Tran, T. V. 1998. Substance abuse among Southeast Asians in the U.S.: Implications for practice and research. *Social Work in Health Care* 26:69–80.

Office of Minority Health 1999. Eliminating racial and ethnic disparities in health. http://www.raceandhealth.omhrc.gov/sidebars/sbinitOver.htm.

Office of Refugee Resettlement 1998a. *Annual report to Congress, FY 1997*. http://www.acf.gov/programs/orr/97arc2.htm.

Office of Refugee Resettlement 1998b. *Highlights from the 1998 ORR survey on refugee economic adjustment*. http://www.acf.dhhs.gov/programs/orr/refsurvey.htm.

Office of Refugee Resettlement 1999a. *Refugee resettlement program*. http://www.acf.dhhs.gov/programs/opa/facts/orr.htm.

Office of Refugee Resettlement 1999b. Functional Statement. http://www.acf.dhhs.gov/programs/orr/orrfunctstate.htm.

Office of Refugee Resettlement 2000a. Community and family strengthening and integration. http://www.acf.dhhs.gov/programs/orr/00-cfsi.htm.

Office of Refugee Resettlement 2000b. *English literacy and civics education initiative*. http://www.acf.dhhs.gov/programs/orr/civicsfac.htm.

Office of Refugee Resettlement 2000c. *Recertification resources*. http://www.acf.dhhs.gov/programs/orr/recreden.htm.

Office of Refugee Resettlement 2000d. *Final notice of allocations to states of FY 2000 funds for refugee social services*. http://www.acf.dhhs.gov/programs/orr/FINSS00.htm.

Office of Refugee Resettlement 2000e. *Individual Development Accounts*. http://www.acf.dhhs.gov/programs/orr/IDA-ANN.htm.

Office of Refugee Resettlement 2000f. *Microenterpise development*. http://www.acf.dhhs.gov/programs/orr/00micro.htm.

Okamura, J. Y., and Agbayani, A. 1991. Filipino Americans. In N. Mokuau, ed., *Handbook of social services for Asian and Pacific Islanders*. New York: Greenwood Press, pp.97–116.

Olness, K. N. 1998. Refugee health. In S. Loue, ed., *Handbook of immigrant health*. New York: Plenum, pp. 227–242.

Ortega, D. M., and Richey, C. A. 1998. Methodological issues in social work research with depressed women of color. In M. Potocky and A. Y. Rodgers-Farmer, eds., *Social work research with minority and oppressed populations: Methodological issues and innovations*. Binghamton, NY: Haworth, pp. 47–70.

Palmer, D. L. 1996. Determinants of Canadian attitudes toward immigration: More than just racism? *Canadian Journal of Behavioural Science* 28:1–12. http://www.cpa.ca/cjbsnew/1996/ful_palmer.html.

Paquin, L. 1983. *The Hatians: Class and color politics*. Brooklyn: Multi-Type.

Parker, M. 1991. Career and employment counseling with Soviet Jewish immigrants: Issues and recommendations. *Journal of Employment Counseling* 28:157–166.

Patterson, C. 1994. Secondary prevention of elder abuse. In Canadian Task Force on the Periodic Health Examination, eds., *The Canadian Guide to Clinical Preventive Health Care*. Ottawa: Minister of Supply and Services Canada, pp. 922–929. http://www.hc-sc.gc.ca/hppb/healthcare/pubs/clinical_preventive/pdf/s11c77e.pdf.

Pérez-Stable, M., and Uriarte, M. 1997. Cubans and the changing economy of Miami. In D. Y. Hamamoto and R. D. Torres, eds., *New American destinies. A reader in contemporary Asian and Latino immigration*. New York: Routledge, pp. 141–162.

Perkins, J., Simon, H., Cheng, F., Olson, K., and Vera, Y. 1998. *Ensuring linguistic access in health care settings: Legal rights and responsibilities*. Washington, DC: National Health Law Program. http://www.healthlaw.org/pubs/19980131ling access.html.

Personal Responsibility and Work Opportunity Reconciliation Act of 1996, P. L. 104–193, 110 Stat. 2105.

Pessar, P. R. 1995. The elusive enclave: Ethnicity, class, and nationality among Latino entrepreneurs in greater Washington, DC. *Human Organization* 54:383–392.

Pettys, G. L., and Balgopal, P. R. 1998. Multigenerational conflicts and new immigrants: An Indo-American experience. *Families in Society* 79:410–423.

Pinderhughes, E. 1989. *Understanding race, ethnicity, and power: The key to efficacy in clinical practice*. New York: Free Press.

Portes, A. 1990. From south of the border: Hispanic minorities in the United States. In V. Yans-McLaughlin, ed., *Immigration reconsidered: History, sociology, and politics*. New York: Oxford University Press.

Portes, A., and Bach, R. L. 1985. *Latin journey: Cuban and Mexican immigrants in the United States*. Berkeley: University of California Press.

Portes, A., and MacLeod, D. 1996. Educational progress of children of immigrants: The roles of class, ethnicity, and school context. *Sociology of Education* 69:255–275.

Portes, A., and Rumbaut, R. G. 1990. *Immigrant America: A portrait*. Berkeley: University of California Press.

Portes, A., and Sensenbrenner, J. 1993. Embeddedness and immigration: Notes on the social determinants of economic action. *American Journal of Sociology* 98:1320–1350.

Portes, A., and Zhou, M. 1993. The new second generation: Segmented assimilation and its variants. *Annals of the American Academy of Political and Social Science* 530:74–96.

Portes, A., Kyle, D., and Eaton, W. W. 1992. Mental illness and help-seeking behavior among Mariel Cuban and Haitian refugees in South Florida. *Journal of Health and Social Behavior* 33:283–298.

Potocky, M. 1996a. Toward a new definition of refugee economic integration. *International Social Work* 39:245–256.

Potocky, M. 1996b. Refugee resettlement in the United States: Implications for international social welfare. *Journal of Sociology and Social Welfare* 23:163–174.

Potocky, M. 1997a. Multicultural social work in the United States: A review and critique. *International Social Work* 40:315–326.

Potocky, M. 1997b. Predictors of Refugee Economic Status: A replication. *Journal of Social Service Research* 23:41–70.

Potocky, M., and McDonald, T. P. 1995. Predictors of economic status of Southeast Asian refugees: Implications for service improvement. *Social Work Research* 19:219–227.

Potocky-Tripodi, M. in press. Micro and macro determinants of refugee economic status. *Journal of Social Service Research*.

Prochaska, J. O., and DiClemente, C. C. 1984. *The transtheoretical approach*. Homewood, IL: Dorsey Press.

Queralt, M. 1984. Understanding Cuban immigrants: A cultural perspective. *Social Work* 29:115–121.

Raiff, N. R., and Shore, B. K. 1993. *Advanced case management: New strategies for the nineties*. Newbury Park, CA: Sage.

Rebhun, L. A. 1998. Substance use among immigrants to the United States. In S. Loue, ed., *Handbook of immigrant health*. New York: Plenum, pp. 493–520.

Refugee Act of 1980, P. L. 96–212, 94 Stat. 102.

Refugee Education Assistance Act of 1980, 94 Stat. 1799.

Refugee Relief Act of 1953, P. L., 67 Stat. 400.

Refugee-Escapee Act of 1957, P. L., 71 Stat. 639.

Rehr, H., Showers, N., Young, A. T., and Blumenfield, S. 1998. Professional accountability and quality improvement through practice-based studies. In H. Rehr, G. Rosenberg, and S. Blumenfield, eds., *Creative social work in health care: Clients, the community, and your organization*. New York: Springer.

Rennie, J., and Marcos, K. 1998. *The effectiveness of bilingual education*. Washington, DC: Center for Applied Linguistics. http:www.cal.org/ericcll/faqs/rgos.bi.html.

Rhee, S. 1996. Effective social work practice with Koran immigrant families. *Journal of Multicultural Social Work* 4:49–61.

Rhee, S. 1997. Domestic violence in the Korean immigrant family. *Journal of Sociology and Social Welfare* 24:63–77.
Riedel, R. L. 1998. Access to health care. In S. Loue, ed., *Handbook of immigrant health*. New York: Plenum Press, pp. 101–124.
Rivera-Batiz, F. 1996. The education of immigrant children in New York City. *ERIC Digest*. http://www.ed.gov/databases/ERIC_Digests/ed402399.html.
Rodríguez, N. 1999. U.S. immigration and intergroup relations in the late 20th century: African Americans and Latinos. In S. Jonas and S. D. Thomas, eds., *Immigration: A civil rights issue for the Americas*. Wilmington, DE: SR Books., pp. 131–144
Rodriguez, R., and DeWolfe, A. 1990. Psychological distress among Mexican-American and Mexican women as related to status on the new immigration law. *Journal of Consulting and Clinical Psychology* 58:548–553.
Roffman, R., Picciano, J., Wickizer, L, Bolan, M., and Ryan, R. 1998. Anonymous enrollment in AIDS prevention telephone group counseling: Facilitating the participation of gay and bisexual men in intervention and research. In M. Potocky and A. Y. Rodgers, eds., *Social work research with minority and oppressed populations: Methodological issues and innovations*. New York: Haworth, pp. 5–22.
Rogers, R., and Copeland, E. 1993. *Forced migration: Policy issues in the post-Cold War world*. Medford, MA: The Fletcher School of Law and Diplomacy, Tufts University.
Rogler, L. H., and Cortes, D. E. 1993. Help-seeking pathways: A unifying concept in mental health care. *American Journal of Psychiatry* 150:554–561.
Romo, H. 1993. Mexican immigrants in high schools: Meeting their needs. *ERIC Digest*. http://www.ed.gov/databases/ERIC_Digests/ed357905.html.
Romo, H. 1997. Improving ethnic and racial relations in the schools. *ERIC Digest*. http://www.ed.gov/databases/ERIC_Digests/ed414113.html.
Root, M. P. P. 1997. Introduction. In M. P. P. Root, ed., *Filipino Americans: Transformation and identity*. Thousand Oaks, CA: Sage, pp. xi-xv.
Rose, S. M. 1992. *Case management and social work practice*. White Plains, NY: Longman.
Rosenberg, G. 1983. Practice roles and functions of the health social worker. In R. S. Miller and H. Rehr, eds., *Social work issues in health care*. Englewood Cliffs, NJ: Prentice-Hall, pp. 121–180.
Roskin, M. 1986. A preventive groupwork intervention with new immigrants to Israel. *Journal of Primary Prevention* 6:181–188.
Ross, H. 1999. Minorities less likely to have employer-sponsored health insurance. *Closing the Gap*, August/September 1999, 4. http://www.omhrc.gov.
Rubin, A., and Babbie, E. 1997. *Research methods for social work* (3rd ed.). Pacific Grove, CA: Brooks/Cole.
Rumbaut, R. 1991. The agony of exile: A study of the migration and adaptation of In-

dochinese refugee adults and children. In F. L. Ahearn and J. L. Athey, eds., *Refugee children: Theory, research, and services*. Baltimore: Johns Hopkins University Press, pp. 53–91.

Rumbaut, R. 1999. Transformations: The post-immigrant generation in an age of diversity, JSRI Research Report #30. East Lansing, MI: The Julian Samora Research Institute, Michigan State University. http://www.jsri.msu.edu/RandS/research/irr/rr30.html.

Sakauye, K. 1992. The elderly Asian patient. *Journal of Geriatric Psychiatry* 25:85–104.

Saleebey, D. 1997. *The strengths perspective in social work practice* (2nd ed.). Boston: Allyn and Bacon.

Salvador, D. S., Omizo, M. M., and Kim, B. S. 1997. Bayanihan: Providing effective counseling strategies for children of Filipino ancestry. *Journal of Multicultural Counseling and Development* 25:201–209.

Sanders, J. M., and Nee, V. 1996. Immigrant self-employment: The family as social capital and the value of human capital. *American Sociological Review* 61: 231–249.

Sandhu, D. S., and Brown, S. P. 1996. Empowering ethnically and racially diverse clients through prejudice reduction: Suggestions and strategies for counselors. *Journal of Multicultural Counseling and Development* 24:202–217.

Santos, S. J., Bohon, L. M., and Sanchez-Sosa, J. J. 1998. Childhood family relationships, marital and work conflict, and mental health distress in Mexican immigrants. *Journal of Community Psychology* 26:491–508.

Schlesinger, E. G. 1985. *Health care social work practice: Concepts and strategies*. St. Louis: Times Mirror/Mosby.

Schlosberg, C. 1998. Non-qualified immigrants' access to public health and emergency services after the welfare law. Washington, DC: National Health Law Program. http://www.healthlaw.org/pubs/19980112immigrant.html.

Schlosberg, C., and Wiley, D. 1998. The impact of INS public charge determinations on immigrant access to health care. Washington, DC: National Health Law Program. http:www.healthlaw.org/pubs/19980522publiccharge.html.

Schnur, E., Koffler, R., Wimpenny, N., Giller, H., and Rafield, E. N. 1995. Family child care and new immigrants: Cultural bridge and support. *Child Welfare* 74:1237–1248.

Schwartz, W. 1994. Anti-bias and conflict resolution curricula: Theory and practice. *ERIC Digest*. http://www.ed.gov/databases/ERIC_Digests/ed377255.html.

Schwartz, W. 1996. Immigrants and their educational attainment: Some facts and findings. *ERIC Digest*. http://www.ed.gov/databases/ERIC_Digests/ed402398.html.

Sewell-Coker, B., Hamilton-Collins, J., and Fein, E. 1985. Social work practice with West Indian immigrants. *Social Casework* 66:563–568.

Shepard, M. 1998. Understanding nonviolence. http://www.markshep.com/nonviolence/Understanding.html.

Sherraden, M., Johnson, L., Clancy, M., Beverly, S., Schreiner, M., Zhan, M., and Curley, J. 2000. *Saving patterns in IDA programs*. St. Louis: Center for Social Development, School of Social Work, Washington University. http://gwbweb.wustl.edu/Users/csd/.

Siegel, D. H. 1984. Defining empirically based practice. *Social Work* 29:325–331.

Siegel, R. J. 1992. Fifty years later: Am I still an immigrant? In E. Cole, O. M. Espin, and E. D. Rothblum, eds., *Refugee women and their mental health: Shattered societies, shattered lives*. Binghamton, NY: Haworth., pp. 105–112.

Simpson, G. E., and Yinger, J. M. 1985. *Racial and cultural minorities: An analysis of prejudice and discrimination* (5th ed.). New York: Plenum.

Smyth, N. J. 1998a. Alcohol abuse. In B. A. Thyer and J. S. Wodarski, eds., *Handbook of empirical social work practice (Vol. I): Mental disorders*. New York: Wiley, pp. 181–204.

Smyth, N. J. 1998b. Substance abuse. In B. A. Thyer and J. S. Wodarski, eds., *Handbook of empirical social work practice (Vol. I): Mental disorders*. New York: Wiley, pp. 123–153.

Solomon, B. B. 1976. *Black empowerment: Social work in oppressed communities*. New York: Columbia University Press.

Song-Kim, Y. I. 1992. Battered Korean women in urban United States. In S. M. Furuto, R. Biswas, D. K. Chung, K. Murase, and F. Ross-Sheriff, eds., *Social work practice with Asian Americans*. Newbury Park, CA: Sage, pp. 213–226.

Sorensen, S., Brewer, D. J., Carroll, S. J., and Bryton, E. 1995. *Increasing Hispanic participation in higher education: A desirable public investment*. Santa Monica, CA: RAND Corp. http://www.rand.org/publications/IP/IP152/.

Spencer, M. S. 1998. Reducing racism in schools: Moving beyond rhetoric. *Social Work in Education* 20:25–36.

Suárez-Orozco, M. M. 1996. California dreaming: Proposition 187 and the cultural psychology of racial and ethnic exclusion. *Anthropology and Education Quarterly* 27:151–167.

Sue, D. W., Arredondo, P., and McDavis, R. J. 1992. Multicultural counseling competencies and standards: A call to the profession. *Journal of Multicultural Counseling and Development* 20:64–88.

Surgeon General 2000. *Mental health: A report of the Surgeon General*. Washington, DC: U.S. Public Health Service. http://www.surgeongeneral.gov/library/mental health/toc.html.

Szapocznik, J., Santisteban, D., Hervis, O., Spencer, F., and Kurtines, W. M. 1981. Treatment of depression among Cuban American elders: Some validational evidence for a life enhancement counseling approach. *Journal of Consulting and Clinical Psychology* 49:619–626.

Szapocznik, J., Scopetta, M. A., and King, O. E. 1978. Theory and practice in matching treatment to the special characteristics and problems of Cuban immigrants. *Journal of Community Psychology* 6:112–122.

Takada, E., Ford, J. M., and Lloyd, L. S. 1998. Asian Pacific Islander health. In S. Loue, ed., *Handbook of immigrant health*. New York: Plenum, pp. 303–328.

Tang, J., and O'Brien, T. P. 1990. Correlates of vocational success in refugee work adaptation. *Journal of Applied Social Psychology* 20:1444–1452.

Tannenbaum, J. 1990. An English conversation group model for Vietnamese adolescent females. *Social Work with Groups* 13:41–55.

Temple-Raston, D. 2000. Immigrants fill critical gap in wide-open job market. *USA Today, June 23*, 1B-2B.

Tran, T. V., Dhooper, S. S., and McInnis-Dittrich, K. 1997. Utilization of community-based social and health services among foreign born Hispanic elderly. *Journal of Gerontological Social Work* 28:23–43.

Tripodi, T. 1994. *A primer on single-subject design for clinical social workers*. Washington, DC: NASW Press.

Tsai, D. T., and Lopez, R. A. 1997. The use of social supports by elderly Chinese immigrants. *Journal of Gerontological Social Work* 29:77–94.

Tsui, A. M., and Sammons, M. T. 1988. Group intervention with adolescent Vietnamese refugees. *Journal for Specialists in Group Work* 13:90–95.

Tyhurst, L. 1951. Displacement and migration: A study in social psychiatry. *American Journal of Psychiatry, 107*, 561–568.

U.S. Bureau of the Census 1993. *1990 census of the population, the foreign-born population* (CP-3–1). Washington, DC: Government Printing Office.

U.S. Bureau of the Census 1997. Country of origin and year of entry into the U.S. of the foreign born. http://www.bls.gov/cps/pub/1997/for_born.htm.

U.S. Bureau of the Census 1998. Selected characteristics of the foreign-born population. http://www.census.gov/population/socdemo/foreign/97.

U.S. Bureau of the Census 2001. *Current Population Survey, March 2000*. http://www.census.gov.

U.S. Committee for Refugees 1998. *World refugee survey 1998*. Washington, DC: Immigration and Refugee Services of America.

U.S. Committee for Refugees 2000. Refugees admitted to the United States, by nationality, FY 1987–2000. *Refugee Reports* 21(12):10–11.

U.S. Department of Health and Human Services 1998. Health care Rx: Access for all. http:www.hrsa.dhhs.gov.

U.S. Department of Labor 1999. Foreign Labor Certification. http://www.doleta.gov/employer/dflc.htm.

U.S. Department of State 1996. Fact sheet: Who is a refugee? http://www.state.gov/www/global/prm/fs_refugee.html

U.S. Department of State 1998a. Latin America and the Caribbean refugee admissions program. http://www.state.gov/www/global/prm/fs_latcar_refu_adm_9807.html.

U.S. Department of State 1998b. Near East and South Asia refugee admissions program. http://www.state.gov/www/global/prm/fs_nesa_refu_adm_9807.html.

U.S. Department of State 1998c. New Independent States and the Baltics refugee admissions program. http://www.state.gov/www/global/prm/fs_nisbal_refu_adm_9807.html.

U.S. Department of State 1998d. Fact sheet: U.S. support for Balkan refugees. http://www.state.gov/www/global/prm/fs_990517_balkan_aid.html.

U.S. Department of State 1998e. African refugee admissions program. http://www.state.gov/www/global/prm/fs_latcar_refu_adm_9807.html.

U.S. Equal Employment Opportunity Commission 1997. Facts about national origin discrimination. http://www.eeoc.gov/facts/fs-nator.html.

U.S. Immigration and Naturalization Service 1996. State population estimates: Legal permanent residents and aliens eligible to apply for naturalization. http://www.ins.usdoj.gov/hqopp/lprest.html.

U.S. Immigration and Naturalization Service 1997a. Glossary. http://www.ins.usdoj.gov/glossary.

U.S. Immigration and Naturalization Service 1997b. Legislative history. http://www.ins.usdoj.gov/graphics/statistics/legishist.

U.S. Immigration and Naturalization Service 1998. Immigration fact sheet. http://www.ins.usdoj.gov/stats.

U.S. Immigration and Naturalization Service 1999a. Annual report: Legal immigration, fiscal year 1998. http://www.ins.usdoj.gov/stats.

U.S. Immigration and Naturalization Service 1999b. General Naturalization Requirements. http://www.ins.usdoj.gov/graphics/services/natz/general.htm.

U.S. Immigration and Naturalization Service 1999c. Laws, Regulations, and Guides. http://www.ins.usdoj.gov/graphics/lawsregs.

U.S. Immigration and Naturalization Service 1999d. Overview. http://www.ins.usdoj.gov/graphics/aboutins/thisisins/overview.htm.

U.S. Preventive Services Task Force 1996. Patient education and counseling for prevention. In *Guide to clinical preventive services (2nd ed)*. Washington, DC: Department of Health and Human Services. http://158.72.20.10/pubs/guidecps/text/iv_edu.txt.

Uba, L., and Chung, R. C. 1991. The relationship between trauma and financial and physical well-being among Cambodians in the United States. *Journal of General Psychology* 118:215–225.

United Nations 1951. Convention relating to the status of refugees. Geneva: Author.

United Nations High Commissioner for Refugees 1997. *The state of the world's refugees, 1997–98: A humanitarian agenda*. Oxford: Oxford University Press.

United Nations High Commissioner for Refugees 1999a. United Nations Instruments. http://www.unhcr.ch/refworld/legal/instrume/regional/un/un.htm.

United Nations High Commissioner for Refugees 1999b. Universal Declaration of Human Rights (abbreviated). http://www.unhcr.ch/teach/tchhr/12-14ud.htm.

United Nations High Commissioner for Refugees 1999c. What is UNHCR?. http://www.unhcr.ch/un&ref/what/what.htm.

van der Veer, G. 1998. *Counselling and therapy with refugees and victims of trauma* (2nd ed.). New York: Wiley.

Van Voorhis, R. 1998. Culturally relevant practices: Addressing the psychosocial dynamics of oppression. In R. R. Greene and M. Watkins, eds., *Serving diverse constituencies: Applying the ecological perspective*. New York: Aldine de Gruyter, pp. 97–112.

Vaznaugh, A. 1995. Dropout intervention and language minority youth. *ERIC Digest*. http://www.cal.org/ericcll/digest/Vaznau01.htm.

Vega, W. A., Kolody, B., Valle, R., and Hough, R. 1986. Depressive symptoms and their correlates among immigrant Mexican women in the United States. *Social Science and Medicine* 22:645–652.

Vernez, G., Abrahamse, A. F., and Quigley, D. 1996. *How immigrants fare in U.S. education*. Santa Monica, CA: RAND Corp. http://www.rand.org/Abstracts/.

Vernez, G., Krop, R. A., and Rydell, C. P. 1999. *Closing the education gap: Benefits and costs*. Santa Monica, CA: RAND Corp. http://www.rand.org/Abstracts/.

Vesti, P., and Kastrup, M. 1995. Treatment of torture survivors: Psychosocial and somatic aspects. In J. R. Freedy and Stevan E. Hobfoll, eds., *Traumatic stress: From theory to practice*. New York: Plenum Press, pp. 339–364.

Vesti, P., and Kastrup, P. 1992. Psychotherapy for torture survivors. In M. Basoglu, ed., *Torture and its consequences: Current treatment approaches*. Cambridge: Cambridge University Press, pp. 348–362.

Vinokurov, A., Birman, D., and Trickett, E. 2000. Psychological and acculturation correlates of work status among Soviet Jewish refugees in the U.S. *International Migration Review* 34:538–559.

Volland, P. J., Berkman, B., Stein, G., and Vaghy, A. 1999. *Social work education for practice in health care: Final report*. New York: New York Academy of Medicine.

Vonk, M. E., and Yegidis, B. L. 1998. Post-traumatic stress disorder. In B. A. Thyer and J. S. Wodarski, eds., *Handbook of empirical social work practice (Vol. I): Mental disorders*. New York: Wiley, pp. 365–383.

Waldinger, R. 1995. *From Ellis Island to LAX: Immigrant prospects in the American city*. New York: Taub Urban Research Center. http://urban.nyu.edu/research/immigrants-waldinger/.

Watzlawick, P., Weakland, J.H., and Fisch, R. 1974. *Change: Principles of problem formation and problem resolution*. New York: W. W. Norton.

Weeks, J. R., and Cuellar, J. B. 1983. Isolation of older persons: The influence of immigration and length of residence. *Research on Aging* 5:369–388.

Weine, S. M., Kulenovic, A. D., Pavkovic, I., and Gibbons, R. 1998. Testimony psychotherapy in Bosnian refugees: A pilot study. *American Journal of Psychiatry* 155:1720–1726.

Wellman, D. 2000. From evil to illness: Medicalizing racism. *American Journal of Orthopsychiatry* 70:28–32.

Westermeyer, J. 1987. Prevention of mental disorder among Hmong refugees in the U.S.: Lessons from the period 1976–1986. *Social Science and Medicine* 25:941–947.

Westermeyer, J. 1990. Motivations for uprooting and migration. In In W. H. Holtzman and T. H. Bornemann, eds., *Mental health of immigrants and refugees*. Austin, TX: Hogg Foundation for Mental Health, pp. 78–89.

Westermeyer, J. 1991a. Models of mental health services. In J. Westermeyer, C. L. Williams, and A. N. Nguyen, eds., *Mental health services for refugees (DHHS Publication No. [ADM] 91–1824)*. Washington, DC: U.S. Government Printing Office, pp. 73–89.

Westermeyer, J. 1991b. Special considerations. In J. Westermeyer, C. L. Williams, and A. N. Nguyen, eds., *Mental health services for refugees* (DHHS Publication No. [ADM] 91–1824). Washington, DC: U.S. Government Printing Office, pp. 56–72.

Westermeyer, J. 1991c. Psychiatric services for refugee children: An overview. In F. L. Ahearn and J. L. Athey, eds., *Refugee children: Theory, research, and services*. Baltimore: Johns Hopkins University Press, pp. 127–162.

Westermeyer, J., and Wahmenholm, K. 1989. Assessing the victimized psychiatric patient. *Hospital and Community Psychiatry* 40:245–249.

Westermeyer, J., Callies, A., and Neider, J. 1990. Welfare status and pscyhosocial adjustment among 100 Hmong refugees. *Journal of Nervous and Mental Disease* 178:300–306.

Western Interstate Coalition on Higher Education 1998. *Cultural competence standards in managed mental health care for four underserved/underrepresented racial/ethnic groups*. http://www.wiche.edu/mentalhealth/CCStandards/ccstoc.htm.

Westwood, M. J., and Ishiyama, F. I. 1991. Challenges to counseling immigrant clients: Understanding intercultural barriers to career adjustment. *Journal of Employment Counseling* 28:130–143.

Wilk, R. J. 1986. The Haitian refugee: Concerns for health care providers. *Social Work in Health Care* 11:61–74.

Williams, C. L., and Berry, J. W. 1991. Primary prevention of acculturative stress among refugees. *American Psychologist* 46:632–641.

Witmer, T. A. P., and Culver, S. M. (in press). Trauma and resilience among Bosnian refugee families: A critical review of the literature. *Journal of Social Work Research and Evaluation*.

Women's Commission for Refugee Women and Children 1997. *Guidelines on the protection of women: A synopsis of the UNHCR guidelines*. http://www.intrescom.org/wcrwc/wc_guidelineswomen.html.

Women's Commission for Refugee Women and Children 2000. *Sexual violence in refugee crises: A synopsis of UNHCR guidelines for prevention and response*. http://www.intrescom.org/wcrwc/wc_guidelinesexviol.html.

Woolf, L. M. 1998. *Elder abuse and neglect.* http://www.webster.edu/woolflm/abuse.html.
Wright, R., Jr., Saleebey, D., Watts, T. D., and Lecca, P. J. 1983. *Transcultural perspectives in the human services.* Springfield, IL: Charles C. Thomas.
Wrigley, H. S. 1993. Innovative programs and promising practices in adult ESL literacy. *ERIC Digest.* http://www.cal.org/ncle/digests/.
Yamashiro, G., and Matsuoka, J. K. 1997. Help-seeking among Asian and Pacific Americans: A multiperspective analysis. *Social Work* 42:176–186.
Yee, B. W. K. 1992a. Elders in Southeast Asian families. *Generations* 16:24–27.
Yee, B. W. K. 1992b. Markers of successful aging among Vietnamese refugee women. In E. Cole, O. M. Espin, and E. D. Rothblum, eds., *Refugee women and their mental health: Shattered societies, shattered lives.* Binghamton, NY: Haworth, pp. 221–238
Ying, Y. 1999. Strengthening intergenerational/intercultural ties in migrant families: A new intervention for parents. *Journal of Community Psychology* 27:89–96.
Zastrow, C. 1995. *The practice of social work* (5th ed.). Pacific Grove, CA: Brooks/Cole.
Zhou, M., and Bankston, C. L. 1994. Social capital and the adaptation of the second generation: The case of Vietnamese youth in New Orleans. *International Migration Review* 28:821–845.
Zimmerman, W., and Tumlin, K. C. 1999. Patchwork policies: State assistance for immigrants under welfare reform. Washington, DC: Urban Institute. http://www.newfederalism.urban.org/html/occa24.html.

INDEX

Abortion, 206–7
Access. *See* Health care access
Acculturation: acculturative stress, 258, 291–298; adolescents, 325–26; defined, 127; and education, 366–67; and health care access, 192; and intergenerational conflict, 315, 318, 319, 321; and marital conflict, 312; models of, 127–28; structural, 128–30
Acculturative stress, 258, 291–98
Adjustment of status, 8–9
Adlerian psychotherapy, 476
Adolescents: interventions for, 348–51; life cycle issues, 325–27. *See also* Children
Adult Education Act (AEA), 384
Advocacy. *See* Case advocacy; Policy advocacy
AEA. *See* Adult Education Act
AFDC. *See* Aid to Families with Dependent Children
Afghanis, 47
African Americans, 191, 427
Africans, 50–51, 288
AFSC. *See* American Friends Service Committee
Age: demographics, 30; and family therapy, 337–38; and migration decisionmaking, 15. *See also* Elderly people
Agriculture Research, Extension, and Education Reform Act (1998), 85
AI. *See* Amnesty International
Aid to Families with Dependent Children (AFDC), 80
Alienation, 267
Aliens, defined, 5, 9
American Friends Service Committee (AFSC), 100

Americanization, 129, 318. *See also* Structural assimilation
American Jewish Joint Distribution Committee (JDC), 100
American Refugee Committee (ARC), 100
Amnesty, 71–72
Amnesty International (AI), 104
Anglo culture. *See* Dominant culture
Anti-immigrant sentiments, 418; causal theories, 421–22; and economic impact, 372–73 , 421–22; and historical policies, 58; and Personal Responsibility and Work Opportunity Reconciliation Act, 74, 77; in U.S.-born minority groups, 427. *See also* Interethnic relations
Antiracist model of social work, 416
Anxiety, 269, 298–301, 350–351
ARC. *See* American Refugee Committee
Arranged marriages, 46
Asian Indians. *See* Indians
Asians, 44–47; case study exercises, 253–54; communication styles, 263; contemporary policies, 67, 68; economic well-being, 45, 47, 191; education, 363–64; family influences, 203; health care access, 184; historical policies, 58–59, 61; and intergenerational conflict, 337; and intimate partner violence, 334; mental health care, 305; naturalization rates, 34; and psychotropic medication, 288–289; traditional healing systems, 197, 198, 199, 231, 321. *See also specific groups*
Assertiveness training, 295–296
Assessment: children/adolescents, 348–49; elderly people, 351–52; health care, 213, 237–39; instruments, 148–50, 161, 285–86; interethnic relations, 429–30;

Culturally competent practice *(continued)*
care, 273, 278, 286–87; summary, 482–83;
terminology, 124–30; theories, 137–41.
See also Cultural competence knowledge
base; Cultural competence skills
Cultural relativity, 261–62
Cultural sensitivity model of social work, 416
Culture, defined, 125
Culture-bound syndromes, 193, 198,
261–63. *See also* Folk illnesses
Culture broker role, 116
Culture shock (acculturative stress), 258,
291–98
Cupping, 200

Data driven systems of mental health care,
275
DED. *See* Deferred Enforced Departure
Defense mechanisms, 475–76
Deferred Enforced Departure (DED), 9, 10
Demographics, 30–36, 143, 179; and health
care access, 192; and migration
stressors, 259–60. *See also* Economic
well-being; Populations
Departure stage of migration. *See*
Premigration/departure stage of
migration
Deportable aliens, defined, 10
Depression, 268–69, 298–300, 351
Derivitave citizenship, defined, 10
Dermabrasion, 200, 321
*Diagnostic and Statistical Manual of
Mental Disorders* (*DSM*), 148–49, 262
Diagnostic systems, 148–49. *See also*
Assessment
Direct services, 118
Discharge planning, 282
Disclosure, 158
Discrimination: causal theories, 419–22;
current incidence, 423–24, 426; defined,
130, 418–19; education about, 473–74;
employment, 382, 414, 433–34. *See also*
Interethnic relations
Displaced Persons Act (1948), 60, 61, 62
Displacement perspective, 427, 475–76
Diverse society concept, 129
"Diversity immigrants," 74
Doctors Without Borders, 101

Documented aliens, defined, 5
Domestic violence. *See* Intimate partner
violence
Dominant culture, 128, 147–48
Dominicans, 42
Drug abuse services, 119
Dysfunctional circular interaction, 323

East Europeans, 49–50; case study
exercises, 254–55; historical policies, 59,
60, 61
Ecological structural family therapy,
344–45
Eco-map, 336–37
Economic gain theory of interethnic
relations, 420
Economic impact of immigrants/refugees,
371–73, 421–22
Economic migrants. *See* Immigrants
Economic/political stratification, 129–30,
417–18
Economic well-being, 31–34, 370–83,
403–14; Asians, 45, 47, 191; British, 48;
and economic impact, 371–73; and
education, 367–68, 378; and financial
capital, 377, 409–12; Haitians, 44; and
health care access, 190–91; and health
status, 196; home ownership, 376, 378,
411–12; and household composition,
379, 407–9; and human capital, 377–79,
403–7; income, 374; Jamaicans, 43; labor
force participation, 373–74, 403–7; and
labor market conditions, 381–83; Latin
Americans, 38, 42; Middle Eastern
people, 48; and migration
decisionmaking, 15; occupations,
374–75; poverty, 375–76; and social
capital, 379–80, 412–13; Soviets/former
Soviets, 49; summary, 486–87; and U.S.
immigration/refugee policies, 380–81
Education, 31–32, 42, 360–70, 387–402;
adults, 360–61, 387–88; children's
achievement, 362–64; community
factors, 369–70; and economic well-
being, 367–68, 378; family factors,
367–68; individual factors, 365–67; and
interethnic relations, 472–75; as life
cycle issue, 326–27; macro-level

practices, 388–90; micro-level practices, 388, 400–2; peer factors, 368–69; school factors, 369; summary, 486. *See also* Meso-level education practices

Elder abuse, 322–23, 347–48

Elderly people: health, 208, 322; and intergenerational conflict, 321–23, 347–48; interventions for, 351–52; Latin Americans, 38; life cycle issues, 328–29; and substance abuse, 306–7. *See also* Age

El Salvador. *See* Salvadorans

Emergency Supplemental Appropriations Act (1997), 85

Emergent conflict resolution, 459–60

Emigrants, defined, 4

Emotional expression: and intergenerational conflict, 323; Latin Americans, 38; Soviets/former Soviets, 49; and traditional healing systems, 197

Empacho, 199, 231

Empirically based practice, 123, 136–37, 151–52; mental health care, 290–91

Employee language banks, 234–35

Employment. *See* Labor force participation

Employment services, 119, 403–7

Empowerment, 168–71; and mental health care, 274, 297; and monitoring, 172; techniques, 169–71; women, 330–31

Enclave economy, 373, 378, 380

Engagement: health care, 236–37; skills for, 152, 155–57

English-as-a-Second-Language (ESL) programs, 357, 384–87, 394

English proficiency. *See* Language issues

Entrants, defined, 8, 9–10

Entrepreneurship. *See* Self-employment

Envy, 198

ESL programs. *See* English-as-a-Second-Language (ESL) programs

Ethical issues, 204, 231

Ethiopians, 51. *See also* Africans

Ethnic agencies, 111

Ethnic enclaves, 45, 373, 378, 380

Ethnic identity: adolescents, 325–26, 349–50; defined, 126; self-awareness, 131–33; self-knowledge, 142–43

Ethnicity, 125, 195. *See also* Ethnic identity

Ethnic sensitivity, 124

Ethnocentrism, 130

Ethnographic interviewing, 158

Ethnopsychopharmacology, 289

Europeans, 48–50

Evaluating responses, 156

Evaluation, 119, 124; community health education, 227; community health planning, 220; health care advocacy, 216–17; and monitoring, 171–72, 175; skills for, 174, 175–79

Evil eye beliefs, 198

Experiential training, 475

Expressive arts therapy, 351

Eye contact, 156

Family dynamics, 310–55; case study exercises, 353–56; family composition, 379; Filipinos, 45; Haitians, 44; and health care, 203; Indians, 46; and interpreter role, 115–16; life cycle issues, 317, 324–29; macro-level practices, 329–31; marital conflict, 311–14, 331–36; meso-level practices, 331–32; Middle Eastern people, 48; and migration decisionmaking, 312; summary, 485–86. *See also* Intergenerational conflict; Micro-level family issues practices

Family influences: Asians, 203; and education, 367–68; and health care, 194, 203, 232, 238; Jamaicans, 42; Latin Americans, 38; and mental health care, 306–7; Soviets/former Soviets, 49. *See also* Chain migration

Family preservation programs, 347

Family reunification policies, 67, 68, 72, 74

Family secrets, 323–24

Family systems theory, 341–42

Family therapy, 337–47; behavioral, 341; Bowen's systems therapy, 342–43; family systems theory, 341–42; general principles, 337–38; Milan systemic approach, 346; psychoeducational, 338–41; strategic, 345; structural, 343–45

Feedback principle of mental health care, 274

Feelings, 176–77. *See also* Emotional expression

Female circumcision. *See* Female genital mutilation
Female genital mutilation, 207, 231
Filial piety, 321–22
Filipinos, 44–45, 366–64
Financial capital, 377, 409–12
Folk illnesses, 193, 198–199, 231, 262–63
Follow-up, 177–78, 179–81
Forced migrants, 7. *See also* Refugees
Foreign-born population, defined, 4
Foreign students, 24–25
Frustration-aggression theory, 419, 422
Future recommendations, 489–91

Garment industry, 383
Gay/lesbian people, 207–8
Gender: demographics, 30; and education, 365; employment discrimination, 382–83. *See also* Gender roles
Gender roles: and family therapy, 337–38; and intergenerational conflict, 316, 319–20; Latin Americans, 38; and marital conflict, 311–12; and meso-level practices, 331–32; and self-esteem problems, 268; and substance abuse, 307. *See also* Women
Genetic traits, 196
Geneva Conventions, 57
Genocide, 129, 417
Genogram, 336–37
Gifted students, 398–400
Goal setting, 162–64, 429–31
Grief, 266
Group consciousness, 170
Guatemalans, 39–40. *See also* Central Americans
Guilt, 270–71

Haitian Refugee Immigration Fairness Act (1998), 94
Haitians, 43–44; entrants, 8, 9–10; traditional healing systems, 197, 199; transit stage of migration, 19; and U.S. immigration/refugee policies, 43, 70, 94
Harmony/balance, 197, 205
Hate crimes, 425, 443–44
Hate groups, 426, 444–45

Health, 183–255; best practices overview, 209–12; case study exercises, 253–55; differential health status, 195–96; and economic well-being, 190–91, 379; elderly people, 207–8, 322; gay/lesbian people, 207–8; psychosocial issues, 201–4, 249–53; summary, 483–84; traditional healing systems, 194, 196–201, 202, 231–32, 238, 286; trends, 212; U.S. government agencies, 107; women, 205–7. *See also* Health care access; Macro-level health practices; Meso-level health practices; Micro-level health practices
Health care access, 183–94; defined, 183–85; financial barriers, 190–91; mental health care, 274, 281; personal/cultural barriers, 192–94; structural barriers, 184–90
Health education: community level, 221–280; micro-level practices, 237, 245–48
Health insurance, 191, 275
Health services, 119
Hierarchy of suffering, 324
Hill-Burton Act (1946), 190
Hispanics: economic well-being, 191; health care access, 184, 191; and psychotropic medication, 288; traditional healing systems, 197, 231. *See also specific groups*
HIV/AIDS, 208
Hmong, 253. *See also* Southeast Asians
Holism in mental health care, 274
Holocaust, 302. *See also* Nazism
Home ownership, 376, 378, 411–12
Homosexuality. *See* Gay/lesbian people
Hondurans, 40. *See also* Central Americans
Hot blood, 199
Hot/cold beliefs, 197, 205
Household composition, 379, 407–9
Housing services, 119
HRW. *See* Human Rights Watch
Human capital, 377–78, 403–7
Human rights perspective, 427
Human Rights Watch (HRW), 104
Hwabyung, 199

ICMC. *See* International Catholic Migration Commission

ICRC. *See* International Committee of the Red Cross
ICVA. *See* International Council of Voluntary Agencies
IDAs. *See* Individual Development Accounts
Idioms of distress, 262
IFRC. *See* International Federation of Red Cross and Red Crescent Societies
IIRIRA. *See* Illegal Immigration Reform and Immigrant Responsibility Act
Illegal immigrants. *See* Undocumented aliens
Illegal Immigration Reform and Immigrant Responsibility Act (IIRIRA) (1996), 66, 92–94, 187–88
Immigrant integration policy, 79
Immigrant policy. *See* Immigrant integration policy
Immigrants: countries of origin, 22, 25–26; defined, 4, 10; premigration/departure stage of migration, 17–18; states of residence, 29. *See also* Immigrants vs. refugees
Immigrants vs. refugees: countries of origin, 22–23; definitions, 4–5, 7–8, 12; stages of migration, 17–18, 19
Immigration Act (1882), 58, 62
Immigration Act (1917), 59, 62
Immigration Act (1924), 59–60, 62
Immigration Act (1990), 65, 72–74, 75–77
Immigration and Nationality Act (1952), 60–61, 63
Immigration and Nationality Act Amendments (1965), 64, 66–67
Immigration and Nationality Act Amendments (1976), 64, 67–68
Immigration and Naturalization Service (INS), 105, 482. *See also* Undocumented aliens
Immigration/legal assistance, 119
Immigration policy. *See* U.S. immigration/refugee policies
Immigration Reform and Control Act (IRCA) (1986), 65, 71–72
Indians, 46
Indigenous helping approaches, 136
Indigenous professionals, 113–14
Indirect services, 118

Individual Development Accounts (IDAs), 409–10
Information gathering, 475
Information/referral, 118
Information/skills training, 293–96, 349–50
INS. *See* Immigration and Naturalization Service
Institutional discrimination/oppression, 130, 418–19
Integration (biculturalism), 128, 326
Integration option for refugees, 98
Integration principle of mental health care, 275
InterAction, 100
Interdisciplinary collaboration, 230–34. *See also* Collaboration
Interest-based negotiation, 463–64
Interethnic relations, 416–78; assessment, 429–31; case study exercises, 477–78; causal theories, 419–22; and cultural competence knowledge base, 142, 146–47; current state of, 422–28; and empowerment, 170; as environmental influence, 146–47; key concepts, 417–19; micro-level practices, 472–76; and problem definition, 159; self-awareness, 132–34; summary, 488; terminology, 130; and trust, 155. *See also* Anti-immigrant sentiments; Conflict resolution; Macro-level interethnic relations practices; Structured interethnic contact
Intergenerational conflict, 314–24, 336–48; assessment, 336–37; behavioral family therapy, 341; Bowen's systems therapy, 342–43; and children, 319–21; and elderly people, 321–23, 347–48; family systems theory, 341–42; family therapy principles, 337–38; Milan systemic family therapy, 346; overview, 315–19; psychoeducational family therapy, 338–41; and refugees, 323–24; strategic family therapy, 345; structural family therapy, 343–45
Intergovernmental organizations, 96–99
Intermarriage, 313
Internally displaced persons, 7
International Catholic Migration Commission (ICMC), 100

International Committee of the Red Cross (ICRC), 101
International Council of Voluntary Agencies (ICVA), 101
International Federation of Red Cross and Red Crescent Societies (IFRC), 101
International humanitarian law, 54, 56–57
International human rights law, 54, 55
International law, 7, 53–57, 70
International migrant worker law, 54
International Organization for Migration (IOM), 97–98, 106, 481
International protection, 98
International refugee law, 54, 70
International Rescue Committee (IRC), 101
International service delivery organizations, 96–105; advocacy, 103–5; intergovernmental, 96–99; private, 99–102
Interpersonal psychotherapy, 251, 298, 300
Interpreters, 114–16, 155; health care, 234–35, 244–45; mental health care, 288
Interpreting responses, 156
Interventions. *See specific areas*
Intimate partner violence, 313–14, 330–31, 333–36
Involuntary migrants. *See* Refugees
IOM. *See* International Organization for Migration
Iranians, 47–48
Iraqis, 48
IRC. *See* International Rescue Committee
IRCA. *See* Immigration Reform and Control Act (IRCA) (1986)
Islam, 48

Jamaicans, 42–43, 363–64
JDC. *See* American Jewish Joint Distribution Committee
Jesuit Refugee Service (JRS), 101
Job coaching, 405
Job development, 413–14
Job search assistance, 404, 412–13
JRS. *See* Jesuit Refugee Service

Kennedy, John F., 67
Key informants, 144
Koreans, 45–46, 199. *See also* Asians

Labor Department, 107
Labor force participation, 373–74; case study exercises, 415; downward mobility, 268, 375; employment discrimination, 382, 414, 433–34; employment services, 119, 403–7; and gender roles, 268, 312; labor market conditions, 381–83; U.S. government agencies, 107
Labor recruitment, 39, 58–59, 60
Language issues: assessment instruments, 148; case study exercises, 414–15; and engagement, 155; Haitians, 44; and health care, 189–90, 229–30, 234–35, 244–45; and intergenerational conflict, 321; interpreter role of service delivery personnel, 113–16; interventions, 384–87; and labor force participation, 268, 377–78; and mental health care, 287–88; research findings, 356–60; summary, 486, 487
Laotians, 47. *See also* Southeast Asians
Latin Americans, 38–40, 67, 364. *See also* Hispanics; *specific groups*
Lawyers Committee for Human Rights (LCHR), 104
LCHR. *See* Lawyers Committee for Human Rights
Lead agency, 218
Legal Immigration Family Equity Act (2000), 94
Legalized aliens, defined, 10
Legal status. *See* U.S. immigration/refugee policies
LEP. *See* Limited English proficiency
Lesbian/gay people. *See* Gay/lesbian people
Liberians, 51. *See also* Africans
Life cycle issues, 317, 324–29
Limited English proficiency (LEP), 357. *See also* Language issues
Loneliness, 267
Loss, 18–19
Lutheran World Relief, 101

MAA. *See* Mutual Assistance Association
Macro-level health practices, 210, 213–28; advocacy, 214–17; community health education, 221–28; community-level

planning, 217–21; community-needs assessment, 213
Macro-level interethnic relations practices, 431–49; community development, 438–46; community education, 446–47; nonviolent resistance, 448–49; policy advocacy, 432–38
Macro-level practices: economic well-being, 408; education, 387, 388–90; family dynamics, 329–31; language issues, 384–85; mental health, 276–78. *See also* Macro-level health practices; Macro-level interethnic relations practices
Mainstream culture. *See* Dominant culture
Mainstream organizations, 110–11, 111–12
Mal aire, 199
Mal de ojo, 199
Mal puesto, 199
Managed care, 273
Marginalization, 128
Marielitos, 41
Marital conflict, 311–14, 332–36
Marital therapy, 333
Marriage, 46. *See also* Family dynamics; Marital conflict
Médecins Sans Frontières (MSF), 101
Mediation, 466–72, 474
Medical interpretation, 235
Melting pot concept, 129, 417
Men. *See* Gender; Gender roles
Mennonite Central Committee, 102
Mental health, 256–309; alienation/loneliness, 267; anxiety, 269; best practice summary, 272–76; case study exercises, 307–9; children, 327, 350–51; cultural factors, 260–64; depression, 268; and economic well-being, 378–79; grief, 266; guilt, 270–71; incidence/prevalence studies, 264–65; macro-level practices, 276–78; meso-level practices, 278–80; migration stressors, 257–60; paranoia, 270; personnel roles, 114–16; post-traumatic stress disorder, 271; self-esteem problems, 268; somatization, 269; substance abuse, 271–72; summary, 484–85; and traditional healing systems, 197. *See also* Micro-level mental health practices

Mentoring, 405, 412
Meso-level education practices, 390–400; gifted students, 398–99; instructional practice, 396–98; limited English proficiency students, 393–96
Meso-level health practices, 210, 229–36; interdisciplinary collaboration, 230–34; organizational development, 234–36, 236
Meso-level practices: economic well-being, 403–7, 408; education, 387; family dynamics, 331–32; language issues, 385–86; mental health, 278–80. *See also* Conflict resolution; Meso-level education practices; Meso-level health practices; Structured interethnic contact
Mexicans, 19, 39; education, 363, 364; folk illnesses, 199, 231; and U.S. immigration/refugee policies, 60, 71. *See also* Hispanics; Latin Americans
Microenterprise development, 410–411
Micro-level family issues practices, 332–52; children, 348–51; elderly people, 351–52; marital conflict, 332–36. *See also* Intergenerational conflict
Micro-level health practices, 210–211, 236–53; case management, 239–45; general principles, 236–38; health education/counseling, 237, 245–48; psychosocial treatment, 249–53
Micro-level mental health practices, 280–307; for acculturative stress, 291–98; assessment, 281, 283–86, 304–5; clinical considerations, 286–91; for depression/anxiety, 298–300; empirically based practice, 290–91; overview, 280–83; for post-traumatic stress disorder, 301–3; for substance abuse, 304–7
Micro-level practices: education, 388, 400–2; interethnic relations, 472–76; language issues, 386–87. *See also* Micro-level family issues practices; Micro-level health practices; Micro-level mental health practices

Middle Eastern people, 47–48, 197, 263
Migration: causes of, 14–16, 480; decisionmaking, 13–17, 312; stages of, 17–20, 480. *See also* Migration stressors
Migration for Employment Convention, 57
Migration stressors, 277, 310; and child abuse, 320–21; and marital conflict, 313; and paranoia, 270; and stages of migration, 257–59
Milan systemic family therapy, 346
Minority groups: defined, 125. *See also* U.S.-born minority groups; *specific groups*
Monitoring, 167, 171–74; and evaluation, 171–72, 175; and follow-up, 180
Mother's milk complications, 199
Moxibustion, 198
MSF. *See* Médecins Sans Frontières
MST. *See* Multisystemic therapy
Multicultural education, 391
Multicultural society concept, 129
Multilevel approach: causes of migration, 14–16; intervention selection, 165; problem definition, 159–61. *See also specific areas*
Multisystemic therapy (MST), 351
Mutual Assistance Association (MAA), 111

National Literacy Act, 384
National origins. *See* Countries of origin
Nationals, defined, 10
Nation of Immigrants, A (Kennedy), 67
Nativism, 418
Naturalization, 85, 86; defined, 9, 11–12; rates, 34, 35. *See also* Citizenship
Natural support in mental health care, 274
Nazism, 50, 60
"Need to know," 238
Negotiation, 461–66
Neo-classical economic theory of international migration, 13–14
Networking, 118
Newcomer schools, 394
"New immigrants," 67. *See also* Asians; Latin Americans
NGOs (nongovernmental organizations). *See* Private voluntary organizations
Nicaraguan Adjustment and Central American Relief Act (NACARA) (1997), 40, 94
Nicaraguans, 40. *See also* Central Americans
Nodding, 156
Noncitizen Benefit Clarification and Other Technical Amendments Act (1998), 85–86
Nongovernmental organizations. *See* Private voluntary organizations
Nonimmigrants: countries of origin, 24–25; defined, 10–11
Non-refoulement, 57, 70, 98
Nonviolent resistance, 448–49
Normative group, 148
Normative theories of interethnic relations, 420, 422

Objectives, 163. *See also* Goal setting
Occupations, 374–75. *See also* Labor force participation
Office of Refugee Resettlement (ORR), 106–7, 330, 482
Open-ended questions, 284
Organizational development, 234–36
Origin, countries of. *See* Countries of origin
ORR. *See* Office of Refugee Resettlement
Outcome principle of mental health care, 275, 279–80
Outreach/community education role, 114
Overprotectiveness, 323–24

Paranoia, 270
Paraprofessionals, 113–17
Parentification, 324
Parolees, defined, 8, 11
Participant observation, 144
Partners for Development, 102
Pathways to health care, 193–94
Peaceable classroom programs, 474
Peaceable school programs, 474
Peer educators/counselors, 246–47, 350, 401–2
People of color. *See* Minority groups; U.S.-born minority groups
Persian Gulf War, 48
Personality characteristics, 16, 260

Personal responsibility, 170
Personal Responsibility and Work Opportunity Reconciliation Act (PRWORA) (1996), 65–66, 74, 77–92; consequences of, 86, 90–92; distinctions under, 81–83; and economic well-being, 380–81; and health care access, 185–88; limits on, 85–86; and Proposition 185, 77–78; provisions of, 80–81; summary table, 87–89; term definitions, 83–84
Personnel, 113–17, 234–35
Pharmacoanthropology, 289
Philippines. *See* Filipinos
Physical therapies, 198
Planning/coordination, 119
Pluralistic society concept, 129, 417
Policy advocacy, 119; health care, 214–17; interethnic relations, 432–38; organizations, 103–5, 109, 110
Populations, 20–29; countries of origin, 21–26; states of residence, 27–29
Post-traumatic stress disorder (PTSD), 271, 301–3; and intergenerational conflict, 323–24
Poverty. *See* Economic well-being
Power-conflict theories of interethnic relations, 420–22
Power issues, 168–71, 316
Powerlessness, 168
Practice evaluation, 124
Prejudice, 130, 418; causal theories, 419–22. *See also* Interethnic relations
Premigration/departure stage of migration, 17–19; acculturative stress interventions, 291; service delivery, 96, 97, 106; stressors, 257, 258–59
Prenatal care, 184, 205–6
Presbyterian Disaster Assistance, 102
Prevention principle of mental health care, 276–277
Principal aliens, defined, 11
Private voluntary organizations (PVOs), 99
PRM. *See* Bureau of Population, Refugees, and Migration
Probing responses, 155
Problem definition, 157–60, 237–39
Process curriculum, 474

Professionals, 113–14, 116
Program evaluation, 124
Projection, 475
Proposition 185, 77–78
Protective services, 119
Protocols. *See* Relationship protocols
PRWORA. *See* Personal Responsibility and Work Opportunity Reconciliation Act
Psychodynamic psychotherapy, 302, 475–76
Psychoeducational family therapy, 336–41
Psychological theories of interethnic relations, 419–20, 422
Psychotherapy: cognitive/behavioral, 251–52, 298–99; and health care, 249–53; and interethnic relations, 475–76; interpersonal, 251, 298, 300; psychodynamic, 302, 475–76; testimonial, 302–3
Psychotropic medication, 288–90
PTSD. *See* Post-traumatic stress disorder
Public benefit eligibility, 69, 93. *See also* Personal Responsibility and Work Opportunity Reconciliation Act; Service utilization
"Public charge" laws, 187–89
Public health education. *See* Community health education
Push-pull theory of international migration, 13
PVOs. *See* Private voluntary organizations

Qualified immigrants, 82–83
Quality principle of mental health care, 275
Questions, 283–84
Quota systems, 59–61, 66

Race, defined, 125
Racism, 130, 418–19; causal theories, 419–22. *See also* Interethnic relations
Rape, 314
Rastafari movement, 42–43
Rational emotive psychotherapy, 476
Reality therapy, 476
Recertification, 406
Referral, 174–75
Refugee Act (1980), 64–65, 68–71, 330, 380–81

Refugee and Migration Service, 102
Refugee Education Assistance Act (1980), 70
Refugee-Escapee Act (1957), 61, 63
Refugee-like situations, 7
Refugee Relief Act (1953), 61, 63
Refugees: countries of origin, 26; defined, 4, 11; economic well-being, 376–77; and health care, 206; and intergenerational conflict, 323–24; and marital conflict, 312; and mental health care, 256, 257, 263–64, 269–71, 284–85, 288–89; microenterprise development, 410–11; Middle Eastern people, 47–48; and Personal Responsibility and Work Opportunity Reconciliation Act, 83, 91; premigration/departure stage of migration, 17; service delivery organizations, 96, 98–99, 105–6; service utilization, 36, 91; Southeast Asians, 46–47; states of residence, 28; and U.S. immigration policy, 7–8, 39, 68–71, 72. *See also* Immigrants vs. refugees
Regions of birth. *See* Countries of origin
Relationship protocols, 156–57, 238, 338
Religion: Asians, 45, 46; and elderly people, 328; Haitians, 44; Jamaicans, 42–43; Latin Americans, 38, 41; Middle Eastern people, 48; Soviets/former Soviets, 49; and traditional healing systems, 197; and twelve-step programs, 306
Reminiscence therapy, 352
Repatriation option for refugees, 98
Reproductive health, 205–7
Research/evaluation, 119, 124
Resettlement agencies, 107–9
Resettlement assistance: international organizations, 98; Refugee Act (1980), 69–70, 71; U.S. national organizations, 106–7; U.S. private organizations, 107–9
Resettlement stage of migration, 17, 18, 20; and guilt, 270–71; mental health practices, 277; stressors, 257–59, 270
Residential segregation, 129–30, 417
Respect, 316, 321–22
Role preparation, 286–87

Salvadorans, 39. *See also* Central Americans

Salvation Army World Service Office (SAWSO), 102
Santería, 41, 197
Satyagraha, 448
Save the Children, 102
SAWSO. *See* Salvation Army World Service Office
Scapegoats, 419, 422, 476
Screening protocols, 237
Seasonal workers, 39
Secondary labor market, 373
Secondary traumatic stress syndrome, 303
Segmented assimilation, 128, 366–67
Segregation, 129–30, 417
Self-awareness, 131–34
Self-blame, 170
Self-definitions, 13, 480
Self-disclosure, 157
Self-efficacy, 170
Self-employment, 46, 375, 405; microenterprise development, 410–11
Self-esteem, 268
Self help groups, 282
Self-knowledge, 142–43
Separation, 127
Service coordination, 240, 241
Service delivery: personnel, 113–17; summary, 481–82; technique overview, 117–20. *See also* Service delivery organizations; *specific areas*
Service delivery organizations: and community health planning, 218–20; culture-bound nature of, 150; summary, 481–82. *See also* International service delivery organizations; U.S. national service delivery organizations
Service utilization, 36–37, 376; and anti-immigrant sentiments, 78; and economic impact, 371–72; mental health care, 263–64; and Personal Responsibility and Work Opportunity Reconciliation Act, 90–92. *See also* Health care access
SES (socioeconomic status). *See* Economic well-being
Settlement policy. *See* Immigrant integration policy
Sexual harassment, 382–83

Sheltered English content programs, 394
Simpson, Alan, 85
Skills training, 293–96, 349–50
Smuggling, 19, 41
Social capital, 379–80, 412–13
Social context of immigration, 318, 320
Social justice, 136
Social maps, 145
Social Security Act, 187
Social skills training, 294–96, 349–50
Socioeconomic status. *See* Economic well-being
Sojourners, 319
Solution-focused intervention, 251
Somalians, 51. *See also* Africans
Somatization, 202–3, 269
Soul loss, 198, 199
South Asians. *See* Indians
Southeast Asians, 46–47; case study exercises, 253; traditional healing systems, 231, 321
South Europeans, 59, 60, 61
Soviets/former Soviets, 49, 68
Split labor market theory of interethnic relations, 420–21
Spouse abuse. *See* Intimate partner violence
States of residence, 27–29; Asians, 45, 46, 47; Dominicans, 42; Haitians, 44; Jamaicans, 43; Latin Americans, 39, 42
Status gain theory of interethnic relations, 421
Statutory law, 94
Stereotyping, 130, 201
Strategic family therapy, 345
Stratification, 129–30, 417–18
Strengths, 160–61
Strengths perspective, 159
Stresses, 160–61
Structural acculturation, 128–30, 417
Structural assimilation, 129, 417
Structural family therapy, 343–45
Structured interethnic contact, 449–59; conducting, 454–57; dialogue characteristics, 451; leadership, 458–59; organizing steps, 451–54; in schools, 473–74
Substance abuse, 271–72, 304–7

Sudanese, 51. *See also* Africans
Supervisors, 116–17
Supportive responses, 155
Survivor guilt, 270
Susto, 199
Sweatshops, 383

TANF. *See* Temporary Assistance to Needy Families
Targeted Assistance Grant Program, 70
Temporary Assistance to Needy Families (TANF), 80
Temporary Protected Status (TPS), 9, 11, 74
Temporary workers, 24
Termination, 174–79
Testimonial psychotherapy, 302–3
Theories, 137, 139–40, 148. *See also specific areas*
Thin blood, 199
Title VII of the Civil Rights Act (1964), 433–34
Title VI of the Civil Rights Act (1964), 190
Torture: case study exercises, 308–9; and psychotropic medication, 289; and survivor guilt, 270. *See also* Refugees
Tossed salad concept, 129
TPS. *See* Temporary Protected Status
Traditional healing systems, 194, 196–201, 202; and interdisciplinary collaboration, 230–31; and mental health, 286; and micro-level health practices, 238
Transit stage of migration, 17, 18, 19; acculturative stress interventions, 291; service delivery, 96, 97–98, 106–7; stressors, 257, 258–59
Translator role, 114
Transnationals, defined, 8, 11
Triangulation, 317, 320
Trust, 155
Twelve-step programs, 306, 476
Two-way immersion programs, 395

UN Convention and Protocol Relating to the Status of Refugees, 57, 68
Understanding responses, 155
Undocumented aliens: anxiety, 269; Central Americans, 39–40; countries of

origin, 23; defined, 5–6; education, 361, 390; Haitians, 43; health care access, 186–87; and Immigration Reform and Control Act (1986), 71–72; labor force participation, 373; and PRWORA, 79; and Refugee Act (1980), 70; states of residence, 29; and transit stage, 19
UNHCR. *See* UN High Commissioner for Refugees
UN High Commissioner for Refugees (UNHCR), 97, 98–99, 481–82
Union organizing, 414
United Nations, 96–97. *See also* International law; *specific organizations and protocols*
Universal coverage principle, 275
Universal Declaration of Human Rights, 54–56
Universality, 261
Unqualified immigrants, 82–83
U.S. Agency for International Development (USAID), 107
USAID. *See* U.S. Agency for International Development
U.S.-born minority groups, 94–95; and acculturation, 128, 366; interethnic relations, 426–28
U.S. Committee for Refugees (USCR), 104
USCR. *See* U.S. Committee for Refugees
U.S. immigration/refugee policies, 57–95; and Central Americans, 39; and Chinese, 45; contemporary goals, 63; and Cubans, 40–41, 61, 70; and economic well-being, 380–82; and Haitians, 43, 70, 94; and health care access, 185–89; historical, 58–63; Illegal Immigration Reform and Immigrant Responsibility Act, 66, 92–94; Immigration Act (1990), 65, 72–74, 75–77; Immigration and Nationality Act Amendments (1965), 64, 66–67; Immigration and Nationality Act Amendments (1976), 64, 67–68; Immigration Reform and Control Act (1986), 65, 71–72; implementation, 95, 105–6; Refugee Act (1980), 64–65, 68–71; and refugees, 7–8, 39; summaries, 62–63, 64–66; summary, 481; and U.S.-born minority groups, 94–95. *See also* Personal Responsibility and Work Opportunity Reconciliation Act; U.S. national service delivery organizations
U.S. national service delivery organizations, 105–12; government agencies, 105–7; local organizations, 110–12; private organizations, 107–10

Vicarious traumatization, 303
Vietnamese, 199. *See also* Southeast Asians
Vietnam War, 46, 68
Violence prevention programs, 474–75
Vital essence, 197
Vocational education, 405–6
Vocational rehabilitation, 119
Voluntary Agency Matching Grant Program, 69–70
Voluntary migrants. *See* Immigrants
Voodoo, 44
Voudou, 197

Wandering womb, 199
WASP culture. *See* Dominant culture
WCC. *See* World Council of Churches
Welfare. *See* Service utilization
White Americans, 126, 191
Women: empowerment programs, 331–32; exploitation of, 383; health, 205–7; Jamaicans, 42. *See also* Gender; Gender roles
Women's Commission for Refugee Women and Children, 105
Work. *See* Labor force participation
World Concern, 102
World Council of Churches (WCC), 102
World Relief, 102
World Vision, 102
World War II, 59

Xenophobia, 130, 418

Yin/yang, 197
Youth services, 119